ORCHIDS
OF AUSTRALIA

ORCHIDS
OF AUSTRALIA

THE COMPLETE EDITION

DRAWN IN NATURAL COLOUR BY

W. H. NICHOLLS

WITH DESCRIPTIVE TEXT

EDITED BY

D. L. JONES, B.Ag.Sc. and T. B. MUIR, B.Sc.

NELSON

THOMAS NELSON (AUSTRALIA) LIMITED
597 Little Collins Street Melbourne 3000
403 George Street Sydney 2000

THOMAS NELSON AND SONS LTD
36 Park Street London W1Y 4DE

THOMAS NELSON AND SONS (SOUTH AFRICA) PTY LTD
P.O. Box 9881 Johannesburg

THOMAS NELSON AND SONS (CANADA) LTD
81 Curlew Drive Don Mills Ontario

National Library of Australia registry number AUS 69-848
SBN 17 001805

Printed in Hong Kong by Dai Nippon Printing Co., (International) Ltd

Preface

S OME YEARS AGO (about 1923), I began to spend my few leisure hours in the pleasurable task of describing, by pen and brush, the orchid wealth of our continent. Some comprehensive book, it was felt, was long overdue: students of these fascinating plants were finding (like myself) great difficulty in the accurate identification of their specimens by reference to published works. Such difficulty might sometimes be attributed to the inadequacy of existing descriptions, sometimes to the tardy interchange of recorded discoveries between authorities working in different States or countries—in the early years of last century, means of communication were extremely meagre. Hence, several names were often applied, in different places, to what later proved one and the same species.

I resolved that my hobby should prepare the way for an authoritative monograph on Australian orchids, and this publication is the outcome of unremitting toil over the past 27 years. I soon realised that mere verbal descriptions, however detailed, and even if accompanied by natural size pictures of the specimens described, could never be wholly satisfactory. So I applied myself to faithful and enlarged colour portrayals of the wonderful, often minute, reproductive organs of these remarkable flowers, in addition to separate delineations of sepals, petals and labella. To collectors of what might seem freaks or variations of well-known species, these details should be helpful. A glance at column or labellum (in large-size portrayal) should greatly assist the identification. . . . [A key has been constructed as a guide to identification of all known Australian genera.—Ed.]

I have used only living specimens as subjects for my drawings and descriptions. Many of the rarer tropical orchids have been grown at my home and encouraged to flower under glass in furtherance of this object. Only thus could I acquire that thorough knowledge of diagnostic characters, of peculiarities in structure and growth that are indispensable to the monographer— dried specimens, however well preserved, could never supply the subtle details of habit, colour and texture.

My entire collection of *exsiccatae*, including types of all the novelties I have described, has been presented to and is now housed at the Victorian National Herbarium, South Yarra.

This present work, while making no pretence at perfection, claims to be absolutely reliable as far as it has gone. Having early resolved never to publish anything that had not been amply tested, I made bold to seek—for corroboration of every statement where necessary—the only fountain-heads of such knowledge, viz. the various National Herbaria of Australia, as well as more important ones overseas (e.g. Kew and the British Museum, where the earlier Australian collections had been deposited). I take this opportunity, therefore, of acknowledging my indebtedness to the custodians of these institutions, without whose unfailing courtesy I would not have been able to encompass my objective.

To that fine old man of Australian orchidology—Dr. Richard Sanders Rogers, M.A., M.D., D.SC., F.L.S., who died in Adelaide on April 30, 1942—I owe much. It was he who finally induced me to take up the study, a decision I never regretted. His advice and his published articles, with such comprehensive descriptions of orchids, were of the utmost value to me in the present work.

I also acknowledge my great indebtedness to the late Mr. Arthur Belgrave Braine, schoolmaster at Cravensville in the Tallangatta Valley, Victoria—one of the State's most enthusiastic students of orchidaceous plants—and to members of the Maud Gibson Trust (Melbourne Botanic Gardens) for a substantial grant which enabled me to visit Western Australia twice, thereby obtaining live material of many localised and rare orchid species; this generous grant served also to defray postage on specimens for delineation from remote parts of other States.

Finally, I desire to record my grateful thanks to Mr. J. H. Willis, of the Melbourne National Herbarium staff, for considerable help in preparing the various keys and in editing the complete manuscript [as originally published]—a task involving much time and patience.

W. H. NICHOLLS
July 1950

v

DEDICATED TO

THE MEMORY OF

MY WIFE, EVELYN JANE

Through her devotion
and her sunny companionship
this work
was rendered possible

Contents

Foreword

TREMENDOUS contributions have been made to scientific literature and art in Australia by amateur workers who were compelled only by love of their hobby and a desire to share it with others. In the botanical field one thinks of men like J. M. Black, a retired Adelaide journalist who set himself to write a 746-page *Flora of South Australia*, published in four parts between 1922 and 1929; at the time of death (1951), in his ninety-seventh year, he had almost completed a new and enlarged edition that appeared posthumously. Black's *Flora* is authoritative, extremely useful and probably the best modern textbook ever to appear on the vegetation of an Australian state. But, whereas Black was able to devote more than forty years of a long retirement exclusively to his pet theme, others have produced scientific masterpieces of sterling value during limited leisure hours from an exacting workaday life. This is particularly true of Australian orchidologists, and the three outstanding figures this century have all been amateurs—Rogers, the doctor; Rupp, the clergyman; and Nicholls, the bookbinder and latterly gardener.

It was my great privilege to know W. H. Nicholls as a personal friend for many years before his death in March 1951, and to go camping with him on several occasions; he was one of nature's truest gentlemen, an admirable companion with a rich fund of anecdotes, a good sense of humour and an exuberant enthusiasm for the bush. His camera went everywhere, recording with great clarity not only flowers and trees, but waterfalls and picturesque old huts which held a particular fascination for him. He never carried normal collecting gear, preferring to 'travel light' and usually brought home any special orchid trophies concealed under the capacious crown of his hat—those were the days before polythene bags.

With only a primary education, Will Nicholls taught himself drawing, painting and enough Latin to concoct formal diagnoses for the many undescribed orchid species that he detected. His keen vision, patience and powers of concentration were quite amazing. Working at great speed, with a lens in one hand and a pencil or paint brush in the other, he would delineate the structural features of such delicate, pinhead-sized flowers as those of an *Oberonia*. Over twenty-five years he built up a gallery of almost five hundred excellent Australian orchid portraits, with anatomical dissections, all painted from life and remarkable for their detailed accuracy. It had long been his dream to have these pictures reproduced in book form, and to this end he carefully prepared a sheet of descriptive text to accompany each plate.

Early in 1950 the Melbourne firm, Georgian House, adventurously undertook to publish the superb water-colours and important manuscripts by Nicholls, involving an expenditure of many thousands of pounds. The plates were to be issued in groups of twenty-four per part, and the estimated twenty-odd parts would be spread over a decade or more. As publication proceeded, Nicholls would continue to paint missing subjects and newly described species. The retail price for each part of the work was £7.10.0 ($15)—a high figure at that time, but it was considered that overseas demand would enable most of the one thousand sets to be sold. Most unfortunately, Nicholls died just before Part I was off the press; so he missed this tangible pleasure of fulfilment. It was then that I accepted editorial responsibility for the remaining parts of the monograph. By the time Part IV appeared, sales had dwindled below profit-level, and further publication had to be suspended as uneconomic. This was indeed a sad blow to a worthy, if ambitious, project. Over the succeeding years, various avenues were explored for getting *Orchids of Australia* 'off the ground' again, but to no avail. Despondency settled on all who were vitally interested in bringing the scheme to completion. Only last year Thomas Nelson (Australia) Limited, keen to produce a major botanical work in colour and acquainted of these languishing orchid plates, made arrangements with Georgian House and the Nicholls family to publish *all* the pictures in a single volume. It was like an answer to prayer! The original format needed considerable modification to reduce bulk, and the ninety-six plates already issued by Georgian House have been repeated in the new book; nevertheless, faithful reproduction of high quality is maintained throughout, and the purchaser is certainly assured of his money's worth. The gratitude of orchidologists everywhere, and of many other plant lovers, goes to this enterprising firm which has timed the appearance of W. H. Nicholls' complete *Orchids of Australia* to coincide with the Sixth World Orchid Conference being held in Sydney during September 1969. At such short notice, it was impossible for me to edit the entire manuscript; but Thomas Nelson was fortunate in securing, as joint text editors, two competent professional botanists of Melbourne—Messrs T. B. Muir and D. L. Jones, who are also specialists in the *Orchidaceae*.

The invitation to provide a Foreword for this *opus magnum*, however, was accepted very gladly, for I deem it both an honour and a delight to be linked thus with the final consummation of my late friend's life-work. Not only will the book serve as a very useful monument to his industry and artistic skill, but it will take its place among the greatest regional floristic monographs of all time. May it also awaken much more interest in our magnificent flora, retreating so rapidly on so many fronts, and stir up a desire to fight for the protection of what yet remains.

J. H. WILLIS
Assistant Government Botanist
Melbourne
June 1969

Editors' Introduction

THE FANTASTIC DIVERSITY and complexity of orchid flowers have long excited popular imagination, and some species have become symbols of luxury and exotic beauty. However, for naturalists and botanists, there are many other species which are equally fascinating. This is not to be wondered at, since the orchid family is not only one of the largest but also one of the most complex among flowering plants. It is world-wide in distribution and, although the majority of species are in the tropics, orchids are also to be found in many other habitats, extending even into the arctic. The Australian orchids are by no means an insignificant group within this family, since they too are found in a wide range of climates and habitats, and have a diversity of flower shapes and sizes. Furthermore they are plentiful and can be readily found, even in close proximity to any of the capital cities.

Epiphytes are most common in the wet tropical and subtropical regions of the east coast. Although some terrestrials also share this environment, they are most abundant in the southern temperate regions. A few extend into the semi-arid parts of the interior and into the Alps where snow lies during winter. Along with the diversity of habitat, there is also a great diversity in flower shapes, from the almost regular *Thelymitra* to the bizarre *Spiculaea*. Others with extraordinary appearance include *Diuris*, *Caleana*, *Pterostylis*, *Caladenia* and *Calochilus*. Saprophytes are well represented in Australia, two of which, *Rhizanthella gardneri* and *Cryptanthemis slateri*, are of particular interest because they are subterranean. Another saprophyte, *Galeola foliata*, is one of the tallest orchids in the world, specimens reaching a height of 14 metres (44 feet). At the other extreme *Bulbophyllum globuliforme* is one of the world's smallest. *Taeniophyllum* and *Chiloschista* are also of interest because they are leafless epiphytes in which the roots, which contain chlorophyll, have taken over the function of leaves

The epiphytes mainly belong to large and widespread genera such as *Dendrobium* and *Bulbophyllum*, although the majority of Australian members are endemic. Because some are attractive and very free flowering, they are widely cultivated in Australia and worthy of a place in overseas collections. There is much interest at present in the use of these species for the production of hybrids. This work has shown that there is a number of natural hybrids amongst the epiphytes, for example *Dendrobium×delicatum*. There is evidence that some terrestrial orchids are also natural hybrids, for example *Pterostylis toveyana*, but this cannot be confirmed until more is known about the germination of terrestrial orchid seed. This is indeed a field for study.

Pollination is another field about which little is known, pollination of the epiphytes particularly requiring further study. Only a few species have been studied in detail, but some fascinating information has come to light. The best known work is that by Mrs Edith Coleman, who found that the flowers of *Cryptostylis* lure insects by a scent. This is discussed in more detail in the text for *Cryptostylis*. Other genera such as *Spiculaea*, *Drakaea*, *Chiloglottis* and *Acianthus* mimic insects in the shape, colour or scent of their flowers. Otherwise there has been no systematic study of pollination and only a few additional facts are known about Australian species.

This book is an excellent introduction to Australian orchids, of which there are about seven hundred and fifty species, most of them being endemic to this country. They are in about ninety genera of which about twenty are endemic. The colour plates illustrate almost four hundred of these species in detail; thus they comprise more than half the total for Australia, and they include most of the common ones.

From the plates it is clear that Australia has many attractive and interesting species. After reading the text it should also become clear that there is much yet to learn about Australian orchids. We hope this book will stimulate interest and further study. However, people must realise that many species are threatened with extinction despite the fact that orchids are plants protected by law. It is vital for their conservation that we have adequate reserves and national parks. Only in this way will orchids and other native species, common or rare, be preserved for the future in their natural state. Failure in this will result in some species becoming extinct, and subsequently known only from illustrations and dried herbarium specimens.

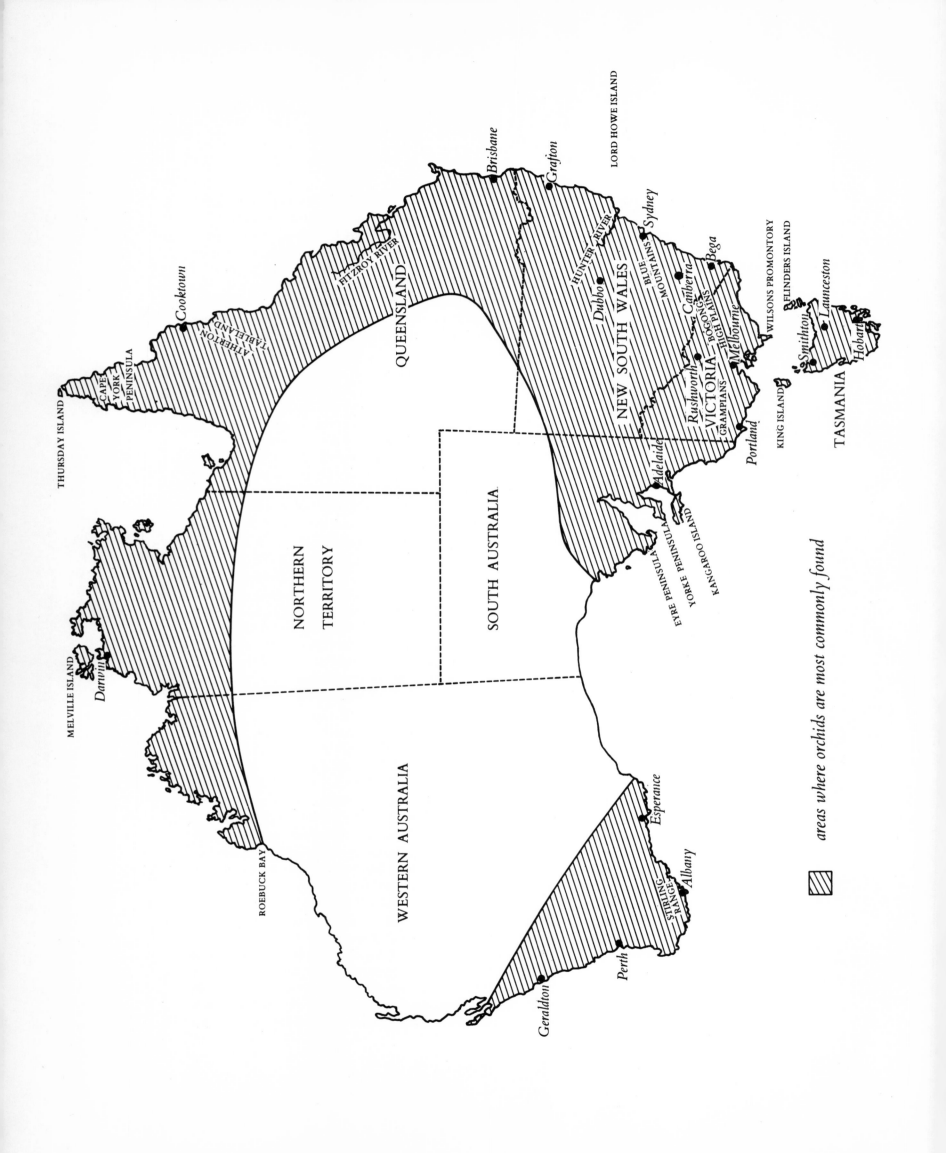

THURSDAY ISLAND

Cooktown

CAPE YORK PENINSULA

ATHERTON TABLELAND

FITZROY RIVER

QUEENSLAND

Brisbane

Grafton

LORD HOWE ISLAND

HUNTER RIVER

Sydney

Dubbo

BLUE MOUNTAINS

Canberra

Bega

NEW SOUTH WALES

BOGONG HIGH PLAINS

WILSONS PROMONTORY

FLINDERS ISLAND

Launceston

Smithton

Hobart

Rushworth

VICTORIA

GRAMPIANS

Melbourne

Portland

KING ISLAND

TASMANIA

MELVILLE ISLAND

Darwin

NORTHERN TERRITORY

SOUTH AUSTRALIA

Adelaide

EYRE PENINSULA

YORKE PENINSULA

KANGAROO ISLAND

ROEBUCK BAY

WESTERN AUSTRALIA

Esperance

STIRLING RANGE

Albany

Geraldton

Perth

areas where orchids are most commonly found

Editorial aims

In editing the text of W. H. Nicholls' manuscript it has been our aim to ensure that it remained a reflection of his opinions, while bringing it up to date in certain details. (For some species there was only a plate and it was necessary to supply the information in these cases.) Thus we have generally made only minor alterations to his descriptions and notes. However, some changes in names and data on distribution and flowering period were needed because more information has become available since the death of W. H. Nicholls in 1951.

To achieve accuracy we have personally checked the original description of each species, with few exceptions, to ensure that the details of the references to volume number, page, date, etc. were correct. For date of publication we have referred frequently to F. A. Stafleu, *Taxonomic Literature, A Selective Guide*. Regnum Vegetabile, vol. *52* (1967).

We have now entered a period in which groups within the orchid family are being studied intensively. As a result there have been changes in nomenclature and there are sure to be more in the next few years. It is certain that a number of varieties included in this book will be reduced to synonymy, as they are based on mere differences in size or flower colour and undoubtedly come within the range of normal variation. Some species also have a doubtful status. However, we have taken a conservative view of these and have allowed them to remain.

Arrangement of genera and species

The systematic arrangement of genera is basically that of E. Pfitzer in *Natürlichen Pflanzenfamilien II⁶* (1889), with some modifications. We have followed H. M. R. Rupp in *Orchids of New South Wales* (1943), in placing *Pterostylis* after *Cryptostylis*, but have placed *Calochilus* near *Thelymitra* as did J. H. Willis in *Handbook to Plants in Victoria* vol. *1* (1962). For the genera in the sub-tribe *Sarcanthinae* (*Phalaenopsis* to *Drymoanthus*) we have followed A. W. Dockrill in *Review of the Australasian Sarcanthinae* (1967). Categories above that of genus have been omitted as the status of some is in doubt and their delimitation is by no means certain.

In arranging species within a genus we have tried to place like species together to facilitate identification and to draw attention to their relationships. Generally we found species could be placed in a series, taking some prominent feature of the plant as a basis. In this we were obliged to rely on our own judgement as literature was of limited assistance. Little has been published on the natural relationships of Australian species and only after research will such become clear.

It is also obvious that much remains to be learnt about the correct names and delimitation of a number of species, consequently we considered it quite impracticable to draw up keys to species at this stage.

Arrangement of text

The name of each genus is in bold type. It is preceded by a generic number and is followed by the citation, consisting of the name of its author and place of publication. The titles of publications throughout the text, together with the volume numbers, are printed in italics, followed by a colon; then comes the page and/or plate number, and lastly the year of publication (in round brackets). After a somewhat brief generic description comes a note on the approximate number of species in the genus, and their distribution.

For each species a uniform pattern has been followed, so that on becoming familiar with it, the reader can readily find any particular details.

The botanic name comes first in bold type, followed by the plate number, then the citation. As is customary the generic name is abbreviated to the initial letter, but for ease of reference it appears in full at the top of the page. Immediately after the citation is a select list of references to publications in which that species has been mentioned. (These will give some details which are not in the text of this book. Those chosen are for the most part comprehensive and recently published, and also readily available either from booksellers or in the larger reference libraries.) The basionym is next, with any other synonyms by which the species may have been known in the more prominent publications on orchids. This list is not exhaustive as we believe that complete synonymy is of more interest to the specialist and better found in monographs and floras.

The main part of the text is taken up with the description. The habit of the plant is dealt with first, followed by details of the leaves, the inflorescence and finally the flower.

Then come the notes in which W. H. Nicholls often expressed his opinions on variation within a species or relationships between species. These notes, which may also mention such things as habitat of a species or its pollination, have been included because of their considerable importance.

Flowering period comes next. Except for a few species, mostly epiphytes from Queensland, Australian orchids have their main flowering restricted to a period of one or two months. Time of flowering will depend on latitude and altitude. Thus species will flower earlier in the north of their range than in the south, and earlier in the lowlands than in the Alps. This explains the apparent lengthy flowering period for some widely distributed species. It should be realised that on occasion plants will be found flowering out of season.

A common name is given only for common or widespread species, or if the name is apt. We have chosen what we believed were the most widely known, but have included some alternative names. However, common names are used loosely and for a particular species may vary from one state to another. We have not given a common name for rare species nor in the case where it is merely a translation of the botanic name.

Lastly, in the distribution the Australian states are listed in order, from Queensland to New South Wales, Victoria and Tasmania, followed by South Australia and Western Australia. For the few species found in the north of Australia, distribution is listed from Western Australia to the Northern Territory and Queensland. Only for rare and localised species are details of localities given. For other species it will be necessary to refer to publications from the select list or to appropriate ones listed for additional reading.

The key to the plate and the plate number are found on the plate itself, together with the number of the page on which the text is printed. Figures which are natural size are listed below the key, the other figures being variously enlarged. In certain cases it was necessary to slightly reduce the Plates. Thus these Figures, which are designated natural size, are actually slightly less, but the difference is insignificant. The Plates concerned are Plates 99, 104, 106, 107, 109, 110, 116, 331, 361, 371, 373 and 406.

Identification of specimens

We expect that the book will often be used for identification. The following notes will be helpful when an unfamiliar specimen is being dealt with.

First go to the key to genera, and having determined the genus turn to the appropriate plates and compare the specimen with the illustrations. If a good match is obtained, turn to the relevant text for any other information required. It may be necessary to check the descriptions of several species and refer to floras mentioned in the select bibliography when a specimen cannot be matched satisfactorily. It should be realised that not all Australian genera or species are illustrated and that atypical specimens may prove difficult to identify. In such cases it would be advisable to consult someone with a specialist knowledge.

The editors would be very pleased to receive information about species not illustrated in this book, or anything else of importance not recorded. Correspondence should be addressed to them through the publishers.

Description of an orchid

This description applies to the majority of orchids. The remainder are exceptional and more comprehensive texts should be consulted for descriptions of these. A few of the terms used in describing an orchid are explained below. For other terms see the Glossary.

Orchids may be *epiphytic* on the branches and trunks of trees, with aerial roots; *lithophytic* on rocks; or *terrestrial* with underground tubers or rhizomes. They are perennials, with leaves absent or reduced to scales in some *saprophytic* species which live on decaying organic matter in association

26 Lateral sepals much larger than all other segments, deflexed, white or
    pink; labellum much recurved   *Eriochilus* (**17**)
    Lateral sepals much narrower and longer than the dorsal one, brown or
    greenish, labellum almost straight   27
    Lateral sepals not differing markedly in shape or length from the dorsal one 28

27 Leaf solitary, rarely two, ovate; petals prominent, linear-clavate; labellum
    with wide reddish-purple fringe   *Leptoceras* (**21**)
    Leaves two to several, linear; flowers on slender pedicels; petals prominent,
    stalked; labellum margins entire   *Diuris* (**6**)
    Leaves several, linear; flowers almost sessile; petals minute, sessile; lateral
    sepals extremely long; labellum margins entire   *Orthoceras* (**7**)

28 Plants with single leaf, sometimes borne on a shoot separate from the
    scape, or absent at flowering time; pseudobulbs absent   29
    Plants with two to several leaves; pseudobulbs sometimes present   44

29 Labellum extremely modified, with long slender claw and lamina
    shaped like a hammer or pick-head   30
    Labellum claw short or absent, lamina never hammer-like   31

30 Labellum lamina pointed towards column, its appendage smooth   *Spiculaea* (**13**)
    Labellum lamina directed away from the column, its appendage covered
    with large warty protuberances   *Drakaea* (**12**)

31 Labellum much larger and longer than all the other segments, covered with
    hairs or papillae, rarely glabrous   *Calochilus* (**5**)
    Labellum shorter than or subequal to the other segments, smooth or
    variously glandular   32

32 Labellum entirely smooth, one or two glands sometimes at very base   33
    Labellum lamina fringed, pubescent, or bearing glandular papillae or calli 37

33 Flowers brightly coloured—purple, pink or white   34
    Flowers wholly green, brown or blackish   36

34 Labellum at least as long as, and broader than other segments; leaf almost
    glabrous   *Nervilia* (**27**)
    Labellum far shorter than other segments; leaf hairy   35

35 Column wings extended to form an entire hood over the anther; labellum
    glabrous, sigmoid or recurved towards apex; perianth glazed within   *Elythranthera* (**24**)
    Column wings terminating below the anther, not forming a hood;
    labellum puberulous towards base; perianth not glazed within   *Glossodia* (**25**)

36 Leaf separate from flowering scape; habit rhizomic; flowers green   *Townsonia* (**16**)
    Leaf attached to base of scape; rhizomes absent; flowers reddish, rarely
    green   *Acianthus* (**15**)

37 Column almost or quite wingless   38
    Column broadly winged   40

38 Labellum almost as long as and broader than all other segments, straight
    and pink   *Nervilia* (**27**)
    Labellum much shorter than the lateral sepals, often recurved   39

39 Labellum much recurved and pale, sometimes striped; floral bracts large   *Lyperanthus* (**19**)
    Labellum almost straight, dark brownish; floral bracts inconspicuous   *Acianthus* (**15**)

40 Labellum fringed, without glands; lateral sepals and petals spathulate   *Leptoceras* (**21**)
    Labellum always bearing calli or papillae; lateral sepals and petals never all
    spathulate   41

41 Plants rhizomic   42
    Plants with tubers, but no rhizomes   43

42 Leaf narrow, as long as the scape; flowers numerous   *Pachystoma*
    Leaf ovate, much shorter than scape; flower solitary   *Adenochilus* (**23**)

43 Leaf usually hairy; floral bracts small, not exceeding the ovary; labellum
    with definite calli   *Caladenia* (**22**)

Leaf always glabrous; floral bracts large, exceeding the ovary; labellum with papillate processes — *Lyperanthus* (**19**)

44 Leaves two, radical, usually petiolate; flower solitary; labellum with dark waxy glands or papillae — *Chiloglottis* (**14**)

Leaves more than two, often cauline and stem clasping; flowers several, rarely solitary; labellum devoid of dark waxy glands, but sometimes with hairs, lamellae or calli — 45

45 Leaves thick, and leathery, cauline; labellum cruciform, fused with the column — **Epidendrum* (**45**)

Leaves not thick and leathery; labellum never cruciform, quite free from the column — 46

46 Labellum never saccate or spurred — 47
Labellum saccate, pouched or spurred at the base — 51

47 Plants with normal tubers; flowers few, usually one to three, rarely up to eight — 48

Plants rhizomic or with pseudobulbs; flowers numerous, exceeding eight (except in *Liparis simmondsii* with wholly dark purplish flowers) — 49

48 Flowers readily and widely expanding; segments not waxy, variously coloured; leaves ovate, green with reddish veins — *Leptoceras* (**21**)

Flowers seldom opening; segments waxy, all white internally; leaves inconspicuous, purplish and bract-like — *Burnettia* (**20**)

49 Leaves 30 cm. or more long, distichous, plicate; perianth segments all broad; labellum deeply trilobed, lateral lobes linear — *Dipodium* (**51**)

Leaves less than 30 cm. long, alternate, cauline, on wiry stems 1 m. long; perianth segments all broad; labellum trilobed, lateral lobes elliptic — *Bromheadia*

Leaves not exceeding 30 cm. in length, neither distichous nor plicate; at least some perianth segments very narrow; labellum entire, rarely trifid at the apex — 50

50 Sepals and lateral petals all long-acuminate, almost filiform and directed forward; odour not apparent — *Rimacola* (**18**)

None of the perianth segments with long filiform tips, all spreading and sometimes reflexed; sometimes with distinct and unpleasant odour — *Liparis* (**39**)

51 Labellum deeply cleft at the apex, forming two equal, wing-like divergent lobes — 52

Labellum not cleft apically into two wing-like lobes (either entire, undulate, slightly laciniate, or prominently trilobed) — 53

52 Perianth segments all small and appressed; labellum margins entire — *Zeuxine* (**35**)

At least the lateral sepals widely spreading; labellum margins variously laciniate — *Anoectochilus*

53 Plants with tubers; labellum with a long slender spur at the base, usually trilobed — *Habenaria* (**1**)

Plants rhizomic; labellum saccate or pouched, but without a long spur; never trilobed — 54

54 Leaves long and linear, absent at flowering time; perianth veined, expanding, variously tinted, at least 9 mm. long — *Eulophia*

Leaves present in a basal rosette, ovate-lanceolate; perianth veinless, campanulate, greenish-white, less than 8 mm. — *Cheirostylis*

55 Tall terrestrial herbs with long, often broad, plicate leaves — 56
Epiphytes with creeping roots; leaves never plicate, sometimes absent — 60

56 Leaves cauline; flowers in axillary panicles, white; labellum spathulate, on a long linear claw adnate to the column — *Corymborchis*

Leaves terminating pseudobulbs; labellum claw short or absent — 57

57 Flowers wholly white or rich purple; labellum deeply trilobed — 58
Flowers variously coloured, white or pink on the back; labellum entire or obscurely lobed — 59

58   Leaves broad and plantain-like; flowers white; mid-lobe of the labellum deeply cleft   *Calanthe* **(42)**
       Leaves linear; flowers purple; labellum mid-lobe entire   *Spathoglottis* **(43)**

59   Leaves several per pseudobulb; raceme erect; perianth segments more than 2 cm. long, variously coloured but always white on the back   *Phaius* **(41)**
       Leaves several per pseudobulb; raceme drooping at apex when flowers mature; perianth segments less than 2 cm. long, wholly pink   *Geodorum* **(44)**
       Leaves one per pseudobulb; raceme erect; perianth segments less than 2 cm. long, greenish-white   *Tainia*

60   Perianth under 5 mm. long, often minute   61
       Perianth always exceeding 5 mm. in length   79

61   Leaf absent   62
       Leaves one to many on each plant   64

62   Flowers with a mentum formed by union of column foot and bases of lateral sepals, but labellum never spurred   *Bulbophyllum* **(50)**
       Flowers without a mentum, but the labellum bearing a conspicuous pouch or spur, lateral sepals free   63

63   Labellum immobile, spurred at the rear; pollinia four, separate   *Taeniophyllum*
       Labellum articulate, spurred in front; pollinia four, in two closely appressed pairs   *Chiloschista*

64   Flowers with a mentum   65
       Flowers without a mentum   68

65   Pollinia four   66
       Pollinia eight   67

66   Leaves many, distichous, on slender stems; pseudobulbs absent   *Podochilus*
       Pseudobulbs present, each bearing one or two leaves   *Bulbophyllum* **(50)**

67   Pseudobulbs present, each bearing one to several long leaves; growth sympodial   *Eria* **(48)**
       Pseudobulbs absent; growth monopodial   *Phreatia* **(49)**

68   Pollinia eight; inflorescence a dense spike of small flowers   *Thelasis*
       Pollinia two or four; inflorescence a few-flowered raceme   69

69   Labellum not spurred, sessile, undivided; sepals and petals green   *Drymoanthus* **(66)**
       Labellum spurred   70

70   Pollinia two   71
       Pollinia four, in two pairs   72

71   Inflorescence long, many-flowered; most flowers open at the one time   *Robiquetia* **(54)**
       Inflorescence short, few-flowered (three to five); flowers developing one or two at a time   *Saccolabium*

72   Labellum hinged   73
       Labellum immobile   75

73   Labellum spurred at rear   *Peristeranthus* **(59)**
       Labellum spurred in front   74

74   Disc of labellum with a large, more or less erect, usually longitudinally grooved callus in centre; and a callus at base of each lateral lobe   *Sarcochilus* **(56)**
       Disc of labellum completely filled with a large callus which is adnate to the lateral lobes   *Mobilabium* **(58)**
       Disc of labellum without calli   *Parasarcochilus* **(57)**

75   Lateral lobes of labellum joined to column foot   *Papillilabium* **(65)**
       Lateral lobes of labellum free from column base or column foot   76

76   Calli within the spur, or overhanging its orifice   77
       Calli absent from the spur and its orifice   78

77   Thickened base of labellum mid-lobe extended partly across the orifice of the spur as a callus   *Schistotylus* **(63)**
       Hirsute finger-like callus within the spur   *Plectorrhiza* **(61)**

78	Labellum with a thick transverse ridge between the spur and the mid-lobe	*Saccolabiopsis* **(64)**
	Labellum without transverse ridges; rostellum extending above the anther	*Schoenorchis*
79	Flowers with a mentum; labellum not spurred	80
	Flowers without a mentum; labellum sometimes spurred	83
80	Pronounced spur formed by union lateral sepals with column foot; column more or less hairy in front	*Cadetia* **(47)**
	Lateral sepals united with column foot, but not forming a prominent spur	81
81	Pollinia eight	*Eria* **(48)**
	Pollinia four	82
82	Labellum indistinctly lobed; leaf solitary; pseudobulbs arising directly from rhizome	*Diplocaulobium*
	Labellum distinctly trilobed; leaf solitary; pseudobulbs separated from rhizome by a short slender aerial shoot	*Ephemerantha*
	Labellum distinctly trilobed; leaves one to several; pseudobulbs arising directly from rhizome	*Dendrobium* **(46)**
83	Lateral sepals united to form a single lobe; labellum fused with the column for half its length	*Acriopsis*
	Sepals free; labellum free from column or united with it only at the very base	84
84	Labellum without a spur or protuberance beneath	85
	Labellum with a hollow spur of fleshy protuberance beneath	87
85	Leaves terete; flowers small, developing one or two at a time on a short, few-flowered spike	*Luisia*
	Leaves flat; flowers conspicuous in long racemes	86
86	Petals more than 2·5 cm. wide, differing from sepals	*Phalaenopsis* **(53)**
	Petals less than 2·5 cm. wide, similar to sepals	*Cymbidium* **(52)**
87	Pollinia two	88
	Pollinia four	90
88	Inflorescence short, crowded, few-flowered; flowers developing one or two at a time	*Saccolabium*
	Inflorescence not crowded, many-flowered (if ever few-flowered, then petals broadly spathulate); most flowers open at the one time	89
89	Mid-lobe of labellum bifid	*Vanda*
	Mid-lobe of labellum not bifid	*Robiquetia* **(54)**
90	Plants leafless	*Chiloschista*
	Plants with leaves	91
91	Labellum hinged	92
	Labellum immobile	94
92	Disc of labellum without calli	*Parasarcochilus* **(57)**
	Disc of labellum with a large grooved callus in the centre, and a callus at the base of each lateral lobe	93
93	Sepals and petals more or less filiform; roots raspy; flowers fugacious	*Rhinerrhiza* **(55)**
	Sepals and petals not filiform; roots smooth; flowers lasting more than two days	*Sarcochilus* **(56)**
94	Labellum spurred in front	95
	Labellum spurred at rear	96
95	Spur with a large bidentate callus	*Camarotis*
	Spur with a glabrous finger-like callus	*Thrixspermum* **(60)**
96	Spur with a hirsute finger-like callus on the anterior wall, and directed towards the apex	*Plectorrhiza* **(61)**
	Spur with a valvate callus on the posterior wall, and directed towards the orifice	*Pomatocalpa* **(62)**

I *Habenaria*

Habenaria Willd. *Spec. Plant. 4*:5, 44 (1805)

[Terrestrial plants growing from tubers, rarely from a short rhizome. Stem erect; leaves along the stem or basal, usually sessile and sheathing at the base. Inflorescence a terminal raceme. Dorsal sepal and petals erect or incurved to form a hood over the column, lateral sepals spreading or reflexed. Lip spurred, simple or trilobed, the divisions entire or variously dissected. Column short, stigmas two, usually separate, often joined to base of lip, with or without papillose processes. Anther two-celled, pollinia two, caudicles enclosed in tubes, separated by a rostellum. Pollinia granular.

A large genus found throughout the world, mainly in the warmer regions.

H. ferdinandii (Plate 1)

H. ferdinandii Schlechter in *Repert. Spec. nov. Regn. veg. 10*:249 (1911)

SYNONYMY: *H. graminea* Benth. *Flor. aust. 6*:394 (1873), non Lindl. (1835); *H. muellerana* Schlechter in *Repert. Spec. nov. Regn. veg. 9*:435 (1911), non Cogniaux (1893)

An erect terrestrial plant with slender stems 20–35 cm. high. Leaves three to five, close together, somewhat spreading, 2–6 cm. long, 3–6 mm. wide, linear, obtuse or acute, glabrous. Raceme many-flowered, 10–20 cm. long, bracts somewhat spreading, lanceolate, acuminate, glabrous, shorter than ovary. Flowers somewhat spreading, glabrous. Dorsal sepal erect, 3 mm. long, broadly ovate, obtuse; lateral sepals deflexed, as long as dorsal sepals, obliquely oblong-lanceolate, somewhat obtuse. Petals erect, as long as dorsal sepal, obliquely ligulate, somewhat obtuse, anterior margins almost lobed and angled at the base. Labellum trilobed, divided almost to the base, lobes linear, acute; mid-lobe projecting forward, slightly longer than the sepals; lateral lobes erect, slightly longer than the mid-lobe, apices slightly hooked; spur cylindrical, about 8 mm. long, sub-acute, constricted at the middle. Anther standing out boldly, circumscribed by short ascending grooves. Rostellum low, triangular, obtuse; stigmatic processes extending outward, almost twice as long as the anthereal grooves. Ovary about 1 cm. long, sub-fusiform to cylindrical, glabrous.

FLOWERING PERIOD: Feb. to May

DISTRIBUTION: Coastal regions in the north-west of WA, the north of NT and the north of Qld—Ed.]

2 *Monadenia*

Monadenia Lindl. *Gen. & Spec. orchid. Pls* 356 (1838)

Terrestrial herbs with simple sessile tubers; leaves usually cauline and gradually reduced upward, or the lower subradical and the upper reduced to short sheaths. Inflorescence usually a long dense spike, sometimes more lax or in short spikes; bracts usually narrow or narrowed from a broad base. Sepals free; dorsal sepal superior, hood-shaped, usually with an oblong or cylindrical spur; lateral sepals spreading. Petals erect, entire or bilobed. Lip anticous, usually small and narrow, without a spur. Column short. Anther erect or reclinate, two-celled, with the cells distinct and parallel; pollinia two, solitary in each cell, granular, attached by short or long caudicles to a single gland. Ovary twisted; rostellum erect, sub-entire, emarginate, or trilobed. Capsule oblong or elliptic-oblong.

A genus of twenty species, endemic in southern Africa. One of the commonest, *M. micrantha*, is naturalised in Western Australia, where it was originally thought to be indigenous and a distinct species.

M. micrantha (Plate 2)

M. micrantha Lindl. *Gen. & Spec. orchid. Pls* 357 (1838); W. H. Nicholls in *Aust. Orchid Rev. 14*:98 (1949); R. Erickson *Orchids West* ed. 2:45 (1965)

SYNONYMY: *Disa micrantha* (Lindl.) H. Bolus in *Trans. S. Afr. phil. Soc. 5*:142 (1888); *Monadenia australiensis* H. M. R. Rupp in *Aust. Orchid Rev. 11*:70, fig. A–D (1946)

An erect glabrous herb 7–40 cm. high, but usually about 20 cm. Tubers large, ovoid; roots numerous. Stem erect, leafy. Leaves erect or spreading-incurved, linear, acuminate, channelled, widened somewhat at the base, 5–15 cm. long. Spike cylindrical, densely many-flowered, 3–20 cm. long; bracts spreading-incurved, ovate, acuminate, exceeding the flowers or equalling the upper ones. Lateral sepals spreading-recurved, obliquely ovate, subacute or obtuse, greenish-white, tipped with red or red-brown, 3 mm. long. Dorsal sepal erect, galeate, oblong, obtuse, as long as the lateral sepals and coloured similarly; the spur pendent, sub-filiform, red or red-brown, about as long as the galea. Petals erect, obliquely obovate in outline, subfalcate, the posterior margin widened at the middle, obtuse, a little shorter than the sepals. Labellum porrect or deflexed, linear-oblong, obtuse, as long as the petals, yellow. Rostellum erect, the arms short, obtuse, a little exceeding the stigma. Anther strongly resupinate, the gland solitary. Ovary 5–7 mm. long.

The appearance of this South African orchid in WA, where it occurs abundantly through a large tract in the south-west, is of more than passing interest. Not only has its origin stimulated speculation, but it was at first thought to be an entirely new species. Its true identity, however, was established later in 1946, when the author visited WA and found it growing *in situ*. The orchid was plentiful in a number of districts some distance from the original Australian habitat, and provides a remarkable instance of natural seed dispersal and acclimatisation.

FLOWERING PERIOD: Sept. to Nov.

DISTRIBUTION: Albany district and Busselton, WA; also South Africa

3 *Thelymitra*

Thelymitra Forst. & Forst. f. *Charact. Gen. Plant.* 97 (1776)

Terrestrial glabrous herbs, very rarely with hairy leaves and with ovoid tubers. Leaf solitary, generally much elongated and fluted, very rarely wide, and ovate-lanceolate or terete. One or two bracts on the stem above. Flowers colourful, one or many in a terminal raceme, the sepals and petals all similar and spreading. Labellum only slightly different and spreading with the other segments. Column erect, with prominent wings which are united shortly in front at the base, produced on each side of the anther into a lateral lobe or appendage. Appendages entire, penicillate, or terminated by a tuft of hairs; wings often extended upward behind the anther to form a hood over it. Anther two-celled, erect or incumbent, its connective often produced into an appendage, entire or bifid. Pollinia two, each deeply bilobed or in two pairs, attached directly or by means of a short caudicle to the disc of the rostellum, or sometimes free from the rostellum; pollen mealy or granular.

Stigma large, borne on a plate, usually below the anther or more or less concealing it. Viscid disc well developed (except in *T. murdochae*), and situated in a slot or depression in the upper border of the stigma.

Species more than fifty, the majority in Australia, but occurring also in NZ, New Caledonia, Indonesia and the Philippines.

T. circumsepta (Plate 3)

T. circumsepta R. D. FitzG. *Aust. Orchids* 1⁴:+t. (1878); H. M. R. Rupp *Orchids N.S.W.* 5 (1943)

A robust or slender plant up to 60 cm. high. Leaf thick and leathery, channelled, prominently keeled. Flowers three to ten, rather small relatively to the size of the plant, pale coloured—greenish-white, pale to deep lilac—opening very shyly. Column wings forming a third penicillate lobe in front, tapering from a broad base to a filiform point as high as the anther, the hairs on either side of the point and behind it pale, rather sparse, in some cases forked. Lateral lobes fringed in front, then bent slightly inward and extending upward into tufts of yellow hairs. Wings forming a hood above, shortly fringed or toothed. Perianth segments all very acute.

FLOWERING PERIOD: Dec.

DISTRIBUTION: NSW, where restricted to the Blue Mountains, New England National Park and Fitzroy Falls

T. retecta (Plate 4)

T. retecta H. M. R. Rupp in *Vict. Nat.* 60:176, fig. A–D (1944); J. H. Willis *Handb. Pls Vict.* 1:351 (1962); M. J. Firth *Native Orchids Tasm.* 37 (1965)

A slender plant, 22–66 cm. high. Leaf thick, channelled, 9–20 cm. long. Stem-bracts two, leaf-like. Flowers three to twenty, 2·5–3 cm. or more in diameter; blue, purple, purplish or pink, or combining these colours. Dorsal sepal sometimes broader than any other segment. Labellum resembling the lateral petals but a little shorter. Column without any hood, very abruptly truncated behind, at or below the base of the anther, but with an erect oblong lateral wing; yellow or orange-coloured on either side, its margins minutely denticulate or crenulate except on the anterior side; the back of the column with a conspicuous dark orange band just below the summit. Lateral lobes erect, with large yellow hair-tufts. Anther with a long filiform point (apex obtuse in my specimens), scarcely as high as the column wings, and conspicuously lower than the hair-tufts.

This interesting species is more closely related to *T. ixioides* and *T. media* than to any other described species. It grows in association with *T. venosa*, and is probably a self-pollinating species. The specific epithet means 'uncovered', in allusion to the total absence of any hood above the anther.

FLOWERING PERIOD: Dec. and Jan.

DISTRIBUTION: Blue Mountains in NSW; Bidwell and Noojee in Vic.; King Island, and northern Tas.

T. ixioides (Plates 5 to 7)

T. ixioides Swartz in *K. svenska VetenskAkad. Handl.* ser. 2, 21:228, t.3 (1800); A. J. Ewart *Flor. Vict.* 329 (1931); J. M. Black *Flor. S. Aust.* ed. 2:213 (1943); H. M. R. Rupp *Orchids N.S.W.* 6 (1943); J. H. Willis *Handb. Pls Vict.* 1:349 (1962); R. Erickson *Orchids West* ed. 2:21 (1965); M. J. Firth *Native Orchids Tasm.* 35 (1965)

SYNONYMY: *T. purpurata* H. M. R. Rupp in *Proc. Linn. Soc. N.S.W.* 70:288, fig. 1 (1946)

A slender or moderately robust plant, 20–60 cm. high. Leaf linear, often exceeding 12 cm. in length, channelled. Flowers on slender pedicels, three to nine; colour variable—violet, mauve, blue, or pink and white. Perianth segments not very acute (except in small, slender specimens), elliptical; sepals more highly-coloured on the outside, 10–15 mm. long, sometimes up to 25 mm. long. Petals 20–23 mm. long. Three upper segments (dorsal sepal and petals) usually marked with darker dots. Column erect, 4–5 mm. long; wings extended upward and forward on either side of anther, ending in white, pink or pale mauve hair-tufts; between the lateral lobes three shorter, truncate denticulate ones. Central lobe much shorter than the others and usually adorned with several rows of calli on the back. Anther slightly above the stigma and rostellum, its blunt point produced a little above the bases of the lateral lobes. Pollinia concealed behind the stigma.

T. ixioides varies from a robust, many-flowered plant to one with slender stems and few flowers. The typical form is recognisable by its *Ixia*-like appearance and characteristic dotting (with deep purple), whence the common name. However, the flower is sometimes unspotted. The column may also vary in shape.

FLOWERING PERIOD: Aug. to Nov., sometimes as late as Jan.

COMMON NAME: Dotted Sun-orchid

DISTRIBUTION: Temperate parts of all Australian states; also NZ and New Caledonia

T. ixioides var. subdifformis (Plate 8)

T. ixioides var. *subdifformis* W. H. Nicholls in *Vict. Nat.* 61:207, fig. N (1945); J. H. Willis *Handb. Pls Vict.* 1:349 (1962)

A rather robust plant with large flowers, distinguished by the green sepals—in striking contrast to the spotted and lavender-coloured petals usually seen.

FLOWERING PERIOD: Oct. and Mar.

DISTRIBUTION: Vic., where known only from Portland and Blackburn

T. ixioides var. truncata (Plate 9)

T. ixioides var. *truncata* (R. S. Rogers) W. H. Nicholls in *Vict. Nat.* 60:55 (1943); J. M. Black *Flor. S. Aust.* ed. 2:213 (1943), as *T. truncata*; J. H. Willis *Handb. Pls Vict.* 1:349 (1962); M. J. Firth *Native Orchids Tasm.* 36 (1965), as *T. truncata*

SYNONYMY: *T. truncata* R. S. Rogers in *Trans. roy. Soc. S. Aust.* 41:343, t. 17 (1917)

A smaller plant than that of the typical form, distinguished by its entire and conspicuously truncate mid-lobe of the column.

Some botanists still consider this to be worthy of specific rank, but its only constant difference from typical *ixioides* lies in the shape of the column mid-lobe. Though usually associated with the latter, the variety sometimes appears in habitats remote from that of *ixioides*.

FLOWERING PERIOD: Sept. to Nov.

DISTRIBUTION: Blue Mountains, NSW; central and north-eastern Vic.; northern Tas.; Myponga, SA

T. ixioides forma merranae (Plate 9)

T. ixioides forma *merranae* (W. H. Nicholls) W. H. Nicholls *Orchids Aust.* 1: facing t. 7 (1951)

SYNONYMY: *T. merranae* W. H. Nicholls in *Vict. Nat.* 46:139, cum icon. (1929)

Intermediate between *T. ixioides* (typical) and the variety *truncata*, having the column mid-lobe widely dilated at the summit and less distinctly truncate than in the latter.

This form is rare. It was first found at Mogg's Creek near Airey's Inlet, by Miss Merran Sutherland in November 1929, and was named in her honour. Miss Sutherland collected further material in October 1931, and E. H. Homann discovered the variety at Wonthaggi in October 1930.

FLOWERING PERIOD: Oct. and Nov.

DISTRIBUTION: Blue Mountains in NSW; Mogg's Creek and Wonthaggi in Vic.

T. irregularis (Plate 10)

T. irregularis W. H. Nicholls in *Vict. Nat. 63*:126, fig. A–C (1946); J. H. Willis *Handb. Pls Vict. 1*:351 (1962)

A slender, glabrous plant, 25–40 cm. high. Leaf narrow-linear, 10–20 cm. long, rather thin, channelled, acute. Stem pink, with a tendency to angulation or nearly straight. Stem-bracts two, subulate, sheathing. Flowers two to four, on slender pedicels, each one subtended by a small sheathing bract. Ovary rather slender, terete. Perianth segments bright rose-pink, similar to those of *T. chasmogama*, expanding freely, elliptical and finely speckled with dots. Column 6–7 mm. long, the lateral wings produced upward into two golden-yellow pencillated processes as in *T. chasmogama*. Hood short and abrupt, not produced forward into a definite tube as in *T. chasmogama*; the apex bright yellow, prominently and irregularly dentate; an erect collar-like fringe of small calli immediately below. Apex of anther obtuse, showing distinctly below the lateral lobes. Anther-case dehiscing freely. Stigma small, with pink upper border.

This *Thelymitra* is clearly related to *T. chasmogama*, but may readily be determined by the very distinct structure of its column mid-lobe and the finely-dotted perianth (dots are present to some extent on the column also). The pollinary mechanism of both species is adapted for cross-pollination. The specific epithet is in allusion to the irregular margins of the column mid-lobe.

FLOWERING PERIOD: Sept. to Nov.

DISTRIBUTION: Port Jackson and Whitebridge in NSW; near-coastal regions of Vic.

T. media (Plates 11 and 12)

T. media R. Br. *Prodr. Flor. Nov. Holl.* 314 (1810); A. J. Ewart *Flor. Vict.* 329 (1931), as *T. canaliculata*; H. M. R. Rupp *Orchids N.S.W.* 6 (1943); J. H. Willis *Handb. Pls Vict. 1*: 349 (1962)

A very slender to tall robust plant, varying in height from 25 cm. to about 90 cm. Leaf linear or lanceolate, channelled, in the large specimens thick and coriaceous, strongly ribbed, 15–30 cm. long. Stem-bracts one to three, very variable in length and character, leaf-like, sheathing at the base, free or closely sheathing. Flowers few or many, varying much in size and colour, 1·5–3·5 cm. in diameter; pale blue to deep blue with purple markings, rarely white; the markings on the sepals brown, pink or green, very prominent on the reverse; perianth segments elliptical lanceolate, the sepals narrower and more acute than the petals. Column erect, 4–6 mm. long on a broad base, not hooded; lobes more or less horizontal, penicillate; mid-lobe yellow, tripartite, the outer sections truncate with denticulate margins; central part varying in height, but usually shorter than the outer sections, and formed by one to several rows of upright calli; a conspicuous collar-like band encircling the mid-lobe. Stigma very prominent. Pollinia four in two pairs, directly attached to the viscid disc.

T. media favours the valleys in undulating open forest as well as the low-lying flats in heavy forest areas. It is a somewhat variable species as the plates show. It is known with certainty from eastern Australia, but is probably absent from the west, where it has been confused with *T. canaliculata*.

FLOWERING PERIOD: Oct. to Jan., rarely earlier

COMMON NAME: Tall Sun-orchid

DISTRIBUTION: Coast and adjacent tablelands of eastern NSW; southern and eastern Vic.; Tas. Possibly in WA and New Caledonia also

T. media var. carneo-lutea (Plate 13)

T. media var. *carneo-lutea* W. H. Nicholls in *Vict. Nat. 60*:56, fig. A–D (1943); J. H. Willis *Handb. Pls Vict. 1*:350 (1962)

A slender plant, 23–40 cm. high. Leaf, stem and bracts delicately glaucous green; leaf linear, channelled, erect, 10–23 cm. long; stem-bracts one or two. Flowers two to five, 1·5–2·5 cm. wide. Perianth segments pale flesh-pink, the sepals yellow externally. Column pink; mid-lobes very prominent. Stigma prominent.

The soft glaucescence of the whole plant, combined with its dainty bicoloured flowers (pale pink and yellow) provides an unusual colour scheme in the genus *Thelymitra*.

FLOWERING PERIOD: Oct. and Nov.

DISTRIBUTION: Restricted to swampy areas at Tynong North, Vic., and in NSW

T. azurea (Plate 14)

T. azurea R. S. Rogers in *Trans. roy. Soc. S. Aust. 41*:342, t. 17 (1917); J. M. Black *Flor. S. Aust.* ed. 2:213 (1943); J. H. Willis *Handb. Pls Vict. 1*:350 (1962); M. J. Firth *Native Orchids Tasm.* 36 (1965)

A slender plant, 10–53 cm. high. Stems rather flexuose. Leaf long, narrow-linear, often filiform. Stem-bracts one or two, cauline. Flowers one to fourteen, brilliant, deep azure blue, 2·5–3 cm. in diameter. Segments of the perianth veined; the labellum narrower than other segments. Column widely winged, with purple or white hair-tufts directed upward and forward; hood between the hair-tufts purple or reddish-purple, with a wide yellow margin, deeply trilobed; the central division denticulate or emarginate, shorter than and often overlapping the adjacent ones, which have smooth or denticulate borders. Anther almost concealed behind the stigma, its point moderately long. Pollinia two, deeply bilobed, connected directly (or by a short caudicle) with the rostellum. Stigma large, ovate. Rostellum prominent.

T. azurea is closely related to *T. ixioides*, from which, however, it differs in its narrow leaf, in the deep azure colour of its flowers, and in the much deeper clefts between the middle and adjacent lobes of the hood; the absence of a crest of two or more rows of calli on the mid-lobe is a further difference from *T. ixioides*.

R. S. Rogers records *T. azurea* as being plentiful only during certain seasons in SA. During the years 1917 and 1932 it occurred 'literally in thousands in a well-frequented place, between Mount Compass and Port Elliot'.

It is possible that this species may prove to be identical with the imperfectly known *T. canaliculata*.

FLOWERING PERIOD: Oct. and Nov.

COMMON NAME: Azure Sun-orchid

DISTRIBUTION: Far west of Vic.; north-western Tas.; south-east of SA

T. murdochae (Plate 15)

T. murdochae W. H. Nicholls in *Vict. Nat.* 50:219, t. 35 (1934); J. H. Willis *Handb. Pls Vict.* 1:350 (1962)

A moderately stout plant, about 45 cm. high. Leaf not seen. Stem bracts two, subulate, lower one 10 cm. long. Flowers 2·3 cm. in diameter, numerous. Inner perianth segments purplish-blue; outer ones deep crimson, ovate-lanceolate. Column about 4 mm. high, purplish-red; lateral lobes long and narrow with a few crimson hairs at the apices; mid-lobe divided into two erect portions with shortly-combed margins. Anther with a short blunt point, situated behind upper portion of stigma. Stigma large, with a long sac-like base. Pollinia four, in two pairs.

T. murdochae was discovered on 7 Nov. 1933 near Wonthaggi, Vic., by E. H. Homann. It was growing in rather marshy country, along the Inverloch road, and only a single specimen was ever located. Superficially *T. murdochae* resembles *T. media*, also the deeper-toned forms of *T. grandiflora*, but the curious column structure, with unique sac-like stigma, is quite distinct from that of any other known species.

FLOWERING PERIOD: Nov.

DISTRIBUTION: Restricted to Wonthaggi, Vic.

T. campanulata (Plate 16)

T. campanulata Lindl. in *Edwards' bot. Reg.* 23: Swan Riv. Append. xlix (1840); R. Erickson *Orchids West* ed. 2:22 (1965)

A slender plant, from 30 cm. to over 50 cm. high. Leaf linear, channelled, about 15–25 cm. long. Stem-bracts acuminate, two or three, 2·5–4 cm. long; those within the raceme rather small and loosely sheathing. Flowers racemose, often numerous, rather small and bell-shaped. Perianth segments rather wide, concave, semi-acute, pale violet-blue or blue with prominent violet and purplish longitudinal stripes, 8–10 mm. long and 5–7 mm. wide. Column erect, stout, 3–4 mm. long; the lateral lobes extended upward and forward on each side of the anther and ending in yellow hair-tufts; between the penicillate lobes are three shorter, stout, blunt, some-times acutely-pointed lobes; the central one with a crest of several rows of calli on the back. Anther higher than the stigma, also the rostellum, its blunt apex produced between the bases of the lateral lobes. Stigma prominent, almost circular. Rostellum situated in the upper depression of stigma. Pollinia attached directly to the disc.

T. campanulata is closely related to *T. ixioides*, but is distinguishable by the very attractively striped perianth segments and more prominently lobed column. The individual flowers also are very different, being smaller and more rigid than those of typical *ixioides*. The specific epithet is in allusion to the bell-shaped appearance of the little blooms.

FLOWERING PERIOD: Sept. and Oct.

DISTRIBUTION: South-western WA

T. crinita (Plate 17)

T. crinita Lindl. in *Edwards' bot. Reg.* 23: Swan Riv. Append. xlix (1840); R. Erickson *Orchids West* ed. 2:22 (1965)

Usually a robust plant, 30–75 cm. high. Leaf ovate-lanceolate or very broad-lanceolate, 4–10 cm. long (not including the sheathing base). Flowers in a loose raceme, rather large. Perianth segments ovate-lanceolate to oblong-lanceolate, the petals narrower than

the sepals. Column 5–6 mm. high; the mid-lobe broadly two-lobed, densely cristate on the back with shortly linear papillae or calli, rising behind and well above the anther; lateral lobes horizontal, penicillate, the hair-tufts purplish and rather dense. Anther visible above the stigma and rostellum, its obtuse apex produced a little above the bases of the lateral lobes. Pollinia concealed behind stigma, and with the disc readily removed intact. Rostellum prominent.

FLOWERING PERIOD: Sept. to Dec.

COMMON NAME: Queen Orchid

DISTRIBUTION: WA, widespread from Perth to Albany

T. fasciculata (Plate 18)

T. fasciculata R. D. FitzG. *Aust. Orchids* 2³:+t. (1888); R. Erickson *Orchids West* ed. 2:22 (1965)

A slender plant, very similar to *T. ixioides*. Leaf linear, channelled, 12–15 cm. long, strongly ribbed. Flowers lilac-blue or light blue, two to five in a very loose raceme, variable in size, 1·5–3·5 cm. in diameter. Sepals and petals elliptical; the sepals strongly marked on the underside with red-brown, the petals shorter and narrower and sometimes finely veined with deeper blue. Column stout; lateral lobes inflated at the base and produced forward and upward into stout linear points, each with a compact tuft of white cilia at the end; mid-lobe prominently truncate and composed of linear glands closely packed together, like a truncated bundle of twigs. Anther produced into a point above the stigma, and remaining behind it. Stigma prominent. Pollinia easily removed without crumbling.

T. fasciculata apparently does not favour any particular habitat, for I have found it growing in dry, clayey soil (on a hillside near Walpole), as well as on the margin of a wet swamp—in black, peaty soil not far north of Manjimup. FitzGerald's specimens grew in sandy soil. Though resembling *T. ixioides* in the field, this species is related morphologically to *T. crinita*—both have densely-crested column mid-lobes.

FLOWERING PERIOD: Sept. and Oct.

DISTRIBUTION: WA, on coastal plain from Perth to Albany

T. luteocilium (Plate 19)

T. luteocilium R. D. FitzG. in *Gdnrs' Chron.* new ser. 17:495 (1882); A. J. Ewart *Flor. Vict.* 330 (1931), as *T. luteo-ciliata*; J. M. Black *Flor. S. Aust.* ed. 2:213 (1943); J. H. Willis *Handb. Pls Vict.* 1:351 (1962)

A slender, almost wholly purplish plant, 15–37 cm. high. Leaf fleshy, narrow-linear to broad-linear, channelled; lamina 10–14 cm. long. Flowers pale pink to light reddish, two to five, on slender pedicels. Stem-bracts usually two, loosely-sheathing; those subtending the floral pedicels smaller. Perianth segments oblong-lanceolate, more or less acute, 7–8 mm. long; the sepals broader than the petals. Column erect, 4–5 mm. long, the wings not very wide, hair-tufts yellow, higher than the mid-lobe; the margins at the base of the hair-tufts shortly and bluntly toothed. Mid-lobe with a convex crenate margin, not forming a very prominent hood. Anther situated above the stigma, its rather blunt triangular point projecting between the hair-tufts; dehiscing in the early bud. Stigma semi-circular, oblique; the lateral wings of column uniting to form a cup-like depression at the base. Rostellum situated in the middle of the upper stigmatic margin. Pollinia four, in two pairs, connected directly by a viscid disc.

The flowers of *T. luteocilium* are self-pollinated while in very early bud, and expand only during extremely humid weather. In its column structure, this species stands almost intermediate between *T. irregularis* and *T. chasmogama*, having neither the abbreviated and irregularly dentate mid-lobe of the former nor the entire globular one of the latter species.

FLOWERING PERIOD: Sept. to Nov.

COMMON NAME: Fringed Sun-orchid

DISTRIBUTION: Woodford, NSW; western and south-central Vic.; southern SA

T. chasmogama (Plate 20)

T. chasmogama R. S. Rogers in *Trans. roy. Soc. S. Aust. 51*:4 (1927); J. M. Black *Flor. S. Aust.* ed. 2:215 (1943); H. M. R. Rupp *Orchids N.S.W.* 6 (1943); J. H. Willis *Handb. Pls Vict. 1*:351 (1962)

A slender glabrous plant, 20–25 cm. high. Leaf narrow-linear, 8–10 cm. long, rather thin, rigid, acute, channelled. Stem pinkish, with a tendency to angulation. Stem-bracts, two subulate, sheathing. Flowers about two, on slender pedicels, each subtended by a small acute sheathing bract. Ovary rather slender, terete. Perianth segments pink, similar to those of *T. rubra*, but slightly larger, expanding freely at moderate temperatures (70°–80° F.), about 1·2–1·3 cm. long, elliptical, the inner ones much wider than the outer. Column about 6·5 mm. long, the lateral lobes carried forward and upward into two yellow penicillated processes (as in *T. luteocilium*); hood dilated, produced forward into a yellow almost globoid tube, the margins of which are entire. Apex of anther prominent and blunt, showing more or less distinctly from the side and front (below the hair-tufts); anther-case carried high above the stigma, dehiscing and leaving the pollinia attached to the viscid disc and partly hidden by the stigma. Stigma semi-oval; viscid disc in a slot on its upper border. Pollinia attached directly to the disc without a caudicle.

T. chasmogama closely resembles *T. luteocilium*, which differs in having a cylindrical, crenated mid-lobe. In *chasmogama* the structure of the pollinarium is adapted for cross-pollination, whereas in *luteocilium* self-pollination is accomplished early in the bud stage, and the flowers very rarely open; then only for a brief period. It is easily separated from *T. carnea* and *T. rubra* by the larger flowers and by the presence of penicillate lateral lobes to the column.

FLOWERING PERIOD: Sept. and Oct.

COMMON NAME: Globe-hood Sun-orchid

DISTRIBUTION: Kurri Kurri, Woodford and Killara in NSW; scattered localities in Gippsland and western Vic.; Golden Grove in SA

T. mucida (Plate 21)

T. mucida R. D. FitzG. in *Gdnrs' Chron.* new ser. *17*:495 (1882); R. Erickson *Orchids West* ed. 2:23 (1965)

A slender species, 25–52 cm. high. Leaf linear, thick, channelled, 9–18 cm. long. Flowers up to five, usually three, lilac-blue. Perianth segments oblong-lanceolate, acute, 8–10 mm. long. Column about 3 mm. long, stout, rather square; mid-lobe deeply and acutely emarginate, with entire margins, very deeply coloured, the apices yellow, covered with a hoary, thickly viscid secretion (resembling mould) which easily rubs off, leaving the dark under-colour apparent. Lateral lobes produced horizontally, the yellow hairs perpendicular, and red at base (sometimes the hairs are white). Stigma situated low down. Anther rather blunt, situated behind

and above the stigma. Pollinia extracted in a somewhat ragged condition.

I found this interesting species growing in association with *Microtis atrata* and *Prasophyllum attenuatum* at Nanarup. In the Upper King River locality it grew with myriads of *Microtis orbicularis* plants. At both places the species favoured very moist situations—often standing in water. It was never plentiful, but occurred as compact, widely separated groups of about four to eight plants. FitzGerald considered it, at least sometimes, self-fertilised, and his epithet ('mouldy') is in allusion to the viscid excretion from the column.

FLOWERING PERIOD: Sept. and Oct.

DISTRIBUTION: South coast of WA, near Albany, and sometimes as far north as Perth

T. pauciflora (Plates 22 to 25)

T. pauciflora R. Br. *Prodr. Flor. Nov. Holl.* 314 (1810); A. J. Ewart *Flor. Vict.* 331 (1931); J. M. Black *Flor. S. Aust.* ed. 2:215 (1943); H. M. R. Rupp *Orchids N.S.W.* 9 (1943); J. H. Willis *Handb. Pls Vict. 1*:347 (1962); R. Erickson *Orchids West* ed. 2:23 (1965); M. J. Firth *Native Orchids Tasm.* 34 (1965)

A plant of variable habit, but commonly slender, 10–50 cm. high. Leaf narrow linear, often thick and fleshy, channelled, very variable in length and width, the width varying from 4 mm. to 2 cm. Stem-bracts one to three, acute, sheathing. Flowers usually few, sometimes as many as fifteen, opening only in very hot weather, 1–2·3 cm. in diameter; variable in colour, from white to deepest purple, other hues being mauve, pale blue or pink. Perianth segments ovate, not very acute, the labellum smaller than the other segments. Column erect, about 5 mm. long, hooded, the hood variable in length, also in colour, but occasionally dilated at the tip (Greensborough, Vic.); hair-tufts usually white, sometimes pink, mauve or yellow, turned upward; mid-lobe cleft to varying degree in depth and width, the divisions rounded and entire.

T. pauciflora is the commonest Sun-orchid throughout Australia, and is a very variable species. It occurs in almost any type of country, but is apparently more plentiful in verdant places bordering sparsely-timbered areas. The species is self-pollinating.

FLOWERING PERIOD: Mainly Aug. to Dec., but later at higher altitudes

COMMON NAME: Slender Sun-orchid

DISTRIBUTION: All Australian states, chiefly in the more temperate coastal regions; also NZ

T. pauciflora var. holmesii (Plate 22)

T. pauciflora var. *holmesii* (W. H. Nicholls) W. H. Nicholls in *Vict. Nat. 60*:56 (1943); J. H. Willis *Handb. Pls Vict. 1*:347 (1962)

SYNONYMY: *T. holmesii* W. H. Nicholls in *Vict. Nat. 49*:263 (1933)

This variety has deep violet flowers, with the perianth often veined, the hood large and the hair-tufts yellow.

FLOWERING PERIOD: Nov. and Dec.

DISTRIBUTION: Known only from Portland, Vic.

T. pauciflora (Plate 26)

[A form in which the plant is wholly a dull sage green with purplish markings, and the flowers yellowish-white, had been named *T. pauciflora* var. *pallida* by W. H. Nicholls in *Orchidol. zeylan. 2*:159 (1935). The date was wrongly given in literature as 1934. The description was in English and hence invalid. However, this form is illustrated here to show further the variation in this species.—Ed.]

FLOWERING PERIOD: Nov.

DISTRIBUTION: Known from Bell in the Blue Mountains, NSW, and Lysterfield, Vic.

T. aristata (Plates 27 to 29)

T. aristata Lindl. *Gen. & Spec. orchid. Pls* 521 (1840); A. J. Ewart *Flor. Vict.* 330 (1931), and l.c. 331, as *T. longifolia*; J. M. Black *Flor. S. Aust.* ed. 2:215 (1943); H. M. R. Rupp *Orchids N.S.W.* 8 (1943); J. H. Willis *Handb. Pls Vict.* 1:348 (1962); R. Erickson *Orchids West* ed. 2:22 (1965); M. J. Firth *Native Orchids Tasm.* 35 (1965)

A variable species: usually slender with one to nine flowers, but sometimes up to thirty-five flowers. Plant 20–100 cm. high. Leaf sheathing towards the base, 15–25 cm. long, broad, lanceolate, somewhat flat. Flowers usually fragrant, in various shades of purple, mauve, or pink. Perianth segments elliptical, lanceolate; occasionally lightly striped, usually 1–2·3 cm. in length, readily expanding in the sunshine. Column erect, hooded, 6–8 mm. high; hair-tufts white (rarely yellow), resembling miniature scrubbing brushes; mid-lobe horizontal, cap-shaped, dilated laterally, dark-coloured towards the back, yellow towards the front (sometimes lightly hued), with a V-shaped notch in the centre, crest reaching to about the level of the hair-tufts. Anther with a short, blunt point, only the extreme base concealed by stigma. Pollinia two, deeply bilobed, attached directly to viscid disc.

Like the majority of its allies, *T. aristata* is dependent upon insects for pollination; but only in certain seasons are capsules of seed produced freely. On sunny days in spring, massed displays of the attractive racemes may be seen in some well-favoured districts. This orchid grows under marshy conditions as well as on dry ridges, often in crevices with little soil, among giant timber of the primeval forest, and often at high altitudes; no wonder it is a variable species. It is few-flowered on open plains, where the habit is more or less gregarious, and also along ridges and on the saddles in many mountain ranges; in verdant places, such as adjacent to streams, specimens are robust. An otherwise typical specimen of *T. aristata*, found in the Ararat district, Vic., by Miss Lorna Banfield (October 1933) is rare, the flowers being dotted in the same manner as those of *T. ixioides*. Material from the basalt plain at St. Albans and Keilor, Vic., is illustrated on Plate 29.

FLOWERING PERIOD: Aug. to Nov.

COMMON NAME: Scented Sun-orchid

DISTRIBUTION: Widespread in temperate parts of all Australian states; also NZ

T. aristata var. megcalyptra (Plate 30)

T. aristata var. *megcalyptra* (R. D. FitzG.) W. H. Nicholls ex J. M. Black *Flor. S. Aust.* ed. 2:215 (1943); A. J. Ewart *Flor. Vict.* 328 (1931), as *T. megcalyptra*; H. M. R. Rupp *Orchids N.S.W.* 8 (1943). in note under *T. aristata*; J. H. Willis *Handb. Pls Vict.* 1:348 (1962)

SYNONYMY: *T. megcalyptra* R. D. FitzG. *Aust. Orchids* 1⁵:+t. (1879)

A form with unusually large and inflated column hood; but all gradations are found, even within a small area, between this condition and the typical Tas. form.

This plate and the preceding three depict something of the species' versatility in its wide range from wet mountain forests (with rainfall of 60 inches) to mallee sandhills (rainfall 11 inches at Hattah, Vic.).

The differences which separate these populations from those of *T. nuda*, *T. pauciflora* and *T. longifolia* are by no means clear-cut, and seem often to be rather trifling. Future more detailed research may prove that all are but variants of a single extremely variable species, in which case the first validly published name of *T. longifolia* Forst. & Forst.f. (of NZ) must be restored for Australian representatives of the complex.

FLOWERING PERIOD: Oct. and Nov.

DISTRIBUTION: Tamworth, Wallerawang, and Mount Kaputar in NSW; western Vic.; Monarto South in SA

T. nuda (Plates 31 and 32)

T. nuda R. Br. *Prodr. Flor. Nov. Holl.* 314 (1810); H. M. R. Rupp *Orchids N.S.W.* 9 (1943); J. H. Willis *Handb. Pls Vict.* 1:348 (1962); R. Erickson *Orchids West* ed. 2:23 (1965); M. J. Firth *Native Orchids Tasm.* 35 (1965)

A rather slender plant 25–60 cm. high. Leaf long, deeply and often widely channelled. Stem-bracts two or three, loosely sheathing, about 5 cm. long, longer towards the base; floral bracts smaller, acuminate. Flowers often numerous, smaller than in *T. aristata*; colour blue, pink or mauve. Perianth segments acute. Column erect about 5 mm. high, hooded; hair-tufts white, pink or mauve, erect and terminal (not scrubbing-brush shaped as in *T. aristata*); mid-lobe yellow towards the tip, emarginate, smooth and bare. Anther point showing at the base of the mid-lobe. Stigma prominent, with the upper border prominently cleft. Rostellum prominent. Pollinia four in two pairs, readily removed with the disc on the point of a needle.

FLOWERING PERIOD: Aug. to Nov.

COMMON NAME: Plain Sun-orchid

DISTRIBUTION: Widespread but uncommon: Burleigh Heads, Qld; eastern NSW; a few scattered localities in Vic. and Tas.; Albany, WA

T. grandiflora (Plates 33 and 34)

T. grandiflora R. D. FitzG. in *Gdnrs' Chron.* new ser. 17:495 (1882); A. J. Ewart *Flor. Vict.* 331 (1931); J. M. Black *Flor. S. Aust.* ed. 2:215 (1943); J. H. Willis *Handb. Pls Vict.* 1:347 (1962); M. J. Firth *Native Orchids Tasm.* 34 (1965)

Often a very robust plant, 35–75 cm. high. Leaf widely-lanceolate, sheathing for several inches at the base, thick, sometimes spotted, sometimes enclosing base of largest bract. Stem-bracts three or four, large, acute, lower ones leafy. Flowers 3–3·5 cm. in diameter, purple-blue or pale blue, usually numerous in a long raceme. Perianth segments rather acute, concave, oblong-lanceolate, 13–20 mm. long, the labellum narrower than the other segments. Column erect, 6–7 mm. high, hooded; wings wide and inflated, hair-tufts white or yellow; mid-lobe arched, bifid, falcate in profile, the segments deeply denticulate, the crest sometimes higher than the hair-tufts. Anther almost wholly concealed behind the stigma. Pollinia in two pairs, lamellar, connected directly to the viscid disc, no caudicle. Stigma ovate, situated unusually low down in the concavity of the column below the middle. Rostellum prominent, viscid.

FLOWERING PERIOD: Oct. and Nov.

COMMON NAME: Great Sun-orchid

DISTRIBUTION: Southern Vic.; north-coastal districts and Lenah Valley, Tas.; south-eastern SA

T. epipactoides (Plate 35)

T. epipactoides F. Muell. *Fragm. Phyt. Aust.* 5:174 (1866); A. J. Ewart *Flor. Vict.* 330 (1931); J. M. Black *Flor. S. Aust.* ed. 2:213 (1943); J. H. Willis *Handb. Pls Vict.* 1:347 (1962)

A robust plant, 20–50 cm. high. Leaf long, fleshy, lanceolate, sheathing with a tubular base. Stem-bracts one or two, leafy. Flowers six to twenty, rather large, on shortish pedicels, variously coloured, often greenish-blue with a metallic lustre, each subtended by a long, acute bract 2–3 cm. long. Perianth segments ovate-lanceolate, 10–15 mm. long. Lateral appendages of column short and broad, the cilia upturned; mid-lobe tripartite; central lobe incurved, truncate, irregularly denticulate at the top; lateral portions of mid-lobe denticulate with oblique apices, inturned and often interlocking. Anther almost concealed behind the stigma. Stigma situated in the cavity at base of column.

T. epipactoides is a most unusual and beautiful sun-orchid. In general aspect it resembles very closely *T. grandiflora*, but usually the flowers are differently coloured. Structurally its closest ally is *T. ixioides*. In the Pomonal area, at the eastern foot of the Grampians, Vic., it favours the sandy 'wildflower flats'. Though comparatively rare, here it often attains its maximum size.

FLOWERING PERIOD: Sept. to Nov.

COMMON NAME: Metallic Sun-orchid

DISTRIBUTION: Lawloit, Grampians, and a few coastal heaths in Vic.; south-eastern SA

T. villosa (Plate 36)

T. villosa Lindl. in *Edwards' bot. Reg.* 23: Swan Riv. Append. xlix, t. 8 fig. C, C¹ (1840); R. Erickson *Orchids West* ed. 2:22 (1965)

A more or less stout species, usually over 23 cm. and occasionally 60 cm. high. Leaf ovate-obovate or ovate-oblong, sometimes rather small, but commonly 9–10 cm. long; villous on both sides, especially underneath, and also on the sheath, the rest of the plant (including the empty sheathing bracts) quite glabrous. Flowers rather large, yellow, dotted with red-brown; raceme loose. Sepals and petals acute, usually about 2 cm. long. Column-wings produced behind and above the anther into a broad hood; the extreme lateral lobes densely cristate or fringed and curved forward, orange-yellow; the mid-lobe prominent, broad and entire, or shortly undulate or fringed, often gland-covered on the back towards the apex, and also with a crest of small calli inside at the base.

I observed this species growing in a natural state in Jarrah country near York (only three specimens were seen); but beyond, in the open country, specimens occurred in fair numbers—these, however, had very small leaves.

FLOWERING PERIOD: Aug. to Oct.

COMMON NAME: Custard Orchid

DISTRIBUTION: Common throughout south-western WA

T. sargentii (Plate 37)

T. sargentii R. S. Rogers in *Trans. roy. Soc. S. Aust.* 54:41 (1930); R. Erickson *Orchids West* ed. 2:22 (1965)

A glabrous, slender to moderately robust plant, reaching a height of 45 cm. Sheath at the base of the stem 3–6 cm. long, loose, cylindrical, membranous. Leaf lanceolate, acuminate, sheathing at the base, reaching beyond middle of scape. Cauline bracts two or three, subulate or acuminate, vaginate at the base. Raceme loose, multi-flowered, 9–14 cm. long. Flowers ten to fourteen, rather

large for the genus, yellow with brown blotches or dots, resembling those of *T. fusco-lutea*. Ovary subconical, about 1 cm. long, on a slender pedicel about 1·3 cm. long. Perianth segments elliptical, subacute, spreading or suberect, about 1·6 cm. long and 0·5 cm. wide. Column elongated, erect, incurved at the apex, about 8 mm. long, yellow, spotted, rather widely winged, produced high above the anther, trilobed at the apex; mid-lobe incurved, not crested on the back, deeply emarginate, the border otherwise entire; lateral lobes ascending, densely papillose-bearded, higher than the middle of the lobe. Anther with a recurved mucro, scarcely higher than the middle of the column. Stigma shield-like, hardly reaching the level of middle of anther.

T. sargentii is more closely allied to *T. villosa* than to other species. Both have the flowers similarly coloured, and each possesses a broad lanceolate basal leaf; but in the latter the leaf is covered with long, soft hairs, while the lobes of the column are very dissimilar.

My first specimens of this orchid were found early in October 1946, growing in association with Feather-myrtles (*Verticordia* spp.) close to Mount Tampia, between Arrowsmith and Narembeen; these were exceptionally fine examples. Other orchids in the vicinity were *T. campanulata* and *Caladenia gemmata*, both in limited numbers. Two years later half a dozen much less robust specimens were observed along the highway between Narembeen and Tandagin, the plants favouring lower levels.

FLOWERING PERIOD: Oct. and Nov.

DISTRIBUTION: Eastern wheatbelt of south-western WA, in the 15 to 20 inch rainfall belt

T. fusco-lutea (Plate 38)

T. fusco-lutea R. Br. *Prodr. Flor. Nov. Holl.* 315 (1810); A. J. Ewart *Flor. Vict.* 328 (1931); J. M. Black *Flor. S. Aust.* ed. 2:215 (1943); J. H. Willis *Handb. Pls Vict.* 1:354 (1962); R. Erickson *Orchids West* ed. 2:23 (1965)

A stout to moderately slender plant, 15–45 cm. high. Stem-bracts one or two, loosely sheathing, the lower about 5 cm. long. Leaf large, about 9 cm. long and 4 cm. wide, ovate-lanceolate to oblong-lanceolate, sheathing at the base. Flowers two or more, rarely exceeding ten, in a loose raceme, yellow or yellowish-green, with dark brown or red-brown spots and blotches, 2·5–3 cm. in diameter, on rather long pedicels, subtended by small acute or acuminate bracts. Perianth segments broad, oblong-lanceolate, acute or shortly acuminate. Column 7–8 mm. long, the wings conspicuous, forming a broad mantle on both sides of the club-shaped dorsal appendage; lateral lobes ill-defined; margins of wings each with a long linear and irregularly dentate fringe, subtending a dense mass (or short crest) of papillate glands. Anther with a long finger-like process, erect or slightly recurved, only its base hidden behind the stigma. Stigma small, situated in the concavity at the base of the column-wings. Rostellum circular, in the upper border of the stigma. Tubers large, obovate.

T. fusco-lutea, is doubtless of western origin, and has migrated eastward. In the well-watered south-west corner of WA it is often frequent. Two unusual specimens from Mrs E. Scouler of Yarloop, received 9 Jan. 1951, had five to eight flowers, their column bases purple, the fringed mantles pure white, and the dorsal crest linear, with a dense mass of pure white glands.

In SA and Vic. this is an uncommon orchid, although recorded as plentiful in the Mount Lofty Range. Eastward from Melbourne it is rarely seen, the most easterly habitat being Wilsons Promontory. A. B. Braine found *T. fusco-lutea* in the Grampians, Vic., 'favouring yellow clayey soil', while in the Jan Juc area, Vic., I found it growing in poor gravelly soil. Sand and weathered granite are other forma-tions on which it grows. Vic. specimens (with the exception of a few found at Pomonal and French Island) are stunted and small-flowered in comparison with WA populations.

Abnormal flowers of *T. fusco-lutea* have been found in Vic. on several occasions by W. L. Williams near the Terraces, Grampians. The abnormality is a curved ligulate process, ascending in front of the column and apically toothed as on the column wings. Viewed from in front, the column hood and abnormal process 'remind the observer of an upper and lower jaw plentifully supplied with dentures'. Thus the column entrance is barred to intruders, much as in *T. circumsepta*.

FLOWERING PERIOD: Sept. to Jan.

COMMON NAME: Blotched Sun-orchid or Leopard Orchid

DISTRIBUTION: Southern Vic. as far east as Wilsons Promontory; south-eastern SA; south-western WA

T. flexuosa (Plate 39)

T. flexuosa Endl. in Endl. & Fenzl *Nov. Stirp.* 23 (1839); A. J. Ewart *Flor. Vict.* 331 (1931); J. M. Black *Flor. S. Aust.* ed. 2:216 (1943); H. M. R. Rupp *Orchids N.S.W.* 9 (1943); J. H. Willis *Handb. Pls Vict.* 1:354 (1962); R. Erickson *Orchids West* ed. 2:25 (1965); M. J. Firth *Native Orchids Tasm.* 37 (1965)

A very slender plant 15–30 cm. high. Leaf terete, clasping below, 5–10 cm. long. Stem pinkish, very wiry, zigzagging several times; stem-bracts two, situated at points of flexion. Flowers one to three, 1–1·5 cm. in diameter, pale yellow, opening only on hot days. Perianth segments obtuse; sepals broad-ovate; petals ovate, the labellum segment shorter and narrower than the others. Column erect, about 4·5 mm. high, not hooded; wings short and broad, rounded and dentate or sub-entire; mid-lobe sometimes slightly notched, all much shorter than the anther. Anther situated entirely above the stigma, apex produced into a large oblong, fleshy, downy process greatly exceeding the lateral lobes. Pollinia four, in two pairs, directly connected with the viscid disc. Stigma somewhat rectangular.

T. flexuosa favours heathland scrubs and damp, grassy places, usually in tufts of several plants or singly in scattered communities. I saw it in great abundance in WA, where at Yarloop it fringed swamps, often growing in several inches of water. These plants, and the flowers themselves, were much larger than one is accustomed to see in Vic. or Tas.

A common species throughout its range from Perth, WA to Orbost, Vic., but the only record available for NSW is based upon a single specimen collected at the head of the Brunswick River by Mrs P. Messmer in August 1936, and some doubt attaches to the identity of this particular sample.

FLOWERING PERIOD: Sept. to Jan.

COMMON NAME: Twisted Sun-orchid

DISTRIBUTION: North coast of NSW; southern Vic.; northern Tas. and Bass Strait islands; south-eastern SA; coastal plain of south-western WA

T. urnalis (Plate 40)

T. urnalis R. D. FitzG. in *Gdnrs' Chron.* new ser. *17*:495 (1882); J. M. Black *Flor. S. Aust.* ed. 2:216 (1943)

A slender plant 10–30 cm. high. Leaf long, linear, channelled, often reaching to base of inflorescence. Flowers small, one or two, yellow inside, the sepals dark red-brown on the outside. Perianth segments

rather wide, acute, about 6 mm. long, opening only in warm sun-shine. Column about 6 mm. long, not hooded, but wings produced above the anther; the lateral lobes not ciliate but broad, horizontal and rugose, the lobe between them undulate or almost denticulate; wings united in front of the column at the base and sometimes produced upward in the form of a central spur in front of the stigma, giving the column an urn-like appearance. Anther two-celled, obtuse, slightly emarginate, protruding above the stigma, after dehiscence carried upward with the growth of the column, leaving the pollinia attached to the rostellum. Pollinia four, in two pairs, attached directly to the viscid disc and easily removed on a needle.

Dr R. S. Rogers found specimens growing alongside those of *T. antennifera* and *T. rubra*. The flowers corresponded in every respect to FitzGerald's description and illustration, except that the tooth in front of the column was not always present. Plants were not numerous, and it is possible that *T. urnalis* may be a natural hybrid between the two species mentioned. The specific epithet refers to its urn-like column.

About 1926 E. Nubling collected near Port Jackson, NSW, an orchid closely resembling FitzGerald's delineation of *T. urnalis*. Drawings were made, but unfortunately no specimen was retained for reference. Workers near Sydney should search the Hawkesbury sandstone areas for a re-occurrence of this plant, which may prove to be a new record for that state.

FLOWERING PERIOD: Sept. and Oct.

DISTRIBUTION: Mount Lofty Range and Bugle Range, SA

T. tigrina (Plate 40)

T. tigrina R. Br. *Prodr. Flor. Nov. Holl.* 315 (1810); R. Erickson *Orchids West* ed. 2:25 (1965)

A very slender plant 25–30 cm. high. Leaf very narrow, channelled. Flowers small, two to four, yellow with a few brown blotches. Perianth segments about 8 mm. long. Column wings broad, pro-duced behind and above the anther; the extreme lateral lobes oblong, densely papillose-bearded, but without the white cilia of the penicillate species; the three mid-lobes broader, shorter and fringed with calli.

In the solitary specimen I have seen of this rare species it was not possible to distinguish the three middle lobes referred to by Bentham. The figure of the column given here is exactly as I saw it.

R. S. Rogers' description of the floral details, in *Trans. roy. Soc. S. Aust.* 44:333 (1920), is not applicable to *T. tigrina* but rather to *T. cucullata*.

FLOWERING PERIOD: Nov. and Dec.

DISTRIBUTION: Between Albany and Perth, WA

T. carnea (Plate 41)

T. carnea R. Br. *Prodr. Flor. Nov. Holl.* 314 (1810); A. J. Ewart *Flor. Vict.* 332 (1931), as *T. elizabethae*; H. M. R. Rupp *Orchids N.S.W.* 9 (1943); J. M. Black *Flor. S. Aust.* ed. 2:256 (1948); J. H. Willis *Handb. Pls Vict.* 1:354 (1962); R. Erickson *Orchids West* ed. 2:24 (1965); M. J. Firth *Native Orchids Tasm.* 40 (1965)

SYNONYMY: *T. elizabethae* F. Muell. in *Vict. Nat.* 7:116 (1890)

A very slender plant, 12–35 cm. high. Stems often markedly flexuose. Leaf reddish at base, linear-terete, erect, slightly channelled, the lamina 10–15 cm. long. Stem-bracts usually two, subulate, closely sheathing, the lowest one longest, 1–1·5 cm. long. Flowers one to four, very small, 1–1·5 cm. in diameter, bright pink, salmon-pink or creamy-white; expanding only during hot, humid weather, and probably self-pollinated. Ovary rather long. Sepals and petals oval-elliptical or oblong, more or less obtuse. Sepals darker in colour than petals. Column about 4 mm. long, pinkish or pale greenish, with a yellow trilobed apex; the mid-lobe short, but longer than in *T. rubra*, imperfectly hooded, arched slightly; lateral lobes more or less denticulate, smooth on the outside, about as high as the anther or a little shorter than it. Anther prominent, only its base concealed behind the stigma, very broad and obtuse.

In general aspect *T. carnea* resembles *T. flexuosa*, but its closest ally is *T. rubra*. From *T. flexuosa* it differs in the red or pinkish perianth and much longer lateral lobes to the column; from *T. rubra* in the less sturdy habit and non-glandular lateral lobes. Dehiscence of the anther takes place during the early bud stage in these three species. *T. carnea* had long been known in Vic., and latterly in NSW, as *T. elizabethae*; but *T. carnea* is correctly interpreted by FitzGerald in *Aust. Orchids* 1⁶:+t. (1880). It is not usually a common orchid, though such a small flower, when the perianth is closed, is difficult to discern amongst grass.

FLOWERING PERIOD: Sept. to Nov.

COMMON NAME: Pink Sun-orchid or Tiny Sun-orchid

DISTRIBUTION: Coastal NSW; southern Vic.; northern and eastern Tas.; Mount Lofty Ranges, SA; south-western WA

T. rubra (Plate 42)

T. rubra R. D. FitzG. in *Gdnrs' Chron.* new ser. *17*:495 (1882); A. J. Ewart *Flor. Vict.* 332 (1931), as *T. carnea*; H. M. R. Rupp *Orchids N.S.W.* 9 (1943), the var. *magnanthera* only; J. M. Black *Flor. S. Aust.* ed. 2:256 (1948); J. H. Willis *Handb. Pls Vict.* 1:353 (1962); M. J. Firth *Native Orchids Tasm.* 39 (1965)

A slender plant, but more robust than *T. carnea*, 15–50 cm. high. Stem often flexuose, deep purplish or crimson. Stem-bracts two or three, the lower one longest and about 7 cm. long, subulate, closely sheathing. Leaf terete or linear-lanceolate, channelled; the lamina 12–21 cm. long, purplish at base. Flowers one to four, ruby-red, salmon or pale pink, rarely pale yellow with reddish markings, 1·5–1·8 cm. in diameter, expanding only in bright sunlight. Ovary comparatively long. Sepals and petals oval-elliptical or elliptical, obtuse. Column about 5 mm. long, not hooded, highly coloured—pink, mauve, brown, yellow and orange; crest orange-yellow; mid-lobe shortly truncate, its margins denticulate; lateral lobes yellow, oblong, hardly erect, normally longer than anther but often very short and broad, covered with rugulose glands, the margins markedly denticulate. Anther stout, very prominent with an obtuse apex, its lower margin hidden behind the upper part of the stigma, its base rather wide.

T. rubra is chiefly a self-pollinated species, and often abundant, growing on heathlands or on low hills, usually in tufts of several plants, as observed by FitzGerald. The tallest and finest examples of *T. rubra* I had ever seen were growing on undisturbed marshy land, beneath low-growing eucalypts around an old homestead at Ocean Grove, Vic. This species has been much confused with the closely-related *T. carnea*, which has smaller paler flowers and non-glandular column lobes. FitzGerald suggested that they may be forms of a single species.

FLOWERING PERIOD: Sept. to Dec., rarely as early as Aug.

COMMON NAME: Salmon Sun-orchid or Pink Sun-orchid

DISTRIBUTION: Central coast of NSW; Vic.; northern and eastern Tas., and King Island; southern and south-eastern SA

T. macmillanii (Plate 43)

T. macmillanii F. Muell. *Fragm. Phyt. Aust.* 5:93 (1865); A. J. Ewart *Flor. Vict.* 333 (1931); J. M. Black *Flor. S. Aust.* ed. 2:216 (1943); J. H. Willis *Handb. Pls Vict.* 1:353 (1962); R. Erickson *Orchids West* ed. 2:24 (1965); M. J. Firth *Native Orchids Tasm.* 39 (1965)

A very slender plant varying in height, 10–20 cm. Stem wiry, flexuose. Leaf erect, narrow-linear, channelled. Flowers one to six, very variable in colour, salmon-pink to crimson, 2–4·5 cm. in diameter, usually expanding freely. Perianth segments elliptical to oblong-elliptical. Column brightly hued, erect, no dorsal crest, 6–7 mm. high, the wings produced laterally into two tall, erect, lanceolate-oblong yellow, red or bi-coloured lobes with irregularly crenulate to intensely rugulose margins but more or less smooth surfaces; not produced behind the anther, where they form a deep sinus. Anther prominent, pubescent, produced forward and above the stigma, apex blunt. Stigma somewhat small, a prominent rostellum situated in the upper depression.

Flowers of *T. macmillanii* vary considerably in different localities according to soil and climatic conditions. Usually they are about 2 cm. in diameter, and salmon-red. One unusual colour combination was salmon-pink on a bright yellow ground, the golden hue showing here and there as brilliant veins. Probably the finest example of this species ever collected was a three-flowered specimen that I received from Maldon, central Vic. in October 1931; its unusually large blooms were rose-pink tipped with salmon, and the columns were purplish.

T. macmillanii diffuses a faint though rare fragrance, somewhat like that of its close ally *T. antennifera*, and the specific name honours Thomas Macmillan of Melbourne (its discoverer, and a keen horticulturist).

FLOWERING PERIOD: Sept. and Oct.

COMMON NAME: Crimson Sun-orchid or Salmon Sun-orchid

DISTRIBUTION: Western and central Vic.; Tas.; south-eastern SA; south-western WA; but nowhere common

T. mackibbinii (Plate 44)

T. mackibbinii F. Muell. in *Chem. & Drugg. Lond. Australas. Suppl.* 42:44 (1881); J. H. Willis *Handb. Pls Vict.* 1:353 (1962)

SYNONYMY: *T. chisholmii* W. H. Nicholls in *Vict. Nat.* 58:98, cum icon. (1941)

A slender purplish plant 15–18 cm. high. Leaf dark green, 7–9 cm. long, the lamina lanceolate or linear, wide at the immediate base, narrowing upward, sometimes very narrow-linear, channelled, the margins inflexed, contracted below to a tubular sheathing base. Stem-bracts one or two, closely sheathing, 1·5–4 cm. long. Flowers one to three, large, 2·5–3 cm. in diameter; violet, or more rarely pink. Perianth segments prominently striped, elliptic-lanceolate, acute; sepals usually purplish, violet towards the base; petals typically violet with purplish tips, slightly shorter and narrower than the sepals. Column 5–7 mm. long, including the upraised lobes; not hooded, deep violet, the upper margins yellow; lateral lobes fleshy, deep golden-yellow, ovoid, flat, pedicellate, about 2 mm. long, their margins glandular-papillate, the outer surface also somewhat rugulose with granulations and (or) papillae, at first in an erect position on both sides and above the anther. Anther large with a broad, rounded apex, almost as broad as long, yellow with some rufous markings, situated well above and to the rear of stigma, its lower margin adnate to the column roof. Anther dehiscing readily when flower expands widely, then relaxing to a position between the now embracing column wings. Stigma small, viscid, circular, oblique, situated in the depression formed at base of column by the lower angles of the wings. Pollinia four, in two pairs, pure white, powdery, connected directly with a prominent viscid disc.

Superficially this orchid may be mistaken for *T. aristata*, but its affinities are with the pink-flowered *T. rubra* and *T. macmillanii*, differing from the former in its freely-expanding larger flowers and much longer papillate lateral lobes, and from the latter species in having shorter lobes that bear crowded finger-like papillae (not obtuse crenulations). *T. mackibbinii* is typically violet-flowered, striped, and broader in leaf than *T. macmillanii*, which never seems to have purplish forms; but both vary considerably in colour. F. Mueller, in attributing it also to SA and WA, was doubtless confusing this very localised Victorian plant with some other species—probably *T. macmillanii*. J. N. McKibbin's original specimens came from 'quartz gravel on hills along the Upper Loddon River', Vic. Recent collections were in Ironbark country amongst shrubs of *Grevillea alpina*; but the habitat of a bright pink form from Port Elliot, SA, is unknown.

FLOWERING PERIOD: Sept. to Nov.

DISTRIBUTION: Maryborough and Smythesdale districts, Vic.; Port Elliot, SA; but rare

T. antennifera (Plate 45)

T. antennifera (Gunn ex Lindl.) Hook. f. *Flor. Tasm.* 2:4, t. 101 fig. A (1858); A. J. Ewart *Flor. Vict.* 332 (1931); J. M. Black *Flor. S. Aust.* ed. 2:216 (1943); R. Erickson *Orchids West* ed. 2:24 (1965); M. J. Firth *Native Orchids Tasm.* 37 (1965)

SYNONYMY: *Macdonaldia antennifera* Gunn ex Lindl. in *Edwards' bot. Reg. 23*: Swan Riv. Append. l, t. 9, fig. C, C¹ (1840)

A slender plant 12–25 cm. high; rather similar to *T. flexuosa*, but less flexuose and bearing larger flowers. Leaf terete, 8–12 cm. long, channelled. Stem pinkish, wiry and zigzagging; stem-bracts two, situated at angles of flexion. Flowers one to three, pale to deep yellow, opening freely, rose-scented in mass. Perianth segments yellow on the inside, the sepals each with a wide reddish-brown stripe externally, elliptical or oblong-elliptical, 13–20 mm. long. Column erect, and broadly winged, not hooded, the wings produced laterally into two erect, dark-brown, spathulate and usually bilobed appendages, much longer than anther; the part between the appendages not produced behind the anther. Anther two-celled, situated above the stigma, its apex produced into a thickened broad, blunt pubescent process. Stigma transversely oval, situated in the basal concavity of the column; rostellum conspicuous in its upper border. Pollinia two, bilobed, attached directly or by a very short caudicle to the viscid disc.

A common species throughout its wide range, favouring open forest country and heathland scrubs. The popular name is often applied in allusion to the pair of dark column appendages, contrasting strongly with the yellowish perianth. Dr Rogers records a form with red flowers, collected by E. E. Pescott near the Grampians, Vic. WA examples sometimes attain large size, with flowers up to 4 cm. wide. Lindley reports that natives of Augusta, WA, ate the bulbs.

FLOWERING PERIOD: Aug. to Dec.

COMMON NAME: Rabbit-ears or Lemon Orchid

DISTRIBUTION: South-western NSW; western and central Vic., also Wilsons Promontory; northern Tas.; SA; south-western WA

T. matthewsii (Plate 46)

T. matthewsii Cheeseman in *Trans. N.Z. Inst.* 43:177 (1910); A. J.

Ewart *Flor. Vict.* 329 (1931), as *T. daltonii*; J. H. Willis *Handb. Pls Vict. 1*:352 (1962); R. Erickson *Orchids West* ed. 2: 25 (1965)

SYNONYMY: *T. daltonii* R. S. Rogers in *Trans. roy. Soc. S. Aust. 54*:42 (1930)

A slender plant 10–22 cm. high. Leaf glabrous, channelled, longitudinally ribbed, subacute, sheathing at the base of the scape; lamina linear, spiral, widely-dilated below. Stem slender, glabrous, erect, with a subulate clasping bract 2·5 cm. long about the middle. Flower single, expanding in hot sunny weather, subtended by a short subacute sheathing bract 2 cm. long. Ovary greenish, obconical, slender, about 1·2 cm. long. Sepals yellowish-green with about seven to nine conspicuous rather wide, dark purplish, longitudinal stripes, ovate-elliptical or elliptic-lanceolate, subacute, concave, about 1 cm. long and 4·5–5 mm. wide; dorsal sepal broader than the lateral ones. Petals shorter and of thinner texture than the sepals, labellum somewhat smaller, rich purple-mauve with prominent stripes as in the sepals. Column rather stout, purplish, about 6 mm. high to apex of anther; lateral lobes bright yellow, broadly elliptical or orbicular in outline, plano-convex, shortly stipitate, erect behind the anther, 1–1·5 cm. long; mid-lobe much shorter and rudimentary, without any dorsal crest, the dorsal margin crowned with grape-like papillae. Anther yellow, incumbent, very conspicuous, oblong or oblong-cuneate, truncate or very obtuse at the apex, bilocular. Stigma prominent, situated just below the anther, orbicular or transversely oval, almost pedicellate, concave, disc-like. A self-pollinating species.

My figures were drawn from specimens collected by A. B. Braine at Pomonal, Vic., where they favoured heavy scrub and were usually well hidden. Mr Braine remarked: 'A blazing hot day late in September or early October gives the best chance of finding specimens, the perianth then being well-expanded to the sun's rays.' The solitary WA specimen from near Armadale has been carefully examined by the author; it is in excellent condition, and constitutes a remarkably isolated record (Sept. 1950).

FLOWERING PERIOD: Sept. and Oct.

COMMON NAME: Spiral Sun-orchid

DISTRIBUTION: South-western and far eastern Vic.; Armadale, WA; also NZ

T. spiralis (Plate 47)

T. spiralis (Lindl.) R. S. Rogers in *Trans. roy. Soc. S. Aust.* 54:43 (1930); R. Erickson *Orchids West* ed. 2:24 (1965)

SYNONYMY: *Macdonaldia spiralis* Lindl. in *Edwards' bot. Reg. 23*: Swan Riv. Append. l (1840)

Typically a slender plant 15–30 cm. high. Leaf with a villous sheath, the lamina usually glabrous, linear, much dilated at the base and often spirally twisted. Stem quite glabrous, erect, a subulate bract near the middle. Flowers one to three, purple or purplish-blue, comparatively small. Perianth segments ovate-lanceolate or elliptical, the labellum segment smaller than the rest, sepals light-coloured and blotched on the underside. Column rather stout, purplish, lateral lobes erect and very prominent, yellow, hatchet-shaped, obtuse, connected by a small obsolete crest behind the anther. Anther conspicuous, bright yellow, more or less incumbent, oblong or oblong-cuneate, very obtuse at the apex, bilocular. Stigma pedicellate, situated just below the anther, more or less prominent, disc-like.

T. spiralis is a widely distributed but rather infrequent species, endemic in WA. It is closely related to *T. matthewsii*, a species which invariably has a single deep violet-blue flower. *T. variegata* is also a close ally, differing in its iridescent sheen and narrowly oblong-elliptic column appendages. Both species may often be observed in the same locality, growing on sandy soil among rushes or grass tussocks, but B. T. Goadby noted (1933) that *T. spiralis* preferred wet clay flats, *T. variegata* the sandy hills.

FLOWERING PERIOD: Aug. to Dec.

DISTRIBUTION: South-western WA

T. spiralis var. **punctata** (Plate 47)

T. spiralis var. *punctata* W. H. Nicholls in *Vict. Nat.* 66:55, fig. F (1949); R. Erickson *Orchids West* ed. 2:25 (1965)

Slender plant 20–25 cm. high. Flowers one or two, large, somewhat purple; perianth segments narrow-lanceolate, copiously marked with spots along the nerves.

DISTRIBUTION: Yarloop, WA

T. spiralis var. **scoulerae** (Plate 47)

T. spiralis var. *scoulerae* W. H. Nicholls in *Vict. Nat.* 66:55, fig. C (1949); R. Erickson *Orchids West* ed. 2:25 (1965)

Slender plant 25–30 cm. high. Flowers two, large; perianth segments purple, broadly ovate, lanceolate, flaccid.

FLOWERING PERIOD: Sept. and Oct.

DISTRIBUTION: Yarloop and Drake Brook, WA

T. spiralis var. **pulchella** (Plate 47)

T. spiralis var. *pulchella* W. H. Nicholls in *Vict. Nat.* 66:56, fig. D, E (1949); R. Erickson *Orchids West* ed. 2:25 (1965)

Very slender plant 15–20 cm. high. Flower variable in size; perianth segments pink, spotted (chiefly on the sepals), more or less flaccid. Lateral lobes of column almost orbicular, orange.

FLOWERING PERIOD: Aug.

DISTRIBUTION: Bolgart, WA

T. spiralis var. **pallida** (Plate 47)

T. spiralis var. *pallida* W. H. Nicholls in *Vict. Nat.* 66:55, fig. B (1949); R. Erickson *Orchids West* ed. 2:25 (1965)

Tall, slender plant 30–35 cm. high. Flowers one or two, large, star-like; perianth segments lanceolate, acute; sepals brownish-green and blotched; petals pale pink.

DISTRIBUTION: Yarloop, WA

T. variegata (Plate 48)

T. variegata (Lindl.) Lindl. ex Benth. *Flor. aust.* 6:323 (1873) pro parte; R. Erickson *Orchids West* ed. 2:24 (1965)

SYNONYMY: *Macdonaldia variegata* Lindl. in *Edwards' bot. Reg. 23*: Swan Riv. Append. l (1840)

A slender plant 30–40 cm. high. Leaf linear, channelled, much dilated at the base, often with a pubescent sheath, erect and usually undulate, occasionally spiral. Flowers two or three, about 4 cm. in diameter. Sepals and petals lanceolate, shortly acuminate, dark-coloured and variegated in shades of violet, purple, red and yellow, the whole giving a brilliantly iridescent effect. Column about 7 mm. long to the anther; lateral wings broad and brilliantly coloured, not produced behind the anther, but with erect lateral lobes 5–6 mm. long, which are narrowly oblong-elliptic, obtuse and connected by a semi-circular crest behind the anther. Anther cells short, the connective produced into a broad obtuse appendage as long as the lateral lobes of the column. Stigma small, pedicellate, situated just below the anther.

Closely allied to *T. spiralis* and previously confused with it, but the ellipsoid lateral lobes and connective are distinguishing features. *T. variegata* is as splendid among our Sun-orchids as the Blue Tinsel Lily (*Calectasia cyanea*) is among our lilies. The rich iridescent sheen of both orchid and lily must be seen to be appreciated.

FLOWERING PERIOD: Aug. to Dec.

COMMON NAME: Queen of Sheba

DISTRIBUTION: Coastal plain of WA, from Jurien Bay to Esperance

T. cucullata (Plate 49)

T. cucullata H. M. R. Rupp in *Aust. Orchid. Rev.* 11:71, fig. A–F (1946); R. Erickson *Orchids West* ed. 2:25 (1965)

A very slender plant up to 45 cm. in height. Leaf lamina 7–9 cm. long, linear channelled. Stem-bracts two, closely sheathing, subulate, 3–4·5 cm. long, those within the floral raceme much smaller. Flowers two to four, fugacious, white, with some green markings and numerous bright purple blotches, about 2 cm. in diameter. Perianth segments spreading, texture very thin, more or less ovate, not very acute, with the exception of the labellum, which is very narrow and acute. Column not hooded, externally marked with upright lines of dark brown dots and blotches; the erect lateral lobes truncate, a little higher than anther, and forming a deep and wide sinus behind the centre of the anther; anther inclined forward to an horizontal position, apex rounded. Stigma transversely oval.

As I saw it in the King River area, *T. cucullata* grew along the margins of peaty bogs.

The specific epithet is unfortunately misleading, for the dorsal sepal is not invariably very broad and conspicuously cucullate as implied in the original description; *nutans* would have been a happier choice.

Conspicuous characters of this species are the nodding or drooping habit of fertilised flowers, the beautifully blotched perianth and the furcate summit of the column.

FLOWERING PERIOD: Aug. to Nov.

DISTRIBUTION: Confined to the Albany district, WA

T. venosa (Plate 50)

T. venosa R. Br. *Prodr. Flor. Nov. Holl.* 314 (1810); A. J. Ewart *Flor. Vict.* 332 (1931); J. M. Black *Flor. S. Aust.* ed. 2:217 (1943); H. M. R. Rupp *Orchids N.S.W.* 10 (1943); J. H. Willis *Handb. Pls Vict.* 1:352 (1962); M. J. Firth *Native Orchids Tasm.* 39 (1965)

A slender plant 15–75 cm. high. Leaf narrow-linear, channelled, often extending beyond the middle of scape. Stem more or less sinuous. Flowers usually one to three, occasionally as many as six, comparatively large, blue, rarely white or pink, on long slender pedicels. Perianth segments rather thin, with conspicuous darker blue veins in most flowers. Sepals longer than the petals, 13–16 mm. long. Labellum differentiated more than in other species, broadly ovate, the anterior margins crisped. Column erect, 5–6 mm. long, widely winged, not hooded; wings produced laterally into two blunt, erect, spirally involute appendages on each side of and above the anther. Anther very protuberant, overhanging the stigma, its apex prolonged and bifid, about as high as the lateral lobes. Pollinia not connected with the rostellum. Stigma placed below the anther, its upper margin bicuspidate.

T. venosa is common in alpine moss beds and morasses, where it sometimes attains a height of 90 cm. The attractive flowers open freely on sunny days; nevertheless they are self-pollinated long before expansion of the perianth.

FLOWERING PERIOD: Oct. to Feb.

COMMON NAME: Veined Sun-orchid

DISTRIBUTION: Coast and near-coastal ranges of NSW; eastern Vic., and Otway Ranges; Tas.; Myponga and Mount Compass, SA; also NZ and New Caledonia

T. venosa var. **magnifica** (Plate 50)

T. venosa var. *magnifica* H. M. R. Rupp in *Aust. Orchid Rev.* 4:81, cum icon. (1939); H. M. R. Rupp *Orchids N.S.W.* 10 (1943)

A large-flowered, showy form from the Blue Mountains and other parts of NSW, it expands even in dull weather, and the blooms remain open at night.

FLOWERING PERIOD: Oct. to Dec.

DISTRIBUTION: Blue Mountains and nearby coastal regions of NSW

T. cyanea (Plate 51)

T. cyanea (Lindl.) Lindl. ex Benth. *Flor. aust.* 6:323 (1873); J. H. Willis *Handb. Pls Vict.* 1:353 (1962); M. J. Firth *Native Orchids Tasm.* 39 (1965)

SYNONYMY: *Macdonaldia cyanea* Lindl. in *Edwards' bot. Reg.* 23: Swan Riv. Append. l (1840)

A very slender plant, 23–60 cm. high. Leaf narrow, thick, deeply channelled, shorter than the stem; leaf lamina thinner on the margins than in *T. venosa*. Stem-bracts usually two, closely sheathing, subulate. Flowers one to four, the slender pedicel often concealed by the floral bract, blue, faintly veined in a darker shade, rarely white. Perianth segments varying in length, from 10–16 mm. long; sepals lanceolate, the dorsal sepal broader than the lateral ones, cucullate. Petals slightly broader, up to 8 mm., nearly ovate, the labellum more nearly obovate or broadly oblanceolate. Column mostly bluish as in the flower, about 6 mm. long and 4 mm. broad, widely winged and trilobed; the broad mid-lobe produced upward behind the anther and slightly hooded, darker coloured, except for the narrow yellow upper margin, which is more or less inturned and usually irregularly and faintly sinuate; lateral lobes horizontal at the height of the anther and about as long as it, or slightly longer, irregularly toothed or jagged at the end. Anther horizontal with a short horizontal apical point, but almost completely concealed by the lateral lobes of the column, unless viewed from directly above the flower. Stigmatic plate conspicuous in the lower half of the column, a small boss in the centre.

W. Hunter remarks of the Bidwell, Vic., occurrence: '*T. cyanea* invariably occurs with *T. venosa*, but I have not yet been able to find it in the places which *T. venosa* seems to favour the most—the sphagnum moss beds of the swamps. I have found it only amongst, or close to, the belts of heath (*Epacris microphylla*), and low heath myrtle (*Baeckea gunniana*) that fringe the wetter parts of the flats or are dotted amongst them, where the soil is comparatively drier and not at all swampy, and then only where *T. venosa* occurs in numbers. My specimens of *T. cyanea* (thirteen) are quite uniform in all their main characters. There is no evidence of any close relationship between the two species, in spite of their similarity in general external appearance and their occurrence together.' Hatch regards this species as a variety—*T. venosa* var. *cyanea* (Lindl.) E. D. Hatch in *Trans. roy. Soc. N.Z.* 79:391, t. 77 fig. F–H (1952).

FLOWERING PERIOD: Nov. to Jan.

DISTRIBUTION: Braidwood, NSW; Bidwell and Maramingo Creek, Vic.; northern Tas.

4 *Epiblema*

Epiblema R. Br. *Prodr. Flor. Nov. Holl.* 315 (1810)

A monotypic genus, similar to *Thelymitra* but having two appendages at the base of the labellum. Endemic in WA.

E. grandiflorum (Plate 52)

E. grandiflorum R. Br. *Prodr. Flor. Nov. Holl.* 315 (1810); R. Erickson *Orchids West* ed. 2:26 (1965)

Terrestrial glabrous plant, slender and erect, 45–60 cm. high. Leaf 12–18 cm. long, narrow-linear, terete, sheathing at the base. Stem bracts two, lower one 4–5 cm. long, acuminate, loosely sheathing, upper one smaller and closely sheathing. Flowers two to eight, in a terminal raceme, lilac to deep mauve, superficially resembling those of *Thelymitra*. Pedicels slender, longer than the ovary, subtended by small floral bracts. Perianth segments spreading, nearly equal, 15–20 mm. long, elliptical or elliptic-lanceolate, veined and blotched along the lines of the longitudinal nerves; lateral petals and labellum more heavily blotched than the other segments; lateral sepals united under the labellum by a broad base. Labellum as long as the sepals, unguiculate, the claw with two erect, rounded, closely parallel appendages; lamina ovate, concave, with a tuft of linear processes near the base; basal processes usually ten, with clavate tips. (Bentham describes two closely parallel appendages on the labellum—however I found only a single appendage although numerous flowers were examined. Whether separate appendages have become fused as one, whether Bentham erred, or whether this character is variable is not known.) Column very short, with erect, thin, petal-like lateral wings, which are 8–10 mm. long, broad, oblique, spotted, and not connected behind the anther. Anther erect or inclined forward, with a short recurved point, the cells distinct. Pollinia granular. Rostellum short.

E. grandiflorum often grows in reedy swamps and similar wet places. At Welshpool I saw it flowering in abundance early in November, the majority of the blooms being then far spent. In other localities this splendid orchid apparently extends its flowering period into March. According to H. Steedman the flowering is erratic—profuse on occasions and then not occurring again for several years.

FLOWERING PERIOD: Oct. to Mar.

COMMON NAME: Babe-in-a-cradle

DISTRIBUTION: South-western WA, from Perth to Esperance

5 *Calochilus*

Calochilus R. Br. *Prodr. Flor. Nov. Holl.* 320 (1810)

Terrestrial glabrous herbs, with (usually) ovoid tubers. Leaf solitary, linear, channelled; bracts sometimes leaf-like. Flowers few or numerous, in a loose raceme. Dorsal sepal erect, broad, concave; lateral sepals broad, acute, somewhat spreading; petals much shorter than sepals, wide, somewhat falcate. Labellum longer than the other segments, sessile, undivided, with an oblong base and triangular lamina, the latter usually densely bearded with long hairs of metallic sheen. Column short and broad, with wide wings produced between but not beyond the anther. Anther terminal, incumbent or horizontal, two-celled, with a blunt beak. Pollinia four or two, each deeply bilobed, granular, not connected with the rostellum.

A small genus of eleven species, of which nine are found in Australia, three in NZ (all Australian forms), an endemic one in New Caledonia (*C. neo-caledonicum* Schlechter), and another in New Guinea (*C. caeruleus* Williams). The popular name of 'Beard-orchid' is in allusion to the long, conspicuously hairy labellum of all species except *C. imberbis* and *C. richae*, which are not known beyond Vic. and Tas.

C. imberbis (Plate 53)

C. imberbis R. S. Rogers in *Trans. roy. Soc. S. Aust.* 51:4 (1927); A. J. Ewart *Flor. Vict.* 324 (1931); J. H. Willis *Handb. Pls Vict.* 1:355 (1962); M. J. Firth *Native Orchids Tasm.* 43 (1965)

Plant rather robust, 20–35 cm. high. Leaf up to 22 cm. long, fleshy, rigid, channelled, linear-lanceolate; a rather long, loose lanceolate bract about the middle of stem. Flowers in a loose raceme, three to five, green with purplish-brown markings (chiefly stripes); pedicels slender, each with a long, loose bract at the base. Dorsal sepal 14–16 mm. long and 8–10 mm. wide, erect, ovate, acute, cucullate; lateral sepals about 15 mm. long and 5–6 mm. wide, ovate, acute, concave, spreading, divaricate. Petals about 7 mm. long, 4–5 mm. wide, triangular, falcate, erect, uncinate, concave, marked with prominent veins. Labellum simple, petaloid, sessile, ovate, acute; margins entire, concave and incurved, with conspicuous purplish nerves; lamina 10–14 mm. long and 6–8 mm. wide, glabrous, entirely devoid of glands, papillae and hairs. Column rather stout and very short; the wings connected in front by a high shield-like plate, a purple gland at the base of each. Anther blunt and short, slightly inclined forward.

C. imberbis is remarkable for its simple beardless labellum, a unique character within the genus, giving the flower a strange appearance and serving to distinguish it from all other forms. Although widely distributed, it has been found in very few localities—a fact which strengthened Dr Rogers' opinion that it may be a pelorial representative of Bentham's frequent species, *C. robertsonii*. *C. imberbis* was discovered on 3 October, 1923, by Mrs Edith Rich, of Rushworth, Vic.

FLOWERING PERIOD: Sept. to Nov.

DISTRIBUTION: Central Vic.; northern and eastern Tas.; chiefly in light sclerophyll forest and uncommon to rare

C. richae (Plate 54)

C. richae W. H. Nicholls in *Vict. Nat.* 45:233, t. 9 (1929); A. J. Ewart *Flor. Vict.* 324 (1931); J. H. Willis *Handb. Pls Vict.* 1:355 (1962)

Plant terrestrial, comparatively slender, up to 25 cm. high. Leaf solitary, linear, channelled. [For convenience in packing, the original collector had separated the leaf from each tall *Calochilus* specimen (about eight in all, representing the present species and *C. imberbis*—of similar stature and appearance). This later caused some confusion, when it was discovered that there were insufficient leaves to go round; so I have purposely omitted the foliage from any plate. One leaf, however, (apparently belonging) accompanied the specimen sent to Dr Rogers.] Stem-bracts one to three, 7–7·5 cm. long, lanceolate. Flowers one to four, more reddish than green, on

long slender crimson pedicels, each subtended by an acuminate bract varying in length from 2 to 4 cm.; the uppermost bract often containing a rudimentary bud; ovary elongated and perianth segments conspicuously veined. Dorsal sepal 15 mm. long, 9 mm. broad, broadly ovate, cucullate, concave, tip acute; lateral sepals 13 mm. long, 4 mm. broad, ovate, lanceolate, widely divergent. Petals widely spread, about as broad as the lateral sepals, 7 mm. long; ovate-falcate, concave. Labellum 13 mm. long, 8 mm. broad, sessile; base rectangular, 3 mm. wide; callus part somewhat orbicular and posterior margins curled below; the base and wide portion of lamina to the margins (except a narrow central strip) rather thickly covered with short, sessile, purplish glands or calli; the apical, almost tubular part of labellum devoid of calli, contracting gradually to an acute point and longitudinally veined; under side of labellum smooth, glabrous, spotted with the reddish bases of the glands, and the apical part correspondingly veined. Column erect, 4 mm. high; wings conspicuous, connected by a purplish ridge; the forward part conical, with a purplish gland on each side of the inner margin; basal part high and smooth. Anther very short, blunt, horizontal. Pollinia as in *C. robertsonii*. Tubers not seen.

The foregoing description is based on the largest of three specimens received from Mrs Edith Rich on 23 October 1928 [and field observations in October 1968—Ed.]. These examples were collected in the vicinity of Whroo (a small township, approximately five miles south of Rushworth). *C. richae*, named after its discoverer, is very rare, and differs from all other recorded species in having the labellum parti-barbate, i.e. two-thirds of the entire lamina is rather densely covered with very short, sessile glands or calli, the apical third being glabrous.

FLOWERING PERIOD: Sept. and Oct.

DISTRIBUTION: Vic., where apparently endemic in Red Ironbark forest, near Rushworth

C. paludosus (Plate 55)

C. paludosus R. Br. *Prodr. Flor. Nov. Holl.* 320 (1810); A. J. Ewart *Flor. Vict.* 327 (1931); J. M. Black *Flor. S. Aust.* ed. 2:211 (1943); H. M. R. Rupp *Orchids N.S.W.* 52 (1943); J. H. Willis *Handb. Pls Vict.* 1:357 (1962); M. J. Firth *Native Orchids Tasm.* 44 (1965)

A slender plant up to 35 cm. high. Leaf up to 18 cm. long, rigid, linear-lanceolate, channelled, keeled. Stem-bracts one or two (usually one), subulate, loose, about 4–6 cm. long. Flowers one to eight, rarely more, reddish. Dorsal sepal about 1·5 cm. long, ovate, acute, prominently cucullate; lateral sepals about 1·3–1·5 cm. long, free, concave, narrowly lanceolate, divaricate, spreading below the labellum. Petals about 8 mm. long, triangular-falcate, erect, uncinate, concave, strongly marked by conspicuous red veins. Labellum sessile on a broad rectangular base, about 2·3–2·6 cm. long (including ligule), the triangular lamina covered with long reddish glabrous hairs; the hairs toward the base reduced to small linear and rounded glands; two auriculate intramarginal, lightly-coloured glands at the base; apex produced into a long flexuose strap-like appendage, almost half as long as the lamina. Column short, very broadly winged and without any basal glands; bases of wings united in front by a more or less prominent tooth-like lobe or band. Stigma prominent, its lower margin prominently marked with purple or red. Anther small, obtuse, as broad as long.

C. paludosus is not restricted to marshy places, as the specific name would suggest. I have found it also on dry hillsides (Portland, Vic.) and in dry sandy parts of heathlands. Pallid green-flowered forms are occasionally found.

FLOWERING PERIOD: Sept. to Dec.

COMMON NAME: Red Beard-orchid

DISTRIBUTION: All Australian States, except WA, but localised in Qld (south-east) and SA (south-east); also NZ

C. grandiflorus (Plate 56)

C. grandiflorus (Benth.) Domin in *Bibl. bot., Stuttgart 20*, Heft 85:551 (1915); H. M. R. Rupp *Orchids N.S.W.* 50 (1943); J. H. Willis *Handb. Pls Vict.* 1:357 (1962)

SYNONYMY: *C. campestris* var. *grandiflorus* Benth. *Flor. Aust.* 6:315 (1873); *C. grandiflorus* H. M. R. Rupp in *Vict. Nat.* 60:240, fig. 1–4 (1934)

A very slender species 30–60 cm. high. Leaf filiform, erect, triangular in section, channelled, green, reddish towards the base, 20–50 cm. long. Stem-bracts two or three, with two scarious, closely-appressed ones also present at base of plant; upper bracts elongate, loosely-sheathing, about 4–8 cm. long. Flowers one to ten, golden-yellow and purple (rarely albino, when pale green and white). Dorsal sepal erect, 16–20 mm. long, widely cucullate, and broadly ovate, acute; lateral sepals widely lanceolate, as long as dorsal sepal, diverging from each side of labellum. Petals 9–10 mm. long, ovate-lanceolate and falcate, finely marked with red stripes. Labellum sessile, 2–2·5 cm. long (excluding the appendage); lamina triangular, the upper surface covered with long purplish-red or red-brown glabrous or papillose hairs, those at the narrow base reduced to sessile and linear calli; anterior half of lamina with long, erect, less dense, pale hairs with sparkling papillae; tip of labellum ending in a long sinuous ribbon-like appendage which is somewhat papillose and commonly as long as the lamina itself. Column 6 mm. high, widely winged, very open at base, with a prominent dark-coloured gland at each lower angle; glands connected by a purplish ridge. Stigma transversely-oblong, the margins conspicuously outlined in purplish-red. Anther comparatively small, with obtuse or emarginate apex.

FLOWERING PERIOD: Sept. to Nov.

DISTRIBUTION: Southern Qld, and northern NSW, in coastal areas, with an isolated occurrence in north-eastern Vic., where it may prove to be more widespread

C. robertsonii (Plate 57)

C. robertsonii Benth. *Flor. aust.* 6:315 (1873); A. J. Ewart *Flor. Vict.* 326 (1931); J. M. Black *Flor. S. Aust.* ed. 2:211 (1943); H. M. R. Rupp *Orchids N.S.W* 50 (1943); J. H. Willis *Handb. Pls Vict.* 1:356 (1962); R. Erickson *Orchids West* ed. 2:28 (1965); M. J. Firth *Native Orchids Tasm.* 44 (1965)

Usually a stout plant 25–45 cm. high. Leaf linear-lanceolate, 20–40 cm. long, thin, triangular in section, erect, channelled. Stem-bracts one to three, about 7–10 cm. long, brown, lanceolate, clasping at the base; the additional bracts, within the floral raceme, gradually becoming smaller upward, 7–15 mm. long. Flowers one to nine, green with purplish or red-brown markings. Dorsal sepal 12–25 mm. long, ovate, acute, cucullate; lateral sepals divergent, spreading below and on each side of the labellum, about as long as the dorsal one. Petals less than half the length of sepals, yellowish, with fine red longitudinal stripes, ovate-falcate, erect. Labellum sessile, 2–3 cm. long; lamina widely triangular, the base fleshy and rectangular, golden-yellow or green, covered with crowded purple glands at the extreme base, otherwise densely bearded with long purple or bronzy glistening hairs; the tip ending in a short glabrous ribbon. Column short, widely winged, a purple gland at each lower angle; the wings united at the base by a transverse raised red or purple ridge. Anther transversely oblong. Rostellum very long

and narrow, not connected with the pollinia. Pollinia two, each deeply bilobed, crescentic, club-shaped.

FLOWERING PERIOD: Sept. to Jan.

COMMON NAME: Purplish Beard-orchid

DISTRIBUTION: All Australian states, but very localised in Qld, SA and WA; also NZ

C. robertsonii (Plate 58)

This pale form was figured by FitzGerald in *Aust. Orchids* 1[4]:+t. (1878) as *C. campestris*, a misconception which I corrected in *Vict. Nat.* 58:93 (1941). G. Lyell, of Gisborne, Vic., remarked: 'It is abundant not far from the north-eastern slopes of Mount Bullengarook; here they favour the sheltered slopes of the hills, under trees and shrubs. The opalescent hue of the flowers may be due to soil conditions; on the other hand, the abundant shade provided by the trees may be the direct cause, as it was noted that those specimens on the fringe of the timber produced flowers of quite normal colouring; colour intermediates are plentiful.' [This form is also found near Rushworth, Vic.—Ed.]

C. gracillimus (Plate 59)

C. gracillimus H. M. R. Rupp in *Vict. Nat.* 60:28 (June, 1943): H. M. R. Rupp *Orchids N.S.W.* 50, t. 7 (Dec., 1943)

A rather slender to moderately robust plant from 20 cm. to over 35 cm. high. Leaf narrow, deeply channelled, of variable length Stem-bracts loosely sheathing, usually two, 8–10 cm. long. Flowers two to eight, reddish-brown or purplish-brown. Dorsal sepal 10–15 mm. long, broadly lanceolate, cucullate; lateral sepals about 10 mm. long, lanceolate, spreading. Petals shorter than sepals, similar to the lateral ones, falcate with dark longitudinal stripes. Labellum similar to that in *C. robertsonii*, but more slender, to 3 cm. long; the lamina with crowded purplish glands at the base and the apex ending in a slender, more or less glabrous ribbon, otherwise densely bearded with long reddish-purple hairs; the individual hairs covered with glistening glands. Column very short, narrow, the wings somewhat inconspicuous, a dark gland at each lower angle. Anther shorter than column, sometimes in a horizontal position, obtusely pointed. Stigma prominent. Pollinia two, bilobed, crescentic and club-shaped.

Very closely allied to *C. robertsonii*, and sometimes equally robust (when it is difficult to differentiate); the more filiform, straighter labellum tip and absence of a coloured ridge between the basal glands of the column are its only distinguishing features.

FLOWERING PERIOD: Nov. to Jan., rarely as early as Sept.

COMMON NAME: Slender Beard-orchid

DISTRIBUTION: South-eastern Qld and eastern NSW, chiefly coastal

C. campestris (Plate 60)

C. campestris R. Br. *Prodr. Flor. Nov. Holl.* 320 (1810); A. J. Ewart *Flor. Vict.* 326 (1931); J. M. Black *Flor. S. Aust.* ed. 2:211 (1943); H. M. R. Rupp *Orchids N.S.W.* 49 (1943); J. H. Willis *Handb. Pls Vict.* 1:356 (1962); M. J. Firth *Native Orchids Tasm.* 43 (1965)

SYNONYMY: *C. cupreus* R. S. Rogers in *Trans. roy. Soc. S. Aust.* 42:24, t. 2 (1918)

A robust plant often 45–60 cm. high. Leaf erect, 12–30 cm. long, rigid, fleshy, triangular in section, deeply channelled, sheathing at the base. Stem-bracts one to three, each 5–8 cm. long, green or copper-coloured, lanceolate, clasping, the floral bracts smaller.

Flowers racemose, comparatively small, seven to fifteen, yellowish-green with reddish-brown, purplish or light rufous markings. Sepals almost equal in length, yellowish-green or green with a reddish-brown central stripe; dorsal sepal broadly ovate, cucullate, shortly acuminate; lateral sepals narrower than the dorsal, dilated (but not widely) on each side of the labellum. Labellum with a fleshy rectangular base and wide triangular lamina, longer than the other segments, golden-yellow or greenish with finely fimbriated margins and reddish-blue, often glandular hairs with metallic lustre; the narrow basal portion entirely smooth (devoid of glands), or bearing brilliant metallic-blue, reddish-blue or purplish-black raised and lustrous lines which are more or less fused and terminate in free hair-points; other hairs on the lamina not dense, and shorter than in *C. robertsonii*; labellum tip recurved, ending in a short, sometimes very brief, strap-like, sinuous appendage with glandular margins. Column short, very wide and open at the base, the lower angles with conspicuous glands which have no connecting ridge as in *C. robertsonii*. Anther long, horizontal, with a wide apex. Stigma transverse, reniform.

C. campestris is pollinated by a scollid wasp, *Campsomeris tasmaniensis*. See article by F. Fordham in *Vict. Nat.* 62:199 (1946). The leafless character of the specimen figured by Hook.f. *Flor. Tasm.* 2:t. 106a (1858) is suggestive of *C. saprophyticus* but the tubers are those of *C. campestris*.

FLOWERING PERIOD: Sept. to Jan.

COMMON NAME: Copper Beard-orchid

DISTRIBUTION: All states except WA, ranging from high rainfall montane forests to arid Mallee sandhills; also NZ

C. saprophyticus (Plate 61)

C. saprophyticus R. S. Rogers in *Trans. roy. Soc. S. Aust.* 54:41 (1930); A. J. Ewart *Flor. Vict.* 325 (1931); J. H. Willis *Handb. Pls Vict.* 1:356 (1962); M. J. Firth *Native Orchids Tasm.* 43 (1965)

A pale leafless or almost leafless saprophyte, often robust, 20–55 cm. high, bearing large thickened tuberous rhizomes in addition to large, often irregularly-shaped tubers. Stem green or yellowish, with two membranous imbricate sheaths at the base, bracts two to four, lanceolate, 6–7 cm. long, yellowish-pink, pale green or copper-coloured, the lowest bract fleshy (actually an aborted leaf lamina). Raceme one to fifteen flowered; flowers subtended by lanceolate bracts 1·5–4 cm. long, the uppermost bract smaller than those towards the base of the inflorescence. Flowers stalked, similar to those of *C. campestris*, pale green, the segments suffused with saffron-yellow and marked with reddish-brown. Dorsal sepal erect or incurved, widely lanceolate, subacute, cucullate, five-nerved; lateral sepals spreading, falco-lanceolate, margins sometimes irregularly notched. Labellum pale yellow-green, spreading, sessile on an oblong base, somewhat rhomboidal, very shortly ligulate at the apex, about 1·3 cm. long (without the ligule which is 2–4 mm.), glabrous at the base, with two, sometimes more, parallel, deep blue, raised metallic plates which are often bifurcated in front and produced into long hairs; the lamina and its margins covered with dark purplish or reddish-purple hairs; lateral margins of yellow-green lamina strongly fringed, or combed, distinctly pruinose and sparkling. Column short, broadly winged, but not so widely as in *C. campestris*, with a dark purple gland at the base of each wing, convex at the back and fleshy. Anther rather long, incumbent, subobtuse, greenish-yellow. Stigma triangular. Rostellum prominent, without a caudicle.

At the close of 1942 about 270 specimens had been recorded in the Portland region. Some of these plants were exceptionally robust, growing chiefly in sandy *Melaleuca* country adjacent to swamps and sometimes actually in the water. Much of the country had been burnt over in the previous summer. Concerning the original Cravensville collection A. B. Braine wrote in his diary: 'Fred Supple found the first specimen (5 October, 1918) in an unsheltered place, a blanched form. The second specimen, found on 7 November, 1920, had two flowers, much smaller than *C. robertsonii*, but the labellum was similarly coloured, and the bracts were flesh-tinted. It was growing at the foot of a tree, just above where the original specimen was found.'

FLOWERING PERIOD: Oct. to Dec.

DISTRIBUTION: NSW, Vic., and Tas., chiefly in sandy coastal scrub but rare, its exact range unknown because of confusion with the closely related *C. campestris*

6   *Diuris*

Diuris Sm. in *Trans. Linn. Soc. Lond.* 4:222 (1798)

Terrestrial glabrous plants with tubers, and several imbricate scales at the base of the scape. Leaves more than one, narrow, arising from the base of the stem, with a few sheathing bracts higher up. Flowers one or more, in a terminal raceme, sometimes large and conspicuous, yellow, purple or white, often spotted or otherwise marked with dark brown or purple. Dorsal sepal erect, rather broad, closely clasping the column at the base, upper part open; lateral sepals narrow-linear, often herbaceous, parallel or crossed, spreading or deflexed. Petals longer than the dorsal sepal, oval, elliptical or orbicular, on slender claws, erect or spreading. Labellum as long as, or longer than the dorsal sepal, deeply tri-lobed, the mid-lobe much contracted at the base, with one or two longitudinal raised lines along the narrow part. Column very short, the wings produced into erect lateral lobes, but not continued behind the anther. Anther erect, often acuminate, two-celled, on a very short filament; margins of the filament produced into erect lateral lobes or wings not adnate to the stigmatic plate. Stigma borne on a broad style in front of the anther, a slot in its upper border representing the rostellum and likewise enclosing the loose viscid disc, the latter attached at maturity to the apices of the pollinia, without intervention of a caudicle. Pollinia two, each deeply bilobed, suspended behind the stigma from the back of the viscid disc. Pollinia mealy.

A genus of over forty species, all of them confined to Australia with the exception of one—*D. fryana* from Timor. The species hybridise readily in nature, which is one of the main reasons for the genus being so difficult to the taxonomist.

D. punctata

D. punctata Sm. *Exot. Bot.* 1:13, t. 8 (1804–5); A. J. Ewart *Flor. Vict.* 356 (1931), and including *D. alba* l.c. 356; J. M. Black *Flor. S. Aust.* ed. 2:237 (1943); H. M. R. Rupp *Orchids N.S.W.* 12 (1943); J. H. Willis *Handb. Pls Vict.* 1:357 (1962)

A slender glabrous plant 20–60 cm. high. Leaves one to four, linear, channelled, 15–30 cm. long. Flowers two to ten, usually lilac or purple, sometimes white or rarely yellow, and sometimes with darker spotting. Stem bracts usually two, loosely sheathing, subulate, about 6–8 cm. long, those within the raceme often very long. Dorsal sepal broadly ovate, erect or recurved at the apex, 1–2·5 cm. high. Lateral sepals 3–9 cm. long, green or brownish, narrow linear, spreading or parallel. Petals 1–3 cm. long, on a short claw, the lamina orbicular to elliptic-oblong, length overall about 3 cm. Labellum about 2 cm. long, trilobed; mid-lobe ovate to semi-circular on a narrow base; lateral lobes less than half as long, oblong-falcate, erect with outwardly curved tips, margins entire or crenulate; two longitudinal raised yellow plates or ridges traversing the labellum from the base to the middle, ending in tooth-like processes, a more or less prominent central ridge extending to the tip, with a corresponding groove underneath. Column short and broad, lateral wings lanceolate and about as high as the anther, the frontal margins yellow, sinuous. Rostellum short, bifid. Pollinia two. Flowers often fragrant.

This species, the Purple Diuris, is the showiest of the genus, the massed flowers presenting quite a wonderful display of rich colour. [It varies considerably throughout its range in eastern and south-eastern Australia. These variations have been discussed in great detail by A. W. Dockrill in *Vict. Nat.* 81:128–138 (1964). Only two of them are illustrated here.—Ed.]

D. punctata forma **blakneyae** (Plate 62)

D. punctata var. *punctata* forma *blakneyae* F. M. Bailey *Compreh. Cat. Qd Pls* 847, fig. 973 E–H (1913)

This form has flowers varying from white to purple, with the labellum occasionally spotted. It is very variable, and is the most common form, being found throughout the range of the species.

FLOWERING PERIOD: Mar. to May, and Aug. to Nov., depending on latitude

DISTRIBUTION: Generally in natural grassland, from the coast to the western plains in eastern Australia. It extends from the Atherton Tableland in Qld., south to Vic. and west as far as Mount Gambier in SA

D. punctata var. **albo-violacea** (Plate 63)

D. punctata var. *albo-violacea* H. M. R. Rupp ex A. W. Dockrill in *Vict. Nat.* 81:137, t. 3 fig. 46–52 (1964); A. J. Ewart *Flor. Vict.* 356 (1931), as *D. alba*; J. H. Willis *Handb. Pls Vict.* 1:358 (1962), in note under *D. alba* sens. A. J. Ewart

The varietal name refers to the colour of the flowers, which are white with violet suffusions. This fragrant variety is found only in the grassland on the basalt plain north-west of Melbourne, where it was once abundant. Due to grazing and cultivation it is now extremely rare. [It has been known as *D. alba* R. Br., but the latter is now regarded as a distinct variety of *D. punctata*, found only in NSW and Qld.—Ed.]

FLOWERING PERIOD: Oct. and Nov.

DISTRIBUTION: Keilor plains between West Footscray and Sydenham, Vic.

D. colemanae (Plate 64)

D. colemanae H. M. R. Rupp in *Vict. Nat.* 57:63, cum icon. +fig. 1–11 (1940); H. M. R. Rupp *Orchids N.S.W.* 13 (1943)

A slender or moderately robust plant 20–35 cm. high, usually with two leaves about as high as the base of the inflorescence; leaves in my specimens rather broad and channelled. Flowers two to seven, in a loose raceme, yellow or pale orange with purple-brown markings; labellum base and raised plates with a white ground. Floral bracts large. Dorsal sepal variable in shape, 8–10 mm. long, broad-ovate to ovate-triangular. Lateral sepals green, slender or moderately stout, 4–6 cm. long, lax. Petals 10–14 mm. long, lamina ovate-lanceolate; claw variable in length, stout or slender. Labellum trilobed from above its base, the lateral lobes small,

sometimes broader than long, the outer margins more or less crenulate; mid-lobe with two longitudinal plates extending beyond the junction of the lateral lobes, its lamina broad-lanceolate or sometimes almost rhomboid. Column-wings never quite as high as the anther. Anther purplish. Stigma very prominent.

This species is closely allied to *D. tricolor* R. D. FitzG., and is regarded by some as synonymous with it.

FLOWERING PERIOD: Sept. and Oct.

DISTRIBUTION: South-eastern Qld; inland slopes of ranges in eastern NSW

D. pedunculata (Plate 65)

D. pedunculata R. Br. *Prodr. Flor. Nov. Holl.* 316 (1810); A. J. Ewart *Flor. Vict.* 357 (1931); J. M. Black *Flor. S. Aust.* ed. 2:237 (1943); H. M. R. Rupp *Orchids N.S.W.* 19 (1943); J. H. Willis *Handb. Pls Vict.* 1:361 (1962); M. J. Firth *Native Orchids Tasm.* 79 (1965)

A slender glabrous plant 18–40 cm. high. Leaves five to seven, narrow-linear, 10–15 cm. long. Flowers racemose, one to four, on very slender pedicels, canary-yellow with brown or greenish-brown tinges on the outer surface of the perianth segments and labellum, and sometimes on the inner surface of the labellum also. Dorsal sepal broadly ovate, erect, much shorter than the other segments, 10–16 mm. long; lateral sepals green, linear-lanceolate, channelled on the inner side, spreading below the labellum, 14–23 mm. long. Petals 15–20 mm., spreading, the lamina elliptical, the claws linear, green, 4–6 mm. long. Labellum 12–18 mm. long and 10–15 mm. wide, almost flat in the mature flower, tip blunt or acute, spreading; lateral lobes 3–7 mm. long, narrow, falco-lanceolate, toothed on the outer margins, curved outward; mid-lobe on a contracted base, ovate-rhomboid or ovate-lanceolate, about three to five times longer than the lateral ones; lamina with two raised, rather widely separated pubescent longitudinal lines on the base, the lines often laminate, ending dentately a little beyond the contracted part, then continued as a single line or fold towards the tip. Anther flat, or almost so, about same height as or somewhat shorter than the viscid disc; lateral appendages narrow, lanceolate, very acuminate, margins toothed, and about same height as anther.

FLOWERING PERIOD: Aug. to Nov., sometimes as late as Feb. in alpine regions

COMMON NAME: Snake Orchid or Golden Moths

DISTRIBUTION: South-eastern Qld; eastern NSW; Vic. generally; northern and eastern Tas. and King Island; south-eastern SA

D. pedunculata var. **gigantea** (Plate 65)

D. pedunculata var. *gigantea* W. H. Nicholls in *Vict. Nat.* 49:174, fig. A (1932); H. M. R. Rupp *Orchids N.S.W.* 19 (1943)

Plants of this variety are usually more robust than in the typical form and flowers are larger, up to 6·5 cm. in diameter.

FLOWERING PERIOD: Oct.

DISTRIBUTION: More or less the same as for the typical form

D. pallens (Plate 66)

D. pallens Benth. *Flor. aust.* 6:329 (1873); H. M. R. Rupp *Orchids N.S.W.* 19 (1943)

A slender plant 10–15 cm. high, very similar to *D. pedunculata*. Leaves two or more, 6–8 cm. long, narrow-linear or filiform, channelled. Flowers one to three, rather small, pale yellow. Dorsal sepal broad-ovate, 5–8 mm. long. Lateral sepals 1–1·5 cm. long, short and broad, green, linear-lanceolate, connate at base. Petals as long as lateral sepals, ovate-lanceolate, on a short broad green claw. Labellum about the same length as petals, trilobed from above the base, the lateral lobes minute, tooth-like; mid-lobe ovate-lanceolate on a wide base, margins entire, sometimes incurved, the raised lines on the callus plate converging or forming a compact mass of callus, which continues as a single narrow raised fold along the lamina to the apex, with two more or less prominent raised fleshy glands on the base. Anther purplish, about as high as viscid disc. Upper margin of stigma deeply emarginate, purplish. Column appendages ovate-lanceolate, shorter than the anther.

FLOWERING PERIOD: Aug. to Nov.

DISTRIBUTION: South-eastern Qld; north-eastern NSW

D. fastidiosa (Plate 67)

D. fastidiosa R. S. Rogers in *Trans. roy. Soc. S. Aust.* 51:6 (1927); A. J. Ewart *Flor. Vict.* 357 (1931); J. H. Willis *Handb. Pls Vict.* 1:361 (1962)

A small, very slender species from 5–20 cm. high. Leaves usually seven or eight, setaceous, about half the height of the scape, slightly twisted; stem glabrous with two bracts, one loose, elongated subulate, the other short, closely sheathing, a membranous cylindrical sheath at the base. Flowers racemose, one to three, on long very slender pedicels, yellow with dark brown markings. Ovary narrow, elongated; bracts loose, subulate, exceeding the pedicels. Dorsal sepal more or less oval, erect, subacute, recurved at the apex, clasping the column at the base, nine-nerved, brown markings in the lower half, about 11 mm. long, 6 mm. wide, equalling the labellum in length; lateral sepals greenish, linear parallel, spreading, channelled above, about 1·75 cm. long. Petals seven-nerved, markedly stipitate, about 1·3 cm. long; lamina yellow, elliptical, claws dark brown, about 4 mm. long. Labellum vertical or sub-vertical, with irregular brown blotches or markings, trilobed, the division well above the base; lateral lobes oblong, blunt, slightly dentate on the outer margins, about 6 mm. long, slightly exceeding half the length of the labellum; mid-lobe obtuse, spathulate, narrowing posteriorly between the lateral lobes into a claw, margins entire, about 11 mm. long; lamina with two pubescent raised parallel lines on the claw of the mid-lobe, succeeded by a single keel to the apex. Anther blunt, equalling in height the rostellum and lateral appendages; lateral appendages membranous, wide with irregular borders and long subulate apex.

The spring of 1925, and that of 1927, are well remembered for the remarkable growth of vegetation. On the Keilor plains, as in more favoured localities, wild flowers were very plentiful. It was under such conditions that *D. fastidiosa*, the 'Proud Diuris', was first seen, and—so it would appear—in such seasons only does it show itself. On a glorious day late in August the author rambled over the plains, visiting those few spots as yet untouched by settlement. The yellow, moth-like flowers of *D. pedunculata* and the dark wall-flower-hued blooms of *D. palustris* were surprisingly plentiful. When first I saw the little flowers of *fastidiosa* wavering in the wind, I imagined them to be those of a pale-coloured form of Lindley's plant, but the 'something strange' invited closer scrutiny.

The proud, erect bearing of *D. fastidiosa* is noticeable, because all the other forms so far described have the twin sepals, to a greater or lesser extent, pendent. Here we have flowers with the sepals directed, more or less, skyward, so suggesting the specific name given to the form by Dr R. S. Rogers to whom the first-found specimens were forwarded.

The author's records show that this species was first collected in August 1923—but one specimen being found. The type specimens were collected during August and September in 1925-6-7. In 1925 there were five small, compact tufts growing in an area of about 10 square feet. During the season of 1926, specimens were again difficult to find, two only being seen. In 1927 the five original tufts were once again in evidence, but since that favoured season the species has not re-appeared. Though the locality has been diligently searched each season, no sign of any growth in connection with this orchid has been detected. Since then the habitat of this species—a railway enclosure—has been covered with gravel.

The characteristics of this species are intermediate between those of *D. palustris* and *D. pedunculata*, and there is a distinct possibility that it was a hybrid from these two.

FLOWERING PERIOD: Aug. and Sept.

DISTRIBUTION: Known only from Tottenham, Vic.

D. palachila (Plate 68)

D. palachila R. S. Rogers in *Trans. roy. Soc. S. Aust.* 31:209 (1907); A. J. Ewart *Flor. Vict.* 358 (1931); J. M. Black *Flor. S. Aust.* ed. 2:239 (1943); H. M. R. Rupp *Orchids N.S.W.* 16 (1943); J. H. Willis *Handb. Pls Vict.* 1:361 (1962); M. J. Firth *Native Orchids Tasm.* 80 (1965)

A slender, glabrous plant 10–40 cm. high. Leaves two to eight, narrow-linear or linear, somewhat lax or setaceous, often reaching a length of 17 cm. Flowers one to three, on long slender pedicels, yellow with few brown markings or conspicuously marked and blotched. Dorsal sepal 10–15 mm. long, more or less ovate, yellow, usually with brown markings or dots, chiefly on the outer surface near the base and around the margins. Lateral sepals 10–25 mm. long, green, more or less marked with brown, linear-acuminate or linear-spathulate, spreading below the labellum, parallel or rarely crossed. Petals yellow or yellowish-brown, the claw greenish-brown or brown, 4–8 mm. long; lamina elliptical, 10–15 mm. long, spreading. Labellum yellow with light brown linear markings, or with dark brown dots or other markings, 11–14 mm. long; lateral lobes usually rather more than half the length of the mid-lobe, narrow-lanceolate, with upturned, usually dentate margins and outwardly curved free ends; mid-lobe spade or shovel-shaped, apex crescentic; lamina with two widely separated raised longitudinal lines on a narrow base, ending abruptly in two teeth or rounded lobes at the expanded part; in some flowers the lines (or plates) are toothed along the inner margins; thereafter merged into a central keel extending to the apex. Anther as high as the viscid disc of rostellum, rather flat, with a very short point. Lateral appendages of column as high as the anther, oblong-falcate, the anterior margins dentate.

D. palachila is a variable species, notably in regard to the size of the flowers and their colour markings; but in the open forest areas, it has established itself as a small slender plant with pale yellow flowers, the brown colour markings inconspicuous. In swampy places, however, it is a moderately robust plant with much larger blooms—up to 4 cm. in diameter, the leaves up to eight and setaceous. In the open spaces it is often very variable in its colour markings, the brown markings predominating. Natural hybridisation is, presumably, responsible for much of this diversity of colour, the parents probably being *D. maculata* and *D. pedunculata*.

FLOWERING PERIOD: Aug. to Nov.

COMMON NAME: Broad-tip Diuris

DISTRIBUTION: Eastern NSW; southern Vic.; northern and eastern Tas.; south-eastern SA

DIURIS

D. aurea (Plate 69)

D. aurea Sm. *Exot. Bot.* 1:15, t. 9 (1804-5); H. M. R. Rupp *Orchids N.S.W.* 18 (1943)

SYNONYMY: *D. spathulata* Swartz in Schrad. *Neues J. Bot.* 1:60 (1805), non R. D. FitzG. (1891)

A slender or moderately robust species, 15-50 cm. high. Leaves two, rather narrow, ribbed and deeply channelled, about half the height of the plant. Flowers two to five in a raceme, golden yellow, with few conspicuous brown markings. Dorsal sepal 10-17 mm. long, recurved; lateral sepals 17-24 mm. long, green, often marked with brown, usually dilated towards the ends and sometimes crossed. Petals 15-22 mm. long, on rather short claws, usually with brown markings; lamina broad lanceolate to almost orbicular. Labellum as long as the dorsal sepal or almost so, trilobed from close to the base; lateral lobes almost half as long as the mid-lobe, obliquely oblong with more or less crenate upper margins, or sometimes almost ovate and entire, splashed with brown or purplish-brown. Mid-lobe with two short brown, yellow or greenish longitudinal plates, the space between them flexed into a keel from near the base and continued to the apex of the lamina, which is nearly orbicular to ovate or almost diamond-shaped, and more or less marked with brown. Column wings dentate and usually higher than the anther, sinuous at the base in front. Stigma ovate.

FLOWERING PERIOD: Apr. to Nov.

DISTRIBUTION: East coast of Qld and NSW, from Atherton Tableland south to Port Jackson

D. abbreviata (Plate 70)

D. abbreviata F. Muell. ex Benth. *Flor. aust.* 6:329 (1873); H. M. R. Rupp *Orchids N.S.W.* 19 (1943)

A very slender plant 15-45 cm. high. Leaves one to three, 12-20 cm. long, narrow-linear, channelled. Flowers three to eight, in a loose raceme, rather small, yellow, more or less blotched with brown. Pedicels long and slender, the rhachis more or less flexuose. Stem-bracts two, 2·5-3 cm. long, closely sheathing, those within the raceme shorter and more acute. Petals ovate or ovate-oblong on long slender claws. Lateral sepals greenish, narrow-linear, slightly exceeding the labellum. Dorsal sepal a little shorter than labellum, erect, ovate-oblong, enclosing the column at its base. Labellum trilobed from above the base, the lateral lobes small, triangular or lanceolate-falcate; mid-lobe much longer than broad, but contracted at the base, tip blunt; callus with two prominent raised lines or plates ending a little beyond the broad part of the mid-lobe, smooth and glabrous. Column wings lanceolate, acuminate, and continuous in front with the raised lines of the labellum, and about as high as the anther. Anther blunt, a little higher than the rostellum.

The author's specimens came from two localities in northern NSW—Woolgoolga—where they grew under eucalypts in fairly dense forest, and Byron Bay where they grew amongst grass tussocks under banksias quite close to the ocean.

FLOWERING PERIOD: Aug. to Nov.

DISTRIBUTION: South-eastern Qld and eastern NSW as far south as the Hunter River

D. sulphurea (Plate 71)

D. sulphurea R. Br. *Prodr. Flor. Nov. Holl.* 316 (1810); A. J. Ewart *Flor. Vict.* 359 (1931); J. M. Black *Flor. S. Aust.* ed. 2:239 (1943); H. M. R. Rupp *Orchids N.S.W.* 18 (1943); J. H. Willis *Handb. Pls Vict.* 1:360 (1962); M. J. Firth *Native Orchids Tasm.* 80 (1965)

A slender to moderately stout plant 25-75 cm. high. Leaves two or three, 18-50 cm. long, linear. Stem-bracts usually two, 5-15 cm. long, closely sheathing, subulate. Flowers three to six on long slender pedicels, 4-5·5 cm. in diameter, yellow with dark brown markings. Dorsal sepal 20-22 mm. long, ovate, often recurved, with two conspicuous dark brown eye-like dots near the middle; lateral sepals 2·5-3 cm. long, linear, acuminate, more brown than green, usually parallel, but sometimes crossed. Petals 2-3 cm. long, spreading; claw 5-8 mm. long; lamina elliptical, recurved. Labellum 12-15 mm. long, sessile, much shorter than dorsal sepal; lateral lobes large, rather wide, obovate, almost half as long as the mid-lobe; mid-lobe rhombo-cuneate, wide, but depressed on each side of the central ridge; lamina with a single conspicuous raised longitudinal ridge from the base to just beyond the middle, where it merges into the fold of the lobe. Anther hardly pointed, its apex as high as, or higher than, the viscid disc of the rostellum. Lateral appendages of column prominent, semi-ovate, incurved. Flowers fragrant.

FLOWERING PERIOD: Aug. to Nov.

COMMON NAME: Tiger Orchid

DISTRIBUTION: South-eastern Qld; eastern NSW; southern and central Vic.; northern and eastern Tas.; south-eastern SA

D. sulphurea—pelorial form (Plate 72)

A pelorial form is one which may appear in a species normally having irregular flowers. It is due to an abnormality which results in the development of symmetrical flowers. Such a form with beautiful pansy-like flowers was collected by the author west of Coimadai, Vic., on 5 November 1929. Hereabouts the normal form was abundant, growing chiefly within the shelter of *Brachyloma daphnoides*. Only three perfect specimens were found. Here also were other specimens showing a gradation to the normal form. In this form there are two raised lines on the callus plate of the labellum.

D. brevifolia (Plate 73)

D. brevifolia R. S. Rogers in *Trans. roy. Soc. S. Aust.* 46:148 (1922); J. M. Black *Flor. S. Aust.* ed. 2:239 (1943); H. M. R. Rupp *Orchids N.S.W.* 16 (1943); J. H. Willis *Handb. Pls Vict.* 1:360 (1962), in note

A slender glabrous plant 15-40 cm. high. Leaves four to eight, linear or setaceous, acuminate, not twisted, very erect, 7-12 cm. long, rarely reaching beyond the middle of the stem. Flowers solitary or in a loose raceme of two to five, on slender pedicels, yellow with a few brown markings. Dorsal sepal 11-15 mm. long, yellow with a dark brown spot on each side of the dorsum near the base, ovate, recurved; lateral sepals 15-23 mm. long, green, linear, acuminate, parallel, sometimes crossed, spreading below the labellum or slightly recurved. Petals 14-23 mm. long, shortly stalked, spreading, recurved; lamina canary-yellow, elliptical. Labellum yellow, at least as long as the dorsal sepal and generally longer; lateral lobes less than half as long as the mid-lobe, generally 5-7 mm. long, rather narrow, margins entire, tips recurved; mid-lobe rhombo-cuneate with depressed antero-lateral margins; lamina with two parallel raised lines on the basal half continuous with the anterior central keel, the lines surrounded in front and on both sides by a conspicuous dark brown border. Anther without a definite point, rather higher than the viscid disc of the rostellum. Lateral appendages of column subulate or linear-falcate, a little higher than the viscid disc.

D. brevifolia has two close allies in *D. setacea* and *D. sulphurea*. From the former it differs chiefly in having flowers of a different yellow colour, different markings, and less numerous leaves, etc.

18

From *D. sulphurea* it differs in the possession of much shorter and relatively more numerous leaves and a larger labellum without any transverse blotch near the apex.

FLOWERING PERIOD: Oct. to Dec.

DISTRIBUTION: Central and south coastal regions of NSW; Mount Lofty Range and localities to the south, also Kangaroo Island, SA

D. emarginata (Plate 74)

D. emarginata R. Br. *Prodr. Flor. Nov. Holl.* 316 (1810); R. Erickson *Orchids West* ed. 2:34 (1965)

Often a tall, somewhat stout plant, 25–90 cm. high. Leaves two or three, 15–20 cm. long, narrow-linear, wider towards the base and there channelled, semi-spiral towards the end. Stem-bracts three or four, loosely sheathing, varying much in length, the longest often 20 cm. long; other bracts 2·5–5 cm. long. Flowers up to seven, in a loose raceme, yellow with red-brown markings chiefly towards the base of the labellum. Pedicels slender, erect; lateral sepals 2·5 cm. long; dorsal sepal shorter, on a firm base and embracing the column, open at the top; petals slightly shorter than lateral sepals, elliptical, contracted on a short claw. Labellum as long as the dorsal sepal, the lateral lobes broad, triangular, entire or toothed, from a third to a half as long as the mid-lobe, and the double raised keel merging into a single broad one on the lamina of the mid-lobe. Column-wings as high as the anther. Tubers long and narrow.

This species, the largest of the western *Diuris*, favours moist, often shady places and grows abundantly and luxuriantly with its roots in water.

FLOWERING PERIOD: Sept. to Dec.

DISTRIBUTION: Coastal regions of south-western WA

D. pauciflora (Plate 75)

D. pauciflora R. Br. *Prodr. Flor. Nov. Holl.* 316 (1810); R. Erickson *Orchids West* ed. 2:35 (1965)

A slender, often attenuated plant from 15–40 cm. high. Leaves usually three, 8–15 cm. long, very narrow. Flowers up to seven, yellow, and marked with brown or purplish-brown. Petals 10–15 mm. long, ovate; lateral sepals about 1·5 cm. long, linear, wider than in most species; dorsal sepal shorter than lateral sepals, dotted on the margins and at apex. Labellum about as long as the dorsal sepal, trilobed from the base, the lateral lobes almost half as long as the mid-lobe, with a single raised line along the centre. Anther higher than viscid disc of rostellum. Lateral appendages of column slightly shorter than anther, oblong-lanceolate, incurved, their lower margins yellow, sinuous. Stigma prominent.

FLOWERING PERIOD: Sept. to Nov.

DISTRIBUTION: Coastal and near-coastal regions of south-western WA

D. carinata (Plate 76)

D. carinata Lindl. *Gen. & Spec. orchid. Pls* 510 (1840); R. Erickson *Orchids West* ed. 2:34 (1965)

Sometimes a very slender plant 20–50 cm. high. Leaves two or three, 3–16 cm. long, narrow-linear or filiform. Stem-bracts two or three, the lowest similar to the leaves, those within the raceme smaller. Flowers one to four, variable in size, pale yellow, with few markings, or bright yellow with red-brown or purplish-brown markings dominating. Dorsal sepal about as long as the labellum,

ovate, oblong or ovate-cuneate. Lateral sepals linear, usually parallel, occasionally crossed. Petals as long as or a little longer than the lateral sepals, oval, stipitate, spreading, reflexed, the claws often stout. Labellum trilobed from a little above the base; the lateral lobes often broad, but variable as to size, usually about half as long as the mid-lobe. Mid-lobe rather broad, sometimes the margins rolled back, semi-circular, the base contracted, the plate along the centre much raised and deeply furrowed, forming a double keel on the claw of the mid-lobe, merging with a single broad keel on the lamina. Lateral lobes of the column narrow, often marked with purple, as high as or a little higher than the anther.

FLOWERING PERIOD: Sept. to Nov.

COMMON NAME: Bee Orchid

DISTRIBUTION: Widespread throughout south-western WA, and abundant in wet places

D. setacea (Plate 77)

D. setacea R. Br. *Prodr. Flor. Nov. Holl.* 316 (1810); R. Erickson *Orchids West* ed. 2:34 (1965)

A slender plant 20–35 cm. high. Leaves seven or eight, 8–10 cm. long, linear, filiform, setaceous, enclosed at their base by a prominent sheath. Stem-bracts two or three, linear-lanceolate, the lower one similar to the leaves; floral bracts subulate, loosely-sheathing. Flowers one to three, yellow with a few reddish markings. Dorsal sepal narrow-lanceolate, triangular; lateral sepals about 4 mm. longer than the labellum, broad-linear, parallel, green and red-brown. Petals 13–15 mm. long, ovate, stipitate. Labellum trilobed, about as long as the petals; the lateral lobes ovate, anterior margin and base marked with red-brown; mid-lobe ovate-rhomboid, margined with red along the posterior margins; callus with two raised plates extending to about half the length of the mid-lobe, then continuing as a single broad, raised ridge to the end, apex rounded. Column wings usually narrow, sometimes rather wide, toothed along the outer margins, shorter than the anther.

FLOWERING PERIOD: Sept. to Nov.

DISTRIBUTION: Albany district, WA

D. purdiei (Plate 78)

D. purdiei Diels in *J. Proc. Mueller bot. Soc. West. Aust.* 1^11:79 (1903); R. Erickson *Orchids West* ed. 2:34 (1965)

A slender to moderately robust plant 12–45 cm. in height. Leaves five to ten, 8–10 cm. long, narrow-linear, filiform on a wide base, spirally-twisted. Stem-bracts one or two, linear-lanceolate, the lower one similar to the leaves. Flowers one to five, pale yellow with red-brown wallflower markings at the base of the labellum, becoming purplish on drying. Dorsal sepal about 1·5 cm. long, broad ovate-triangular. Lateral sepals about 1 cm. longer than the labellum, stout, linear-lanceolate. Lateral petals golden-yellow above, often with wallflower markings on the reverse, orbicular or elliptical, on a claw two-thirds the length of the labellum. Labellum with two short raised lines situated widely apart at the base of the lamina (the lines somewhat rugose), and extending as a single ridge to the apex. Mid-lobe very wide, almost rhomboid, and more than twice as long as the lateral lobes; lateral lobes semi-ovate, deeply cleft on the outer margin and toothed along the upper, the margins red-lined. Column appendages narrow, almost as high as the anther.

In the Busselton district this species attained a height of 45 cm. and over, with three to five flowers, the soil being sandy; elsewhere, on granite slopes, it was of low stature, with one to three blooms.

DIURIS

FLOWERING PERIOD: Oct. and Nov.

DISTRIBUTION: Coastal and near-coastal regions of south-western WA

D. laevis (Plate 79)

D. laevis R. D. FitzG. in *Gdnrs' Chron.* new ser. *17*:495 (1882); R. Erickson *Orchids West* ed. 2:33 (1965)

A slender plant 20–35 cm. in height. Leaves three to seven, 8–10 cm. long, narrow-linear, spirally twisted, enclosed at their base by a prominent sheath. Stem-bracts one or two, linear-lanceolate, the lower one similar to the leaves; floral-bracts loosely sheathing. Flowers one to five, pale yellow, with brown blotchings on the underside of dorsal sepal, petals and labellum. Dorsal sepal small, about half the length of the other segments, almost triangular or narrow-lanceolate, embracing the column. Lateral sepals green, about 1·5 cm. long, narrow-linear, parallel; petals about 1·3 cm. long, stipitate, lamina oval or oval-oblong, often somewhat angular. Labellum trilobed, about same length as the petals, the lateral lobes half the length of the mid-lobe, somewhat falcate, but variable in shape, and fringed or denticulate along the upper margin; mid-lobe ovate-rhomboid or triangular, callus with two raised smooth plates, which extend about a third or halfway along the lamina, then continue as a single raised ridge to the apex. Column wings broad, toothed, and about as high as or a little higher than the anther.

FLOWERING PERIOD: Sept. and Oct.

DISTRIBUTION: Coastal regions of south-western WA

D. venosa (Plate 80)

D. venosa H. M. R. Rupp in *Proc. Linn. Soc. N.S.W.* *51*:313, fig. 1–6 (1926); H. M. R. Rupp *Orchids N.S.W.* 15 (1943)

A rather robust plant 10–40 cm. high, often with a dark purplish-red stem and three to five rather short leaves. Flowers two to four, lilac or greyish-blue, very fragrant. Dorsal sepal 10–12 mm. long, very dark at the base (in the author's specimens hardly so), and with conspicuous dark veins on the back. Lateral sepals greenish, about as long as the petals. Petals 12–13 mm. long, the lamina lanceolate to broad-ovate, veined on the back, claw very dark. Labellum strongly veined below, trilobed from near the base; lateral lobes short and obtuse, obliquely ovate, crenulate; mid-lobe with two longitudinal ridges, its lamina usually more or less cordate. Column wings about as high as the anther.

FLOWERING PERIOD: Nov. to Jan.

DISTRIBUTION: Confined to the Barrington Tops, NSW

D. palustris (Plate 81)

D. palustris Lindl. *Gen. & Spec. orchid. Pls* 507 (1840); A. J. Ewart *Flor. Vict.* 357 (1931); J. M. Black *Flor. S. Aust.* ed. 2:238 (1943); J. H. Willis *Handb. Pls Vict.* 1:358 (1962); M. J. Firth *Native Orchids Tasm.* 77 (1965)

A small glabrous plant 10–18 cm. high. Leaves eight to ten, erect, usually more than half the length of scape, channelled, setaceous and twisted, or very narrow linear, dark green, crimson below. Flowers rather small, one to four, on long slender pedicels, yellow, variously blotched with dark brown, the dark colour prevailing on the outside, pervaded by faint odour of spice or nutmeg. Dorsal sepal about 8 mm. long, ovate or oblong-cuneate, recurved in the upper half or erect, purple or dark brown behind the anther, yellowish beyond this. Lateral sepals 15–18 mm. long, green or green-brown, free, linear, parallel, spreading below the labellum. Petals 6–10 mm.

long and 4–6 mm. wide, clawed, the claw purplish, recurved. Labellum 6–10 mm. long; lateral lobes 4–6 mm. long, erect, oblong with rounded crenate anterior margins, margins otherwise entire, yellow on inner surface, much blotched with brown outside; mid-lobe oblong, the lamina (which occasionally is transversely oblong) with two thick fleshy parallel longitudinal raised lines from the base to beyond the middle, thereafter merging into a single short raised line dilating at the anterior margin into a rounded emarginate eminence; dark brown markings at the end of the two raised lines and also at the tip, sometimes the extreme apex marked with white. Anther blunt, rather narrow, a little higher than rostellum. Column wings higher than anther, very rugose.

D. palustris frequents grass-covered, usually marshy, places. Specimens from Portland, Vic., however, were found on the summit of a high hill. Sept. is the best month for it in Vic. and SA; in Tas. it appears later, from Oct. to Dec. It usually grows in compact tufts.

FLOWERING PERIOD: July to Dec.

COMMON NAME: Swamp Diuris

DISTRIBUTION: Western Vic.; northern and eastern Tas., also Macquarie Harbour; southern SA

D. longifolia (Plate 82)

D. longifolia R. Br. *Prodr. Flor. Nov. Holl.* 316 (1810); A. J. Ewart *Flor. Vict.* 358 (1931); J. M. Black *Flor. S. Aust.* ed. 2:238 (1943); H. M. R. Rupp *Orchids N.S.W.* 14 (1943); J. H. Willis *Handb. Pls Vict.* 1:359 (1962); R. Erickson *Orchids West* ed. 2:34 (1965); M. J. Firth *Native Orchids Tasm.* 79 (1965)

Often a stout plant, 10–45 cm. high. Leaves two or three, 7–20 cm. long and 4–12 mm. wide, linear or lanceolate, channelled, usually of unequal length. Flowers usually large, one to eight, on slender pedicels, in a loose raceme, yellow and brown, occasionally a tinge of mauve on the lip (WA flowers sometimes with the labellum mid-lobe almost wholly mauve), the colours suffusing into each other as in the wallflower, some flowers wholly yellow. Dorsal sepal 10–12 mm. long, very broad and rounded. Lateral sepals green, 18–25 mm. long, linear, rather broadly dilated at the tips, parallel or crossed. Petals stalked, recurved or spreading, the claw 4–5 mm. long; lamina oval or elliptical, about 16 mm. long. Labellum about 10 mm. long, dark brown and yellow blended, or rich mauve; lateral lobes nearly as long as the mid-lobe, in some forms noticeably longer, oblong-cuneate, margins entire; mid-lobe 10 mm. long, rounded, recurved, lanceolate to broad-ovate, its anterior border retuse; lamina with a single (very rarely double), raised line at its extreme base merging into a central one extending to the tip. Anther without a point, a little higher than the viscid disc of the rostellum. Lateral appendages about the same height, linear-falcate, anterior margins irregular.

D. longifolia is a common species throughout its range. The most attractive flowers are to be found in sheltered places in fairly heavily timbered country. WA flowers are often intensely coloured.

FLOWERING PERIOD: July to Nov.

COMMON NAME: Wallflower Orchid or Donkey Orchid

DISTRIBUTION: Timbillica in NSW; southern Vic.; northern Tas.; SA; south-western WA

D. longifolia var. parviflora (Plate 82)

D. longifolia var. *parviflora* W. H. Nicholls in *Vict. Nat. 64*:115, fig. I (1947); R. Erickson *Orchids West* ed. 2:34 (1965)

This variety differs from the typical in its small flowers.

FLOWERING PERIOD: Sept.

DISTRIBUTION: Darling Range, WA

D. maculata (Plate 83)

D. maculata Sm. *Exot. Bot. 1*:57, t. 30 (1804–5); A. J. Ewart *Flor. Vict.* 358 (1931); J. M. Black *Flor. S. Aust.* ed. 2:238 (1943); H. M. R. Rupp *Orchids N.S.W.* 14 (1943); J. H. Willis *Handb. Pls Vict. 1*:359 (1962); M. J. Firth *Native Orchids Tasm.* 79 (1965)

Plant usually slender, 18–30 cm. high. Leaves two or three, 10–24 cm. long, narrow-lanceolate, channelled. Flowers two to eight, in a flexuose raceme, yellow, heavily spotted with distinct dark brown spots, underside of perianth more deeply spotted than the upper; pedicels slender. Dorsal sepal 9–11 mm. long, more or less ovate, margins irregularly sinuous, apex usually bent forward; lateral sepals 12–20 mm. long, green with dark purplish markings, stoutly linear with oblique tips, falcate and crossed in the mature flower. Petals 15–20 mm. long; lamina orbicular or broadly ovate, upper surface yellow, often with a few brownish spots or blotches, the lower surface much blotched with dark brown; claw almost as long as the lamina, dark brown, linear, reflexed. Labellum 6–7 mm. long, trilobed from well above the base, lateral lobes upturned with wide crescentic, crenate, recurved anterior margins, as long or almost as long as the mid-lobe; mid-lobe obcuneate with widely retuse truncate apex; lamina with two rather widely separated, fleshy, prominent raised lines, ending near the middle in two acute teeth. Anther with a short point about as high as the viscid disc.

An abundant species throughout its range—in scrub lands, open forest and comparatively heavily timbered country, also in rocky places.

Bentham has described a variety in which the flowers are yellow with few or no spots: *D. maculata* var. *concolor* Benth. *Flor. aust.* 6:328 (1873). Yellow forms are common in western Vic., especially in the Grampians.

FLOWERING PERIOD: July to Nov.

COMMON NAME: Leopard Orchid

DISTRIBUTION: South-eastern Qld; NSW east of the Darling River; Vic.; northern and eastern Tas.; southern SA

D. brevissima (Plate 84)

D. brevissima R. D. FitzG. [ut tabula separata (? 1894)]; H. M. R. Rupp *Orchids N.S.W.* 15 (1943); J. H. Willis *Handb. Pls Vict. 1*:359 (1962)

Plant slender, about 35 cm. high. Leaves usually two, linear, channelled, about 20 cm. long. Flowers six to nine in a flexuose raceme, on long slender pedicels and subtended by long, usually purplish sheathing bracts; yellow, conspicuously blotched with dark red-brown, the markings similar to those in *D. maculata* though more pronounced. Dorsal sepal 8–10 mm. long, broadly ovate, prominently marked with deep red-brown, and dotted along the upper margin. Lateral sepals 1 cm. long, broad-linear, obliquely pointed, parallel. Petals with a claw shorter than the lamina, lamina more or less orbicular, irregularly blotched on the under surface. Labellum about 1 cm. long, a brighter yellow than the other segments, with prominent dark red-brown markings; lateral lobes obliquely oblong, almost as long as the mid-lobe; mid-lobe oblong-cuneate, wider towards the tip than in *D. maculata*, tip retuse; lamina with two raised, parallel, incurved plates ending near the middle in two blunt teeth, a more or less broad keel extending to the apex. Anther with an obtuse point, as high as or a little above the viscid disc.

Among *Diuris* species *D. brevissima* is, in my opinion, an outstanding and beautifully marked form, and despite its obvious affinity with *D. maculata*, it is well deserving of specific recognition, for it is an established form throughout the Ararat district of Vic. It is more robust than *D. maculata*, and the flowers are more attractively marked. *D. brevissima* was observed by the author growing in McDonald Park, Ararat, on 14 October 1939. It was growing in association with abundant specimens of *Glossodia major* and *D. maculata*, with *D. sulphurea* in lesser quantity. It now appears that this species has been known in the Ararat and Pomonal districts for a long period, having been passed over as a robust form of *D. maculata*, and in some instances as *D. palachila*.

FLOWERING PERIOD: Oct. and Nov.

DISTRIBUTION: Central and south-eastern NSW; western Vic. and Mount Timbertop; Penola, SA

D. flavopurpurea (Plate 85)

D. flavopurpurea P. R. Messmer in H. M. R. Rupp *Orchids N.S.W.* 141 (1943); M. J. Firth *Native Orchids Tasm.* 80 (1965)

[Slender plant 30–50 cm. high, the upper part of the stem dark purple. Leaves two or three, about 18 cm. long, linear, rather rigid. Stem-bracts two, closely appressed. Flowers four to ten, in a flexuose raceme, yellow with brownish-purple markings, on long pedicels with very short bracts. Dorsal sepal about 10 mm. long, somewhat ovate, yellow with a brownish-purple marginal line, or sometimes dotted, two prominent purple blotches on the inner surface near the back of the column, the outer surface with a large furcate purple blotch toward the base, margins undulate. Lateral sepals 10–14 mm. long, acute, green and brown. Petals about 10 mm. long, ovate, on dark brown claws 8 mm. long; lamina yellow with heavy brownish-purple blotches on the underside near the base. Labellum 8–10 mm. long; mid-lobe obovate-cresentic, dark brownish-purple with a yellow apex; lateral lobes 6 mm. long, acute, yellow with brown blotches, margins more or less crenate. Labellum ridges brown along the outer edges, yellow along the inner, the central ridge almost as high as the two lateral ridges and very distinct from the keel of the lamina. Column short and broad with incurved margins and a dark marginal line; wings not as high as the anther, deeply dentate, invisible from the front.

D. flavopurpurea is probably a hybrid of *D. maculata* and another species.

FLOWERING PERIOD: Oct.

DISTRIBUTION: Mount Victoria, NSW; Beauty Point and Austin's Ferry, Tas.—Ed.]

D. citrina (Plate 86)

D. citrina W. H. Nicholls in *Vict. Nat.* 66:211, fig. A–C (1950)

A very slender plant 20–30 cm. high. Leaves two, very slender, elongated, 10–20 cm. long; stem-bracts one or two. Flowers three or four, in a loose raceme, on long slender pedicels, pale lemon-yellow, with very dark brown, almost black markings; ovary much elongated; bracts loose, subulate and exceeding the pedicels. Dorsal sepal somewhat ovate-lanceolate with conspicuous markings, the apex recurved but occasionally decurved, clasping the column at the base, about 8 mm. long, and about equal to the labellum in length. Lateral sepals greenish, linear, parallel or sometimes crossed, channelled above, about 12 mm. long. Petals about 1·5 cm. long, ovate on slender claws. Labellum trilobed from well above the base, the lateral lobes crescent-shaped, attenuated at the apex, about 4 mm. long, inner margins lacerated or fimbriated; mid-lobe about 10 mm. long, sub-orbicular or orbicular, narrowing towards the base, between the lateral lobes, into a claw, the margins entire; lamina with two well-separated parallel raised plates on the claw of the mid-lobe, a single keel continuing to the apex. Anther obtuse, about as high as the rostellum and lateral wings. Lateral wings narrow, with irregular margins and subulate apex.

FLOWERING PERIOD: Oct.

DISTRIBUTION: Dripstone and Katoomba, NSW

D. althoferi (Plate 87)

D. althoferi H. M. Rupp in *Proc. Linn. Soc. N.S.W.* 73:133, t. 2 fig. 1 (1948)

[A slender plant, up to 35 cm. high. Leaves two or three, about 22 cm. long. Flowers three to seven, in a flexuose raceme, clear lemon yellow. Dorsal sepal about 1 cm. long, more or less erect, with a large dusky forked blotch near the base; margins reflexed, apex very obtuse. Lateral sepals 16–20 mm. long, narrow but slightly dilated towards the apex, often crossed, green and brown. Petals 12–13 mm. long on a dark claw 4–6 mm. long, spreading, neither spotted nor blotched, the lamina ovate. Labellum about as long as the lamina of the petal, trilobed; lateral lobes almost lanceolate, about half as long as the mid-lobe, obtuse or shortly acute, spreading and sometimes reflexed, upper margins minutely crenulate or denticulate, mid-lobe with a short disc; callus plates separated by a low keel; lamina usually orbicular, but sometimes broadly ovate, neither spotted nor blotched, or occasionally with two or three short brownish markings above. Column appendages obscure from the front, nearly triangular, slightly denticulate, shorter than the anther.

This species may be only a form of *D. platichila*.

FLOWERING PERIOD: Sept. and Oct.

DISTRIBUTION: Apparently confined to the Mudgee district, NSW —Ed.]

D. platichila (Plate 88)

D. platichila R. D. FitzG. *Aust. Orchids* 2⁴:+t. (1891); H. M. R. Rupp *Orchids N.S.W.* 16 (1943)

[A slender plant up to 60 cm. high, with two linear leaves about 30 cm. long. Stem-bracts two or three, 5–8 cm. long, terminating in a fine point; floral bracts 1 cm. long. Flowers two to seven, on long pedicels, pale yellow. Dorsal sepal about 6 mm. long, ovate-lanceolate, recurved. Lateral sepals about 13 mm. long, linear, acute, greenish-brown. Petals about 6 mm. long, ovate, yellow, with green claws about 5 mm. long. Labellum about 8 mm. long, pale yellow, spotted brown, trilobed; lateral lobes about 6 mm. long, linear-lanceolate, spreading; mid-lobe narrow for half its length, then widening and becoming as broad as long; a smooth ridge running down the centre for the whole length, with two prominent side-lines for half the length. Anther shorter than stigma; the wings as long as the stigma, broad, linear, denticulate. Stigma shallow, triangular, contracting to a point downward. Rostellum large.

FLOWERING PERIOD: Oct.

DISTRIBUTION: South-eastern Qld; mountains of central-eastern NSW—Ed.]

D. lineata (Plate 89)

D. lineata P. R. Messmer in H. M. R. Rupp *Orchids N.S.W.* 142 (1943)

A slender plant 20–30 cm. high, with a light purple stem. Leaves two, up to 12 cm. long. Stem-bracts two, the lower one leafy, the

upper one almost immediately above it, appressed. Floral bracts purple, 2·5–3 cm. long. Flowers several, pale sulphur yellow to chrome yellow, with red-brown linear markings, pedicels about 4 cm. Dorsal sepal spathulate, with more or less crenate margins, and occasionally brown marginal dots; two prominent brown blotches on the inner surface, and a large brown furcate blotch on the outer surface near the base. Lateral sepals brownish-green or green, expanded anteriorly and often crossed. Petals 7–10 mm. long, ovate to broad-lanceolate, on dark brown claws 6 mm. long; the lamina yellow, sometimes with light brown streaks. Labellum at least 6 mm. long, trilobed; mid-lobe rhomboidal or obtusely spathulate, with short, thick brown striae radiating towards the margins; basal ridges three, prominent, obtuse, yellow with brown spots, central ridge broad, not extending as a laminal keel (although the keel was prominent in the author's specimens). Lateral lobes three-fourths as long as the mid-lobe, spreading, broad, with crenate or entire anterior margins. Column short, with broad, irregularly triangular wings, acuminate and denticulate, shorter than the anther. Anther narrow, as high as the broad stigma, disc prominent.

This species bears some resemblance to *D. platichila*, and it may be a form of the latter.

FLOWERING PERIOD: Oct.

DISTRIBUTION: Central eastern NSW

7 *Orthoceras*

Orthoceras R. Br. *Prodr. Flor. Nov. Holl.* 316 (1810)

Terrestrial plants, similar to *Diuris*, but differing in the almost sessile flowers, the minute sessile petals, and the filiform erect lateral sepals. A monotypic genus found in Australia, New Zealand and New Caledonia.

O. strictum (Plate 90)

O strictum R. Br. *Prodr. Flor. Nov. Holl.* 317 (1810); A. J. Ewart *Flor. Vict.* 359 (1931); J. M. Black *Flor. S. Aust.* ed. 2:240 (1943); H. M. R. Rupp *Orchids N.S.W.* 20 (1943); J. H. Willis *Handb. Pls Vict.* 1:362 (1962); M. J. Firth *Native Orchids Tasm.* 82 (1965)

Glabrous terrestrial plants with ovoid tubers. Leaves radical, two to five, 15–30 cm. long, narrow-linear, channelled, sheathing at the base and passing gradually above into one or two stem-bracts. Inflorescence 15–60 cm. high, a narrow rigid raceme; flowers one to nine, green to yellowish-brown, almost sessile within erect floral bracts 2–4 cm. long. Dorsal sepal broadly ovate, more or less acute, 8–12 mm. long, hooded; lateral sepals narrow-linear to filiform, 2–4 cm. long, erect or somewhat spreading. Petals 5–8 mm. long, oblong, blunt and the tips often notched, hidden under the dorsal sepal. Labellum reddish-brown, trilobed, 8–12 mm. long, the mid-lobe elliptic-oblong, contracted at the base, the margins entire and more or less incurved, the apex truncate; lateral lobes 4–5 mm. long, erect; lamina yellow-centred, smooth except for a large callus at the base. Column about 4 mm. long, with two lateral wings that are shorter than the anther. Anther blunt, incurved, two-celled; stigma erect in front of it. Pollinia two, bilobed, lacking a caudicle, mealy and friable.

FLOWERING PERIOD: Oct. to Jan.

COMMON NAME: Horned Orchid

DISTRIBUTION: South-eastern Qld; eastern NSW; southern and north-eastern Vic.; St Helens, Rosebery and Trial Harbour, Tas.; south-eastern SA

8 *Microtis*

Microtis R. Br. *Prodr. Flor. Nov. Holl.* 321 (1810)

Terrestrial glabrous herbs, with small underground tubers. Leaf solitary, lamina elongate or terete. Flowers small, numerous, in a terminal spike or raceme. Dorsal sepal hooded, erect, broad; lateral sepals as long or shorter, lanceolate or oblong, spreading or recurved; petals usually narrower, incurved or spreading. Labellum sessile, oblong, ovate or orbicular, obtuse, truncate or emarginate; lamina with callosities at the base or along the centre, or quite smooth. Column very short, nearly terete, with two small auricles behind the stigma. Anther erect, two-celled; pollinia granular, caudicle often very short or sometimes absent. Stigma obtuse or with a rostellum shorter than the anther.

The genus has representatives in New Zealand, New Caledonia, Indonesia, Philippines, Taiwan, and China. Fourteen species have been recorded in Australia, twelve of these being endemic.

M. atrata (Plate 91)

M. atrata Lindl. in *Edwards' bot. Reg. 23*: Swan Riv. Append. liv (1840); A. J. Ewart *Flor. Vict.* 333 (1931); J. M. Black *Flor. S. Aust.* ed. 2:218 (1943); J. H. Willis *Handb. Pls Vict.* 1:362 (1962); R. Erickson *Orchids West* ed. 2:50 (1965); M. J. Firth *Native Orchids Tasm.* 54 (1965)

A small plant, 4–15 cm. high. Leaf-fistula close to the inflorescence; lamina variable in length, often exceeding it. The whole plant, including the flowers, yellowish-green. Flowers minute in a somewhat dense spike which is usually 1–3 cm. long. Ovary tumid, sessile. Dorsal sepal up to 1 mm. long, obtuse, widely galeate; lateral sepals oblong, blunt, spreading, but not recurved, as long as the dorsal sepal. Petals shorter than lateral sepals, similar in shape, spreading. Labellum about as long as the dorsal sepal, oblong, the tip quite blunt; its margins practically entire and beset with minute glands; lamina with two spreading longitudinal lines of small glands, no prominent callosities present. Column shorter than the labellum, its appendages (auricles) higher than the anther. Anther hemispherical, two-celled. Pollinia two, each bilobed, connected directly with viscid disc; caudicle absent. Stigma semilunar, rostellum in upper border.

M. atrata is commonly found in great abundance in moist situations, where it often grows nearly submerged. It is often especially abundant in WA.

FLOWERING PERIOD: Sept. to Dec.

COMMON NAME: Yellow Onion-orchid

DISTRIBUTION: Scattered through swampy areas of Vic., Tas., SA, and WA, usually in coastal heaths

M. orbicularis (Plate 92)

M. orbicularis R. S. Rogers in *Trans. roy. Soc. S. Aust.* 31:63, t. 20 fig. 1 (1907); J. M. Black *Flor. S. Aust.* ed. 2:218 (1943); J. H. Willis *Handb. Pls Vict.* 1:363 (1962); R. Erickson *Orchids West* ed. 2:50 (1965); M. J. Firth *Native Orchids Tasm.* 54 (1965)

A slender plant 15–30 cm. high. Leaf lamina generally shorter than the inflorescence, the fistula just below the flowers, at a characteristic angulation in the stem. Spike not crowded, and often more flattened than in other species. Flowers small, green, sessile. Dorsal sepal obtuse, galeate, gradually narrowing towards the base, about 1·25 mm. long; lateral sepals about same length, linear-oblong, blunt, concealed below the labellum. Petals narrower than the lateral sepals, about 1·25 mm. long, spreading transversely, slightly recurved. Labellum orbicular, its margins entire; lamina concave, reflexed, about as long as the lateral sepals. Column very minute, about 0·75 mm. high, with distinct linear auricles. Rostellum protuberant, as a dark green dot. Anther two-celled, galeate. Pollinia attached to rostellum by a long caudicle.

M. orbicularis favours swampy ground, often growing in great abundance in the water. Sometimes the flowers are more brown than green and crowded on the spike.

FLOWERING PERIOD: Sept. to Dec.

DISTRIBUTION: Confined to a few swampy areas in southern Vic., south-eastern SA, and south-western WA, but often extremely abundant; also in Tas., where confined to the north coast and rare

M. holmesii (Plate 93)

M. holmesii W. H. Nicholls in *Vict. Nat.* 66:94, fig. J–L (1949); J. H. Willis *Handb. Pls Vict.* 1:364 (1962)

Plant more or less robust, from 25–30 cm. high. Leaf sheathing at the base; lamina slender, 9–12 cm. long. Inflorescence in a compact but not crowded raceme of 8–12 cm. Flowers numerous, with large ovaries, green, the pedicels short. Dorsal sepal erect, concave, minutely apiculate, about 2·5 mm. long. Lateral sepals oblong-lanceolate, often tightly-revolute, about 3·5 mm. long. Petals oblong-linear, erect, apices obtuse or somewhat acute, often concealed within the dorsal hood, or quite free and prominent, about 2 mm. long. Labellum sessile, cordate, recurved, about 3 mm. long; its margins entire, undulate; two dark green callosities at the base, and a minute pale green one at the tip. Column short. Anther obtuse; the auricles comparatively large. Viscid disc prominent.

I have named this outstanding addition to *Microtis* after its discoverer, N. Holmes of Moe, Gippsland. Some of his specimens were remarkable for their splendid symmetrical spike of flowers. *M. holmesii* is quite a late-flowering species, often being in bloom when flowers of both *M. unifolia* and *M. parviflora* are withered in the same association. It was found along the railway enclosure on the western outskirts of the town, in grey and rather clayey soil.

FLOWERING PERIOD: Nov. to Jan.

DISTRIBUTION: Vic., where apparently endemic at Moe

M. parviflora (Plate 94)

M. parviflora R. Br. *Prodr. Flor. Nov. Holl.* 321 (1810); A. J. Ewart *Flor. Vict.* 334 (1931); J. M. Black *Flor. S. Aust.* ed. 2:217 (1943); H. M. R. Rupp *Orchids N.S.W.* 21 (1943); J. H. Willis *Handb. Pls Vict.* 1:364 (1962); R. Erickson *Orchids West* ed. 2:50 (1965); M. J. Firth *Native Orchids Tasm.* 53 (1965)

Plant generally slender, occasionally robust, 7–60 cm. high. Leaf lamina usually longer than the spike. Flowers green, sometimes golden-green, on short pedicels, smaller than those of *M. unifolia*, commonly in a dense raceme which is often elongated; subtending bracteoles long, acuminate. Dorsal sepal galeate, ovate with a short recurved point, about 2 mm. long; lateral sepals variable in length, sometimes shorter than the dorsal sepal, oblong, acute, recurved or revolute. Petals blunt, about 1·3 mm. long, linear to oblong-linear, erect, partly hidden by the dorsal sepal. Labellum oblong, ovate-oblong or ovate, widest at the base, with a rounded, rectangular or shortly acuminate tip, about 1·5 mm. long; recurved, simply reflexed or occasionally inflexed; lamina with two narrow transverse callosities at the base, its margins more or less smooth; callus thickened only towards the apex where it sometimes forms a papillose protuberance. Column hardly 1 mm. long, with a distinct and rather prominently rounded auricle on each side of the anther. Anther hemispherical. Pollinia two, each bilobed, attached to a viscid disc by a very short caudicle. Stigma semilunar, situated between the auricles.

FLOWERING PERIOD: Oct. to Feb., depending on altitude

COMMON NAME: Slender Onion-orchid

DISTRIBUTION: Temperate parts of all Australian states, but in WA confined to the Albany area; also NZ, New Caledonia, and extending through the islands to China

M. bipulvinaris (Plate 95)

M. bipulvinaris W. H. Nicholls in *Vict. Nat.* 66:92, fig. A–F (1949); J. H. Willis *Handb. Pls Vict.* 1:365 (1962); M. J. Firth *Native Orchids Tasm.* 54 (1965)

A slender plant 25–40 cm. high. Leaf sheathing at base; lamina variable in length, but usually longer than raceme. Inflorescence a somewhat lax raceme 12–15 cm. long; flowers numerous, green, the pedicels 1–2 mm. long, suberect. Dorsal sepal erect, wide, concave over the column, somewhat hemispherical, with a minute point at the apex about 2 mm. long. Lateral sepals free, lanceolate, diverging on each side of the labellum, sometimes recurved, about 2·5 mm. long. Petals erect, 1·5 mm. long, oblong-linear, acute to obtuse, the apices sometimes reflexed. Labellum sessile, linguiform, channelled, apiculate, about 1·5 mm. long; its lateral margins entire or somewhat crenulate; lamina marked near the tip with a slightly raised mass of granulations, and bearing towards the base two conspicuous cushion-like elevations, at the extreme base with two inconspicuous horizontal glands (in a few flowers examined these glands were obsolete). Column very short, terete. Anther hemispherical, obtuse; the auricles conspicuous.

This species has close affinities with *M. parviflora*, with which it is often associated in the field.

FLOWERING PERIOD: Mainly Sept. to Nov., but even as late as Jan. in some Vic. swamps, e.g. Portland

DISTRIBUTION: Central eastern NSW; scattered localities in Vic.; and possibly Tas.

M. unifolia (Plate 96)

M. unifolia (Forst.f.) Reichenb.f. *Beitr. syst. Pflk.* 62 (1871); A. J. Ewart *Flor. Vict.* 334 (1931), as *M. porrifolia*; J. M. Black *Flor. S. Aust.* ed. 2:217 (1943), as *M. uniflora*; H. M. R. Rupp *Orchids N.S.W.* 21 (1943); J. H. Willis *Handb. Pls Vict.* 1:363 (1962); R. Erickson *Orchids West* ed. 2:49 (1965); M. J. Firth *Native Orchids Tasm.* 53 (1965)

SYNONYMY: *Ophrys unifolia* Forst.f. *Flor. Ins. Aust. Prodr.* 59 (1786); *Microtis rara* R. Br. *Prodr. Flor. Nov. Holl.* 321 (1810); *M. porrifolia* (Swartz) R. Br. ex Spreng. *Syst. Veg.* 3:713 (1826); *Epipactis porrifolia* Swartz in *K. svenska VetenskAkad. Handl.* ser. 2, 21:233 (1800)

An extremely variable plant, sometimes short, but commonly upward of 20 cm. Leaf lamina terete, elongated, often exceeding the inflorescence. Flowers green, small, numerous in a dense terminal raceme, but occasionally distant and slender. Dorsal sepal erect,

shortly acuminate, galeate, broadly ovate, usually exceeding 2 mm. Lateral sepals shorter, spreading, recurved, oblong, acute or rather blunt. Petals oblong, erect, partly concealed by the dorsal sepal, shorter and narrower than the lateral sepals. Labellum about the same length as lateral sepals, sessile, oblong with crisped or irregular margins; tip blunt or emarginate; lamina with two raised callosities at the base and a central one near the apex. Column about 1 mm. long. Anther hemispherical, two-celled, with a minute point, the auricles distinct, blunt, reaching about halfway up the anther. Stigma prominent, semi-orbicular. Rostellum viscid, conspicuous. Pollinia two, each deeply bilobed, friable, attached directly, or via a long caudicle to the rostellum, easily detached with the disc when fresh.

A common plant of many different habitats, but favouring moist open grassland communities. Several specimens observed *in situ* at Ocean Grove, Vic. in Oct. 1931 were approximately 90 cm. tall and very robust, reminiscent of a sturdy *Prasophyllum elatum*. As well, they possessed the purplish hue at the base of the scape so characteristic of that species.

FLOWERING PERIOD: Oct. to Jan.

COMMON NAME: Common Onion-orchid

DISTRIBUTION: Temperate parts of all Australian states, often locally common; also NZ, New Caledonia, Indonesia, China and Japan

M. biloba (Plate 97)

M. biloba W. H. Nicholls in *Vict. Nat.* 66:94, fig. G–I (1949); J. H. Willis *Handb. Pls Vict.* 1:364 (1962); M. J. Firth *Native Orchids Tasm.* 54 (1965)

A slender species up to 25 cm. high, similar in habit to *M. unifolia*. Inflorescence often rather short, 4–5 cm. long. Dorsal sepal erect, concave, with a prominent acuminate apex, about 3 mm. long. Lateral sepals free, revolute, oblong-lanceolate, obtuse, about 3·5 mm. long. Petals erect, linear, obtuse, about 2·5 mm. long. Labellum oblong-quadrate, 3·5 mm. long; lamina green, margins irregular, pale yellow; apex prominently bilobed, the lobes angular; two large dark green callosities at the base and a minute one near the tip. Column short. Anther obtuse. Auricles small.

Characteristic features of this species are the yellowish tinge pervading the whole plant, and the curious bifid labellum from which it derives its name. In all respects it is close to *M. unifolia*.

FLOWERING PERIOD: Nov. to Jan.

DISTRIBUTION: Known with certainty only from widely scattered localities in Vic., but probably also in NSW and Tas.

M. oblonga (Plate 98)

M. oblonga R. S. Rogers in *Trans. roy. Soc. S. Aust.* 47:339 (1923); A. J. Ewart *Flor. Vict.* 334 (1931); J. M. Black *Flor. S. Aust.* ed. 2:218 (1943); H. M. R. Rupp *Orchids N.S.W.* 21 (1943); J. H. Willis *Handb. Pls Vict.* 1:363 (1962); M. J. Firth *Native Orchids Tasm.* 54 (1965)

Plant very slender, up to 45 cm. high. Leaf thin, often taller than the inflorescence. Raceme lax, 4–22 cm. long. Flowers very small, distant, on short slender pedicels; ovary slender, oblong-elliptical. Dorsal sepal 3–5 mm. long, almost erect, broadly hooded, acute, the apex slightly recurved; lateral sepals tightly revolute. Petals 2–3 mm. long, erect or widely spread, obtuse or truncate, linear-falcate, the posterior margins overlapped by the dorsal sepal. Labellum 3–6 mm. long, reflexed, narrowly oblong, with crenulate margins, two large callosities at the base, and one near the apex. Column stout, short, with relatively large auricles. Caudicle of variable length (long in the original description but short in many of my specimens). Flowers fragrant.

This species is also extremely variable, especially in the length of the labellum, and coiling of the lateral sepals; often it is difficult to separate from *M. unifolia*.

FLOWERING PERIOD: Oct. to Jan. depending on altitude

COMMON NAME: Sweet Onion-orchid

DISTRIBUTION: Distributed through the temperate parts of all Australian states except WA, but in Qld confined to the south-east

M. alba (Plate 99)

M. alba R. Br. *Prodr. Flor. Nov. Holl.* 321 (1810); R. Erickson *Orchids West* ed. 2:50 (1965)

A slender to robust plant from 16 cm. to almost 60 cm. high. Leaf with a long sheath, the lamina often exceeding the inflorescence. Flowers numerous, incurved, snowy white or whitish-green in a compact or slender, loose raceme. Dorsal sepal very prominent, lanceolate-falcate, acute, concave, sometimes broad, contracted at the base, variable in length. Lateral sepals nearly as long as the dorsal sepal, oblong, at first erect and spreading, but becoming revolute at maturity. Petals shorter and narrower than lateral sepals. Labellum as long as the sepals, narrow at the base, the upper half expanded into two lobes, either large and broad, or long, narrow and divaricate, the margins undulate and crisped, crenate or fringed, the callus with an oblong or somewhat irregular callosity along the centre, and sometimes a pair of marginal calli below it. Column with prominent narrow auricles. Stigma prominent.

FLOWERING PERIOD: Oct. to Jan.

COMMON NAME: White Mignonette-orchid

DISTRIBUTION: Endemic in WA where it is widely distributed over the coastal plain in the south-west, and often abundant

9   *Prasophyllum*

Prasophyllum R. Br. *Prodr. Flor. Nov. Holl.* 317 (1810)

Terrestrial glabrous herbs with ovoid or globular tubers. Leaf solitary, usually with a long sheath, the lamina terete, but in the diminutive members of the genus reduced to a bract in the flowering season. Flowers several in a terminal spike or raceme, usually inconspicuous in colour, commonly greenish, white or purple, sometimes fragrant. Flowers reversed. Dorsal sepal lanceolate, or broad and acute, concave, either erect and arched over the column, or recurved; lateral sepals as long as or longer than dorsal sepal, usually more or less lanceolate, free or partially united. Petals usually shorter, but sometimes as long as the sepals, lanceolate or linear. Labellum sessile or on a short claw attached to the basal projection of the column; ovate, oblong or lanceolate; undivided; margins of lamina crisped, ciliate, denticulate or entire; callus with an adnate plate sometimes broad with free margins, sometimes reduced to a central longitudinal thickening; usually erect and concave at the base, recurved towards the end. Ovary turgid, erect, sessile or pedicellate, subtended by a bract. Column very short below the anther; its margins produced into two erect lateral appendages, usually adnate to the basal margins of the stigmatic-plate. Anther two-celled, erect behind the stigma; the rostellum often produced beyond it, but sometimes shorter. Pollinia two, each bilobed,

sectile, attached by a linear caudicle to the glandular disc of the rostellum.

The genus has representatives in NZ, but is otherwise exclusively Australian. About eighty species have been recorded.

Bentham conveniently divided the genus into three sections: (i) *Euprasophyllum*, in which the labellum is sessile at the base of the column; (ii) *Podochilus*, in which the labellum is connected to the column by a short rigid claw, but is not articulate or movable; and (iii) *Genoplesium*, in which the labellum is articulate and movable on a conspicuous claw attached to the column-foot. Rupp in *Orchids N.S.W.* 22–23 (1943) widened the definition of the section *Euprasophyllum* to cover *Podochilus*. As well, in the *Vict. Nat.* 66:75–79 (1949), he reinstated the genus *Genoplesium*, thus rendering the name of that section invalid. In the same article he suggested the name *Micranthum* to replace it. Thus under present considerations the genus *Prasophyllum* is divided into two sections: (1) *Euprasophyllum* (Plates 100–45); and (2) *Micranthum* (Plates 146–70).

P. striatum (Plate 100)

P. striatum R. Br. *Prodr. Flor. Nov. Holl.* 318 (1810); H. M. R. Rupp *Orchids N.S.W.* 30 (1943)

A very slender plant from 9 to 19 cm. high; a sheathing leaf above the middle of the stem, the lamina usually short, 1·5–2 cm., rarely reaching 6 cm.; subulate or linear acuminate. Flowers two to ten, in a loose raceme 2–5 cm. long. Ovary oblong-cylindrical, about 5 mm. long. Lateral sepals connate to near the apex, narrow, cuneate, about 8 mm. long. Petals shorter than the sepals, lanceolate. Labellum about 8 mm. long on a narrow horizontal claw, ovate-oblong, concave, the lower half erect; upper half recurved, with undulate margins; callus plate broad in the lower half, reduced upward to a thick double raised line, reaching almost to the apex. Column appendages narrow-linear, as long as the slender pointed rostellum. Anther very short, blunt; caudicle long, filiform.

P. striatum is very like a small edition of *P. australe*, but unlike that delightfully fragrant species it has rather an unpleasant scent.

FLOWERING PERIOD: Mar. to June

DISTRIBUTION: Endemic in NSW where it is widespread from the central coast to the tablelands

P. parvifolium (Plate 101)

P. parvifolium Lindl. in *Edwards' bot. Reg.* 23: Swan Riv. Append. liv (1840); R. Erickson *Orchids West* ed. 2:59 (1965)

A slender plant 23 cm. to over 40 cm. high, the leaf splitting above the middle of the stem, with a short slender lamina. Flowers resembling those of *P. striatum*, in a loose raceme of 5–8 cm. Ovary narrow-oblong. Sepals 7–10 mm. long, the lateral ones dilated at the base and adnate to the basal projection of the column, forming a short pouch, but otherwise free; dorsal sepal lanceolate, concave. Petals narrower and rather shorter. Labellum stipitate at the end of the basal projection, but apparently continuous with it, the total length of the projection and claw nearly 5 mm., lamina lanceolate, concave, recurved, as long as the sepals; the callus plate nearly as broad as the lamina, and ending about the middle. Column appendages entire, shorter than the rostellum. Anther short, light brown. Caudicle of the pollinia long and linear.

This species is generally the first of the genus to flower in WA, where it is often called the Autumn Leek-orchid.

FLOWERING PERIOD: Apr. to Sept.

DISTRIBUTION: Endemic in WA where it is widespread through coastal areas in the south-west

P. cyphochilum (Plate 102)

P. cyphochilum Benth. *Flor. aust.* 6:340 (1873); R. Erickson *Orchids West* ed. 2:58 (1965)

A slender plant ranging in height from 25 cm. to 60 cm. Leaf lamina slender, usually 4–6 cm. long. Flowers small, pedicellate, yellowish or whitish-green, with chocolate stripes down the centre of the dorsal sepal and petals. Ovary oblong or oblong-turbinate. Sepals 4–5 mm. long, the lateral ones quite free. Petals shorter. Labellum sessile, gibbous at the base, forming a short pouch protruding between the lateral sepals, the erect part concave, not broad, tapering upwards, recurved for half its length and undulate; callus plate reduced to parallel, slightly raised lines along the centre. Column appendages linear-falcate, shorter than the rostellum. Anther short, brown, shortly and obtusely acuminate. Caudicle comparatively long and stout.

FLOWERING PERIOD: Sept. and Oct.

COMMON NAME: Pouched Leek-orchid

DISTRIBUTION: Endemic in WA where it is widespread over a range of habitats in the south-west

P. cucullatum (Plate 103)

P. cucullatum Reichenb.f. *Beitr. syst. Pflk.* 59 (1871); R. Erickson *Orchids West* ed. 2:58 (1965)

A small species, 12–22 cm. high. Leaf narrow-linear, dilated at the base. Flowers from one to over fifty in a much crowded blunt spike resembling that of *Orchis pyramidalis*, white with bright purple markings, sweetly scented. Dorsal sepal purple, lanceolate, reflexed, about 6 mm. long; lateral sepals connate to the extreme tips, the conjoined laminae widely dilated, and erect with incurved tips forming a hood above and in front of the labellum, about 6 mm. long. Petals contracted, purple at the base, otherwise white with a central purple stripe; inflated towards the tips, spreading, and about 6 mm. long. Labellum attached to a long narrow claw, longer than other segments, erect for three-quarters of its length above the claw, the tip bent forward almost at right angles; the erect portion at first narrow, wider towards the bend; the horizontal part dilated into a semicircular tip with crenulate margins; lamina with two wide, raised, slightly pubescent callus plates on the erect part, terminating just beyond the bend. Column appendages variable in length, oblong-falcate with the tips bent backwards. Anther small. Caudicle long.

This small terrestrial orchid was found in considerable abundance on the margins of an extensive swamp just north of the Upper King River State School. It was growing in association with *Diuris laevis*, *Caladenia unita* and *Caladenia paniculata* and was just as plentiful on the very wet black soil bogs. In the Nanarup district only a few specimens were seen, growing in association with *Microtis atrata*.

FLOWERING PERIOD: Sept. and Oct.

COMMON NAME: Hooded Leek-orchid

DISTRIBUTION: Endemic in WA where it is confined to coastal areas in the south-west but often locally abundant

P. fimbria (Plate 104)

P. fimbria Reichenb.f. *Beitr. syst. Pflk.* 60 (1871); R. Erickson *Orchids West* ed. 2:56 (1965)

SYNONYMY: *P. giganteum* Endl. in Lehm. *Plant. Preiss.* 2:12 (1946), non Lindl. (1840)

A tall plant with the habit of *P. elatum*, usually of green hues in

robust plants, purplish-black in others. Leaf lamina longer than in *P. elatum*. Ovary elongated. Flowers green with red-brown markings or deep purplish-black, very fragrant. Sepals 10–12 mm. long, the lateral ones free at the base and often connate above the middle; dorsal sepal deeply concave, the tip reflexed. Petals linear or linear-falcate, shorter than the sepals. Labellum as long as or longer than sepals, glistening white, truncate at base, on a distinct narrow, horizontal claw; lamina broadly oblong, slightly contracted at the bend, the upper part broad with crisped margins; two callus plates present, the inner one wide with two broad callosities at the base and ending in a broad, free, densely fringed, purple margin; within it a more or less conspicuous second plate with scarcely prominent entire margins. Column appendages falcate on a wide base, as long as the rostellum, with a small tooth on the outer margin. Anther short, brown. Caudicle of medium length.

[This species is often tall, up to 120 cm. (4 ft.), and most flowering specimens exceed 60 cm.]

FLOWERING PERIOD: Sept. to Dec.

COMMON NAME: Fringed Leek-orchid

DISTRIBUTION: Endemic in WA where it is widespread throughout the coastal areas of the south-west

P. triangulare (Plate 105)

P. triangulare R. D. FitzG. in *Gdnrs' Chron.* new ser. 17:495 (1882); R. Erickson *Orchids West* ed. 2:57 (1965)

Plant more or less robust, from 20 cm. to over 40 cm. in height, the whole plant very darkly coloured. Leaf slender, terete, 20–26 cm. long, the lamina 12–16 cm. Flowers darkly coloured, nineteen to thirty in a long raceme. Lateral sepals connate throughout, the tips free, ovate, acuminate, glandular at the base and along the conjoined margins; dorsal sepal often longer than the lateral sepals, 6–7 mm. long. Petals lanceolate, shorter than the sepals; labellum on a prominent claw, triangular, very slightly recurved, margins entire and slightly undulate; the callus forming a raised triangular plate which occupies almost the whole labellum. It is somewhat swollen towards the points and irregularly covered with small sessile calli. Column appendages broad at the base, falcate, acuminate, equal in length to the rostellum, thickened on the outer margin into three or more callosities. Anther shorter than the rostellum, more or less acuminate.

P. triangulare was a difficult species to locate. We found it growing, somewhat sparingly, among the blackened ruins of what had been a fine Jarrah forest covering a red ironstone hill crest.

FLOWERING PERIOD: Oct.

COMMON NAME: Dark Leek-orchid

DISTRIBUTION: Endemic in south-western WA, where it favours the coastal plain

P. elatum (Plate 106)

P. elatum R. Br. *Prodr. Flor. Nov. Holl.* 318 (1810); A. J. Ewart *Flor. Vict.* 314 (1931); J. M. Black *Flor. S. Aust.* ed. 2:220 (1943); H. M. R. Rupp *Orchids N.S.W.* 26 (1943); J. H. Willis *Handb. Pls Vict.* 1:370 (1962); R. Erickson *Orchids West* ed. 2:56 (1965); M. J. Firth *Native Orchids Tasm.* 21 (1965)

A robust plant usually from 45 cm. to 140 cm. in height. Leaf lamina generally short, but sometimes exceeding the inflorescence, the whole plant varying in colour from pale yellowish-green to greenish or purplish-black. Flowers large, sessile on a narrow, elongated, terete ovary. Dorsal sepal lanceolate, about 11 mm. long, acute, concave, erect or recurved. Lateral sepals connate from the middle almost to the tips, but often free, falco-lanceolate, 10–11 mm. long. Petals almost as long as sepals, narrower, falco-lanceolate, spreading or incurved. Labellum sessile, ovate, 8–9 mm. long and 6·5–7 mm. wide, slightly recurved from the middle, basal margins entire, upper margins corrugated, callus plate ovate, occupying most of the lamina, ending midway between the bend and the tip, the free crenulate margins united anteriorly. Anther erect, two-celled, with a short acute, variable point, usually the same height as the rostellum. Rostellum long and narrow with a prominent disc. Pollinia two, deeply bilobed, attached to the disc by a caudicle of medium length. Column appendages blunt, linear falcate, exceeding the rostellum in most flowers, with a small thickened basal lobe, free from the stigmatic plate. Stigma prominent, rounded or shield-like.

This species is often abundant in coastal areas, and flowers in profusion after bush fires. It attains its maximum development in WA where it often reaches a height of 140 cm. (4 ft. 6 in.) and over, with a stem 2·5 cm. in diameter.

FLOWERING PERIOD: Aug. to Dec.

COMMON NAME: Tall Leek-orchid

DISTRIBUTION: Temperate parts of all Australian states, but in Qld restricted to the south-east; often abundant in coastal areas

P. muelleri (Plates 107 and 108)

P. muelleri C. R. P. Andrews in *J. Proc. Mueller bot. Soc. West. Aust. 1⁹*:19 (1902); R. Erickson *Orchids West* ed. 2:57 (1965)

SYNONYMY: *P. paludosum* W. H. Nicholls in *Vict. Nat. 64*:172 (1948); *P. elatum* var. *muelleri* W. H. Nicholls in *Vict. Nat. 65*:270 (1949)

A slender to moderately robust plant from about 40 to 60 cm. high. Leaf lamina not exceeding the inflorescence. Flowers fragrant, not crowded, wholly pale yellowish to greenish-yellow with pale red or purplish markings. Ovary long and slender, 7–8 mm. long, sessile or almost so. Dorsal sepal lanceolate, usually with a recurved acuminate apex, 7–8 mm. long. Lateral sepals connate almost to the apex, occasionally quite free, 7–8 mm. long, the margins incurved. Petals narrow-lanceolate, erect, widely dilated, shorter and narrower than the sepals. Labellum on the short basal claw of the column, narrow-lanceolate, abruptly reflexed about the middle in mature flowers, 7–8 mm. long; membranous part narrow, creamy-white in colour, crisped, margins incurved; callus plate green, its margins free only towards the base and hardly raised beyond the bend; margins entire throughout, the plate narrowing gradually and continuing almost to the extreme apex, deeply channelled below. Column stout, lateral appendages about 5 mm. high, extending well above the rostellum, linear-falcate, with a large double lobe at the base. Anther ovate with a recurved apex, much shorter than the rostellum. Pollinia attached by a short caudicle to a prominent disc.

[The above description was drawn up for *P. paludosum* but close examination by A. S. George has shown it to be identical with *P. muelleri*. See *West. Aust. Nat. 8*:38 (1961). The description should be amended on the following points to allow for normal variation: (i) leaf blade can be shorter, as long as, or longer than the inflorescence; (ii) petals can be narrower or broader than the sepals; (iii) anther can be shorter or as long as the rostellum.

In reference to *P. elatum* var. *muelleri* he states: 'P. muelleri has for some years been confused with *P. elatum*, but is actually a distinct species. Nicholls made it a variety of Robert Brown's plant, but it differs considerably in the floral details, especially of the column and labellum.'—Ed.]

This species is a frequenter of reedy swamps and boggy places. Near Perth it grows luxuriantly in 15 cm. of water, while near Busselton it was plentiful in *Melaleuca* country, where the location was discovered by chance, because of this orchid's powerful fragrance. [Of the two plates depicting this species, Plate 107 is referable to *P. elatum* var. *muelleri* and Plate 108 to *P. paludosum*. —Ed.]

FLOWERING PERIOD: Sept. and Oct.

COMMON NAME: Swamp Leek-orchid

DISTRIBUTION: Endemic in WA, where it is widespread through the coastal areas in the south-west

P. regium (Plate 109)

P. regium R. S. Rogers in *Trans. roy. Soc. S. Aust. 42*:27 (1918); R. Erickson *Orchids West* ed. 2:57 (1965)

A robust species ranging in height from 75 cm. to 180 cm. Leaf not as tall as the inflorescence; bracts subtending the flowers acute, about one-third length of ovary. Flowers in a loose raceme which is sometimes over 45 cm. long, and comprising upward of sixty flowers; lower flowers distant; ovaries long and attenuated. Sepals acute, often narrow, equal in length, 6–9 mm. long, lateral sepals free at the extreme base and tips, connate elsewhere; dorsal sepal reflexed in the mature flower. Petals narrow, falcate-lanceolate, usually shorter than the sepals. Labellum on a distinct narrow claw, oblong-lanceolate, with crenulate margins, erect in the basal third, horizontal in its anterior part, equal to or slightly longer than the petals, inner callus plate with a wide orbicular base, margins free, entire, suddenly contracting at the bend into a bluntly lanceolate part with entire margins, extending nearly to the tip. (In a few individual flowers the labellum was suddenly constricted towards the tip as in *P. frenchii*.) Column with a blunt sessile anther; the long, narrow rostellum greatly exceeding it in length; caudicle long and strap-like; column appendages blunt, oblong-falcate, membranous, with a basal thickening on the dorsal margin, much higher than rostellum.

The tallest specimens of *P. regium* were seen near Cookernup and at Oyster Cove. Individual plants measured 180 cm. (6 ft.) in height. Many of the King River specimens were exceedingly fine examples; in bud stage 135 cm. high, the stem measuring 2 cm. through. These giants of the undergrowth were by no means rare along the roadsides west of the King River and at Cookernup.

FLOWERING PERIOD: Oct. to Dec.

COMMON NAME: King Leek-orchid

DISTRIBUTION: Endemic in WA where it is confined to the cool moist parts of the south-west

P. grimwadeanum (Plate 110)

P. grimwadeanum W. H. Nicholls in *Vict. Nat. 64*:174, fig. D–F (1948); R. Erickson *Orchids West* ed. 2:56 (1965)

A robust greenish-bronze plant up to 65 cm. high. Leaf lamina variable, about 18 cm. long. Flowers in a crowded inflorescence 18–24 cm. high, with forty to sixty flowers, which are brightly coloured—yellow, green, crimson, purple, mauve, etc., merging in a delightful colour scheme. Ovaries slender on very short pedicels, the subtending bracteoles lanceolate, acute. Dorsal sepal lanceolate, acuminate, incurved, the apex sometimes recurved, about 12 mm. long. Lateral sepals connate, the tips free, narrow-lanceolate, falcate, recurved, longer than the dorsal one. Petals linear to narrow-lanceolate, erect, incurved, about 10 mm. long. Labellum on a very short claw, about 12 mm. long, not abruptly reflexed; membranous part wide, crisped, dull mauve in colour; the callus plate with a wide deeply channelled base, the margins elevated, free and entire, contracting at the bend into a slightly raised, rounded green section, oblong in shape, terminating some distance from the apex. Column stout, about 3 mm. long, the appendages linear, apices angular, higher than the rostellum, a small lobe situated at the base of each appendage. Anther dark red-brown, shorter than the rostellum, apiculate. Caudicle short.

This species, the most gaily coloured of all the *Prasophyllums*, was found growing in thick scrub on the lee side of sand dunes adjacent to Middleton's Beach, near Albany. It was discovered when the writer penetrated the scrub, which is about 4·5 m.(15 ft.) high, while endeavouring to regain the open beach. Only six specimens were seen, two of which were in perfect condition, the remainder being well past their prime with only the uppermost flowers expanded. I have named this attractively-coloured species in honour of W. Russell Grimwade of Melbourne, who has taken a keen interest in Australian orchids.

This species is closely related to *P. ellipticum*, but differs in having brightly-hued flowers, as opposed to the wholly pale-yellowish blooms of the latter, also in several important particulars of the floral structure. It is also allied to *P. regium* and to *P. lanceolatum*, but again it is readily recognised by the crisped nature of the outer, membranous part of the labellum; both *P. regium* and *P. lanceolatum* possess entire or almost entire outer margins.

P. grimwadeanum is apparently a littoral species, for it was not observed elsewhere other than in heavy scrub near the beach. The peak of flowering is apparently during September.

FLOWERING PERIOD: Sept. and Oct.

COMMON NAME: Bronze Leek-orchid

DISTRIBUTION: Endemic in WA where it is confined to the coastal south-west and uncommon

P. flavum (Plate 111)

P. flavum R. Br. *Prodr. Flor. Nov. Holl.* 318 (1810); A. J. Ewart *Flor. Vict.* 315 (1931); H. M. R. Rupp *Orchids N.S.W.* 25 (1943); J. H. Willis *Handb. Pls Vict.* 1:370 (1962); M. J. Firth *Native Orchids Tasm.* 21 (1965)

Plant usually robust, 30–90 cm. or more in height. Leaf closely-sheathing with a very short terete lamina, 1–2·5 cm. long. Stem and leaf dark purplish-black to greenish-black. Flowers six to fifty, in a long raceme, more or less crowded, yellow or green with purplish-brown markings. Ovary elongate, green. Lateral sepals and petals lanceolate; petals narrower than the sepals; lateral sepals connate, except towards the base (in dry weather some are quite free). Dorsal sepal broad-lanceolate. All perianth segments about 1 cm. long, concave. Labellum sessile, oblong-lanceolate, deeply concave, erect or depressed, recurved slightly beyond the middle, 6–8 mm. long; basal margins entire; lamina green with white or yellowish crenulate margins and a more or less prominent callus plate arising from near the base and extending to the bend. Column appendages adnate for most of their length, broad and thick, inconspicuously bilobed and much shorter than the bifid rostellum. Stigma prominent. Anther much shorter than the rostellum. Pollinia two, bilobed, the caudicle short. Tuber large, of irregular formation.

This somewhat rare species was first found in the vicinity of Port Jackson, NSW. It is a most interesting terrestrial form, not only on account of certain characteristics, unique in themselves, but also because it is rarely collected, despite its wide distribution throughout the four states.

P. flavum favours forest country where amid the dense undergrowth it is usually well hidden. The plant itself is dark coloured, and its inconspicuous spike harmonises with the surroundings; in such seclusion it grows, usually solitary, or in small groups of four to five plants. The root system is unique within the genus, consisting of fleshy rhizomes and swollen tubers, paralleling in this respect *Calochilus saprophyticus*. These leafless or partly leafless forms were once thought to be parasitic on the roots of trees; but they are now known to be holo-saprophytes, strange plants which live in symbiotic relationship with a fungus known as *Mycorrhiza*. Many other plant species have such relationships. *P. flavum* prefers somewhat high and dry, though not necessarily arid, situations. I have even found it growing in the very hard soil bordering a main highway, but these were poor examples when compared with those growing in unmolested spots in the natural forest.

FLOWERING PERIOD: Oct. to Feb., depending on altitude

COMMON NAME: Yellow Leek-orchid

DISTRIBUTION: Scattered from south-eastern Qld, through NSW and Vic. to Tas., generally along the coast or in near-coastal ranges, but uncommon and rarely collected

P. australe (Plate 112)

P. australe R. Br. *Prodr. Flor. Nov. Holl.* 318 (1810); A. J. Ewart *Flor. Vict.* 316 (1931); J. M. Black *Flor. S. Aust.* ed. 2:219 (1943); H. M. R. Rupp *Orchids N.S.W.* 25 (1943); J. H. Willis *Handb. Pls Vict.* 1:369 (1962); R. Erickson *Orchids West* ed. 2:55 (1965); M. J. Firth *Native Orchids Tasm.* 21 (1965). (Illust. on p. 52=*P. brevilabre*)

A slender plant from 25 cm. to over 75 cm. high. Leaf lamina usually shorter than the inflorescence. Flowers sessile, on very slender, terete, elongated ovaries, often 10 mm. or more long, in a loose spike, with prevailing tints of white, brown and green; perianth segments all acute; sepals yellowish-green and all nearly equal in length; the dorsal one about 8 mm. long, erect or recurved, concave, ovate-lanceolate; the lateral ones sometimes free at the extreme base, united beyond this almost to the tips. Petals erect, yellowish-green with wide reddish-brown stripes down the centre, narrower and shorter than the lateral sepals. Labellum conspicuously white, sessile with a bulging erect base; acutely reflexed about the middle; the free end voluminous, crisped, with undulate margins; callus plate ending abruptly in two elevated knuckles near the bend. Anther erect, with a short point, two-celled, not as tall as the rostellum. Column appendages lanceolate-falcate, adnate in front to the pedicel of the stigmatic plate, the basal lobes thickened and sinuous, about equal in height to the rostellum. Viscid disc large, ovate, situated in a triangular depression on the anterior apex of the rostellum. Stigma large, prominent, somewhat pentagonal. Caudicle long. Pollinia two, bilobed. Flowers strongly fragrant.

This species favours swamps or moist grassland habitats, where the normally conspicuous racemes are camouflaged and difficult to detect amongst the tall panicles of *Themeda*, *Danthonia*, etc. It has a delightful scent, which on a warm day amongst a colony of flowering plants can become almost overpowering.

FLOWERING PERIOD: Sept. to Jan., being earliest in Qld

COMMON NAME: Austral Leek-orchid

DISTRIBUTION: A widespread component of near-coastal swamps in all Australian states, but in Qld restricted to a few south-eastern localities

P. australe var. sargentii (Plate 113)

P. australe var. *sargentii* W. H. Nicholls in *Vict. Nat.* 65:268 (1949);
R. Erickson *Orchids West* ed. 2:55 (1965)

A robust, almost wholly deep prune-coloured plant. Flowers in a compact raceme. Lateral sepals pure white, labellum not so markedly voluminous or crisped as in the typical form, the membranous part sometimes entire.

Unlike the typical form this plant seems to be restricted to high and often very dry areas.

FLOWERING PERIOD: Sept.

DISTRIBUTION: Endemic in south-western WA

P. hians (Plate 114)

P. hians Reichenb.f. *Beitr. syst. Pflk.* 61 (1871); R. Erickson *Orchids West* ed. 2:58 (1965)

A slender plant 10–60 cm. high. Leaf-sheath loose, the lamina 7–15 cm. long. Flowers white, tinged with red-brown or purplish markings, in a more or less dense raceme. Dorsal sepal erect, incurved, lanceolate, acuminate, 6–8 mm. long. Lateral sepals connate except near the tip, shorter than the petals, gibbous below, thin and white where they join. Petals white, 6–8 mm. long, dilated. Labellum sessile, broad at the base but not gibbous, recurved above the middle, the margins prominently undulate; the callus plate tinted olive green, narrower, forming a longitudinal central thickening, ending at the bend or a little beyond it in a thick tomentose fringe which contains two raised knuckles. Column long, the lateral appendages adnate on one side, falcate, acute, entire with a short lobe at the base. Anther short, dark brown. Pollinia with a long stout caudicle.

FLOWERING PERIOD: Sept. and Oct.

COMMON NAME: Yawning Leek-orchid

DISTRIBUTION: Endemic in south-western WA where it is widely distributed and often common

P. plumaeforme (Plate 115)

P. plumaeforme R. D. FitzG. in *Gdnrs' Chron.* new ser. 17:495 (1882); R. Erickson *Orchids West* ed. 2:59 (1965)

A slender species, from 23 cm. to 45 cm. high. Leaf comparatively short, 14–15 cm. long, the lamina 5–8 cm. long. Flowers ten to forty, in a feathery inflorescence. Perianth segments oblong, about 5 mm. long; lateral sepals white with a green or yellowish stripe; dorsal sepal yellowish, edged with white, and with purplish-brown nerves; petals white with a purplish-brown stripe; lateral sepals free; labellum white, not gibbous, oblong, tapering slightly, reflexed for about two-thirds of its length; two parallel, slightly raised longitudinal callus plates on the lamina. Column appendages falcate, the lobes unequal in length. Rostellum larger than the appendages. Anther short, red-brown. Pollinia with a stout caudicle.

This species was seen by the writer growing in moist places, in the valleys, amongst Mallee gums, where *Pterostylis sargentii* grew in abundance. Several specimens were also collected near Jam Wattles (*Acacia acuminata*) on the granite slopes, amongst myriads of pink everlastings.

FLOWERING PERIOD: Aug. and Sept.

COMMON NAME: Feathery Leek-orchid

DISTRIBUTION: Endemic in WA where it is confined to the south-west

P. brevilabre (Plate 116)

P. brevilabre (Lindl.) Hook.f. *Flor. Tasm.* 2:11, t. 110 fig. A (1858); A. J. Ewart *Flor. Vict.* 314 (1931); H. M. R. Rupp *Orchids N.S.W.* 26 (1943); J. H. Willis *Handb. Pls Vict.* 1:369 (1962); M. J. Firth *Native Orchids. Tasm.* 20 (1965)

SYNONYMY: *P. lutescens* Lindl. var. *brevilabre* Lindl. *Gen. & Spec. orchid. Pls* 514 (1840)

A slender to stout plant 10–48 cm. high, the peduncle within the inflorescence sometimes having a fasciated appearance, especially obvious in robust specimens. Leaf lamina short, loosely sheathing. Flowers eight to thirty-two, not crowded, green with red to red-brown markings or purplish-black, labellum white or stained with pink. Ovary obovoid to oblong, sessile or almost so, 5–6·5 mm. long, a small, broad, acute bracteole at the base. Dorsal sepal ovate-lanceolate, acuminate, about 8 mm. long. Petals spreading or incurved, narrow-lanceolate to linear, tips varying from acuminate to broad-obtuse, crisped, about 8 mm. long. Lateral sepals as long as, or longer and broader than the dorsal sepal, the degree of union extremely variable, tips acuminate to acute, margins folded inward. Labellum sessile or almost so, oblong-lanceolate, 9–10·5 mm. long, very abruptly reflexed about the middle, often bringing both sections in contact, but the angle of flexion varying; upper portion of lamina brief; membranous part with crisped-undulate margins; callus plate narrower than the membranous part, except towards the base, either abruptly terminated just beyond the bend, or continuing towards the apex, channelled along the centre. Column appendages 3–4 mm. high, slightly exceeding the rostellum, falcate, with a small irregular lobe at the base. Anther dark-red to brown, much shorter than the rostellum; rostellum bifid, after removal of disc; disc variable, usually ovate. Pollinia two, bilobed, caudicle broad, long, stigma reniform.

P. brevilabre is frequently plentiful in sub-alpine and alpine regions; far more so, it would appear, than on the lowlands. It is a well-defined species, though, like many other members of this perplexing genus, variable to a marked degree. I have seen individual specimens, chiefly from NSW habitats, with unusual flowers: the labellum abnormally wide and short, the crisped margins of the flexed part embracing the lower portion.

FLOWERING PERIOD: Aug. to Jan., depending on altitude

COMMON NAME: Short-lip Leek-orchid

DISTRIBUTION: Confined to the eastern parts of Australia, and there extending from south-eastern Qld through NSW and Vic. to Tas.

P. odoratum (Plate 117)

P. odoratum R. S. Rogers in *Trans. roy. Soc. S. Aust.* 33:209, t. 9B (1909); A. J. Ewart *Flor. Vict.* 316 (1931); J. M. Black *Flor. S. Aust.* ed. 2:221 (1943); H. M. R. Rupp *Orchids N.S.W.* 27 (1943); J. H. Willis *Handb. Pls Vict.* 1:371 (1962); M. J. Firth *Native Orchids Tasm.* 22 (1965)

A slender to robust plant, 25–90 cm. high. Leaf lamina varying in length, often exceeding the inflorescence. Flowers pink and white, strongly perfumed. Dorsal sepal 7–13 mm. long, ovate-lanceolate, often recurved in mature flowers, but incurved in young flowers; lateral sepals 7–13 mm. long, dilated at the base, with conical, acute or bidentate points, usually divergent. Petals shorter than the lateral sepals, pinkish with white tips or white with red to brown stripes, linear-lanceolate, spreading or incurved. Labellum as long as or slightly longer than the sepals, conspicuously white, sessile or nearly so, oblong-lanceolate, acutely reflexed about the middle, the tip extending through the lateral sepals; erect part bulging, the margins entire; reflexed part bluntly triangular with crenulate margins;

lamina with a large pyramidal green callus at its base; the callus plate not very thick in the erect part but prominent where it terminates just beyond the bend; membranous portion very voluminous and exceeding the callus. Anther shorter than the rostellum. Rostellum elongated, triangular.

This species has a delightful spicy perfume which is very apparent on a warm day. It is a common plant that responds actively to bush fires, the specimens being robust, large flowered and often numerous.

FLOWERING PERIOD: Aug. to Feb., depending on the locality

COMMON NAME: Scented Leek-orchid

DISTRIBUTION: Temperate parts of all Australian states except WA, but in Qld restricted to the south-east

P. odoratum var. album (Plate 118)

P. odoratum var. *album* (R. S. Rogers) R. S. Rogers in J. M. Black *Flor. S. Aust.* ed. 1:126 (1922); J. M. Black *Flor. S. Aust.* ed. 2:221 (1943); J. H. Willis *Handb. Pls Vict.* 1:371 (1962)

Usually a smaller plant, with flowers smaller than the type, and with fewer pink tints, otherwise with similar colouring. The flexion of the labellum is seldom as acute as in the species, and the reflexed part is usually shorter than the erect part. In Vic. the var. *album* is highly fragrant and sometimes is an extremely robust plant with numerous densely-clustered flowers. Often it is very abundant and occasionally the inflorescence reaches a length of 15 cm. So perfectly symmetrical is the spike of bloom, that it has the appearance of having been turned on a lathe.

When var. *album* occurs in the same locality as the species, it flowers when the latter has withered off.

Remarkable colour forms of var. *album*, also of the typical form, were collected by C. French jnr in the Anglesea district, Vic., during Nov. 1934.

FLOWERING PERIOD: Sept. to Dec., reaching a peak in Nov.

DISTRIBUTION: Recorded definitely only from a few localities in southern Vic. and SA, but perhaps also extending into Tas.

P. suttonii (Plate 119)

P. suttonii R. S. Rogers & B. Rees in *Proc. roy. Soc. Vict.* new ser. 25:112, t. 6 fig. A–C (1912); A. J. Ewart *Flor. Vict.* 317 (1931); H. M. R. Rupp *Orchids N.S.W.* 30 (1943); J. H. Willis *Handb. Pls Vict.* 1:368 (1962); M. J. Firth *Native Orchids Tasm.* 20 (1965)

Plant often stout, 17–25 cm. high. Leaf lamina 7–12 cm. long, sometimes exceeding the inflorescence; fistula some distance below the raceme. Flowers in a short raceme, 3–11 cm., usually about 6 cm., shortly stalked and subtended by a small stout bracteole, as broad as is long. Lateral sepals 6–7 mm. long, often connate, not gibbous, narrow-lanceolate, the points blunt. Dorsal sepal 6–7 mm. long, narrow, slightly incurved, pointed; petals broader, as long as or longer than the lateral sepals, broadly linear with acute triangular tips, membranous, white with a purple-mauve or crimson stripe down the centre; margins undulate-crisped. Labellum on a short broad claw, obovate, comparatively large with undulate-crisped margins; recurved at a 60° angle about the middle, the proximal part erect, with entire margins, the tip broadly blunt and rounded, margins and surface almost entirely membranous; callus plate narrow, channelled, increasing in thickness towards the bend, and ending slightly beyond it in two raised lines. Anther blunt, hidden behind the rostellum and much shorter than it. Column appendages large, reaching to the level of the rostellum,

falcate, with a small basal ovate lobe, adnate to base of column. Rostellum voluminous, purple, higher than the anther, triangular, stigmatic surface large. Ovary short, pyriform. Flowers fragrant only during the warmer hours of the day.

The rich purple-mauve markings, the broad labellum and petals are the characteristic features of the species and easily distinguish it from *P. odoratum*, its nearest ally, and other forms.

On Talbot Peak in the Baw Baw Range, Vic., *P. suttonii* favours the black, peaty soil of the morass, the root system in the accompanying plate being drawn from a plant collected here, and differing from those collected in grass-covered places.

An undoubted specimen of *P. suttonii* is in the National Herbarium, Melbourne, labelled '*P. purpurosuis* F. Muell.' collected 'C. Stuart, remitted from herb. W. Sonder'. Mueller, however, did not publish a description.

FLOWERING PERIOD: Dec. to Mar.

COMMON NAME: Mauve Leek-orchid

DISTRIBUTION: Confined to alpine and sub-alpine areas of NSW, Vic. and Tas., generally above 900 m. (3,000 ft.) and often locally common

P. colemanae (Plate 120)

P. colemanae R. S. Rogers in *Trans. roy. Soc. S. Aust.* 47:337 (1923); A. J. Ewart *Flor. Vict.* 315 (1931); J. H. Willis *Handb. Pls Vict.* 1:372 (1962)

A moderately stout species with a loose raceme of up to twenty lavender or lilac flowers. Each flower is subtended by a short, wide, blunt, appressed bracteole, pedicels very short; ovaries short and turgid, not markedly retracted from the floral axis. Dorsal sepal greenish, about 7 mm. long, oblong-concave in the lower two-thirds, contracted above this into a conical point, recurved or erect; lateral sepals green, stout, conical, fluted above, about 8 mm. long, divergent. Petals lavender with a narrow green central stripe; 7·5 mm. long and 1·75 mm. wide at widest point, narrowly oblong, blunt, spreading. Labellum lavender, nearly as long as the lateral sepals, widely ovate, sessile or nearly so, the upper surface flat; slightly flexed in the middle; anterior margins crenate; the callus plate thin, greenish, ending in two inconspicuous knuckles just beyond the bend; the membranous part very wide; tip blunt. Column short; lateral appendages oblong-falcate with blunt often truncate tips and small basal lobes, shorter than the rostellum, usually lavender tinted, adnate to the stigma; anther purplish, shorter than the appendages and much shorter than the rostellum; caudicle long.

FLOWERING PERIOD: Nov.

DISTRIBUTION: Endemic in Vic., where it has not been seen since the original collection was made at Bayswater in Nov. 1922

P. ovale (Plate 121)

P. ovale Lindl. in *Edwards' bot. Reg.* 23: Swan Riv. Append. liv (1840); R. Erickson *Orchids West* ed. 2:59 (1965)

A very slender species from 25 cm. to over 40 cm. in height. Leaf-sheath and lamina long. Flowers small, white, in a loose spike 7–15 cm. long. Ovary narrow. Sepals about 5 mm. long, generally blunt. Petals about 5 mm. long, blunt, almost truncate. Lateral sepals usually free, and not gibbous; dorsal sepal wider than the other segments, cucullate, or reflexed. Labellum as long as the lateral sepals, sessile, oval to broadly elliptical, concave, reflexed; membranous part broad, white, the erect part with entire margins, slightly crenulate towards the tip; callus plate smooth, shiny, conspicuous, triangular or oval, often divided by a deep channel into two parts, extending from the base to slightly beyond the middle. Column appendages broad, falcate, as long as the rostellum. Rostellum higher than the anther. Caudicle long.

FLOWERING PERIOD: Sept. and Oct.

COMMON NAME: Little Leek-orchid

DISTRIBUTION: Widespread throughout south-western WA where it is endemic

P. ovale var. **triglochin** (Plate 121)

P. ovale var. *triglochin* Reichenb.f. *Beitr. syst. Pflk.* 60 (1871); R. Erickson *Orchids West* ed. 2:59 (1965)

Leaf lamina short. Flowers smaller with conspicuous dark reddish markings. Lateral sepals free; the callus plate of the labellum ending less abruptly than in the typical form.

FLOWERING PERIOD AND DISTRIBUTION: This variety is also confined to south-western WA where it apparently favours wetter areas than the typical form. It flowers during Sept. and Oct.

P. gracillimum (Plate 122)

P. gracillimum W. H. Nicholls in *Vict. Nat.* 64:175 (1948); R. Erickson *Orchids West* ed. 2:56 (1965)

A very slender elongated species, 40–60 cm. high. Leaf lamina erect, slender, terete, shorter than the inflorescence. Flowers in a loose raceme 18–25 cm. long, small, green with brown markings, the labellum pure white. Ovaries long and slender, the pedicels short, subtending bracteoles shortly acuminate. Perianth segments acuminate, equal in length, about 7 mm. long, dorsal sepal lanceolate, concave, apex incurved; lateral sepals connate, free at the apices, narrow-lanceolate, shortly acuminate; petals spreading, narrow-lanceolate, falcate; labellum on a long slender claw, semi-circularly recurved, ovate-lanceolate, shortly acuminate; membranous part white, prominently crisped; the callus plate thin, indistinct, with undulate white margins, channelled, and terminating beyond the middle. Column appendages stout, obtuse, falcate, with a small lobe some distance above the base. Rostellum higher than the column appendages, with an emarginate apex. Anther shorter than the rostellum, light brown. Caudicle of medium length.

[Note the flowering period; in the original paper this was inadvertently given as Oct.—Ed.]

FLOWERING PERIOD: Aug.

COMMON NAME: Slender Leek-orchid

DISTRIBUTION: Endemic in south-western WA

P. patens (Plate 123)

P. patens R. Br. *Prodr. Flor. Nov. Holl.* 318 (1810); A. J. Ewart *Flor. Vict.* 315 (1931); J. M. Black *Flor. S. Aust.* ed. 2:221 (1943); H. M. R. Rupp *Orchids N.S.W.* 27 (1943); J. H. Willis *Handb. Pls Vict.* 1:375 (1962); M. J. Firth *Native Orchids Tasm.* 23 (1965)

A slender plant from 10–40 cm. high. Leaf erect, lamina terete, varying in length, the base sheathing. Flowers more or less sessile, often numerous, in a loose or crowded spike. Ovary turgid, appressed against the stem. Dorsal sepal green with brown markings, about 7 mm. long, ovate-lanceolate, more or less recurved; lateral sepals 7–8 mm. long, free, lanceolate, usually slightly bidentate, not inflated at the base, almost parallel, green. Petals 5·5–6 mm. long, blunt, linear, spreading in the mature flower; light green with a

reddish to brown central stripe. Labellum almost sessile, ovate-lanceolate, not abruptly reflexed, margins crenulate to crenate; membranous border whitish, pinkish or light prune, more extensive than the callus plate; callus green, not prominent, terminating just beyond the bend, not or hardly channelled. Column about 2 mm. high. Anther dark red-brown, with a short point, shorter than the rostellum. Pollinia two, caudicle short, linear, attached to a narrow triangular disc. Column appendages narrow-oblong with smooth blunt or notched tips and small rounded basal lobes, shorter than the rostellum. Rostellum erect, bifid at tip. Stigma reniform.

This species is often common in coastal scrub areas; its closest congener is *P. odoratum* with which it often grows in the field.

FLOWERING PERIOD: Sept. to Feb., depending on proximity to coast, and on altitude

COMMON NAME: Broad-lip Leek-orchid

DISTRIBUTION: Widely scattered through a variety of habitats in all Australian states except WA, but in Qld confined to the south-east

P. patens var. **robustum** (Plate 124)

P. patens var. *robustum* W. H. Nicholls in *Vict. Nat.* 57:84 (1940)

Plant robust, about 40 cm. high. Flowers 2 cm. in diameter, in a loose spike of about 14 cm. Perianth segments widely spreading. Ovary very large for the size of the flower, 1–2 cm. long. Petals narrow-linear. Other particulars of flowers more or less typical.

FLOWERING PERIOD: Oct. and Nov.

DISTRIBUTION: Apparently confined to Tas., the original collection being from Smithton

P. fitzgeraldii (Plate 125)

P. fitzgeraldii R. S. Rogers & Maiden in *Trans. roy. Soc. S. Aust.* 33:216, t. 7 fig. 1–9 (1909); J. M. Black *Flor. S. Aust.* ed. 2:222 (1943)

A stout plant 15–45 cm. high. Flowers more or less sessile, green to prune-coloured, very fragrant; standing well out from the vertical axis; ovary turgid; expansion often beginning in middle of inflorescence, extending upward and downward. Dorsal sepal about 6 mm. long, broadly lanceolate, flat, retracted, recurved at the apex in the mature flower; lateral sepals free, 6–6·5 mm. long, lanceolate. Petals bluntly linear 4–5 mm. long, slightly divergent. Labellum prune-coloured, sessile, slightly contracted at the base; recurved almost at right angles about the middle; the erect portion with entire margins, rather bulging; recurved portion broadly triangular with crisped margins; callus deep prune-coloured, inconspicuous in the basal half, becoming raised and pubescent at the bend, ending abruptly near the tip; membranous part lighter coloured and smaller in extent. Anther reddish-brown with a blunt point, erect, but recurved after removal of the pollinia. Rostellum about the same height as column appendages, higher than the anther. Pollinia two, bilobed. Caudicle short. Column appendages membranous, very wide with truncate tips, more or less quadrangular with the basal lobes reaching to the middle, adnate only to the stigmatic plate at the extreme base. Stigma wide, almost rectangular.

This species' closest ally is *P. pallidum*, but it differs in the colour of the flowers, and the pubescent callus plate. R. D. FitzGerald had painted an unpublished plate of this species.

FLOWERING PERIOD: Oct.

DISTRIBUTION: Walleragang, NSW; also SA where it is confined to the south and rarely collected

P. rogersii (Plate 126)

P. rogersii H. M. R. Rupp in *Proc. Linn. Soc. N.S.W.* 53:340 (1928); H. M. R. Rupp *Orchids N.S.W.* 28 (1943); J. H. Willis *Handb. Pls Vict.* 1:373 (1962); M. J. Firth *Native Orchids Tasm.* 23 (1965)

Plant slender, 20–30 cm. high. Leaf lamina sometimes exceeding the inflorescence. Flowers not numerous, in a loose raceme, on short pedicels, greenish, faintly perfumed. Dorsal sepal nearly straight, broad-ovate, acute, 5·5 mm. long, with three prominent nerves and a finer one on each side; lateral sepals free, more or less spreading, lanceolate, longer than the dorsal sepal, hardly acute, three-nerved. Petals erect, slightly spreading, obtuse, broad. Labellum erect for two-thirds of its length from the base; the anterior third curved, not sharply reflexed; the whole labellum broad-ovate, but contracted towards the apex; the membranous part white, sometimes flushed with pink towards the apex, margins entire; the greatest width about 2·75 mm.; callus plate prominent, especially just beyond the curve, broader towards the base, tinged with pink. Column short, the lateral appendages broad and comparatively large. Anther broad, dark red-brown.

The above description was compiled from Tasmanian specimens. *P. rogersii* appears to be more closely related to *P. patens* than to other described forms. This comparatively rare orchid was first found in 1928 by H. M. R. Rupp on Barrington Tops in NSW at 1,500 m. (5,000 ft.) altitude. Concerning the Tasmanian plants Olsen writes: 'The specimens were found on 2/12/1939, growing at the 360 m. (1,200 ft.) level on Knocklofty, near Hobart, a dolerite outcrop of the upper Mesozoic period. I found this orchid for the first time in 1936, but in each succeeding year I have missed its flowering season, and found it only in fruit. On the 2 Dec. 1939 I found two perfect specimens, and later in the month plenty in a localised area. The dominant vegetation is *Eucalyptus*, the undergrowth mainly grass and various species of orchids. It was growing with *P. brevilabre*, being readily distinguished by the greenish-yellow stalk and flowers.'

In the specimens from Barrington Tops, the lateral appendages of the column are referred to as 'small'; and the 'anther higher than the lateral appendages'. I have examined Tas. and Vic., and NSW plants from the Barrington Tops, and find that the appendages are almost as high as the rostellum, and the anther only about two-thirds the height of the appendages.

FLOWERING PERIOD: Dec. and Jan.

COMMON NAME: Marsh Leek-orchid

DISTRIBUTION: NSW where confined to the Barrington Tops; far south-western and eastern Vic., and Tas., where localised and rarely collected; also NZ

P. diversiflorum (Plate 127)

P. diversiflorum W. H. Nicholls in *Vict. Nat.* 59:8, fig. A–L (1942); J. H. Willis *Handb. Pls Vict.* 1:375 (1962)

A moderately robust to slender plant 30–60 cm. high. Leaf lamina withered in all the specimens seen, but apparently slender, terete, varying in length, but often exceeding the inflorescence. Flowers variable in size, numbering ten to forty, green with red-brown markings, in a more or less crowded raceme, ovary pear-shaped, pedicels short, the subtending bracteoles small and depressed; expansion begins in the middle of the raceme and extends upward and downward. Dorsal sepal ovate-lanceolate, usually incurved, five-nerved, tip shortly acuminate; lateral sepals prominent, lanceolate, concave, the outer margins incurved, free, erect, divergent, three-nerved, tips usually bidentate. Petals linear, incurved, acute, in some flowers prominently falcate, obtuse, three-nerved. All perianth segments about 5–9 mm. long. Labellum

on a short broad movable claw, oblong-cuneate, deeply concave throughout, often very broad towards the base, reflexed just beyond the middle, tip narrow, the apex either emarginate, obtuse, or acuminate; membranous portion white, suffused with pink, about as broad as the callus plate; in some flowers there is a horizontal fold at the flexion, the whole depressed from the bend upward; margins crisped or undulate, rarely smooth, or laterally pinched beyond the flexion; callus plate green, not prominently raised except towards the tip, divided by a furrow which may extend to the tip, or terminate just beyond the bend, the furrow widening to a definite channel below the bend. In some flowers the callus plate also is constricted near the tip, the apical portion appearing as a separate raised somewhat wrinkled callosity as in some species of *Microtis*. Occasionally this raised portion is superimposed over the larger callus plate, extending downward to the bend. Column short, appendages large, with more or less hatchet-shaped oblique tips, a small rounded lobe at the base. Anther shorter than rostellum, reniform, red. Rostellum triangular, higher than the appendages, tip emarginate after removal of disc. Pollinia two, bilobed, caudicle linear, of medium length; pollen grains small, depressed. Stigma reniform, viscid.

P. diversiflorum is probably one of the most variable species, in regard to the floral characters, on record; yet *P. patens* appears to be its nearest affinity. During the winter months the area of several hundred acres, known locally as Malseeds, where this orchid flourishes, is covered to a depth of two or more feet of water. It is a wide creek bed, a natural watercourse, and a favourite feeding-ground for emus and kangaroos. That the season of 1941 was the driest for twenty-five years probably explains why this orchid had not been recorded before. Other ground orchids that occur here include *Pterostylis falcata*, *Caladenia carnea* and some *Microtis* species. The soil is black and loamy, the country flat and heavily timbered.

[The habitat of the type of this orchid as described here has long since been destroyed by conversion to agricultural land and the species is apparently extinct. However South Australian collector, R. Nash has found in SA specimens closely agreeing with the description, and further examination may prove them to be this species.—Ed.]

FLOWERING PERIOD: Dec. to Mar.

DISTRIBUTION: Apparently confined to south-western Vic., where now presumed to be extinct, but possibly also extending into SA (record awaiting confirmation)

P. gracile (Plates 128 and 129)

P. gracile R. S. Rogers in *Trans. roy. Soc. S. Aust.* 33:213, t. 12A (1909); A. J. Ewart *Flor. Vict.* 316 (1931); J. M. Black *Flor. S. Aust.* ed. 2:220 (1943); H. M. R. Rupp *Orchids N.S.W.* 26 (1943); J. H. Willis *Handb. Pls Vict.* 1:376 (1962); M. J. Firth *Native Orchids Tasm.* 24 (1965)

SYNONYMY: *P. pyriforme* E. Coleman in *Vict. Nat.* 49:195, t. 14 (1932)

A slender plant from 25 cm. to over 50 cm. high. Leaf lamina shorter than the inflorescence. Flowers often numerous, usually in a loose raceme, yellowish-green, brownish, or even dark-purple. Dorsal sepal 7–12 mm. long, ovate-lanceolate, often incurved; lateral sepals 10–15 mm. long, more or less united, or free, or in some flowers connate in their basal third, concave on top, the tips bidentate, narrow, ovate-lanceolate. Petals 9–12 mm. long, linear-lanceolate, tips incurved, often meeting each other and also the tip of dorsal sepal. Labellum on a well-marked claw, recurved near the middle, the degree of flexion variable; erect part deeply concave, the margins entire; lamina in front of the bend narrow-triangular with a sharp point, margins slightly undulate with a more or less well-marked constriction beyond the bend; membranous part white, pinkish or purplish, glandular, the width varying from flower to flower, but normally slightly narrower than the callus plate; callus plate raised in front of the bend and ending abruptly just beyond the constriction, but not reaching the tip. Column appendages shorter than rostellum, hardly falcate with blunt tips, and a narrow basal lobe reaching almost to the middle. Anther case with a short erect point, shorter than rostellum. Pollinia two, each longitudinally furrowed. Caudicle of medium length. Stigma reniform.

Dr Rogers first recorded this species from Sandergrove, a place about fifty miles from Adelaide, SA. He writes: 'Although thorough searches have been made, no further specimens have been discovered in that locality since that date (1908). In 1912, it appeared in thousands at Bridgewater, about thirteen miles from Adelaide, a locality almost as familiar to me as the parks in the city. It was found on every hill in that neighbourhood in vast quantities. The following season I desired to check a matter in regard to its pollination and visited the place for that purpose. I could not find a single specimen although the scrub remained intact. Every season since then I have searched for it, but without success. The season which has just passed was so similar to that of 1912, that I made an intensive search, but without finding the slightest indication of the plant.'

P. gracile inhabits a wide variety of habitats. It is found on open grassy plains (Bairnsdale), in poor sandy soil on stony mountain spurs (Suggan Buggan), in somewhat heavily-timbered country (Grampians); also in lightly-timbered areas (Airey's Inlet) and on high mountain ranges (near Cobungra, 4,500 ft. altitude), all these localities being in Vic.

P. gracile is an extremely variable species, the lateral sepals alone can vary from being fully united to completely free and divergent, with all intermediates. After careful examination I consider that *P. pyriforme* is only one of the many forms of *P. gracile*.

FLOWERING PERIOD: Sept. to Jan.

COMMON NAME: Graceful Leek-orchid

DISTRIBUTION: East-central NSW; Vic.; Rocky Cape, Tas.; south-eastern SA; widely distributed and often locally common

P. frenchii (Plate 130)

P. frenchii F. Muell. in *Vict. Nat.* 6:126 (1889); A. J. Ewart *Flor. Vict.* 315 (1931); H. M. R. Rupp *Orchids N.S.W.* 30 (1943); J. H. Willis *Handb. Pls Vict.* 1:375 (1962); M. J. Firth *Native Orchids Tasm.* 24 (1965)

A slender to stout plant 30–45 cm. high. Leaf lamina slender, cylindrical, rarely exceeding the inflorescence. Flowers often numerous, shortly pedicellate, delicately shaded in varying tones of yellow, pink, brown and green or sometimes wholly purplish. Dorsal sepal ovate-lanceolate, 7–8 mm. long, the point reflexed. Lateral sepals free, falco-lanceolate, the tips usually bidentate, concave, erect, recurved or spreading, about 7–8 mm. long. Petals shorter than the sepals, elliptic-lanceolate or linear-lanceolate, spreading, the tips sometimes incurved. Labellum sessile, longer than the petals, reflexed beyond the middle, ovate-cuneate; terminal portion with a prominently raised callus plate extending almost to the extreme apex, the point more or less acute; the basal part of lamina not markedly raised, channelled; membranous part narrow, usually pink, not crisped, often with a very definite constriction beyond the bend. Anther minutely pointed, red or brown. Column appendages erect, oblong, shorter than, or as high as the rostellum; basal lobes small and rounded, adnate to the column base. Flowers fragrant.

The Keilor plains specimens found by the author adjacent to Tottenham railway station and near Sunshine, Vic., during the seasons 1924–7 were remarkably stout, but the total absence of any constriction on the labellum segments and the wholly green colour, suggested a distinct species. During the two following seasons the plants remained dormant owing to lack of rain, but during the seasons 1930–1 the specimens were abundant and the greater number of plants produced flowers with the labella constriction, so often a characteristic of *P. frenchii*. In fact some spikes of flowers showed almost every conceivable variation both in form and colour.

FLOWERING PERIOD: Sept. to Jan.

COMMON NAME: Slaty Leek-orchid

DISTRIBUTION: Coastal and inland forest tracts of south-eastern NSW, where rare; Vic.; and northern Tas.; often locally common

P. validum (Plate 131)

P. validum R. S. Rogers in *Trans. roy. Soc. S. Aust.* 51:7 (1926); J. M. Black *Flor. S. Aust.* ed. 2:220 (1943)

A robust plant up to about 60 cm. high. Leaf in a faded condition at flowering time. Inflorescence very robust, with about thirty flowers. Flowers amongst the largest in the genus, ovary 1–1·3 cm. long, dark green, sessile, subtended by a small, though comparatively long, acute, appressed bracteole; perianth segments a clear greenish-yellow; the labellum greenish-white, with a light green callus plate; dorsal sepal erect, ovate, acute, incurved, later recurved, about 1·3 cm. long and 4·75 mm. wide; lateral sepals spreading, arched, more or less connate, about 1·35 cm. long and 5 mm. wide, acute. Petals erect, incurved, linear-lanceolate, narrower and shorter than the sepals. Labellum shortly clawed, ovate, in some flowers constricted towards the tip; tip subacute or acute, lamina contracted at base; the lower half erect, concave, thereafter recurved at right angles; callus plate conspicuous, triangular from the base, elevated, ending abruptly near the apex; margins voluminous, entire in the lower half, thereafter crenulate, laterally contracted at the bend. Anther reddish-brown or pale coloured, apiculate, apex retracted, much shorter than the rostellum; column appendages oblong, shortly bifid at the apex, erect, with a conspicuous rounded basal lobe, shorter than the rostellum, about equal to or slightly longer than the anther; rostellum erect, slender, with a distinct disc at its apex; caudicle long.

The plants illustrated were obtained from Melrose, SA. 'The specimens were growing in *Ixodia* country at Mount Remarkable; four or five specimens were growing in the colony, the soil light chocolate, of a granite nature.'

This plant has the robust habit of *P. elatum*, but with a very different labellum. The flower in its structure most closely approaches the prune-coloured *P. constrictum*, but the flowers are very much larger and differ in colour, the column, etc.

FLOWERING PERIOD: Oct. and Nov.

DISTRIBUTION: Endemic in SA where it is apparently confined to the Flinders Ranges

P. occidentale (Plate 132)

P. occidentale R. S. Rogers in *Trans. roy. Soc. S. Aust.* 32:11 (1908); J. M. Black *Flor. S. Aust.* ed. 2:219 (1943)

A dwarf plant 12–20 cm. high. Fistula of leaf high up, sometimes just below the inflorescence, the lamina usually exceeding the inflorescence. Flowers green, more or less sessile, ovary short and turgid, in a loose raceme of ten to eighteen flowers, rarely more. Dorsal sepal erect or retracted, ovate-lanceolate, 5–6 mm. long, very acute, concave; lateral sepals lanceolate, slightly bidentate, a little longer than the dorsal sepal, concave on their inner surfaces, united for half to three-quarters of their length in the freshly expanded flower, but sometimes free in the older flower, especially in very hot weather. Petals nearly as long as the dorsal sepal, lanceolate, erect or slightly spreading. Labellum sessile, acutely or abruptly reflexed about the middle, ovate-cuneate, 5–6 mm. long and 2–6 mm. wide; erect portion almost orbicular with entire margins, slightly bulging at the base; reflexed part oblong-cuneate with crisped or crenulate margins and acute tip; callus plate not prominent until beyond the bend, then contracted into a narrower and more elevated apical extension, ending abruptly midway between the bend and the tip; membranous part about equal in extent to the callus. Column short and wide. Anther with a short point, about the same height as the rostellum. Column appendages erect, oblong, with obliquely truncated tips, about as high as the rostellum, the basal lobes reaching to about the middle, adnate below the stigma to the stigmatic plate. Stigma transversely reniform. Caudicle of medium length.

In my specimens the leaf lamina varied much in its length; the same applies to the callus plate of the labellum. In the majority of specimens the lateral sepals are connate for about half their length.

FLOWERING PERIOD: Sept. and Oct.

DISTRIBUTION: Apparently endemic in SA, where found only in a few southern localities

P. pallidum (Plate 133)

P. pallidum W. H. Nicholls in *Proc. roy. Soc. Vict.* new ser. 46:33, fig. P–U (1933); J. M. Black *Flor. S. Aust.* ed. 2:221 (1943); J. H. Willis *Handb. Pls Vict.* 1:372 (1962)

A slender species, almost wholly green or yellowish-green, 15–30cm. in height. Leaf terete, erect, of varying length. Flowers fifteen to thirty, green or yellowish-green, in a long loose spike, pedicels short, ovary turgid, standing well out from axis. Perianth segments glandular; dorsal sepal erect, ovate-lanceolate, somewhat concave, acuminate, 5–6 mm. long. Lateral sepals parallel, lanceolate-concave, connate at the extreme base or in some flowers quite free, 6·5–7 mm. long. Petals semi-erect, spreading or incurved, tips more or less obtuse, 4–5 mm. long. Labellum sessile, erect, then recurved abruptly about the middle, ovate-cuneate, margins crenulate, very shortly ciliate; callus plate ovate-lanceolate, green, not conspicuously raised, extending to within a short distance of the tip; membranous part comparatively broad, white; base of labellum lamina with a long, subulate-lanceolate appendage. (Though not recorded by R. S. Rogers in his review of SA *Prasophyllum*, in *Trans. roy. Soc. S.A.* 33:213 (1909), this unique feature is mentioned in his more comprehensive description under the name of *P. fuscum* in J. M. Black *Flor. S. Aust.* ed. 1:127 (1922).) Column appendages broadly oblong, tips obtuse, oblique. Anther shorter than rostellum. Pollinia very granular, with a long caudicle. Rostellum with an emarginate apex. Fragrant.

FLOWERING PERIOD: Sept. to Nov.

COMMON NAME: Pale Leek-orchid

DISTRIBUTION: Confined to Pomonal district and rarely collected in Vic., but extending to SA where it is widespread and more common

P. brainei (Plate 134)

P. brainei R. S. Rogers in *Trans. roy. Soc. S. Aust.* 46:149 (1922); A. J. Ewart *Flor. Vict.* 313 (1931); J. H. Willis *Handb. Pls Vict.* 1:372 (1962); M. J. Firth *Native Orchids Tasm.* 22 (1965)

A slender wholly green plant 12–35 cm. high. Leaf lamina dilated at the base, setaceous or narrowly linear. Flowers often numerous on very short pedicels, in a comparatively loose raceme. Dorsal sepal erect or recurved, concave, ovate-lanceolate, acuminate, contracted at the base, 5–7 mm. long. Lateral sepals free, spreading, slightly divergent; tips slightly recurved, concave on upper surface, narrow-lanceolate, 6–8 mm. long. Petals erect, narrowly oblong or linear-lanceolate, not acute, shorter than the sepals. Labellum sessile, gibbous at the base, not protruding between the sepals, 6–8 mm. long, the base erect against the column, margins entire, then recurved forming a complete sigmoid flexure, laterally contracted towards the apex, the margins crenulate, and very shortly papillate-ciliate from the first bend to the extreme tip; callus plate dark green, ovate-lanceolate, extending from the base to just beyond the first flexure, its margins shortly ciliate; membranous part wide, whitish, smooth in the entire part, rugose anteriorly, very glandular, tomentose towards the tip. Column appendages large, broadly oblong with blunt oblique tips; basal lobes distinct, exceeding the column in height. Anther shorter than the rostellum. Flowers fragrant.

This fragrant species was named after A. B. Braine, an ardent student of Victorian orchids. The species grows in a variety of habitats—amongst rushes and sedges in western Vic., amongst grass and herbs in eastern Vic., and extending to sub-alpine grassland.

FLOWERING PERIOD: Sept. to Jan., depending on altitude

COMMON NAME: Green Leek-orchid

DISTRIBUTION: Scattered throughout Vic. and eastern Tas., but inconspicuous and not often collected

P. parviflorum (Plate 135)

P. parviflorum (R. S. Rogers) W. H. Nicholls in *Vict. Nat.* 57:191, fig. A–I (1941); J. H. Willis *Handb. Pls Vict.* 1:373 (1962); M. J. Firth *Native Orchids Tasm.* 23 (1965)

SYNONYMY: *P. hartii* var. *parviflorum* R. S. Rogers in *Trans. roy. Soc. S. Aust.* 54:44 (1930)

A slender to moderately-robust plant, 18–45 cm. high. Leaf lamina slender, not generally exceeding the inflorescence. Flowers ten to forty, small, somewhat globular in form (only noticeable in fresh flowers), on short pedicels, subtended at the base by a short acute bracteole; in a long loose spike, standing well out from the axis; green or green with purplish-brown markings or almost wholly purplish. Dorsal sepal ovate-acuminate, incurved, about 3 mm. long; lateral sepals elliptic-falcate, concave, parallel, about 4 mm. long; connate to the middle, or at base only, rarely free. Petals erect, incurved, linear-falcate, about 3 mm. long. Labellum sub-sessile, erect at the base, more or less recurved in its distal third; membranous part wide with entire margins, but appreciably narrowed upward; in some flowers constricted towards the tip, as in *P. frenchii*; callus plate prominently raised, especially beyond the bend, and extending to within a short distance of the extreme tip; at the base traversed by a wide channel, which continues as a narrow groove upward beyond the bend. Column short; appendages about as high as the rostellum, oblong with oblique tips; basal lobes small, compressed and oblique. Stigmatic surface wide. Anther dark red. Pollinia granular; caudicle of medium length.

This plant differs from *P. hartii* in its more slender habit, smaller more globuliform flowers and a different labellum (having a different form of callus plate), also entirely different column appendages, and stouter lateral sepals, which are invariably connate, and not prominently bidentate at the tips. It appears to be more closely allied to *P. frenchii* than to *P. hartii*.

This species was first forwarded to the writer by A. J. Tadgell in 1922–3 from Port Albert, Vic. It is reported as favouring damp situations, and being plentiful through its distribution. It is a variable species in details of flowers, yet easily distinguished in the field from other described forms by the slender character of the inflorescence—the flowers are well-spaced and usually the spike is long. The shape of the labellum is variable to some degree.

[M. J. Firth in *Native Orchids Tasm.* gives a tentative record of this species in Tas. Since then the identity of these specimens has been confirmed and the range extended.—Ed.]

FLOWERING PERIOD: Oct. to Feb., depending on altitude

DISTRIBUTION: Vic., where it is widespread and often locally common along the coast, from the south-west to East Gippsland; also sub-alpine areas in Tas. Its extension into SA and southern NSW is highly probable

P. hartii (Plate 136)

P. hartii R. S. Rogers in *Trans. roy. Soc. S. Aust.* 51:8 (1927); A. J. Ewart *Flor. Vict.* 318 (1931); J. H. Willis *Handb. Pls Vict.* 1:374 (1962)

Plant often robust, up to 60 cm. in height. Leaf lamina often exceeding the inflorescence. Flowers numerous, more or less crowded, greenish to green with brown or red markings or prune coloured. Flowers subsessile, subtended at the base by a short very obtuse bracteole. Ovary relatively large, green and turgid. Dorsal sepal erect, but recurved at the apex, ovate, acute, concave, glandular on the outside, about 8 mm. long. Lateral sepals elliptic-falcate, acuminate, free, 10 mm. long, concave, spreading, parallel. Petals erect, elliptic-falcate, rather blunt, 8 mm. long. Labellum shortly and broadly clawed, the basal two-thirds more or less erect, voluminous, ventricose, concave, the margins wide, rounded and entire; thereafter recurved at right angles into a triangular acute tip with crenulate narrow margins, callus plate conspicuously raised, hastate, with thickened very glandular margins, extending just beyond the bend. Column short and wide. Anther dark red or brown, ovate, erect, flat, not apiculate, distinctly shorter than the rostellum and lateral appendages. Lateral appendages widely oblong, erect or incurved; apices truncate, notched or lacerated, with a small subulate tooth posteriorly; basal lobe rounded, small. Rostellum erect, bifid. Caudicle slender of medium length.

A very beautiful species but an extremely variable one also. The labellum is most characteristic and unique. It is becoming rare because of conversion of its habitats into farmland.

FLOWERING PERIOD: Oct. to Dec.

COMMON NAME: Maroon Leek-orchid

DISTRIBUTION: Vic., scattered along the coast; also SA where confined to the south-east, favouring moist grassland in open forest areas

P. subbisectum (Plate 137)

P. subbisectum W. H. Nicholls in *Vict. Nat.* 53:72, fig. A–H (1936); J. H. Willis *Handb. Pls Vict.* 1:372 (1962)

A slender, rather diminutive plant 12–16 cm. high. Leaf terete, sometimes in a withered condition at flowering time; lamina shorter than the inflorescence, fistula a short distance below the flowers. Flowers seven to fourteen, in a loose spike, green with brown markings, sometimes more brown than green. Ovary oblong-ovate on a short, more or less horizontal pedicel subtended by a small acute bracteole. Dorsal sepal 2·5–3 mm. long, erect, ovate-lanceolate, with a short point. Lateral sepals lanceolate, about 4 mm.

long, free, erect, spreading, concave on the inner side, the tips more or less bidentate. Petals linear, widely spread, about 3 mm. long, a prominent longitudinal stripe down the centre. Labellum about 4 mm. long, ovate-cuneate, on a short claw, very wide at base, recurved at right angles about the middle; membranous part narrow, greenish, with crenulate margins; callus plate hardly raised, reaching to within a short distance of the tip, deeply and widely divided at base by a green channel viscid only at the base, the channel appreciably narrowing upward to a fine point; margins of callus ridges undulate, purplish. Column appendages broad linear, with a short broad depressed basal lobe. Rostellum emarginate. Anther purplish; pollinia granular, the caudicle short.

This interesting species was discovered at Pomonal by Miss Laura Banfield, of Ararat, Vic., in 1932. It bears a closer resemblance to *P. fuscum* than to other described forms, but is well defined by its slender and lowly habit, and entirely different labellum, which possesses a callus plate hardly raised above the membranous portion and almost completely divided into two separate portions, a character suggesting the specific name. Apparently it is a local form.

FLOWERING PERIOD: Oct. and Nov.

DISTRIBUTION: Endemic in Vic., where it is localised and rare, being only known from the type collection from Pomonal

P. alpinum (Plate 138)

P. alpinum R. Br. *Prodr. Flor. Nov. Holl.* 318 (1810); A. J. Ewart *Flor. Vict.* 314 (1931), as *P. tadgellianum*; H. M. R. Rupp *Orchids N.S.W.* 28 (1943); J. H. Willis *Handb. Pls Vict.* 1:369 (1962); M. J. Firth *Native Orchids Tasm.* 21 (1965)

SYNONYMY: *P. frenchii* var. *tadgellianum* R. S. Rogers in *Trans. roy. Soc. S. Aust.* 46:153 (1922); *P. tadgellianum* (R. S. Rogers) R. S. Rogers l.c. 47:338 (1923)

A stout dwarf plant 10–23 cm. high. Leaf lamina usually shorter than the inflorescence. Flowers in a loose or dense raceme, usually 4–10 cm. long, green or yellowish with chocolate-brown markings. Dorsal sepal lanceolate to broad lanceolate, acuminate, 5–6 mm. long. Lateral sepals connate in the basal half, 5–6 mm. long. Petals shorter than the sepals, lanceolate to falco-lanceolate. Labellum sessile, the lower part almost orbicular, erect against the column, semi circularly recurved, narrowly cuneate beyond the bend; callus plate widely triangular at the base, prominently raised and extending almost to the tip of the distal half; membranous part narrow throughout. Column appendages as high as the rostellum, falcate with truncate or obtuse tips. Stigma very oblique, reniform. Anther slightly shorter than the rostellum.

P. alpinum is to be found growing, often abundantly, on all our southern and eastern alpine regions. On three separate occasions I have found it, very plentifully distributed over the area, between Mount Erica and Mount Whitelaw, on the Baw Baw plateau at about 5,000 ft. altitude.

This fragrant ground orchid grows in almost any situation: on the margins of the morasses, on the dry open levels, and sometimes on the rock-strewn rises, where individual plants were found growing in the crevices of the boulders. It also flourishes among the Snow gums. Some of the specimens are wholly pale yellowish, others practically colourless. It is closely allied to *P. fuscum*. The accompanying plate of figures was drawn from material collected on Talbot Peak in the Baw Baw Range, at 1,500 m. (5,000 ft.).

FLOWERING PERIOD: Dec. to Mar., depending on altitude

COMMON NAME: Alpine Leek-orchid

DISTRIBUTION: Widespread in alpine communities above 4,500 ft.

altitude and often locally abundant in NSW, where restricted to the south, Vic. and Tas.

P. fuscum (Plate 139)

P. fuscum R. Br. *Prodr. Flor. Nov. Holl.* 318 (1810); A. J. Ewart *Flor. Vict.* 313 (1931); H. M. R. Rupp *Orchids N.S.W.* 28 (1943); J. H. Willis *Handb. Pls Vict.* 1:373 (1962); M. J. Firth *Native Orchids Tasm.* 22 (1965)

A slender to moderately robust plant 14–30 cm. high; leaf lamina of variable length, erect, terete, dilated at the union of the stem. Flowers in a moderately loose raceme, usually one-third the length of plant, expanding in an irregular manner, often from the centre outward; green and brown, rarely wholly pale green; ovary oblong-ovate to ovate on a short pedicel, subtended by a small acute bracteole, which is often pink. Dorsal sepal erect, oblong-lanceolate, acuminate, the tip usually slightly deflexed, about 5·5 mm. long; lateral sepals about 5·5 mm. long, free, or united at the extreme base only, occasionally the whole length united by a thin filament; spreading widely when free, margins incurved, tips bidentate. Petals 4–5 mm. long, linear, spreading, tips more or less obtuse; labellum on a broad claw, oblong-cuneate, recurved abruptly in its distal third; membranous part narrow, with entire margins, pink or greenish-white; callus plate viscid, green, conspicuously raised, especially beyond the bend, and extending to within a short distance of the apex, occupying almost the whole width in some flowers. Column appendages with obtuse tips, shorter than the rostellum; rostellum with a bifid apex; anther brownish to red-brown, broadly ovate, reaching to about the same height as the appendages; pollinia granular, very friable, easily removed; caudicle short.

This is a delightfully fragrant species, the scent being detectable for several yards on a warm day. It favours open grassy habitats.

FLOWERING PERIOD: Sept. to Dec.

COMMON NAME: Tawny Leek-orchid

DISTRIBUTION: Central tablelands of NSW, where rare; western Vic. and Tas., where scattered through the drier open areas and uncommonly collected

P. concinnum (Plate 140)

P. concinnum W. H. Nicholls in *Vict. Nat.* 64:232 (1948); M. J. Firth *Native Orchids Tasm.* 24 (1965)

A slender species, 30–40 cm. high. Leaf slender, terete, sheathing at the base, erect, the lamina not exceeding the inflorescence. Flowers in a lax raceme of 10–14 cm., green or yellowish-green with brown markings. Pedicels short. Ovaries turgid. Dorsal sepal about 10 mm. long, narrow-lanceolate, erect, acuminate, the tip often incurved. Lateral sepals about 10 mm. long, parallel, lanceolate, falcate-recurved; the outer margins prominently incurved, connate only for about 1 mm. from the base. Petals about 8 mm. long, spreading or incurved, linear, acute. Labellum rigid on a stout claw, erect, recurved in its distal third, ovate-cuneate, about 8 mm. long; membranous part pale coloured, wide towards the base, and narrow beyond the bend, the margins entire throughout; callus plate prominently raised upward, narrow, green, extending from the bend almost to the extreme apex; a prominent channel towards the base, with two lateral lobes, the outer margins of which are raised and entire. Column appendages very short and stout, obtuse, with an emarginate apex, a small lobe at base. Anther small. Caudicle short.

This attractive species is closely allied to *P. fuscum* and *P. alpinum*, but it differs from both in a number of important particulars. The chief difference is the presence of lateral lobes towards the base of the labellum, a feature not readily discernible in such small flowers without the aid of a lens. The specific epithet is in allusion to the neat, immaculate appearance of the plant when in bloom.

FLOWERING PERIOD: Nov. and Dec., extending to Mar. in alpine areas

COMMON NAME: Trim Leek-orchid

DISTRIBUTION: Endemic in Tas., where it extends from sandy heathlands to sub-alpine areas

P. macrostachyum (Plate 141)

P. macrostachyum R. Br. *Prodr. Flor. Nov. Holl.* 318 (1810); R. Erickson *Orchids West* ed. 2:59 (1965)

SYNONYMY: *P. gracile* Lindl. in *Edwards' bot. Reg. 23*: Swan Riv. Append. liv (1840), non R. S. Rogers (1909); *P. nigricans* Endl. in Lehm. *Plant. Preiss.* 2:12 (1846), non R. Br. (1810)

A slender plant usually not so tall as *P. ovale*, but sometimes resembling it in habit. Flowers small, green or greenish-yellow, shortly pedicellate and usually rather distant in a long raceme. Ovary narrow-turbinate or oblong. Lateral sepals 4–5 mm. long, lanceolate-subulate, acute, broad and shortly united at the base, connate to about the middle or free only at the apex. Dorsal sepal shorter. Petals shorter than the sepals, lanceolate, acute, or almost so. Labellum sessile, or nearly so, shorter than the sepals and narrow in the most common form, the erect part concave, the reflexed part as long, ovate, almost acuminate; the callus plate nearly as broad as the erect part, channelled and terminating a short distance from the apex; membranous part narrow. Column appendages shorter than the anther, stout.

Bentham in his description of the callus plate of the labellum writes: 'forming two calli at the bend and shortly continued along the centre of the reflexed part'. The calli were not apparent in the flowers which the writer examined, but are present in the flowers of *P. attenuatum*, which bears a superficial resemblance to *P. macrostachyum*.

R. S. Rogers refers to an interesting form of *P. macrostachyum*: 'At Lake Chockerup, in the Albany district, in swampy country, a form was found in which the labellum and the petals were a deep purple in colour, giving the plant a very unfamiliar appearance.' (See *Trans. roy. Soc. S. Aust.* 44:336 (1920).) This form was very prolific and was not associated with others of the common colour. It may be Endlicher's *P. nigricans*. This dark form was also found near Denmark by the author.

FLOWERING PERIOD: July to Oct.

DISTRIBUTION: Endemic in WA where it is widespread and often locally common in the south-west

P. uroglossum (Plate 142)

P. uroglossum H. M. R. Rupp in *Vict. Nat.* 64:3 (1947); M. J. Firth *Native Orchids Tasm.* 22 (1965)

A moderately robust plant 30–45 cm. high. Leaf lamina emerging high up the stem and usually extending far above the inflorescence. Flowers numerous in a rather dense raceme 7–12 cm. long, dark brown with prune tints, the buds opening from the middle, upward and downward. Dorsal sepal up to 8 mm. long, very broadly lanceolate, margins often inturned, primary veins three, conspicuous. Lateral sepals about 8 mm. long, free, linear, hardly gibbous at the base, shortly divaricate there, then almost parallel. Petals shorter and paler. Labellum very dark, not much shorter than the sepals, abruptly reflexed at a right angle about the middle, then somewhat rigidly protruding between the lateral sepals like a tail; callus plate extending well beyond the bend, not quite as dark as the rest of the labellum, and almost devoid of any membrane. Column about 3·5 mm. high, with rather wide appendages, higher than the column (4–4·5 mm.). Ovary rather slender, very shortly stalked, forming an acute angle with the axis.

This species was first discovered within fifty miles of Sydney in Nov. 1946, which is quite remarkable. It has affinities with *P. fuscum*, but is distinguished by the labellum and long column appendages.

FLOWERING PERIOD: Nov.

DISTRIBUTION: Burrawang, NSW, and Tas., but rarely collected

P. appendiculatum (Plate 143)

P. appendiculatum W. H. Nicholls in *Vict. Nat.* 66:212, fig. F–I (1950); J. H. Willis *Handb. Pls Vict.* 1:374 (1962)

A very slender species 25–40 cm. high. Leaf erect, 8–12 cm. long. Inflorescence comparatively short, 5–12 cm. long. Flowers small, not crowded, somewhat globular in form, subsessile, the prevailing colour purplish. Dorsal sepal 6 mm. long, ovate-lanceolate, usually incurved; lateral sepals 6 mm. long, connate to about the middle in all flowers examined, finely acuminate and parallel at the apices. Petals 5 mm. long, linear or linear-falcate, incurved in the majority of flowers, acute at the tips. Labellum not movable, conspicuously orbicular and concave; margins entire or minutely crenulate; apical part narrow, acute and sharply flexed; callus plate inconspicuous at the base of the flexed part. Column short. Anther brownish, equal or almost equal to the rostellum and column appendages. Column appendages broad.

The species has superficial affinities with *P. hartii*, but though the colour scheme of the flowers is very similar, the brief inflorescence and distinct squat labellum with the curious appendix-like apex separate it immediately.

FLOWERING PERIOD: Nov.

DISTRIBUTION: Apparently endemic in Vic., where it is confined to moist heathy grass-tree flats in the Cann River, Genoa district. It probably also extends into similar country in NSW

P. morganii (Plate 144)

P. morganii W. H. Nicholls in *Vict. Nat.* 46:179, t. 7 (1930); A. J. Ewart *Flor. Vict.* 319 (1931); J. H. Willis *Handb. Pls Vict.* 1:371 (1962)

A plant of robust habit 14–25 cm. high. Leaf terete, sheathing at the base. Inflorescence crowded, very compact, fifty to eighty flowers in a spike of 7–8 cm.; flowers sessile, green, variegated with prune or purple markings. Ovary green, rather large, turgid, with a broad appressed bracteole at the base. Lateral sepals, dorsal sepal and petals almost equal in length, 4–5 mm. long; dorsal sepal erect, concave, broadly ovate, acuminate, contracted at the base. Lateral sepals free, spreading, glandular, elliptic-falcate, curving upward and inward over the labellum, inwardly concave, inflated towards the base, apices slightly bidentate. Petals spreading, narrowly oblong, recurved, broader towards the tips, where they are blunt. Labellum small, reniform-cordate, on a broad claw, almost as broad as long, purplish; at its widest part 2–3 mm., contracting abruptly to an acute, often recurved apex; membranous part slightly wider than the callus plate; margins entire, crenulate; callus plate not prominent, dark prune, somewhat papillose, reaching almost to the tip; apex sometimes bifid. Column erect, very short and broad, a

little over 1 mm. high. Anther small, orbicular, pale coloured; column appendages about as high as the rostellum, tips rounded, oblique, prune coloured; basal lobe small, ill-defined, botryoidal. Rostellum bifid. Pollinia two, bilobed, caudicle short. Tubers ovate-oblong.

Specimens of this rare species were sent by Henry Morgan of Cobungra, north-eastern Vic. Concerning his find he writes: 'They were growing on the sunny side of a small ridge running down to Spring Creek; the soil is inclined to be clayey, with a little quartz and sandstone among it.' Growing in association with *P. morganii* were *P. brevilabre* and *P. suttonii*.

P. morganii is a well-defined species and hardly likely to be confused with any other recorded form. It is pleasantly fragrant. A robust many-flowered specimen of this species resembles to a marked degree a spike of the well-known garden flower—the Mignonette.

FLOWERING PERIOD: Oct. and Nov.

DISTRIBUTION: Endemic in Vic., where it is extremely localised and known only from Cobungra

P. attenuatum (Plate 145)

P. attenuatum R. D. FitzG. in *Gdnrs' Chron.* new ser. 17:495 (1882); R. Erickson *Orchids West* ed. 2:58 (1965)

A very slender, wiry plant from 12 cm. to over 30 cm. high. Leaf green, the lamina linear, channelled, 4–10 cm. in length. Flowers from fifteen to forty, in a comparatively loose, often attenuated raceme, green with pale edges or green and red-brown. Lateral sepals connate, except at the extreme tips, oblong, cucullate with obtuse tips, 3–4 mm. long. Dorsal sepal 2·5–3 mm. long, oblong, obtuse, slightly recurved in some flowers. Petals about 2 mm. long, green with red-brown margins and a central stripe, oblong, very obtuse at the apices. Labellum 3–4 mm. long, ovate-oblong, saccate at the end; callus plate about two-thirds the length of the labellum, slightly raised with five raised ridges towards the apex. Column appendages falcate, acuminate, usually bilobed, the small lobe obtuse. Anther shorter than rostellum, obtuse. Pollinia with a short caudicle.

Found by the author in swamps, growing in association with *Microtis atrata* and *Thelymitra mucida*. There exists in the flowers of this species a small cone-like protuberance, just below the middle at the rear of the conjoined sepals, which forms on the reverse side a circular depression, into which fits the labellum base—a feature not referred to in the original description.

FLOWERING PERIOD: Sept. to Nov.

COMMON NAME: Thin Leek-orchid

DISTRIBUTION: Endemic in WA where it is confined to coastal areas of the south-west

P. despectans (Plate 146)

P. despectans Hook. f. *Flor. Tasm.* 2:13, t. 113 fig. A (1858); A. J. Ewart *Flor. Vict.* 319 (1931); J. H. Willis *Handb. Pls Vict.* 1:365 (1962); M. J. Firth *Native Orchids Tasm.* 26 (1965)

SYNONYMY: *P. brachystachyum* sens. A. J. Ewart *Flor. Vict.* 320 (1931) non Lindl. (1840)

A very slender plant 10–20 cm. high, but occasional specimens attain a height of 40 cm. Leafless, except for a narrow sheathing, acute bract below the inflorescence. Flowers very small, one to forty-five, usually in a dense, pyramidal raceme, variable in colour, pale yellowish-green, purplish or brownish. Ovary ovate to narrow-oblong, convex, very shortly stalked, a small bracteole at the base. Lateral sepals 2·5–4·5 mm. long, falco-lanceolate, acuminate, cylindrical, united at the base, which is rather broad. Dorsal sepal broadly ovate, acuminate, deeply concave, about 2 mm. long. Petals ovate-lanceolate, very acute, 2–3 mm. long. Labellum inconspicuous, articulate on a short broad claw, attached to the dark coloured projecting base of the column, narrow-lanceolate or lanceolate; tip acuminate, recurved, 3–3·5 mm. long; callus plate raised, comparatively broad, occupying the full width of the narrow upper portion, a narrow central longitudinal channel sometimes traversing the centre; membranous part very narrow, thin, margins minutely and irregularly serrulate, or quite entire. Column appendages subulate, falcate, glabrous, usually exceeding the anther, with a small rounded inner lobe of variable size at the base. Anther point of medium length, mucronate. Pollinia two, bilobed; caudicle about half the length of pollinia; rostellum bifid, much shorter than the anther; stigma ovate.

FLOWERING PERIOD: Mainly Mar. to June, but in alpine areas flowering Jan. and Feb., and occasional lowland specimens have been noted during July to Sept.

COMMON NAME: Sharp Midge-orchid

DISTRIBUTION: Extending from central coast of NSW where it is very rare, into western Vic. and Tas. where it is widespread and common. It is often locally abundant in open forest country

P. nichollsianum (Plate 147)

P. nichollsianum H. M. R. Rupp in *Vict. Nat. 59*:123 (1942); H. M. R. Rupp *Orchids N.S.W.* 31 (1943)

[A moderately robust plant 12–18 cm. high. Lamina of the bract emerging at the base of the lowest ovary in the inflorescence, long, sometimes exceeding the latter. Flowers few or occasionally numerous, brownish-red or yellowish-green, on long and prominent ovaries. Dorsal sepal about 3 mm. long, cucullate, almost oblong, with a short linear gland at the apex. Lateral sepals 5–6 mm. long, broad-linear, usually gland tipped. Petals shorter, unusually broad, generally with a broad stripe along the median line and a gland at the tip. Labellum narrowly oblong, suddenly contracting to an almost acute apex. Callus plate large, darker than the lamina, its posterior half with upturned margins which terminate very abruptly. Column appendages whitish with faint red tints, wide, bilobed; anterior lobe narrow and acuminate, posterior lobe large, obtuse, sometimes emarginate. Anther with a flat top, oblong, a rather long filament emerging from the apex. Rostellum small; stigma broadly ovate.

This species was named in honour of the author of this work. Its main distinction from other species is the unusual anther; its closest congener is probably *P. longisepalum*.

FLOWERING PERIOD: May

DISTRIBUTION: Endemic in NSW where it is apparently confined to the central coast area and rare.—Ed.]

P. trifidum (Plate 148)

P. trifidum H. M. R. Rupp in *Vict. Nat. 58*:21 (1941); H. M. R. Rupp *Orchids N.S.W.* 31 (1943)

A very slender plant, 10–30 cm. high. Bract close to the flowers, short, or in small few-flowered specimens exceeding the raceme. Flowers either few, or numerous in a crowded spicate raceme; the buds often green, the mature flowers deep purplish-red. Dorsal sepal rather broad, but acuminate, 1·5 mm. long; lateral sepals longer, oblong, widely divergent, acute. Petals flagelliform, conspicuously tipped with a linear or twisted translucent gland. Labellum ovate,

acute, with minutely-serrulate anterior margins, and a thick channelled raised callus plate along its whole length. Column greenish, with broad, bifid or trifid appendages, the points very dark at the tips.

This species was originally discovered at La Perouse by E. Nubling, long before it was found and described by Rupp. These first-found specimens were forwarded to R. S. Rogers of Adelaide prior to his death, with a view to its being described as a new species. Nubling suggested a name which was descriptive of the characteristic flask-like petals, but the present name alludes to the column-appendages, which are frequently, but not invariably trifid.

FLOWERING PERIOD: Apr. to June

DISTRIBUTION: Endemic in NSW where it is scattered throughout the central coast area

P. aureoviride (Plate 149)

P. aureoviride H. M. R. Rupp in *Vict. Nat. 58*:22 (1941); H. M. R. Rupp *Orchids N.S.W.* 32 (1943)

A slender to moderately robust plant 9–18 cm. high. Leaf bract close under the inflorescence and occasionally exceeding it. Flowers few to twenty, golden-green, the raceme not very dense. Sepals 2–3·5 mm. long, the lateral ones connate at the base and slightly longer than the dorsal sepal, all more or less gland-tipped. Petals shorter than the sepals, broadly lanceolate, sometimes tipped with a gland. Labellum ovate-acute with entire margins, membranous part very narrow, pale-coloured; callus plate conspicuously broad and extending to the apex, golden-yellow, channelled towards the base and prominently raised, the claw purple. Column appendages unequally bilobed, the anterior one narrower than the posterior. Stigma broad-ovate.

The author's specimens of *P. aureoviride* came from Burleigh Heads in Qld.

FLOWERING PERIOD: Mar. to May

DISTRIBUTION: Chiefly coastal, from north Qld to central NSW

P. aureoviride var. elmae (Plate 149)

P. aureoviride var. *elmae* (H. M. R. Rupp) H. M. R. Rupp in T. E. Hunt in *Aust. Orchid Rev. 11*:92 (1946); H. M. R. Rupp in *Orchids N.S.W.* 32 (1943), as *P. elmae*

SYNONYMY: *P. elmae* H. M. R. Rupp in *Vict. Nat. 59*:122 (1942)

Resembles *P. viride* but the labellum is quite different. It is a more robust plant than the typical form, with crimson markings on the perianth segments.

The material of this variety came from La Perouse in NSW. [A. W. Dockrill does not recognise the varietal status of this orchid and includes it as a synonym of *P. aureoviride* var. *aureoviride*. See *Checklist orchid. Pls trop. Qd 2* (1966).—Ed.]

FLOWERING PERIOD: Mar. to May

DISTRIBUTION: Co-extensive with the typical form throughout its range

P. nigricans (Plate 150)

P. nigricans R. Br. *Prodr. Flor. Nov. Holl.* 319 (1810); A. J. Ewart *Flor. Vict.* 319 (1931); J. M. Black *Flor. S. Aust.* ed. 2:222 (1943); H. M. R. Rupp *Orchids N.S.W.* 33 (1943); J. H. Willis *Handb. Pls Vict.* 1:366 (1962); M. J. Firth *Native Orchids Tasm.* 26 (1965)

SYNONYMY: *P. dixonii* F. Muell. in *Vict. Nat. 9*:44 (1892)

A very slender plant 6–24 cm. high, a small sheathing bract some distance below the inflorescence. Flowers three to thirty-five, green with purplish markings or wholly purplish-black, rarely green with red markings, in a more or less dense raceme 5–45 mm. long, pyramidal in appearance, owing to the very regular expansion of the flowers from below upward. Flowers on short pedicels, the ovary usually oblong, convex, a minute bracteole at the base. Lateral sepals free, or united at the extreme base which is slightly gibbous, triangular-lanceolate or lanceolate, cylindrical, often very divergent, the tips erect, 3–3·5 mm. long. In occasional specimens the tips have poorly developed glands at the apices. Dorsal sepal broadly cucullate, the tip recurved, green with purple linear markings or wholly purplish, about 2·5 mm. long. Petals same colour as dorsal sepal with a prominent central stripe, triangular-lanceolate, equal to or shorter than the dorsal sepal. Labellum dark purple, glandular, articulate on a narrow claw from the extreme base of column, about 2·5 mm. long, ovate-oblong or oblong; apex acute or shortly acuminate, usually recurved; the margins entire at the base, then upward irregularly crenulate or serrate; in occasional specimens the margins of the labella are irregularly ciliate; callus plate oblong, slightly raised and reaching to the extreme tip in some flowers, more or less channelled; membranous part narrow. Column appendages triangular, chelate, the lobes sometimes almost equal in length. Anther point very short, incurved. Pollinia two, bilobed, disc viscid; caudicle short. Rostellum shorter than the anther, the depression in the apex cup-shaped. Stigma ovate or oval. Tubers globular, these and the underground portion of plant encased in a dense fibrous sheath.

FLOWERING PERIOD: Jan. to May

COMMON NAME: Midge-orchid

DISTRIBUTION: Widespread through dry sclerophyll forests in all Australian states except WA, but in Qld restricted to the south-east

P. rufum (Plate 151)

P. rufum R. Br. *Prodr. Flor. Nov. Holl.* 319 (1810); A. J. Ewart *Flor. Vict.* 319 (1931); H. M. R. Rupp *Orchids N.S.W.* 33 (1943); J. H. Willis *Handb. Pls Vict.* 1:366 (1962); M. J. Firth *Native Orchids Tasm.* 26 (1965)

A very slender, somewhat variable species from 4 cm. to more than 30 cm. high. Stem-bract below the inflorescence 10–30 mm. long, closely sheathing or with a free lamina. Flowers very small, few or numerous in a dense spike of about 2–6 cm.; flowers in the mature specimen deflexed, green and reddish-brown to dark purplish-red, sometimes grey-green and red. Dorsal sepal 2–3 mm. long, broad-ovate, acute, deeply cucullate. Lateral sepals broad-lanceolate, widely diverging, longer than the dorsal sepal, often gland-tipped. Petals shorter than the dorsal sepal, lanceolate to triangular, the anterior margins sometimes irregular. Labellum deep purplish, obovate-cuneate; the anterior margins denticulate or shortly serrate, suggestive of cilia in some instances; apex shortly acuminate; posterior margins entire; callus plate prominently raised, very dark, extending from the shortly channelled base to the apex. Column appendages unequally bifid, the posterior lobe short and rounded, lightly hued; the anterior lobe long, darkly hued, often minutely serrate. Anther incurved, commonly with a long point. Pollinia two, bilobed; caudicle sometimes purple. Stigma prominent.

[The actual identity of *P. rufum* was for a long time in doubt. The confusion was caused by R. D. FitzGerald's interpretation of Robert Brown's species and his depiction of it in *Aust. Orchids* 2⁴:+t. (1891). Today the status of this species is in doubt because it is so close to *P. nigricans*. J. H. Willis feels that the two would be best treated as geographical variants of the one species rather than distinct species.

See his *Handb. Pls Vict.* 1:366 (1962). A comparison of the Plates 150 and 151 will show how close they are.—Ed.]

P. rufum is an abundant species on the *Melaleuca* grasslands near Hobart. Tas., and is also plentiful in many parts of NSW. Rupp records it as 'literally in millions' in the Weston scrub. Mueller's ostensible 'rufum' from Station Peak, You Yangs Range, Vic., is unquestionably *P. nigricans*.

FLOWERING PERIOD: Jan. to May

COMMON NAME: Red Midge-orchid

DISTRIBUTION: Widespread and often common in southern Qld, NSW and Tas., but absent from Vic., and apparently not extending westward; also NZ

P. fusco-viride (Plates 152 and 153)

P. fusco-viride F. M. Reader in *Vict. Nat.* 14:163 (1898); A. J. Ewart *Flor. Vict.* 318 (1931); J. M. Black *Flor. S. Aust.* ed. 2:222 (1943); J. H. Willis *Handb. Pls Vict.* 1:366 (1962)

SYNONYMY: *P. horburyanum* H. M. R. Rupp in *Vict. Nat.* 59:122 (1942)

A slender to comparatively robust plant 12–30 cm. high. Bract 1·5–2 cm. long, subulate, closely sheathing, immediately below the inflorescence. Flowers very small, green or yellowish-green, with dark purple or brownish labella, sessile, deflexed, the subtending bracteole often long; spike more or less crowded, especially in the larger specimens, flowers expanding from below upward in a spiral manner. Dorsal sepal about 3 mm. long, green, broadly ovate, concave, acute; lateral sepals slightly longer than the dorsal sepal, united at the extreme base only, lanceolate, divergent, green. Petals about 3 mm. long, lightly coloured, with a prominent purple central stripe, linear or lanceolate, tipped with a small stalked gland. Labellum varying in shape, broadly ovate or oblong-ovate, sometimes narrow towards the base, curved; dark reddish-brown or purple, sometimes almost black; 2–3 mm. long; on a movable claw attached to the basal projection of column; tip sometimes slightly recurved, with a gland inset; margins almost entire; callus plate reaching almost to the tip, not prominently raised, with a distinct groove or channel down the centre, about equal in width to the membranous part, which is rather thick. Anther with a very short point, pollinia two, caudicle short (often described as being as long as the pollinia). Column appendages deeply bifid, reddish-brown, triangular-lanceolate, slightly higher than anther. Capsule shortly oblong, oblique.

[A. S. George has made a careful study of this and the WA species *P. horburyanum* and found them to be conspecific. See *West. Aust. Nat.* 8:39 (1961). Of the two plates illustrating this species, Plate 152 is referable to *P. fusco-viride* and Plate 153 to *P. horburyanum*.—Ed.]

FLOWERING PERIOD: Mainly from Mar. to May, but occasionally as late as Aug.

COMMON NAME: Mallee Midge-orchid

DISTRIBUTION: Scattered from NSW (where it is rare), through the drier parts of Vic., southern SA, and south-western WA, often locally common

P. brachystachyum (Plate 154)

P. brachystachyum Lindl. *Gen. & Spec. orchid. Pls* 513 (1840); M. J. Firth *Native Orchids Tasm.* 25 (1965)

A slender, comparatively dwarf plant 9–12 cm. high. Closely allied to *P. rufum*, but readily distinguished by its short spike of larger and lighter coloured flowers. Flowers from five to nine, green with purplish markings, or green with very deep purplish and red markings, occasionally the lateral sepals bright yellow and green. Dorsal sepal cucullate, acute or acuminate, 3·5–4 mm. long; lateral sepals 4–5 mm. long, broadly lanceolate, united at the base, occasionally with small green glands at the apex (most apparent in the bud), widely spreading. Petals lanceolate, acuminate, about 3 mm. long. Labellum articulate on a short basal claw, lanceolate with entire margins; the membranous part comparatively wide; callus plate dark coloured above, green below, where it is prominently raised and broad, channelled, and extending to the tip, which is acute and about as long as the petals. Column about 1 mm. long, the lateral appendages unequally bilobed, the lobes very short. Rostellum shorter than the anther, prominent. Stigma prominent, ovate. Anther with a short point.

Authentic specimens of *P. brachystachyum* have been rarely collected since the days of R. C. Gunn, the able collector of Tas. plants. The author had long sought this elusive little orchid, but without success, until 1946, when it arrived from H. Trethewie, who found it growing at Stanley, Tas. He writes: 'In the field it is often mistaken for *P. archeri*, owing to its short spike of flowers'—a characteristic of both species. [During April 1966, M. J. Firth collected it at Rocky Cape, on the north coast of Tas. This is the same locality from which Gunn collected it in 1837.—Ed.] Specimens of *P. nigricans* from Green Gully, near Newstead, Vic., collected by G. Weindorfer and Dr Sutton, have been incorrectly referred to this species.

FLOWERING PERIOD: Jan. to July

DISTRIBUTION: This rare species now appears to be endemic in Tas., although once incorrectly recorded from Vic.

P. densum (Plate 155)

P. densum R. D. FitzG. in *J. Bot., Lond.* 23:135 (1885); H. M. R. Rupp *Orchids N.S.W.* 34 (1943); J. H. Willis *Handb. Pls Vict.* 1:367 (1962)

A diminutive compact plant 6–10 cm. high. Flowers numerous, in a short crowded raceme of 1·5–2 cm., light brown to dark brown with green markings. Perianth segments, including the labellum, often gland-tipped. Bract terete, 1–2 cm. long, in a more or less horizontal position and protruding from within the inflorescence. Dorsal sepal ovate, cucullate over the column, with a short point. Lateral sepals connate at the base, lanceolate, divergent, with an acute sinus, concave on the inner sides, about 4 mm. long. Petals lanceolate, much shorter and narrower than the lateral sepals. Labellum small, on a prominent movable claw, oblong with entire margins, obscurely ciliate towards the tip which is recurved and very short; callus plate not markedly raised, smooth, channelled, occupying almost the whole surface of the lamina, even to the extreme tip. Column very short and broad, the appendages entire, or more or less cleft at their apices. Anther incurved with a short point. Stigma ovate. Pollinia two; caudicle short. Tuber large, the remains of old tubers attached.

FLOWERING PERIOD: Dec. to May

DISTRIBUTION: Scattered through coastal and montane areas of south-eastern Qld, NSW, and Vic. (where represented by a single collection from Mount Wellington) and generally rare

P. viride (Plate 156)

P. viride R. D. FitzG. in *J. Bot., Lond.* 23:135 (1885); H. M. R. Rupp *Orchids N.S.W.* 34 (1943); J. H. Willis *Handb. Pls Vict.* 1:367 (1962)

A slender, wholly green plant 10–22 cm. high. Lamina of the bract immediately below the inflorescence, acuminate. Flowers very

small, in a more or less dense raceme, eight to fourteen in number; the perianth not widely expanding. Dorsal sepal broad-lanceolate, 1·5–2 mm. long, green and yellowish; lateral sepals gibbous at the base, longer than the dorsal sepal, slightly divergent. Petals almost as long as the dorsal sepal, very acute, with a transparent hook-like gland at the apex. Labellum yellowish, on a long curved red claw, ovate to ovate-oblong, with an acute point; callus plate often wide, occupying the major portion of the lamina and extending to the extreme apex, papillose, channelled at the base only; margins entire at the base, then minutely dentate to the tip. Column appendages unequally bilobed, the anterior one red in the majority of flowers examined, the lobes somewhat variable. Stigma broadly ovate. Anther with a moderately long point.

FLOWERING PERIOD: Mar. to June

COMMON NAME: Green Midge-orchid

DISTRIBUTION: Extending from south-eastern Qld, where rare, through NSW, where widespread in central coast and tablelands, into Vic., where also rare and confined to coastal grass-tree plains in the east

P. mollissimum (Plate 157)

P. mollissimum H. M. R. Rupp in *Vict. Nat.* 65:146 (1948)

A slender plant up to 36 cm. high. Bract broad and remote from the inflorescence. Flowers five to twenty, in a short raceme, hardly crowded. Dorsal sepal cymbiform, about 3 mm. long, green and brown, with minutely fimbriate margins. Lateral sepals about 4 mm. long, falcate-lanceolate, nearly flat, divergent, united at their bases, brown and green. Petals falcate to broad-lanceolate, acuminate, about 3 mm. long, green and brown, with minutely fimbriate anterior margins. Labellum broadly oblong, acute, recurved, rich chestnut brown, densely pubescent on the upper surface and having the appearance of velvet, articulate on a moderately long claw, margins minutely fimbriate; callus plate obscured by the pubescence, channelled. Column appendages conspicuous, deeply and unequally bilobed; the outer lobe slender, acuminate, dark, with minute fimbriae, the inner one pale, obtuse. Anther often with a prominent mucro. Rostellum conspicuous. Stigma nearly circular. Tubers large.

FLOWERING PERIOD: Feb. to Apr.

DISTRIBUTION: Apparently endemic in NSW where known only from Heathcote National Park

P. beaugleholei (Plate 158)

P. beaugleholei W. H. Nicholls in *Vict. Nat.* 59:11, fig. M–U (1942); H. M. R. Rupp *Orchids N.S.W.* 35 (1943); J. H. Willis *Handb. Pls Vict.* 1:368 (1962); M. J. Firth *Native Orchids Tasm.* 25 (1965)

A very slender plant, usually 10–16 cm. high, but robust specimens up to 20 cm. Fruiting specimens often attain a length of 30–35 cm. Tuber globular or of irregular shape. Base of scape with a fibrous sheath, often with the remains of old tubers attached. Stem usually wiry, in robust specimens 3 mm. thick. Bract below the inflorescence, sheathing, 2–3 cm. long. Flowers very small, five to forty, sessile, green and red-brown or purplish-black, somewhat deflexed. Ovary long, curved, a minute blunt bracteole at the base. Dorsal sepal conspicuously cucullate, erect 1·5–3 mm. long, with a gland at the apex; lateral sepals connate at the base, 2·5–3 mm. long, lanceolate, concave, erect, divergent, the tips with a prominent gland. Petals slightly shorter than the dorsal sepal, triangular-lanceolate, acuminate. Labellum ovate with a short acute apex, semi-recurved, fleshy, the surface raised, papillose, green with deep red-brown or purplish-brown markings, 1·5–3 mm. long; attached to a prominent columnar projection by a movable claw; margins shortly ciliate, the cilia inclined towards the tip, individual cilia glandular; callus plate raised, divided into two parallel sections by a narrow groove, which is wider at the base, each section lanceolate, uniting at the tip in a dark coloured blotch; membranous part about same width as raised sections. Anther with a moderately long point. Pollinia two, lacking a caudicle. Rostellum shorter than the anther. Column appendages prominent, the outer lobes purplish, narrower and slightly longer than the inner lobes, outer margins minutely ciliate. Inner lobes broad, rounded, not coloured, margins entire. Stigma circular, concave.

In the south-west of Vic. this species favours swampy areas, amongst sphagnum, *Nertera*, etc., but it has also been collected from open grassy situations.

FLOWERING PERIOD: Feb. to Apr.

DISTRIBUTION: Extending from central tableland of NSW, through a few localities in south-west and east of Vic. to Tas., but generally uncommon and difficult to locate

P. archeri (Plate 159)

P. archeri Hook. f. *Flor. Tasm.* 2:14, t. 113 fig. B (1858); A. J. Ewart *Flor. Vict.* 320 (1931); J. M. Black *Flor. S. Aust.* ed. 2:222 (1943); H. M. R. Rupp *Orchids N.S.W.* 35 (1943); J. H. Willis *Handb. Pls Vict.* 1:367 (1962); M. J. Firth *Native Orchids Tasm.* 25 (1965)

SYNONYMY: *P. intricatum* C. Stuart ex Benth. *Flor. aust.* 6:346 (1873); *P. ciliatum* A. J. Ewart & B. Rees in *Proc. roy. Soc. Vict.* new ser. 25:111, t. 6 fig. d–g (1912)

A slender plant 5–20 cm. high; leafless except for a long subulate bract below the short squat inflorescence of two to fifteen flowers; flowers pale yellow or green with light brown, red or purplish markings or almost wholly purplish-black. Ovary oblong to ovate, slightly recurved; pedicels very short, with a small acute bracteole at the base. Lateral sepals connate at the extreme base, rarely free, oblong-lanceolate, falcate, somewhat undulate, narrowing to an acute tip, concave towards the front, widely divergent, 4–7 mm. long; dorsal sepal broadly ovate to oblong, deeply cucullate, the tip acute or acuminate, 4–6·5 mm. long. Petals narrowly ovate, falcate, spreading widely, acuminate, 4–5 mm. long. Labellum articulate on a short broad claw, as long as the dorsal sepal, broadly obovate or oblong, sometimes convex, and contracted towards the base, the tip acute or finely acuminate, recurved, deep purple or brownish; the margins entire, minutely crenulate, anterior margins sparsely and irregularly fringed with short cilia, the raised callus plate and the outer margins usually dark coloured; triangularly divided at the base then gradually narrowing upward to the extreme tip. Anther point variable, often long. Column appendages bifid, anterior margins of the outer lobe fringed with pink cilia, tip acute, the inner lobe glabrous, obtuse, but sometimes divided and marked with cilia. Stigma oblong. Pollinia easily detached, granular, very friable; caudicle short. Base of plant, including tubers, encased in a fibrous sheath, remains of old tubers often present.

P. archeri, like many of its congeners has a tendency to vary considerably; thus we find it has been, in the past, described under other names.

The finest specimens so far seen by the author were found in the foothills of Mount Cobbler, Vic. Among the grass tussocks they grew in clusters, looking very like 'Mulberries on sticks', as the cattlemen call them. The colour of the plant—flowers and stem—is wholly very dark purplish. In this locality the flowering peduncle is

invariably attended by a slender leaf which arises from the sheath. Some few blooms possessed fringed margins to the lateral petals—a remarkable occurrence not previously recorded in this species.

FLOWERING PERIOD: Dec. to June

COMMON NAME: Variable Midge-orchid

DISTRIBUTION: All Australian states except WA, but localised and rare in south-eastern Qld, and SA, where known only from Mount Compass

P. archeri var. deirdrae (Plate 159)

P. archeri var. *deirdrae* W. H. Nicholls in *Vict. Nat.* 49:114 (1932)

Flowers pale yellow with conspicuous red and inconspicuous green markings, all with a pronounced drooping habit. Labellum very small and masked by other perianth segments. Only a solitary specimen was collected from Maryborough, Vic., by A. Chisholm in April 1932. I have named it var. *deirdrae* in honour of his daughter.

P. wilsoniense (Plate 160)

P. wilsoniense H. M. R. Rupp in *Vict. Nat.* 59:126, fig. E, 1–4 (1942); H. M. R. Rupp *Orchids N.S.W.* 37 (1943)

A slender plant 10–22 cm. high. Lamina of the stem-bract 2–4 cm. below the inflorescence. Flowers from five to twenty-five, usually conspicuously bent over, but the ovaries less prominent than in other species. Flowers dark brownish-red, occasionally paler. All the floral segments with ciliate, fimbriate, or toothed glandular margins. Dorsal sepal more than 2 mm. long, cucullate, acute, or acuminate. Lateral sepals longer than dorsal sepal, usually widely divergent, gibbous at the base. Petals shorter than the dorsal sepal, acuminate. Labellum on a claw, broadly ovate with an apiculate upturned apex; margins irregularly fimbriate or sometimes regularly and densely ciliate; callus plate variable, but commonly narrowly bipartite, sometimes occupying the greater part of the upper surface of the lamina. Column appendages variable, but always deeply bilobed, the anterior lobe dark and shortly ciliate or almost serrate. Anther cordiform; stigma ovate.

Rupp remarks: 'a very interesting species, with all floral segments and the column appendages variably decorated along the margins with glandular fringes.'

FLOWERING PERIOD: Nov. and Dec.

DISTRIBUTION: Endemic in NSW where it is confined to the Blue Mountains (Mount Wilson)

P. woollsii (Plate 161)

P. woollsii F. Muell. *Fragm. Phyt. Aust.* 5:100 (1865); H. M. R. Rupp *Orchids N.S.W.* 38 (1943)

A slender plant 18–26 cm. high. Bract some distance below the inflorescence, subulate, 1·5–2·5 cm. long. Flowers numerous in a dense spike of about 2·5 cm., green with dark red-brown markings, the dark colour often intense; more or less pendent due to the oblong ovary being curved. Dorsal sepal cucullate, very broad, the apex shortly acuminate, about 2·5 mm. long, the margins sometimes sparsely ciliate; lateral sepals longer than the dorsal one, oblong, gibbous, divergent, margins prominently incurved, apices acute, united at the base. Petals ovate-lanceolate, a little shorter than the dorsal sepal, acuminate, the margins shortly ciliate. Labellum articulate on a prominent claw, broadly obovate, acute; callus plate very dark, fleshy, raised, occupying the major part of the lamina, papillose, channelled, with shortly ciliate margins (sometimes cilia present along the anterior portion only); the cilia mostly glandular.

Column short, with very prominent chelate appendages which exceed the anther; lobes unequal, the inner lobes pale; outer, or anterior lobes longest, dark red-brown, the outer margins very shortly ciliate; the column-foot prominent, red-brown. Anther pale with a short point. Stigma almost orbicular.

Rupp writes in reference to *P. woollsii*: 'Cilia are present not only on the labellum and petals, but also on the dorsal sepal and the column appendages. Hitherto *P. woollsii* has been described as possessing cilia only on the margins of the labellum and petals.'

I am indebted to Rupp for my specimens of this species, in some of which I have observed flowers with a few short cilia on the lateral sepals. One such flower I have figured.

FLOWERING PERIOD: Nov. to Mar.

DISTRIBUTION: South-eastern Qld, also central coast and tableland of NSW; of local occurrence and rare

P. nublingii (Plate 162)

P. nublingii R. S. Rogers in *Trans. roy. Soc. S. Aust.* 51:293 (1927); H. M. R. Rupp *Orchids N.S.W.* 38 (1943)

A slender plant 11–27 cm. high, with a subulate bract above the middle of the stem. Inflorescence a lax raceme, with five to twenty small reddish-brown or greenish flowers. Dorsal sepal ovate, acuminate, cucullate, recurved at the apex, three-nerved, about 4 mm. long and 2 mm. wide, the margins shortly ciliate. Lateral sepals spreading, lanceolate, divaricate at an angle of about sixty degrees, slightly gibbous, concave, shortly connate at the base, three-nerved, nearly 5 mm. long. Petals ovate-lanceolate, acuminate, erect, about 3·5 mm. long and 0·8 mm. in the widest part, three-nerved, the margins shortly ciliate. Labellum on an irritable claw, somewhat rectangular, narrower at the base and widening towards the apex, shortly apiculate, flat, not recurved at the tip, the margins shortly ciliate, about 4 mm. long and 2 mm. wide; lamina with two raised, fleshy, parallel, papillose, dark, longitudinal bands coalescing and widening in front and terminating slightly beyond the middle; decorated towards the apex with dark purple radial veins. Column short; anther incumbent with a very acute mucro, shorter than the appendages, but a little higher than the rostellum; column appendages bifid, the chelae almost equal in length, anterior margins minutely ciliate.

[The shape of the flat labellum—rectangular at the base, widening towards the front, with its peculiar double callosity and radial veins on the lamina—is quite distinctive, and easily separates this from other ciliate species.]

FLOWERING PERIOD: Jan. to Mar.

DISTRIBUTION: Endemic in NSW where it is found in the central coast region

P. ruppii (Plate 163)

P. ruppii R. S. Rogers in *Trans. roy. Soc. S. Aust.* 51:292 (1927); H. M. R. Rupp *Orchids N.S.W.* 38 (1943)

A slender species 10–30 cm. high. Lamina of the bract some distance below the inflorescence. Raceme of flowers 3–3·5 cm. long, rather dense; flowers more or less deflexed, ovaries slender, red-brown, the lateral sepals green with red-brown flecks or almost wholly bright green. Dorsal sepal broadly ovate but acute, cucullate, shortly ciliate, three-nerved, about 3 mm. long. Lateral sepals gibbous at the base, oblong-lanceolate, divergent, about 4 mm. long. Petals shorter than the dorsal sepal, triangular-acuminate, shortly ciliate. Labellum oblong-ovate, apiculate, not recurved, under 3 mm. long, the margins shortly ciliate, the cilia

crowded, from near the base to the apex; callus plate inconspicuous, channelled, but occupying the greater part of the lamina. Cilia on the labellum, dorsal sepal and petals gland-tipped. Column appendages darkly coloured, shortly bilobed, the anterior lobe sparsely ciliate. Anther with a conspicuous mucro. Stigma ovate.

FLOWERING PERIOD: Jan. to Apr.

DISTRIBUTION: Endemic in NSW where it is scattered through the central and southern coastal districts, extending into the tablelands, generally uncommon

P. acuminatum (Plate 164)

P. acuminatum R. S. Rogers in *Trans. roy. Soc. S. Aust.* 51:291 (1927); H. M. R. Rupp *Orchids N.S.W.* 37 (1943)

Stem very slender, up to 22 cm. high, with a leafy, linear, subulate bract well above the middle. Flowers in a moderately lax spike of six to sixteen, dark reddish-brown, striated with purple lines. Dorsal sepal ovate, erect, cucullate, very acuminate, with three distinct longitudinal nerves and sometimes also two indistinct marginal ones; margins ciliate, about 4–5 mm. long and 1·75 mm. at widest part. Lateral sepals free, elongate, spreading, slender, not gibbous, divaricate, lanceolate, with a gland at each apex, concave above, about ·5 mm. long. Petals triangular, erect, markedly acuminate, striated, with three distinct longitudinal nerves, shorter than the dorsal sepal, about 3·5 mm. long and 1·0 mm. wide, margins ciliate. Labellum on a movable claw, ovate, apex acuminate, much recurved, the margins ciliate, about 2·5 mm. long and 1·25 mm. wide, three-nerved, upper surface of lamina glabrous, a dark purple thickened inner plate extending beyond the middle. Anther with an elongated terete point about 0·5 mm. long. Column appendages erect, ciliate, about 1·5 mm. long, notched; anterior segment elongated, subulate; posterior segment very short, wide and rounded.

Among a number of specimens received from M. W. Nichols (Mar. 1939) were several short segmented forms—they were minus the glands at the apices of the lateral sepals.

FLOWERING PERIOD: Dec. to May

DISTRIBUTION: Scattered from southern Qld where rare, to the north coast of NSW

P. morrisii (Plate 165)

P. morrisii W. H. Nicholls in *Vict. Nat.* 48:108, fig. d–g, i, j, n, o, r, s (1931); H. M. R. Rupp *Orchids N.S.W.* 37 (1943); J. H. Willis *Handb. Pls Vict.* 1:367 (1962); M. J. Firth *Native Orchids Tasm.* 24 (1965)

SYNONYMY: *P. fimbriatum* sens. A. J. Ewart *Flor. Vict.* 321 (1931), non R. Br. (1810)

Plant slender, usually more robust than *P. fimbriatum*, 9–36 cm. high; leafless except for a small subulate bract below the spike. Flowers three to twenty-five, almost wholly very dark purple or prune, or green with purplish markings, rarely green with rufous markings; flowers not crowded, raceme from 5 mm. to 5·5 cm. long. Ovary oblong, recurved; pedicel short, subtending bracteole small. Lateral sepals united at the base only, oblong-lanceolate, falcate, concave, narrowing to a minute acuminate apex, widely spread, 4·5–5·5 mm. long, dark purplish, lighter on the concave side, or greenish; dorsal sepal 4–5 mm. long and 3–4 mm. wide, broad-ovate, cucullate, with a long acuminate point, margins deeply coloured, with purple or purplish-brown hairs. Petals triangular, acuminate, deeply hued, except towards the base, fringed with hairs as in the dorsal sepal, 4–4·5 mm. long. Labellum 4–5 mm.

long, and 2–2·5 mm. wide, articulate on a small claw, oblong-ovate, conspicuously narrowing towards the base; the apex abruptly acute, recurved; margins densely fringed with long undulate or bristly, purplish to purple-brown hairs, those towards the tip sometimes very long, up to 3 mm.; lamina surface towards the tip entirely smooth, almost black, and raised above the margins in a few specimens; two raised pubescent bands extending to the base. Column 1–2 mm. high; the appendages acutely bifid, anterior lobe longest, acute or acuminate, somewhat densely fringed with minute cilia or a few marginal cilia only; posterior lobe smooth, pale coloured, obtuse or acuminate. Anther with a long point. Pollinia granular; caudicle about half as long. Stigma narrowly ovate, sometimes with a basal appendage which is variable in length.

This beautiful species is often abundant on heavy clay washes in dry sclerophyll forests. In some specimens from Mount Irvine, NSW, the cilia on the perianth segments were absent.

FLOWERING PERIOD: Dec. to May

COMMON NAME: Bearded Midge-orchid

DISTRIBUTION: From coastal and inland districts of the Blue Mountains, NSW, into southern Vic. and Tas.

P. morrisii var. contortum (Plate 166)

P. morrisii var. *contortum* W. H. Nicholls in *Vict. Nat.* 59:14 (1942)

A comparatively robust plant 30–35 cm. high. Flowers larger than those of the typical form. Labellum ovate-cuneate, the base very wide; apex of labellum with a peculiar undulate, somewhat contorted twist.

This unusual form was found in the Pyrete Ranges, near Gisborne, Vic., on rocky ledges in Ironbark country, growing with *Caleana major*.

FLOWERING PERIOD: Apr. to May

DISTRIBUTION: Apparently endemic in Vic., where rare, being only known by the type collection from Pyrete Ranges

P. plumosum (Plate 167)

P. plumosum H. M. R. Rupp in *Vict. Nat.* 59:127, fig. G, 1–3 (1947); H. M. R. Rupp *Orchids N.S.W.* 34 (1943)

A slender to moderately robust species 12–28 cm. high. Lamina of bract a little below the inflorescence. Flowers three to nine, at first deflexed, but later becoming more or less horizontal, green and pale yellowish-green with red markings. Dorsal sepal broadly lanceolate, sometimes with a filiform point, but more commonly acuminate, about 7 mm. long. Lateral sepals slightly longer than the dorsal sepal, broad-linear, green, more or less spreading. Petals narrow-lanceolate, acuminate, about 5 mm. long. Labellum red-brown, on a short claw, oblong or narrowly shield-shaped, the callus plate not markedly raised, extending almost to the extreme tip of the lamina, channelled throughout; the margins entire from the base for about half their length, then densely fringed with long white cilia to the apex. Column appendages deeply bilobed with almost equal lobes; anterior lobe pink, plumose with long densely packed curled white cilia; posterior lobe pale, not ciliate. Rostellum very thick and prominent. Stigma ovate. Anther with a short point.

E. Nubling writes: 'I considered this a very distinctive species, it struck me as such at once in the field when discovered, it grows somewhat sparingly among low scrub on the soakage flats.'

It is closely allied to *P. archeri*, but is separated from this species by the very characteristic plume-like fringes of the column appendages, also in the different labellum, etc.

FLOWERING PERIOD: Jan. to Mar.

COMMON NAME: Plumed Midge-orchid

DISTRIBUTION: South-eastern Qld and central coast of NSW, uncommon and rarely collected

P. fimbriatum (Plate 168)

P. fimbriatum R. Br. *Prodr. Flor. Nov. Holl.* 319 (1810); H. M. R. Rupp *Orchids N.S.W.* 37 (1943)

A very slender, often attenuated plant 11–38 cm. high. A sheathing bract about 2 cm. long subtending the inflorescence. Flowers often fairly numerous—up to twenty-seven in my specimens—in a comparatively loose spike. Ovary curved, oblong, cylindrical. Dorsal sepal about 5 mm. long, lanceolate, acute, deeply concave, marked with crimson striae and fringed with short cilia. Lateral sepals 5–6 mm. long with a very short claw and gibbous at the base, linear-falcate, widely divergent, concave. Petals shorter than the sepals, acuminate, marked with prominent longitudinal crimson striae. Labellum linear-oblong, contracted into a short erect claw, articulate, recurved in the upper part, slightly dilated at the end and densely fringed with long fine cilia; callus plate forming two raised thick lines extending along the claw and narrow part at the base of the swelling. Column appendages nearly as long as the anther, acutely bifid, the column below the anther very short.

Rupp states: 'Recorded also from Vic. (rare)'. No specimens are in evidence and it is apparent the species has been confused with another.

FLOWERING PERIOD: Jan. to May

COMMON NAME: Fringed Midge-orchid

DISTRIBUTION: Apparently endemic in NSW where it is wide-spread and often locally common in central and south-eastern districts

P. bowdenae (Plate 169)

P. bowdenae H. M. R. Rupp in *Vict. Nat.* 65:144, fig. 8–9 (1948)

A somewhat slender to robust plant, up to 55 cm. high. Bract remote from the inflorescence; raceme 7–8·5 cm. long. Stem below the lamina terete, above it strikingly angular. Flowers six to twenty, never crowded, green or greenish-brown, sub-sessile but standing well out from the axis; labellum and lateral sepals developed out of all proportion to the rest of the flower. Dorsal sepal minute, rarely 3 mm. long, ovate-acute, cucullate. Lateral sepals up to 1 cm. long, free, broad-linear, concave, at first divergent but soon becoming parallel or even crossed, gibbous at the base. Petals up to 2·5 mm. long, lanceolate, ciliate (non-ciliate in my specimens), veined longitudinally. Labellum articulate on a long curved claw, oblong but acute at the recurved tip, up to 1 cm. long, undulate, slightly constricted about the middle, pale with some purple or reddish markings, especially about the apex; densely beset with long tangled grey to purplish cilia; callus plate ill-defined, but large and conspicuously channelled. Column diminutive, abnormal in structure; appendages deeply bilobed; the outer lobe ciliate in some flowers, acuminate; the inner one shorter, sometimes obtuse. Rostellum large; stigma either brown or green; anther with a filiform point.

This plant was found in abundance, and is apparently a self-fertile species.

FLOWERING PERIOD: Feb. to Apr.

DISTRIBUTION: Apparently endemic in NSW where it is found on the eastern slopes of the Blue Mountains

P. anomalum (Plate 170)

P. anomalum H. M. R. Rupp in *Vict. Nat.* 65:142, fig. 1–6 (1948)

A slender plant up to 30 cm. high. Bract 2–3 cm. or more below the inflorescence. Flowers five to twenty, green, not crowded, standing out prominently from the axis on shortly stalked ovaries, the bracteole mucronate. Dorsal sepal about 5 mm. long, ciliate, cucullate, broadly lanceolate. Lateral sepals 7–8 mm. long, free, spreading, almost acuminate, sometimes hooked at the apices. Petals about 4 mm. long, ciliate, most frequently articulate on short claws, but rarely sessile and smaller. Labellum about 6 mm. long, articulate on a claw, oblong, almost straight and somewhat constricted about the middle, reflexed at the apex, acute or shortly acuminate, pale green, blotched with red towards the tip, densely fringed with long purple or reddish cilia which may be reversed; callus plate obscure. Column anomalous; anther stalked, separate from the stigma, often, but not always abortive; stigma on a flat stalk, usually leaning against the base of the anther; rostellum obscure or obsolete; column appendages rudimentary, or sometimes filiform and glabrous, entire or occasionally unequally furcate.

In many flowers of this unusual orchid the anther is abortive, neither pollinia nor caudicle being present. In some flowers there was an imperfect anther sac with a few pollen grains, and in a few instances the anther was perfect. In many flowers the appendages of the column are rudimentary, one on each side with what appears to be a third rudiment in front, but occasionally the two laterals are developed into glabrous filaments of varying length; in some cases these were unequally furcate. The flowers open very shyly, and few are out at the same time.

It is a remarkable fact that the unusual nature of the petals in *P. anomalum* was not observed, until the author had drawn Rupp's attention to it. Apparently the majority of the flowers he examined had fixed petals. In the material forwarded to me by Miss Bowden most of those inspected possessed the articulate type.

FLOWERING PERIOD: Feb. to Apr.

DISTRIBUTION: Apparently endemic in NSW where confined to the Blue Mountains, and found in considerable numbers along a range of several miles on the eastern slopes

G. baueri (Plates 171 and 172)

G. baueri R. Br. *Prodr. Flor. Nov. Holl.* 319 (1810); H. M. R. Rupp *Orchids N.S.W.* 30 (1943), as *Prasophyllum baueri*, and l.c. 31, as *P. deaneanum*

SYNONYMY: *Prasophyllum baueri* (R. Br.) Poir. *Encycl. meth. Bot. Suppl.* 4:547 (1816); *P. deaneanum* R. D. FitzG. in *Aust. Orchids* 2³:+t. (1888)

A small, slender to robust species 4–15 cm. high, stem greenish, purplish towards the base, base enclosed in a scarious sheath. Leaf reduced to a small sheathing bract a little distance below the inflorescence. An unusual bracteole subtending the ovary. Flowers two to six, green and red. Dorsal sepal short, broad at the base, suddenly contracting towards the apex, margins inturned, about 4 mm. long. Lateral sepals green, very long, concave on the inner side, widely divergent, united towards the base. Petals very short, notched or unequally bidentate, incurved, colourless with red margins, 4 mm. long. Labellum lanceolate, thick and fleshy, constricted in the basal portion by the inturned margins; anterior portion deflexed. Callus plate and its membrane extending nearly to the extreme apex; the central portion with free, entire margins folded inwards, upper margins of labellum minutely and irregularly undulate. Column appendages claw-like, widely diverging, not exceeding the anther. Anther acuminate, purplish. Stigma prominent. Pollinia oval. Caudicle short, purplish.

A comparison of my own drawings of *P. baueri* and those in *Aust. Orchids*, which FitzGerald states were copied from the original work of Ferdinand Bauer, shows some difference in the floral structure. However, I have carefully checked, and rechecked, with the aid of a powerful magnifier, every detail to ensure its accuracy.

[The species is notoriously variable. Rupp in the article where he reinstates the genus *Genoplesium* states: 'After watching the development of a number of racemes, it appears to me that the labellum from the time when the flower first opens, to the time of its full maturity, gradually passes from the form shown by FitzGerald to that shown by Bauer.' See *Vict. Nat.* 66:75 (1949). Thus any depictions of the species are unlikely to be identical in all respects.

Of the two plates depicting this species, Plate 171 is referable to *P. Baueri* and Plate 172 to its synonym *P. deaneanum*.—Ed.]

FLOWERING PERIOD: Feb. to May

DISTRIBUTION: Apparently endemic in NSW where it is of scattered occurrence on the central coast and rarely collected

10   *Genoplesium*

Genoplesium R. Br. *Prodr. Flor. Nov. Holl.* 319 (1810)

A monotypic genus very close to *Prasophyllum*, endemic in NSW.

[Rupp sets out the differences as follows: (1) The very succulent, brittle and tender substance of the whole plant has no parallel in *Prasophyllum*, least of all in the section *Micranthum*. (2) The form commonly taken by the floral bract is unique. (3) No species of *Prasophyllum* can be found with petals in any way resembling those shown by Bauer, which are characteristic of many plants examined. (4) The labellum, whether Bauer's form or FitzGerald's, is unlike that of a *Prasophyllum*. (5) The same remark applies to the column appendages. (6) The leaf lamina shows no tendency to become terete.—Ed.]

11   *Caleana*

Caleana R. Br. *Prodr. Flor. Nov. Holl.* 329 (1810)

Terrestrial glabrous slender herbs, with two oval or elongated tubers. Leaf solitary, radical, linear or narrow-lanceolate—in one species (*C. nigrita*) broad-lanceolate. Flowers one to eight on slender pedicels. Flowers reversed; sepals and petals linear; the dorsal sepal slightly incurved over the column; the lateral sepals spreading or reflexed; the petals erect or incurved against the column. Labellum articulate on a movable claw at the base of the column; the lamina peltate, ovate, its surface convex, smooth or tuberculate. Column elongated, its margins broadly winged throughout their length. Anther valvate, two-celled; pollinia granular. Caudicle and viscid disc absent.

This small genus of five species is confined to Australia and New Zealand; all of them are found in Australia, one, *C. minor*, extending into New Zealand.

C. major (Plate 173)

C. major R. Br. *Prodr. Flor. Nov. Holl.* 329 (1810); A. J. Ewart *Flor. Vict.* 323 (1931); J. M. Black *Flor. S. Aust.* ed. 2:223 (1943); H. M. R. Rupp *Orchids N.S.W.* 41 (1943); J. H. Willis *Handb. Pls Vict.* 1:376 (1962); M. J. Firth *Native Orchids Tasm.* 13 (1965)

SYNONYMY: *Caleya major* (R. Br.) R. Br. in Ait. f. *Hort. kew.* ed. 2, 5:204 (1813)

A slender glabrous plant usually 15–35 cm. high. Leaf solitary, 5–12 cm. long, glabrous, narrow-lanceolate, more or less reddish. Stem reddish-brown or green, wiry. Flowers reversed, more or less reddish-brown, one to five on very slender pedicels, the upper bracteole including a floral rudiment. Dorsal sepal 12–15 mm. long, linear-spathulate, acuminate on a contracted base, erect or incurved, the tip sometimes reflexed, channelled; lateral sepals as long or slightly longer, reflexed, channelled, slightly divergent, contracted about the middle, then narrowly tubular or pointed. Petals 9–13 mm. long, narrow-linear, erect against the wings of the column. Labellum 5–8 mm. long, attached to base of column by a long semi-circular strap-like claw, which is extremely sensitive; lamina obovate, peltate on the claw, 8–9 mm. long, smooth, the centre inflated and hollow, cavity open below, produced on the columnar side into a beak-like process and a flattened blunt appendage at the other end. Column incurved, larger than the other segments, very broadly winged from anther to base; wings slightly adnate to claw of labellum. Anther erect, not pointed. Stigma circular, prominent, concave. Pollinia free, a pair in each cell, elongated, laminate, no caudicle or viscid disc. Rostellum rudimentary.

C. major is at times plentiful in thick scrub areas in coastal districts, also far inland in open forest country. As well it has been found on dry rocky ridges but in such places it occurs sparingly. Atkinson records Tas. specimens of a height of 60 cm. (2 ft.) with six to eight flowers. Mueller also records a Tas. specimen with eight flowers.

FLOWERING PERIOD: Sept. to Feb., depending on altitude

COMMON NAME: Flying Duck-orchid

DISTRIBUTION: South-eastern Qld; eastern NSW; Vic.; northern and eastern Tas.; south-eastern SA

C. nigrita (Plate 174)

C. nigrita Lindl. in *Edwards' bot. Reg.* 23: Swan Riv. Append. liv (1840); R. Erickson *Orchids West* ed. 2:65 (1965)

Leaf ovate to broadly lanceolate, clasping at the base, about 2 cm. long and 1 cm. broad; green, purplish beneath. Stem 10–15 cm. long, bracts absent. Flowers one to three, light green with reddish-brown or purplish markings, on pedicels about 1·3–2·5 cm. long, the subtending bracteoles small. Sepals and petals linear-spathulate 1·3–1·5 cm. long; dorsal sepal appressed to the back of the column; lateral sepals incurved and clasping the dilated wings of the column and attached to the extremity of the columnar foot. Labellum with a curved strap-like claw about 6 mm. long; lamina peltate, oblong, very convex, 1·2–1·5 cm. long; tuberculate on the surface, the upper end, or lobe twice as long as the lower lobe or appendage; both ends obtuse or emarginate. Column nearly as long as the sepals, the wings wide and adnate to the basal projection of the column forming a broad sac as in *C. minor*. Anther small. Stigma reniform.

It was found growing in sandy soil often in association with *Drakaea*.

In some flowers the tuberculate portion of the labellum-lamina is reddish-brown; in others quite black—hence the specific name of the plant.

FLOWERING PERIOD: Sept. and Oct.

DISTRIBUTION: Endemic in WA where it is most abundant in the south-west

C. minor (Plate 175)

C. minor R. Br. *Prodr. Flor. Nov. Holl.* 329 (1810); A. J. Ewart *Flor. Vict.* 324 (1931); J. M. Black *Flor. S. Aust.* ed. 2:223 (1943); H. M. R. Rupp *Orchids N.S.W.* 42 (1943); J. H. Willis *Handb. Pls Vict.* 1:377 (1962); M. J. Firth *Native Orchids Tasm.* 14 (1965)

SYNONYMY: *Caleya minor* (R. Br.) Sweet *Hort. brit.* ed. 1:385 (1827)

A very slender plant ranging in height from 6–17 cm. Stem almost filiform, wiry, only occasionally with a minute bract about the middle. Leaf 3–9 cm., very narrow-linear, channelled, often withered at flowering time. Flowers one to seven, much smaller than those of *C. major*; green, tinged with red or red-brown; a rudimentary bud often at the head of the raceme. Ovary on a slender pedicel, subtending bracteole reddish, 3–4 mm. long. Sepals and petals narrow-linear, channelled on the anterior surface, the petals incurved against the sides of the column, and a little shorter than the sepals; lateral sepals wide at base, and attached to the base of column; dorsal sepal spathulate, erect and incurved, exceeding the column by 1·5–2 mm. Dorsal sepal and petals attached at base of column. Labellum peltately attached by a long rather wide convex, curved elastic strap to the elongated foot of column; lamina broadly ovate or ovate-lanceolate, 5–6 mm. long, the upper convex surface covered with closely set darkly hued tubercules, those towards the margins largest; widest part of lamina contracting to a narrow bifid apex; reverse side of lamina concave, smooth, except for marginal tubercules and a few encroaching ones; base of lamina with a somewhat blunt point. Column 5–7 mm. long, broadly winged throughout, the base elongated. Anther obtuse. Pollinia four, long and narrow.

C. minor can be found on scrublands, rocky timbered slopes, and at the base of trees in forest country. I have seen flowers of *C. minor* with two perfectly shaped labella. More strangely fashioned flowers could scarcely be imagined.

FLOWERING PERIOD: Nov. to Jan.

COMMON NAME: Small Duck-orchid

DISTRIBUTION: Temperate parts of all Australian states except WA, but in Qld restricted to the south-east, and rare in south-eastern SA; also in NZ

C. sullivanii (Plate 176)

C. sullivanii (F. Muell.) E. E. Pescott in *Vict. Nat.* 43:228 (1926); A. J. Ewart *Flor. Vict.* 323 (1931); J. H. Willis *Handb. Pls Vict.* 1:377 (1965)

SYNONYMY: *Caleya sullivanii* F. Muell. in *Chem. & Drugg, Lond. Australas. Suppl.* 4: 44 (1882)

A very slender plant 9–10·5 cm. high; stem wiry, reddish. Leaf narrow-linear, 7–8 cm. long, arising from the base of the stem, usually in a withered condition at flowering time. No bract present on the stem. Flowers usually two or three, very small, pale green with reddish markings; ovaries on slender pedicels, subtending bracteoles small, reddish; sepals and petals narrow-linear, channelled on the inner surface; petals shorter than the sepals; labellum lanceolate-ovate, pointed at the apex, attached to the column by a long, curved, rather narrow strap; lamina surface raised, beset with irregular papillular, sessile glands towards the centre; under surface concave; column 7–8 mm. long, greenish; broadly winged throughout; stigma small, situated below the anther; anther imperfect.

Very few botanists have been fortunate enough to examine a specimen of this duck-orchid in a fresh condition. On 12 December 1926, I received specimens from C. W. D'Alton, collected in the Wonderland Range, Grampians, approximately eighteen miles from Mount Zero, where the species was originally found in 1882.

This orchid bears a superficial resemblance to *C. minor*, which was in fair abundance in the immediate vicinity of the Wonderland colony. *C. sullivanii* was first discovered in this particular locality by D'Alton in 1924. Owing to its small stature, it is very difficult to locate. It favours open spaces facing the sun, on rock ledges and in mossy crevices. The flowers are paler than in other species of the genus.

Other interesting collections of the species have been made in south-western Vic. The first specimens were received from A. J. Swaby who writes as follows: 'The plants were collected on the south-west slopes near the summit of Mount Byron in the Black Range. We found the specimens in depressions and soaks, always in mossy places—the tubers on the rocks. They were growing in association with *C. minor* and species of other genera.'

Additional specimens were forwarded to the author by Miss Lorna Banfield, collected from Moyston West, near Mount William (10 Jan. 1937). The specimens were 16–20 cm. high, and bore as many as eight flowers.

In the prior descriptions of *C. sullivanii* there is no reference to the pollinia and none existed in the flowers of my specimens, the stalked anther in all instances being abortive. Swaby also mentions the vagueness of the reproductive organs in what he refers to as 'freak flowers' . . . 'the end of the column never could form an anther, and the labellum has no inclination to move.'

I cannot trace prior records of antherless orchids; probably *C. sullivanii* and its ally *C. nublingii*, are unique in this respect. The simply-constructed labellum of *C. sullivanii* constitutes—in the absence of pollen sacs—a useless appendage. It is not irritable as in all other recorded species, but is only slightly sensitive, and owing to its form does not close effectively. The stigmas in the mature blooms are misshapen by the formation of irregular granulations which may be the result of insect action—probably the agent concerned in pollination. A strong lens brought to light traces of, presumably, pollen grains immersed in the dry secretion around the margins of the stigma.

FLOWERING PERIOD: Nov. to Jan.

DISTRIBUTION: Endemic in Vic., where it is confined to the moist depressions of the Grampians and Black Range, and rarely collected

C. nublingii (Plate 177)

C. nublingii W. H. Nicholls in *Vict. Nat.* 48:15 (1931); H. M. R. Rupp *Orchids N.S.W.* 42 (1943)

A very slender glabrous species about 10 cm. high. Stem reddish-brown, wiry. Leaf very narrow-linear, almost filiform, 2–5 cm. in length. Flowers one or two (two specimens only found), green with red and purplish markings. Pedicels slender, a very small, acute bracteole at the base. Ovary short. Dorsal sepal narrow-linear, spathulate, channelled on the inner side, incurved and exceeding the column slightly. Lateral petals narrow-linear, not channelled, embracing the wings of column and a little shorter than the sepals.

Dorsal sepal and petals arising from the posterior base of column; the lateral sepals from the anterior base. Labellum somewhat pyriform, gibbous; peltate as in other species of the genus; the connecting strap wide, semi-circular, concave on the underside, very irritable and attached to the projecting foot of the column; lamina 3.5–4 mm. long, and 2.5 mm. wide; the entire surface, outer and lower margins covered with numerous, small greenish-purplish tubercules of irregular shape; lamina centrally divided by a narrow longitudinal groove which gradually widens below to a definite bilobed, emarginate or retuse-truncate ending; apices broad and rounded; upper margins crenulate, thin, the apex cuneate-acute; underside deeply concave, two-celled. Column about 6.5 mm. high, encumbent, very similar to that in *C. nigrita*, light green, very widely winged throughout, the projecting basal foot extending along the labellum-strap and adnate to it, forming a cup-like cavity. Stigma somewhat circular, concave. Anther erect with an obtuse or emarginate apex. Pollinia not observed.

Anther rudimentary in two flowers examined, the inner surface marked by raised callosities (see Plate 177 Fig. **e**). In the remaining flower the anther was comparatively well-formed, but lacked the pollinia.

This curious and intriguing form is named after E. Nubling, who discovered it at Bell, in the Blue Mountains. Nubling writes as follows: 'found on 27 Dec. 1930 on a rocky and sandy spur (Hawkesbury sandstone formation) at about 3,500 feet altitude. The spur extends for some considerable distance towards the Grose River, though probably some 1,500 feet above it. *C. major* and *C. minor* found not far from them.'

FLOWERING PERIOD: Nov. and Dec.

DISTRIBUTION: Endemic in NSW where it is apparently confined to the Blue Mountains and rare

12   *Drakaea*

Drakaea Lindl. in *Edwards' bot. Reg. 23*: Swan Riv. Append. lv (1840)

Slender plants with rounded fleshy basal tubers. Leaf solitary, basal, ovate to ovate-cordate, often fleshy. Flower solitary, shortly pedicellate. Perianth segments all about equal in length, narrow linear. Dorsal sepal erect or retroflexed. Lateral sepals acutely reflexed downward and backward. Petals acutely reflexed downward, often crossing the lateral sepals. Labellum very irritable on a claw to which it is peltately attached, generally ovate in shape with revolute margins, beset with glands or hairs in various arrangements, bilobed. Column slender, abruptly incurved near the middle, narrowly winged, with a linear basal claw.

A small genus of four species, all confined to WA.

D. elastica (Plate 178)

D. elastica Lindl. in *Edwards' bot. Reg. 23*: Swan Riv. Append. lvi (1840); R. Erickson *Orchids West* ed. 2:67 (1965)

A very slender plant 15–20 cm. high. Leaf ovate-cordate, thick and fleshy, dark green, net-veined above, sometimes the nerves dark-purplish; rugose white below, the margins dark purplish, incurved, 1–1.5 cm. long. Stem green with a small sheathing bract below the middle; lower section of stem thinner, wiry purplish. Flower solitary. Sepals and petals linear, golden-red, 5–8 mm. long, the petals shorter than the sepals, all reflexed below and to the rear of the ovary; dorsal sepal slightly longer than the lateral sepals, erect, the tip retroflexed. Labellum purplish, articulate on the end of the basal projection of the column, and 'moving at the joint with every breeze', the claw narrow-linear, 4–5 mm. long; lamina more or less hammer-shaped, peltately attached, broadly ovate but very convex, the sides completely folded back so as to conceal the under surface; the upper surface covered with short thick hairs and calli, except the smooth tip, the lower lobe, or appendage (head) solid and fleshy (mulberry-like) with a few short hairs interspersed between the glands; half as long as the upper one. Column about as long as the petals, abruptly incurved in the middle, fleshy below the middle, the narrow wings produced into narrow auricles at the base; the basal projection of the column supporting the labellum, 4–5 mm. long, and linear like the claw. Anther large, blunt, horizontal, 3–4 mm. long. Rostellum point prolonged beyond the anther. Stigma rather small.

FLOWERING PERIOD: Sept. and Oct.

COMMON NAME: Praying Virgin

DISTRIBUTION: Endemic in WA where it is widespread throughout the south-west

D. fitzgeraldii (Plate 179)

D. fitzgeraldii Schlechter in *Repert. Spec. nov. Regn. veg.* 17:81 (1921); R. Erickson *Orchids West* ed. 2:67 (1965)

A very slender plant 9–30 cm. high. Stem very slender, glabrous, green, a small clasping bract 5–8 mm. long well below the middle, a portion of the stem below the bract, wiry, and purplish. Leaf roundly ovate, somewhat reniform, acute, pale greyish-green marked with red-brown chiefly along the margins, 8–25 mm. long. Flower solitary. Ovary green club-shaped, the pedicel short, subtending bracteole ovate-lanceolate, 8–10 mm. long. Perianth segments approximately equal, 10–15 mm. long, narrow-linear, yellow marked with red; lateral sepals expanded at their insertion near the base of the columnar-foot, acutely-reflexed downward and backward behind the ovary, occasionally in the opposite direction; dorsal sepal retroflexed behind the column; lateral petals acutely reflexed, often crossing the lateral sepals. Labellum very mobile, articulate by a narrow-linear, spotted claw to the distal end of the columnar-foot, peltately attached to the claw where it is constricted into two unequal lobes; the constriction or neck very glandular and hairy; the longer lobe with a greenish and prune coloured oblong foot-like base covered with prominent blackish wart-like glands and some short branched hairs especially abundant in the vicinity of the claw; anterior part with an emarginate apex abruptly turned upward; the shorter lobe (or head) mulberry-like with glistening blackish glands and short hairs. Column very slender, 8–10 mm. high (without the columnar-foot), retracted backward at the base, but incurved near the middle; very narrowly winged in the lower third, the wings small, triangular, 3–4 mm. long. Rostellum point prolonged beyond the anther. Stigma prominent.

D. fitzgeraldii grows in sandy peaty soil on the margin of swamps. My specimens, some far more robust than specimens of other species, were collected on the Porongorups, Peel Estate, and from Yarloop.

The species was illustrated as *D. elastica* by R. D. FitzGerald in *Aust. Orchids* 2¹: (1884).

FLOWERING PERIOD: Sept. and Oct.

COMMON NAME: Warty Hammer-orchid

DISTRIBUTION: Endemic in WA where it is confined to the coastal plain of the south-west

D. glyptodon (Plate 180)

D. glyptodon R. D. FitzG. in *Gdnrs' Chron.* new ser. 17:494 (1882); R. Erickson *Orchids West* ed. 2:67 (1965)

A slender plant 15–32 cm. high. Stem green, the lower four centimetres thinner, wiry, purplish; a minute, closely-sheathing bract well below the middle. Leaf ovate-cordate, thick, 1·3–2 cm. in diameter. Flower solitary. Perianth segments narrow-linear; dorsal sepal erect, 8–10 mm. long; lateral sepals acutely reflexed downward, 8–10 mm. long. Petals a little shorter than the sepals, acutely reflexed behind the ovary. Ovary pyriform. Labellum dark red-brown, articulated at the end of the columnar projection, on a linear claw of 4–5 mm.; the central part of the labellum ovate-convex, produced towards the end into an emarginate projection, and at the other extremity, into a dark glandular appendage, resembling the head of the extinct Armadillo, *Glyptodon*; the recurved under surface and basal part of the upper surface covered with branching hairs. Column 6–8 mm. high, curved, the wings forming two ovate auricles at the base; basal projection linear, about 4 mm. long. Stigma not produced into a long point as in *D. fitzgeraldii*; the anther not pointed.

FLOWERING PERIOD: Sept. and Oct.

COMMON NAME: King-in-his-carriage

DISTRIBUTION: Endemic in WA, where it prefers sandy areas particularly of the south-west

D. jeanensis (Plate 181)

D. jeanensis R. S. Rogers in *Trans. roy. Soc. S. Aust.* 44:322 (1920); R. Erickson *Orchids West* ed. 2:68 (1965)

Plant slender, 18–32 cm. high. Leaf orbicular to broadly ovate, cordate, about 2·5 cm. in diameter, rather rigid, glabrous, the upper surface emerald-green. Stem very slender, glabrous, resilient; a small clasping acuminate bract about 5 mm. long considerably below the middle. Flower solitary on a slender pedicel 9–10 mm. long, subtended by a small ovate-lanceolate clasping bracteole about 5 mm. long. Ovary somewhat pyramidal, about half the length of the pedicel. Segments of the perianth subequal, narrow-linear, yellowish-green, about 12 mm. long. Lateral sepals expanded at their insertion into the base of the columnar-foot, acutely reflexed downward and backward, their tips crossed behind the ovary; dorsal sepal retroflexed behind the column. Petals acutely reflexed downward, their tips crossed behind the ovary. Labellum very mobile, articulated on a narrow-linear claw about 9 mm. long to the distal end of the columnar-foot; peltately attached to the claw where it is constricted into two unequal lobes; the constriction or neck encircled by a shaggy leonine mane of reddish-purple hairs with tufted bifurcated tips; the longer lobe with a yellowish-green and reddish-purple orbicular base, hairless except in the vicinity of the claw, and a convex somewhat ovate reddish-brown smooth extremity with revolute margins; the shorter lobe a more or less globular mass of glistening purplish-black mulberry-like glands interspersed with hairs similar to those on the neck; the two lobes almost in a straight line; lamina about 12 mm. long, insectiform in appearance. Column very slender, retracted backward at the base but incurved about the middle; about 9 mm. long (without the foot); very narrowly, and somewhat triangularly winged in its lower part; produced beyond the wings into a narrow-linear horizontal foot about 10 mm. long. Anther relatively large, blunt, incurved, about 4·5 mm. long. Rostellar point not prolonged beyond the anther.

FLOWERING PERIOD: Oct. and Nov.

COMMON NAME: Hammer-orchid

DISTRIBUTION: Endemic in WA where it is confined to the coastal plain of the south-west

13   *Spiculaea*

Spiculaea Lindl. in *Edwards' bot. Reg.* 23: Swan Riv. Append. lvi (1840)

Terrestrial glabrous herbs, with small underground tubers. Usually leafless at flowering time or leaf in a withered condition; or sometimes present as a lateral growth, rarely present at base of the stem. Stem more or less fleshy. Flowers racemose, sometimes numerous, reversed. Sepals and petals linear, the dorsal sepal erect, the lateral sepals and petals spreading or reflexed. Labellum articulate at the base of the column or at the end of its basal projection and movable with a linear claw; the lamina narrow, peltate, hammer-shaped, convex, shorter below than above its insertion. Column elongated, narrow, incurved; the wings represented by one or two pairs of narrow auricles variously placed. Anther erect, bilocular, quite blunt. Rostellum rudimentary. Pollinia granular.

A small genus of three species, closely allied to *Drakaea* and *Caleana*, endemic in Australia.

S. ciliata (Plate 182)

S. ciliata Lindl. in *Edwards' bot. Reg.* 23: Swan Riv. Append. lvi (1840); R. Erickson *Orchids West* ed. 2:66 (1965)

Plant from 6–17 cm. in height; stem rigid, purplish, withering from the base upward—the upper portion fleshy—often swollen. Leaf a little above the base, lanceolate or ovate-lanceolate, dark green above, purplish beneath; complicate, shortly sheathing and erect at the base, recurved upward, 2–2·5 cm. long. A single leaf-like bract about the middle, sheathing at the base. Flowers two to six on short pedicels, greenish-red. Ovary slender, terete, the subtending bracteole sheathing, rather blunt, 7–10 mm. long. Sepals and petals narrow-linear; dorsal sepal erect, slightly incurved, about 1·5 cm. long; the lateral sepals and petals a little shorter than the dorsal sepal, spreading and reflexed. Labellum shorter than the sepals, articulated by a movable joint to the forward, very brief projection of the column; lamina hammer-like, peltately attached, the upper lobe recurved, about 3 mm. long, tapering to a blunt tip; lower part of lamina smooth with a narrow curved lobe projecting upward, margins incurved; upper portion of lamina with concave margins fringed with red glandular hairs; tip dark coloured, blunt. Column erect, incurved, narrow, the very narrow wings dilated into two linear abruptly falcate upturned auricles, serrate on the inner margins, a red spot at the 'elbow', and at the anther dilated into two smaller recurved auricles with a short triangular lobe at the base of each on the upper side. Stigma often with a very short point.

O. H. Sargent reports this small xerophytic plant as occurring in the Darling Range about twenty miles from the coast, and extending eastwards, probably 150 miles to the vicinity of Merriden.

B. T. Goadby writes in reference to the habitat: 'granite shelf with a few inches of soil overlay, wet during the winter from seepage from the higher slopes of rocky hillsides. After October the soil becomes very dry and hot—no shade—basal leaf withers early—flower spike withers from base upwards, last flower opening on a withered stem. Associated with liver worts, and *Ophioglossum*, all dying off in summer.'

FLOWERING PERIOD: Oct. to Jan.

COMMON NAME: Elbow-orchid

DISTRIBUTION: Endemic in WA where it is widespread and often common on granitic outcrops of the south-west

S. irritabilis (Plate 183)

S. irritabilis (F. Muell.) Schlechter in *Repert. Spec. nov. Regn. veg.* 17:82 (1921); H. M. R. Rupp *Orchids N.S.W.* 43 (1943)

SYNONYMY: *Arthrochilus irritabilis* F. Muell. *Fragm. Phyt. Aust.* 1:43 (1858); *Drakaea irritabilis* (F. Muell.) Reichenb. f. *Beitr. syst. Pflk.* 68 (1871)

A slender plant with a flowering stem from 5–37 cm. high. Leaves two to five, basal or towards the base of stem, often occurring as lateral growths, ovate-oblong to lanceolate, 3–10 cm. long, the mid-rib prominent. Flowers numerous, or few, in a loose raceme, insectiform, light green with reddish spots and other markings; pedicels short, the bracteoles narrow, acute. Dorsal sepal erect or slightly incurved behind the column, linear, 12–14 mm. long; lateral sepals shorter, sharply deflexed. Petals almost filiform, as long as the lateral sepals and similarly deflexed. Labellum articulate at the end of the basal projection of the column; the linear claw about 5 mm. long above the articulation; the lamina hammer-shaped and peltately attached, densely ciliate with rather long hairs on its upper surface; the upper lobe emarginate, glandular, rough; the lower lobe or appendage linear. Column incurved, the lower auricles prominent, triangular with shortly acute points; the auricles on either side of the anther short and blunt.

Rupp, when stationed at Bulahdelah recorded this orchid as occurring 'literally in myriads on the lower slopes of Alum Mountain.'

FLOWERING PERIOD: Dec. to Apr.

COMMON NAME: Leafy Elbow-orchid

DISTRIBUTION: Eastern Qld, extending to eastern NSW at least as far south as Sydney, mainly coastal; once erroneously recorded from Vic.

S. huntiana (Plate 184)

S. huntiana (F. Muell.) Schlechter in *Repert. Spec. nov. Regn. veg.* 17:83 (1921); A. J. Ewart *Flor. Vict.* 311 (1931), as *Drakaea huntiana*; H. M. R. Rupp *Orchids N.S.W.* 43 (1943); J. H. Willis *Handb. Pls Vict.* 1:377 (1962)

SYNONYMY: *Drakaea huntiana* F. Muell. in *Vict. Nat.* 5:174 (1889)

A slender or moderately stout leafless plant 9–18 cm. high; stem reddish or green, with two or three small clasping bracts, and an additional small sheathing one at the base. Flowers insectiform, reddish-green, or green, two to ten, reversed on slender pedicels about 1·3 cm. long, each embraced by a short blunt bracteole. Ovary more or less slender, terete. Segments of perianth equal in length about 5 mm., all reflexed against the ovary; lateral sepals oblong-spathulate, convex on the outer surface, concave on inner, and reflexed against the ovary; dorsal sepal blunt, about same width as lateral sepals, concave, reflexed and slightly incurved towards the column; lateral petals narrow-linear, much narrower than the sepals, rather blunt, reflexed against the ovary. Column acutely reflexed from its base towards the ovary, about the same length as the perianth segments. The upper half expanded in a concave disc-like surface, from the margins of which proceed two pairs of appendages, about equal in length; the upper pair narrow-lanceolate, divergent, curving forward on each side of the apex of the anther;

the inferior pair falcate-lanceolate, divergent, curving upward and forward on each side of the stigma. Rostellum rudimentary. Stigma prominent, reniform, the concave border immediately below and in contact with the anther. Labellum articulated by a movable joint to a linear projection of the column; peltate on a linear claw about as long as the column-foot. Lamina reddish-purple, insectiform, about as long as the claw (6 mm.); anteriorly giving origin to a pair of stalked processes, each terminating in a globular purple gland; posteriorly dividing into two long narrow-lanceolate divergent tails, from which proceed numerous long-jointed purplish, reddish or pale green hairs; an intermediate portion, on the undersurface of which is inserted the claw, fringed with numerous long purple hairs, on its undersurface a large purple triangular gland situated at the base of the anterior pedicels.

Originally described from material found in NSW, *Spiculaea huntiana* long remained a rarity among the orchids of Australia. Until a few years ago it was known in Vic. from Cravensville only. In Dec. 1929 it was found in the Pyrete Range, near Gisborne, and was later discovered near Harrietville, Mount Kent, and Mount Cobbler. Crossing Holmes Plains, near Mount Howitt in Dec. 1934 the author saw this orchid in many places. Revisiting Mount Cobbler (Dec. 1935) we found it plentiful on the rocky ramparts of the mountain, close to Cobbler Hut; also on the heavily-timbered saddles facing Dondangadale Gorge, within sight of Buffalo. It has since been collected on the plateau itself.

FLOWERING PERIOD: Nov. to Mar.

COMMON NAME: Elbow-orchid

DISTRIBUTION: Extending from the Blue Mountains area in NSW south into Vic. where it is widespread and often locally common

14 *Chiloglottis*

Chiloglottis R. Br. *Prodr. Flor. Nov. Holl.* 322 (1810)

Terrestrial herbs, with small underground tubers. Leaves two, radical or nearly so. Scape one-flowered, without any bract below the bracteole subtending the terminal pedicel. Dorsal sepal erect, incurved, concave, contracted at the base; lateral sepals narrow-linear or terete; petals lanceolate-falcate. Labellum on a very short claw, broadly ovate, obovate or oblong, undivided, the lamina with variously arranged calli. Column elongated, incurved, winged. Anther terminal, erect, two-celled; pollinia granular.

A small genus of eight species, six endemic in Australia, with two extending to New Zealand.

C. cornuta (Plate 185)

C. cornuta Hook. f. *Flor. antarct.* 1:69 (1844); A. J. Ewart *Flor. Vict.* 353 (1931), as *C. muelleri*; J. H. Willis *Handb. Pls Vict.* 1:379 (1943); M. J. Firth *Native Orchids Tasm.* 83 (1965)

SYNONYMY: *C. muelleri* R. D. FitzG. *Aust. Orchids* 2²:+t. (1885)

A wholly green plant. Stem very short at flowering time, rarely exceeding 4 cm., but often elongating after fertilisation to 15–23 cm. Leaves lanceolate, occasionally broadly ovate, petiolate, the margins undulate or crisped, 3–7 cm. long and 1·5–4 cm. wide. Flower solitary, 2·2 cm. in diameter, in robust specimens up to 3 cm.; rarely 4 cm. as occurring on the Baw Baw Range, Vic. Dorsal sepal cucullate over the column, enclosing it, broadly ovate with a short point, contracted at the base. Lateral sepals linear, longer than the

dorsal one, recurved or deflexed. Petals erect, falco-lanceolate, sometimes longer than the sepals, spreading or incurved. Labellum on a very short claw, usually broadly ovate; calli very variable in shape and arrangement, usually green and sessile, those at the tip often brown or purplish. Column widely winged, the points higher than the anther.

This terrestrial is recorded by E. E. Pescott as 'practically an epiphyte', but not according to observations made by the author and F. J. Bishop, when we traversed the Baw Baw plateau. We found this orchid growing on Mount Erica, beneath *Melaleuca* and other bushes, even among grass tussocks, also between rocks, right out in the open. It was plentiful at 5,000 feet altitude. On the morasses it was unusually robust, much larger in the leaf than *C. gunnii*, with the flower almost as large. The day's journey across Mount St Phillach (5,140 feet) to Fall's Creek, (twenty-four miles), revealed this plant as a terrestrial. On the Thomson River headwaters, in the fern gullies, it was noted in thousands. We made a special search of the tree fern trunks, but did not discover a solitary plant. In Tas. Mrs Needham records it as a terrestrial. In NZ it occurs on the decaying roots of trees in shaded places. However, on the Dandenong Ranges I have seen it crowning the tops of dead tree ferns. [For a record of this species in NSW see *Orchadian* 2:76 (1967).—Ed.]

FLOWERING PERIOD: Oct. to Jan., depending on altitude

COMMON NAME: Green Bird-orchid

DISTRIBUTION: Extending from southern NSW through southern Vic., to Tas., inhabiting sub-alpine grassland and sphagnum bogs, and densely shaded lowland areas, often locally abundant; also NZ

C. gunnii (Plate 186)

C. gunnii Lindl. *Gen. & Spec. orchid. Pls* 387 (1840); A. J. Ewart *Flor. Vict.* 353 (1931); H. M. R. Rupp *Orchids N.S.W.* 45 (1943); J. H. Willis *Handb. Pls Vict.* 1:378 (1962); M. J. Firth *Native Orchids Tasm.* 83 (1965)

SYNONYMY: *Caladenia gunnii* (Lindl.) Reichenb.f. *Beitr. syst. Pflk.* 67 (1871)

A robust plant usually 5–8 cm. high; among undergrowth sometimes drawn up to 18–25 cm. Leaves large, petiolate, ovate to ovate-oblong, spreading, up to 10 cm. long. Flower solitary, rarely two, dark purplish-brown or green, 2·5–4 cm. in diameter. Ovary shortly pedicellate, the subtending bract large, loosely sheathing; peduncle elongating considerably after fertilisation. Dorsal sepal erect, incurved, broadly oblong, acuminate, or acute. Petals spreading, broad-lanceolate, falcate, acuminate. Lateral sepals narrow-linear, acuminate. Labellum large, on a short irritable claw, broadly ovate, acute, usually with a long erect callus near the base, a large sessile one in the centre and a more or less regular line of small glands on either side. (In some Cobungra, Vic., specimens, the larger glands only were in evidence. Grampians, Vic., flowers occasionally possess three large stalked glands at the base in addition to four smaller ones between them; the two in the centre are small—one shortly stalked, the other sessile.) Column erect, broadly winged above, the upper angle of wings extending above the anther. Pollinia mealy.

C. gunnii is a fairly widely distributed plant of gregarious habits. It is found in heavily timbered country, extending from the low-lying areas to the summits of the high mountains.

FLOWERING PERIOD: Sept. to Jan., depending on altitude

COMMON NAME: Common Bird-orchid

DISTRIBUTION: Extending from southern NSW through Vic., to Tas., inhabiting sub-alpine sphagnum bogs and open lowland forests, often locally common

C. pescottiana (Plate 187)

C. pescottiana R. S. Rogers in *Proc. roy. Soc. Vict.* new ser. *30*:139, t. 25 (1918); A. J. Ewart *Flor. Vict.* 354 (1931); J. H. Willis *Handb. Pls Vict.* 1:379 (1962); M. J. Firth *Native Orchids Tasm.* 84 (1965)

A slender plant, 8–18 cm. high. Leaves 4–6 cm. long, basal, on long petioles, oblong-lanceolate, or ovate in occasional specimens; a sheathing acuminate bract about 2 cm. long situated about the middle of the stem. Flower solitary, greenish-bronze or wholly purplish, with dark almost black calli. Lateral sepals linear-lanceolate, recurved, connate at the extreme base; dorsal sepal spathulate-acuminate, more or less incurved over the column and about the same length as the lateral sepals, 1·4–1·6 cm. long. Petals spreading, lanceolate, much wider, but also about 1·5 cm. long. Labellum oblong, rounded at the tip, on a very short irritable claw, shorter than the lateral sepals, slightly recurved about the middle of lamina. Calli distributed as follows: (1) one large crescentic sessile callus in mid-line in advance of all others; (2) a large bilobed stalked callus about midway between this and base of lamina; (3) numerous stalked calli, small and medium sized, between (1) and (2); (4) a somewhat irregular row of small stalked calli running on either side of the mid-line from the bend in the lamina to its base. Column shorter than dorsal sepal, winged, especially in its upper part, the wings being produced into two short falcate processes above and behind the anther; anther blunt, situated on apex of column immediately above the circular stigma as in a *Caladenia*.

This orchid is restricted to a few spots adjacent the Bucheen Creek, near the old township of Cravensville in north-eastern Vic.

How necessary it is to view orchids in their wild state ! I had examined quite a number of specimens of *C. pescottiana* received from residents of the district where it grows, but not until Nov. 1930, did I, in the company of A. B. Braine, the original discoverer of this orchid in 1907, realise what a stately little species it really is. The stem is rigidly erect and the plants are of sturdy appearance. The labellum of this orchid is unique—bearing as it does from a side view a somewhat striking resemblance to an aborigine's bark canoe.

C. pescottiana is easily singled out among the other species with which it is always associated in Vic., i.e. *C. trapeziformis* and *C. gunnii*. There seems little reason to doubt the theory that this form originated from a cross between its two allies, for, although the majority of the plants possess the twin light green, narrowly-oblong leaves, similar to those of *trapeziformis*, specimens have been found with the dark-green broadly ovate leaves so characteristic of *gunnii*. However in Tas. it was found in a gully on Mount Barrow. Large colonies of it were interposed between *C. gunnii* and *C. cornuta*. *C. trapeziformis* is not recorded for Tas.

Our visit to Cravensville was indeed a fortunate one, as we found the three Vic. representatives in bloom. They love the moist and well-sheltered positions between the buttresses of giant Eucalypts, and another patch was located on the other side of the creek.

It is to be regretted that the home of this—and other rare orchids—is now given over to sheep. Signs of their depredations were to be observed throughout the valley slopes.

In the original description, the author refers to the colour of the flowers as 'greenish-bronze'. Those observed *in situ* were wholly of a very rich purplish-black, thus harmonising with their shady retreat, but when the sun shone through the forest at early morning the plants were given an added touch of crimson !

FLOWERING PERIOD: Sept. to Dec.

DISTRIBUTION: Extremely rare and localised—known only from Cravensville, Vic., and Mount Barrow, Tas.

C. trapeziformis (Plate 188)

C. trapeziformis R. D. FitzG. *Aust. Orchids* 1³:+t. (1877); A. J. Ewart *Flor. Vict.* 353 (1931); H. M. R. Rupp *Orchids N.S.W.* 44 (1943); J. H. Willis *Handb. Pls Vict.* 1:380 (1962)

Leaves basal, narrow-oblong, acute, varying in size, but normally 6–8 cm. long; narrowed at the base into a petiole 1·5–2 cm. long. Stem 7–10 cm. slender, erect, often pinkish. Pedicel, including ovary, 3–5 cm. long, a sheathing green bract 1·3–2 cm. long at the base. Flower solitary, usually more purplish than green—sometimes the whole plant is verdant green. Dorsal sepal erect, incurved, 1·2–1·5 cm. long, lanceolate, sometimes broad, much narrowed downward, apex with a short point. Lateral sepals narrow-linear, curved, 1–1·2 cm. long. Petals reflexed to a position in line with the ovary, linear-lanceolate, curved, about 1·2 cm. long. Labellum trapeze- or rhomb-shaped, 1–1·2 cm. long, on a very short claw; lamina with a prominent dark coloured group of calli about the centre, and some small ones distributed around. Column usually shorter than the labellum, green, widely-winged above the centre, the rounded apices of the wings reaching above the anther.

This species is often remarkably gregarious, the plants covering a wide area. It is regarded as a comparatively rare form, for it flowers only under the most favourable conditions. The main characteristic feature of *C. trapeziformis* is the peculiarly arranged mass of glands on the labellum.

FLOWERING PERIOD: Sept. to Nov.

COMMON NAME: Broad-lip Bird-orchid

DISTRIBUTION: Extending from south-eastern Qld through eastern NSW to eastern Vic., widespread and often locally common

C. formicifera (Plate 189)

C. formicifera R. D. FitzG. *Aust. Orchids* 1³:+t. (1877); H. M. R. Rupp *Orchids N.S.W.* 44 (1943)

A small, comparatively slender to robust plant up to 12 cm. high. Leaves broadly ovate or oblong, about 5 cm. long, the margins undulate-crisped, contracted into a petiole about 1 cm. long. Stem-bract sheathing at the base of the terminal pedicel. Flower solitary, small, green with brown or purplish markings. Dorsal sepal, erect, curved, cuneate, shortly acuminate, much contracted in its lower half, 1–1·2 cm. long. Lateral sepals linear, terete, reflexed, about the same length as the dorsal sepal. Petals lanceolate, spreading or reflexed, attached by a broad base, acute, slightly shorter than the sepals, transparent. Labellum nearly rhomb-shaped, the apex recurved; calli prominent, of variable size, numerous (the whole somewhat ant-shaped, the mass of calli resembling the abdomen), extending to tip; lamina about same length as petals. Column incurved, winged throughout, the upper angle of wings forming a hood over the anther.

FLOWERING PERIOD: Sept. and Oct.

COMMON NAME: Ant Orchid

DISTRIBUTION: In Australia restricted to NSW where it is chiefly in the central east coast; also NZ

C. reflexa (Plate 190)

C. reflexa (Labill.) Druce in *Rep. bot. (Soc.) Exch. Cl. Manchr 1916*:614 (1917); A. J. Ewart *Flor. Vict.* 353 (1931); H. M. R. Rupp

Orchids N.S.W. 44 (1943); J. H. Willis Handb. Pls Vict. 1:379 (1962); M. J. Firth Native Orchids Tasm. 83 (1965)

SYNONYMY: *Epipactis reflexa* Labill. *Nov. Holl. Pl. Specim.* 2:60, t. 211 fig. 1 (1806); *Acianthus bifolius* R. Br. *Prodr. Flor. Nov. Holl.* 322 (1810); *Chiloglottis diphylla* R. Br. *Prodr. Flor. Nov. Holl.* 323 (1810)

A slender plant 8–15 cm. high with a small sheathing bract at the base, and a longer one below the floral pedicel. Leaves two, 1·2–4·5 cm. long, ovate-elliptic to oblong-lanceolate, acute, net-veined, margins crisped and undulate. Petioles often very short and stout. Flower small, solitary, green with claret markings or wholly prune coloured. Dorsal sepal cuneate, 1·2–1·5 cm. long, normally shortly acuminate, much contracted towards the base. Lateral sepals linear-terete, spreading and reflexed, very slender or somewhat thickened in the upper half, and as long as or longer than the dorsal sepal. Petals lanceolate, attached by a broad base, acute, rather shorter than the sepals, transparent and reflexed. Labellum more or less obovate, obtuse or acute, 8–14 mm. long, contracted at the base into a distinct claw—the claw variable in length; calli on the disc mostly shortly linear, the central ones larger and thicker, arranged more or less in two rows, and one or two at the base of lamina; the calli sometimes covering the greater portion of the lamina, very variable as to number and form. Column about same length as petals, winged above and extending, as a hood, behind and above the anther.

C. reflexa is normally an autumnal species, but when conditions are favourable, it extends its flowering throughout the year. It is a gregarious plant and a shy bloomer, favouring cool, shady situations, but not necessarily wet places. The fruiting scape often attains a length of 20–30 cm.

FLOWERING PERIOD: Chiefly **Mar.** to May but recorded in flower for every month of the year

COMMON NAME: Autumn Bird-orchid

DISTRIBUTION: Extending the length of the east coast from north Qld through NSW and extending across southern Vic., also Tas.; often locally abundant in large colonies, and chiefly coastal

15 *Acianthus*

Acianthus R. Br. *Prodr. Flor. Nov. Holl.* 321 (1810)

Terrestrial glabrous herbs, with small rounded tubers. Leaf solitary, immediately above the basal sheath or higher up the stem; broadly ovate-cordate, entire, lobed or rarely deeply dissected. Flowers usually in a terminal raceme, occasionally solitary, on a scape or stem without scales above the leaf, except the small bracteoles within the raceme. Dorsal sepal erect or incurved over the column, concave, not very broad and often produced into a fine point; lateral sepals narrow, spreading or upwardly curved, petals almost equal in length to the dorsal sepal, sometimes very short. Labellum sessile, undivided, spreading, with two basal calli or tubercles. Column incurved or reflexed, rarely winged. Anther erect, two-celled. Pollinia granular or mealy, four, two in each cell, each pair connected to a separate disc of the rostellum, no caudicle present.

A comparatively small genus of approximately twenty species, seven of which occur in Australia, two in NZ and twelve others in New Caledonia.

This description includes *Cyrtostylis* R. Br., a genus which has been included in *Acianthus* by Schlechter.

A. caudatus (Plate 191)

A. caudatus R. Br. *Prodr. Flor. Nov. Holl.* 321 (1810); A. J. Ewart *Flor. Vict.* 337 (1931); J. M. Black *Flor. S. Aust.* ed. 2:226 (1943); H. M. R. Rupp *Orchids N.S.W.* 46 (1943); J. H. Willis *Handb. Pls Vict.* 1:380 (1962); M. J. Firth *Native Orchids Tasm.* 49 (1965)

A slender glabrous plant 7–22 cm. high. Leaf at or near the base, cordate-ovate, purplish below, reticulate-veined, 1–4 cm. long. Flowers one to nine, wholly prune coloured, on short pedicels; the subtending bracteoles narrow. Dorsal sepal more or less inflexed, dilated over the anther, then tapering to a filiform point 2–3·5 cm. long; the dilated part concave, base narrow. Lateral sepals free, sometimes as long as the dorsal one, but usually shorter, tapering into filiform points, curving upward at their ends. Petals falco-lanceolate, reflexed or spreading, 4–5 mm. long. Labellum sessile, crimson or prune-coloured; base erect, semi-orbicular, embracing the column, thereafter broadly but very acutely lanceolate, at first horizontal then abruptly recurved near the tip; the margins entire; lamina glandular with smooth surface, except for two tooth-like or triangular calli at the extreme base. Column about 4 mm. long, inflexed on the summit of the ovary; almost terete in its lower two-thirds, dilated above, very narrowly winged in the terete part, widening shortly on each side of the stigma and continued upward as a kind of arillus behind the anther. Anther pointless. Pollinia two in each cell, granular, each pair connected to a separate viscid disc in the upper border of stigma. Stigma rather prominent, hemispherical. Rostellum double; each part tooth-like, bearing a rather large viscid disc.

This curious terrestrial is invariably found in well-sheltered positions under trees and shrubs. In many coastal districts it is, at times, exceedingly plentiful. An unpleasant odour is diffused by the flowers—similar to that resulting from the wet coat of a dog. Children refer to it as 'Doggie'!

FLOWERING PERIOD: Aug. to Oct.

COMMON NAME: Mayfly Orchid

DISTRIBUTION: Extending south from the Manning River, NSW, to southern Vic., eastern Tas., and south-eastern SA, where it is rare

A. exsertus (Plate 192)

A. exsertus R. Br. *Prodr. Flor. Nov. Holl.* 321 (1810); A. J. Ewart *Flor. Vict.* 337 (1931); J. M. Black *Flor. S. Aust.* ed. 2:226 (1943); H. M. R. Rupp *Orchids N.S.W.* 48 (1943); J. H. Willis *Handb. Pls Vict.* 1:381 (1962); R. Erickson *Orchids West* ed. 2:68 (1965); M. J. Firth *Native Orchids Tasm.* 49 (1965)

SYNONYMY: *A. brunonis* F. Muell. *Fragm. Phyt. Aust.* 5:96 (1865), pro parte

A slender glabrous plant 7–21 cm. high. Leaf 1·5–4·5 cm. long, at or near the base, sessile, margins entire, sinuous, broad, ovate-cordate, often bilobed, dark green above, purplish beneath; veins conspicuous, reticulated. Flowers three to twenty on very short pedicels, racemose, sometimes crowded, reddish-green or purplish, sometimes wholly verdant green or almost colourless. Bracteoles subtending the flowers broad-ovate, acute, the lowest ones larger. In occasional specimens, one or two similar bracts or even a solitary flower appear just above the leaf. Dorsal sepal ovate-acuminate, incurved, concave, the base contracted, 5–8 mm. long. Lateral sepals subulate, almost parallel or spreading with the points diverging, 7–9 mm. long. Apices of sepals varying from acute to clavate. Petals lanceolate, spreading or acutely reflexed, 2–5 mm. long. Labellum on a short contracted claw, ovate-lanceolate 3–6 mm. long, concave towards the base, tip thickened, quite smooth, or with numerous minute glands; frontal margins depressed, the base contracted, with two large smooth comma-shaped callosities present. Column 2·5–4 mm. high, exserted, incurved, not winged, semi-terete, the base thickened; tip cup-shaped, broad, upper margin sometimes markedly fornicate. Anther blunt, erect, two-celled. Pollinia two in each cell, semi-circular, clavate, each set with a separate viscid disc. Stigma prominent, very concave, broad-ovate, the rostellum represented by two subulate-falcate points.

Experiments carried out by the author on a large colony of this species growing in a pot proved that it is pollinated by insect agency. Of approximately 400 flowers, not one capsule matured under glass. In the habitats of *A. exsertus* the author has often noted specimens with the majority of capsules fully developed.

Under adverse conditions this species is a shy bloomer, often extensive congregations of the plants are noted without even a solitary flower.

FLOWERING PERIOD: Mar. to Aug.

COMMON NAME: Mosquito Orchid

DISTRIBUTION: Temperate parts of all Australian states except WA, but in Qld confined to the south-east; often locally abundant

A. fornicatus (Plate 193)

A. fornicatus R. Br. *Prodr. Flor. Nov. Holl.* 321 (1810); H. M. R. Rupp *Orchids N.S.W.* 46 (1943); J. H. Willis *Handb. Pls Vict.* 1:381 (1962)

SYNONYMY: *A. brunonis* F. Muell. *Fragm. Phyt. Aust.* 5:96 (1865), pro parte

Stem slender 15–30 cm. high. Leaf 2·5–5 cm. long, basal or below the middle, broadly ovate to orbicular, deeply cordate and stem-clasping with broad rounded auricles, sometimes sinuate or deeply three-lobed. Flowers four to fourteen, on short pedicels, the sub-tending bracteoles ovate or lanceolate, acute. Dorsal sepal ovate-lanceolate, about 1 cm. or more in length, erect, incurved, concave, acute, the mid-rib produced into a fine point about 3 mm. long; lateral sepals about 1 mm. long, close together or shortly united under the labellum, sometimes with a tendency to become trilobed. Petals lanceolate, about half as long as the sepals, with a short point. Labellum much shorter than the sepals, but variable in length, on a very short claw, oblong-lanceolate, acuminate, concave at the base with two very short raised longitudinal plates or calli; smooth along the channelled centre with two very prominent, broad, raised papillose lines parallel to the reflexed margins, the point short. Column short, incurved, semiterete, not winged, often concealed in the dorsal sepal, but sometimes bent forward as in *A. exsertus*. Anther with a very short point. Pollinia four in each cell. Stigma prominent.

This species is widespread in eastern Qld and NSW where it often forms colonies. In NZ a different form, the var. *sinclairii* (Hook.f.) E. D. Hatch, is found, which is exceedingly abundant in many parts.

FLOWERING PERIOD: May to Sept.

COMMON NAME: Pixie Caps

DISTRIBUTION: Extending from the Endeavour River in north Qld as far south as the Clyde River in NSW, generally coastal; also NZ, as var. *sinclairii*

A. ledwardii (Plate 194)

A. ledwardii H. M. R. Rupp in *Qd Nat.* 10:113, cum icon. (1938)

Plant about 5 cm. high. Leaf pale green above. Flowers two to six, somewhat depressed. Dorsal sepal deeply cucullate, mucronate at the apex, with a short depressed point. Lateral sepals linear, parallel (not divergent as in *A. fornicatus*), the apex shortly and prominently trifid, the outer divisions shorter than the middle one. Petals broadly lanceolate, short. Labellum ovate, convex below, with incurved serrulate margins. Disc smooth towards the base, papillose towards the blunt apex. Column as in *A. fornicatus*.

The author of *A. ledwardii* writes: 'Some doubt has been felt, both by the discoverer and myself, whether this interesting little orchid might not be included in *A. fornicatus*, to which it is very obviously related. The gynostemium is identical in almost every particular, but the labellum is so strikingly different, and other features of the flower give it such a distinctive appearance, that it could only be placed in *A. fornicatus* by extending the description of the latter to cover far greater variability than seems desirable. *A. fornicatus* is an exceedingly common terrestrial from southern Qld to southern NSW and in the latter state is found as far west as Molong. Among the thousands of plants I have seen over many years, there was never one with a labellum like that of Dr Ledward's plant.'

Dr. Ledward states: 'So far I have only seen dark coloured forms of the new species. Both *A. fornicatus* and *A. ledwardii* grow together —within a few feet of each other. I found the new species in June 1934 and then only in one small colony. It did not appear again till June 1938, when I found one plant only in flower in exactly the same spot as previously. And now it has appeared for the third time in exactly the same spot. This year six plants only have flowered. It is growing on a sheltered slope close to rain forest. Each year it has flowered the autumn and early winter have been mild with good rains—so it may be a form that would be more plentiful further north.'

FLOWERING PERIOD: June and July

DISTRIBUTION: Endemic in Qld, where it is apparently confined to the south-east, at Burleigh Heads, and extremely rare

A. reniformis (Plate 195)

A. reniformis (R. Br.) Schlechter in *Bot. Jb.* 39:39 (1906); A. J. Ewart *Flor. Vict.* 338 (1931), as *Cyrtostylis reniformis*; J. M. Black *Flor. S. Aust.* ed. 2:227 (1943); H. M. R. Rupp *Orchids N.S.W.* 48 (1943); J. H. Willis *Handb. Pls Vict.* 1:380 (1962); R. Erickson *Orchids West* ed. 2:68 (1965); M. J. Firth *Native Orchids Tasm.* 47 (1965)

SYNONYMY: *Cyrtostylis reniformis* R. Br. *Prodr. Flor. Nov. Holl.* 322 (1810); *Caladenia reniformis* (R. Br.) Reichenb.f. *Beitr. syst. Pflk.* 67 (1871)

A slender plant 5–19 cm. high. Leaf orbicular-cordate, 1·5–4 cm. long, green on both sides. Flowers one to seven, reddish-brown, rarely verdant-green, sessile or very shortly pedicellate. Dorsal sepal linear-lanceolate, erect, incurved, concave, 9–15 mm. long; lateral sepals a little shorter, linear, spreading. Petals similar, about the same length but narrower. Labellum 9–15 mm. long and 4–5 mm. wide, sessile, flat, broadly oblong, contracted at its insertion; tip varying from obtuse to acuminate; two erect bead-like calli at the base, produced into raised plates along the lamina. Column elongated, incurved, winged in its upper part, 5–8 mm. long. Anther almost globose, without a point. Stigma small.

A. reniformis is a common gregarious plant throughout its distribution. It is found chiefly in forest country, and scrub-covered hills and plateaux, but is abundant also in coastal areas. The colour of the flowers varies from a deep prune colour through green to yellow-orange. It extends to NZ as the var. *oblongus* (Hook.f.) H. M. R. Rupp et E. D. Hatch.

FLOWERING PERIOD: May to Oct.

COMMON NAME: Gnat Orchid

DISTRIBUTION: South-eastern Qld; eastern NSW; Vic.; northern and eastern Tas.; southern SA; south-western WA; widespread in a variety of habitats; also in NZ, as the var. *oblongus*

A. huegelii (Plate 196)

A. huegelii (Endl.) W. H. Nicholls & B. T. Goadby in *Vict. Nat.* 50:106 (1933); R. Erickson *Orchids West* ed. 2:68 (1965)

SYNONYMY: *Cyrtostylis huegelii* Endl. in Lehm. *Plant. Preiss* 2:6 (1845)

An extremely slender plant 10–18 cm. high. Leaf at, or near the base of stem, fleshy, orbicular-cordate, variable in size and resembling that of *A. reniformis*. Inflorescence a loose spike, the flowers small, two to twelve (or more), green or green with purplish markings. Ovary elongated, the subtending bracteole small, ovate-acuminate, concave, 5–6 mm. long; no bract on the stem below the inflorescence. Dorsal sepal narrow-linear, erect or projected forward, concave, abruptly acuminate, 8–9 mm. long and about 1 mm. wide, sometimes recurved at the apex; lateral sepals and petals linear, about 9 mm. and 7 mm. long respectively; the petals spreading or reflexed. Labellum sessile, cuneate-lanceolate, broad at the base where it embraces the column, about 5 mm. long and 3 mm. wide; lamina flat, the margins reflexed, terminating in a short point, two prominent conical glands at base; apices of glands black; two parallel lines traversing the lamina from base to tip. Column 4–4·5 mm. long, erect for two-thirds of its length, then abruptly incurved, the tip terminating in a knob.

[This species is botanically very close to *A. reniformis* and further examination may prove separation from the latter variable species to be unwarranted.—Ed.]

A. huegelii grows in large colonies in thick scrub, the soil wet and peaty. The finding of such a rare orchid on the mainland, so close to Perth, after its discovery on Rottnest Island well over half a century ago is of great botanical interest.

FLOWERING PERIOD: Sept. and Oct.

DISTRIBUTION: Apparently endemic in WA where it is confined to the vicinity of Perth (Bayswater, Rottnest Island) and rare

16 *Townsonia*

Townsonia Cheeseman *Man. N.Z. Flor.* ed. 1:691 (1906)

[A monotypic genus found in Australia, where it is restricted to Tas., and also in NZ. It is botanically close to *Acianthus*, differing chiefly in the creeping root system and obscure basal calli of the labellum.—Ed.]

T. viridis (Plate 197)

T. viridis (Hook.f.) Schlechter in *Repert. Spec. nov. Regn. veg.* 9:250 (1911); M. J. Firth *Native Orchids Tasm.* 7 (1965)

SYNONYMY: *Acianthus viridis* Hook.f. *Flor. Tasm.* 2:372 (1859); *Townsonia deflexa* Cheeseman *Man. N.Z. Flor.* ed. 1:692 (1906)

[Plant 8–12 cm. high. Flowering stem and leaves arising from a creeping rhizome or caudicle, thickened at intervals into tubers, with a few short fibrous roots, the whole underground system

more or less covered with short hairs except at the growing point. Radical leaves scattered at intervals along the rhizome, prominently petiolate, sometimes one at the base of the flowering stem. Leaf lamina ovate-orbicular or cordate with crenulate margins, light green to yellowish-green, about 1 cm. long. Petioles slender, 1–5 cm. long. A solitary sheathing bract present about the middle of the peduncle, 3–5 mm. long, sessile, acute at the apex, the margins crenulate or entire. Flowers one to four, pale green to reddish, soon becoming horizontal or deflexed, the perianth segments acute or obtuse. Petals very minute, 1–2 mm. long, erect or somewhat reflexed, linear. Dorsal sepal cucullate, ovate-lanceolate, acute, 4–5 mm. long. Lateral sepals deflexed, often incurved, linear, about 5 mm. long. Labellum sessile, ovate-orbicular to cordate, the apex broad and hardly acute, 4–5 mm. long. Basal calli obscure and reduced to two flat ridges or absent. Column erect, incurved, about 4 mm. high, prominently winged.

This species grows amongst moss and leaf litter in the dense shade of Myrtle Beech forests. The creeping rhizomes are completely covered and all that is visible of the plant are the leaves and flowers. It is a shy flowerer, few racemes being obvious amongst the leaves.

FLOWERING PERIOD: Dec. and Jan.

COMMON NAME: Beech-orchid

DISTRIBUTION: In Australia confined to Tas., where it is apparently only found in Beech forests but often locally common; also NZ—Ed.]

17 *Eriochilus*

Eriochilus R. Br. *Prodr. Flor. Nov. Holl.* 323 (1810)

Slender glabrous or hairy terrestrial herbs, with fleshy underground tubers. Leaf solitary, basal, ovate to ovate-lanceolate, present or absent at flowering time. Peduncle slender, bearing from one to six pale pedicillate flowers, each subtended by a bracteole. Dorsal sepal narrow, erect, often contracted in the lower part; lateral sepals narrow, spreading or deflexed, usually longer than other segments. Petals shorter than or as long as the sepals, narrow, erect. Labellum shorter than the lateral sepals, the upper part of the lamina strongly recurved. Column erect, shorter than the dorsal sepal, narrowly winged or entire.

A small genus of four or five species, endemic in Australia.

E. dilatatus (Plate 198)

E. dilatatus Lindl. in *Edwards' bot. Reg. 23*: Swan Riv. Append. liii (1840); R. Erickson *Orchids West* ed. 2:63 (1965)

SYNONYMY: *E. latifolius* Lindl. in *Edwards' bot. Reg. 23*: Swan Riv. Append. liii (1840); *E. dilatatus* var. *latifolius* (Lindl.) Benth. *Flor. aust. 6*:373 (1873); *E. dilatatus* var. *brevifolius* Benth. *Flor. aust. 6*:373 (1873)

A slender glabrous or hirsute plant, very variable. Plant slender, usually above 15 cm. high. Leaf at or below the middle of stem, sometimes reduced to a small acute bract, or distinctly ovate to ovate-lanceolate, acute, up to 6 cm. long, sessile and clasping the stem. Flowers usually one to three, but sometimes as many as eight, rarely ten to thirteen; resembling those of *E. cucullatus*. Dorsal sepal 1–1·3 cm. long, oblong in the upper part, contracted below the middle; lateral sepals oblong-lanceolate, acute, 1·3–1·5 cm. long, contracted into a slender claw; petals about as long as the dorsal sepal but much narrower, linear or dilated at the tips. Labellum very variable, much shorter than the lateral sepals, the claw erect, with slightly prominent rounded lateral lobes; the lamina or mid-lobe ovate-oblong, usually longer than broad, very convex and recurved, pubescent above. Column not winged.

This species is extremely variable, resulting in a confused botanical history. The following forms have been named: var. *latifolius* with leaves lanceolate, flowers large; var. *brevifolius* with leaves small, ovate-lanceolate. However these differences seem slight.

Dr Rogers in his notes, writes: 'All these variations are to be found in plants collected from the same group, and even in flowers on the same raceme variations in the labellum are to be observed. I have never seen any specimens of *Eriochilus* which I could definitely label *E. multiflorus* Lindl., and it is doubtful whether this species should be separated from *E. dilatatus* on the characters assigned to it by Lindley and Bentham.' *E. tenuis* Lindl. is also perhaps a form of this species.

FLOWERING PERIOD: Mar. to June

COMMON NAME: White Bunny Orchid

DISTRIBUTION: Endemic in WA where it is widespread over a range of habitats and often locally common in the south-west

E. cucullatus (Plate 199)

E. cucullatus (Labill.) Reichenb.f. *Beitr. syst. Pflk.* 27 (1871); A. J. Ewart *Flor. Vict.* 339 (1931); J. M. Black *Flor. S. Aust.* ed. 2:227 (1943); H. M. R. Rupp *Orchids N.S.W.* 53 (1943); J. H. Willis *Handb. Pls Vict.* 1:381 (1962); M. J. Firth *Native Orchids Tasm.* 41 (1965)

SYNONYMY: *Epipactis cucullata* Labill. *Nov. Holl. Plant Specim.* 2:61, t. 211 (1806); *Eriochilus autumnalis* R. Br. *Prodr. Flor. Nov. Holl.* 323 (1810)

A very slender plant, 5–25 cm. high. Leaf ovate-acute, often undeveloped at flowering time, basal, 5 mm. to over 3·5 cm. long. Flowers one to five, white or pale to bright pink. Dorsal sepal 7–12 mm. long, slightly incurved, narrow to broad-lanceolate, acute. Lateral sepals 11–17 mm. long, spreading horizontally or slightly deflexed, the lamina elliptic-lanceolate, contracted into a slender claw. Petals as long as or a little shorter than the dorsal sepal, linear to linear-spathulate. Labellum about half as long as the lateral sepals, with an erect, concave, narrow claw, sometimes showing at the apex minute lateral lobes or angles; lamina or mid-lobe recurved, oval-oblong, convex and hairy but without prominent calli. Column shorter than the dorsal sepal, narrowly winged below the very broad concave stigma.

The leaf of this orchid is characteristically undeveloped and sheathing at flowering time, but as the season progresses it expands and flattens on the ground. Late in the season it is common to see these small dark green leaves with the wispy remains of the flowering stalk attached.

FLOWERING PERIOD: Dec. to May

COMMON NAME: Parsons Bands

DISTRIBUTION: Widespread in all Australian states except WA, but in Qld restricted to the south-east; extending from coastal scrubs to sub-alpine sphagnum bogs and common throughout its range

E. scaber (Plate 200)

E. scaber Lindl. in *Edwards' bot. Reg.* 23: Swan Riv. Append. liii (1840); R. Erickson *Orchids West* ed. 2:63 (1965)

Plant closely allied to *E. cucullatus*, usually, but not always shorter; slender, and hairy with articulate transparent hairs. Leaf ovate to cordate, acute, usually persisting at the base of the flowering stem. Flowers one to three, pink or mauve, the bracts broad and mostly acute. Dorsal sepal erect behind the column, narrow-lanceolate, 1–1·3 cm. long; lateral sepals elliptic-lanceolate, spreading, usually wider than in *E. cucullatus*, and 1·3–1·5 cm. long. Petals erect, linear-spathulate, shorter than the sepals. Labellum-claw distinctly produced into small erect lateral lobes, the lamina or mid-lobe almost orbicular, very convex and densely hairy. Column not winged, but the two angles ciliate as well as the outer valves of the anther. Pollinia distinct and almost contracted into caudicles as in *E. cucullatus*.

Solitary or in small groups, this species prefers the higher rainfall areas. It is seen at its best after fires.

FLOWERING PERIOD: July to Sept.

COMMON NAME: Pink Bunny Orchid

DISTRIBUTION: Endemic in WA where it is widespread in the south-west but uncommon

18   *Rimacola*

Rimacola H. M. R. Rupp in *Vict. Nat.* 58:188 (1942)

A monotypic genus confined to NSW where it is found only in the crevices of sandstone cliffs. It was originally included under *Lyperanthus* but differs in the numerous leaves and numerous flowers of the plant.

R. elliptica (Plate 201)

R. elliptica (R. Br.) H. M. R. Rupp in *Vict. Nat.* 58:188 (1942); H. M. R. Rupp *Orchids N.S.W.* 53 (1943)

SYNONYMY: *Lyperanthus ellipticus* R. Br. *Prodr. Flor. Nov. Holl.* 325 (1810); *Caladenia elliptica* (R. Br.) Reichenb.f. *Beitr. syst. Pflk.* 67 (1871)

Stems slender, drooping, 15–25 cm. long, with two to five small elliptical clasping leaves of variable size along the stem; basal leaves elliptical to ovate, 3–10 cm. long, conspicuously petiolate. Tuberous roots terete, very brittle, rasp-like. Flowers numerous, six to fifteen, in a weak terminal raceme, often drooping, pale green to yellowish-green with brown markings. Sepals and petals acuminate with fine points, the dorsal sepal broad-lanceolate, cucullate; about 2 cm. long; lateral sepals 2·5–3 cm. long; petals about 2 cm. long; the lateral sepals and petals linear to linear-lanceolate, flat, slightly falcate, spreading or recurved. Labellum white, about half as long as the sepals, on a short broad concave claw; lateral lobes obsolete, the mid-lobe with lamina raised, veined, the margins entire, the surface with a few raised papillae at the base, but sometimes absent. Column incurved, very narrowly winged, slender. Anther acute; pollinia four in two pairs; stigma prominent.

R. elliptica grows on cliff faces in rather stiff clay, intermixed with the rhizomes of Coral fern (*Gleichenia*). The clay is lodged in narrow horizontal fissures of wet sandstone, often not more than two fingers high, so that it is rather difficult to dislodge the brittle plants without breaking off the leaves, particularly as the stiff-rhizomed fern occurs in front of the clay.

The species appears to be intermediate in character between epiphytic and terrestrial orchids, the habit suggesting the epiphyte, whereas the flower has affinities with that of the terrestrial.

FLOWERING PERIOD: Nov. and Dec.

DISTRIBUTION: Endemic in NSW where it is apparently confined to the Blue Mountains area

19 *Lyperanthus*

Lyperanthus R. Br. *Prodr. Flor. Nov. Holl.* 325 (1810)

Terresrial glabrous herbs, with fleshy tubers, sometimes drying black. Leaf solitary (in the Australian forms), basal, broad and thick or long and narrow. Bracts often large. Dorsal sepal usually broad, erect, or incurved over the column; other segments narrow erect or spreading, and about equal in length to the dorsal segment. Labellum shorter, undivided or trilobed; lamina somewhat papillose, sometimes bearing raised longitudinal lines. Column erect, incurved, winged, the wings sometimes small, about the same length as labellum. Anther terminal, two-celled. Pollinia four, a bilobed mass in each cell, granular or mealy.

A small genus of twelve species. All of the four Australian species are endemic, while of the remainder one is found in NZ and the other seven in New Caledonia.

L. forrestii (Plate 202)

L. forrestii F. Muell. in *Sth. Sci. Rec.* 2:55 (1882); R. Erickson *Orchids West* ed. 2:75 (1965)

Plant 12–23 cm. high; the tubers oblong-ellipsoidal to oblong, about 1·3 cm. long; a sheath surrounding the stem below the leaves. Leaves three, light green tending to turn yellow as the flower matures, sessile at or near the base but clasping the stem at their insertion; the lowest leaf ovate-lanceolate, coriaceous, 5–5·5 cm. long and 2·3–3 cm. broad, spreading, and overlapping the base of the second leaf which is smaller, lanceolate and more vertical than the one below, 2–4 cm. long and in turn overlapping the base of the upper leaf which is very similar to the middle one; sometimes an acute lanceolate bract near the middle of the stem. Flowers one to four, on long, slender pedicels, each subtended by a large lanceolate bracteole (a floral rudiment sometimes arising alongside the upper-most pedicel); flowers white with pink shading and deep crimson marks and dots. Perianth segments about equal, 2·5 cm. long; lateral sepals spreading, obfalcate, the bases very attenuated, three-nerved, spotted in some flowers; dorsal sepal erect, wider, very concave, cucullate, contracted at the base; petals falcate-lanceolate, contracted at the base, three-nerved and often spotted. Labellum almost obovate, with a long attenuated base; erect in the lower half then gradually recurved forward above the middle; margins crenulate but not fringed; about 2 cm. long; the lamina traversed for its entire length with numerous prominent longitudinal nerves, and scattered sessile glands numerous towards the tip. Column erect, slightly winged, about 15 mm. long. Anther incumbent with narrow sharp point. Stigma large, prominent, situated just below the anther.

FLOWERING PERIOD: Nov.

DISTRIBUTION: Endemic in WA where it is confined to swampy areas of the south-west, flowering mainly after fires

L. nigricans (Plate 203)

L. nigricans R. Br. *Prodr. Flor. Nov. Holl.* 325 (1810); A. J. Ewart *Flor. Vict.* 340 (1931); J. M. Black *Flor. S. Aust.* ed. 2:227 (1943); H. M. R. Rupp *Orchids N.S.W.* 54 (1943); J. H. Willis *Handb. Pls Vict.* 1:382 (1962); R. Erickson *Orchids West* ed. 2:75 (1965); M. J. Firth *Native Orchids Tasm.* 51 (1965)

SYNONYMY: *Leptoceras pectinatum* Endl. in Lehm. *Plant. Preiss.* 2:6 (1846) non Lindl. (1840); *Caladenia nigricans* (R. Br.) Reichenb.f. *Beitr. syst. Pflk.* 67 (1871)

A stout fleshy plant 8–20 cm. high, rarely more. Leaf broadly ovate-cordate, fleshy, of variable size, 3–9 cm. long. The whole plant drying black. Stem-bracts two or three, leaf-like, loose, sheathing, rather blunt, 2·5–4 cm. long. Flowers large, two to eight, marked with crimson lines on a white ground, the tips of the segments very dark red-brown. Ovary and pedicel enclosed in a large subtending bracteole which often envelopes the lower part of the perianth. Dorsal sepal broadly lanceolate, incurved, 2–3·5 cm. long. Lateral sepals spreading or deflexed, sometimes darker than the other segments, linear, 2–3·5 cm. long. Petals similar to the lateral sepals, recurved or spreading. Labellum lighter coloured with crimson veins and purple markings on the tip, sessile, obovate-lanceolate, 1·5–2 cm. long, trilobed, the lateral lobes erect, clasping the column; mid-lobe with a blunt tip, which is recurved, margins fringed or deeply denticulate; lamina with a wide smooth longitudinal raised plate between the lateral lobes and a few minute sessile calli on the undersurface. Column erect, then incurved, from 12 mm. to 2 cm. long, very narrowly winged. Anther incumbent with a blunt tip. Pollinia two, elongated, bilobed, powdery. Stigma prominent, circular or lobulate, its upper margin thickened into a convex rostellum.

L. nigricans 'often grows in great carpets, standing as thick as could be possible'. 'Last season a fire passed over the spot—an area of about 1 m. square—this small space contained approximately one hundred flowering plants.' Such reports are frequent during the flowering season. Yet in some localities the flowers of this orchid are absent, although in the majority of its haunts 'Red Beaks' is an abundant plant, the leaves being seen more often than the flowers. Some such stimulant as a fire is necessary to induce the plant to bloom. It is as much at home in dense forest, as in the sandy stretches of the sea shore. Albino specimens were collected near Mount Barker, WA, in Oct. 1948 by the author—three plants were found amongst innumerable plants of normal colour.

FLOWERING PERIOD: Aug. to Nov.

COMMON NAME: Red Beaks

DISTRIBUTION: Eastern NSW; southern and western Vic.; northern Tas.; south-eastern SA; south-western WA; often abundant in dense colonies.

L. serratus (Plate 204)

L. serratus Lindl. *Gen. & Spec. orchid. Pls* 393 (1840); R. Erickson *Orchids West* ed. 2:75 (1965)

SYNONYMY: *Caladenia serrata* (Lindl.) Reichenb.f. *Beitr. syst. Pflk.* 67 (1871)

A stout plant over 30 cm. high. Leaf broadly linear, 25–35 cm. long and 1·3–1·5 cm. wide, flat, channelled towards the base, the margins incurved. Stem-bracts two, lanceolate, sheathing, 3–6 cm. long, the upper one and those within the raceme streaked and otherwise marked with red or brown, acuminate; two sheathing scales at the base of stem. Flowers four to seven, sessile or almost so, pale green to yellow, streaked and suffused with crimson or brown. Dorsal sepal lanceolate, cucullate over the column, about 2 cm. long, contracted at the base; lateral sepals and petals linear-lanceolate or falco-lanceolate, spreading, channelled, deeply coloured red-brown on the concave surface, 2–3 cm. long, the petals sometimes longer than sepals. Labellum much shorter than the other segments, obovate on a sessile base, the lateral lobes not prominent, margins entire, and embracing the column-wings, inner surface studded with irregular sessile glands or merely rugose, the whole mottled red; calli in two or more rows, stout, fleshy, pyramidal or falcate; mid-lobe recurved, brush-like at the tip with prominent crowded calli, the apex acute. Column erect, incurved, narrowly winged, mottled with red. Anther incumbent with a long point.

FLOWERING PERIOD: Sept. and Oct.

COMMON NAME: Rattle Beaks

DISTRIBUTION: Endemic in WA where it is widespread through the south-west

L. suaveolens (Plate 205)

L. suaveolens R. Br. Prodr. Flor. Nov. Holl. 325 (1810); A. J. Ewart Flor. Vict. 341 (1931); H. M. R. Rupp Orchids N.S.W. 54 (1943); J. H. Willis Handb. Pls Vict. 1:383 (1962); M. J. Firth Native Orchids Tasm. 51 (1965)

SYNONYMY: Caladenia sulphurea A. Cunn. in Field Geogr. Mem. N.S.W. 361 (1825); Leptoceras sulphureum (A. Cunn.) Lindl. Gen. & Spec. orchid. Pls 416 (1840); Caladenia suaveolens (R. Br.) Reichenb.f. Beitr. syst. Pflk. 67 (1871)

A glabrous plant 30–45 cm. high. Tubers large, globose, about 2 cm. in diameter, the roots fleshy. Leaf green, the inner surface whitish, linear-lanceolate, concave, the margins incurved, 15–20 cm. long, apex acute. Stem-bracts closely sheathing, a long brownish one at the base, two shorter ones along the stem and short acuminate bracteoles within the raceme. Flowers two to eight in an extended raceme, sometimes sweetly scented, dark reddish to brownish, almost sessile. Ovary green. Dorsal sepal cucullate over the column, acuminate, 2–2·3 cm. long, broader than the other segments, the tip sometimes recurved. Lateral sepals and petals about equal in length, slightly longer than the dorsal sepal, linear, spreading or recurved. Labellum much shorter than the sepals, the erect part broad with entire incurved margins; the lateral lobes rounded, not very prominent; mid-lobe ovate-oblong, obtuse, recurved; lamina covered throughout with papillae-like glands in several rows or irregular, confluent scale-like glands, with smaller rounded glands on each side. Column erect, incurved, winged throughout, fleshy. Anther with a prominent point.

L. suaveolens favours the lower forest areas and more or less open scrub country. Occasionally large clumps are formed at the base of trees. There are many colour forms of this species.

FLOWERING PERIOD: Aug. to Nov.

COMMON NAME: Brown Beaks

DISTRIBUTION: Extending from south-eastern Qld along the east coast to eastern Tas.; widespread but not generally common

20   *Burnettia*

Burnettia Lindl. Gen. & Spec. orchid. Pls 517 (1840)

A monotypic genus, endemic in Australia. It differs from Caladenia in the habit of the plant, the longitudinal plates on the labellum, the thick consistency of the perianth and its connivent segments.

B. cuneata (Plate 206)

B. cuneata Lindl. Gen. & Spec. orchid. Pls 518 (1840); A. J. Ewart

Flor. Vict. 341 (1931); H. M. R. Rupp Orchids N.S.W. 56 (1943); J. H. Willis Handb. Pls Vict. 1:383 (1962); M. J. Firth Native Orchids Tasm. 31 (1965)

SYNONYMY: Lyperanthus burnettii F. Muell. Fragm. Phyt. Aust. 5:96 (1865); Caladenia cuneata (Lindl.) Reichenb.f. Beitr. syst. Pflk. 67 (1871)

Terrestrial herbs with small underground tubers, apparently leafless, except for empty sheathing scales. Stems 5–13 cm. high, with several sheathing empty scales, the lower ones short and imbricate, the upper ones distant, loose, often small, but sometimes 2 cm. in length, fleshy, red-brown, sometimes well-developed, ovate-lanceolate in shape. Flowers usually one to three, but occasionally as many as seven, on pedicels of variable length, erect or incurved, almost wholly red-brown or white with red-brown markings outside, pure white within, rarely pink. Sepals and petals 8–13 mm. long, linear-lanceolate to ovate-lanceolate, falcate, acute, 1–1·5 cm. long, erect or connivent, of a thicker consistency than in Caladenia. Dorsal sepal incurved, concave. Labellum 3–6 mm. long, broad, sessile, truncate or obscurely sinuate, erect at the base, recurved towards the end with two longitudinal plates, which are shortly lobed or broken up in a few calli above the middle, often extending to the margins, the reverse side and also scattered over the broad expanse of the side lobes. Column erect, 7 mm. long, concave, narrowly winged upward. Another erect, two-celled, the outer valves broad. Pollinia granular, two.

B. cuneata should be looked for in wet boggy country where Melaleuca squarrosa grows. I have found it more abundant on land which has been burnt over the previous season.

FLOWERING PERIOD: Sept. to Dec.

COMMON NAME: Lizard Orchid

DISTRIBUTION: Wet coastal swamps of NSW (south of the Blue Mountains), Vic., and Tas.; rarely collected, but occasionally locally abundant

21   *Leptoceras*

Leptoceras (R. Br.) Lindl. in Edwards' bot. Reg. 23: Swan Riv. Append. liii (1840)

A monotypic genus, endemic in Australia. It is closely related to Caladenia menziesii from which it differs in the sepals; and is also related to the genus Eriochilus which has a recurved labellum whereas in Leptoceras it is straight. The genus however has been included under Caladenia by some botanists, e.g. Bentham. Robert Brown included it thus and placed it in a section Leptoceras. See Prodr. Flor. Nov. Holl. 325 (1810).

L. fimbriatum (Plate 207)

L. fimbriatum Lindl. in Edwards' bot. Reg. 23: Swan Riv. Append. liii (1840); A. J. Ewart Flor. Vict. 339 (1931); J. M. Black Flor. S. Aust. ed. 2:228 (1943); J. H. Willis Handb. Pls Vict. 1:384 (1962); R. Erickson Orchids West ed. 2:61 (1965)

SYNONYMY: Caladenia fimbriata (Lindl.) Reichenb.f. Beitr. syst. Pflk. 67 (1871); Eriochilus fimbriatus F. Muell. in Sth. Sci. Rec. 2:152 (1882)

Terrestrial glabrous herbs, originating from a rounded tuber with fibrous roots. Very slender, 15–25 cm. high. Leaf basal, solitary or occasionally two, overlapping, bluish-green with prominent red veins, ovate to oblong-lanceolate, sheathing (in dry seasons leaf often minute), subtended by a comparatively large bract. Stem-bracts small, usually one. Flowers one to three, rarely more, yellowish with reddish-brown or purplish markings, the pedicels slender. Dorsal sepal incurved, concave, broadly ovate, 9–11 mm. long, the tip acute. Lateral sepals spathulate, acute, narrow, deflexed, 10–12 mm. long. Petals erect, pointed, linear-clavate, the tips very glandular, longer than the lateral sepals. Labellum on a short movable claw, wider than long, trilobed, the lateral lobes large and dome-shaped, fringed deeply, combed anteriorly, with pubescent spots on their upper convex surface; the mid-lobe much smaller, rounded, not recurved, less deeply combed, its upper surface smooth or almost so; yellowish-green with reddish-brown or purplish markings, 5–6 mm. long and 9–12 mm. wide; margins of fringe minutely ciliate. Column 6–7 mm. high, incurved, prominently winged. Anther bent forward, blunt at apex, two-celled, valvate. Pollinia four in two pairs, lamellate. Stigma triangular, its apex deeply sunk between the divergent lobes of the anther. Rostellum poorly developed; no viscid disc or caudicle.

In good seasons in the coastal districts of Vic. this orchid is very plentiful. The flowers are extremely difficult to locate amongst the camouflaging heathland flora. The colonies are stimulated into mass flowerings by fire, this being especially so in WA.

FLOWERING PERIOD: Mar. to Aug.

COMMON NAME: Fringed Hare Orchid

DISTRIBUTION: Scattered through heath and sandplain country of southern Vic., south-eastern SA, and south-western WA, often locally abundant

22 *Caladenia*

Caladenia R. Br. *Prodr. Flor. Nov. Holl.* 323 (1810)

Terrestrial herbs, usually hairy, but sometimes only slightly so, with small rounded tubers. Leaf solitary, generally linear-lanceolate or oblong, from within a scarious sheathing scale close to the ground. Flowers solitary, or in a loose raceme or panicle of not more than eight, on an erect scape with an empty bract or sheathing scale about the middle and a similar bract under each pedicel; flowers usually erect and variously coloured. Dorsal sepal erect, incurved over the column or more rarely retracted, usually narrow; lateral sepals similar to it, flat, spreading or reflexed. Petals narrow, erect, spreading or reflexed. Labellum often on a movable claw and generally erect at the base; undivided or trilobed; the lateral lobes when present erect; the mid-lobe or lamina of the labellum recurved; the margins often fringed or toothed; the lamina with sessile or stalked calli, arranged in two or more longitudinal rows or irregularly scattered or crowded. Column erect or incurved, more or less two-winged in the upper part. Anther terminal, more or less oblique, usually pointed, two-celled, valvate. Pollinia four, lamellate, commonly leg-of-mutton shape, granular. Stigma immediately below the anther, circular and disc-like. Rostellum poorly developed. Viscid disc and caudicle absent.

A rather large genus of seventy or more species, most of which are endemic in Australia. Several are found in NZ, New Caledonia and Malaysia. The species are most abundant in WA.

Generally the genus is divided into two sections: (1) *Calonema*, in which the sepals and petals are elongated and often filiform, the species being commonly known as Spider Orchids; (2) *Eucaladenia*,

in which the sepals and petals are short, their apices not produced. This division however is not altogether satisfactory.

C. menziesii (Plate 208)

C. menziesii R. Br. *Prodr. Flor. Nov. Holl.* 325 (1810); A. J. Ewart *Flor. Vict.* 344 (1931); J. M. Black *Flor. S. Aust.* ed. 2:233 (1943); J. H. Willis *Handb. Pls Vict.* 1:384 (1962); R. Erickson *Orchids West* ed. 2:87 (1965); M. J. Firth *Native Orchids Tasm.* 59 (1965)

A slender plant 6–20 cm. or more in height. Leaf glabrous or nearly so, of variable shape and size; usually ovate-lanceolate or broad oblong-lanceolate, 3–9 cm. long. Flowers one to three, white and pink, sometimes pure white. Dorsal sepal reddish, glandular-hairy on the back, spathulate-lanceolate, contracted gradually towards the base, rather blunt, cucullate, 11–15 mm. long, entirely enveloping the column. Lateral sepals 11–15 mm. long, spreading, white or pink, traversed by a pink stripe on the lower surface, crescentic, wide in the middle, contracted towards both ends. Petals purplish-red, very narrow-linear in the lower half, clavate and closely-glandular above, erect, channelled, 15–20 mm. long. Labellum on a short claw, 7–10 mm. long, white with conspicuous transverse pink markings, orbicular-ovate, undivided, erect at the base, tip white, narrow, blunt, recurved; margins entire or nearly so; calli slender with large rounded heads, in two to four rows, not extending to the tip. Column 7–10 mm. long, erect, slightly incurved, with transverse pink stripes, winged rather widely throughout. Anther compressed laterally, shortly pointed. Pollinia four, lamellate, unlike those prevailing in other species of the genus, angular like a try-square.

FLOWERING PERIOD: Aug. to Nov.

COMMON NAME: Hare Orchid, or Rabbit Orchid

DISTRIBUTION: Southern Vic.; northern and eastern Tas.; south-eastern SA; south-western WA Usually in light forests of sandy coastal districts, and flowering freely after bush-fires

C. flava (Plate 209)

C. flava R. Br. *Prodr. Flor. Nov. Holl.* 324 (1810); R. Erickson *Orchids West* ed. 2:95 (1965)

A hairy plant, more glandular than most species, usually less than 30 cm. high, the underground stems very woolly and knotty. Leaf lanceolate, and often rather large for the plant. Flowers large, yellow, usually two to four, up to 4·5 cm. in diameter, on a flexuose rhachis. Sepals and petals broad-lanceolate, rather acute or almost acuminate, contracted at the base, the lateral sepals longer than the other segments, often more than 2·5 cm. long; dorsal sepal rather smaller with a more or less distinct scarlet line or red blotches along the centre. Petals shorter than dorsal sepal. Labellum about 1 cm. long and broad, with a very short broad, concave claw, the broad lamina cordate at the base, deeply trilobed, the lateral lobes ovate, shortly acuminate, the mid-lobe rather longer and lanceolate, bordered on each side by two or three linear-clavate calli; calli of the lamina linear-clavate in two rows almost converging into a semi-circle. Column winged from the base. Anther with a long point.

FLOWERING PERIOD: Aug. to Oct.

COMMON NAME: Cowslip Orchid

DISTRIBUTION: Widespread throughout south-western WA

C. paniculata (Plate 210)

C. paniculata R. D. FitzG. in *Gdnrs' Chron.* new ser. 17:461 (1882); R. Erickson *Orchids West* ed. 2:96 (1965)

SYNONYMY: *C. purdieana* C. R. P. Andrews in *J. Proc. Mueller bot. Soc. West. Aust.* 1[10]:39 (1902)

A slender hairy species 10–20 cm. high. Leaf oblong-lanceolate, hairy, 2–11 cm. long and 5–20 mm. wide. Flowers white or pink with dusky reddish-brown on lower surface of the perianth segments, and many glandular hairs on all segments; two to six in a raceme. Perianth segments narrow-lanceolate to lanceolate, 1·2–2 cm. long. Labellum much shorter than the other segments, erect, trilobed, the lateral lobes large and erect, their anterior margins more or less fringed and everted; the mid-lobe rather large, recurved, margins fringed throughout. Calli forming a plate in two converging rows in middle of lamina. Column erect, incurved. Anther with a long point. Stigma prominent.

C. paniculata grows on grassy flats, around paper-barks (*Melaleuca* spp.) and around the base of eucalypts. Often it occurs in clustered masses, which look like flocks of white pigeons, in miniature.

[This species and *C. purdieana* were formerly believed to be distinct. After investigating the matter, A. S. George has found that there is no difference between them and has relegated *C. purdieana* to synonymy. See *West. Aust. Nat. 8*:40 (1961).—Ed.]

FLOWERING PERIOD: Sept. and Oct.

COMMON NAME: White Fairy Orchid

DISTRIBUTION: South-western WA

C. unita (Plate 211)

C. unita R. D. FitzG. in *Gdnrs' Chron.* new ser. *17*:461 (1882); R. Erickson *Orchids West* ed. 2:96 (1965)

A slender shortly-hairy plant 8–30 cm. high. Leaf linear-lanceolate, 7–15 cm. long. Flowers pink or pinkish-mauve, about 2·5 cm. in diameter, hairy on the outside, two or three on long or short pedicels. Dorsal sepal erect, incurved, lanceolate; lateral sepals lanceolate-falcate, united for one-third to two-thirds of their length. Petals lanceolate, acute, widely spread, contracted towards the base. Labellum ovate, on a long claw, markedly recurved, margins fringed with long and short linear calli; calli of the lamina linear, in two converging rows, united at the base into a plate. Column winged to the base, the wings produced into oblong lobes on each side of the stigma; anther with a comparatively long narrow point.

FLOWERING PERIOD: Sept. and Oct.

DISTRIBUTION: South-western WA

C. latifolia (Plate 212)

C. latifolia R. Br. *Prodr. Flor. Nov. Holl.* 324 (1810); A. J. Ewart *Flor. Vict.* 348 (1931); J. M. Black *Flor. S. Aust.* ed. 2:233 (1943); H. M. R. Rupp *Orchids N.S.W.* 63 (1943); J. H. Willis *Handb. Pls Vict.* 1:391 (1962); R. Erickson *Orchids West* ed. 2:96 (1965); M. J. Firth *Native Orchids Tasm.* 62 (1965)

A moderately robust plant 10–30 cm. high. Leaf large, very hairy, oblong-lanceolate to lanceolate, 4–10 cm. long. Flowers one to four, 1·5–3·5 cm. in diameter, pink or white, or both, distant on short pedicels, subtending bracts prominent, sheathing; perianth segments paler on the reverse, glandular-hairy, spreading handwise with the exception of the dorsal one which is erect. Lateral sepals oblong-lanceolate, obtuse; dorsal sepal shorter and more acute; petals shorter and more lanceolate. Labellum sessile, deeply trilobed; lateral lobes oblong, banded with pink; margins entire or shortly serrate; mid-lobe broad and long with a prominent pink central blotch; the long calli of the lamina linear or clavate, in two short rows, more or less converging in a semi-circle. Column erect,

winged throughout, rather broadly so at the apex. Anther with a long point, pollinia four, deeply bilobed, lamellate.

C. latifolia is chiefly a littoral plant. On the sand hills along our extensive coastline, it may be seen, during a normal season, in countless numbers; it also occurs, but less extensively, far inland. Although recorded for Qld and NSW, no specimens are known from these states, but it may extend from Vic. into southern NSW.

FLOWERING PERIOD: Sept. to Dec.

COMMON NAME: Pink Fairies

DISTRIBUTION: Southern Vic.; Tas.; south-eastern SA; south-western WA; generally near the coast

C. reptans (Plate 213)

C. reptans Lindl. in *Edwards' bot. Reg. 23*: Swan Riv. Append. lii (1840); R. Erickson *Orchids West* ed. 2:96 (1965)

A comparatively small, slender plant 12–18 cm. high, closely allied to *C. latifolia*, but apparently with a creeping underground stem. Leaf oblong or lanceolate, green, frequently purplish underneath. Flowers one or two, pink, 2–3 cm. in diameter. Perianth segments similar to those in *C. latifolia*. Labellum contracted into a long claw, deeply trilobed, the mid-lobe not recurved, the margins variously combed or crenate; lateral lobes prominent, 5–6 mm. long, oblong-falcate, entire with three prominent longitudinal stripes; the calli of the lamina long and thick, more or less united at the base into two deeply-lobed plates, forming two short converging rows placed in a semi-circle or almost transverse. Column erect, 6–8 mm. high, very shortly hairy, prominently winged above and below. Anther with a long point.

[*C. nana* Endl. is very much like this species and is considered to be synonymous with it by some botanists.—Ed.]

FLOWERING PERIOD: July to Sept.

DISTRIBUTION: South-western WA, but uncommon

C. sericea (Plate 214)

C. sericea Lindl. in *Edwards' bot. Reg. 23*: Swan Riv. Append. lii (1840); R. Erickson *Orchids West* ed. 2:87 (1965)

Usually softly villous; the hairs, especially on the leaves, shorter, more dense and silky than in any other species. Leaf oblong-lanceolate, often rather broad, 2·5–8 cm. long. Stem 15–35 cm. high, with one or two rather large blue or mauve flowers, much incurved in the bud. Sepals and petals nearly equal, 2–3 cm. long, oblong-lanceolate, obtuse or nearly acute, the dorsal one more erect than the others and concave. Labellum 1–2 cm. long, contracted at the base, cuneate upward, nearly equally trilobed at the end; lateral lobes erect, shortly oblong, incurved and obtuse; mid-lobe recurved, shortly fringed with a few calli; calli of the lamina short, linear or slightly clavate, in four to six rows, with a few long linear-clavate ones at the base of the limb, the lowest ones sometimes united in linear or oblong plates. Column a little shorter than the labellum, narrowly winged throughout. Anther with a short point.

FLOWERING PERIOD: July to Oct.

DISTRIBUTION: South-western WA

C. gemmata (Plate 215)

C. gemmata Lindl. in *Edwards' bot. Reg. 23*: Swan Riv. Append. lii (1840); R. Erickson *Orchids West* ed. 2:90 (1965)

A dwarf hairy species 10–25 cm. high. Stem-bracts one, besides those subtending the floral pedicels, subulate, sheathing, 1·5–2·5 cm.

long, situated in the upper part of the stem. Leaf ovate or ovate-lanceolate, 3–3·5 cm. long, purplish beneath, hairy. Flowers one or two, rather large, 4–7 cm. in diameter, of a soft deep blue, rarely white. Sepals and petals broadly elliptical-oblong, obtuse or acute, contracted at the base and almost clawed. Dorsal sepal erect, tip recurved. Labellum broadly ovate, undivided, comparatively small, erect at the base, but scarcely contracted into a claw, recurved at the end and obtuse, about 1 cm. long; calli numerous, gem-like, small and clavate, those at the base usually longer, in longitudinal rows occupying almost the entire surface of the lamina. Column about as long as the labellum, narrowly winged throughout. Anther with a prominent point.

FLOWERING PERIOD: Aug. to Oct.

COMMON NAME: Blue China Orchid

DISTRIBUTION: Widespread through south-western WA

C. gemmata forma lutea (Plate 215)

C. gemmata forma *lutea* S. C. Clemesha in *Orchadian* 2:118 (1967); R. Erickson *Orchids West* ed. 2:90 (1965), as *C. gemmata* var. *ixioides*

SYNONYMY: *C. ixioides* Lindl. in *Edwards' bot. Reg.* 23: Swan Riv. Append. lii (1840)

[This form has been mentioned in literature as var. *ixioides*, but this name had not been validly published. It differs from the typical only in the flowers being yellow.—Ed.]

DISTRIBUTION: Apparently found only in Perth–Northam area of WA

C. saccharata (Plate 216)

C. saccharata Reichenb.f. *Beitr. syst. Pflk.* 63 (1871); R. Erickson *Orchids West* ed. 2:87 (1965)

A very slender species 5–20 cm. high, similar in size and habit to *C. caerulea*. Leaf linear, sparsely hairy. Flower solitary, segments of perianth white on their upper surfaces, violet with glandular-tipped hairs on the reverse. Lateral sepals spreading, broader than the petals; dorsal sepal erect or slightly incurved. Labellum tri-lobed; mid-lobe large and rounded, yellow or white, recurved but not revolute, apex blunt, margins entire; lateral lobes prominent, violet or partially violet on outer surface, violet with purple stripes on the inside, erect with entire margins; lamina with a double row of yellow, linear, clavate calli extending almost to the extreme tip. Column reddish-purple, incurved. Anther with a short, or comparatively short point. Stigma small.

FLOWERING PERIOD: Aug. and Sept.

COMMON NAME: Sugar Orchid

DISTRIBUTION: Widespread and fairly common in south-western WA

C. alba (Plate 217)

C. alba R. Br. *Prodr. Flor. Nov. Holl.* 323 (1810); A. J. Ewart *Flor. Vict.* 349 (1931); H.M.R. Rupp *Orchids N.S.W.* 64 (1943); J. H. Willis *Handb. Pls Vict.* 1:391 (1962)

SYNONYMY: *C. carnea* var. *alba* (R. Br.) Benth. *Flor. aust.* 6:387 (1873)

A slender species similar to *C. carnea*. Plant 7–30 cm. high, with a long linear, sparsely hirsute leaf. Flowers usually solitary, occasionally two, up to 5 cm. in diameter, pure white or pink, except for the yellow or orange tip of the labellum and the often yellow-headed calli. Perianth segments similar to those of *C. carnea*, 12–20 mm.

long. Labellum white, with two rows of white or yellow-headed calli on the lamina, trilobed; the lateral lobes prominently rounded and stained with purple or crimson; mid-lobe small with fringed and undulate margins. Neither labellum nor column barred with red lines as in *C. carnea*. Column whitish or green.

FLOWERING PERIOD: May to Oct., being earlier in the northern localities

COMMON NAME: White Caladenia

DISTRIBUTION: South-eastern Qld; near-coastal regions of NSW; south-eastern Vic.

C. alba var. picta (Plate 217)

C. alba var. *picta* W. H. Nicholls in *Vict. Nat.* 47:157, fig. 7 (1931); H. M. R. Rupp *Orchids N.S.W.* 66 (1943); J. H. Willis *Handb. Pls Vict.* 1:391 (1962)

Calli slender, tall; column tricoloured; upper part deep olive-green, middle part deep red; lower part white.

FLOWERING PERIOD: May to Sept.

DISTRIBUTION: Known only from several localities in the Newcastle–Sydney area of NSW, and Ringwood in Vic.

C. caerulea (Plate 218)

C. caerulea R. Br. *Prodr. Flor. Nov. Holl.* 324 (1810); A. J. Ewart *Flor. Vict.* 349 (1931); J. M. Black *Flor. S. Aust.* ed. 2:235 (1943); H. M. R. Rupp *Orchids N.S.W.* 68 (1943); J. H. Willis *Handb. Pls Vict.* 1:393 (1962); R. Erickson *Orchids West* ed. 2:86 (1965)

A very slender, sparsely hairy plant similar to *C. carnea*, 8–17 cm. high. Leaf linear-lanceolate, 2–7 cm. long, only slightly hairy, the hairs short. Flower solitary, bright violet-blue, very rarely white. Perianth segments lighter coloured on the reverse, and beset with minute dark blue glands and glandular hairs, contracted towards the base. Dorsal sepal 10–20 mm. long, narrower than the lateral sepals, erect, concave, slightly incurved, rather blunt; lateral sepals 13–24 mm. long, elliptic-lanceolate, acute, spreading. Petals about same length as lateral sepals, but narrower, spreading. Labellum on a short claw, distinctly trilobed; lateral lobes erect and embracing the column, broad and rounded with entire margins; mid-lobe much recurved, narrow, cuneate, more or less acute with entire margins; lamina with transverse, linear, dark blue bands on a lighter ground; calli linear, yellow, clubbed, in two rows extending to the extreme tip, the forward calli sessile. Column 7–10 mm. long, much incurved, moderately winged throughout. Anther with a prominent point.

FLOWERING PERIOD: June to Sept., being earlier in the north

COMMON NAME: Blue Caladenia

DISTRIBUTION: South-eastern Qld; eastern NSW; southern Vic.; Bugle Ranges, SA; south-western WA. Often abundant, and favouring dry stony ground

C. carnea (Plate 219)

C. carnea R. Br. *Prodr. Flor. Nov. Holl.* 324 (1810); A. J. Ewart *Flor. Vict.* 348 (1931); J. M. Black *Flor. S. Aust.* ed. 2:233 (1943); H. M. R. Rupp *Orchids N.S.W.* 63 (1943); J. H. Willis *Handb. Pls Vict.* 1:392 (1962); M. J. Firth *Native Orchids Tasm.* 63 (1965)

A very slender species 8–20 cm. high. Leaf slightly hairy, narrow linear, often as long as the scape. Flowers one to three, pink, more rarely white. Perianth segments a dusky-green with glandular-hairs and pink stripes on the back, pink and glabrous on the inner surface;

tips generally acute, but sometimes blunt. Dorsal sepal erect or slightly incurved, linear, 11–16 mm. long; lateral sepals free, spreading, generally longer than the dorsal sepal, 11–20 mm. long, lanceolate or falco-lanceolate. Petals narrower than the sepals, but about the same length, spreading, falco-lanceolate; sometimes all the segments of the perianth equal. Labellum sessile, trilobed, erect at the base, recurved; lateral lobes prominent, broad, erect, with rounded anterior border and entire margins; mid-lobe lanceolate, more or less dentate or fringed with a few calli; lamina 6–8 mm. long, with two rows of stalked clubbed calli, which are sometimes larger and in four rows at the base, not extending beyond the bend, with interrupted transverse red linear bands. Column 6–8 mm. long, incurved, rather narrowly winged, with transverse linear red markings anteriorly. Anther with rather a long point.

The flowers of several forms of *C. carnea* diffuse their surroundings with a strong musk-like scent. So powerful is this under certain weather conditions, that one form in particular, diffusing its scent at night and apparently a moth-pollinated form, must be included among the most strongly scented orchids we have. This form, which I consider should be included under var. *gigantea*, occurs in the Airey's Inlet district, Vic. On one occasion our party of naturalists had arrived well after midnight at a convenient spot there for a camp-out, when the gentle breezes wafted a mysterious sweet fragrance in our direction. Immediate investigation was decided on, resulting in the finding of over thirty specimens of this form of *C. carnea*.

[This is a very variable species. Several of the named varieties are illustrated and in the following section of text their characteristic features are described.—Ed.]

FLOWERING PERIOD: Aug. to Dec.

COMMON NAME: Pink Fingers

DISTRIBUTION: South-eastern Qld; eastern NSW; Vic.; Tas.; south-eastern SA; also NZ and New Caledonia

C. carnea var. **pygmaea** (Plate 219)

C. carnea var. *pygmaea* R. S. Rogers in *Trans. roy. Soc. S. Aust.* 51:13 (1927); J. M. Black *Flor. S. Aust.* ed. 2:235 (1943); H. M. R. Rupp *Orchids N.S.W.* 64 (1943); J. H. Willis *Handb. Pls Vict.* 1:392 (1962); M. J. Firth *Native Orchids Tasm.* 63 (1965)

A diminutive plant up to 9 cm. high, with very small perianth segments 5–8 mm. long but comparatively broad. Flowers with deep reddish tints, rarely pale.

FLOWERING PERIOD: Sept. and Oct.

DISTRIBUTION: Eastern NSW; coastal Vic.; coastal Tas. and King Island; Mount Lofty Range, SA

C. carnea var. **gigantea** (Plate 220)

C. carnea var. *gigantea* R. S. Rogers in *Proc. roy. Soc. S. Aust.* 51:13 (1927); H. M. R. Rupp *Orchids N.S.W.* 64 (1943); J. H. Willis *Handb. Pls Vict.* 1:392 (1962)

Robust plant up to 60 cm. high. Flowers usually bright rose-pink, large; sepals up to 2 cm. long and 8 mm. wide. Mid-lobe of labellum orange, calli sometimes in four to six rows. Flowers often with a strong musky perfume.

FLOWERING PERIOD: July to Sept., being earlier in the north

DISTRIBUTION: Confined to the coast, from northern Qld, south through NSW to Cann River in eastern Vic.

C. carnea var. **subulata** (Plate 221)

C. carnea var. *subulata* W. H. Nicholls in *Vict. Nat.* 62:61, fig. A–F (1945); J. H. Willis *Handb. Pls Vict.* 1:393 (1962)

Perianth segments very narrow, pale pink shaded to green, each with a prominent longitudinal red-brown stripe along the centre. Lateral sepals reflexed, often embracing the ovary, sometimes crossed. Labellum erect; the mid-lobe yellow, narrow-subulate, the margins entire; lamina with narrow red-brown horizontal stripes; calli usually two, restricted to the immediate base only.

FLOWERING PERIOD: Oct. and Nov.

DISTRIBUTION: Known only from Portland, Vic., where it is reported to be plentiful in good seasons

C. carnea var. **ornata** (Plate 221)

C. carnea var. *ornata* W. H. Nicholls in *Vict. Nat.* 62:61, fig. G–J (1945); J. H. Willis *Handb. Pls Vict.* 1:392 (1962)

Perianth segments pink, somewhat yellowish on the back. Whole of the upper surface of the labellum bright red and conspicuously ornamented with broad transverse stripes of a deeper colour. Lateral sepals often united at the base.

FLOWERING PERIOD: Oct.

DISTRIBUTION: Known only from Gorae, near Portland, Vic.

C. **aurantiaca** (Plate 222)

C. aurantiaca (R. S. Rogers) H. M. R. Rupp in *Proc. Linn. Soc. N.S.W.* 71:280 (1947); J. H. Willis *Handb. Pls Vict.* 1:392 (1962)

SYNONYMY: *C. carnea* var. *aurantiaca* R. S. Rogers in *Trans. roy. Soc. S. Aust.* 46:154 (1922)

A slender plant 12–17 cm. high, with a narrow-linear leaf a little more than half as long as the stem. Flowers one or two, the second on a filiform pedicel. Perianth segments 7–10 mm. long, acute, white inside, conspicuously striped with green outside. Labellum white except for the tip and the calli, which are deep orange; entire or obscurely lobed. Margins entire, or denticulate near the tip, the teeth irregular. Calli in two rows, with relatively large clavate heads and slender stalks. Column broader than in either *C. alba* or *C. carnea*, the wings also wider. No transverse striation on either labellum or column.

FLOWERING PERIOD: Aug. to Nov.

COMMON NAME: Orange-tip Caladenia

DISTRIBUTION: Central to northern coastal districts, NSW; a few coastal localities in eastern Vic.

C. **deformis** (Plate 223)

C. deformis R. Br. *Pròdr. Flor. Nov. Holl.* 324 (1810); A. J. Ewart *Flor. Vict.* 348 (1931); J. M. Black *Flor. S. Aust.* ed. 2:235 (1943); H. M. R. Rupp *Orchids N.S.W.* 68 (1943); J. H. Willis *Handb. Pls Vict.* 1:390 (1962); R. Erickson *Orchids West* ed. 2:87 (1965); M. J. Firth *Native Orchids Tasm.* 62 (1965)

A slightly hairy species 6–17 cm. high. Leaf almost glabrous, linear-lanceolate, 4–10 cm. long and 2–5 mm. wide. Flower solitary, deep blue, occasionally white, pink or yellow. Perianth segments lightly coloured on the outside with many scattered minute purple glands, spreading, with the exception of the dorsal sepal, which is usually erect and recurved. Dorsal sepal 12–25 mm. long, more or less acute, elliptic-lanceolate; lateral sepals shorter, falco-lanceolate. Petals sometimes erect and spreading, obliquely oblong-lanceolate, same length as lateral sepals. Labellum contracted towards the base, sessile, 10–15 mm. long when extended, and 5–8 mm. wide, obcuneate; its lower two-thirds erect, clasping the sides of the column, obscurely trilobed, the lateral lobes toothed anteriorly, their margins otherwise entire, not very prominent; mid-lobe triangular, recurved, dark purple, fringed with dentate calli; calli of lamina linear or slightly clubbed, bristly, in four to six more or less ill-defined rows, not quite extending to the extreme tip, somewhat crowded and presenting a tomentose appearance. Column 8–12 mm. long, incurved, winged throughout, broadly so in its upper half, the wings united in front at the base, more or less marked with deep red or purple dots and other markings. Anther with a long acute point. Pollinia four, free, lamellate, elongate, crescentic.

C. deformis often grows in tufts, favouring chiefly the base of hills and damp, somewhat sheltered situations under trees and shrubs.

Although the flowers are generally blue, a group of several plants was collected on 22 August 1920 at Cheltenham, Vic., with bright canary-yellow flowers.

FLOWERING PEROD: June to Oct.

COMMON NAME: Bluebeard Caladenia, or Blue Fairies

DISTRIBUTION: Central eastern NSW; southern and central Vic.; northern and eastern Tas.; south-eastern SA; south-western WA

C. congesta (Plate 224)

C. congesta R. Br. *Prodr. Flor. Nov. Holl.* 324 (1810); A. J. Ewart *Flor. Vict.* 350 (1931); J. M. Black *Flor. S. Aust.* ed. 2:235 (1943); H. M. R. Rupp *Orchids N.S.W.* 66 (1943); J. H. Willis *Handb. Pls Vict.* 1:393 (1962); M. J. Firth *Native Orchids Tasm.* 63 (1965)

[A slender, slightly hairy plant 15–60 cm. high. Leaf 7–12 cm. long, linear. Flowers one to three, pink, glandular-hairy outside, pedicels slender. Dorsal sepal about 12 mm. long, lanceolate, cucullate; lateral sepals about 18 mm. long, elliptic-lanceolate, spreading. Petals about 14 mm. long, falcate, spreading. Labellum about 9 mm. long when extended, pink, on a rather long and narrow claw, basal-half erect against the column then gradually curved forward, trilobed. Lateral lobes falcate, acute, margins entire, extending beyond middle of labellum; mid-lobe long-acuminate, much recurved, margins entire. Calli dark crimson, imbricate, completely covering middle of labellum and becoming congested towards the tip; at first placed longitudinally in two rather obscure rows, the two nearest the claw being stalked, the others sessile, large, flat-topped, more or less oblong. Column about 8 mm. long, incurved, with rather wide wings, especially in the upper part, blotched with pink markings, anther pointed.

FLOWERING PERIOD: Oct. to Dec.

COMMON NAME: Black-tongue Caladenia

DISTRIBUTION: South-eastern NSW; Vic.; northern Tas.; Mount Gambier, SA; generally uncommon—Ed.]

C. cucullata (Plate 225)

C. cucullata R. D. FitzG. *Aust. Orchids* 1²:+t. (1876); A. J. Ewart *Flor. Vict.* 351 (1931); H. M. R. Rupp *Orchids N.S.W.* 67 (1943); J. H. Willis *Handb. Pls Vict.* 1:394 (1962); M. J. Firth *Native Orchids Tasm.* 64 (1965)

A very slender, often wiry-stemmed plant 10–25 cm. high. Leaf linear, sparsely hairy, 9–24 cm. long. Flowers one to five, 2–3 cm. in diameter, white with greenish-brown markings. Perianth segments of similar appearance, widely spread, sepals often broader, especially towards the tip; dorsal sepal remarkably cucullate. Labellum trilobed, of flat appearance, the sides spotted with pink, the surface minutely scabrous-denticulate; lateral lobes somewhat broad and rounded with the frontal margins crenulate, stained deep-mauve; mid-lobe broad, the margins crenulate or deeply toothed often to the extreme tip, the teeth minutely scabrous-denticulate; tip acute, wholly deep purple-mauve. Calli in four regular rows, very stout, clavate, the heads granular, basal calli yellow-headed; intermediate calli deep-purple or mauve; the anterior ones varying in colour, either purple, pink or white, sessile, often crowded, extending almost to the apex. Column widely winged, red-spotted, abruptly bent forward in the upper third.

FLOWERING PERIOD: Sept. to Nov.

COMMON NAME: Hooded Caladenia

DISTRIBUTION: Eastern NSW; western Vic.; Tas.

C. lyallii (Plate 226)

C. lyallii Hook.f. *Flor. N.-Z.* 1:247 (1853); A. J. Ewart *Flor. Vict.* 349 (1931), as *C. alpina*; H. M. R. Rupp *Orchids N.S.W.* 63 (1943), as *C. alpina*; J. H. Willis *Handb. Pls Vict.* 1:394 (1962); M. J. Firth *Native Orchids Tasm.* 63 (1965)

SYNONYMY: *C. alpina* R. S. Rogers in *Trans. roy. Soc. S. Aust.* 51:12 (1927)

Plant moderately robust 12–29 cm. high. Leaf elliptic-lanceolate to oblong or falco-lanceolate, suberect, sparsely hairy, ribbed, 8–22 cm. long and 5–12 mm. wide, stem often reddish, hairy, a loose or sheathing acute bract about the middle. Flowers usually one or two, rarely three, 2–3·5 cm. in diameter, white or pale pink, pedicels long and slender, the subtending bract prominent, acute, under-surface of segments of perianth minutely glandular hairy. Dorsal sepal broadly ovate, cucullate over the column, blunt at the apex; lateral sepals elliptic-lanceolate, spreading. Petals widespread, narrower than the sepals. Labellum on a short claw, broadly ovate, about 9 mm. long and 7 mm. wide, erect against the column, then recurved, obscurely trilobed; lateral lobes erect, not well defined, their margins entire, except for a few small anterior crenulations; mid-lobe shortly triangular, much recurved, dentate or serrate; lamina with transverse interrupted red or purple stripes or sometimes spotted; calli linear or golf-stick type, yellow or white, in four rows, gradually becoming sessile and irregular, extending almost to the tip; apex not very acute. Column hidden by the dorsal sepal, about 7 mm. long, dorsum red-spotted, incurved, rather widely winged. Anther incumbent, mucronate.

This species was first discovered in Vic. by A. J. Tadgell in 1921, on Mounts Bogong and Hotham. It is often very abundant at high altitudes, and in some places such as Middleton's Gap in the Grampians, Vic., it occurs in small tufts on the rock ledges and cliff faces, in other places growing in sheltered positions on the lee side of the hills. The characteristic features are the wide leaf and the exceptionally wide dorsal sepal.

FLOWERING PERIOD: Oct. to Jan.

COMMON NAME: Mountain Caladenia

DISTRIBUTION: South-eastern alps, NSW; alpine areas and Grampians, Vic.; alpine areas, Tas.; also NZ

C. dimorpha (Plate 227)

C. dimorpha R. D. FitzG. *Aust. Orchids* 1¹:+t. (1875); H. M. R. Rupp *Orchids N.S.W.* 66 (1943)

A comparatively large though slender plant 8–30 cm. high. Stem and bracts shortly hairy. Leaf linear, often long, sparsely hairy. Flowers one to three, large, white or white with pink or purplish markings, 3–3·5 cm. in diameter. Perianth segments widespread, somewhat broad, lanceolate, acute; dorsal sepal shorter than the lateral sepals, cucullate; lateral sepals up to 2 cm. long; petals narrower than the sepals. Labellum broadly ovate, sometimes spotted with red, margins entire in erect part, then fringed with numerous very regular, short clubbed calli which extend in some flowers almost to the apex; often the margins gradually becoming irregularly dentate. Calli in four rows, moderately stout, with purple, pink, yellow or white granular heads, extending in some cases almost to the tip; apex acute or somewhat obtuse. Labellum apex reddish-purple or marked with a purplish blotch. Column moderately stout, striped with red, widely winged. Anther acuminate, papillose.

FLOWERING PERIOD: Oct. and Nov.

DISTRIBUTION: Endemic in NSW where found in the central eastern tablelands

C. angustata (Plate 228, also Plate 227 Figs a–e)

C. angustata Lindl. *Gen. & Spec. orchid. Pls* 420 (1840); A. J. Ewart *Flor. Vict.* 351 (1931), as *C. testacea*; J. M. Black *Flor. S. Aust.* ed. 2:235 (1943); H. M. R. Rupp *Orchids N.S.W.* 66 (1943); J. H. Willis *Handb. Pls Vict.* 1:394 (1962), including *C. praecox*; M. J. Firth *Native Orchids Tasm.* 64 (1965)

A slender, often moderately robust, sparsely hairy plant 15–45 cm. high. Leaf narrow-linear, slightly hairy, 7–30 cm. long. Flowers one to eight, 2–3·5 cm. in diameter, on slender pedicels, white with pink or bronze markings. Lower perianth segments widely spreading, lanceolate, acute; under surface of segments often a rich bronze-brown or purplish-brown, covered with sessile glands and hairs. Dorsal sepal cucullate; lateral sepals elliptic-lanceolate; petals falcate. Labellum obscurely trilobed, occasionally well-lobed in robust specimens, often spotted red or purple; lateral lobes, when present, prominent, entire, or represented by short marginal calli; mid-lobe shortly fringed, towards the tip crenulate, sometimes prominently blotched with pink or purple, occasionally wholly yellow at the tip. Calli of the lamina usually in four rows, rather stout and short, a few sessile, especially those towards the tip, club-shaped with red, yellow or white heads. Column moderately stout, winged throughout, blotched with red. Flowers usually diffusing a strong musk-like fragrance.

C. angustata has been included in *C. testacea*, but a careful examination of the duplicate of Lindley's type (from Circular Head, Tas.), sent to me from the Royal Botanic Gardens, Kew, proves this orchid to be distinct from *C. testacea*.

The figures of *C. angustata* on Plate 227 were painted from specimens that had been collected near Bell in the Blue Mountains, NSW, and wrongly identified as *C. dimorpha*. These specimens represent the first record of the species for NSW.

Throughout its range it is sometimes remarkably abundant. It seems to prefer dry hillsides and high hilltops, which are often heavily covered with trees and scrub. The musky odour of the flowers, though pleasant at first, is apt to become somewhat nauseating because of its strength and persistence.

FLOWERING PERIOD: Sept. to Nov.

COMMON NAME: Musky Caladenia

DISTRIBUTION: Central eastern NSW; Vic.; Tas.; far south-east of SA

C. praecox (Plate 229)

C. praecox W. H. Nicholls in *Vict. Nat.* 43:156, fig. a–j (1926); H. M. R. Rupp *Orchids N.S.W.* 68 (1943); J. H. Willis *Handb. Pls Vict.* 1:395 (1962), in note

SYNONYMY: *C. testacea* var. *praecox* (W. H. Nicholls) W. H. Nicholls in *Vict. Nat.* 55:168 (1939)

A dwarf plant, usually 8–15 cm. high. Leaf narrow-linear, sparsely hairy, occasionally longer than the flowering-stem. Flowers one to four, comparatively large, 20–35 mm. in diameter, white with pink or green markings, rarely deep pink, with some green markings. Perianth segments widely spread; dorsal sepal cucullate; lateral sepals and petals narrow-lanceolate, elliptic or falcate; undersurface glandular-pubescent. Labellum obscurely trilobed, narrow, about as long as the dorsal sepal, white, sometimes pink-spotted; margins entire in erect portion, the mid-lobe deeply fringed, the fringe abruptly shorter towards the tip then crenulate to the end; marginal fringe erect, slender, white or yellow-headed; tip of labellum narrowly cuneate, often marked with a purple blotch. Calli of the lamina in four to six rows, short and stout, oblong-clavate, with yellow or white granular heads, those on the tip depressed and irregular. Column slender, narrowly winged throughout, irregularly blotched with pink. Anther with a short point.

C. praecox is often exceedingly abundant during August, on hillsides, open grasslands and in light forest. Prior to being described, this species was regarded as a form of *C. carnea*, but it differs mainly in having a cucullate dorsal sepal. It has most affinities however with *C. testacea*. [In fact, the author reduced it to a variety of the latter, but Rupp and others did not accept this change, and later re-established it as a species.—Ed.]

FLOWERING PERIOD: Aug. to Oct.

DISTRIBUTION: South-east coast, NSW; eastern and central Vic.; Tas.

C. testacea (Plate 230)

C. testacea R. Br. *Prodr. Flor. Nov. Holl.* 324 (1810); A. J. Ewart *Flor. Vict.* 352 (1931), as *C. hildae*; H. M. R. Rupp *Orchids N.S.W.* 67 (1943); J. H. Willis *Handb. Pls Vict.* 1:395 (1962)

An extremely slender, sparsely hairy plant 10–22 cm. high. Leaf narrow-linear, sparsely hairy, 8–21 cm. long. Flowers one to six, on short pedicels, 10–18 mm. in diameter. Perianth segments (except the dorsal sepal) widespread, varying in colour, but usually yellow or greenish-yellow and brown, sometimes uniformly pale green inside and red-brown towards the tips on the hairy extremity of the segments, pale greenish-white only or white with pink or mauve markings. Dorsal sepal erect, incurved, concave, acute, contracted at the base; lateral sepals elliptic-lanceolate, falcate. Petals slightly narrower than sepals, but otherwise similar. Labellum white with deep purple markings, 6–8 mm. long, on a short movable claw, narrow, obscurely trilobed, margins entire in erect part, then deeply toothed or fringed, shorter towards the tip, then crenate to the end; fringe erect, yellow or purple headed; tip broadly cuneate, wholly dark purple; calli in four rows, white, the granular heads oblong-clavate, much crowded and depressed towards the apex. Column moderately stout, upper angle broadly winged, conspicuously striped with pink. Flowers honey-scented.

FLOWERING PERIOD: Sept. to Feb., being later in alpine regions

COMMON NAME: Honey Caladenia

DISTRIBUTION: Central eastern and south-eastern NSW; eastern Vic.

C. testacea var. hildae (Plate 230)

C. testacea var. *hildae* (E. E. Pescott & W. H. Nicholls) W. H. Nicholls in *Vict. Nat.* 55:168 (1939)

SYNONYMY: *C. hildae* E. E. Pescott & W. H. Nicholls in *Vict. Nat.* 45:235, fig. a–j (1929)

Plant 12–15 cm. high, flowers 2·5 cm. in diameter, a rich golden yellow with light brown and pink markings.

Specimens of this variety were first collected at Cobungra, Vic., growing in soil which was apparently derived from an old basalt. They were described as *C. hildae* but were later reduced to a variety. They apparently owed their robust habit and rich colour to the rich soil of the habitat. Specimens of *C. testacea* growing elsewhere in the district are normal in size and colouring.

FLOWERING PERIOD: Dec.

DISTRIBUTION: Known only from Cobungra, Vic.

C. iridescens (Plate 231)

C. iridescens R. S. Rogers in *Trans. roy. Soc. S. Aust.* 44:328, t. 13 (1920); A. J. Ewart *Flor. Vict.* 350 (1931); H. M. R. Rupp *Orchids N.S.W.* 68 (1943); J. H. Willis *Handb. Pls Vict.* 1:395 (1962); M. J. Firth *Native Orchids Tasm.* 64 (1965)

A very slender plant 8–25 cm. in height. Stem often purplish, beset with very short fine hairs, a small clasping subulate bract about the middle. Leaf narrow-linear, 7–12 cm. long, occasionally longer, sparsely hirsute. Flowers one to four, a dusky red mingled with iridescent golden tints, to wholly purplish-crimson, often with green tips to the segments, occasionally the segments whitish; 2–2·5 cm. in diameter. Ovary narrow-elongated, hirsute, on a slender pedicel, subtended by a narrow acute lanceolate bract. Dorsal sepal erect, but much incurved, sometimes cucullate, spathulate-lanceolate. Lateral sepals spreading, falco-lanceolate, upper surface in some flowers a deep red, almost a claret colour, sometimes passing into a greenish-gold at the tips; lower surface dull gold, iridescent, studded with dark reddish or purplish glands. Petals narrower than the other segments, shorter than lateral sepals. Labellum ovate on a short claw, about 5 mm. long, trilobed; the lateral lobes erect, rather acute with entire margins and transverse red stripes, anteriorly merging into two or three blunt or clavate teeth; the mid-lobe rather broadly triangular, recurved, dark crimson or purple and very glandular with long clavate glandular calli on its margins; lamina between the lateral lobes entirely covered with (usually) crowded wide-headed, shortly stalked dark purple calli arranged in two or four rows, irregular or regular, often imbricate; calli becoming sessile towards the tip. Column about 6 mm. long, much incurved above, rather widely winged, marked with red. Anther pointed, incumbent; pollinia in two lamellate triangular pairs. Stigma concave, the lower margin semi-circular, the upper border passing into a viscid triangular rostellum.

The colouring of this small Caladenia is very distinctive and often unusually striking. From its closer allies *C. congesta*, *C. cucullata*, and *C. angustata*, it differs in a number of important particulars, chiefly in its smaller size, different colouring of the flowers, also in the details of the labellum, the calli of which extend almost to the extreme tip.

FLOWERING PERIOD: Sept. to Nov.

COMMON NAME: Bronze Caladenia

DISTRIBUTION: South-eastern NSW; western Vic., also South Belgrave and Healesville districts; Circular Head, Tas.

C. aphylla (Plate 232)

C. aphylla Benth. *Flor. aust.* 6:387 (1873); R. Erickson *Orchids West* ed. 2:87 (1965)

Stem slender, almost filiform, glabrous, attaining a length of 30–45 cm. Tuber large, ovoid. No leaf present at time of flowering; one or two short scarious scales at base, and sometimes a small bract higher up; the bract subtending the flowering pedicel somewhat larger. Flower solitary, slightly papillose or quite glabrous, 4–4·5 cm. in diameter, whitish or pale yellow. Sepals and petals narrow-lanceolate, tapering at the base, acutely but very shortly acuminate; dorsal sepal erect and concave. Labellum trilobed, more than half as long as the sepals, yellowish-white, mottled with red-brown and some mauve; the base contracted into a claw; lateral lobes erect, incurved, almost acute; mid-lobe longer with a recurved yellow tip, which is constricted and coloured mauve on its basal portion, the margins entire, undulate. Calli of the lamina rather long, linear-clavate, marked with mauve, the tips yellow, numerous or few, in two rows, sometimes extending beyond the lateral lobes and reaching halfway along the mid-lobe. Column winged conspicuously, mottled with red bands. Anther with a short point.

FLOWERING PERIOD: Mar. and Apr.

DISTRIBUTION: South-western WA, favouring the coastal plain

C. hirta (Plate 233)

C. hirta Lindl. in *Edwards' bot. Reg.* 23: Swan Riv. Append. lii (1840); R. Erickson *Orchids West* ed. 2:96 (1965)

SYNONYMY: *C. tenuis* R. D. FitzG. in *Gndrs' Chron.* new ser. 17:462 (1882)

Plant very hairy and often above 30 cm. high, the root system more creeping than in other species. Leaf oblong or lanceolate, 5–13 cm. long. Flowers one to three, white and pink or wholly pink. Sepals and petals 2–3 cm. long, irregularly acuminate, but the points much shorter than in *C. patersonii* and always shorter than the dilated portion. Labellum at least half as long as the sepals, ovate-oblong or ovate-lanceolate, obtuse, undivided but more or less fringed from the middle upward, contracted and erect at the base, recurved towards the end; calli linear, more or less regularly placed in four to six rows. Column winged upward. Anther with a prominent point.

[A. S. George states in *West. Aust. Nat.* 8:39 (1961) that an unpublished plate by FitzGerald of *C. tenuis* was clearly an illustration of *C. hirta*. There was no significant difference between the descriptions of these species, so *C. tenuis* becomes a synonym of *C. hirta.*—Ed.]

FLOWERING PERIOD: Aug. to Oct.

COMMON NAME: Sugar-candy Orchid

DISTRIBUTION: Common in south-western WA

C. roei (Plate 234)

C. roei Benth. *Flor. aust.* 6:383 (1873); R. Erickson *Orchids West* ed. 2:86 (1965)

A shortly hairy plant 13–20 cm. high. Leaf narrow-linear, the empty bract near the middle of stem about 1·5 cm. long and sometimes leaf-like. Flower solitary, greenish or greenish-yellow, 3–4 cm. in diameter. Sepals and petals dilated in their proximal ends, thereafter contracted into filiform or acute points; the lateral sepals with clavate points. Labellum comparatively large, on a distinct unwinged claw of about 1 mm. or less, the lateral lobes very large and broad, light coloured, not fringed; the whole labellum expanding to a breadth of about 1·3 cm.; the mid-lobe much smaller, recurved, dark coloured and denticulate or fringed with short calli; one large, or several long calli between the lateral lobes at the top of the claw, and small obtuse calli compactly crowded, or in three to four rows along the central line. Column long, incurved, broadly and shortly winged under the anther, two yellow stalked glands at the base.

It is a curious and intriguing plant, this Caladenia, with its oversized labellum. We found this species abundantly distributed over the low, granite-strewn slopes around Arrowsmith, via Narembeen. It was interesting to note the diverse character and colouring of the lip; also the sepals and petals.

FLOWERING PERIOD: Aug. to Oct.

COMMON NAME: Jack-in-the-box

DISTRIBUTION: South-western WA

C. cairnsiana (Plate 235)

C. cairnsiana F. Muell. *Fragm. Phyt. Aust.* 7:31 (1869); R. Erickson *Orchids West* ed. 2:90 (1965)

A slender wiry-stemmed hairy species 10–30 cm. high. Leaf linear, reddish, 5–12 cm. long. Flowers one or two, pale yellowish with reddish or purplish markings. Sepals and petals narrow linear, 1–1·5 cm. long, often glandular tipped at the apices, hairy on the undersurface; dorsal sepal erect and slightly recurved over the column but not always against it; lateral sepals and petals acutely and closely reflexed against the ovary. Labellum erect or nearly vertical, broadly ovate, margins entire, about same length as the sepals; claw short, elegantly marked with deep reddish or purplish divergent veins, the apex edged by a narrow dark callus border as in *C. tessellata*. Calli of the lamina in two rows, those on the claw and at the base linear-clavate, those in front thick and depressed. Column widely winged above, much curved, no glands at the base. Anther blunt, without a point.

Near Greenbushes *C. cairnsiana* was seen by the author growing plentifully in Ironstone country in association with *C. longiclavata*; near Mount Willyung in the Upper King River district it was quite as numerous on granite slopes, and Mueller records it from the 'base of the Stirling Range in basaltic valleys'. It is a very difficult orchid to locate by reason of the characteristic posture of the floral segments, the lateral sepals and petals being closely appressed against the ovary, the dorsal erect and the labellum in a more or less vertical position. The large labellum is beautifully marked.

FLOWERING PERIOD: Aug. to Oct.

COMMON NAME: Zebra Orchid

DISTRIBUTION: South-western WA, where widespread

C. discoidea (Plate 236)

C. discoidea Lindl. in *Edwards' bot. Reg.* 23: Swan Riv. Append. lii (1840); R. Erickson *Orchids West* ed. 2:95 (1965)

[Usually a very hairy plant about 30 cm. high. Leaf broadly linear or lanceolate, usually long and sometimes more than 15 cm. long. Flowers one to three, yellowish-green streaked with red. Sepals about 1 cm. long, shortly or acutely acuminate; dorsal sepal narrow, erect, incurved, and concave; lateral sepals lanceolate, somewhat falcate, spreading. Petals rather longer and narrower. Labellum not much shorter than sepals, broadly ovate or orbicular, marked with dark red diverging forked veins and fringed with rather long cilia, on a short claw; calli irregularly crowded along or near the centre, thick, obovoid or oblong, the lower ones often longer and clavate. Column narrow and incurved at the base, broadly winged in the upper half.

FLOWERING PERIOD: Aug. to Nov.

COMMON NAME: Dancing Orchid

DISTRIBUTION: Widely distributed through south-western WA—Ed.]

C. tessellata (Plates 237 and 238)

C. tessellata R. D. FitzG. *Aust. Orchids* 1²:+t. (1876); A. J. Ewart *Flor. Vict.* 345 (1931), as *C. cardiochila*; J. M. Black *Flor. S. Aust.* ed. 2:230 (1943), as *C. cardiochila*; H. M. R. Rupp *Orchids N.S.W.* 58 (1943), including *C. cardiochila*; J. H. Willis *Handb. Pls Vict.* 1:389 (1962)

SYNONYMY: *C. cardiochila* R. Tate in *Trans. roy. Soc. S. Aust.* 9:60, t. 2 (1887)

Slender plant 10–30 cm. high, hairy. Leaf linear-lanceolate, hairy, 4–12 cm. long. Flowers one or two, yellow or yellowish-green with red-brown or dark brown markings. Segments of perianth acuminate with glandular tips, not clavate. Dorsal sepal linear-lanceolate, erect, slightly incurved, 1·5–3 cm. long. Lateral sepals about same length as dorsal sepal but much wider, usually pendent, often crossed, falco-lanceolate; sometimes contracted at the base, dilated in the middle, then abruptly acuminate. Petals narrower than lateral sepals, about 3 cm. long. Labellum cordate or broad-ovate, 1–2 cm. wide and 1–1·5 cm. long, on a narrow movable claw, undivided; margin entire or almost so, with a conspicuous dark brown thickening toward the apex; rather flat, usually erect at the base then spreading with a recurved tip. Calli reddish-brown or yellow with dark divergent veins; in two or four rows; clavate and stalked towards the base; sessile, and congested towards the tip; sometimes a cluster of slender calli at the base of the lamina. Column 1–1·5 cm. long, incurved, widely winged above, the base with two yellow, sessile glands.

C. tessellata favours sandy somewhat swampy positions, often growing under shrubs in association with *C. reticulata* and *Burnettia cuneata*.

[It was formerly considered to be distinct from *C. cardiochila*. Of the two plates here, Plate 237 is referable to *C. tessellata* in the narrow sense, and Plate 238 is referable to *C. cardiochila*.—Ed.]

FLOWERING PERIOD: Sept. to Nov.

COMMON NAME: Thick-lip Spider-orchid

DISTRIBUTION: South-eastern NSW; southern and western Vic.; south-eastern SA

C. clavigera (Plate 239)

C. clavigera A. Cunn. ex Lindl. *Gen. & Spec. orchid. Pls* 422 (1840); A. J. Ewart *Flor. Vict.* 347 (1931), including *C. cordiformis*; J. M. Black *Flor. S. Aust.* ed. 2:230 (1943); H. M. R. Rupp *Orchids N.S.W.* 62 (1943); J. H. Willis *Handb. Pls Vict.* 1:388 (1962); M. J. Firth *Native Orchids Tasm.* 60 (1965)

SYNONYMY: *C. cordiformis* R. S. Rogers in *Trans. roy. Soc. S. Aust.* 44:330 (1929)

A variable plant, chiefly in regard to height of plant and size of flowers, 11–40 cm. high. Leaf linear to oblong-lanceolate, hairy. Stem hairy, erect, usually slender, a loose narrow-lanceolate bract about the middle. Flower usually solitary, yellowish with dark reddish-brown markings. Sepals sub-equal, 3–5 cm. long, wider towards the base, narrowing into fine points, usually clavate, yellowish, traversed by a prominent reddish-brown longitudinal stripe; dorsal sepal erect, incurved; lateral ones spreading horizontally or drooping. Petals similar, rarely clavate, and rather shorter. Labellum shortly clawed, more or less ovate, recurved, the lateral lobes yellowish or emerald green, rounded, entire; mid-lobe dark reddish-brown, triangular, subacute with entire or slightly irregular margins towards the base; calli linear, golf-stick type, reddish-brown, in four to six longitudinal rows along the posterior half of lamina. Column rather widely winged in upper part, two yellow oval glands at the base. Anther with a minute mucro.

FLOWERING PERIOD: Sept. to Dec.

COMMON NAME: Plain-lip Spider-orchid

DISTRIBUTION: NSW, where confined to a few localities in the south-east; southern and central Vic.; north-eastern and eastern Tas.; far south-east of SA

C. leptochila (Plate 240)

C. leptochila R. D. FitzG. in *Gdnrs' Chron.* new ser. *17*:462 (1882); A. J. Ewart *Flor. Vict.* 345 (1931); J. M. Black *Flor. S. Aust.* ed. 2:231 (1943)

A slender hairy plant 15–45 cm. high. Leaf hairy, narrow-lanceolate to oblong or elliptical-lanceolate, sheathing at the base. Flowers one or two, about 5·5 cm. in diameter, yellowish-green, marked with reddish-brown; perianth segments with a central reddish-brown stripe, spreading (with the exception of the dorsal sepal). Sepals clavate, sub-equal; dorsal sepal incurved, 2·5–3 cm. long, tapering from the base to a fine clavate point; lateral sepals dilated in basal half, thereafter constricted into fine upturned clavate points. Petals falco-lanceolate, tapering into fine non-clavate points, 2–2·5 cm. long. Labellum oblong or broad-lanceolate, 11–13 mm. long and 4·5 mm. wide, on a movable claw, undivided, dark reddish-brown; erect in lower half, thereafter recurved; margins practically entire; tip generally acute, sometimes blunt; lamina almost flat; calli sessile except near the claw, in two to four rows, rarely extending beyond the bend. Column 10–12 mm. long, retracted at base, thereafter erect, or incurved, widely winged above, more narrowly below; two sessile or short-stalked yellow calli at the base. Anther with a straight sharp point.

FLOWERING PERIOD: Oct.

COMMON NAME: Narrow-lip Spider-orchid

DISTRIBUTION: Vic. where known only from a few localities in the south; south-eastern SA

C. sigmoidea (Plate 241)

C. sigmoidea R. S. Rogers in *Trans. roy. Soc. S. Aust.* 62:12 (1938); R. Erickson *Orchids West* ed. 2:85 (1965)

An erect and rather slender species, 4–8 cm. high. Leaf linear-lanceolate, slightly hairy, usually as long as or sometimes much longer than the inflorescence, strongly three-nerved with numerous smaller veins. Stem hairy, an acute linear slender bract 1–2 cm. long near the middle. Flowers relatively large, one or two, yellowish with dark reddish-brown veinings, 2·5–3 cm. in diameter, on short slender pedicels subtended by a subulate bract 1–1·5 cm. long. Segments of perianth similar, about 1·5 cm. or more long, yellowish with a longitudinal reddish-brown median nerve, tapering to a filamentous conspicuously clavate point; dorsal sepal incurved over the column; lateral sepals projecting forward; lateral petals erect, or somewhat spreading. Labellum mobile on a distinct claw, sigmoid, yellowish, somewhat narrowly ovate when spread out, with dark red veinings; margins entire or often bidentate on each side, the tip obtusely uncinate; lamina traversed by dark red divergent and longitudinal veins, and provided in its proximal half with two parallel median rows of dark reddish fleshy calli. Column winged, elongated, slightly incurved at the apex. Anther quite blunt. Stigma semilunar, just below the anther.

FLOWERING PERIOD: Aug.

DISTRIBUTION: South-western WA, where found only in the Salmon Gums and Lake King districts

C. bicalliata (Plate 242)

C. bicalliata R. S. Rogers in *Trans. roy. Soc. S. Aust. 33*:17 (1909); J. M. Black *Flor. S. Aust.* ed. 2:233 (1943)

A slender hairy plant about 10 cm. high. Leaf very hairy, linear-lanceolate, about 6 cm. long, three-nerved. Flower solitary, cream coloured, with red veinings, pedicel shorter than the ovary. Perianth segments similar, dilated in their basal parts, then suddenly contracted into rather coarse cylindrical hairy filaments. Dorsal sepal about 2 cm. long, one-third of which is dilated, incurved over the column; the lateral sepals about 1·8 cm., one-half of which is dilated, spreading. Petals more or less spreading, gradually contracted into caudae. Labellum cream coloured, about 7 mm. long and 5 mm. wide, ovate, on a short movable claw; erect in the lower part, then recurved to a rather blunt apex; margins very shortly and bluntly serrate except the posterior one, which is entire; lamina marked by conspicuous red divergent veins; calli of the golf-stick type, in two well-defined rows, extending to within 3 mm. of the extreme tip. Column about 8 mm. long, erect, then incurved, widely winged in its upper third, narrowly below. Anther without a point.

This diminutive Caladenia is one I had long wished to see in a fresh condition. It has obvious affinities with *C. filamentosa*, possessing as it does a similar labellum, but lacking the very long filamentous points of the latter. The accompanying figures were drawn from material collected at Coffin Bay. It is, I think, our smallest spider orchid flower.

The first specimen of *C. bicalliata* was found by Mrs R. S. Rogers near Kingscote 'growing in rather sandy soil on the margin of the scrub'.

FLOWERING PERIOD: Sept.

DISTRIBUTION: SA, where known only from Kingscote on Kangaroo Island, Coffin Bay and Warooka

C. macrostylis (Plate 243)

C. macrostylis R. D. FitzG. in *Gdnrs' Chron.* new ser. *17*:462 (1882); R. Erickson *Orchids West* ed. 2:92 (1965)

A slender hairy species, about 18 cm. high. Leaf linear-lanceolate, sheathing at the base, 10–13 cm. long. Flower solitary. Perianth segments light yellow, with one to three red lines down the centre; petals 2·5–3 cm. long, lanceolate, tapering to a fine point, turned up, sometimes with a slight clavate point. Sepals slightly longer and broader, lanceolate, tapering to a fine point, with slightly clavate tips; dorsal sepal erect for three-fourths of its length. Labellum on a short claw, ovate-lanceolate, about 1·5 cm. long, yellow or light purple, veined with a deeper shade, the edges thickened for about one-third towards the point, undulate, darkly coloured, red-brown or black. Calli of the lamina dark red-brown or black, in a broad band, extending from the base to within a short distance of the point, linear, clavate, closely packed together; three or five calli at the base, linear, twice clavate. Column 1–1·3 cm. long, and rather broadly winged on each side of the stigma. Anther with a short point. Two orbicular, shortly stalked glands at the base of the column.

Dr Rogers says: 'This orchid chooses the most barren of ironstone country on which to grow. On the Upper Kalgan River a few specimens occupied a small area of ground shunned by every other living plant. At Mount Barker it was quite numerous amid scrub almost equally inhospitable.' FitzGerald found his specimens 'at St Werberg, on the edge of a swamp'. It also grows in forest country.

FLOWERING PERIOD: Sept. to Dec.

COMMON NAME: Leaping Spider

DISTRIBUTION: South-western WA, where it favours bare Ironstone country

C. ericksonae (Plate 244)

C. ericksonae W. H. Nicholls in *Vict. Nat.* 66:214, fig. E (1950); R. Erickson *Orchids West* ed. 2:90 (1965)

A very slender, shortly hairy plant 12–18 cm. high. Leaf narrow-lanceolate, hairy, channelled, about 7 cm. long; a short acuminate bract near the middle of the stem. Flower solitary, dark brown on a light ground or wholly deep blood-red. Perianth segments about equal in length, 2·5–3 cm. long, horizontally spreading or deflexed (with the exception of the dorsal one, which is erect and incurved), dilated in the lower part, the filiform points glandular-hairy. Petals projecting outward, narrower than the sepals. Labellum cordiform, mobile on a short broad claw; margins entire in the erect portion, then combed with short stout calli to the apex; apex shortly recurved; lamina boldly marked with dark crimson radial nerves. Calli in two rows, dark red-brown, the anterior ones stout, of golf-stick type, not extending beyond the bend. Column erect, incurved, 7–8 mm. long, widely winged above, almost wholly blood-red, white toward the base. Anther extremely blunt.

I have named this WA Caladenia after its discoverer, Mrs Rica Erickson, who is a very keen botanist and an artist of exceptional talent. The species is an interesting addition to the section Calonema. Though closely related to *C. reticulata*, it has affinities also with *C. cristata*. From the former it may be differentiated by the presence of hairy points to the perianth segments, and by the labellum, which is of thicker consistency, and boldly ornamentated with radial lines, similar to those in *C. cairnsiana*. From *C. cristata* it is readily distinguished by the labellum margins, which are entire in *C. cristata*, also by a very different arrangement of the calli.

FLOWERING PERIOD: Aug. and Sept.

COMMON NAME: Prisoner Orchid

DISTRIBUTION: South-western WA

C. ensata (Plate 245)

C. ensata W. H. Nicholls in *Vict. Nat.* 64:138, fig. G–I (1947)

A fairly robust hairy plant 30–45 cm. high. Leaf oblong-lanceolate, very hairy, 15–20 cm. long. Stem very hairy with a non-clasping subulate bract about the middle of stem. Flowers two to four, about 6 cm. in diameter, segments yellow, each with three longitudinal purplish lines and blotches, three-nerved, dilated in the proximal half, then contracted into long subulate, fluted sword-like points which are yellow and finely glandular. Ovary with dark glandular hairs. Dorsal sepal erect, incurved, 4–5 cm. long; lateral sepals similar, spreading and reflexed; petals shorter and narrower than the sepals, horizontally spreading or reflexed. Labellum on a short claw, somewhat oblong, apex much recurved; margins entire in the erect part, then very shortly and irregularly serrate; lamina decorated with red or purplish radial nerves and blotches; calli darkly coloured, linear, golf-stick type, densely crowded in four to six rows, and terminating just beyond the bend. Column erect, incurved, about 1·3 cm. long, widely winged on each side of stigma, with two stalked calli at the base. Anther obtuse.

This species has affinities with *C. gladiolata* from SA. It is also closely related to *C. longiclavata*, with which it may be synonymous.

FLOWERING PERIOD: Oct.

DISTRIBUTION: South-western WA, where it is confined to the King River district

C. longiclavata (Plates 246 and 247)

C. longiclavata E. Coleman in *Vict. Nat.* 46:196, fig. A–C (1930); R. Erickson *Orchids West* ed. 2:95 (1965)

A moderately robust to robust, hairy plant 15–40 cm. high. Leaf very hairy, lanceolate, 10–15 cm. long. Stem-bracts usually two, the one near the middle of the stem loosely sheathing, 1·2–3·5 cm. long. Flowers one or two, maroon and yellow. Perianth segments slightly spreading, except the dorsal sepal which is erect and incurved, yellowish with wide, deep red central stripes; sepals and petals heavily clavate for more than one-third their length; lateral sepals 3·5–4 cm. long, widely dilated for about one-third their length, scarcely spreading, often pendent; dorsal sepal same length as the lateral ones, the petals a little shorter and narrower. Labellum ovate, yellowish; apex and calli maroon; not tremulous, lacking lateral lobes as in *C. dilatata*; lateral margins pectinate except towards the base, gradually shortening into dentate or serrate margins towards the tip; apex recurved. Calli in four rows, rarely six, rather short, golf-stick type, not extending beyond the bend. Column erect, incurved, widely winged above, more narrowly below, two yellow stalked glands at the base. Anther with a short point.

C. longiclavata is an abundant species in many localities. The typical form is highly coloured and easily distinguished from all its congeners by the colour scheme alone. The first specimens of this rugged species collected by the author were seen in dense Karri country near Manjimup. They were of pale hue, the perianth widely spreading and of delicate texture, in keeping with the colour scheme so typical of flowers from dark forest glades. The typical form was observed in Oct. in Ironstone country, growing in association with other species including numerous specimens of *C. cairnsiana*.

FLOWERING PERIOD: Aug. to Nov.

COMMON NAME: Clubbed Spider-orchid

DISTRIBUTION: South-western WA

C. magniclavata (Plate 248)

C. magniclavata W. H. Nicholls in *Vict. Nat.* 64:135, fig. A–C (1947); R. Erickson *Orchids West* ed. 2:95 (1965)

A robust hairy plant, 30–35 cm. high. Leaf lamina linear to linear-lanceolate, hairy, 25–30 cm. long; a loose subulate bract about the middle of the stem. Ovary rather large, green, with fine silky hairs. Flowers one or two, 7–8 cm. in diameter. Perianth segments lanceolate, yellow to yellowish-green, with a broad crimson or purplish stripe, dilated towards the base, then contracted into a long clavate point which is yellow, with minute darkly coloured glands; dorsal sepal erect, incurved, the lamina lanceolate, 4·5–5 cm. long; lateral sepals similar to the dorsal sepal, spreading. Petals a little shorter and narrower than sepals. Labellum yellowish with reddish-purple markings, shortly clawed, ovate, the tip purplish, very dark, recurved, margins finely combed, purplish, anterior margins denticulate; lamina concave with fine divergent purplish veinings; calli in four rows, linear, golf-stick type, those towards the tip sessile. Column erect, incurved, 1–1·3 cm. long, two yellow stalked glands at the base, rather widely winged throughout, more so above. Anther with a short point.

This Caladenia bears a superficial resemblance to *C. longiclavata*, but it differs in many particulars. It is a much more robust plant, the flowers are larger and coloured differently, the labellum is smaller and more prominently pectinate, the perianth segments are more prominently clavate, and the clavate portion is, in some flowers, fully half the length of the segments. It was found growing in limited numbers in gravelly Ironstone country, amongst heavy scrub of the Jarrah forest, and reported as being in greater numbers early in Aug.

FLOWERING PERIOD: Aug. and Sept.

DISTRIBUTION: South-western WA, where known only from Lesmurdie

C. caudata (Plate 249)

C. caudata W. H. Nicholls in *Vict. Nat.* 64:231, fig. F–I (1948); M. J. Firth *Native Orchids Tasm.* 60 (1965)

A moderately robust or slender hairy plant 10–12 cm. high. Leaf lanceolate, hairy, channelled, about 9 cm. long, with a subulate bract near the middle of the stem. Flower solitary, yellowish-green with purplish and red markings, about 4 cm. in diameter (segments not spread out). Perianth segments dilated at the base, then narrowing gradually to purplish-black tail-like points, the tips very glandular, glands invading to some extent the laminal portion. Dorsal sepal 3 cm. long, erect, incurved; lateral sepals 3 cm. long, similar to the dorsal one; petals narrower and a little shorter. Labellum on a movable claw, subovate-cuneate with a tail-like, very glandular, decurved apex 6–8 mm. long; margins pectinate, more or less regular, dentate towards the tip. Calli linear, curved, some foot-like, almost black, in six rows ending at the bend. Column erect, incurved, about 1·2 cm. long, winged widely on each side of the stigma; two stalked glands at base. Anther short.

C. caudata is more closely allied to *C. reticulata* than to other species, but the stout tail-like points to all the segments are very characteristic. Outwardly it resembles also *C. echidnachila*, but in this rare form the labellum fringe is different and the points of all the segments are slender and longer.

FLOWERING PERIOD: Sept. and Oct.

DISTRIBUTION: Tas., where it is found in a few localities in the north and the south-east

C. reticulata (Plate 250)

C. reticulata R. D. FitzG. in *Gdnrs' Chron.* new ser. 17:462 (1882); A. J. Ewart *Flor. Vict.* 346 (1931); J. M. Black *Flor. S. Aust.* ed. 2:231 (1943); H. M. R. Rupp *Orchids N.S.W.* 59 (1943); J. H. Willis *Handb. Pls Vict.* 1:389 (1962); M. J. Firth *Native Orchids Tasm.* 62 (1965)

SYNONYMY: *C. fitzgeraldii* H. M. R. Rupp in *Vict. Nat.* 58:199 (1942)

A slender hairy plant 10–30 cm. high. Leaf very hairy, linear or narrow-lanceolate, channelled, 4–11 cm. long. Flowers large, usually one or two, pale yellowish-green and crimson, sometimes wholly crimson. Sepals yellowish-green with a red central stripe, usually with a clavate tip, of equal length, 3·5–6 cm. long, dilated in basal half, the upper portion filamentous; dorsal sepal erect, incurved; the lateral ones spreading. Petals lanceolate, shorter and narrower than sepals, usually not clavate, spreading, narrowing to a fine point. Labellum on a movable claw, usually yellowish with crimson markings, ovate, 12–18 mm. long, erect in the basal part; margins entire, then dentate, the teeth linear; recurved portion narrowing to a point with shortly denticulate or sometimes entire

margins; calli of the lamina fleshy, in four to six rows, crimson, golf-stick type, sometimes extending almost to the extreme tip, but the calli on the tip usually sessile. Lamina generally with crimson veins. Column 9–15 mm. high, retracted at the base, thereafter erect and incurved; widely-winged above, two usually sessile yellow calli at the base. Anther with a straight sharp point.

This Caladenia is often prolific in many places in Vic., but is a variable one in many respects. The reticulate markings on the labellum, a feature which suggested the specific name, are sometimes absent, as also is the clubbing at the points of the sepals and petals. On the other hand this latter feature may be most pronounced.

FLOWERING PERIOD: Sept. to Nov.

COMMON NAME: Veined Spider-orchid

DISTRIBUTION: South-eastern Qld; central eastern NSW; southern and central Vic.; eastern Tas.; south-eastern SA

C. reticulata var. valida (Plate 251)

C. reticulata var. *valida* W. H. Nicholls in *Vict. Nat.* 59:189 (1943)

The leaf of this variety is often very large, more so than in sturdy specimens of *C. latifolia*. Specimens often attain a height of 45 cm. with the stem 3–4 mm. thick. Flowers usually two or three, pale yellow, with the labellum tip deep red-brown; sepals strongly clavate; labellum more or less strongly reticulate-veined.

[*C. reticulata* being such a variable species, it is probably better to regard this simply as a form, rather than a named variety.—Ed.]

FLOWERING PERIOD: Sept. and Oct.

DISTRIBUTION: Vic., where it is known only from heathlands at Portland, but often in great abundance there

C. pectinata (Plate 252)

C. pectinata R. S. Rogers in *Trans. roy. Soc. S. Aust.* 44:352 (1920); R. Erickson *Orchids West* ed. 2:94 (1965)

A robust plant reaching 60 cm. or more in height. Stem hairy with one acute bract. Leaf narrow-linear, very hairy. Flowers 6–9 cm. in diameter, yellowish with reddish markings on the perianth segments and labellum. Lateral sepals spreading, dilated in their proximal ends, thereafter contracted into long and rather rigid clavate points, total length 5–7 cm., dilated part 2–3 cm., greatest breadth 5–7 mm.; a light reddish stripe down the middle of the dilated part, with often a subsidiary one on either side; dilated part almost glabrous, clubs dark and glandular. Dorsal sepal erect or slightly incurved; its proximal end dilated and concave, but narrower than in the case of the lateral sepals; points clavate; in other respects and measurements similar to the lateral sepals. Lateral petals spreading or deflexed backwards, narrow-lanceolate; yellowish with a red stripe down the centre; points very acuminate, but not clavate; 3·5–4·5 cm. long and 4–6 mm. in the widest part. Labellum on a short claw, erect in lower half with a recurved tip; yellow in posterior two-thirds with crimson or dark reddish-brown apex; ovate-oblong or broadly ovate-lanceolate, 2–3·5 cm. long when extended and 11–15 mm. wide (without fringe); lateral lobes indefinite, their margins deeply pectinate with reddish linear or filamentous calli, which are often forked or dentate at their free ends; mid-lobe triangular, or somewhat oblong with blunt tip, recurved, with shortly denticulate margins; calli arranged on the lamina in four rows, increasing to six or eight rows near the tip, light coloured and stalked near the base, crimson and almost sessile anteriorly, their apices often darker than their stalks, mostly of the golf-stick variety, not very fleshy. Column about 2 cm. high, much incurved, moderately winged below with wide triangular membranous expansion on each side near the stigma; two yellow sessile glands on anterior near the base. Anther reddish, shortly mucronate. Stigma concave, more or less circular, situated just below the anther, its upper margin projected into a small triangular rudimentary rostellum. No caudicle or gland.

This beautiful Caladenia is fairly common and apparently hybridises freely with *C. patersonii* var. *longicauda*, giving rise to perplexing intermediate forms. These hybrids generally resemble this species in coloration and in the peculiar winging of the column, but the flowers are larger and the tentacles longer and unclubbed as in the var. *longicauda*.

FLOWERING PERIOD: Sept. and Oct.

COMMON NAME: King Spider-orchid

DISTRIBUTION: WA, where generally found on the coastal plain in the south-west

C. species (Plate 253)

[There was no text for this plate, and no information on the origin of the specimen, although it probably came from WA. It is such a striking plate, however, that it is worth including, in the hope that someone will recognise it.—Ed.]

C. ferruginea (Plate 254)

C. ferruginea W. H. Nicholls in *Vict. Nat.* 64:136, fig. D–F (1947); R. Erickson *Orchids West* ed. 2:95 (1965)

A slender, very hairy plant 25–35 cm. high. Leaf lanceolate, channelled, 10–15 cm. long, a single loose subulate bract about the middle of the stem. Flowers one or two, about 6 cm. in diameter. Perianth segments almost wholly red-brown, widely spreading (except the dorsal sepal); lamina dilated, then narrowing abruptly into fine acuminate points on the petals, and shortly clavate points on the sepals. Petals a little narrower than sepals. Labellum on a movable claw, red-brown and white, broadly ovate or oblong, obscurely trilobed, 2–2·3 cm. long and 1–1·3 cm. wide (without the fringe); margins entire near the base then prominently fringed, except towards the tip where they are denticulate to the apex; lamina conspicuously marked with red-brown divergent lines and fine blotches, the tip wholly red-brown. Calli linear, golf-stick type, in six rows, extending a little beyond the bend, calli darkly coloured. Column erect, incurved, about 1·3 cm. long, widely winged on each side of the stigma, two sessile glands at the base. Anther with a short fine point.

This species was found growing in fair numbers in scrub country. Other orchids found in association were *C. patersonii*, *Thelymitra crinita* and *T. aristata*. It has affinities with *C. reticulata*, but differs in the much more prominent labellum fringe, which is in keeping with its rigidly spread, spider-like perianth segments.

FLOWERING PERIOD: Sept. and Oct.

COMMON NAME: Rusty Spider-orchid

DISTRIBUTION: WA, where confined to the Armadale–Bunbury area

C. pallida (Plates 255 and 256)

C. pallida Lindl. *Gen. & Spec. orchid. Pls* 421 (1840); J. H. Willis *Handb. Pls Vict.* 1:388 (1962); M. J. Firth *Native Orchids Tasm.* 61 (1965)

A slender hairy species 30–40 cm. high. Leaf linear-lanceolate, channelled, 12–20 cm. long; somewhat withered at flowering time.

Leaf and stem covered with very fine, soft hairs. Flowers large, one or two, usually wholly pale greenish-yellow, or yellow with either a deep red-brown or brown tip to the labellum, the last-mentioned being very rare, and sometimes with light brown marked calli on the lamina and fringe. Perianth segments regularly brief, rigidly spreading, the lamina broad-lanceolate to lanceolate, contracted into rather brief, often thickened caudate points, very rarely clavate. Sepals 3·5–5 cm. long, the dorsal one erect, incurved over the column. Petals similar but shorter and narrower than the sepals, the minute, not very crowded glands on the segments (at the tips) somewhat dome-shaped and quite unlike those in *C. reticulata* and *C. patersonii*. Labellum on a distinct movable claw, broadly ovate, undivided, the basal half erect, usually with entire margins; anterior portion recurved, somewhat acute, almost wholly red-brown in some localities, the marginal fringe long, gradually becoming short and tooth-like to the extreme apex; anterior margins sometimes quite entire; marginal fringe composed of irregular-tipped, recurved calli. Calli of the lamina in four to six rows, of irregular golf-stick shape, or club-like, rarely extending beyond the bend. Column erect, incurved, widely winged above, narrowly below, 12–15 mm. high, two shortly stalked, golden calli at the base. Anther with a short point.

FLOWERING PERIOD: Nov. to Jan.

COMMON NAME: Summer Spider-orchid

DISTRIBUTION: Eastern and southern Vic.; Tas. where scattered through the north and east

C. pumila (Plate 257)

C. pumila R. S. Rogers in *Trans. roy. Soc. S. Aust.* 46:152 (1922); A. J. Ewart *Flor. Vict.* 351 (1931); J. H. Willis *Handb. Pls Vict.* 1:388 (1962)

A very hairy plant 5–15 cm. high. Leaf 6–8 cm. long, linear or oblong-lanceolate, clasping at the base. Stem rather stout, with a large free acute bract close to that subtending the terminal pedicel. Flower solitary, white, sometimes with pink markings on the perianth segments; perianth segments spreading, lanceolate, nearly equal in length, 3·5–4 cm. long, not contracted into filaments, but finely acuminate, with (usually) non-clavate points, rarely glandular; dorsal sepal erect, incurved. Labellum white with narrow pink margins, obscurely trilobed, a few pink splashes on the lateral lobes, ovate, somewhat blunt at the apex, about 1·7 cm. long; lower half erect with entire margins, thereafter recurved with finely serrulate or crenulate margins, the lamina flattened transversely; calli pink, narrowly linear in four to six rows, ending near the middle. Column incurved, about as long as the labellum, finely speckled with pink, widely winged in its upper half. Anther shortly mucronate. Stigma circular. Pollinia in two pairs.

This species is very localised in its distribution and is known only from its original habitat, where it grows in association with other terrestrial species such as *C. dilatata*, *Thelymitra macmillanii*, *T. carnea*, etc. It was discovered by Miss B. Pilloud in 1922. *C. pumila* is easily distinguished from other somewhat similar forms. The pinkish-white, spider-like flower seems rather large, owing to the shortness of the stem, yet the segments of the perianth are comparatively short. But the labellum shows the most important characteristics, the margins often quite entire throughout. The tubers are small and naked, and above them are often numerous remains of withered tubers, interwoven through which are the fine rootlets of grasses growing in the vicinity.

FLOWERING PERIOD: Sept.

DISTRIBUTION: Vic., where known only from Bannockburn

C. filamentosa (Plate 258)

C. filamentosa R. Br. Prodr. Flor. Nov. Holl. 324 (1810); A. J. Ewart Flor. Vict. 351 (1931); J. M. Black Flor. S. Aust. ed. 2:232 (1943); H. M. R. Rupp Orchids N.S.W. 62 (1943); J. H. Willis Handb. Pls Vict. 1:386 (1962); R. Erickson Orchids West ed. 2:90 (1965); M. J. Firth Native Orchids Tasm. 61 (1965)

A very slender shortly hairy plant 15–40 cm. high. Leaf narrow-linear, shortly hairy, 7–18 cm. long, a loose subulate bract about the middle of stem. Flowers one to four, greenish-white, red or deep-crimson, sometimes yellow and brown. Perianth segments dilated in their basal fourth, thereafter produced into long hairy filaments. Dorsal sepal erect, incurved, about 5 cm. long but up to 12 cm. long in WA specimens; lateral sepals spreading, as long as the dorsal one. Petals spreading, a little shorter and narrower than the sepals. Labellum ovate or oblong, about 6 mm. long and 3 mm. wide, but much larger in some WA specimens, on a short claw, erect against the column with entire margins; anterior margins shortly serrate with stout calli, occasionally with short linear calli, thereafter recurved; margins near the tip sometimes entire, thick and sinuous, the tip more or less acute; lamina white, usually marked with divergent veins or almost wholly crimson; calli in two to four rows, usually closely set and extending to about the bend, short, thick and fleshy with a tendency to become imbricate, rarely linear. Column about 7 mm. to 2 cm. long, with wide hatchet-like wings above, and less widely winged below. Anther without a point or the point very short.

In Vic., as elsewhere throughout its range, C. filamentosa is a very polymorphic species. Often it occurs in compact tufts, the underground systems entwined; when in bloom these tufts are a striking picture of floral daintiness. In WA some of the flowers are large, and the colouring varies considerably. Though occasionally there is some degree of variation in the shape of the labellum and in the number of rows of calli, etc. it is doubtful if the differences are sufficiently pronounced to warrant specific or even varietal distinction.

C. dorrienii Domin, a species from WA, is possibly a form of C. filamentosa.

FLOWERING PERIOD: July to Oct.

COMMON NAME: Daddy-long-legs

DISTRIBUTION: South-eastern Qld; NSW; Vic.; St Helens, Tas.; Kangaroo Island and Monarto South, SA; south-western WA

C. filamentosa var. tentaculata (Plate 258)

C. filamentosa var. tentaculata R. S. Rogers in J. M. Black Flor. S. Aust. ed. 1:138 (1922); J. M. Black Flor. S. Aust. ed. 2:232 (1943); J. H. Willis Handb. Pls Vict. 1:386 (1962); R. Erickson Orchids West ed. 2:90 (1965)

SYNONYMY: C. tentaculata R. Tate in Trans. roy. Soc. S. Aust. 12:130 (1889), non Schlechter (1847)

This variety is morphologically identical with the typical, but has cream or yellowish flowers with reddish markings.

DISTRIBUTION: Western Vic.; south-eastern SA; south-western WA

C. patersonii (Plate 259)

C. patersonii R. Br. Prodr. Flor. Nov. Holl. 324 (1810); A. J. Ewart Flor. Vict. 347 (1931); J. M. Black Flor. S. Aust. ed. 2:232 (1943); H. M. R. Rupp Orchids N.S.W. 59 (1943); J. H. Willis Handb. Pls Vict. 1:387 (1962); R. Erickson Orchids West ed. 2:94 (1965); M. J. Firth Native Orchids Tasm. 61 (1965)

A hairy species 20–40 cm. high. Leaf hairy, oblong to linear-lanceolate, sometimes short, 10–20 cm. long. Flowers large, but very variable in size, usually solitary, occasionally two or four, generally white or creamy with dark points on the perianth segments and labellum, more rarely crimson or yellow, yellowish-green and brown, often 10–20 cm. in diameter. Perianth segments spreading, the dorsal sepal erect or incurved over the column, the lower part dilated, then produced into a long tentacular point 4–10 cm. long; lateral sepals similar but spreading and drooping, rather longer, with a wider and longer dilated portion. Petals shorter, gradually tapering to fine points. Labellum 1·5–3 cm. long when extended, usually with a purple or crimson tip and calli; ovate-lanceolate, on a short claw, undivided; the basal half commonly light coloured, erect, with acutely toothed margins, anterior part recurved, generally purple or crimson, the margins bluntly toothed or serrate with a more or less acute tip; calli of lamina rarely extending beyond the bend, linear-golf-stick in the typical form, in four to eight rows. Column incurved, 12–20 mm. long; winged narrowly in lower part, widely above; two yellow sessile calli at the base. Anther pointed.

An extremely variable species throughout its wide distribution. At any one locality it is difficult to find two plants that are exactly alike.

FLOWERING PERIOD: Aug. to Nov.

COMMON NAME: Common Spider-orchid

DISTRIBUTION: South-eastern Qld; eastern NSW; Vic.; northern and eastern Tas.; SA; south-western WA

C. patersonii var. arenaria (Plate 260)

C. patersonii var. arenaria (R. D. FitzG.) W. H. Nicholls in Vict. Nat. 59:189 (1943); H. M. R. Rupp Orchids N.S.W. 60 (1943), as C. arenaria; J. H. Willis Handb. Pls Vict. 1:387 (1962), as C. arenaria, in note

SYNONYMY: C. arenaria R. D. FitzG. Aust. Orchids 1⁷:+t. (1882)

Plant up to 34 cm. high. Leaf linear or linear-lanceolate, densely clothed with very short fine hairs, almost blanket-like. Flowers one or two. Sepals 7 cm. long. Petals 5·5 cm. long. The colour a light biscuit-yellow with a touch of grey; the markings confined to obscure reddish lines, chiefly on the petals and on the reverse of the perianth segments; the long caudae dark reddish with minute glands. Labellum margins crenulate or runcinate. (FitzGerald describes the labellum margins as crenate, but they may be referred to much better as runcinate. They are very regular and extend to the extreme apex, and each is marked with a dark coloured collar-like band. These features are alone sufficient to differentiate this form from others.) Calli in six rows, golf-stick type, varying in degrees of stoutness, those towards the base longest. Column stoutly winged, marked sparingly with minute longitudinal red blotches, two conspicuous sessile yellow glands at base.

This attractive Spider-orchid has been plentiful in the Portland district, Vic., from Oct. to Dec. The individual blooms are not consistently very large as figured herewith, or by FitzGerald, and the colour in the Portland flowers varies from pale yellowish to a beautiful light olive-green. The labellum margins do not always have the neat saw-edge fringe. Indeed they vary from this to those long calli-combings which are often quite a feature of the larger specimens of C. patersonii.

[This variety differs from typical C. patersonii mainly in its general greyish flowers. Although placed here as a variety of C. patersonii, it is sometimes regarded as a distinct species.—Ed.]

FLOWERING PERIOD: Sept. to Dec.

DISTRIBUTION: South-eastern NSW and southern Vic., but nowhere common

C. patersonii var. longicauda (Plate 261)

C. patersonii var. *longicauda* (Lindl.) R. S. Rogers in *Trans. roy. Soc. S. Aust.* 44:351 (1920); R. Erickson *Orchids West* ed. 2:94 (1965)

SYNONYMY: *C. longicauda* Lindl. in *Edwards' bot. Reg. 23*: Swan Riv. Append. lii, t. 8 fig. A (1840)

A robust plant reaching 75 cm. in height. Flowers up to 25 cm. in diameter, white; perianth segments with tails covered with glandular hairs. Labellum ovate-oblong, apex obtuse, lateral margins with long combings as far as middle, then margins serrate to the apex. Calli linear, in four to six rows.

This is the largest and one of the most beautiful Caladenias.

FLOWERING PERIOD: Sept. and Oct.

DISTRIBUTION: South-western WA

C. patersonii var. magnifica (Plate 262)

C. patersonii var. *magnifica* W. H. Nicholls in *Vict. Nat.* 52:167, fig. A–C[1] (1936); J. H. Willis *Handb. Pls Vict.* 1:387 (1962), in note

A fairly robust plant about 30 cm. high. Flower solitary, large; the perianth segments yellow, generously streaked and speckled with crimson, the filiform points glandular, purplish-black; sepals and petals about equal in length, up to 10 cm.; the labellum oblong-cuneate, irritable on a broad crimson claw, almost wholly purplish-black; the lateral lobes densely veined, marginal fringe long and recurved; calli in six to eight rows extending to just beyond the bend; mid-lobe thick and fleshy, often circinate, very long; margins undulate-crisped. Column yellow, richly marked with crimson.

This is a particularly attractive orchid, recalling the var. *longicauda* from WA. It was first collected at a locality called 'Rising Shrine', where it grew in alluvial soil.

FLOWERING PERIOD: Oct. and Nov.

DISTRIBUTION: Vic., where known only from Clydesdale

C. patersonii var. suaveolens (Plate 263)

C. patersonii var. *suaveolens* W. H. Nicholls in *Vict. Nat.* 57:83 (1940); J. H. Willis *Handb. Pls Vict.* 1:387 (1962), in note

A comparatively robust hairy plant 15–30 cm. high. Leaf 10–12 cm. long. Flowers one to three, large, pale olive-green with very deep markings of intense chocolate-brown, restricted in the main to the long gland-covered filaments. Sepals 5–8 cm. long. Petals 4–7 cm. long. Labellum as in the typical form. Flowers very fragrant.

This variety is distinguished by its brownish-green exceptionally fragrant flowers.

FLOWERING PERIOD: Sept. to Nov.

DISTRIBUTION: Vic., where confined to Portland district

C. echidnachila (Plate 264)

C. echidnachila W. H. Nicholls in *Proc. roy. Soc. Tasm.* 1932:13, t. 6 fig. A–G (1933); M. J. Firth *Native Orchids Tasm.* 60 (1965)

A slender moderately hairy species with the habit of *Caladenia patersonii*. Leaf hairy, linear-lanceolate, channelled. Flowers one or two, yellowish with crimson veinings, and dark filamentous glandular filaments to the segments; filaments 4–5 cm. long. Ovary

covered with dense gland-tipped hairs. Lateral sepals and petals narrow-lanceolate, spreading, pendent, with three narrow longitudinal central lines; sepals and petals about equal in length; petals narrower than the sepals; dorsal sepal erect, incurved. Labellum 3·5–4 cm. long, erect on a small movable claw, ovate-lanceolate, acuminate, yellowish with pale diffused crimson veinings; tip wholly dark crimson, lower part of lamina with entire margins, then deeply fringed; anterior margins serrulate; apex produced into a long, tapering filamentous-glandular process, twice as long as the broad portion of lamina; calli fleshy, slender, clavate, golf-stick type, in six rows; forward calli short and stout, not extending beyond the bend; five conspicuous longitudinal ridges continuing from between the rows of calli towards the tip. Column erect, incurved, about 1·3 cm. long, widely winged above; two yellow sessile glands at the base; anther with a short point.

This interesting species is closely related to *C. patersonii*, but differs from it, and also from all other closely-related species, chiefly in having a long filamentous apex to the labellum.

FLOWERING PERIOD: Oct. and Nov.

COMMON NAME: Spiny-tongued Caladenia

DISTRIBUTION: Endemic in Tas., where found in the north and the east

C. dilatata (Plate 265)

C. dilatata R. Br. *Prodr. Flor. Nov. Holl.* 325 (1810); A. J. Ewart *Flor. Vict.* 346 (1931); J. M. Black *Flor. S. Aust.* ed. 2:232 (1943); H. M. R. Rupp *Orchids N.S.W.* 60 (1943); J. H. Willis *Handb. Pls Vict.* 1:385 (1962); R. Erickson *Orchids West* ed. 2:93 (1965); M. J. Firth *Native Orchids Tasm.* 59 (1965)

A moderately robust or slender plant 15–45 cm. high, hairy. Leaf very hairy, oblong to elliptical-lanceolate, often rather wide, 5–12 cm. long. Flower solitary, often 10 cm. in diameter, prevailing tints green, yellow, and maroon. Perianth segments all spreading except dorsal sepal, yellowish-green with red central stripe; sepals often clavate, subequal; petals narrower and shorter, rarely clavate. Dorsal sepal erect, lower third dilated, thereafter contracted into a filiform, often clubbed point, 5–5·5 cm. long; lateral sepals similar, the basal part deflexed, the points thereafter spreading and sometimes crossed. Petals falco-lanceolate, gradually tapering into fine points, 3–4 cm. long. Labellum maroon, green, and yellowish-white, tremulous on a movable claw; trilobed, somewhat ovate, 2–3 cm. wide; recurved about the middle; the lateral lobes green, erect, their side margins entire, their anterior margins deeply combed or fringed; mid-lobe recurved, widely lanceolate, margins toothed or serrate with maroon acute tip; calli maroon, golf-stick type, in four rows hardly extending beyond the bend, those towards the base large, thick and fleshy, the others small and linear. Column much incurved, about 15 mm. long, widely winged in the upper part, more or less constricted towards the base; two yellow calli at the base. Anther with a sharp point.

C. dilatata is probably our best-known Spider-orchid, occurring abundantly not only on the sandy areas of the coastal districts, but also far inland to the timbered hills, where often very fine specimens, sometimes two-flowered, may be found. The finest examples seen by the author, however, came from the Sandringham district, in Vic. Albino (really semi-albino) flowers are not uncommon.

FLOWERING PERIOD: Aug. to Jan., being later in Tas.

COMMON NAME: Green-comb Spider-orchid

DISTRIBUTION: South-eastern Qld; NSW; Vic.; northern and eastern Tas.; south-eastern SA; south-western WA

C. dilatata var. concinna (Plate 265)

C. dilatata var. *concinna* H. M. R. Rupp in *Proc. Linn. Soc. N.S.W.* 53:554, fig. 4 (1928); J. M. Black *Flor. S. Aust.* ed. 2:232 (1943); H. M. R. Rupp *Orchids N.S.W.* 60 (1943); J. H. Willis *Handb. Pls Vict.* 1:385 (1962), in note

This variety differs from the typical in its dwarf size, shorter non-caudiform perianth segments, and very shortly-toothed or almost entire lateral margins of the labellum.

FLOWERING PERIOD: Aug. and Sept.

DISTRIBUTION: Central-southern NSW; northern SA; Bicheno, Tas.; perhaps northern and western Vic., where some specimens close to this variety have been found. [The specimens from Greensborough, Plate 265, Figs **e** and **f**, are unlikely to be the var. *concinna*, probably being an abnormal form.—Ed.]

C. dilatata × patersonii (Plate 266)

This fine Spider-orchid is distributed throughout most parts of Vic. It appears to be a well-established form and during bounteous seasons it is always plentiful. Albino forms have been collected in the Portland district. It combines the features of both parents, and probably occurs in states other than Vic.

C. radiata (Plate 267)

C. radiata W. H. Nicholls in *Vict. Nat.* 65:267, fig. A–E (1949); R. Erickson *Orchids West* ed. 2:94 (1965)

A slender hairy plant 15–30 cm. high. Stem blotched red. Leaf hairy, narrow-lanceolate, 12–18 cm. long. Flower solitary, 7–9 cm. in diameter, green with reddish and deep maroon markings. Perianth segments rather narrow, green, with three fused reddish longitudinal stripes; dorsal sepal erect, incurved, dilated at the base, narrow-lanceolate, filiform with a clavate point, 6–7 cm. long; lateral sepals similar but wider towards the base, the filiform indefinite clavate points often crossed at the tips; petals similar to the sepals, 4–5 cm. long, horizontally spreading, not clavate. Labellum large, trilobed, green with a deep maroon tip, the tip recurved, cordiform on a broad movable crimson claw, erect against the column, margins prominently fringed or deeply combed from the extreme base to the recurved tip, the fringe filiform and radiating outward; lateral lobes green, the mid-lobe deep maroon; calli in four rows, deep maroon, linear, of golf-stick type, not extending beyond the bend. Column incurved, 1·5–2 cm. long, widely winged, more widely above, two stalked, yellow glands at the base; anther with a prominent point.

This notable addition to the *Orchidaceae* was found growing in water six inches deep, on the swampy areas a few miles west from Yarloop, and at Pinjarra, in association with *C. pectinata. C. radiata* has affinities with *C. lobata* and *C. dilatata*, but differs from both in the following important particulars: smaller stature; a smaller, more perfectly fringed labellum, with long fimbriae to the extreme base; a different column and different perianth segments. The only other Caladenia with such a perfectly fringed labellum is *C. plicata*, a comparatively short-segmented species with folded tip to the labellum.

FLOWERING PERIOD: Oct.

DISTRIBUTION: South-western WA

C. lobata (Plate 268)

C. lobata R. D. FitzG. in *Gdnrs' Chron.* new ser. 17:461 (1882); R. Erickson *Orchids West* ed. 2:93 (1965)

A moderately robust or slender hairy plant, 25–45 cm. high. Leaf oblong-lanceolate, sheathing at the base, very hairy, 12–15 cm. long, a loose subulate bract about 3 cm. long near the middle of stem. Flowers one or two, but usually solitary, large, yellowish or yellowish-green with red markings. Dorsal sepal erect, incurved, clavate, 6–8 cm. long. Lateral sepals sharply curved upward, widely dilated in the basal half; longer than the dorsal sepal, the tips clavate. Petals shorter than sepals, dilated in the basal portion, then narrowing into fine filamentous points. Labellum over 3 cm. long and 2·5–3·5 cm. wide, on a long narrow tremulous claw, trilobed, the mid-lobe deep maroon, lanceolate, acute, reflexed; margins denticulate; much inflated at the base; lateral lobes green, narrow, acute, fringed with long, linear calli; the calli of the lamina linear, very darkly coloured, and crowded for about one-third of the labellum in two rows, which unite into one towards the base. Column 2–2·5 cm. high, erect and curved near the anther, the wings dilated into peculiar lobes, similar to those in *Drakaea*, near the centre of the column, no glands at the base. Anther with a short, sharp point.

At Yarloop this beautiful Caladenia was found growing in sandy soil, the flowers much smaller than those seen near Waterloo, where it grew in abundance in very hard clayey soil. These specimens were just as I have figured them. No wonder FitzGerald remarked that this 'is the largest and in every way the finest of what are known as Spider-orchids'. *C. patersonii* var. *longicauda* is however the largest species known, though *C. lobata* excels it in beauty.

FLOWERING PERIOD: Sept. and Oct.

COMMON NAME: Butterfly Orchid

DISTRIBUTION: South-western WA

C. integra (Plate 269)

C. integra E. Coleman in *Vict. Nat.* 49:246, cum icon. (1933); R. Erickson *Orchids West* ed. 2:93 (1965)

A hairy terrestrial 35–40 cm. high. Leaf broadly lanceolate or lanceolate, very hairy, 10–20 cm. long. Stem erect, with two conspicuous bracts 1–3 cm. long. Flower large, solitary; perianth segments cream and green, the central portions longitudinally suffused with red; sepals widely dilated for nearly half their length, the apices clubbed; dorsal sepal erect, then more or less incurved or reflexed, 5–9 cm. long; the lateral ones longer, often crossed, and falcate, curved upward on each side of the labellum; petals narrowly lanceolate, about 4·5 cm. long and about 3 mm. wide towards the base, then gradually narrowing to fine filiform points. Labellum trilobed, tremulous on a short, narrow claw; lateral lobes somewhat erect; green or tawny-green, delicately veined with red, apex deep velvety-maroon; margins entire, the apex obscurely dentate; calli clubbed, tall at the base, short, fleshy and crowded for less than half the length of the lamina, diminishing into two or more irregular rows, a few only extending as far as the mid-lobe. Column incurved, widely winged in the upper half; margins of the lower half more or less crenulate; no glands at the base. Anther broad, blunt, mucronate.

C. integra was found by the author growing on the crest of the Mount Bakewell range. It was abundant in thick, rather tall scrub and flourished under the most arid conditions. These specimens were taller and bore larger flowers than those originally described by Mrs Coleman. *C. integra* is a most elegant Spider-orchid.

FLOWERING PERIOD: Sept. and Oct.

COMMON NAME: Smooth-lipped Spider-orchid

DISTRIBUTION: South-western WA

23 Adenochilus

Adenochilus Hook.f. *Flor. N.-Z.* 1:246 (1853)

Small, slender, glabrous terrestrial herbs with fleshy rhizomes. Leaf solitary, ovate to cordate, either sessile on the flowering stem or on a long petiole arising from the rhizome. Flower solitary, with a subtending sheathing bract well below the ovary, the bract usually furnished between its margins at the base with a conspicuous filament, spathulate at the apex. Dorsal sepal broad but acute, more or less cucullate. Lateral sepals narrower, acuminate, and longer. Petals narrower and shorter than the sepals. Labellum on a claw, trilobed, the surface covered with calli except towards the tip; the lateral lobes erect. Column erect, widely winged, the wings higher than the anther. Anther erect; pollinia eight, granular.

A genus consisting of two species, one in NSW and the other in NZ.

A. nortonii (Plate 270)

A. nortonii R. D. FitzG. *Aust. Orchids 1²*:+t. (1876); H. M. R. Rupp *Orchids N.S.W.* 70 (1943)

A slender very delicate plant 10–25 cm. high, arising from a creeping rhizome. Leaf about 3 cm. long, on a slender petiole 3–8 cm. long; when cauline almost half-way up the stem, which in its lower parts is usually lightly spotted with red. Flower white, 1–2 cm. in diameter. Sepals and petals with a few short cilia on the margins, under surface covered with minute reddish glands. Labellum marked with red, a band of long clavate yellow and white calli down the centre and a few smaller ones on the side lobes. Column and wings spotted red; wings irregularly crenulate-dentate on top. Stigma broadly cordate or nearly circular.

A. nortonii grows in wet dripping cavelets and in sphagnum moss in the mountains at about 3,000 ft. altitude.

FLOWERING PERIOD: Nov. and Dec.

DISTRIBUTION: Endemic in NSW, where found only in the Blue Mountains and the Barrington Tops

24 Elythranthera

Elythranthera (Lindl.) A. S. George in *West Aust. Nat.* 9:6 (1963)

[A genus closely allied to *Caladenia* and *Glossodia*. Terrestrial herbs with small tubers. Leaf solitary, basal, lanceolate, glandular-hairy. Flowers one to four, pink or purple, inner surface shining, outer surface spotted, on an erect scape. Perianth segments more or less equal, oblong-lanceolate, spreading. Labellum membranous, re-curved or sigmoid towards the apex, glabrous, sessile; two calli at the base, hinged and individually movable. Column erect, with lateral wings extended to form a hood over the anther. Stigma reniform.

A genus of two species, confined to WA. Previously the genus *Glossodia* was believed to extend to the west, although past botanists thought that these western species were anomalous in *Glossodia*. After examining and comparing fresh specimens of the eastern and western species, A. S. George concluded that the differences were sufficiently important to warrant placing the western species in a separate genus. See his discussion in *West. Aust. Nat.* 9:3–9 (1963).—Ed.]

E. brunonis (Plate 271)

E. brunonis (Endl.) A. S. George in *West. Aust. Nat.* 9:7 (1963); R. Erickson *Orchids West* ed. 2:77 (1965)

SYNONYMY: *Glossodia brunonis* Endl. *Nov. Stirp.* 16 (1839)

A very glandular-hairy plant 15–30 cm. high. Leaf narrow-lanceolate, 2·5–8 cm. long, glandular-hairy, green, purplish towards base. Flowers one to three, upper surface of perianth purple, shining; under surface lighter, prominently purple-blotched. Sepals and petals 12–20 mm. long, spreading, oblong to oblong-lanceolate; dorsal sepal erect, the apex recurved; lateral sepals and petals somewhat falcate. Labellum inconspicuous, white or white flushed or purple marked towards the base, abruptly recurved in its anterior third, shorter than the column; lamina lanceolate, or linear, entire, without calli, but at its base two long, thick, linear, obtuse calli, often as long as the lamina, sometimes united at the base, erect against the column. Column half as long as sepals, with a broad wing produced beyond the anther into a concave hood. Anther case pubescent, shortly acuminate.

FLOWERING PERIOD: Aug. to Dec.

COMMON NAME: Purple Enamel-orchid

DISTRIBUTION: South-western WA, a widespread and common species, particularly on the coastal plain and on sandplains

E. emarginata (Plates 272 and 273)

E. emarginata (Lindl.) A. S. George in *West. Aust. Nat.* 9:7 (1963); R. Erickson *Orchids West* ed. 2:77 (1965)

SYNONYMY: *Glossodia emarginata* Lindl. *Gen. & Spec. orchid.* Pls 424 (1840); *G. intermedia* R. D. FitzG. in *Gdnrs' Chron.* new ser. 17:462 (1882)

A slender or moderately robust softly hairy plant 12–30 cm. high. Leaf narrow-lanceolate or lanceolate, softly hairy, the hairs short and glandular, 6–10 cm. long, stem-bracts acute, two, including the one subtending the lowest floral pedicel. Flowers one to four, 3–4 cm. in diameter, rose-pink, spotted underneath. Perianth segments highly polished, oblong-lanceolate. Labellum incon-spicuous, linear or oblong-linear, whitish, blotched and otherwise marked with rose-purple, the lamina re-complicate about the middle, very obtuse or truncate and usually emarginate at the apex; basal calli or appendages linear, slightly clavate and almost as long as the labellum. Column with a hood-shaped wing extending beyond the anther, about 1 cm. long.

[The plant formerly known as *Glossodia intermedia* is now regarded as a form of *E. emarginata*. Plate 272 is referable to *G. emarginata* and Plate 273 to *G. intermedia.*—Ed.]

FLOWERING PERIOD: Aug. to Dec.

COMMON NAME: Pink Enamel-orchid

DISTRIBUTION: South-western WA, most common in swampy soils on the coastal plain or clay and granite soils in the forests

25 Glossodia

Glossodia R. Br. *Prodr. Flor. Nov. Holl.* 325 (1810)

Terrestrial herbs, more or less hairy, growing from small under-ground tubers. Leaf solitary, radical, oblong or lanceolate, emerging from within a scarious sheath close to the ground. Flowers one or two, blue or purple, on an erect scape with a sheathing bract at or near the middle and a similar bract under each pedicel. Perianth segments nearly equal, spreading. Labellum almost sessile, movable on a short claw, undivided, margin entire, its lamina without glands, calli or plates, but at its base two (sometimes fused) linear clubbed calli or appendages erect against the column, and from half to nearly its whole length. Column erect, incurved, two-winged. Anther erect, terminal, two-celled, the outer valves broad, the inner much smaller, the connective produced into a small point. Pollinia four, lamellate, unconnected with the rostellum, granular.

A genus of two species which are confined to eastern Australia.

G. major (Plate 274)

G. major R. Br. *Prodr. Flor. Nov. Holl.* 326 (1810); A. J. Ewart *Flor. Vict.* 342 (1931); J. M. Black *Flor. S. Aust.* ed. 2:236 (1943); H. M. R. Rupp *Orchids N.S.W.* 70 (1943); J. H. Willis *Handb. Pls Vict.* 1:396 (1962); M. J. Firth *Native Orchids Tasm.* 55 (1965)

A slender hairy plant 10–30 cm. high. Leaf oblong to oblong-lanceolate, hairy, 3–10 cm. long and 1–2 cm. wide. Flowers one or two, usually purple or mauve, rarely white. Perianth segments spreading, subequal, 20–25 mm. long, rarely longer, their bases white with purple dots, elliptic-lanceolate, not very acute, outer surface light coloured and glandular-hairy. Labellum sessile, on a contracted base, ovate-lanceolate, usually 10–11 mm. long and 5 mm. wide; the posterior part white and pubescent; at first erect, but soon recurved forward, dilated laterally into two convexities or bosses with a furrow between them; the anterior half purple, glabrous, margins entire; a large purple sigmoid linear appendage with a broad fleshy-yellow bilobed head at the extreme base, erect against the column. Column erect in its lower part, incurved above, 9–10 mm. long; broadly winged throughout, especially so in its upper part. Anther with an acute point. Flowers scented.

This is often a very common species in scrub or lightly timbered country, where it may form sheets of colour. The finest examples I have ever seen were found on the elevated levels of the Brisbane Ranges in the spring of 1933. The flowers, one or two, were up to 7 cm. in diameter.

FLOWERING PERIOD: Aug. to Nov.

COMMON NAME: Wax-lip Orchid, or Parson-in-the-pulpit

DISTRIBUTION: South-eastern Qld; eastern NSW; Vic.; Tas.; south-eastern SA

G. minor (Plate 275)

G. minor R. Br. *Prodr. Flor. Nov. Holl.* 326 (1810); A. J. Ewart *Flor. Vict.* 343 (1931); H. M. R. Rupp *Orchids N.S.W.* 70 (1943); J. H. Willis *Handb. Pls Vict.* 1:396 (1962)

A small slender hirsute species normally 6–14 cm. high, similar in general appearance to *G. major* but smaller in all its parts. Leaf lanceolate, with a small sheathing, green or pinkish bract about the middle of stem. Flower solitary, rarely two, mauve, occasionally pure white, 2–3 cm. in diameter. Sepals and petals oblong-lanceolate, about equal in length and width. Labellum about one-third the length of sepals, broad, biconvex and pubescent with white hairs or papillae in the lower half, the spreading upper half triangular, acute, flat, glabrous, the basal calli or appendages two, linear, flattened, clavate at the end, rather shorter than the column, very shortly united at the base. Column nearly as long as the labellum, broadly winged but the wing not produced on the anther. Pollinia four.

An attractive little species, very numerous in the majority of its haunts. It is often found in the company of *G. major*, and intermediate forms are not uncommon. Its small stature, combined with the distinct calli, and differences in the labellum and column, separate it from its larger sister.

FLOWERING PERIOD: July to Nov.

COMMON NAME: Small Wax-lip Orchid

DISTRIBUTION: South-eastern Qld; coastal regions of NSW; far eastern Vic.

26   *Corybas*

Corybas Salisb. *Parad. lond.* t. 83 (1805)

SYNONYMY: *Corysanthes* R. Br. *Prodr. Flor. Nov. Holl.* 328 (1810)

Dwarf terrestrial herbs with small underground tubers, and a single ovate-cordate, orbicular or reniform leaf with a scarious sheathing bract below it. Flower solitary, sessile within the leaf or very shortly pedicellate, with a small subtending bract usually close to the leaf. Pedicel elongated in the fruiting stage. Dorsal sepal erect, very much incurved and concave, hood-shaped or contracted into a stipe; lateral sepals and petals small, linear, sometimes minute. Labellum erect under the galea, broadly tubular, the margin of the oblique orifice either shortly recurved and denticulate, or produced into a large concave denticulate or fringed lamina closely reflexed. Column short, erect, variously thickened under the stigma, or winged. Anther erect, two-celled, the outer valves large, the inner small; pollinia granular, without any caudicle.

An extensive genus of about fifty species, ranging from Australia, with eight species, and NZ, with ten, northward through New Guinea, with nineteen species, to the Philippines and west as far as the Himalayas.

C. pruinosus (Plate 276)

C. pruinosus (R. Cunn.) Reichenb.f. in *Beitr. syst. Pflk.* 42 (1871); H. M. R. Rupp *Orchids N.S.W.* 73 (1943)

SYNONYMY: *Corysanthes pruinosa* R. Cunn. in *N.S.W. Mag.* 1:41 (1833)

Leaf ovate, orbicular or orbicular-cordate, often lobed, 2–3 cm. long; apex often mucronate; green on both sides, but paler beneath. Flower variable in size, usually small, loosely set, the distance from the leaf varying; greyish-green with purplish-red markings. (Rare white forms have been collected on the Hawkesbury River.) Dorsal sepal narrow, paddle-shaped, concave over the labellum, the apex projecting beyond the dilated lamina, greyish or greyish-green, finely and sparsely blotched and streaked with purplish-red along the spine. Labellum contracted towards the base into a narrow split tube, its upper portion, or lamina, curved forward and in the majority of specimens shorter than the tube; the lamina dilated with fringed margins, hardly incurved, with both pale and dark fimbria— the margins imperfectly veined. Central boss small, orbicular, pale but with a dusky red central patch, the calli in the lower region spur-like, numerous but inconspicuous. Auricles at the lower end of the labellum with small apertures; from beneath these arise the fili-form lateral sepals and petals which have entire margins; the sepals often erect, about 2 cm. long, among the lower labellum fringe; petals only 1 mm. long, not erect. Column very small, 2 mm. long, wings small, ovary short.

[This species was originally recorded from all Australian states but is now known only from NSW. The early botanists confused it with *C. diemenicus*, *C. dilatatus* and *C. fimbriatus*.—Ed.]

E. Nubling reports that seeding specimens of *C. pruinosus*, with green ovaries, were placed in water to keep fresh. In three weeks the pedicel on one of them had elongated to 3 cm. and the seed had ripened.

FLOWERING PERIOD: Apr. to July

DISTRIBUTION: Apparently endemic in NSW, from the coast to the tablelands, and from the Manning River south as far as Illawarra

C. fimbriatus (Plate 277)

C. fimbriatus (R. Br.) Reichenb.f. *Beitr. syst. Pflk.* 42 (1871); A. J. Ewart *Flor. Vict.* 336 (1931), as *Corysanthes fimbriata*; H. M. R. Rupp *Orchids N.S.W.* 73 (1943); J. H. Willis *Handb. Pls Vict.* 1:397 (1962); M. J. Firth *Native Orchids Tasm.* 46 (1965)

SYNONYMY: *Corysanthes fimbriata* R. Br. *Prodr. Flor. Nov. Holl.* 328 (1810)

A small plant, 1·5-2·5 cm. high. Leaf orbicular-cordate, 2-4 cm. in diameter, texture thick. Flower, the largest of the Australian forms, purplish-red or crimson, sessile or almost so above the leaf, with a small acute bract, ovary short; dorsal sepal broad-cuneate, much contracted in the lower half, transparent with numerous purplish-red spots, cucullate over the labellum; lateral sepals and petals linear, very small, appressed behind the lower part of the labellum, rarely chelate; sepals usually connate and longer than the petals; labellum lamina reflexed, widely expanded, large, longer than the tube, the margins often inflexed, fimbriate, reticulate and covered with minute glands, chiefly around the boss; boss usually purplish-red; labellum tube split and enclosing the column, erect against the dorsal sepal, usually with two very prominent ear-like auricles at the base. Column short, not winged. Fruiting plants more or less elongated.

The species favours sandy ground near the coast and grows in loose colonies amongst *C. diemenicus*, *Pterostylis concinna* and *P. obtusa*.

FRUITING PERIOD: May to Aug.

COMMON NAME: Fringed Helmet-orchid

DISTRIBUTION: Extending along the east coast from northern Qld through NSW and eastern Vic. to eastern Tas., generally coastal

C. dilatatus (Plate 278)

C. dilatatus (H. M. R. Rupp & W. H. Nicholls) H. M. R. Rupp & W. H. Nicholls ex H. M. R. Rupp in *Vict. Nat.* 59:61 (1942); A. J. Ewart *Flor. Vict.* 337 (1931), as *Corysanthes dilatata*; J. M. Black *Flor. S. Aust.* ed. 2:224 (1943); J. H. Willis *Handb. Pls Vict.* 1:397 (1962); R. Erickson *Orchids West* ed. 2:71 (1965); M. J. Firth *Native Orchids Tasm.* 46 (1965)

SYNONYMY: *Corysanthes dilatata* H. M. R. Rupp & W. H. Nicholls in *Proc. Linn. Soc. N.S.W.* 35:87 (1928)

Plant slender, 2·5-3 cm. high above the leaf. Flower in the typical form rather large, standing erect from the leaf above a very long ovary of about 7 mm. Leaf of variable size and shape, commonly orbicular-cordate, with a tendency to lobation, green, frosty beneath. Dorsal sepal very broad and low-set, concave; lower portion erect, then recurved, the apex projecting over and beyond the lamina of the labellum; width at broadest part about 1·5 cm.; colour dark reddish-purple over pale green. Lamina of labellum always shorter than the tube, often much so; margins widely expanding at maturity,

boldly and coarsely toothed. Veins between margins and central boss irregularly blotched, prominent, purplish, ending at the apices of the teeth. Central boss large and conspicuous, whitish, almost circular, but usually with two posterior ear-shaped extensions; calli round the base, red, acuminate. Auricles often very conspicuous, translucent, with two purplish-red marks above them; openings much dilated, facing downward and forward, most frequently below the lamina. Beneath them are the sepals (5 mm.) and the petals (2-3 mm.) projecting forward, all frequently with bifid tips and purplish markings. Column about 2 mm., not conspicuously winged. Stem often elongated after fertilisation, occasionally attaining 25 cm. or more in height.

C. dilatatus grows, often abundantly, on mossy rock surfaces and moist mountain slopes, as well as on tree-fern trunks in fern gullies, and also extends to coastal areas.

FLOWERING PERIOD: June to Sept.

COMMON NAME: Veined Helmet-orchid

DISTRIBUTION: Cool and sheltered places, in NSW (where known only from Batlow), Vic., Tas., SA and WA; often locally abundant

C. diemenicus (Plate 279)

C. diemenicus (Lindl.) H. M. R. Rupp & W. H. Nicholls ex H. M. R. Rupp in *Vict. Nat.* 59:61 (1942); A. J. Ewart *Flor. Vict.* 336 (1931), as *Corysanthes diemenica*; J. M. Black *Flor. S. Aust.* ed. 2:226 (1943); H. M. R. Rupp *Orchids N.S.W.* 73 (1943); J. H. Willis *Handb. Pls Vict.* 1:397 (1962); M. J. Firth *Native Orchids Tasm.* 46 (1965)

SYNONYMY: *Corysanthes diemenica* Lindl. *Gen. & Spec. orchid. Pls* 393 (1840); *Corysanthes fimbriata* R. Br. var. *diemenica* (Lindl.) Benth. *Flor. aust.* 6:351 (1873)

Leaf broadly ovate or ovate-cordate with a tendency to become lobed, apex mucronate, green above, frosty beneath, about 2·5-3 cm. long. Flower smaller than in *C. fimbriatus*, and stiffly set on a very short stalk, (after fertilisation is effected the fruiting stalk often elongates, sometimes attaining a length of over 14 cm.), dark prune coloured, sometimes with crimson veining on the labellum lamina. Dorsal sepal comparatively narrow, greenish-grey, marked and otherwise spotted over its entire surface with dark purple or purplish-brown; lamina broadly ovate, and concave over the labellum lamina, but not exceeding it; apex obtuse. Labellum not so closely recurved as in *C. pruinosus*, the pulvinate central boss large, channelled, yellowish or white; the calli on the lower portion tooth-like, minute but numerous. Labellum lamina 1-1·6 cm. in diameter, about equal to the tube, which is often broad; margins very dark and usually much incurved, denticulate, the teeth variable in size, but always blunt. Openings to the auricles at the base of the labellum tube not conspicuous, below these are the sepals and petals; the sepals about 2 mm. long, the petals shorter and broader in some flowers (in some Tasmanian flowers the petals were almost twice the length of the sepals); the apices often irregularly bidentate. Column about 2 mm. long, the wings small.

This species is often exceptionally abundant, especially on near-coastal heaths, where it forms congested colonies. The number of plants flowering is generally very small compared with the size of the colony.

FLOWERING PERIOD: June to Sept.

COMMON NAME: Slaty Helmet-orchid

DISTRIBUTION: Extending from NSW, where it is rare and known only from Mudgee, into Vic., Tas., and SA, where known only from Mount Lofty Range; widespread and often locally abundant

C. undulatus (Plate 280)

C. undulatus (R. Cunn.) H. M. R. Rupp in *Proc. Linn. Soc. N.S.W.* 53:551 (1928); H. M. R. Rupp *Orchids N.S.W.* 74 (1943)

SYNONYMY: *Corysanthes undulata* R. Cunn. in *N.S.W. Mag.* 1:41 (1833)

A diminutive plant about 2 cm. high. Leaf variable in size, cordate with a tendency to lobation, upper surface green with a prominent mid-rib; under surface pale green, often tinged with purple. Ovary ovate, subtended by a long acuminate bract. Flower dark purplish-red with prominent veins. Dorsal sepal erect, galeate, deeply concave, apex blunt or minutely apiculate, 6–12 mm. long, base much narrowed. Lateral sepals linear, erect from between the spurs, 2·5–3·5 mm. long, petals abortive, or about 1 mm. long. Labellum large, tubular in the basal half, a prominent rounded protuberance on the anterior margin immediately below the lamina, the tube at the rear longitudinally divided; two small bicalcarate spurs at the base, enclosing the column; lamina circular with a prominent raised central glandular pubescent boss, diffused with purple, or whitish. The entire surface studded with numerous wart-like glands, with a few tall ones towards the margins; the margins irregularly undulate-dentate with a conspicuous mucronate apex. Column minute, 2·5–3 mm. high; wings prominent, acute. Stigma conspicuous, almost circular, viscid. Anther with a short blunt point, glandular. Pollinia bilobed, mealy, pale yellow, attached to a rounded viscid disc. The flowering stem elongates after fertilisation.

C. undulatus is the smallest member of the genus in Australia. After its discovery in NSW it was lost to science for nearly a century, when it was again found at Bulahdelah—on the slopes of Alum Mountain. It grows in moist soil—usually clay under scrub of *Melaleuca nodosa*, etc.

FLOWERING PERIOD: May to July

DISTRIBUTION: South-eastern Qld and north-eastern NSW, of very limited occurrence and rare

C. aconitiflorus (Plate 281)

C. aconitiflorus Salisb. *Parad. lond.* t. 83 (1805); A. J. Ewart *Flor. Vict.* 335 (1931), as *Corysanthes bicalcarata*; H. M. R. Rupp *Orchids N.S.W.* 74 (1943); J. H. Willis *Handb. Pls Vict.* 1:398 (1962); M. J. Firth *Native Orchids Tasm.* 45 (1965)

SYNONYMY: *Corysanthes bicalcarata* R. Br. *Prodr. Flor. Nov. Holl.* 328 (1810); *Corysanthes cheesemanii* Hook.f. ex T. Kirk in *Trans. N.Z. Inst.* 3:180 (1871)

Plant varying considerably in height according to habitat conditions, but usually 2·5–4 cm. Leaf membranous, orbicular-cordate, reticulate-veined, grey-green above, usually purplish or reddish below; in the flowering plant 1·5–3·5 cm. long. Pedicel very short, the subtending bract comparatively long, linear. Ovary long, cylindrical. Dorsal sepal large, dark prune coloured, reddish or greyish, rarely whitish; overarching and enclosing the labellum lamina, very convex, acute, not markedly contracted at the base; the apex often upturned, 1·5–2·5 cm. long. Lateral sepals and petals minute, linear-subulate, the sepals longer than the petals. Labellum lamina whitish, often marked with red or purple; margins recurved, convex, often undulate and sometimes minutely ciliate; the tubular base extended below into two conspicuous horn-like hollow spurs, or auricles produced forward. Column short, very narrowly winged; a prominent gibbosity at the anterior base. Stigma prominent.

This species forms dense colonies, usually in thick scrub. The flowers are very delicate and easily damaged.

FLOWERING PERIOD: Mar. to July

COMMON NAME: Spurred Helmet-orchid

DISTRIBUTION: From northern Qld through NSW to Vic., and Tas., widespread over a wide range of habitats on the coast and near-coastal ranges; also NZ

C. unguiculatus (Plate 282)

C. unguiculatus (R. Br.) Reichenb.f. *Beitr. syst. Pflk.* 43 (1871); A. J. Ewart *Flor. Vict.* 335 (1931), as *Corysanthes unguiculata*; J. M. Black *Flor. S. Aust.* ed. 2:224 (1943); H. M. R. Rupp *Orchids N.S.W.* 76 (1943); J. H. Willis *Handb. Pls Vict.* 1:398 (1962); R. Erickson *Orchids West* ed. 2:72 (1965); M. J. Firth *Native Orchids Tasm.* 46 (1965)

SYNONYMY: *Corysanthes unguiculata* R. Br. *Prodr. Flor. Nov. Holl.* 328 (1810); *Corybas matthewsii* (Cheeseman) Schlechter in *Repert. Spec. nov. Regn. veg.* 19:23 (1923); *Corysanthes matthewsii* Cheeseman in *Trans. N.Z. Inst.* 31:351 (1899)

A small plant rarely exceeding 3 cm. high. Leaf ovate-cordate, often with a tendency to become trilobed, strongly ribbed; under surface of leaf usually purplish tinted, this colour often invading the upper surface along the margins; 1–3 cm. long (in the non-flowering plant up to 4 cm.). Flower solitary, pedicellate, almost wholly deep reddish-purple, recurved or reflexed against the ovary; ovary 3–5 mm. long. Dorsal sepal suddenly contracted into a narrow claw about the same length as the hooded lamina; lamina orbicular, deeply concave; lateral sepals filiform, often chelate, 4·5 mm.–1 cm. long, spreading below the labellum; petals similar but shorter, 2·5–5 mm. long, spreading on each side of the labellum; sepals and petals often marked with a central red line. Labellum exceeding the dorsal sepal in length, tubular, inflated in the middle and much narrowed towards the base, and towards the orifice; the lateral margins meeting along the dorsum in the mid-line; the orifice oblique, directed downward and forward, margins with minute cilia; a longitudinal mass of inturned glistening calli along the centre of the lamina from the orifice almost to the extreme base. Column very small and short, incurved, two-winged. Anther two-celled, valvate. Pollinia four, in two pairs, attached directly to a circular disc. Stigma prominent. Flowering stem often elongating after fertilisation.

The largest colony seen by the author was in the neighbourhood of Oakleigh, Vic. (since destroyed). Within the close shelter of *Melaleuca* scrub over a score of flowering plants were seen; some of the specimens were very fine, far larger than those received from Tas. and SA habitats. Its curious flowers make it one of the most intriguing species.

FLOWERING PERIOD: May to Oct.

COMMON NAME: Small Helmet-orchid

DISTRIBUTION: Extending from just north of Sydney, NSW, south to Vic. and Tas., then west to south-eastern SA and south-western WA, generally coastal; also NZ

C. fordhamii (Plate 283)

C. fordhamii (H. M. R. Rupp) H. M. R. Rupp in *Vict. Nat.* 59:61 (1942); H. M. R. Rupp *Orchids N.S.W.* 76 (1943)

SYNONYMY: *Corysanthes fordhamii* H. M. R. Rupp in *Vict. Nat.* 58:83 (1941)

A small plant usually 2–4 cm. high, growing in boggy ground. Leaf ovate-cordate, quite green on both sides, usually well up from the soil. Flower slender, on a very slender ovary, pedicel conspicuous and about 1 cm. long or more. Dorsal sepal 13–14 mm. long, reddish-purple from the base to near the pallid apex; narrowly cuneate, not abruptly contracted into a claw; the narrow posterior part gradually recurved; the lamina ovate-oblong, scarcely exceeding 3 mm. at its widest part, convex above, the apex emarginate. Lateral sepals narrow-linear, often tinged pale purple, 7–8 mm. long, closely appressed to the sides of the labellum. Petals much shorter, filamentose, appressed to the labellum between the dorsal and lateral sepals. Labellum shorter than the dorsal sepal, conspicuously striped with dark reddish-purple lines, except for the dark purple basal third; a transparent auricle close to the base, through which the column is clearly visible; tubular, but not appreciably diminishing in calibre till quite close to the base; in front contracting to a rather small orifice, which is directed horizontally; lower lip of the orifice striate, with a large reddish-purple blotch immediately behind the broadly emarginate apex. At the base of this patch and of the stripes are irregular fimbriae directed inward. No row of calli leading from the orifice to the base of labellum, as in *C. unguiculatus*. Column rather long and slender for the genus (3 mm. long in dissected specimen), much incurved close to the summit; wings obscure, but their membranes in front almost concealing the stigma. Anther valvate, two-celled, obtuse; pollinia four.

[This species is closely allied to the Australian *C. unguiculatus* and the NZ species *C. carsei* Cheeseman. It was collected in SA for the first time in 1968 by R. C. Nash.—Ed.]

FLOWERING PERIOD: July and Aug.

DISTRIBUTION: Extending from south-eastern Qld to NSW and south-eastern SA, and probably also entering Vic.; chiefly coastal

27 *Nervilia*

Nervilia Commerson ex Gaudich. in Freyc. *Voy. aut. Monde* (*Bot.*) 421, t. 35 (1829)

Plants growing from round underground tubers, the leaf and inflorescence appearing at different times. Leaf solitary, short or long, stalked, broadly heart-shaped; inflorescence erect, bearing one to several flowers. Sepals and petals similar, spreading, rather long and narrow, lip not spurred, usually trilobed, the base embracing the column. Column rather long, straight, thickened at the top; anther almost horizontal; pollinia two, divided, granular.

A fairly extensive genus of about forty species, widespread throughout tropical areas from Africa to India, China and south-east Asia, and reaching Australia where there are about four species.

N. holochila (Plate 284)

N. holochila (F. Muell.) Schlechter in *Bot. Jb. 39*:48 (1906)

SYNONYMY: *Pogonia holochila* F. Muell. *Fragm. Phyt. Aust. 6*:200 (1866)

Flowering stems slender, 15–28 cm. high, with a few rather long sheathing scarious bracts, the upper ones sometimes almost leafy at the end. Flowers two to six, on slender, rather short pedicels, light rose-purple (labellum), and light green (sepals and petals). Bracteoles subtending the pedicels linear, rather long, 1–2·5 cm. long. Sepals and petals 2·5–3 cm. long, the lateral sepals oblong-linear, the dorsal sepal and petals narrow-linear, the petals more contracted at the base. Labellum nearly as long as the sepals, broadly

ovate, shortly sinuate, trilobed, the lateral lobes broadly rounded, the mid-lobe smaller, rather broader than long with a bearded line extending halfway along it. Column slender, very shortly winged at the apex.

FLOWERING PERIOD: Dec. to Feb.

DISTRIBUTION: Apparently endemic in Australia, extending northward from the Burdekin River near Townsville, northern Qld, and generally coastal

28 *Cryptostylis*

Cryptostylis R. Br. *Prodr. Flor. Nov. Holl.* 317 (1810)

Terrestrial glabrous herbs with fleshy rhizomes. Leaves few, radical, on long petioles, erect, lanceolate to ovate. Flowers reversed, often rather large, several in a terminal raceme, green except for the large labellum which is variously coloured. Sepals and petals linear, the sepals about equal in length, the petals shorter. Labellum undivided, sessile, the base enclosing the column, the lamina sometimes very broad, concave on the upper surface, or convex through reflexion of the margins, longitudinally ridged or furnished with sessile calli. Column very short and broad, with lateral appendages forming auricles or produced posteriorly into a glandular or membranous process with fringed margins behind the anther. Anther erect or incumbent, two-celled; pollinia four, granular. Stigma large, its upper border forming a triangular rostellum with viscid disc.

A genus of about eighteen species with representatives in Malaya, Taiwan, Philippines, Fiji, Samoa, New Caledonia, New Guinea and Australia. In Australia there are five species, all endemic.

[The pollination of the Australian species has received world-wide attention, for the remarkable adaptation of the plants to lure and use the unwary insect. Very briefly, the flowers emit a scent which sexually attracts male ichneumon wasps. In the act of pseudo-copulation with the flower the wasp (*Lissopimpla semipunctata*) removes the pollinia and transfers them to the next flower that attracts it.

This phenomenon was was first queried by the scientific world, when a paper was published by its discoverer, Mrs Edith Coleman, in 1927. However, it soon became widely recognised and has since been observed in other orchid genera, though the actual details vary.—Ed.]

C. erecta (Plate 285)

C. erecta R. Br. *Prodr. Flor. Nov. Holl.* 317 (1810); H. M. R. Rupp *Orchids N.S.W.* 77 (1943); J. H. Willis *Handb. Pls Vict.* 1:399 (1962)

A slender to moderately robust plant, 20–45 cm. high. Leaves one to three, ovate-lanceolate, 7–14 cm. long on moderately long petioles, arising from a thickened scape. Stem-bracts two or three, small, clasping, acute. Flowers in a loose raceme, large, two to twelve, green with purplish and red-brown stripes and other markings. Sepals and petals narrow-linear, subulate, greenish; sepals 2·5–3 cm. long; petals 1·2–1·5 cm. long. Labellum large, forming a broad erect cucullate hood, towards the base a marked posterior constriction, the horizontal base enclosing the column; lamina very broad-ovate, 3–3·5 cm. long, deeply concave, more or less obtuse; membranous part with a network of conspicuous purplish, reticulate veins arising from a purplish base, the central longitudinal callus plate green, with a few large purplish spots near the centre. Lateral lobes of column comparatively large, colourless, with denticulate-glandular margins. Stigma prominent. Anther shortly rostrate, shorter than the rostellum. Pollinia four, in two sections, granular, no caudicle; disc brownish, viscid.

In NSW *C. erecta* is still a common plant, about Sydney, and in parts of the Blue Mountains, where it grows on the slopes of the sandstone gullies, either on mossy rock ledges, or by creeks in damp situations, or up the dry sandy sides to the crest of the hills. It is apparently not at all particular as to the degree of moisture in the soil where it grows. In Vic. it occurs only in parts of East Gippsland, where it was discovered in 1936.

FLOWERING PERIOD: Sept. to Feb.

COMMON NAME: Bonnet Orchid

DISTRIBUTION: Widespread from south-eastern Qld through NSW to far eastern Vic., where rare; chiefly coastal and often locally common

C. ovata (Plate 286)

C. ovata R. Br. *Prodr. Flor. Nov. Holl.* 317 (1810); R. Erickson *Orchids West* ed. 2:30 (1965)

Habit similar to *C. subulata*, but the leaves much larger, and varying from ovate to oblong, 8–15 cm. long and 3·5–6·5 cm. broad, strongly ribbed, green, purplish on the reverse surface, the upper surface in the larger leaves often traversed by a more or less irregular white median line. Petiole 5–8 cm. long. Flowers about six, similar to those of *C. subulata*. Labellum also similar, but finely net-veined, the callus plates less prominent, and lamina differently coloured, the surface of which is finely pubescent. Column lobes continuous in front of the anther as in *C. subulata*. Pollinia four, in two irregular pairs.

According to the observations of B. T. Goadby and O. Sargent *C. ovata* is pollinated by the same species of wasp as the other members of this genus (see article by Sargent in *The West Australian*, 14 December 1929).

During October and November 1946 the author saw this orchid in abundance at Little Grove, near Albany. Colonies of the plants were situated under the Willow Myrtles (*Agonis flexuosa*) adjacent to the beach.

FLOWERING PERIOD: Oct. to Feb.

COMMON NAME: Slipper Orchid

DISTRIBUTION: Endemic in WA where it is confined to the south-west but there widespread and often locally common, especially in swampy situations

C. leptochila (Plate 287)

C. leptochila F. Muell. ex Benth. *Flor. aust.* 6:334 (1873); A. J. Ewart *Flor. Vict.* 361 (1931); H. M. R. Rupp *Orchids N.S.W.* 78 (1943); J. H. Willis *Handb. Pls Vict.* 1:400 (1962)

A slender to moderately stout plant, 15–35 cm. high. Leaves ovate, on petioles 3–6 cm. long, green, the under surface brown, purplish or wholly deep red. Flowers smaller than those of *C. subulata*, also more numerous than in other Australian species, nine to twelve. Labellum with the short broad base of the other forms, abruptly contracted above it into an oblong-linear, somewhat thick pubescent lamina, tip recurved, occasionally decurved; a thick longitudinal raised, often interrupted callus plate along the centre of the lamina, and on either side of this line a row of dark, shining, domed asterisk-like calli. Column appendages with two broad denticulate lobes interrupted behind the nearly erect anther as in *C. erecta*.

C. leptochila is mostly confined to heavy scrub lands. At Lockwood, near Belgrave, Vic., I have counted over eighty plants in a radius of approximately thirty square yards. Here and also near Mount Erica, Vic., it appears to be partial to the upper slopes and crests of the low hills.

FLOWERING PERIOD: Mainly Dec. to Feb., but sometimes as late as May

COMMON NAME: Small Tongue-orchid

DISTRIBUTION: Extending from the New England Tableland in NSW, south to Vic., where it is widespread in eastern highland forests

C. hunterana (Plate 288)

C. hunterana W. H. Nicholls in *Vict. Nat.* 54:182, t. 18 (1938); J. H. Willis *Handb. Pls Vict.* 1:399 (1962)

A comparatively slender plant, 15–45 cm. high. Leafless in all the specimens seen. Stem-bracts appressed, acute, six to eight, not including those subtending the flowers. Flowers five to ten, rather large, apparently sessile, reversed. Labellum conspicuous, in a more or less erect position, narrow-oblong, convex, markedly glandular; margins recurved; about 3·3 cm. long; the lower portion yellowish-green with red markings, upper portion light red merging into the black furred centre; five conspicuous, more or less interrupted black lines arising from the concave base, which encloses the column, extending upward and merging into a broad longitudinal, slightly raised central ridge resembling closely woven black wool or fur, which reaches almost to the tip; apex recurved. Sepals and petals subulate, very narrow, yellow; sepals about 2 cm. long, the petals only half as long. Column inconspicuous, resembling that in *C. subulata*.

For detailed data relating to this orchid I am indebted to a resident of Orbost, Master Norman A. Wakefield. He writes: 'Accompanied by my father I visited the localities where this orchid was found. Wherever we looked we found *C. hunterana* in the country off the old Bemm Road, from Cape Conran to Orbost. It grows on the coastal grass-tree plains which extend from Marlo eastward, from the coast one to six miles. *C. subulata* invariably in association. None of the specimens had leaves and scores of plants were seen.'

FLOWERING PERIOD: Dec. to Feb.

DISTRIBUTION: Extending from Broken Bay, north of Sydney, NSW, south to East Gippsland, Vic., generally near the coast; uncommon and rarely collected

29 Pterostylis

Pterostylis R. Br. *Prodr. Flor. Nov. Holl.* 326 (1810)

Terrestrial herbs with small underground tubers. Leaves broad, in a radical rosette, or narrow and cauline, occasionally crowded at the base and passing into bracts on the stem. Flowers usually green, sometimes marked with red, brown or purplish stripes, less frequently tinted reddish throughout, large and solitary or several together in a raceme on shortish pedicels. Dorsal sepal arcuate and incurved, the lateral petals appressed to it, and forming a hood, or galea, which conceals the column. Lateral sepals more or less united into a lower lip, either deflexed, or erect and embracing the galea. Labellum attached by a movable, often irritable claw, frequently bearing at its base a simple or penicillate appendage. Column elongated and curved within the galea, winged on each side. Stigma situated on the face of the column below the wings. Anther two-celled. Pollinia granular.

A genus of about seventy species, chiefly Australian, but extending also to NZ, New Caledonia and New Guinea.

P. falcata (Plate 289)

P. falcata R. S. Rogers in *Proc. roy. Soc. Vict.* new ser. *28*:106, t. 9 (1915); A. J. Ewart *Flor. Vict.* 368 (1931); H. M. R. Rupp *Orchids N.S.W.* 86 (1943); J. H. Willis *Handb. Pls Vict.* 1:403 (1962); M. J. Firth *Native Orchids Tasm.* 70 (1965)

Plant comparatively slender, 15–30 cm. high. Leaves four or five, basal (occasionally absent), 2–6 cm. or more in length, ovate-lanceolate to oblong-lanceolate, shortly petiolate, passing gradually into the stem-bracts. Stem-bracts two to four, large and leaf-like, lanceolate, sheathing. Flower solitary, very large with a short ovary; galea 4–6 cm. long, white with green lines and light brown markings toward the apex, erect, very acuminate and boldly sickle-shaped; lower lip cuneate, the sinus wide; apices of conjoined sepals prolonged into filamentous caudae of about same length as the galea, curving forward high above it, each one sometimes bifid at the tip. Labellum dark green, lanceolate; tip blunt and, when relaxed, protruding far beyond the sinus of the lower lip; lamina curved, 2–2·5 cm. long, a prominent raised longitudinal ridge along the centre, with a corresponding narrow groove on the under side; upper surface of lamina convex in section; appendage linear, curved, densely penicillate. Column shorter than labellum, the upper angle of lobes with an upright tooth; lower lobes oblong with inturned ciliate margins. Stigma rather long and narrow, oblong-lanceolate, pointed at the upper angle and rounded below.

P. falcata is most aptly named, all segments of the flower being sickle-shaped. Flowers in some favoured localities attain a very large size for the genus—a galea may even measure 8 cm. around the curve. This species is usually confined to shady, moist situations, e.g. stream banks and low-lying ground, where it may be often inundated. As with *P. alpina*, it had long been confused in Vic. with the very different species *P. cucullata*.

FLOWERING PERIOD: Sept. to Jan., according to altitude and environment

COMMON NAME: Sickle Greenhood

DISTRIBUTION: Central-eastern NSW, where uncommon; extending into Vic. where it is widespread and often locally abundant; also northern Tas., where rare

P. acuminata (Plate 290)

P. acuminata R. Br. *Prodr. Flor. Nov. Holl.* 326 (1810); H. M. R. Rupp *Orchids N.S.W.* 84 (1943); J. H. Willis *Handb. Pls Vict.* 1:405 (1962), in note

A slender glabrous plant, 10–20 cm. high. Leaves in a basal rosette, petiolate, 1·5–3·5 cm. long, ovate to broad-lanceolate. Stem-bracts one or two, very small. Flower solitary, greenish-white, at the apex often light reddish; galea about 2·5 cm. long, erect or slightly inclined forward; dorsal sepal erect for half its length, then more or less horizontal, the apex finely acuminate; petals a little shorter, also acuminate; lower sepals connate in the lower third, the sinus rather widely acute, lobes lanceolate and produced into long filiform points which embrace and far exceed the galea. Labellum on a movable claw, the lamina about 15 mm. long, oblong-linear, tapering to a long recurved acuminate point; a prominent raised ridge throughout its length; basal appendage linear, curved, with a penicillate apex. Column erect, about 1·5 cm. long; upper angle of

wings with an erect subulate point at each angle; lower lobes linear-oblong with very sparsely ciliate inturned margins. Stigma narrow, oblong-lanceolate.

FLOWERING PERIOD: Mar. to July

COMMON NAME: Sharp Greenhood

DISTRIBUTION: NSW and Qld where often abundant in coastal areas, also New Caledonia and New Guinea

P. acuminata var. ingens (Plate 291)

P. acuminata var. *ingens* H. M. R. Rupp in *Proc. Linn. Soc. N.S.W.* 53:552 (1928); A. J. Ewart *Flor. Vict.* 371 (1931), as *P. acuminata*; J. H. Willis *Handb. Pls Vict.* 1:404 (1962); M. J. Firth *Native Orchids Tasm.* 71 (1965), as *P. acuminata*

Typically a robust, larger-flowered plant (galea to 3·5 cm. long) than the common NSW form of the species, from which it differs also in the pubescent labellum, with blunt apex, and in the flowering time which is at least three months later.

Since describing the var. *ingens*, Rupp is of opinion that this Vic. plant is sufficiently distinct to warrant recognition as a species. I first collected it at Bayswater, Vic., where it flourished on damp ground beside the railway line. Later it was observed growing luxuriantly along Bucheen Creek, which flows through the Cravensville reserve in north-eastern Vic. Although never recorded by SA botanists, *P. acuminata* var. *ingens* is represented in Melbourne Herbarium by a single, but well preserved, old specimen from the Port Elliot district.

FLOWERING PERIOD: Sept. to Nov., sometimes as early as Aug. or as late as Dec.

COMMON NAME: Pointed Greenhood

DISTRIBUTION: Southern tablelands of NSW to eastern Vic.; Mount Barrow Road, Tas.; Port Elliot, SA. Represented from NSW and SA by single collections

P. nutans (Plate 292)

P. nutans R. Br. *Prodr. Flor. Nov. Holl.* 327 (1810); A. J. Ewart *Flor. Vict.* 374 (1931); J. M. Black *Flor. S. Aust.* ed. 2:243 (1943); H. M. R. Rupp *Orchids N.S.W.* 83 (1943); J. H. Willis *Handb. Pls Vict.* 1:412 (1962); M. J. Firth *Native Orchids Tasm.* 74 (1965)

A slender plant, 10–30 cm. high. Leaves about five in a basal rosette, up to 9 cm. long, petiolate, ovoid to oblong, with undulate or crisped margins. Stem-bracts two to four, loosely sheathing. Flower rather large, usually solitary, wholly green except for the pale reddish-brown tips of segments. Galea 1·5–3 cm. long, curved forward for almost its whole length, so that the interior faces the ground, the apex of dorsal sepal shortly acuminate and often a little upturned. Lateral sepals conjoined for more than a third of their length, forming a broadly acute sinus, sweeping downward and then almost horizontal (from the nodding habit of the flower); free lobes narrow-linear, shortly acuminate, divergent and slightly exceeding the tip of the galea. Labellum on a movable claw, 12–16 mm. long, oblong-linear, almost semi-circularly decurved, projecting far beyond the sinus; apex obtuse; lamina pubescent, green, with a red central ridge; appendage linear, curved, penicillate. Column about 16 mm. long, much incurved; upper angle of wings rounded, each prolonged into a linear tooth; lower lobes bluntly oblong-falcate, the anterior margins incurved and ciliate; anther incumbent, very blunt. Stigma long and narrow, pointed at both ends, not viscid. Rostellum very viscid.

Except at the extremities of its range, *P. nutans* is a common orchid throughout eastern temperate Australia. It avoids open plains and mallee scrubs, but favours sheltered positions among light-forest undergrowth, especially in sandy areas near the coast. Huge colonies may develop, and flowering is usually prolific. The fruiting capsule is large, oblong-ellipsoid in shape, and, toward maturity, it gradually assumes an erect position, with the stalk often much elongated. Nodding Greenhood is the name widely applied to this familiar orchid; but in NSW it is often called Parrot's-beak Orchid, while such fanciful names as Cow-horns are used by country children.

A small slender form with hispid flowers, from NSW, is known as *P. nutans* var. *hispidula* (R. D. FitzG.) H. M. R. Rupp.

FLOWERING PERIOD: July to Oct.; but sometimes even as late as Dec. in the mountains, or as early as May and June in coastal districts of NSW (var. *hispidula*)

COMMON NAME: Nodding Greenhood

DISTRIBUTION: Temperate parts of all Australian states except WA, but in Qld restricted to the south-east; also NZ

P. pedoglossa (Plate 293)

P. pedoglossa R. D. FitzG. *Aust. Orchids* 1³:+t. (1877); A. J. Ewart *Flor. Vict.* 368 (1931); H. M. R. Rupp *Orchids N.S.W.* 85 (1943); J. H. Willis *Handb. Pls Vict.* 1:410 (1962); M. J. Firth *Native Orchids Tasm.* 73 (1965)

A very slender plant 5-15 cm. high, excluding the sepal prolongations. Leaves three to six in a radical rosette, or not strictly rosulate, 15-25 mm. long, ovate or oblong and petiolate. Stem bracts one or two, the lower sometimes leaf-like. Flower solitary, almost wholly green, the apex sometimes adorned with a touch of red-brown. Galea about 15 mm. long, erect for about half its length, then curving forward into the long-acuminate or filiform point of the dorsal sepal which is sometimes 2-4 cm. and as long as those of the conjoined sepals. Petals about half as long as galea and shortly acute. Lateral sepals erect, united for about a quarter of their length, narrowly cuneate and forming an acute, rather inflexed sinus; the lobes gradually attenuated into long, somewhat divergent filiform points which far exceed the galea. Labellum on a long claw, very short; lamina 3-4 mm. long, ovate-oblong, cordate, rather thick, tip sometimes emarginate; basal appendage linear, curved, nearly as long as the lamina, excluding the tripartite, penicillate apex. Column somewhat cuneate, very straight and more than thrice the length of the labellum; upper angles of wings produced into two erect, stout, subulate teeth almost as high as the anther; lower lobes narrow, ciliate at the apices.

P. pedoglossa is a fragile and very dainty autumn orchid, to be looked for in damp heathland thickets, where usually it is well hidden. The delicate prolongations of the sepals, when erect, give height to the plant, and add to the attractive appearance. Large colonies may occur, but the known centres of distribution are very isolated R. D. FitzGerald named *P. pedoglossa* from the likeness of the labellum to an ancient rudder.

FLOWERING PERIOD: Mar. to July

COMMON NAME: Prawn Greenhood

DISTRIBUTION: Coastal areas of central eastern NSW, eastern Vic., and eastern Tas.

P. nana (Plate 294)

P. nana R. Br. *Prodr. Flor. Nov. Holl.* 327 (1810); A. J. Ewart *Flor. Vict.* 373 (1931); J. M. Black *Flor. S. Aust.* ed. 2:245 (1943); H. M. R. Rupp *Orchids N.S.W.* 85 (1943); J. H. Willis *Handb. Pls Vict.* 1:411 (1962); R. Erickson *Orchids West* ed. 2:40 (1965); M. J. Firth *Native Orchids Tasm.* 74 (1965)

A rather diminutive species, normally about 10 cm. high but varying from 3 to more than 20 cm. Leaves ovate, three to eight in a rosulate cluster at the base, 1-3 cm. long with petioles 5-15 mm. Stem bracts two or three, sometimes absent, usually loose, acute, often leaf-like, sheathing at the base. Flower solitary, rarely two, light green. Galea normally erect for two-thirds, 1-2 cm. long, the horizontal apex broad and obtuse. Lower sepals forming an erect lip with broad, truncated sinus and a prominent green, inflexed, denticular lobule on the inner margin; the linear to filiform lobes erect, 1·5-2·5 cm. long, embracing the galea and exceeding it, usually with clavate points. Labellum oblong on a short movable claw; surface slightly rough; tip blunt and slightly decurved; lamina 4-10 mm. long, with a central longitudinal ridge; appendage at the base linear, curved, with trifid apex. Column erect, 8-15 mm. high; the upper angle of wings produced into an erect tooth; lower lobes oblong with short incurved marginal cilia. Stigma elliptical.

This species is found in lightly timbered country, where it grows often in sheltered positions under trees and shrubs, tolerating a wide range of soils—from heavy clay to desert sands (as in the mallee scrub of far north-western Vic.); sometimes it appears in rock crevices. [It was once thought to be exceedingly rare in NSW but has been collected frequently since 1964.—Ed.] In WA and SA and northern Tas. *P. nana* is very widespread and commonly seen; advancing settlement has destroyed many habitats where it was once abundant—as in parts of the North Island of NZ. Occurrences usually consist of scattered colonies or small compact groups over wide areas, but the flowering is prolific and seed freely produced.

In a few specimens I have noted several prominent bead-like papillae on the lower margins of the labellum lamina—a feature not previously observed in any other species of this large genus—see Plate 294, Fig. **n**.

FLOWERING PERIOD: July to Oct.

COMMON NAME: Dwarf Greenhood

DISTRIBUTION: All Australian states, except Qld, and confined to the south-west in WA; occupying a wide range of habitats and often abundant; also NZ

P. pyramidalis (Plate 295)

P. pyramidalis Lindl. in *Edwards' bot. Reg.* 23: Swan Riv. Append. liii (1840); R. Erickson *Orchids West* ed. 2:40 (1965), under *P. nana*

Plant slender or moderately robust, occasionally reaching a height of 30 cm. Leaves (the differentiating feature of this species) usually crowded at base of stem, passing gradually into sessile stem leaves and empty bracts; but the basal leaves are not always present. Flowers similar in every respect to that of *P. nana*, but the general aspect of the foliage places this form in a different division of the genus.

Undoubtedly typical forms differ appreciably in foliage and robustness from those of *P. nana*, but in some localities, where both forms occur, they interbreed so freely that segregation is impossible. It is probable that *P. nana* in WA has developed along lines which ultimately produced the form *pyramidalis*, and I lack any evidence to suggest that the latter originated as a hybrid between *nana* and some third species. *P. foliata* provides a parallel instance in which the normal form has prominent cauline leaves, yet I have observed specimens of this greenhood with a definite basal rosette of leaves. Thus there seems no satisfactory reason for dividing the variants of *P. nana* and I consider that *P. pyramidalis* should be regarded as a remarkable western variant of it. [R. Erickson in the second edition of her *Orchids of the West* includes *P. pyramidalis* with *P. nana*.—Ed.]

FLOWERING PERIOD: Aug. to Nov.

COMMON NAME: Snail Orchid

DISTRIBUTION: WA where widespread in the south-west, especially on coastal plains

P. celans (Plate 296)

P. celans H. M. R. Rupp in *Vict. Nat.* 61:106 (1944); J. H. Willis *Handb. Pls Vict.* 1:412 (1962)

A diminutive, slender plant, 3·5–11 cm. high. Leaves three to six in a basal cluster, orbicular to ovate, 10–15 mm. long, stoutly petiolate, the petioles up to 10 mm. long. Stem bracts two, leafy, ovate, acute, 1–2 cm. long. Flower solitary, green, on a long pedicel; ovary robust. Galea about 15 mm. long, erect for about two-thirds of its length, then arched forward to an acute and slightly decurved point. Lateral conjoined sepals erect, with a very narrow sinus, suddenly contracting into the filiform lobes which curve forward high above the galea. Petals entirely free from the dorsal sepal, very broad. Labellum immobile on a narrow claw, broadly lanceolate, about 11 mm. long, erect, concave, decurved about the middle, extending to the tip of the galea and (with the petals) completely concealing the interior of the flower, thin membranous; the longitudinal ridge narrow, green on a white ground, with a parallel green line on each side; apex minutely truncate, basal appendage vestigial, acute. Column 7–10 mm. long, erect; each upper angle of wings produced into an erect, rather blunt tooth; lower lobes broad with incurved shortly ciliate margins. Stigma very conspicuous ovate, much wider than the column.

When described, *P. celans* was known from a single colony in dense scrub country, then being cleared for agriculture near Portland. It flowered in two successive seasons, viz. Oct. 1943 and Oct. 1944. Since then an additional colony has been located. In the field this plant is associated with *P. nana*, which it outwardly resembles closely; in fact, it may eventually prove to be an abnormal form of the latter species, having the labellum modified into a membranous petaloid structure which conceals the whole interior of the galea. *P. celans* is, in my opinion, self-pollinated; thereby, with *P. crypta*, it is unique in the genus. This conclusion was supported by the examination of undeveloped flowers; even at a very early stage of development, the pollinia had dehisced, to some extent, over the surface of the stigma.

FLOWERING PERIOD: Sept. and Oct.

DISTRIBUTION: Vic., where endemic in coastal areas of the south-west

P. concinna (Plate 297)

P. concinna R. Br. *Prodr. Flor. Nov. Holl.* 326 (1810); A. J. Ewart *Flor. Vict.* 375 (1931); H. M. R. Rupp *Orchids N.S.W.* 82 (1943); J. H. Willis *Handb. Pls Vict.* 1:410 (1962); M. J. Firth *Native Orchids Tasm.* 73 (1965)

A slender glabrous plant, 4–30 cm. high. Leaves in a basal rosette, usually on fairly long petioles; lamina 1–3 cm. long, ovate to oblong-elliptic. Stem bracts usually two, small. Flower solitary, rarely two, green with darker green longitudinal stripes and some brown markings; galea erect, 1–2 cm. long, curved forward in the anterior third, with acute and depressed apex; lower lip erect with a very wide sinus, the lobes terminating in erect filiform tips high above the galea (tips often slightly clavate). Labellum up to 10 mm. long, on a narrow claw, irritable, attached to the basal projection of the column; lamina oblong, broadly bidentate or acutely

emarginate, almost straight with a wide raised ridge along the centre and a corresponding narrow groove on the under side; appendage slender, curved, with penicillate tip. Column erect, about 10 mm. long, the upper angle of wings produced into a long erect lobe; lower lobes rounded, the margins inturned, ciliate. Stigma tumid, oval.

Sandy coastal scrublands are favoured by this common gregarious orchid, but it occurs as far inland as the northern Grampians and Cravensville in Vic.

FLOWERING PERIOD: May to early Oct.

COMMON NAME: Trim Greenhood

DISTRIBUTION: All eastern states, from south-eastern Qld to Tas., generally coastal, but doubtfully recorded from SA and absent from WA

P. ophioglossa (Plate 298)

P. ophioglossa R. Br. *Prodr. Flor. Nov. Holl.* 326 (1810); H. M. R. Rupp *Orchids N.S.W.* 80 (1943)

Scape glabrous, one-flowered, rarely two, 4–25 cm. long. Leaves in a radical rosette, shortly petiolate, 2–3·5 cm. long, ovate or broadly oblong, obtuse and often mucronate. Stem with a single empty bract near the base, rarely ebracteate, the terminal pedicel subtended by a rather broad, very acute bract. Flower rather large in relation to the usual length of stem; galea 2–3 cm. long, sometimes more, erect, incurved, acuminate, rather broad, green and white with brown longitudinal stripes; lower lip erect, broadly cuneate, deeply two-lobed, the lobes narrowing to long subulate points which embrace the galea and far exceed it. Labellum 12–16 mm. long, irritable on a narrow claw; lamina oblong-linear, ending in two narrow lobes which are produced forward beyond the sinus of the lower lip; basal appendage linear-subulate, curved, the apex penicillate. Column about as long as the labellum, the upper angle of wings produced into an erect tooth; lower lobes oblong and obtuse; inner margins with inturned cilia.

FLOWERING PERIOD: Apr. to July

COMMON NAME: Snake-tongue Greenhood

DISTRIBUTION: Qld and NSW, chiefly coastal and often abundant; also New Caledonia

P. ophioglossa var. collina (Plate 298)

P. ophioglossa var. *collina* H. M. R. Rupp in *Proc. Linn. Soc. N.S.W.* 54:552, fig. 2B (1929); H. M. R. Rupp *Orchids N.S.W.* 82 (1943)

It differs from the typical form in having smaller flowers with conspicuous reddish-brown striae, very shortly acute galea, shorter-pointed lateral sepals and more recurved labellum.

FLOWERING PERIOD: Mar. to Aug.

DISTRIBUTION: Extending from northern Qld at least as far south as Paterson, NSW, often in low coastal ranges

P. allantoidea (Plate 299)

P. allantoidea R. S. Rogers in *Trans. roy. Soc. S. Aust.* 64:139 (1940); R. Erickson *Orchids West* ed. 2:41 (1965)

A very slender plant, 6–10 cm. high. Leaves radical and rosulate, on rather long petioles; lamina 10–15 mm. long, ovate, reticulate, margins slightly crenulate. Stem bract solitary, close to the rosette, ovate with long-acuminate apex, minutely ciliate on margins. Flower solitary, erect, about 10 mm. long; galea markedly acute and de-curved, green with dark purplish longitudinal stripes and markings; junction of the lateral sepals dark-coloured and very gibbous, their apices prolonged into filamentous points which are erect or reflexed and greatly exceed the galea. Labellum about 4·5 mm. long, mobile, unguiculate, semi-cylindrical, fleshy, channelled above, slightly curved, pubescent in the anterior part and protruding a little at the sinus; appendage trifid. Column erect; upper angle of wings with short, erect lobes; lower lobes hatchet-shaped. Stigma prominent, ovate.

The specific epithet is in allusion to the sausage-like labellum of this little greenhood. In his original diagnosis, R. S. Rogers describes the stem bract as 'subulate'; but in the duplicate type specimens, which I received from C. A. Gardner, the bract is ovate with a long fine point.

FLOWERING PERIOD: Sept.

COMMON NAME: Shy Greenhood

DISTRIBUTION: WA, where endemic in the south-west

P. baptistii (Plate 300)

P. baptistii R. D. FitzG. *Aust. Orchids* 1¹:+t. (1875); H. M. R. Rupp *Orchids N.S.W.* 84 (1943); J. H. Willis *Handb. Pls Vict.* 1:413 (1962)

Plant usually 30–35 cm. high. Leaves basal, elliptical to lanceolate on petioles 5–7 cm. long. Stem bracts up to five, 4–6 cm. long. Flower large, solitary, translucent, white with green lines and brown markings; galea inflated at the base, erect then incurved, 4–5 cm. long, with a short acuminate apex, the petals dilated. Lower lip erect, cuneate with a wide sinus, the filiform lobes reflexed and exceeding the galea. Labellum broad-linear, compressed for about one-fifth of its length into a point; lamina 1·5–2 cm. long, almost straight but curving at the tip, a broad ridge running along the centre with a corresponding channel on the under side. Basal appendage shortly penicillate, linear, curved. Column erect, 1·7–2·5 cm. long, a subulate tooth present in the upper angle of wings; the lower lobes oblong with inturned ciliate margins. Stigma ovate-elliptical.

P. baptistii favours the dense scrubs, usually in the vicinity of streams or swamps. It is one of the largest representatives of the genus and often forms extensive colonies.

FLOWERING PERIOD: Aug. to Nov.

COMMON NAME: King Greenhood

DISTRIBUTION: From northern Qld, through NSW, to eastern Vic.; usually coastal and often common

P. curta (Plate 301)

P. curta R. Br. *Prodr. Flor. Nov. Holl.* 326 (1810); A. J. Ewart *Flor. Vict.* 373 (1931); J. M. Black *Flor. S. Aust.* ed. 2:243 (1943); H. M. R. Rupp *Orchids N.S.W.* 82 (1943); J. H. Willis *Handb. Pls Vict.* 1:412 (1962); M. J. Firth *Native Orchids Tasm.* 74 (1965)

A rather sturdy glabrous plant, 10–30 cm. high, although in dry areas specimens may attain only 5 cm. Basal leaves usually two to five in a radical rosette, 3–9 cm. long, on petioles of variable length, ovate or oblong-elliptical; margins often crisped. Stem bracts two or three (including the terminal one), loosely sheathing. Flower usually solitary, green with pale red-brown markings; galea erect, 2–3·5 cm. high; lower lip cuneate, with a very wide sinus and the shortly acuminate lobes not, or rarely, exceeding the galea. Labellum red-brown, on a short irritable claw, somewhat obtuse, recurved slightly and protruding through the sinus; lamina about

2 cm. long, oblong-linear, very narrow at the base, the anterior portion curiously twisted; under surface with a narrow groove, corresponding to the broad raised longitudinal ridge above; basal appendage stout, curved, fimbriate. Column about 18 mm. high, upper angle of wings broad, with fine erect subulate setae; lower lobes oblong, with short inturned marginal cilia. Anther horizontal, obtuse. Stigma oblong-lanceolate, viscid. (In J. M. Black's *Flor. S. Aust.* Rogers describes the stigma as 'not viscid'. In the very numerous specimens of *P. curta* which I have examined from Vic. and NSW I have found the stigma definitely viscid, though not to the degree obtaining in some other species of the genus.)

P. curta is a very common terrestrial orchid of temperate wood-lands; the finest examples form extensive colonies in cool, moist and shaded gullies, and the species is absent from all dry inland areas.

FLOWERING PERIOD: July to Oct., sometimes as late as Nov.

COMMON NAME: Blunt Greenhood

DISTRIBUTION: Widespread in all states except WA, but in Qld confined to the south-east and in SA also confined to the south-east; also New Caledonia

P. hildae (Plate 302)

P. hildae W. H. Nicholls in *Qd Nat.* 10:39, t. 3 (1937); H. M. R. Rupp *Orchids N.S.W.* 83 (1943)

A slender glabrous plant, 10–15 cm. high. Leaves basal, two or three, rather large; laminae 2–4 cm. long, ovate or oblong, on long petioles. Stem bracts small, two to four. Flower solitary, rather small, almost wholly green, the apex tinged with light brown; galea about 2 cm. long, erect, incurved for upper third, sub-acute; conjoined sepals erect with acute sinus, the finely subulate points embracing the galea but not exceeding it. Labellum spathulate or oblong-elliptical, comparatively large, 9–11 mm. long, almost straight and not twisting as in *P. curta*, irritable on a short movable claw; apex shortly obtuse, protruding through the sinus of the lower lip; lamina traversed by a central raised longitudinal line; appendage at base linear, curved, penicillate. Column 12–14 mm. long, the upper angle of wings produced into long erect processes; lower angles somewhat narrow, obtuse, the inner margins ciliate. Stigma narrow, prominent. Anther prominent with a short mucro.

Very similar to *P. curta*, but with smaller flowers, narrower sinus and labellum never twisting. There is little doubt that the form figured by FitzGerald in *Aust. Orchids* 1⁵: (1879), and there referred to as a probable hybrid between *P. curta* and *P. pedunculata*, is in reality identical with *P. hildae*. It grows in small colonies among the rich black humus accumulated in subtropical rain forests, and, because it favours shady places on the edge of thick scrub, it is easily overlooked.

FLOWERING PERIOD: Mar. to Oct., earlier in the north

DISTRIBUTION: Qld, and NSW as far south as Wollongong, generally on or near the coast

P. alpina (Plate 303)

P. alpina R. S. Rogers in *Proc. roy. Soc. Vict.* new ser. 28:108, t. 9 (1915); A. J. Ewart *Flor. Vict.* 370 (1931); H. M. R. Rupp *Orchids N.S.W.* 88 (1943); J. H. Willis *Handb. Pls Vict.* 1:404 (1962); M. J. Firth *Native Orchids Tasm.* 70 (1965)

A slender glabrous plant, varying much in height, 10–45 cm. high. Leaves cauline, not forming a radical rosette, varying in size and shape, 2–6 cm. long, lanceolate to oblong-lanceolate, elliptical or ovate, stem-clasping at the base; margins often crenulate; one or two small scale-like bracts at base of stem. Flower solitary, large, pale green; galea erect, 2·5–3·5 cm. long, gradually curved forward near the apex which is rather blunt; lower lip narrowly cuneate at the base with very broad sinus, the lobes ending in rather short fine points which are sharply reflexed across both sides of the galea so that they lie more or less horizontally. Labellum usually greenish, sometimes red-brown, about 12 mm. long, linear-lanceolate, curved towards the tip which is blunt; lamina tapering at the apex, convex, traversed by a prominent raised central ridge and corresponding channel on the under side; curved linear basal appendage densely penicillate. Column shorter than the labellum; upper angle of wings toothed; lower angle narrow, obtuse, with inturned shortly ciliate margins. Stigma prominent, ovate-lanceolate, the points directed upward. Anther small, oblique.

P. alpina was at one time considered to be a variant of what is now called *P. falcata*, when the latter was erroneously identified with *P. cucullata*, but there is really little resemblance to *P. cucullata*. Two notable features distinguishing *P. alpina* are the soft blending of green and white in the galea and the pronounced backward sweep of the lateral sepals. It is not strictly an alpine orchid, though often abundant at high elevations, and is usually met with in damp forest country and along the banks of mountain streams. The tip of the labellum not infrequently exhibits a decided twist, as in *P. curta*.

FLOWERING PERIOD: Aug. to Nov., extending to the end of summer at high altitudes

COMMON NAME: Alpine Greenhood

DISTRIBUTION: NSW, where localised and uncommon, at Kosciusko, Mount Wilson in the Blue Mountains and the head of the Macleay River; also Vic. and Tas., where often abundant in cool montane situations

P. furcata (Plate 304)

P. furcata Lindl. *Gen. & Spec. orchid. Pls* 390 (1840); A. J. Ewart *Flor. Vict.* 372 (1931); J. M. Black *Flor. S. Aust.* ed. 2:246 (1943); H. M. R. Rupp *Orchids N.S.W.* 86 (1943); J. H. Willis *Handb. Pls Vict.* 1:403 (1962); M. J. Firth *Native Orchids Tasm.* 71 (1965)

Plant moderately robust or slender, glabrous, 15–30 cm. high. Basal leaves two or three, shortly petiolate, 1·5–3·5 cm. long, ovate or ovate-lanceolate, margins entire or crenate. Stem bracts two or three, leaf-like, loosely sheathing, 2–2·5 cm. long. Flower solitary and erect; galea 2·5–3 cm. long, curved forward and beaked; dorsal sepal and petals usually equal in length, wholly green and white, the petals simple, leaf-like; lower lip erect, with acute sinus, the filamentous points directed forward, embracing the galea and exceeding it by 4–5 mm. Labellum oblong or broadly linear, wide at the base, gradually narrowing upwards to a narrowly obtuse tip, erect, curved forward in its anterior third, with apex protruding slightly through the sinus; appendage curved, trifid, the central lobe tufted. Column shorter than labellum; upper lobes wide, with an erect subulate tooth at each upper angle; lower lobes rather acute; margins with inturned cilia. Stigma narrow-elliptical.

The first living specimens that I had seen of *P. furcata* came from the National Park about forty miles north-west of Hobart, Tas. These were growing in fairly heavy black soil amongst native grass, in open spaces on the northern bank of the Russell River. These plants differ from herbarium material of more typical *P. furcata* in having smaller flowers with more filiform lateral sepals; indeed, Rupp suggests that they approach *P. foliata* more closely than *P. furcata*, which he regards as a kind of link between *P. falcata* and *P. alpina*. In January 1950 I received fairly typical fresh specimens

of *P. furcata* from the southern end of Lake St Clair, Tas. In NZ is a variable assemblage that has been referred to *P. micromega* Hook.f. and some of the forms are too close to the Tasmanian *P. furcata* to be distinguishable. Rupp and E. D. Hatch have expressed the opinion that *P. micromega* should be synonymised under *P. furcata*, to which a far greater variability attaches than I had at first supposed.

FLOWERING PERIOD: Oct. to Jan.

COMMON NAME: Forked Greenhood

DISTRIBUTION: Uncommon and seldom collected in NSW (Kosciusko region), Vic. (Condah), and SA (Mount Gambier), but often locally abundant in Tas., usually in cool hilly situations; also NZ

P. vereenae (Plate 305)

P. vereenae R. S. Rogers in *Trans. roy. Soc. S. Aust.* 38:360, t. 18 (1914); J. M. Black *Flor. S. Aust.* ed. 2:245 (1943); M. J. Firth *Native Orchids Tasm.* 71 (1965)

A plant of slender or moderately robust habit, 7–15 cm. high. Leaves three to five in a radical rosette, 3–5 cm. long, almost sessile, lanceolate-ovate, often rather fleshy. Bracts one or two, about the middle of the stem or below the ovary, very large and leaf-like, broadly lanceolate, sheathing at the base. Flower solitary; galea 2–3 cm. long, green and white, erect but abruptly curved forward near the apex, terminating in a rather acute point; conjoined sepals making an acute sinus, then tapering into fine points which embrace the sides of the galea and curve forward above it. Labellum on a movable claw about 12–14 mm. long, linear-oblong or lanceolate, higher than the anther, slightly recurved towards the subacute tip which protrudes through the sinus; lamina traversed throughout its length by a raised central ridge, with two or three longitudinal veins on each side, the under surface with a deep furrow corresponding to the ridge; basal appendage curved, its tip trifid and penicillate. Column about 1·5 cm. long; upper angles of wings produced into an acute tooth, the lower angles forming blunt, linear-oblong ciliate lobes. Stigma narrow-lanceolate, occupying the middle third of column, its upper angle toothed.

This species appears to be more closely related to *P. furcata*, although having affinities also with *P. pedunculata* and *P. nana*. Tasmanian specimens are all much more robust than those described and figured by Rogers, while the labellum also departs in shape. However, after examining Atkinson's Mount Bischoff collection, Rogers agreed in placing it with his *P. vereenae*. The Mount Bischoff specimens were growing under peaty conditions in a morass, but shaded beech forests are the usual habitat for this species in Tas.

FLOWERING PERIOD: Sept. to Dec.

DISTRIBUTION: Apparently confined to Cherry Gardens, SA, and Mount Bischoff, Tas.; uncommon and rarely collected

P. foliata (Plates 306 and 307)

P. foliata Hook.f. *Flor. N.-Z.* 1:249 (1853); J. H. Willis *Handb. Pls Vict.* 1:403 (1962); M. J. Firth *Native Orchids Tasm.* 70 (1965)

SYNONYMY: *P. gracilis* W. H. Nicholls in *Vict. Nat.* 43:324 (1927)

A very slender plant, 12–30 cm. high. Stem leaves varying in size and shape, but usually oblong-lanceolate, on slender petioles, the margins often crisped. Stem bracts three or four, sessile, lanceolate, acuminate, clasping at the base, 2–4 cm. long, the lowest bract scarious. Flower solitary, rather small, green with the apex of galea brown. Galea about 2 cm. long, erect, incurved, the apices of dorsal sepal and petals about equal in length, shortly acuminate. Lateral sepals forming an erect, narrowly cuneate lip, the lobes prolonged into filiform points which embrace the galea and exceed it by about 8 mm. Labellum oblong, the obtuse apex, which is sometimes decurved, protruding beyond the sinus of the lower lip; under side of lamina slightly concave towards the tip; upper surface slightly concave towards the base, and traversed by a raised longitudinal ridge with corresponding narrow furrow beneath; basal appendage stout, curved, thickly and shortly penicillate. Column a little shorter than labellum, the upper angle of wings toothed; lower lobes narrow, obtuse, with incurved ciliate margins. Stigma narrow, the point directed upwards.

P. foliata varies considerably in height and robustness. Specimens from south-western Vic. (Portland district) show heights from 5–30 cm. In the majority of my specimens the foliage is well-developed, and clothes the stem toward its base, though not strictly basal; these are typical, but some specimens from grasslands possess a definite basal rosette of leaves as in *P. nutans*. *P. foliata* approaches somewhat closely to *P. alpina*, but is much more slender than that species, and the flower is smaller. The large leaves and stout labellum are similar to those of *P. cucullata*, but in no other respect does it resemble that well-marked species.

In the field this greenhood has been mistaken, on first glance, for *P. pedunculata*, with which it is sometimes found growing; but the resemblance is only superficial, heightened, no doubt, by the dark coloration in the forepart of the galea and the slender character of both plants. *P. pedunculata* is even more slender, with leaves strictly basal and stem leaves smaller; the flower also is smaller, and the labellum of different shape—bluntly ovate. [For the first record from NSW see J. A. P. Blackmore in *Orchadian* 2:76 (1967).—Ed.]

FLOWERING PERIOD: Mainly Aug. to Nov. but as late as Feb. in Tas. mountains

COMMON NAME: Slender Greenhood

DISTRIBUTION: Southern NSW at Batlow, Vic. and Tas.; widespread through a variety of habitats, but generally uncommon

P. cucullata (Plate 308)

P. cucullata R. Br. *Prodr. Flor. Nov. Holl.* 327 (1810); A. J. Ewart *Flor. Vict.* 372 (1931); J. M. Black *Flor. S. Aust.* ed. 2:245 (1943); J. H. Willis *Handb. Pls Vict.* 1:402 (1962); M. J. Firth *Native Orchids Tasm.* 69 (1965)

A stout glabrous plant 5–30 cm. in height. Leaves large, up to 10 cm. long, ovate-oblong to elliptical, stoutly petiolate; in dwarf specimens crowded towards the base, in taller plants somewhat scattered upward with the longest towards the middle. Stem bracts similar to the leaves, but smaller and clasping at their bases. Flower large, solitary, enveloped by the uppermost bract, pubescent, green with brown or cayenne markings towards the front. Galea erect, about 3 cm. high; tip abruptly decurved, shortly acuminate or merely acute. Lower sepals forming an erect lip with acute sinus, the lobes shortly acuminate and in some specimens not exceeding the galea. Labellum oblong-elliptical on a movable claw, about 1·5 cm. long, with the tip obtuse and only slightly recurved, usually dark reddish-brown; upper surface convex, with a broad central ridge; basal appendage stout, linear, curved, thickly penicillate. Column about 2 cm. long, the upper angle of wings with a short subulate process; lower lobes oblong, the margins with short inturned cilia. Stigma ovate-lanceolate or elliptical.

P. cucullata is a well-marked species, having large, usually crowded, somewhat spathe-like leaves. The specific epithet alludes to the large cowl-like upper bract, which in many specimens, envelops the

ovary and portion of the flower. Rogers, in his admirable booklet *An Introduction to the Study of South Australian Orchids* 19, Fig. 13 (1911), refers to the characteristics of this interesting greenhood thus: 'It feels the cold badly, because you will notice that it is muffled up, sometimes to the ears, in an overcoat of big leaves'. In Victoria, the species favours sandy coastal tracts in shade, and is not commonly observed.

FLOWERING PERIOD: Normally Aug. to Oct., but as late as Jan. in Tas. mountains

COMMON NAME: Leafy Greenhood

DISTRIBUTION: Vic. and SA, usually on southern coastal heaths; also Tas. where it extends to alpine areas

P. pedunculata (Plate 309)

P. pedunculata R. Br. *Prodr. Flor. Nov. Holl.* 327 (1810); A. J. Ewart *Flor. Vict.* 369 (1931); J. M. Black *Flor. S. Aust.* ed. 2:245 (1943); H. M. R. Rupp *Orchids N.S.W.* 86 (1943); J. H. Willis *Handb. Pls Vict.* 1:411 (1962); M. J. Firth *Native Orchids Tasm.* 73 (1965)

Typically a very slender plant 10–25 cm. high. Leaves three to six in a basal rosette, 2–4 cm. long, ovate or oblong on long petioles, often with undulate margins. Stem bracts small, one to four, the uppermost often remote from the flower. Flower normally solitary, up to 2 cm. long, green with brown or deep reddish-brown markings which are restricted to the forepart of the galea, sometimes almost wholly dark red-brown. Galea erect for almost two-thirds of its length, then becoming horizontal and terminating in a short acute, often slightly upturned point. Conjoined sepals united for less than half their length, forming an acute and slightly gibbous sinus, the free portions produced into erect, divergent, subulate points far exceeding the galea. Labellum dark reddish-brown, bluntly ovate on a movable claw, shorter than the column; lamina about 5 mm. long, with a longitudinal central ridge and corresponding channel on the under side (channel varying in length in individual flowers); basal appendage long, linear, curved, trifid at the apex. Column erect, about 11 mm. long, the upper angle of wings produced into a filiform process; lower lobes lanceolate, obtuse, the margins with incurved cilia. Stigma elliptical, not viscid.

P. pedunculata is more abundant in tea-tree scrubs near the coast than in open forest or shaded gullies. In Vic. fern gullies, e.g. Dandenong and Otway Ranges, it has been found ascending the trunks of tree-ferns.

FLOWERING PERIOD: July to Oct., sometimes as late as Nov. in sub-alpine regions

COMMON NAME: Maroonhood

DISTRIBUTION: Fairly common in temperate parts of all Australian states except WA, and in Qld confined to the south-east

P. recurva (Plate 310)

P. recurva Benth. *Flor. aust.* 6:360 (1873); R. Erickson *Orchids West* ed. 2:41 (1965)

A slender, somewhat rigid plant, usually 20–30 cm. high but occasionally reaching a height of 45–50 cm., without any radical rosette of leaves during the flowering period. Stem bracts leaf-like, alternate, linear to linear-lanceolate, 2–5 cm. long, the lowest ones scale-like, those subtending the pedicels usually more lanceolate and shorter. Flowers one to three, whitish with prominent longitudinal green and red-brown or greyish stripes. Galea erect, hardly curved, 3–5 cm. long (excluding the points of the perianth), somewhat funnel-shaped at the apex; dorsal sepal as well as the petals ending in short recurved points. Lateral sepals forming an erect lip as long as or longer than the galea, cuneate with acute sinus; lobes erect, then recurved and terminating in terete reflexed points 1·5–2 cm. long. Labellum on a short claw; lamina oblong, dilated about the middle, narrowed towards the base, concave, with shortly ciliate margins, abruptly narrowed in the upper third to a comparatively long linear point and with a narrow longitudinal raised line traversing the centre; apex blunt, grooved, its margins with short cilia; appendage linear, with a long subulate point and two short lateral ones. Column erect, with upper angle of wings ciliate in front, at the rear produced into a short process; lower lobes narrow-oblong with short cilia. Stigma long and narrow; anther with a short point.

P. recurva is readily distinguished from all other species in the genus by the unusual form and outline of the flower—attributable to the decurved lateral sepals, etc. It chiefly favours the near-coastal sandy soils and grows among low scrub. Brown and Recurved Shell Orchid are other names commonly applied. The type was from the Upper Hay River, WA.

FLOWERING PERIOD: Aug. to Oct.

COMMON NAME: Jug Orchid

DISTRIBUTION: WA where it is widespread, and often common in the south-west; also NT

P. alata (Plate 311)

P. alata (Labill.) Reichenb.f. *Beitr. syst. Pflk.* 70 (1871); A. J. Ewart *Flor. Vict.* 370 (1931); J. M. Black *Flor. S. Aust.* ed. 2:246 (1943); H. M. R. Rupp *Orchids N.S.W.* 91 (1943); J. H. Willis *Handb. Pls Vict.* 1:409 (1962); M. J. Firth *Native Orchids Tasm.* 74 (1965)

SYNONYMY: *Disperis alata* Labill. *Nov. Holl. Plant. Specim.* 2:59, t. 210 (1806); *Pterostylis praecox* Lindl. *Gen. & Spec. orchid. Pls* 388 (1840); *P. striata* R. D. FitzG. *Aust. Orchids* 1³:+t. (1877)

A slender plant usually 10–25 cm. high. No rosulate leaves present at flowering time. Stem leaves three or four, small and bract-like, clasping, sometimes well-developed, rarely longer than 3 cm. Flower usually solitary, white with dark green longitudinal stripes and some purplish or brown markings (occasionally with sage-green stripes on a grey ground and other markings light rufous-brown). Galea erect, then gradually curved forward, 2–3 cm. long; apex rather blunt, ending in a short point about 2 mm. Conjoined sepals erect; the filiform points separated by a wide, truncate and notched sinus, erect, far exceeding the galea and hooked forward at the tips. Labellum about 10 mm. long, narrow-lanceolate, brownish, marked with longitudinal stripes; lamina concave with a prominent central ridge, almost straight; apex acute, not protruding beyond the wide, abrupt sinus of the conjoined sepals; basal appendage narrow-linear, curved, penicillate. Column robust, erect, green, 10–14 mm. long; upper angle of wings falcate; lower lobes oblong, blunt, with incurved ciliate margins. Stigma prominent, elliptical, bilobed.

A common orchid on sandy scrublands near the coast, but ranging inland through sclerophyll forest, usually on the drier Palaeozoic sedimentary formation. On hungry open terrain and during dry seasons, small three-leaved and flowerless plants often appear—these would doubtless have flowered in a normal season. In April 1947 H. Goldsack collected at Wolseley, SA, a remarkable plant which seems to be a hybrid between *P. alata* and *P. robusta*.

FLOWERING PERIOD: Apr. to Aug.

COMMON NAME: Striped Greenhood

DISTRIBUTION: Localised and rare in NSW, at Yass, but common and often forming dense colonies in Vic., Tas. and south-eastern SA

P. toveyana (Plate 312)

P. toveyana A. J. Ewart & Sharman in *Proc. roy. Soc. Vict.* new ser. 28:235, t. 28 (1916); A. J. Ewart *Flor. Vict.* 369 (1931); J. H. Willis *Handb. Pls Vict.* 1:402 (1962); M. J. Firth *Native Orchids Tasm.* 69 (1965)

A slender glabrous plant 8–16 cm. high. Leaves 1·5–3 cm. long, cauline, alternate, occasionally strictly basal, when on rather long petioles, or even absent; ovate or ovate-oblong, acuminate. Stem bracts lanceolate, acuminate. Flower solitary, whitish, prominently striped with green and dark brown, the other markings red-brown and red; galea 1·5–2·5 cm. long, erect, gibbous at base, moderately incurved upward; dorsal sepal with a short acuminate point, usually decurved; petals falcate with broadly acute points; lower lip erect, with wide sinus, the entire part broadly cuneate, the erect curved filiform points embracing the galea and far exceeding it. Labellum dark red-brown, lanceolate, very broad at base of lamina, gradually narrowing to a truncate bifid apex; lamina about 9 mm. long, with a longitudinal central ridge throughout and a corresponding channel beneath; basal appendage curved, penicillate. Column about half the length of galea, the upper angle of wings with an erect subulate tooth; lower lobes obtuse, with short inturned marginal cilia. Stigma ovate, deeply channelled.

P. toveyana exists nowhere abundantly, but it is usually found in close association with *P. concinna* and *P. alata*, and is presumed to be a natural hybrid between these species. Rodway records that hybridisation is common between *P. concinna* and *P. alata* when they grow together. When *P. toveyana* was found originally at Mentone, Vic., intermediates were also in evidence; but colonies found since, in widely separated localities, show that such transitions are rather uncommon.

FLOWERING PERIOD: May to Aug.

COMMON NAME: Mentone Greenhood

DISTRIBUTION: Vic. and Tas. generally in coastal heathlands or near coastal ranges

P. robusta (Plate 313)

P. robusta (A. J. Ewart & Sharman) R. S. Rogers in *Trans. roy. Soc. S. Aust.* 51:296 (1927); A. J. Ewart *Flor. Vict.* 370 (1931); J. M. Black *Flor. S. Aust.* ed. 2:246 (1943); J. H. Willis *Handb. Pls Vict.* 1:409 (1962); R. Erickson *Orchids West* ed. 2:41 (1965)

SYNONYMY: *P. praecox* Lindl. var. *robusta* A. J. Ewart & Sharman in *Proc. roy. Soc. Vict.* new ser. 28:234, t. 27 fig. 7 (1916)

A slender glabrous plant 5–15 cm. in height. Radical leaves broadly ovate, stellate, absent in the flowering plant. Stem-leaves four to seven, including the uppermost bract, alternate, clasping, broadly lanceolate, acuminate, increasing in size up the stem to about 5 cm. in length. Flower large, solitary, greenish with dark green longitudinal stripes and lines; galea 3–4 cm. long, erect, then gradually curved forward towards the apex; apex of dorsal sepal with a very short point; conjoined sepals with a broad sinus, the filiform points embracing and far exceeding the galea. Labellum on an irritable claw, almost straight, up to 15 mm. long, lanceolate, slightly longer than the column, the tip produced into a comparatively short acute point, not protruding beyond the sinus; lamina traversed by a narrow raised ridge down the centre, appendage curved, linear, penicillate. Column erect, 15 mm. long, an erect tooth-like appendage in the upper angle of the column wings; the lower lobes broad, obtuse, the inner margins shortly ciliate. Stigma small, ovate.

P. robusta prefers sheltered positions under trees and shrubs, but may also be found in exposed places. In some of its forms, it closely approaches *P. alata*, differing mainly in the larger flower, broader and shorter labellum and longer stem-leaves. The labellum varies much in colour, from pink to dark brown, or green with brownish markings. In WA this species readily colonises pine plantations.

FLOWERING PERIOD: Apr. to Aug.

COMMON NAME: Sharp-leaf Greenhood

DISTRIBUTION: Widespread through northern and western Vic., south-eastern SA, and south-western WA, often common in dry inland areas

P. hamiltonii (Plate 314)

P. hamiltonii W. H. Nicholls in *Vict. Nat.* 50:89 (1933); J. M. Black *Flor. S. Aust.* ed. 2:246 (1943); R. Erickson *Orchids West* ed. 2:38 (1965)

A moderately slender plant, 8–15 cm. high. Radical leaves not present during the flowering period, rosulate and often numerous, dull green, frosty, broadly ovate, on very short petioles. Stem leaves four to eight, linear-lanceolate to oblong-lanceolate, acuminate, rather spreading, stem-clasping, gradually increasing in length upward to about 3 cm., the basal one or two reduced to small bracts. Flower solitary, large, with longitudinal and very narrow red stripes on a translucent-white ground. Galea erect, 2·5–3 cm. long; apex decurved and shortly acuminate. Conjoined sepals erect, with broad sinus; the very long filiform points falcate, embracing the galea and far exceeding it. Labellum on a short irritable claw, almost wholly red, strap-like, almost straight; apex only slightly curved forward, and showing well beyond the sinus of the lower lip (when relaxed); lamina 1·8–2 cm. long, oblong-linear, tapering to a very long obtuse point, the broad basal part deeply channelled and a narrow raised line traversing the centre; basal appendage linear, much curved, the apex beset with short barbellate setae. Column erect, 1·2–1·4 cm. long, almost wholly red to very dark brown (sepia); upper lobes with a short erect subulate tooth; lower lobes oblong, obtuse, margins with very short incurved cilia.

The only material which I have seen of this rather uncommon orchid is that collected at Boyup Brook by Miss E. Corker in July 1930. *P. hamiltonii* more closely approaches *P. rogersii* and *P. robusta* than any other species, but affinities with *P. constricta* are also obvious. The sinus of the conjoined sepals, forming the lower lip, is very acute in *P. rogersii*, while in *P. hamiltonii* it is flat, with a notch in the centre; in the latter the labellum also has a different shape—almost straight and strap-like—whereas with *P. rogersii* it is more curved (often circinnate), with a shorter point. In *P. robusta* we find a comparatively broad labellum, hardly exceeding the column in length and thus too short for the tip to be seen beyond the sinus of the lower lip.

FLOWERING PERIOD: May to July

DISTRIBUTION: SA, near Naracoorte, and on the Eyre and York Peninsulas; and WA where apparently widespread in the south-west

P. truncata (Plate 315)

P. truncata R. D. FitzG. *Aust. Orchids* 1⁴:+t. (1878); A. J. Ewart *Flor. Vict.* 369 (1931); H. M. R. Rupp *Orchids N.S.W.* 89 (1943); J. H. Willis *Handb. Pls Vict.* 1:407 (1962)

A dwarf species, 5–10 cm. high, rarely to 16 cm. Radical leaves rosulate, not produced on the flowering plant, obovate or ovate, occasionally varying from ovate-acuminate to linear and on petioles of variable length. Stem leaves two to five, clasping, lanceolate or almost linear, sometimes even ovate, acuminate. Flower large, 3·5–5 cm. long, solitary (sometimes two-flowered), translucent-green and longitudinally striped with darker green or reddish bands. Galea erect, then gradually decurving, with widely expanded forepart. Dorsal sepal usually exceeding the petals by about 2–6 mm. its apex acute or shortly acuminate, rarely truncate. Lateral sepals erect, united for less than a quarter of their length, slightly gibbous at the acute sinus; filiform lobes erect, embracing the galea and exceeding it by about 3 cm. Petals falcate, broadly truncate. Labellum red or brown, 15–20 mm. long; lamina broadly linear to lanceolate, the tapering portion decurved; tip varying from acuminate to mucronate, often with a slight twist, protruding well beyond the sinus of the lower lip; appendage curved, penicillate. Column erect, slightly curved, about 1·3 cm. long; upper angle of wings with an erect subulate tooth; lower angle comparatively narrow, with short cilia along the margin, the wings marked with a conspicuous brown spot towards the front. Stigma lanceolate, projecting at the base, situated about half way up the column.

P. truncata is very distinctive and remarkable for the enormous expansion of the decurved forepart of the galea, also for its comparatively large flower, often half the total height in this dwarf plant. R. D. FitzGerald apparently had scanty material for his description, and the specific epithet—derived from the truncate character of the dorsal sepal—is inappropriate. I have examined hundreds of flowers from both states, and have seen only ten in which the dorsal sepal was conspicuously shorter than the petals; only in three of these could the dorsal be called 'truncate'. The galea, being very easily damaged, has earned its species the apt vernacular name; it is also referred to as Little Dumpy.

Until its discovery on the granitic You Yangs, Vic., by the author in 1924, *P. truncata* had remained practically unknown for almost fifty years. Subsequently, this orchid was found in quantity near Melbourne, on the open grassland of the basalt plains at Tottenham, also among grass tussocks in light forest at Coimadai East and on the eastern heathlands of Port Phillip Bay.

FLOWERING PERIOD: Apr. to July, occasionally as early as Feb.

COMMON NAME: Brittle Greenhood

DISTRIBUTION: North-eastern NSW and south-central Vic., localised and discontinuous but abundant where colonies occur; in Vic. it is restricted to localities within a forty-mile radius of Melbourne

P. rogersii (Plate 316)

P. rogersii E. Coleman in *Vict. Nat.* 46:100, t. 5 (1929); R. Erickson *Orchids West* ed. 2:41 (1965)

A slender plant, 10–20 cm. high; stem papillose. Radical leaves not present at flowering time. Stem leaves four to seven, lanceolate, rather spreading, clasping at the base, bract-like below, the upper ones 5 cm. long. Flower large, single, translucent-white or grey with rufous longitudinal stripes on all the segments and column. Galea about 4 cm. long, the three segments about equal in length, slightly but not abruptly curved. Conjoined sepals forming an erect lip with acute sinus; lobes 5–6 cm. long, produced into erect filiform points embracing the galea. Labellum on a broad claw, very irritable, markedly recurved, with the tip sometimes circinnate and protruding through the sinus of the lateral sepals; lamina about 2 cm. long, channelled above, with a longitudinal ridge traversing the centre, tapering to a long obtuse point; apex usually emarginate or truncate, its margins shortly ciliate; basal appendage obscurely trilobed, penicillate, markedly recurved. Column erect; upper angle of wings produced into short, erect obtuse teeth, scarcely higher than anther; lower lobes elongated oblong-obtuse, margins with short cilia. Stigma cushion-shaped, elongated, oblong-ovate or elliptical.

In general appearance *P. rogersii* approaches somewhat closely *P. robusta*, but the much longer, hairy-tipped labellum and very acute sinus between the lower sepals well separate it. This species readily colonises pine plantations in WA.

FLOWERING PERIOD: June and July

DISTRIBUTION: Endemic in WA where it is confined to the south-west

P. constricta (Plate 317)

P. constricta O. H. Sargent in *J. West Aust. nat. Hist. Soc. 2⁴*:24 (1907); R. Erickson *Orchids West* ed. 2:41 (1965)

A slender plant 7–15 cm. high; stem sometimes flexuose, minutely papillate. Radical leaves forming a rosette not attached to the flowering stem, ovate-lanceolate, shortly petiolate. Stem bracts four or five, narrow-lanceolate, acute or acuminate, about 1–3·5 cm. long, becoming longer upward; a small sheathing bract at the base. Flower solitary, translucent-white with green and dark brown stripes and other markings. Galea erect, incurved, 2–4 cm. long, the apices curved and shortly acuminate. Conjoined sepals erect, cuneate, with broad sinus; the lobes erect, filiform, embracing the galea and extending well beyond it, the tips curved forward. Labellum on a short irritable claw; lamina oblong-lanceolate, blunt, 1·5–2·5 cm. long, with margins abruptly constricted in the upper half and just beyond this constriction markedly decurved, with a narrow longitudinal central ridge, concave on either side below the contraction; tip long and clavate; basal appendage curved, penicillate. Column 1·3–2 cm. long, abruptly bent towards the base; upper margin of wings produced into an acute tooth; the lower lobes hatchet-shaped with incurved shortly ciliate margins. Stigma ovate, the points directed upward.

O. H. Sargent described his plant as 'usually about 8 cm. high', but my material was up to 15 cm. tall; he also described the stem as 'flexuose'—a feature not apparent in my specimens, but apparently present in some individuals.

FLOWERING PERIOD: June to Sept.

DISTRIBUTION: Endemic in WA where it is widely distributed through inland areas in the south-west

P. grandiflora (Plate 318)

P. grandiflora R. Br. *Prodr. Flor. Nov. Holl.* 327 (1810); A. J. Ewart *Flor. Vict.* 371 (1931); H. M. R. Rupp *Orchids N.S.W.* 88 (1943); J. H. Willis *Handb. Pls Vict.* 1:405 (1962); M. J. Firth *Native Orchids Tasm.* 72 (1965)

A very slender plant 15–35 cm. high, without basal leaves (in occasional specimens a small lateral growth of leaves is present). Radical leaves on a separate shoot, often absent at flowering time, ovate or oblong, shortly petiolate. Stem leaves usually six to nine, including the one subtending the pedicel, lanceolate, acuminate, 4–6 cm. long, those towards the base being reduced to sheathing scales. Flower translucent-white, with fine green stripes and rich red-brown markings. Galea 3–3·5 cm. high, erect for half its length then abruptly but gracefully curved forward, the forepart expanding into a wide hood and somewhat decurved; apices acute and darker in colour, the point of the dorsal sepal about 1 cm. long. Petals falcate-lanceolate and very broad, prominently veined, sometimes nearly as long as the dorsal sepal to which their inner margins are hooked. Lower sepals erect, united to form a slender cuneate lip about 2 cm. high, delicately but firmly marked with green stripes; sinus broad with a projecting lip; filiform points erect, embracing and exceeding the galea by about 4 cm., the tips outwardly inclined.

Labellum erect on an irritable claw; lamina oblong-linear in its basal part, then somewhat abruptly narrowing to a long filiform point with clavate apex, projecting far beyond the sinus (when relaxed) and almost in contact with the decurved part of the galea; a narrow raised longitudinal ridge traverses the centre; basal appendage slender, curved, penicillate. Column erect, about 2 cm. high, the upper lobes with an acute tooth; lower lobes oblong, obtuse with incurved marginal hairs. Stigma high up, ovate, short and broad.

With its comparatively large, elegant blooms and vivid red-brown markings, this orchid is probably the most beautiful among all species of *Pterostylis*. It is also known as the Long-tongue Greenhood, or sometimes Cobra Greenhood—from the dilated apex of the galea. Specimens collected by W. Hunter (Aug. 1941) between Mount Raymond and the Brodribb River, eastern Vic., exceeded 50 cm. in height; these grew in sand amongst bracken in moderately timbered country, and had flowers of exceptional size—6 cm. around the curve of the galea.

FLOWERING PERIOD: Normally May to July, but in Tas. sometimes extending into Oct.

COMMON NAME: Superb Greenhood

DISTRIBUTION: Extending from the cooler parts of northern Qld to NSW, Vic., and eastern Tas.; generally coastal

P. revoluta (Plate 319)

P. revoluta R. Br. *Prodr. Flor. Nov. Holl.* 327 (1810); A. J. Ewart *Flor. Vict.* 371 (1931); H. M. R. Rupp *Orchids N.S.W.* 90 (1943); J. H. Willis *Handb. Pls Vict.* 1:405 (1962)

A slender plant rarely with basal leaves, 10–25 cm. high. Radical leaves forming a rosette distinct from the flowering stem, obovate or ovate, rarely lanceolate, on rather long slender petioles. Stem bracts three to five, usually small, clasping at the base, lanceolate, acuminate, the lowermost small and scarious (in damp situations the stem bracts may attain a length of 4·5 cm.). Flower usually solitary, large, green and white with fine longitudinal darker green lines and some light brown markings (absent in succulent forms). Galea erect or inclined forward, 4–4·5 cm. long, sometimes 7 cm. around the curve; gibbous at the base, thereafter gracefully arching over the column and well over the lower lip; the filiform points of both petals and dorsal sepal directed downward, the sepal being much longer than petals. Petals falcate, acuminate, their inner margins hooked to the dorsal sepal. Lateral sepals conjoined to form a lower lip which is erect and cuneate at the base, the very slender upright and outwardly-inclined filiform points much exceeding the galea. Labellum irritable on a narrow claw, arising from the column base, glabrous, gracefully curved and protruding through the widely acute sinus of the lower lip; lamina about 2 cm. long, ovate-lanceolate, gradually contracting to a fairly long acute point, with a narrow raised longitudinal ridge traversing the centre; the curved linear extension at the base ending in a penicillate tuft. Column erect, the wings hatchet-shaped with incurved ciliate margins; upper angle of wings with an erect subulate tooth. Stigma narrow-lanceolate.

P. revoluta is a very graceful species of the autumn flowering group, and is very close to *P. reflexa*. It is widely dispersed throughout its range, and after good late summer rains it flowers abundantly, sometimes occurring in fairly large though scattered communities. The stem in hardier examples is almost leafless, and the best specimens are found along dryish hilltops, often on rocky ledges or ridges. Lowland specimens, though usually bearing a larger flower, very often lack the firmness and dainty colour markings of the hardy hilltop examples. R. D. FitzGerald in *Aust. Orchids 1⁵* (1879) includes this plant under *P. reflexa*—a much smaller species. Bentham, Mueller and other botanists, would not accept them as variants, and included this and other similar forms—including *P. robusta*—under this same specific name, the differences being thought insufficient to justify separation. Close acquaintance with these greenhoods in a fresh state has convinced me that Robert Brown was fully justified in his decisions regarding speciation.

FLOWERING PERIOD: Mar. to June

COMMON NAME: Autumn Greenhood

DISTRIBUTION: Extending from south-eastern Qld, through eastern NSW to Vic.; often abundant in dry situations

P. reflexa (Plate 320)

P. reflexa R. Br. *Prodr. Flor. Nov. Holl.* 327 (1810); H. M. R. Rupp *Orchids N.S.W.* 90 (1943); J. H. Willis *Handb. Pls Vict.* 1:407 (1962)

A very slender glabrous plant up to 24 cm. high. Radical rosette of leaves not present at flowering time, on a separate shoot, ovate and shortly petiolate. Stem leaves four to six, distant, 1–3 cm. long, lanceolate, acuminate, usually increasing in length from base upward, the lowest reduced to clasping bracts. Flower solitary, very rarely two, rather large but hardly half the size of that of *P. revoluta*, green with red-brown markings, sometimes more red-brown than green. Galea gibbous at the erect base, then curving forward for the whole of its length (up to 4 cm.); tips of dorsal sepal and petals produced into fine points, that of the sepal being longer. Conjoined lateral sepals forming a wide sinus at less than a third of their length, erect, narrowly cuneate, the filiform lobes embracing the galea and far exceeding it. Labellum very dark, up to 15 mm. long, narrow-lanceolate, gradually contracting to a long fine point, with a narrow longitudinal ridge traversing the lamina and the gracefully decurved portion protruding well beyond the sinus of the lower lip; basal appendage curved, with penicillate apex. Column about 1 cm. long; upper angle of wings with narrow erect lobes, the lower lobes broad and rounded with short inturned marginal cilia. Stigma narrow-lanceolate.

The outstanding characteristic of *P. reflexa* is the comparative length of the labellum to the galea—about three-sevenths of its total length, which is exceptional. Prior to A. J. Ewart's *Flor. Vict.* (1931), *P. robusta* was known and erroneously recorded in that state as *P. reflexa*.

P. reflexa is sometimes associated with moss covered hill-slopes in NSW, and has been called Moss Greenhood; it is far less common in that state than its close congener, *P. revoluta*. At Mounts Raymond and Kaye, Vic., it occurs on fairly dry granitic slopes.

FLOWERING PERIOD: Mar. to June

COMMON NAME: Small Autumn Greenhood

DISTRIBUTION: South-eastern Qld, eastern NSW and eastern Vic., in scattered loose colonies

P. coccinea (Plate 321)

P. coccinea R. D. FitzG. *Aust. Orchids* 1⁴:+t. (1878); H. M. R. Rupp *Orchids N.S.W.* 89 (1943)

A slender plant, 12–22 cm. high. Radical rosette usually absent at flowering time. Stem leaves bract-like, alternate, very acute. Flower solitary, large, up to 4 cm. long, green with bright red suffusions or sometimes with green bands, only occasionally with red bands (the typical form). Galea variable, up to 7 cm. round the curve, but sometimes less than 5 cm., erect for about one-third of its length, then arching over and tapering into a filiform or merely acuminate point, dorsal sepal much longer than the petals.

Lateral sepals erect, connate for about one-third of their length, conspicuously gibbous at the junction to form a very wide and obtusely angled sinus; free portions rather suddenly contracting into long filiform points which extend high above the galea. Labellum sometimes exceeding 20 mm. long, linear, curving above into a slender but hardly acute point. Column variable in length; upper angles of wide wings produced into erect teeth; the lower angle narrow, obtuse, with margins hardly ciliate. Stigma at the middle of column, ovate-oblong, prominent.

FLOWERING PERIOD: Jan. to Mar.

DISTRIBUTION: Endemic in eastern NSW where found in open grassy situations on the tablelands

P. pulchella (Plate 322)

P. pulchella P. R. Messmer in *Proc. Linn. Soc. N.S.W.* 58:429, fig. 1–10 (1933); H. M. R. Rupp *Orchids N.S.W.* 88 (1943)

A slender plant 10–16 cm. high. Radical leaves, when present, attached by a separate scape to the base of the stem. Stem leaves broad-linear to broad-lanceolate, clasping at the base, 2–4 cm. long. Flower solitary, comparatively large, 2–3·5 cm. long, translucent-white with green stripes at the base and prominent reddish markings above. Galea gently curving upward for half its length, then sweeping forward and downward to an acuminate apex. Petals falcate, with shortly acuminate points. Lateral sepals erect and united for about a third of their length, with a broad and gibbous sinus; free portions very divergent, their long filamentous points embracing the galea and exceeding it. Labellum linear-oblong, 14–17 mm. long, usually widely bifid at the apex which is pubescent on the under margins; appendage curved, penicillate. Column a little shorter than the labellum, the wings with an erect subulate tooth at each upper angle; lower lobes narrow, with incurved, very shortly ciliate margins. Stigma long, narrow, obscure.

Concerning *P. pulchella* Mrs Pearl Messmer, the author, writes: 'Though like no other known *Pterostylis*, it suggests affinities with *P. grandiflora*, *P. ophioglossa* and *P. reflexa*, and may even have originated as a natural hybrid between *P. grandiflora* and *P. ophioglossa*, as the first specimens examined suggested; but more material has placed it in the rank of a constant species. The distinguishing features, though variable, are constant in their distinction, i.e. the shape and set of the apex of the galea, the labellum and the appendage at the base of the labellum. In dissection the dorsal sepal approaches that of *P. ophioglossa*, the lower sepals those of *P. grandiflora*. The column appears to be intermediate between that of *P. ophioglossa* and that of *P. grandiflora*, whilst the petals and base of the labellum are nearer to those of *P. reflexa*.'

To me, the affinities of this dainty Greenhood appear to be more with those of *P. obtusa* and *P. ophioglossa*. These two species are plentiful during April, whereas *P. grandiflora* does not appear until late in May. The pubescent nature of the apex of the labellum—a feature not embodied in the original description—seems to be quite unique.

FLOWERING PERIOD: Apr. and May

DISTRIBUTION: Endemic in eastern NSW, where it is confined to the central tablelands

P. obtusa (Plate 323)

P. obtusa R. Br. *Prodr. Flor. Nov. Holl.* 327 (1810); A. J. Ewart *Flor. Vict.* 373 (1931); J. M. Black *Flor. S. Aust.* ed. 2:246 (1943); H. M. R. Rupp *Orchids N.S.W.* 92 (1943); J. H. Willis *Handb. Pls Vict.* 1:408 (1962)

A very slender glabrous species, 12–25 cm. in height, occasionally much taller. Radical leaves petiolate or almost sessile, ovate and more acute than those of *P. decurva*, on a separate shoot and sometimes present at flowering time. Stem leaves somewhat variable in shape and size, 1–4 cm. long, often bract-like, three to five including the uppermost one, linear to oblong-lanceolate, occasionally ovate, clasping at the base. Flower solitary, rarely two, green and white, sometimes with brown markings chiefly towards the apex. Galea (including the apex) 1·8–3 cm. long, erect for half its length, then gradually decurving, the apex ending in a fine point which is often 5 mm. long in larger specimens. Conjoined lateral sepals cuneate, erect, forming a prominent gibbous lip at the very wide sinus, up to halfway from the base; the free lobes suddenly contracted and produced into long erect filiform points, embracing the galea and exceeding it by 1–2 cm. Labellum slightly exceeding the column, reddish-brown, oblong-linear; the tip very obtuse and slightly recurved; lamina about 10 mm. long, with a longitudinal central ridge and corresponding narrow channel on the under side; appendage linear, curved, penicillate. Column erect, about 10 mm. long, upper angle of wings produced into an acute tooth; the lower lobes bluntly oblong with short incurved marginal cilia. Stigma broad-lanceolate, tumid.

A widespread species, occurring in a variety of habitats, but most commonly on rocky timbered hill slopes—it may be found plentifully among ferns and on mossy slopes in sheltered, often dense, forest areas, also on sandy scrublands. Along the banks of streams in deep valleys I have seen it, sometimes with two flowers, drawn up to a height of over 60 cm. (3 ft.). Specimens from the Glenbrook district in NSW are exceedingly attractive, both in form and bright colouring. It does not extend into Tas., although recorded there by early botanists. The mistake apparently arose when *P. decurva* was wrongly identified as this species.

In a number of mountain retreats (up to 3,000 ft. altitude), where *P. obtusa* and *P. decurva* intermingle and flower simultaneously, hybrid forms occur. This has been noted on Mount Macedon, the range of hills north of Riddell and many areas in far eastern Vic.

FLOWERING PERIOD: Feb. to June, rarely as early as Jan.

COMMON NAME: Blunt-tongue Greenhood

DISTRIBUTION: Temperate parts of south-eastern Qld, NSW, Vic. and south-eastern SA; often locally common. [It has been collected recently from Flinders Island, Tas.—Ed.]

P. alveata (Plate 323)

P. alveata J. R. Garnet in *Vict. Nat.* 56:91, fig. a–n (1939); J. H. Willis *Handb. Pls Vict.* 1:408 (1962)

A small coastal form occurring in dense colonies, usually in moist sandy areas. The labellum is emarginate at the apex.

[In NSW where *P. obtusa* reaches its best development, a range of intermediates between it and *P. alveata* can be found, rendering separation of the two difficult. These two are discussed by S. C. Clemesha in *Orchadian* 2:72–73 (1966).—Ed.]

FLOWERING PERIOD: May to July

DISTRIBUTION: South-eastern NSW and eastern Vic.; generally coastal and uncommon

P. crypta (Plate 324)

P. crypta W. H. Nicholls in *Vict. Nat.* 61:207 (1945); J. H. Willis *Handb. Pls Vict.* 1:408 (1962)

A slender plant about 10 cm. high. Radical leaves not seen. Stem leaves as in *P. obtusa*, 15–25 mm. long. Flower solitary, green with rufous markings. Galea 13–20 mm. high, erect for about half its length, then curved forward, with a short deflexed apex. Petals acute, not exceeding the tip of the galea. Conjoined portion of erect lateral sepals conspicuously adnate to base of galea for fully half its height; upper part widely dilated from its free base, the lobes produced into fine erect points, only slightly exceeding the galea. Labellum on a prominent immobile claw, almost straight, its shortly decurved apex extending right to the tip of the galea, thus (with the petals) completely sealing off the galea entrance; lamina oblong-lanceolate, somewhat constricted about the middle, 1·5–2 cm. long, the lower margins incurved, forming a deep pouch-like cavity below the constricted part; median ridge not prominent; appendage filiform, curved, arising from the base of claw, with a small cordate apex. Column erect, on a stout base, 8–13 mm. long, each angle of upper lobes produced into an acute tooth; lower lobes oblong. Stigma prominent, situated immediately behind the lower lobes, cordiform.

P. crypta is known only from a single collection of three specimens made by Miss Ruth Clarke during May 1941 'in sandy soil along Waratah Bay' under a heavy canopy of tea-tree scrub. This colony grew in association with *P. obtusa*, and may represent a curious teratological form of that widespread species. The specific epithet 'hidden' refers both to the habitat, in dense scrub, and to the hood which is perfectly sealed off by the rigid, unusually long, lid-like labellum (cf. *P. obtusa*).

FLOWERING PERIOD: May

DISTRIBUTION: Vic., where endemic in sandy scrubland at Waratah Bay, South Gippsland

P. fischii (Plate 325)

P. fischii W. H. Nicholls in *Vict. Nat.* 67:45, fig. a–j (1950); J. H. Willis *Handb. Pls Vict.* 1:406 (1962)

A slender plant, 15–20 cm. high. Radical leaves up to five in a rosette distinct from the flowering stem, elliptic to broadly ovate and petiolate. Stem bracts up to five, small, 0·5–2 cm. long, leaf-like, sessile, acuminate. Flower solitary, rather large, with green and rufous stripes on a translucent whitish ground. Galea about 2·5 cm. high, rigidly erect for the greater part, then sharply curved forward to a long and abruptly decurved filiform apex (the dorsal sepal). Conjoined lateral sepals erect, with narrowly acute sinus the base of which is gibbous, pouch-like and protruding; the filiform points erect, embracing the upper portion of galea and exceeding it by 2–2·5 cm. Petals rather short, bluntish, the tips abruptly decurved on each side of the dorsal sepal and almost meeting the lower lip. Labellum less than 1 cm. long, much shorter than the column, almost straight, broadly ovate-lanceolate, on a comparatively long movable claw, sometimes with a constriction about the centre; lamina deeply concave, with a raised longitudinal central ridge and corresponding narrow groove on the under side; apex obtuse or faintly emarginate. Column rigidly erect, about 12 mm. long; the upper portion of each wing with a subulate divergent tooth; lower wings oblong, rounded, with soft hairy incurved margins. Stigma lanceolate; anther with a short point.

[This orchid, only discovered in 1949, was believed to be confined to two localities, but since then it has been collected several times and its range greatly extended.—Ed.] The species bears a close affinity to *P. obtusa* and *P. decurva*. It differs from the former in having a shorter broader labellum and more filiform sepal-points, from the latter in its much shorter labellum and winter flowering time, and from both in the stiffly 'proud', almost martial bearing. In Vic. the habitat is sandy soil in undulating, near coastal, light forest country, the plants growing singly or in small groups of four or five.

FLOWERING PERIOD: From early Mar. to May

DISTRIBUTION: Eastern NSW, where widely distributed through the highlands; eastern Vic., where it is chiefly coastal

P. decurva (Plates 326 and 327)

P. decurva R. S. Rogers in *Trans. roy. Soc. S. Aust.* 47:339, t. 27 (1923); A. J. Ewart *Flor. Vict.* 372 (1931); H. M. R. Rupp *Orchids N.S.W.* 92 (1943); J. H. Willis *Handb. Pls Vict.* 1:406 (1962); M. J. Firth *Native Orchids Tasm.* 72 (1965)

A very slender plant, 10–30 cm. high. Radical leaves absent during flowering, two to five on a separate shoot, ovate or obovate, usually on long petioles. Stem bracts small, four or five, clasping, linear-lanceolate, acuminate, the floral bract often with a filiform point. Flower solitary, variable in size, translucent-white with green longitudinal stripes, often reddish-brown towards the apex. Galea erect for about half its length, then curving forward through a semi-circle and extended at the apex into a long filiform and usually much decurved point, sometimes 6 cm. around the complete curve. Lateral sepals conjoined for about one-third of their length, forming an erect lower lip, cuneate with a very wide gibbous sinus; the lobes 4–5 cm. long, suddenly contracted on each side of the galea into filiform points which rise high above it. Labellum reddish-brown on an irritable claw, up to 17 mm. long but usually about 12 mm.; lamina linear-oblong, with longitudinal ridge traversing the centre, very obtuse at the apex which protrudes from the sinus, sometimes glandular-papillose; appendix trifid, curved, penicillate. Column 11–15 mm. long, erect; the upper angle of darkish wings produced into an acute linear tooth; lower lobes oblong, obtuse, with incurved cilia. Stigma elliptical, in the centre of column.

P. decurva favours montane habitats and is one of the most graceful members of the genus. It has formerly been confused with *P. obtusa* which it closely resembles; but there are important differences—viz. much longer filamentous perianth segments, smaller stem bracts, a longer labellum and a different flowering period in the same localities as *P. obtusa*. Records of the latter species for Tasmania refer to *P. decurva*.

[Plate 326 illustrates typical *P. decurva*, but the specimens illustrated on Plate 327 were determined by Dr Rogers as a form of *P. decurva*. H. M. R. Rupp had commented on this species as follows: 'Both W.H.N. and I were disposed to think it a distinct species, but, there are many intermediates and neither of us took any action'. These comments were pencilled on the back of the original illustration. This form is apparently confined to NSW, flowering Jan.—Ed.]

FLOWERING PERIOD: Oct. to Feb., sometimes as late as Apr. at higher altitudes

COMMON NAME: Summer Greenhood

DISTRIBUTION: NSW, where uncommon and confined to the tablelands; widespread in Vic. and Tas. but seldom abundant

P. furcillata (Plate 328)

P. furcillata H. M. R. Rupp in *Proc. Linn. Soc. N.S.W.* 55:415 (1930); H. M. R. Rupp *Orchids N.S.W.* 88 (1943)

A very slender plant, 10–20 cm. high. Radical leaves one to four, but usually two in flowering plants or occasionally absent. Leaves shortly petiolate, broadly lanceolate or in some instances nearly ovate, acuminate and with crisped margins; stem bracts one or two, similar to the leaves, that on the lower part of stem clasping only at its base, but a more appressed bract subtending the ovary. Flower solitary, 2–3 cm. long, vivid green with somewhat darker bands.

Galea much curved, deflexed, up to 5 cm. long around the curve and extending in a fine point 8–10 mm. beyond the petals. Lateral sepals erect, forming a protruding lip (less marked than in *P. obtusa*) at the very wide sinus, thence prolonged into filaments far beyond the galea. (In a specimen found at Kurri Kurri, NSW, the lower sepals were very much abbreviated.) Labellum about 15 mm. long, broad-linear, shortly bifid at the apex with obtuse points, very dark but paler at the base. Column very slender, a little shorter than the labellum, the lower wing-lobes obtuse and scarcely ciliate, the upper ones acuminate. Stigma narrow, prominent.

This localised species was first discovered in 1930, in *Melaleuca* scrub on a slope at Kurri Kurri, and subsequently near Abermain some three miles away. In general appearance it is not unlike *P. decurva*, but differs from that species in having a notched labellum and basal leaves. About fifteen flowering specimens were found in the two localities, both plant colonies being fairly large. The discoverer, H. M. R. Rupp, considered that *P. furcillata* may have originated by hybridisation between *P. obtusa* and *P. ophioglossa* or perhaps *P. concinna*, but all the flowers obtained were true to type, except for shorter sepals in one. The cleft in the labellum, although very small like that in *P. toveyana*, is quite definite in every flower.

FLOWERING PERIOD: Mar. to May

DISTRIBUTION: NSW, where apparently endemic in the north coast region, and rare

P. parviflora (Plate 329)

P. parviflora R. Br. *Prodr. Flor. Nov. Holl.* 327 (1810); A. J. Ewart *Flor. Vict.* 368 (1931); J. M. Black *Flor. S. Aust.* ed. 2:247 (1943); H. M. R. Rupp *Orchids N.S.W.* 94 (1943); J. H. Willis *Handb. Pls Vict.* 1:401 (1962); M. J. Firth *Native Orchids Tasm.* 69 (1965)

A very slender plant, 5–60 cm. high. Radical leaves absent, or represented by one or more lateral growths at the base of scape. Stem-leaves small, bract-like, acute. Flowers from one to thirteen, small, green with darker green stripes, or brown; galea erect, 5–9 mm. high, incurved, apex more or less obtuse; tip of dorsal sepal often recurved and occasionally much abbreviated; petals brown or red towards the apex. Labellum oblong or oblong-linear, on an irritable claw, tip obtuse and curved forward; lamina 3–5 mm. long, with a prominent raised central ridge; basal appendage curved, tripartite. Column 3·5–7 mm. long, prominently winged, an erect subulate tooth at the upper angle of each column-wing, lobes oblong with inturned ciliate margins. Stigma winged above, cordate. Anther with a short obtuse point.

P. parviflora roughly embraces three forms, coastal, inland and alpine. The coastal form is a small slender plant, rarely exceeding 18 cm.; flowers few and pale-coloured. The inland form is often tall, up to 60 cm., sometimes with many flowers—the stripes on the galea are dark green, the other markings yellowish-brown or bright crimson. The alpine form is usually quite stout, of low stature and rather fleshy, with few slightly scabrous blooms, which often face each other. [This latter form is regarded as a distinct variety by some authors (var. *aphylla*) and was once assigned to specific rank. Some still regard it as a good species and the situation is not clear. It may well be that two species do exist, at least in Tas., the confusion arising because of the various forms assumed by *P. parviflora*.—Ed.]

The finest specimens of *P. parviflora* I have seen came from the Everton district in north-eastern Vic.—tall-growing plants with the individual blooms measuring exactly 12 mm. from base of galea to apex. At the base of the flowering scape many rosettes of leaves were clustered. *P. parviflora* is often very abundant in open forest areas. Minute seedlings are sometimes plentiful during the months of May and June.

FLOWERING PERIOD: From Jan. to Dec., depending on altitude

COMMON NAME: Tiny Greenhood

DISTRIBUTION: All Australian states except WA, but confined to south-east of Qld, and south-east of SA; widespread and often locally common

P. daintreana (Plate 330)

P. daintreana F. Muell. ex Benth. *Flor. aust.* 6:360 (1873); H. M. R. Rupp *Orchids N.S.W.* 94 (1943)

Habit similar to *P. parviflora*. Plant usually slender, 15–30 cm. high. Leaves small, ovate, in a green radical rosette, separate or as one or more lateral tufts at the base of scape. Stem-bracts three to five, small, closely appressed, subulate, 1–2 cm. long. Flowers three to ten, rather small in a loose raceme, white with fine longitudinal green stripes. Ovary on a short pedicel. Galea erect, incurved, 1 cm. long, obtusely hooded, the apex produced into a fine point 5–8 mm. long; the sinus between the lobes very narrow, margins incurved. Labellum 5 mm. long, narrow, obtuse, with an entire tip, sagittate at the base with obtuse auricles, a small obtuse entire appendage between them. Column as long as the galea, the wings very broad with a small point in the angle of each; the lower part of the column winged. Stigma scarcely prominent.

P. daintreana grows in close proximity to shrubs (*Banksia*, *Leptospermum*, etc.) and sometimes in very shallow soil on high sandstone outcrops, often in extensive colonies.

FLOWERING PERIOD: Mar. to July

DISTRIBUTION: South-eastern Qld, and NSW where it is most abundant in the Blue Mountains and adjacent coastal region

P. vittata (Plate 331)

P. vittata Lindl. in *Edwards' bot. Reg.* 23: Swan Riv. Append. liii (1840); A. J. Ewart *Flor. Vict.* 365 (1931); J. M. Black *Flor. S. Aust.* ed. 2:249 (1943); J. H. Willis *Handb. Pls Vict.* 1:414 (1962); R. Erickson *Orchids West* ed. 2:43 (1965); M. J. Firth *Native Orchids Tasm.* 75 (1965)

Flowering plant 8–35 cm. high. Generally without basal leaves but in occasional specimens a lateral growth is present. Stem leaves well developed, lanceolate, clasping at the base, variable in length, 6–8 cm. long and 1–1·5 cm. wide, the longest leaves in the middle of stem; leaves within the floral raceme well-developed, while those at the base are small and scale-like. Radical leaves ovate or obovate on very short petioles. Flowers one to eight, occasionally more, variable in size and colour, green with bold red-brown stripes, or wholly red-brown, greyish or green; galea broad at the base, more or less declined, prominently ribbed, narrowing somewhat abruptly towards the short acute tip. Petals often transparent, with bold longitudinal veins, or almost wholly red-brown, the upper margins beset with many setae. Conjoined sepals pendent, much wider than galea, orbicular, reflexed or cup-shaped; lobes shortly acute, red in the common forms. Labellum ovate-oblong or broadly ovate, on a broad irritable claw, somewhat concave; tip upturned, bifid; lamina with a single hairy or bristly spike arising from the much thickened base, which is usually directed forward, the whole labellum beset with hairs; lamina with a broad longitudinal ridge down the centre, and a corresponding channel on the reverse. Column about as long as the galea, its base almost horizontal, wings markedly ciliate, the cilia within the upper margins somewhat clavate, a small ill-defined tooth in the upper angle of column wings; lower lobes very narrow, margins with inturned or projecting cilia. Stigma oblong-ovate, widely winged.

An extremely variable species often forming spectacular displays in the light coastal scrub which it prefers.

FLOWERING PERIOD: May to Sept.

COMMON NAME: Banded Greenhood

DISTRIBUTION: Extending from western Vic. to south-eastern SA; also in south-western WA where it is abundant; also Tas. where it is confined to the Bass Strait Islands

P. vittata var. viridiflora (Plate 332)

P. vittata var. *viridiflora* W. H. Nicholls in *Vict. Nat.* 49:254 (1933); R. Erickson *Orchids West* ed. 2:43 (1965)

A semi-robust plant, up to 27 cm. in height; stem leaves up to twelve, obovate to lanceolate; flowers smaller than in the typical form, two to nine, in a declined position, greenish or with prominent dark green stripes on a translucent-white ground; galea about 1 cm. from base to apex; conjoined sepals barely longer than the galea; labellum appendage long, directed forward. Grows in gravelly soil amongst rocks.

FLOWERING PERIOD: July and Aug.

DISTRIBUTION: Apparently confined to WA

P. vittata var. subdifformis (Plate 332)

P. vittata var. *subdifformis* W. H. Nicholls in *Vict. Nat.* 49:253 (1933); R. Erickson *Orchids West* ed. 2:43 (1965)

Plant rarely exceeding 18 cm. in height. Leaves variable, from obovate to lanceolate, 2–5 cm. long. Flowers one to six, but generally two, in a terminal raceme, more or less erect, deep red-brown, larger and more strikingly banded than those of the typical form; galea 1·5–2 cm. from base to apex. Conjoined sepals 2–2·5 cm. long, consistently broad and concave, occasionally cleft to the middle or even beyond. Labellum appendage reflexed or erect, the point directed inward, compared with the forward-inclined point of the typical form. Grows in gravelly soil amongst rocks.

FLOWERING PERIOD: July to Aug.

DISTRIBUTION: Apparently confined to WA

P. longifolia (Plates 333 and 334)

P. longifolia R. Br. *Prodr. Flor. Nov. Holl.* 327 (1810); A. J. Ewart *Flor. Vict.* 364 (1931); J. M. Black *Flor. S. Aust.* ed. 2:249 (1943); H. M. R. Rupp *Orchids N.S.W.* 143 (1943); J. H. Willis *Handb. Pls Vict.* 1:413 (1962); M. J. Firth *Native Orchids Tasm.* 75 (1965)

A slender plant 10–90 cm. high. Basal rosette of leaves absent at flowering time, stem-leaves narrow-lanceolate, acute, clasping, reduced to small scales near the base, 1–10 cm. long above the middle, alternate, rarely a lateral tuft present at the base of the stem. Flowers one to fifteen, in a raceme, green, an acute bracteole subtending each pedicel. Galea 12–20 mm. from base to tip in the typical form, gradually incurved, apex acute but not prolonged into a fine point; lower lip reflexed in the mature flower, narrow, the lobes with short acuminate tips. Labellum on a short very irritable claw, oblong, slightly trilobed towards the apex, the lateral lobes very small; the mid-lobe upturned, bifid; lamina 6–8 mm. long, papillose-glandular, convex and much thickened at the base with a short pyramidal appendage, the remainder concave, channelled below. Column incurved, as long as the galea; wings almost square, the upper margin crescentic with a short rather blunt tooth in the middle; front margin beset with inturned hairs. Stigma lanceolate.

P. longifolia favours moist, well-sheltered gullies and shady places in our woodlands but is also found in drier situations. It often grows among almost impenetrable scrub and the branches of fallen trees. The occurrence of exceptionally large-flowered plants of this well-known orchid is not generally known, but I have collected a robust form near Mount Wallace in the Brisbane Ranges, Vic., with flowers almost twice as large as in the typical condition. This form is found also in Were's Paddock, near Greensborough, Vic. In both localities, so widely separated, the normal form is also present, and fairly abundant. On the lower slopes of the Serra Range in south-western Vic., *P. longifolia* grows in the depressions, on the sandstone rocks. In such situations the plants do not attain normal size. Several specimens were noted with a solitary flower, two leaves, the tubers malformed and large. Total height of these plants about 5 cm.

FLOWERING PERIOD: Apr. to Nov., depending on altitude

COMMON NAME: Tall Greenhood

DISTRIBUTION: Recorded from the temperate parts of all Australian states except WA, and in Qld confined to the south

P. sargentii (Plate 335)

P. sargentii C. R. P. Andrews in *J. West Aust. nat. Hist. Soc.* 2²:57 (1905); R. Erickson *Orchids West* ed. 2:43 (1965)

A slender plant, 8–20 cm. high. Basal leaves in a radical rosette, ovate, shortly petiolate, separate from the flowering plants. Cauline leaves narrow-lanceolate, acute, clasping, alternate, 1–6 cm. long, reduced to small scales at the base. Flowers one to three, rarely up to six, green and white with brown markings; galea 1–1·5 cm. from base to tip, incurved; apex acute with a short upturned point; lateral petals shortly pointed, their junction with the dorsal sepal marked by lines of white hairs inside the galea; lower lip reflexed, the lobes ending in very short points and separated by an acute sinus. Labellum on a broad, very irritable claw, glabrous; the mid-lobe triangular, with a ridge down the centre; lateral lobes linear-lanceolate, curved, produced at the base into thick fleshy club-shaped dark brown appendages, which are covered with numerous short cilia. Column shorter than the galea, rostellum flanked by almost orbicular wings which have a very short point at the upper angle. Anther short, not acuminate.

In the country around Mount Tampia and Arrowsmith (Narembeen district), the author found *P. sargentii* growing at the bases of Mallee Eucalypts. Perfectly fresh specimens were secured in the moist, low-lying areas, but those growing on the higher elevations were in fruit. This *Pterostylis* is apparently abundant in this area, judging from the number of specimens seen in a single day's outing. It is a species with unique features, especially in the labellum which is divided into three lobes, the lateral ones having large, basal appendages, and the whole constituting a ready and certain guide to its identification. In every specimen found by the author, the labellum lobes were more or less densely hirsute but subsequent flowers grown from collected tubers possessed labella with glabrous lobes.

FLOWERING PERIOD: July to Oct.

COMMON NAME: Frog Greenhood

DISTRIBUTION: Endemic in WA where it is widespread through inland areas of the south-west

P. cycnocephala (Plate 336)

P. cycnocephala R. D. FitzG. *Aust. Orchids* 1²:+t. (1876); A. J. Ewart *Flor. Vict.* 366 (1931); J. M. Black *Flor. S. Aust.* ed. 2:247 (1943); H. M. R. Rupp *Orchids N.S.W.* 100 (1943); J. H. Willis *Handb. Pls Vict.* 1:414 (1962); M. J. Firth *Native Orchids Tasm.* 75 (1965)

A glabrous plant, generally slender, 3–20 cm. high. Leaves often crowded and numerous in a basal rosette, shortly petiolate or sessile, ovate-lanceolate, often withered at flowering time. Stem-bracts one to five, with additional smaller acute bracteoles subtending the pedicels. Flowers small, two to sixteen, in a crowded or loose or occasionally spiral raceme, usually a brighter green than in *P. mutica*; galea broad at the base, incurved, shortly acute or blunt, 5–8 mm. high; lower lip reflexed, about 6 mm. long, deeply concave, lobes united, except at the tips, which are hardly acute. Labellum irritable on a broad claw, the apex shortly emarginate; lamina 4–4·5 mm. long, somewhat quadrate, a raised ridge on the upper side with a corresponding groove on the reverse; appendage broad, dark green, a pubescent pyramidal process at the end which is directed inward towards the apex. Column incurved, about 7 mm. high, wings hatchet-shaped, upper margins somewhat botryoidal, anterior margins ciliate, lower lobes rounded with inturned cilia. Stigma ovate-lanceolate, channelled, the points directed upward.

FitzGerald named this species from the likeness of the labellum appendage to the head and neck of a swan. His specimens were collected at Malong and Boorowa in NSW. He gives no description of *P. cycnocephala* in his work, confining his remarks chiefly to its salient characteristics, the largest specimen examined by him having had twenty-four flowers.

P. cycnocephala is well separated from *P. mutica* by the different shape of the labellum appendage, but there are other points of differentiation also. *P. cycnocephala* is a common species on open grassy sub-alpine and alpine tablelands. On the lowlands it also favours grass covered areas, either open places, or in open forest country. The tubers are often large, up to 3 cm. in diameter.

FLOWERING PERIOD: Aug. to Jan., depending on altitude

COMMON NAME: Swan Greenhood

DISTRIBUTION: Widespread in NSW, Vic., north-eastern Tas., south-eastern SA; extending into a wide variety of habitats, sparsely distributed although often locally common; also NZ

P. mutica (Plate 337)

P. mutica R. Br. *Prodr. Flor. Nov. Holl.* 328 (1810); A. J. Ewart *Flor. Vict.* 366 (1931); J. M. Black *Flor. S. Aust.* ed. 2:247 (1943); H. M. R. Rupp *Orchids N.S.W.* 100 (1943); J. H. Willis *Handb. Pls Vict.* 1:415 (1962); R. Erickson *Orchids West* ed. 2:43 (1965); M. J. Firth *Native Orchids Tasm.* 75 (1965)

A glabrous plant which may be robust, and 5–16 cm. high, but usually slender, up to 36 cm. high. Leaves sometimes numerous, on short petioles, ovate or elliptical, 1–2 cm. long, in a radical rosette which is often withered at flowering time. Stems slender or robust, with one to nine acute sheathing bracts, which are variable in size and often rather large. Flowers from two to twenty, crowded or loose in a slightly spiral raceme, occasionally the flowers facing the stem; galea about 8 mm. high, gibbous at the base, erect, incurved, somewhat obtuse or sub-acute at the tip; lower lip reflexed, concave, shorter than the galea, the lobes short and broad, hardly acute. Labellum 3·5 mm. long, on a wide irritable claw, apex rounded and slightly emarginate; lamina orbicular-ovate with a raised central ridge; appendage large, oblong, club-shaped, dark green, turned backward toward the claw. Column erect, 5–6 mm. high, the wings broad, each upper angle with an erect, shortly obtuse tooth; lower lobes oblong with short inturned cilia. Stigma narrow-elliptical.

FLOWERING PERIOD: July to Jan., depending on altitude

COMMON NAME: Midget Greenhood

DISTRIBUTION: Widespread in all Australian states, but restricted in Qld to the south-east, in Tas. to Circular Head, in SA to the south-east, and in WA to the south-west; sparsely distributed; also in NZ

P. woollsii (Plate 338)

P. woollsii R. D. FitzG. *Aust. Orchids* 1²:+t. (1876); A. J. Ewart *Flor. Vict.* 367 (1931); H. M. R. Rupp *Orchids N.S.W.* 96 (1943); J. H. Willis *Handb. Pls Vict.* 1:415 (1962); J. A. P. Blackmore & S. C. Clemesha in *Orchadian* 2:150 (1968)

Plant slender, 12–20 cm. high. Basal rosette often withered at flowering time; leaves broadly ovate, acute; stem-bracts two, excluding those subtending the pedicels. Flowers one to four, large, on slender pedicels, green with rufous markings; galea 1·5–2 cm. high, its apex with a filiform point, 1·5–3 cm. long; lower lip 2 cm. long, pendent, concave, the margins involute, its apices produced into fine points up to 9·5 cm. long; labellum 1–1·3 cm. long, ligulate, very sensitive; appendage ligulate, shortly ciliate; the lamina broadly ovate with a bifid apex, its margins beset with long cilia; a broad ridge running along the upper surface of the labellum with a corresponding longitudinal channel on the reverse side. Column erect, curved, 1–1·5 cm. long, the upper angle of the wings produced into a short point; lower lobes narrow, blunt; the inturned margins ciliate; stigma narrow, bifid on top; anther rugose, very short with a blunt point.

[This and the following five species, on Plates 338 to 344, were discussed by J. A. P. Blackmore and S. C. Clemesha when they published their 'Review of the so-called "Rufous group" of the genus *Pterostylis*' in *Orchadian* 2:148–166 (1968).—Ed.]

FitzGerald's specimens came from Richmond and Boorowa in NSW. There are a few minor differences between them and the solitary specimen so far collected in Vic. This plant had but a single flower and the stigma did not form a hood, as described by FitzGerald, as well the upper angles of the column-wings were shortly ciliate. It was collected near Rushworth in northern Vic. and forwarded to the author by Mrs Edith Rich, a local orchid collector. It was growing in an exposed position where many accompanying species of terrestrial orchids occur, including *Calochilus imberbis* and *Caleana major*.

FLOWERING PERIOD: Oct. to Dec.

COMMON NAME: Long-tail Greenhood

DISTRIBUTION: In Qld confined to the south-east, but scattered through NSW to Vic., where it is known only by a single collection from Rushworth

P. biseta (Plate 339)

P. biseta J. A. P. Blackmore & S. C. Clemesha in *Orchadian* 2:150, cum icon. (1968)

A lowly plant with the principal characters of the typical form, but having smaller flowers, which are pale translucent grey. The long pedicels are consistently and conspicuously deflexed—so much so that the galea, in some instances, actually touches the ground and the filiform points of the conjoined sepals are covered with the loose soil of the habitat.

[W. H. Nicholls described the plant illustrated on this plate as *P. rufa* var. *despectans* in *Vict. Nat.* 66:215 (1950). In their review of the 'rufa' group of *Pterostylis*, Blackmore and Clemesha regard this form as aberrant and within the range of variation of *P. biseta*. This form is unusual, but it is noteworthy that it has been collected in several places in Vic., and also that it maintains its unusual

habit in cultivation. The typical form is illustrated on the next plate, Plate 340.—Ed.].

FLOWERING PERIOD: Nov.

DISTRIBUTION: An unusual form apparently confined to central Vic., although typical *P. biseta* extends into NSW, SA, and perhaps WA

P. biseta (Plate 340)

P. biseta J. A. P. Blackmore & S. C. Clemesha in *Orchadian* 2:150, cum icon. (1968)

Plant robust, 10–35 cm. high. Basal leaves often withered at flowering time, shortly petiolate, the lamina 1–3·5 cm. long, more or less acute, ovate to oblong; stem-bracts two to six, acute, scarious, loosely sheathing, additional bracteoles subtending the pedicels. Flowers large, two to seven, rarely one, on long slender pedicels, reddish or green. Galea 10–20 mm. from base to crest, broad, incurved, the apex produced into a fine point, 2 cm. long. Lower lip recurved or reflexed, as long as the galea; the lobes elliptical, produced into fine points, varying from 5 to 45 mm. in length. Labellum, on a long, very sensitive claw, membranous, narrow-oblong, the tip entire, blunt and turned upward; lamina about 6 mm. long, the posterior margin thickened and forming a transverse ridge in front of the claw, a central longitudinal ridge on the upper surface of the lamina, deeply channelled below; generally two long setae on the basal swelling, the lateral margins and tip sparsely ciliate; appendage almost obsolete and represented by the thickened posterior margin. Column incurved, 8–15 mm. long, reaching to the top of the galea, wings quadrangular, the upper angle acute, ciliate; anterior margins inturned, ciliate; the lower lobe rather blunt and ciliate. Stigma narrow-elliptical.

[This species was originally included under *P. rufa* but according to Blackmore and Clemesha it is distinct. It is a hardy plant, with large tubers, and is often found thriving in very arid situations.—Ed.]

FLOWERING PERIOD: Sept. to Jan.

DISTRIBUTION: Eastern NSW, northern and central Vic., south-eastern SA, and perhaps extending into WA; at times abundant

P. gibbosa ssp. mitchellii (Plate 340)

P. gibbosa ssp. *mitchellii* (Lindl.) J. A. P. Blackmore & S. C. Clemesha in *Orchadian* 2:161, cum icon. (1968)

SYNONYMY: *P. mitchellii* Lindl. in Mitch. *J. Exped. trop. Aust.* 365 (1848)

Plant slender, to 30 cm. high, leaves basal, shortly petiolate, ovate to oblong, often withered at flowering time; stem bracts two to five, acute. Flowers one to five, reddish, erect. Galea 2·5 cm. long, curved, ending in a filiform point about 7 mm. long. Lower lip reflexed, filiform for about half its length, light brown to red-brown. Labellum 6 mm. long, deep red-brown, broadly lanceolate, the margins upturned and beset with twelve to fourteen setae, a slight ridge only on the lamina. Appendage an obsolete swelling at the base of the labellum, beset with setae. Column incurved, 8–10 mm. long, wings quadrangular with dense cilia on the anterior margins. Stigma lanceolate.

[Close study of this ssp. has shown its affinities with *P. gibbosa* and it is the opinion of Blackmore and Clemesha that it be included under the latter. They state that records under the name *P. mitchellii*, from Vic., SA, and WA all refer to other species.—Ed.]

FLOWERING PERIOD: Aug. to Nov.

DISTRIBUTION: South-eastern Qld and north-eastern NSW

P. boormanii (Plate 341)

P. boormanii H. M. R. Rupp *Orchids N.S.W.* 98 (1943); J. A. P. Blackmore & S. C. Clemesha in *Orchadian* 2:152 (1968)

Plant slender, 7–27 cm. high. Basal leaves in a green or withered rosette, almost sessile, more or less acute; leaf lamina 20–30 mm. long, elliptical. Stem-bracts one to four, closely sheathing; additional bracteoles subtending the pedicels. Flowers three to eight, in a loose raceme, variable in size, green with reddish tints or almost wholly red-brown and crimson, usually much darker than in other members of this group. Galea about 12 mm. long, its apex produced into a fine recurved point 8–10 mm. long. Lower lip reflexed, the lobes ovate, produced into fine diverging filiform points 10–17 mm. long. Labellum about 3.5 mm. long, thick and fleshy-glandular, very irritable, on a long movable semi-circular claw, narrow-oblong, the tip rounded or cleft below and turning slightly downward, contracted towards the base; lamina with the basal margin thickened and slightly raised, usually without hairs; hollow in front of this thickening, under surface deeply channelled from base to tip; lateral margins with long setae; appendage obsolete, represented by the raised basal margin. Column about 9 mm. long, incurved, as long as the galea; wings quadrangular, the upper angle rather acute, ciliate, the lower lobes blunt, ciliate; anterior margins with inturned hairs. Stigma semi-elliptical, winged, and toothed in its upper margin. Anther blunt, oblique or horizontal.

[It has only been realised recently that *P. boormanii* occurs in Vic. However as early as 1945 W. H. Nicholls compared fresh specimens of the Vic. 'P. mitchellii' and *P. boormanii* from the type area in NSW. Here are his comments: 'I have very carefully examined numerous specimens of freshly gathered *P. mitchellii* from the Rushworth district in Vic. and have completed coloured drawings of every essential detail. The same applies to specimens of *P. boormanii* which I received from G. W. Althofer of Dripstone in NSW (this material came from the original locality of Peak Hill). The Vic. specimens referred to above are of shorter stature than those collected at Peak Hill, but the essential details of the floral structure are alike in every particular.'—Ed.]

FLOWERING PERIOD: Aug. to Nov.

DISTRIBUTION: Central and western NSW; northern and western Vic., but rare; Grangeville, SA; but perhaps extending to Qld and WA

P. boormanii (Plate 342)

[The form of *P. boormanii* illustrated on Plate 342 was originally described by W. H. Nicholls as *P. squamata* var. *valida* in *Vict. Nat.* 58:115 (1941). In their review of the 'rufa' group, Blackmore and Clemesha regard it as having most of the characteristics of *P. boormanii* and have included it under that species.—Ed.]

A robust plant about 14 cm. high, wholly green. Flowers large, similar in general appearance to those of *P. biseta*. Sepal points longer and not hooked inward as in the typical form of *P. hamata*, the points about 2 cm. long.

FLOWERING PERIOD: Oct. and Nov.

DISTRIBUTION: This form is apparently confined to Vic., where it is only found in the Maldon area and rare

P. rufa (Plate 343)

P. rufa R. Br. *Prodr. Flor. Nov. Holl.* 327 (1810); J. A. P. Blackmore & S. C. Clemesha in *Orchadian* 2:163 (1968)

SYNONYMY: *P. pusilla* R. S. Rogers in *Trans. roy. Soc. S. Aust.* 42:26, t. 3 (1918)

A species with two subspecies.

P. rufa ssp. rufa (Plate 343)

SYNONYMY: *P. pusilla* var. *prominens* H. M. R. Rupp in *Proc. Linn. Soc. N.S.W.* 56:137, fig. 2 (1931)

A slender glabrous plant usually 6–15 cm. high but sometimes more than 30 cm. Stem-bracts two to six, closely sheathing, additional bracteoles subtending each floral pedicel. Leaves shortly petiolate, oblong-lanceolate, in a green or withered basal rosette. Flowers one to ten, on long slender pedicels, small, green with brown, grey or red-brown markings; galea from ovary to extreme point of dorsal sepal 1–1.5 cm. long, point short, recurved. Lateral sepals conjoined, subulate, reflexed, margins involute, shorter or as long as galea. Labellum 5 mm. long, fleshy, irritable on a wide claw, green and brown or red-brown, oblong-ovate, concave on its upper surface, with a thickened posterior margin; tip straight, lamina under surface with a deep channel from base to tip, between two pyriform swellings whose apices are directed forward, but rarely reach the tip; a few long hairs present on the lateral margins but absent from the posterior margin; lower channel beset with very stiff transverse hairs. Column incurved, much shorter than galea, wings membranous, quadrangular, with rounded or obtuse angles, anterior margins and the lower lobes beset with cilia; stigma narrow, oblong-elliptical, flanged on either side by a secondary expansion ovate-lanceolate in shape.

FLOWERING PERIOD: Sept. to Dec.

COMMON NAME: Ruddy Hood

DISTRIBUTION: From south-eastern Qld, through central and eastern NSW to Vic.; also northern and eastern Tas., where rare; widely distributed over a range of habitats

P. rufa ssp. aciculiformis (Plate 343)

P. rufa ssp. *aciculiformis* (W. H. Nicholls) J. A. P. Blackmore & S. C. Clemesha in *Orchadian* 2:164, cum icon. (1968)

SYNONYMY: *P. pusilla* var. *aciculiformis* W. H. Nicholls in *Vict. Nat.* 52:167 (1936)

Flowers up to ten, erect, glaucous-green with pale rusty-brown markings; galea compressed laterally; the apices of sepals produced into points of needle-like appearance.

FLOWERING PERIOD: Sept. to Dec.

DISTRIBUTION: Central and eastern NSW, extending into western Vic. and south-eastern SA; but probably also in WA

P. hamata (Plate 344)

P. hamata J. A. P. Blackmore & S. C. Clemesha in *Orchadian* 2:154, cum icon. (1968)

Plant glabrous, robust, usually under 25 cm. in height, but occasionally attaining 40 cm. Flowers two to nine, green with rufous markings or wholly verdant green. Stem-bracts five to eight, seldom fewer, sheathing, closely appressed, the lower ones partially imbricate, additional bracteoles subtending the pedicels. Basal leaves often withered at flowering time. Galea 10–18 mm. from base to crest, the apex produced into a fine point, 5–7 mm. long. Lower lip reflexed, as long as the galea, the lobes produced into fine hooked points about 1 cm. long. Labellum ovate-oblong, fleshy, markedly glandular, extremely irritable, deeply channelled on the upper surface; tip straight, bifid, or slightly emarginate in some Vic. specimens, lateral margins of the labellum and the thickened base beset with long setae. Column-wings almost quadrangular, the upper margins not toothed or ciliate; lower lobes blunt, ciliate, the anterior margins with inturned cilia. Stigma oblong-elliptical.

[This species was formerly known as *P. squamata* R. Br. but after examining photographs of the type, Blackmore and Clemesha stated that *P. squamata* was synonymous with *P. rufa* R. Br. and the species previously known as *P. squamata* was undescribed.—Ed.]

In the Benalla district, Vic., *P. hamata* grows in fair numbers on dry and rocky hillsides in open country, also under trees in thick leaf-mould.

FLOWERING PERIOD: Aug. to Nov.

DISTRIBUTION: Extending from central and eastern NSW, to northern Vic., also Halbury, SA; possibly also in southern Qld

P. barbata (Plates 345 and 346)

P. barbata Lindl. in *Edwards' bot. Reg. 23:* Swan Riv. Append. liii (1840); A. J. Ewart *Flor. Vict.* 365 (1931); J. M. Black *Flor. S. Aust.* ed. 2:247 (1943); H. M. R. Rupp *Orchids N.S.W.* 101 (1943); J. H. Willis *Handb. Pls Vict.* 1:401 (1962); R. Erickson *Orchids West* ed. 2:42 (1965); M. J. Firth *Native Orchids Tasm.* 68 (1965)

SYNONYMY: *P. turfosa* Endl. in Lehm. *Plant. Preiss.* 2:5 (1846)

A comparatively slender plant 12–20 cm. high. Leaves short, imbricate, often numerous, ovate-lanceolate, acuminate, crowded at the base and often extending up the scape, a prominent bract in the middle and another subtending the floral pedicel. Flower usually solitary, green, finely net-veined. Galea erect, often with a long filiform point; lower sepals linear, often with long points to the lobes. Labellum about 2·5 cm. long, filiform, beset with long golden lateral hairs and terminated by a dark green or brown clavate knob; basal appendage short, oblong-linear. Column upright, the upper angle of wings produced into erect, often crossed, filiform points; the lower lobes narrow with inturned cilia.

The floral development of this species to ensure cross pollination by the right species of insect, and its entry in the right way, is amazing. It has been discussed in detail elsewhere.

[The plant illustrated on Plate 345 is from WA and was formerly known as *P. turfosa*. However A. S. George has made an intensive study of this species and *P. barbata*, and says there is only one species actually involved. As the type of *P. barbata* was from WA and as it was named first, *P. turfosa* becomes a synonym. The orchid illustrated on Plate 346 is representative of the species from the eastern states. A. S. George remarks that *P. barbata* also remains the correct name for the eastern states species, 'unless the study of fresh specimens reveals sufficient differences to warrant a new name for it'. See *West. Aust. Nat.* 8:3 (1961) for his discussion of this matter. However, L. I. Cady considers the two populations are specifically distinct and has named the eastern one *P. plumosa*. See *Aust. Pls* 5:138, fig. B-D (1969).—Ed.]

FLOWERING PERIOD: Aug. to Nov.

COMMON NAME: Bearded Greenhood

DISTRIBUTION: Temperate parts of all Australian states except Qld, but rare in NSW; widespread but uncommon over a range of habitats; also NZ

30 *Galeola*

Galeola Lour. *Flor. cochinch.* 520 (1790)

Leafless epiphytes or saprophytes, sometimes climbing to a great extent, the branches flexuose. Flowers in terminal usually pendulous panicles. Bracts at the base of the branches and panicles small or large, but always concave and half stem-clasping. Sepals and petals nearly equal in length, connivent or free, the dorsal sepal incurved, the petals narrow. Labellum, sessile, broad, curved round the column; lateral lobes very short and erect or obsolete; mid-lobe short and broad, undulate-crisped, the lamina with two raised longitudinal lines, the intervening space pubescent or glabrous. Column elongated, erect, scarcely winged, or entire. Anther lid-like, incumbent, with a broad, flat or convex dorsal appendage, two-celled. Pollinia granular-farinaceous or almost waxy, in two deeply bilobed distinct masses, without any caudicle or gland.

A genus of about seventy species distributed through India, Malaysia, Indonesia, New Guinea and New Caledonia to Australia, where there are two endemic species.

G. cassythoides (Plate 347)

G. cassythoides (A. Cunn.) Reichenb.f. *Xenia orchid.* 2:77 (1862); H. M. R. Rupp *Orchids N.S.W.* 101 (1943)

SYNONYMY: *Dendrobium cassythoides* A. Cunn. in *Edwards' bot. Reg. 21:* sub t. 1828 (1836); *Ledgeria aphylla* F. Muell. *Fragm. Phyt. Aust.* 1:239 (1859)

Stems leafless, terminating in long pendulous panicles, deep chocolate-brown in colour, climbing 360–460 cm. (12–15 ft.), and closely adhering to the bark of trees by short light brown spreading adventitious rootlets, which penetrate and become firmly imbedded. Panicles and rootlets from the nodes, often opposite each other. Flowers very numerous, pale yellow with greenish-brown markings, quite glabrous and smooth. Buds more greenish than yellow. Bracts at the base of pedicels and branches ovate-lanceolate, acute, 2–3 mm. long; those on the stem and subtending the panicles 5–8 mm. long; those subtending the rootlets 4–5 mm. long; pedicels, including ovary, 6–10 mm. long. Sepals 1·5–1·8 cm. long, oblong-lanceolate, the dorsal one incurved, lateral sepals slightly falcate. Petals as long as the sepals, but much narrower, linear. Labellum white with transverse bands, scarcely as long as the sepals, sessile, very broad, erect, concave, almost convolute, obscurely trilobed; the lateral lobes short, erect and entire; mid-lobe very short and broad, spreading, undulate-crenate, the erect part with two raised longitudinal lines separated by a broad pubescent centre and ending in a transverse callus, the lamina pubescent on the surface at the base and often bearing irregular undulate calli. Anther with a large broad convex or almost hood-like dorsal appendage, two-celled in front; pollinia two, without caudicles, deeply bilobed, but the lobes closely approximate and in consistency almost as waxy as in *Dendrobium*.

This species is a saprophyte depending essentially on rotting wood and a fungal symbiosis in its roots for survival. A plant in full bloom is an unforgettable sight.

FLOWERING PERIOD: Sept. to Nov.

COMMON NAME: Climbing Orchid

DISTRIBUTION: Inland and coastal districts of southern Qld, also eastern coast of NSW at least as far south as Illawarra

G. foliata (Plate 348)

G. foliata (F. Muell.) F. Muell. *Fragm. Phyt. Aust.* 8:31 (1873); H. M. R. Rupp *Orchids N.S.W.* 102 (1943)

SYNONYMY: *Ledgeria foliata* F. Muell. *Fragm. Phyt. Aust.* 2:167 (1861); *Galeola ledgeri* R. D. FitzG. *Aust. Orchids* 2²:+t. (1885)

Climbing habit the same as *G. cassythoides*, but much more robust. Panicle or flowering portion of the plant much larger; the bracts subtending the branches often 3–5 cm. long, ovate-lanceolate in shape, and with the colour and consistency of bracts rather than of true leaves. Sepals and petals lanceolate, about 2·5 cm. long, yellow, the petals much narrower than the sepals. Labellum broadly obovate, orange-scarlet, more contracted at the base than in *G. cassythoides*, the erect part broadly cuneate, with two raised crimson-margined lines along the centre, converging into a single one on the lamina, glabrous between them; lamina very broad, the margins white, undulate-crisped; surface of the whole labellum on each side of the smooth centre fringed with several lines of small, more or less irregular linear calli; the lines transverse on the claw, longitudinal or diverging on the lamina, strongly scented like wild bee honey. Calli variously tinted, in shades of yellow, scarlet, and white. Anther with the broad dorsal appendage of *G. cassythoides*, but flatter, pollinia distinctly granular, in two masses deeply divided into somewhat distant oblong lobes, giving each mass a horseshoe shape. Capsule 18–24 cm. long. Seed widely-winged.

G. foliata is the tallest-growing orchid in the world, for it grows to a height of 6–15 m. (20–50 ft.) by means of brownish sucker-like roots which attach themselves to giant forest trees and bite deeply into the bark. The plant has no true leaves, as the specific name would imply, but large bracts which arise at the nodes. Often the panicles of flowers are extensive, sometimes measuring as much as 180 cm. (6 ft.) in length, and almost as broad. It is an inhabitant of dense coastal scrubs and rain forests.

FLOWERING PERIOD: Nov. to Jan.

COMMON NAME: Great Climbing-orchid

DISTRIBUTION: From the Endeavour River in northern Qld to the north coast of NSW, often locally common but becoming rare due to the extensive clearing of its habitat

31 *Epipogium*

Epipogium R. Br. *Prodr. Flor. Nov. Holl.* 330 (1810)

Leafless terrestrial herbs, with a thick fleshy or a branching and coral-like rhizome. Scapes simple, ascending or erect, with a few scarious scales, not green. Flowers white or otherwise pale-coloured, in a terminal raceme, usually nodding or pendulous. Sepals and petals free, nearly equal, narrow, erect or spreading. Labellum sessile, large, ovate, concave, with a short obtuse spur at the base. Column very short, the margin membranous. Anther lid-like, with a large thick terminal appendage. Pollinia two, granular, attached to the gland by long caudicles.

A small genus scattered throughout Europe, Africa, Asia and extending through Malaysia to Australia, where there is a solitary species.

E. roseum (Plate 349)

E. roseum (D. Don) Lindl. in *J. Linn. Soc. (Bot.)* 1:177 (1857); H. M. R. Rupp *Orchids N.S.W.* 102 (1943)

SYNONYMY: *Limodorum roseum* D. Don *Prodr. Flor. nepal.* 30 (1825)

Stem ascending from a thick rhizome-like tuber 3–5 cm. long, 15–25 cm. high, with several closely appressed scarious bracts beside those within the raceme, ovate-lanceolate, acute. Flowers racemose, in a more or less drooping position, or erect, pale straw-coloured, on slender pedicels, the buds silky-white, often flushed with rose. Dorsal sepal and petals lanceolate, 1–1·3 cm. long, connivent. Lateral sepals slightly longer and narrower. Labellum sessile, adnate to the column base, as long or longer than the sepals, broadly ovate, deeply concave; margins entire or somewhat undulate, the tip acute; spur 3–6 mm. long, very obtuse; lamina broad with two rows of marginal papillae. Column small, visor-like, with a very prominent appendage at the end of the anther. (In specimens from Tambourine North, Qld, the flowers were more or less suffused with rose.)

A saprophytic species with a characteristic drooping habit during the early stages of growth of the inflorescence. Later the peduncle assumes an erect position which is followed by a pronounced elongation as the capsules ripen.

FLOWERING PERIOD: Oct. to Jan.

DISTRIBUTION: From the Endeavour River in northern Qld to the north coast of NSW, chiefly coastal and uncommon; also Africa and Asia

32 *Gastrodia*

Gastrodia R. Br. *Prodr. Flor. Nov. Holl.* 330 (1810)

Leafless saprophytic herbs; flowers in a loose raceme. Perianth segments united into a five-lobed bell-shaped flower. Labellum slightly shorter, movable on a wide claw adnate to the base of the sepals, ovate-oblong or obscurely trilobed; apex truncate; margins upraised, lacerated or fringed; lamina with conspicuous raised mesial line from the apex to centre, bifurcating posteriorly; at the base and on the claw two undulate callosities. Column elongated, erect; stigma at its extreme base; anther hemispherical, lid-like; pollinia four, granular.

A small genus of about seventeen species, chiefly Indo-Malaysian in origin. Australia has two species, one of which is confined to northern Qld, the other widespread and extending to NZ, which has a further two species.

G. sesamoides (Plate 350)

G. sesamoides R. Br. *Prodr. Flor. Nov. Holl.* 330 (1810); A. J. Ewart *Flor. Vict.* 321 (1931); J. M. Black *Flor. S. Aust.* ed. 2:210 (1943); H. M. R. Rupp *Orchids N.S.W.* 104 (1943); J. H. Willis *Handb. Pls Vict.* 1:417 (1962); R. Erickson *Orchids West* ed. 2:97 (1965); M. J. Firth *Native Orchids Tasm.* 12 (1965)

Plant slender to moderately robust with thick fleshy, succulent, scaly, tuberous rhizomes. Stems dark brown, 30–80 cm. high. Sheathing scales loose and very obtuse, shortly acute, sometimes acuminate, about 1 cm. long, crowded at the base, distant higher up. Racemes erect, rarely drooping, 2·5–10 cm. long, but in large specimens up to 25 cm. long. Bracts subtending the pedicels as long as or slightly longer than them. Flowers few to as many as seventy-five, bell-shaped, brown, white towards the apices, reversed; exterior surface often very rough, perianth 1·3–2 cm. long. Pedicels 3–10 mm. long. Ovary comparatively small. Lateral sepals united for a little more than half their length, gibbous at the base, their apices diverging; dorsal sepal and petals united, their apices free, the dorsal sepal sometimes a little longer than the other segments. Labellum mobile on a broad claw, which is adnate to the basal projection of the lateral sepals; shorter than the perianth, broadly oblong, somewhat obscurely trilobed; lateral lobes very small, the margins upturned and undulate or lacerated; apex of mid-lobe truncate; lamina suffused with yellow or orange, a raised somewhat irregular yellow ridge extending from the apex of the mid-lobe to about the middle of the lamina, then divided into two prominent divergent ridges which continue somewhat obscurely to the base; claw with two large undulate, sigmoid yellow callosities. Column slender, erect, traversed by a wide canal, with a small angular, viscid stigma at the base. Anther lid-like. Pollinia in two pairs, very granular, united by mucus at their apices. Capsule large, obovoid, turbinate.

G. sesamoides is a leafless saprophyte which favours well drained areas rich in accumulated organic matter. It is at its best in cool moist mountain gullies where large colonies are not uncommon. On a warm day the flowers exude a delightful spicy cinnamon scent. The plant was accidentally introduced into South Africa (Kirstenbosch near Capetown) in 1944, from Australia.

FLOWERING PERIOD: Sept. to Feb., depending on altitude

COMMON NAME: Cinnamon Bells or Potato Orchid

DISTRIBUTION: A widespread species favouring the cooler moist areas of all Australian states, but restricted to south-east of Qld and in WA restricted to Karri forests of the south-west; also NZ, and introduced into South Africa

33 *Rhizanthella*

Rhizanthella R. S. Rogers in *Proc. roy. Soc. S. Aust.* 15:1 (1928)

Subterranean saprophytic plants with rootless rhizomes. Inflorescence a capitulum which terminates the rhizome. Petals and sepals joined to form a tube. Labellum on a mobile claw, larger than the other perianth segments.

A monotypic genus endemic in WA. The solitary species is closely related to *Cryptanthemis slateri*, from NSW and Qld. The latter differs in having the perianth segments free, the dorsal sepal longer than the lateral sepals and petals, and the labellum about the same length as the petals.

R. gardneri (Plate 351)

R. gardneri R. S. Rogers in *Proc. roy. Soc. S. Aust.* 15:1 (1928); R. Erickson *Orchids West* ed. 2:98 (1965)

[A rather small subterranean saprophytic plant with short, branching, rootless, thickened rhizomes. Inflorescence a capitulum, erect, subsessile, terminal, those on the smaller lateral rhizomes with well developed bracteate stems. Capitulum up to 5 cm. in diameter; bracts about twelve, rather large, ovate or oblong-lanceolate, imbricate, up to 5 cm. long, slightly spreading at the apices. Flowers numerous, small, sessile, dark purple, crowded, facing the centre and arranged in four or five whorls. Sepals and petals about 4 mm. long, erect, joined to form a split tube, trilobed at the apex. Dorsal sepal cucullate, adnate in its lower half with the petals and back of the column, triangular-ovate, abruptly incurved at the apex; lateral sepals fleshy, connate in their lower half, widely triangular; petals oblong-falcate, acute, membranous, shorter and narrower than the sepals, hidden, adnate in the lower half to the dorsal sepal and column. Labellum reddish, attached to the column-foot by a mobile claw, very large in comparison with the rest of the flower, erect against the column then recurved, glandular, undivided, very fleshy, the tip protruding from the galea. Column about 4 mm. high, erect, not winged, terete, produced into a short

foot at the base. Anther two-celled, rather obtuse. Pollinia four, granular, almost sessile.

This remarkable orchid was accidentally discovered in 1928 by a farmer ploughing land. The thick fleshy white rhizomes were near a decaying *Melaleuca uncinata* stump. The species does not possess chlorophyll in any form and is in fact a saprophyte depending for its existence on the symbiotic activity of an associated fungus. The inflorescence itself, at least in the plants seen, is buried, and this raises some interesting queries on its possible pollination and seed dispersal. The plant is apparently completely subterranean and has only been noted through exposure during cultivation.

FLOWERING PERIOD: Apparently May and June

DISTRIBUTION: Endemic in WA where it is only known from Goomalling, Corrigin and Babakin in the wheat-belt of the south-west.—Ed.]

34 *Spiranthes*

Spiranthes L. C. Rich. *Orchid. Eur. Annot.* 20, 28, 36 (1817)

Terrestrial herbs with elongated underground tubers. Flowers small, sessile in a spiral spike. Leaves narrow or linear, several, basal or nearly so. Perianth segments subequal. Dorsal sepal erect or incurved over the column, ovate, concave; lateral sepals free, ovate-lanceolate, erect or spreading. Petals truncate, erect, their posterior margins concealed by the dorsal sepal and forming with it a hood. Labellum about as long as the sepals, on a very short claw, undivided; the lower half erect with entire margins embracing the column; the tip recurved; the lamina with two rounded glandular bodies at the base. Column erect, very short, contracted in the lower half, clinandrium expanded. Anther blunt or very minutely apiculate, incumbent against the back of the stigma, valvate, two-celled. Column wings membranous, stretching between the anther-filament and the stigmatic-plate, adnate to the latter; forming a pouch between the male and female organs. Stigmatic surface large, about the same length as the rostellum. Rostellum forming with the viscid disc a long membranous structure, exceeding the anther in height. The disc accommodated in the fork of the rostellum and covered by a membranous capsule. Pollinia in two pairs, granular, the apices of the pairs lightly united, exposed above the anther and attached by a short caudicle to the back of the disc.

A rather extensive genus of about fifty species, widely distributed throughout the world, with one species extending to Australia.

S. sinensis (Plate 352)

S. sinensis (Pers.) Ames *Orchidaceae* 2:53 (1908); A. J. Ewart *Flor. Vict.* 360 (1931), as *S. australis*; J. M. Black *Flor. S. Aust.* ed. 2:240 (1943); H. M. R. Rupp *Orchids N.S.W.* 105 (1943); J. H. Willis *Handb. Pls Vict.* 1:418 (1962); M. J. Firth *Native Orchids Tasm.* 29 (1965)

SYNONYMY: *Neottia sinensis* Pers. *Synops. Plant.* 2:511 (1807); *Neottia australis* R. Br. *Prodr. Flor. Nov. Holl.* 319 (1810); *Spiranthes australis* (R. Br.) Lindl. in *Edwards' bot. Reg.* 10: sub t. 823 (1824)

A more or less robust plant 15–45 cm. high, arising from a number of elongated conical or terete tubers. Stem glabrous below the inflorescence. Leaves three to five, 4–16 cm. long, linear or narrow-lanceolate, basal. Stem-bracts three to five, the lower ones large and loosely sheathing, the upper ones closely sheathing and rather small. Spike usually spiral, flowers pink or white, the ovary pubescent, shortly ovoid; subtending bracts ovate, shortly acuminate or acute, 5–8 mm. long. Perianth segments 4–5 mm. long, the petals wider at the tips than at the base. Labellum white, more or less rectangular, the lower half bulging at the base, the tip truncate; margins fringed or glandularly dentate; a large ovoid gland on each side of the base of the lamina. Column about 3 mm. long, fleshy. Anther reaching to about the base of rostellum. Stigmatic surface U-shaped. Disc of rostellum slate-coloured, long, narrow-elliptical, covered by a membranous capsule derived from the rostellum. Pollinia lamellate, pyriform. Flowers fragrant.

This lovely plant could perhaps be the most widely ranging orchid in the world. In Australia it grows in moist boggy patches or adjacent to streams, often under water, and forming extensive colonies. The normal colour of the flowers is pink with a white labellum but plants with all-white flowers are not uncommon. The species is pollinated by native bees.

FLOWERING PERIOD: Oct. to Mar., depending on latitude and altitude

COMMON NAME: Austral Ladies Tresses

DISTRIBUTION: Temperate parts of all Australian states except WA, but in Qld and SA confined to the south-east; also NZ and spreading through Malaysia to Asia and Siberia, extending to 2,500 m. (8,000 ft.) altitude in the Himalayas

spike 4–7·5 cm. long; 3–3·5 mm. long (not including the ovary); bracts hairy, awn-like, shorter than the ovary. Perianth segments nearly equal, the dorsal sepal connate with the petals to form a galea over the column; lateral sepals free, broadly lanceolate, rather blunt, 3–3·5 mm. long, one-nerved; galea erect on a wide base or slightly inclined forward, blunt, about 3 mm. long. Labellum inferior, sessile, adnate to the base of the column; cymbiform in its lower half, suddenly contracted about its middle, then abruptly dilated into a terminal expansion with two large divaricate entire oblong lobes, lamina traversed by three longitudinal lines or nerves, a claw-like callus on each side within the saccate portion near the base. Column very short, two-keeled anteriorly. Anther ovate-lanceolate, rostrate, the beak reaching as high as the rostellum. Rostellum deeply bipartite, segments slender, erect, surmounted by a long vertical linear-elliptical gland. Pollinia two, connected to a gland by a common linear caudicle with inflexed margins; gland readily detached from between the segments of the rostellum. Stigmas two, one on each side of the upper part of the column, separated by the base of the rostellum, relatively large.

FLOWERING PERIOD: July to Sept.

DISTRIBUTION: Confined to the rain forests of coastal north Qld between the Fitzroy and Endeavour Rivers

35 *Zeuxine*

Zeuxine Lindl. *Coll. Bot.* Append. no. 18 (1825)

Slender terrestrial herbs, with a creeping rhizome. Leaves with petioles, expanding at their bases into loose membranous sheaths. Flowers small, sessile, in a dense or lax spike. Sepals nearly equal; the dorsal sepal erect, concave; the lateral ones spreading, free. Petals narrow, cohering with the dorsal sepal into a galea. Labellum very shortly adnate to the base of the column, erect, cymbiform or saccate in its lower half, two calli or spurs within the sac near the base, contracted beyond the sac, and then dilated into a shortly clawed or sessile entire two-winged terminal lobe. Column very short, two-winged or keeled in front; stigmatic lobes two, lateral. Anther erect or inclined forward with contiguous cells; pollinia two, pyriform, attached by an oblong or elliptical gland to the erect rostellum with often an intermediate or linear caudicle. Pollen coarsely granular. Capsule small, erect, ovoid or nearly globular.

A large genus of approximately sixty species found in Africa, India, and Malaysia, extending through the islands of south-east Asia and the Pacific to New Guinea and Australia, where a solitary species is found.

Z. oblonga (Plate 353)

Z. oblonga R. S. Rogers & C. T. White in *Proc. roy. Soc. Qd 32*:121, t. 2 pro parte (1920)

Plant about 30 cm. in height, slender with a hairy stem on a creeping rhizome. Leaves four to seven, alternate, on the lower half or third of the stem, the base of the petiole dilated into a loose membranous tubular sheath; elliptic to oblong-elliptic, 2·5–7·5 cm. long, with a tendency to become deciduous above the expanded portion of the petiole. Stem-bracts two or three, slightly hairy, acuminate, membranous, forming a loose tubular sheath towards their bases. Flowers small, sessile, hairy on the outside, in a moderately crowded

36 *Hetaeria*

Hetaeria Blume *Bijdr. Flor. Ned. Indie* 409 (1825)

Plants in flower 25–60 cm. high. Leaves relatively broad, asymmetric, petiolate, green. Inflorescence a raceme or spike, consisting of many rather small dull flowers which have the labellum uppermost. Dorsal sepal and petals united to form a galea; lateral sepals enclosing the saccate base of the labellum; labellum concave, shallow and narrowed towards the tip which may or may not be flattened, its base almost always containing papillae or glands of various sizes. Column short with two parallel wing-like appendages on the front; anther usually short; stigmas two, convex.

A fairly large genus of about thirty species, chiefly Malaysian but extending to India and Fiji, and to Australia where there are two species confined to the tropics.

H. polygonoides (Plate 354)

H. polygonoides (F. Muell.) A. W. Dockrill in *Aust. Pls 3*:350, cum icon. (1966)

SYNONYMY: *Goodyera polygonoides* F. Muell. *Fragm Phyt. Aust.* 8:29 (1873)

[A slender plant 15–30 cm. high. Leaves three to five in a rosette above the base, with two or three smaller leaves scattered along the stem below these. Leaves narrow-ovate, acute, dark green with a broad white longitudinal stripe. Bracts two, the lower one sheathing the peduncle, the upper one subtending the inflorescence. Flowers five to fourteen, dull green, small on sessile slender ovaries 5–7 mm. long. Dorsal sepal and petals united to form a galea; lateral sepals widely spreading, up to 5·5 mm. long, oblong to narrow-obovate, apiculate and gibbous at the base where they form a backing for the labellum pouch. Petals up to 5·0 mm. long, translucent white, triangular. Labellum up to 4·5 mm. long, saccate, broad in the proximal half and then sharply constricted and narrow; lamina with a high keel inside and grooved below; finger-like glands on the lamina just inside the pouch. Saccate portion broadest near the front where it is deeply cleft down the middle, the basal portion produced past the column to form a pouch. Column short, about 1 mm. high, its wings very large and parallel.

Adapted from A. W. Dockrill in *Aust. Pls* 3:350 (1966).

In the plant illustrated the flowers are not fully open.

FLOWERING PERIOD: June to Aug.

DISTRIBUTION: Confined to the ranges of north Qld at an elevation of about 600 m. (2,000 ft.), but the precise range is unknown.—Ed.]

37 *Malaxis*

Malaxis Soland. ex Swartz *Nov. Gen. & Spec.* 8:119 (1788)

Terrestrial or epiphytic, pseudobulbous or not. Leaves one or more continuous with the sheath. Flowers small in terminal racemes, resupinate. Sepals spreading or recurved. Petals slender, as long as sepals. Labellum adnate to the base of the column, usually flat, sides often produced upward beyond the column as broad or long auricles. Column very short, with short spreading arms; anther subterminal. Pollinia four.

A large genus of about two hundred and fifty species, widely spread over the tropical regions of the world, with two species extending to Australia.

M. latifolia (Plate 355)

M. latifolia Sm. in Rees *Cyclopaedia* 22: sub *Malaxis* no. 3 (1812)

SYNONYMY: *Dienia congesta* Lindl. in *Edwards' bot. Reg. 10*: sub t. 825 (1824); *Microstylis congesta* (Lindl.) Reichenb.f. in Walp. *Ann. Bot. syst.* 6:206 (1861)

Stems stout, 10–20 cm. high, tuberous at the base. Roots numerous, fleshy. Leaves five or six, 8–23 cm. long and 4–6·5 cm. wide, broadly lanceolate, fluted, margins undulate-crisped, apex acute or shortly acuminate, sessile or petiolate. Bracts about five, loosely sheathing. Peduncle with raceme 15–23 cm. long, bracts much longer than ovary, narrow-lanceolate, acuminate. Flowers in distinct whorls, nearly sessile, very numerous, minute, greenish with red-brown or purplish markings; buds green. Sepals about equal; dorsal sepal erect, narrow-oblong, apex obtuse or emarginate, incurved; lateral sepals oblong or broad-ovate, spreading, sometimes connate. Petals as long as but narrower than the sepals, inner margins sometimes undulate towards the base, very obtuse. Labellum sub-quadrately ovate, concave, with a fold under the column, apex three-lobed, the mid-lobe longer than the lateral lobes; callus with minute glands. Ovary grooved. Column with or without prominent wings. Pollinia free, oblique-ovate.

The flowers of this orchid open green and fade to purplish after a few days. The raceme of blooms is absurdly small for such a profusion of foliage.

FLOWERING PERIOD: Dec. to Apr.

DISTRIBUTION: Confined to northern Qld between the Annan and Burdekin Rivers, ranging from 300–1100 m. (1,000–3,500 ft.) altitude

38 *Pholidota*

Pholidota Lindl. ex Hook. *Exot. Flor.* 2:138 (1825)

Epiphytic herbs, the rhizome usually shortly creeping, bearing short flowering stems or pseudobulbs, with a single terminal leaf. Flowers rather small, in terminal pedunculate racemes, usually recurved. Bracts often rather broad and imbricate in the young raceme. Flowers subglobose. Sepals nearly equal, free. Petals smaller. Labellum sessile at the base of the column, concave or almost saccate at the base, entire or trilobed, the lateral lobes erect, the mid-lobe recurved. Column erect, somewhat hood-shaped at the top and winged in front. Anther terminal, lid-like, two-celled, the valves almost transverse. Pollinia four, waxy, globular, without any caudicle.

A relatively small genus of about thirty-five species, chiefly Asian with one species found in Australia.

P. pallida (Plate 356)

P. pallida Lindl. in *Edwards' bot. Reg. 21*: sub t. 1777 (1836)

SYNONYMY: *P. imbricata* Lindl. in *Edwards' bot. Reg. 21*: t. 1777 (1836), non Hook. (1825)

Epiphytic on trees. Stems short with a few brown sheathing scales and a single leaf; the older stems thickened into pseudobulbs. Leaf broadly lanceolate or oblong-acuminate, contracted and convolute at the base, prominently ribbed, often above 30 cm. long; peduncle flexuose, long and very slender, from within the convolute base of the leaf, the flowering part recurved, 10–25 cm. long. Bracts broadly ovate, obtuse or almost acute; those within the raceme acuminate, 1–1·5 cm. long, complicate and imbricate at first, spreading from the peduncle when the flowers are blooming. Pedicels about 1 cm. long. Sepals ovate-lanceolate, about 1 cm. long; petals shorter and narrower; labellum about as long as the sepals, the concave, almost globular part erect, bordered by the short broad lateral lobes, the mid-lobe broader than long, the margin undulate and more or less distinctly trilobed. Column short, the margins winged upward. Capsule obovate, about 1·3 cm. long.

The aboriginal name for this plant is 'Jarra-ronga-ronga'.

FLOWERING PERIOD: Mainly Mar. to May, but erratic

COMMON NAME: Banana Orchid

DISTRIBUTION: In Australia confined to north Qld where it extends from the Burdekin River to Cape York Peninsula. Its range beyond Australia is uncertain owing to confusion with other species

39 *Liparis*

Liparis L. C. Rich. *Orchid. Eur. Annot.* 21, 30, 38 (1817)

Terrestrial or epiphytic plants, the stems sometimes thickened at the base into large pseudobulbs. Leaves at or near the apex of the stem. Flowers small, in a terminal pedunculate raceme. Sepals and petals all free and spreading, equal and similar, or the petals and dorsal sepal narrower. Labellum shortly embracing or united with the column at the base, erect or ascending, entire. Column elongated, incurved, the apex winged. Anther terminal, lid-like. Pollinia four, waxy, obovoid, equal in pairs in the two cells, which are sometimes not closely contiguous.

A large genus of more than one hundred species, widely distributed through tropical and temperate regions of the northern and southern hemispheres. The nine Australian species are apparently endemic.

L. coelogynoides (Plate 357)

L. coelogynoides (F. Muell.) Benth. *Flor. aust.* 6:273 (1873); H. M. R. Rupp *Orchids N.S.W.* 107 (1943)

SYNONYMY: *Sturmia coelogynoides* F. Muell. *Fragm. Phyt. Aust.* 2:71 (1860)

Habit somewhat similar to *L. reflexa*, but the leaves less flaccid, and acute, and more contracted at the base, 8–14 cm. long. Racemes more slender than in *L. reflexa*, and the flowers smaller, the peduncle flattened and winged. Bracts lanceolate, acuminate, 2·5–3 mm. long. Ovary and pedicel about 7 mm. long. Flowers very delicate, pale translucent green with orange tints, scent unpleasant or absent. Labellum wedge-shaped, its front margin irregularly denticulate, the short narrow base embracing the column, 5–6 mm. long and 5 mm. wide. Sepals linear, dorsal sepal 6–6·5 mm. long, lateral sepals 7 mm. long. Petals linear, slightly shorter and narrower than the sepals. Column slender, erect, incurved, two-winged at the summit, 3·5–4 mm. high. Pollinia very hard.

FLOWERING PERIOD: Aug. to Feb.

DISTRIBUTION: From Thorntons Peak in coastal northern Qld to the north coast of NSW, scattered on tree trunks

L. reflexa (Plate 358)

L. reflexa (R. Br.) Lindl. in *Edwards' bot. Reg.* 11: sub t. 882 (1825); H. M. R. Rupp *Orchids N.S.W.* 107 (1943)

SYNONYMY: *Cymbidium reflexum* R.Br. *Prodr. Flor. Nov. Holl.* 331 (1810); *Sturmia reflexa* (R.Br.) F. Muell. *Fragm. Phyt. Aust.* 2:72 (1860)

Pseudobulbs pear-shaped, the barren ones more or less globose, arising from a shortly creeping rhizome. Leaves almost distichous, ensiform, the lower ones scale-like, often sheathing, subulate; upper ones carinate, rather thick, often flaccid, 8–30 cm. long and about 2 cm. broad. Flowers pale greenish-white or yellowish-green, rather small, numerous in erect somewhat loose racemes. Sepals narrow-lanceolate; petals linear; these segments at first widespread, falcate, then assuming a definite reflexed position about the ovary. Labellum broadly oblong, sharply reflexed about the middle, the apex obtuse or retuse; margins in front irregularly indented; lamina with two broad orange curved lines, hardly raised into plates at the base. Column green or almost white, slender, slightly incurved, dilated above into membranous wings. Flowers diffusing an unpleasant sickly odour.

This species is found in dense clumps on rock ledges and crevices, from the coast to inland tablelands and ranges.

FLOWERING PERIOD: Mar. to May

COMMON NAME: Yellow Rock-orchid

DISTRIBUTION: Southern Qld, and NSW at least as far south as Port Jackson, widespread and common along the coast and in nearby ranges

L. reflexa var. parviflora (Plate 358)

L. reflexa var. *parviflora* W. H. Nicholls in *Vict. Nat.* 57:111, fig. C, D (1940)

Flowers numerous, smaller than in the common form, racemes much longer, the perianth segments always widely dilated, linear, obtuse.

FLOWERING PERIOD AND DISTRIBUTION: Collected from the Night Cap Range near Brunswick in northern NSW, flowering in Sept.

L. cuneilabris (Plate 359)

L. cuneilabris F. Muell. ex Benth. *Flor. aust.* 6:273 (1873)

SYNONYMY: *Sturmia angustilabris* F. Muell. *Fragm. Phyt. Aust.* 4:164 (1864)

Habit and general appearance similar to *L. reflexa*, but leaves longer, 30–60 cm. long; sinus of lamina less acute, almost flat; pseudobulbs more slender and compressed laterally. Flowers yellow, smaller than those of *L. reflexa*. Racemes erect, compact. Labellum more or less cuneate, the apical part broad, the apex apiculate; lamina with two dark curved lines noticeably raised into plates at the base. Dorsal sepal and petals narrower than lateral sepals; petals only half as wide. Column yellow, only slightly incurved; base broad, the upper part winged. In the mature flower the segments reflex even more decidedly than in *L. reflexa*.

[With the exception of F. M. Bailey's line drawing in *Compreh. Cat. Qd Pls* (1909) this species has not been figured in a botanical publication before. It is taxonomically close to *L. reflexa*.—Ed.]

FLOWERING PERIOD: Mar. to Aug.

DISTRIBUTION: Confined to elevations above 600 m. (2,000 ft.) between the Burdekin and Bloomfield Rivers, northern Qld.

L. fleckeri (Plate 360)

L. fleckeri W. H. Nicholls in *N. Qd Nat.* 6:1 (1938)

Rhizome shortly creeping, the roots numerous and fibrous. Pseudobulbs pyriform, longitudinally grooved. Leaves linear-spathulate, rather long, and thinner in texture than those of *L. cuneilabris*, the lamina quite flat. Racemes erect, the flowers small, light green, rather numerous, about 1 cm. in diameter. Dorsal sepal erect, concave; lateral sepals narrow-lanceolate, falcate. Petals narrow-linear, widely spreading. Labellum oblong-cuneate, recurved, green, deeply channelled; lamina without the prominent orange curved lines of other Australian species; but two conspicuous, conjoined orange glands at its base. Column green, erect, slightly incurved. Anther inconspicuous.

This species is closely related to *L. cuneilabris* and *L. bracteata*. The plant illustrated was growing in clumps on rocks at about 1200 m. (4,000 ft.) above sea level on Mount Bellenden Ker in northern Qld.

FLOWERING PERIOD: May

DISTRIBUTION: Confined to the Bellenden Ker Range of northern Qld

L. bracteata (Plate 361)

L. bracteata T. E. Hunt in *N. Qd Nat.* 14:9 (1946)

[Pseudobulbs 4–5 cm. high, pyriform, laterally compressed, wrinkled, arising from a shortly creeping rhizome. Leaves two, narrowly spathulate, about 30 cm. long and 1–1·5 cm. broad, sharply keeled, channelled, a prominent nerve on each side of the mid-rib. Peduncle erect, bearing about nine pale greenish-yellow flowers. Pedicels including ovary about 1 cm. long. Sepals about 1 cm. long, linear-acute with revolute margins and a prominent medial nerve; petals shorter than the sepals, narrow-linear, the margins revolute. Labellum about 1 cm. long and 3 mm. wide, erect for about half its length, then sharply recurved, margins entire; two inconspicuous rounded green conjoined calli at the base of the lamina with two orange markings on the lamina in front of them. Column erect, slightly incurved, slender.

The species is named from the persistent foliaceous bracts which remain for several years.

FLOWERING PERIOD: July to Sept.

DISTRIBUTION: Confined to the Bellenden Ker and nearby ranges of northern Qld, above 600 m. (2,000 ft.).—Ed.]

L. nugentae (Plate 362)

L. nugentae F. M. Bailey in *Qd Dep. Agric. Bot. Bull.* 14:11, t. 3 (1896)

Plant epiphytic with a creeping rhizome, producing scape-like stems, the lower parts of which are covered with equitant leaves, but ultimately thickening into compressed rather large green pseudo-bulbs 5–6 cm. high and 3–4 cm. broad; leaves usually two, linear, channelled, of firm texture, 14–30 cm. long and 2·5–3 cm. broad, sharply keeled and showing on each side of the mid-rib one or two well-marked longitudinal nerves; sheathing base short, apex somewhat abruptly acuminate, the pseudobulb always bearing on its crown the peduncle-remains. Peduncle quadrangular, bearing nine to twenty-four flowers. Bracts fugacious and very narrow. Pedicels, including ovary, about 1·2 cm. long. Buds orange. Sepals 1–1·3 cm. long and 2 mm. broad, linear with revolute margins. Petals about as long as the sepals and 1 mm. broad. Sepals and petals reflexed and somewhat curled, pale cream, no markings or veins visible. Labellum somewhat rhomboid when flattened out, erect for about half its length, then suddenly recurved, widening at the bend and almost forming a tooth on either side, otherwise the margins entire; apex obtuse-apiculate; lamina with two thickened ridges stained a deep orange, but scarcely raised into plates, except at the base. Column 6 mm. long, white, incurved, base rather broad, the upper part slightly expanding into wings. Anther small, apiculate in front like the rostellum. Pollinia yellow. Flowers emitting a strong unpleasant odour.

This plant is the largest of the Australian *Liparis* species.

FLOWERING PERIOD: Sept. to Jan.

DISTRIBUTION: Confined to northern Qld, between the Eungella Range and the Big Tableland, above 600 m. (2,000 ft.) altitude

L. habenarina (Plate 363)

L. habenarina (F. Muell.) Benth. *Flor. aust.* 6:273 (1873); H. M. R. Rupp *Orchids N.S.W.* 108 (1943)

SYNONYMY: *Sturmia habenarina* F. Muell. *Fragm. Phyt. Aust.* 4:131 (1864)

A semi-robust, glabrous terrestrial plant 30–60 cm. high. Leaves short, three to four, rigid, 6–18 cm. long and 1·3–3·5 cm. wide, lanceolate, acute, prominently ribbed, plicate, sheathing at the base; two loosely sheathing bracts at the base of the plant, the upper one about 6 cm. long, the lower bract small. Flowers in a long terminal raceme, smaller than those of *L. reflexa*, pale yellowish to green with brownish markings; raceme rigid, the peduncle thick, grooved, a minute bract towards the base; ovary pedicillate, ribbed and twisted. Dorsal sepal broad-linear, base rather wide and prominently ribbed, tip acute and rough-glandular on the upper surface, 6–7 mm. long; lateral sepals broadly oblong, falcate, obtuse, connate except at the tips, about 5 mm. long. Petals narrower than the dorsal sepal, narrow-linear, spathulate, about 6 mm. long. Labellum about 3 mm. long and 2·5 mm. wide, recurved from the middle, broadly oblong, channelled, shortly embracing and adnate to the column base; tip obtuse or retuse; the lamina with two

rather inconspicuous callosities at the base. Column erect, incurved, pale greenish-white. Anther cells at some distance from each other in the anther case. Pollinia four in two pairs.

This plant grows in loose scattered colonies over rocky, granitic, open forest country, often favouring the tops of low ridges.

FLOWERING PERIOD: Jan. to Mar.

DISTRIBUTION: Extending from the Barron River in northern Qld to the north coast of NSW, at least as far south as Byron Bay

40   *Oberonia*

Oberonia Lindl. *Gen. & Spec. orchid. Pls* 15 (1830)

Epiphytic plants with very short or, in non-Australian species, elongated stems, not usually thickened into pseudobulbs. Leaves distichous, equitant. Flowers very small, in terminal pedunculate dense racemes, the pedicels short, the bracts small. Sepals free, nearly equal and erect, or the dorsal one smaller and reflexed. Petals narrower and shorter than the sepals. Labellum sessile, concave, entire or variously divided, often cushion-like or keeled at the base and usually embracing the column. Column very short, terete, contracted at the base, the apex with angular margins. Anther terminal, lid-like. Pollinia four, waxy, closely contiguous in pairs and often falling away in one mass, sometimes oblique and unequal.

A large genus of about one hundred species, widely distributed from tropical Asia and islands of the South Pacific to Australia, where three species are found.

O. muellerana (Plate 364)

O. muellerana Schlechter in *Bot. Jb.* 39:61 (1907); H. M. R. Rupp *Orchids N.S.W.* 108 (1943), as *O. iridifolia*

SYNONYMY: *O. iridifolia* F. Muell. *Fragm. Phyt. Aust.* 5:96 (1865), non Lindl. (1830); *O. fitzgeraldiana* Schlechter in *Bot. Jb.* 58:63 (1922)

Leafy stems very short and thick, rarely lengthening to 2·5 cm. Leaves five to seven, sometimes less than 7 cm. long, but generally 9–15 cm. long and 1·2–2 cm. broad. Peduncle flattened and winged, with one or two scarious bracts. Racemes longer than the leaves, rather dense, very slender when in flower, the minute flowers more or less distinctly arranged in closely approximate whorls. Bracts ovate or oblong, scarious, with denticulate or fringed margins. Pedicels 1·5 mm. long. Sepals broadly ovate, the dorsal one much longer than the lateral sepals. Petals longer than the lateral sepals, and narrower, the margins with coarse irregular teeth. Labellum almost broadly triangular, not perceptibly lobed, bifid at the apex, the margins with coarse irregular teeth. Column very short and broad, the wings short. Stigma broader than long. Capsule 3 mm. long, prominently angled.
This species has previously been confused with *O. iridifolia* Lindl., an Asian species.

FLOWERING PERIOD: Very erratic, recorded for every month.

DISTRIBUTION: From the Endeavour River in northern Qld to the north coast of NSW, extending to 1100 m. (3,500 ft.) altitude and often locally common; also Pacific islands

O. palmicola (Plate 365)

O. palmicola F. Muell. *Fragm. Phyt. Aust.* 2:24 (1860); H. M. R. Rupp *Orchids N.S.W.* 109 (1943)

SYNONYMY: *Malaxis palmicola* (F. Muell.) F. Muell. *Fragm. Phyt. Aust.* 7:30 (1869); *Oberonia titania* H. M. R. Rupp *Guide Orchids N.S.W.* 14 (1930), non Lindl. (1859)

A very small, somewhat delicate, almost stemless plant, often growing in clusters. Roots thread-like and numerous. Leaves five to seven, alternate, lanceolate, clasping at the base, 3–8 cm. long. Racemes very slender, 5–15 cm. long, the minute flowers very numerous, clustered in distinct whorls. Bracts usually as long as the flower, occasionally shorter, lanceolate, with fine, often ciliate points. Sepals and petals about 0·25 mm. long, ovate-lanceolate or lanceolate, acute; dorsal sepal usually much narrower than the petals; lateral sepals sometimes twice as wide as the dorsal one. Labellum about as long as the lateral sepals, with two prominent lateral lobes; mid-lobe rhomboidal, sometimes broader than long. Column urn-like with the wings prominent. Anther incumbent. Fruiting pedicel 0·5 mm. long; capsule 1 mm. long.

FLOWERING PERIOD: Feb. to May in Qld, Aug. to Oct. in NSW

DISTRIBUTION: From the Endeavour River in northern Qld to the north coast of NSW, extending to 1100 m. (3,500 ft.) altitude and often locally common

41 *Phaius*

Phaius Lour. *Flor. cochinch.* 517, 529 (1790)

Terrestrial herbs, the leafy stems short and thickened into pseudobulbs, or almost stemless. Leaves large. Scapes radical, tall, erect, leafless except for sheathing scales imbricate at the base, distant on the stem and passing into the bracts. Flowers large and showy. Sepals and petals nearly equal, free, spreading. Labellum broad, produced into a spur at the base, erect and convolute round the column, entire or trilobed and more or less spreading at the top. Column semi-cylindrical, elongated. Anther lid-like. Pollinia eight, nearly equal, or four shorter, waxy, attached to the branches of a dichotomous caudicle, but no gland.

A small genus of about twenty species extending from tropical Asia through Malaysia and the islands of south-east Asia to New Guinea, and to Australia where there are three species

P. australis (Plate 366)

P. australis F. Muell. *Fragm. Phyt. Aust.* 1:42 (1858)

SYNONYMY: *P. grandifolius* Benth. *Flor. aust.* 6:304 (1873) pro parte; *P. grandifolius* var. *rowanae* F. M. Bailey in *Qd agric. J.* 28:74 (1912)

A large terrestrial species with short leafy stems thickened at the base into small ovate pseudobulbs. Leaves several, large, thin, on long petioles, oblong to ovate-lanceolate, strongly fluted and ribbed. Flowers large, often numerous, usually 8–10 cm. in diameter. Racemes rather loose, produced on long radical scapes 60–160 cm. or more in height. Sepals and petals oblong-lanceolate, about 6 cm. and 5 cm. long respectively, silvery-white on the reverse side, about as long as the sepals, broad-ovate, trilobed; lateral lobes broad chocolate-brown on the inner side, sometimes mottled. Labellum about as long as the sepals broad-ovate, trilobed; lateral lobes broad and rounded, loosely enclosing the column, fluted and veined with crimson on both sides; mid-lobe shortly acute, the margins undulate crisped, white; stained with yellow on the broad lamina, and veined with deep crimson. Spur short and narrow, somewhat curved. Column about 2·3 cm. high, stained with yellow, wings fleshy.

Anther lid-like, tomentose, the stigmatic cavity V-shaped. Pollinia in four pairs, each mass ovate, plano-convex with a short acute apex. Lateral margins of the stigmatic cavity produced into two triangular appendages of a greenish hue.

This is the largest terrestrial orchid native to Australia. Even when not in flower it is a prominent plant in the well sheltered boggy places that it frequents. The flowers are self-pollinating, dehiscence taking place in the bud. The species has a tendency to produce additional anthers (staminodes).

FLOWERING PERIOD: Sept. and Oct.

DISTRIBUTION: Scattered from the Atherton Tableland in northern Qld to the north coast of NSW, generally in moist boggy areas

P. australis var bernaysii (Plate 367)

P. australis var. *bernaysii* (F. Muell. ex Reichenb.f.) W. H. Nicholls in *Vict. Nat.* 67:10 (1950)

SYNONYMY: *P. bernaysii* F. Muell. ex Reichenb.f. in *Gdnrs' Chron.* 1873:361 (1873)

A plant of similar habit and foliage to *P. australis* but flowers pale sulphur-yellow inside, labellum also similarly coloured. The stigmatic cavity is quadrilateral in form and much smaller than in the typical. The attachment of the pollinia is also different.

This lovely variety also favours protected swampy areas and was once locally common in its habitat, but is now rare because of extensive collecting.

FLOWERING PERIOD: Sept. to Nov.

DISTRIBUTION: Confined to swamps of south-eastern Qld

P. tankervilliae (Plate 368)

P. tankervilliae (Banks ex L'Hérit.) Blume *Mus. bot. Lugd.-Bat.* 2:177 (1856); H. M. R. Rupp *Orchids N.S.W.* 109 (1943)

SYNONYMY: *Limodorum tankervilliae* Banks ex L'Hérit. *Sert. Angl.* 28 (1789); *P. grandifolius* Lindl. *Gen. & Spec. orchid. Pls* 126 (1831), non Benth. (1873); *P. blumei* Lindl. *Gen. & Spec. orchid. Pls* 127 (1831); *P. wallichii* Hook.f. *Flor. Brit. Ind.* 5:816 (1890)

A large terrestrial plant. Leaves several, 50–120 cm. long, plicate, lanceolate, narrowing to a rather long petiole. Peduncle up to 200 cm. (6 ft.) tall, bearing from four to twelve flowers, which may be up to 10 cm. in diameter. Perianth segments lanceolate, whitish on the outside, red-brown or densely mottled with brown on the inside. Dorsal sepal and petals about equal. Labellum magenta, bright purple or red, as long as the dorsal sepal, trumpet shaped, obovate when flattened out, obscurely trilobate; margins crisped.

FLOWERING PERIOD: Aug. to Oct.

DISTRIBUTION: Extending from northern Qld to NSW, as far south as the Richmond River, chiefly in wet coastal situations

42 *Calanthe*

Calanthe R.Br. in *Edwards' bot. Reg.* 7: sub t. 573 (1821)

Terrestrial herbs, stemless or nearly so. Leaves large, plicate, usually in tufts of two or three. Scapes in the axils of the outer leaves, tall, erect, and many-flowered. Flowers often showy, white or lilac. Sepals and petals nearly equal, free, spreading, the lateral sepals sometimes shortly adnate to the labellum base. Labellum connate at the base with the column, forming a sort of cup, usually produced into a spur at the base, the lamina spreading, lobed or undivided, with several tubercles or callosities opposite the anther. Column erect, the margins connate with the labellum, the rostellum usually rostrate. Anther lid-like. Pollinia eight, tapering to the base and there affixed to a divisible gland.

A large genus of about one hundred and twenty species, widely distributed through tropical regions of the world, one species only extending to Australia.

C. triplicata (Plate 369)

C. triplicata (Willemet) Ames in *Philipp. J. Sci. (Bot.)* 2:326 (1907); H.M.R. Rupp *Orchids N.S.W.* 110 (1943), as *C. veratrifolia*

SYNONYMY: *Orchis triplicata* Willemet in Usteri *Ann. Bot. 18*:52 (1796); *Limodorum veratrifolium* Willd. *Spec. Plant.* 4:122 (1805); *Calanthe veratrifolia* (Willd.) R.Br. in *Edwards' bot. Reg. 9*: t. 720 (1823)

Rhizome shortly creeping, with tufts of two or three broad leaves, forming a very short stem or pseudobulb at the base. Leaves 30–60 cm. long, ovate-lanceolate, plicate, undulate and strongly ribbed, tapering into a petiole which is dilated at the base. Scapes 30–120 cm. high, usually in the axil of the outer leaf, the flowers rather crowded near the summit. Pedicels spreading, 1·3–2·5 cm. long, recurved after flowering. Sepals and petals white, obovate-oblong, 1–1·8 cm. long, the petals usually broader and more contracted at the base than the sepals. Labellum much longer, the spur slender, 2 cm. long, and usually pubescent, the lamina trilobed with the mid-lobe deeply bifid, the four lobes oblong and sometimes nearly equal, but variable in breadth as well as in the relative depth to which they are divided, the callosities of the lamina yellow. Capsule obovoid-oblong, about 4 cm. long.

This terrestrial orchid favours cool shady situations where it is often abundant. A large plant in flower is a beautiful sight, the flowers themselves being very delicate and blackening readily with handling.

FLOWERING PERIOD: Oct. to Mar.

DISTRIBUTION: Extending from the Bloomfield River in northern Qld almost to Sydney in NSW, both coastal and inland; climbing to 1200 m. (4,000 ft.) altitude and common

43   *Spathoglottis*

Spathoglottis Blume *Bijdr. Flor. Ned. Indie* 400 (1825)

Terrestrial herbs with subterranean tuberous rhizomes. Leaves usually long, plicate and strongly ribbed. Racemes on erect scapes, leafless except for sheathing scales. Bracts usually rather large. Sepals and petals nearly equal, free, spreading. Labellum articulate on the base of the column, concave or saccate at the base, deeply trilobed, the mid-lobe contracted at the base and bearing prominent tubercles or calli. Column erect, free, more or less dilated or two-winged upward. Anthers terminal, lid-like, two-celled. Pollinia eight, four of which are usually smaller; waxy, with very short separate caudicles without any common gland.

A small genus of about fifteen species scattered through tropical Asia, with two extending to Australia, one of which is apparently undescribed.

S. paulinae (Plates 370 and 371)

S. paulinae F. Muell. *Fragm. Phyt. Aust. 6*:95 (1867)

SYNONYMY: *S. soutteriana* F. M. Bailey in *Proc. roy. Soc. Qd 11*:15 (1895)

Leaves six or seven, crowning the pseudobulb, the outer one without any lamina, the others increasing in length, the centre one 45 cm. to 60 cm. long and about 2 cm. wide, but usually less, tapering to fine points, and prominently marked with numerous rib-like nerves. Scape slender, raceme 8–16 cm. long, bearing eight or more light purple flowers, each about 2·3 cm in diameter. Bracts lanceolate, 10–20 mm. long, pedicels about 2·5 cm. long, but increasing to over 3 cm. after fertilisation. Sepals and petals about 1·5 cm. long. Labellum about 1·1 cm. long, articulate on the base of column, trilobed; lateral lobes oblong or slightly spathulate, and somewhat incurved, with two or three large, thick, erect, rather spreading glabrous calli between them; mid-lobe with a rather long claw, expanding into a flabelliform blade, the claw with densely woolly margins. Column incurved, dilated upward, presenting, with the anther, an almost hooded appearance.

[The species grows on hillsides and tablelands in grassland or open forest country, preferring moist well-drained patches and creek beds. For a comprehensive treatment see A. W. Dockrill in *Orchadian 2*:2–4 (1965).—Ed.]

FLOWERING PERIOD: Erratically from July to Mar. reaching a peak in Nov. and Dec.

DISTRIBUTION: Confined to north-eastern Qld between Rockingham Bay and the Endeavour River, generally uncommon

44   *Geodorum*

Geodorum G. Jackson in Andr. *Bot. Repos. 10*: sub t. 626 (1810)

Terrestrial herbs with a shortly creeping rhizome. Leafy stems short, pseudobulbous at the base. Leaves rather large, plicate and strongly-ribbed, the lower ones reduced to membranous sheathing scales. Scapes arising from an outer leaf-base, leafless except for the sheathing scales, terminating in a rather dense, usually nodding raceme. Sepals and petals nearly equal, free, erect. Labellum erect, sessile at the base of the column but free from it; broad, concave and slightly saccate at the base, entire or scarcely lobed. Column short erect, semiterete. Anther terminal, lid-like, very concave. Pollinia two, bilobed, waxy, attached by a very short caudicle to a transverse gland.

A small genus of about twelve species, chiefly Indo-Malaysian, with two extending to Australia.

G. pictum (Plate 372)

G. pictum (R.Br.) Lindl. *Gen. & Spec. orchid. Pls* 175 (1833); H. M. R. Rupp *Orchids N.S.W.* 110 (1943)

SYNONYMY: *Cymbidium pictum* R.Br. *Prodr. Flor. Nov. Holl.* 331 (1810)

Leafy stems 8–10 cm. high, arising from a short creeping rhizome to which persist the dormant remains of previous seasons' stems. Leaves two or three, 10–18 cm. long, oblong-lanceolate, plicate and strongly ribbed. Pseudobulb with several bracts towards the base, the lowest ones reduced to sheathing scales. Scapes arising from the axil of a basal bract, usually longer than the leaves, bearing membranous sheathing scales, large and crowded at the base, distant higher up. Flowers pink, fairly numerous in a terminal raceme that is reflexed only after the flowers have begun to expand. Pedicels short. Bracts linear. Sepals and petals oblong, nearly 1 cm. long. Labellum broadly ovate, darkly veined, obtuse or emarginate or very shortly bilobed at the apex, the margins somewhat undulate; lamina saccate at the base, with two double raised lines, becoming evanescent upward or confluent into two single ones and terminating into a toothed or entire transverse callus below the labellum apex. Column short, erect, the wings small. Pollinia ovoid-globular, waxy, bilobed with a short caudicle. Peduncle straightening as seed-capsules mature.

This plant formed an important article of diet of the aboriginals, to whom it was known as 'Yeenga' or 'Uine'.

FLOWERING PERIOD: Erratic, but mainly Dec. to Feb.

DISTRIBUTION: From north of the Endeavour River in northern Qld to the north coast of NSW, generally common and extending to 900 m (3,000 ft.) altitude; also NT

45   *Epidendrum*

Epidendrum L. *Spec. Plant.* ed. 2:1347 (1763)

[Plants epiphytic, lithophytic or rarely terrestrial, small to large and robust, with or without a conspicuous rhizome. Stems thickened into pseudobulbs with leaves only at the summit, or slender, leafy throughout and branched. Leaves terete or flattened, varying from linear to oval, rounded to long acuminate at the apex. Inflorescence racemose, terminal, rarely axillary, erect or nodding, one- to many-flowered. Flowers minute to rather large. Perianth segments spreading, petals usually much narrower than the sepals. Labellum slightly adnate to the column, entire or trilobed, smooth or callose. Column short to elongate, wingless or prominently winged. Pollinia four, waxy.

A very extensive genus of about eight hundred species, widely distributed through North, Central and South America, and the West Indies. One hybrid has become naturalised in northern Australia.

E. × obrienianum (Plate 373)

E.×obrienianum R. A. Rolfe in *Gdnrs' Chron.* ser. 3, *3*:770 (1888)

Stems not pseudobulbous, scandent, up to 180 cm. (6 ft.) or more, often branched near the base. Roots numerous, cord-like, branching, arising from opposite the leaves and descending to the ground. Leaves up to 5 cm. long, numerous up the stem, ovate-oblong, emarginate. Peduncles slender, sheathed by imbricate adherent bracts and terminating in a many-flowered corymbiform raceme. Flowers numerous, about 3 cm. in diameter, of a uniform bright orange, the calli on the mid-lobe bright yellow. Sepals and petals oblong-lanceolate, narrowed at the base. Labellum trilobed, all lobes fringed; mid-lobe bipartite; the callus consisting of two large, erect teeth with two smaller ones behind them and a rounded keel in front and between them.

This orchid is an artificial hybrid between *E. radicans* of Guatemala and *E. evectum* of New Granada. It was raised in Veitch's nurseries, England, in the 1890's and is now a widespread and commonly cultivated plant.

FLOWERING PERIOD: Almost continuous throughout the year

COMMON NAME: Crucifix Orchid

DISTRIBUTION: Naturalised in some Qld scrubs.—Ed.]

46   *Dendrobium*

Dendrobium Swartz. in *Nova Acta Soc. Sci. upsal.* 6:82 (1799)

Epiphytes or lithophytes, rarely terrestrial plants. Rhizomes tufted or creeping. Stems elongated and branching or short and thick, erect, creeping, or pendulous; stout and rigid or slender and lax; reduced to short pseudobulbs, or pseudobulbous at the base. Leaves variable. Flowers racemose, rarely solitary. Sepals more or less equal, variable; lateral sepals obliquely dilated at the base and connate with the column foot to form a spur (mentum) under the labellum. Petals as long as or longer than the dorsal sepal. Labellum in Australian species articulate on the apex of the column foot, erect, concave near the base, trilobed or occasionally entire; lateral lobes variable, usually embracing the column; mid-lobe recurved or spreading, acute or occasionally obtuse, usually beset with longitudinal callus ridges. Column variable, usually shorter than the labellum, winged or toothed. Anther operculate. Pollinia four in two pairs, waxy.

A very large genus of about one thousand species, widespread through southern and eastern Asia, Japan, Malaysia and various Pacific islands to New Guinea, Australia and New Zealand. In Australia there are about forty-five recorded species and many described varieties. A comprehensive review is necessary to clear up much of the confusion that exists regarding the Australian species.

D. lichenastrum (Plate 374)

D. lichenastrum (F. Muell.) Kraenzlin in *Pflanzenreich iv 50* (Heft 45): 289 (1910)

SYNONYMY: *Bulbophyllum lichenastrum* F. Muell. *Fragm. Phyt. Aust.* 7:60 (1869)

[The text for this species and its varieties is based largely on the publications of A. W. Dockrill.—Ed.]

Rhizomes short, creeping and branching, flexuose, forming dense patches on bark or rocks. Leaves thick, more or less sessile, 4–10 cm. long and 3–6 cm. broad, extremely variable, from ovate-oblong to almost circular. Flower solitary, 4–7 mm. across, white, cream or pink with red stripes and an orange or yellow labellum. Dorsal sepal ovate, up to 5 mm. long. Lateral sepals joined at the base to the column foot, free portion 3–5 mm. long, triangular; mentum 2–4 mm. long, broad obtuse-truncate. Petals 2–5 mm. long, linear, obtuse or acute. Labellum oblong, ovate to obovate, usually constricted in the middle, the apex more or less decurved, obtuse or apiculate, hinged to the column foot by a broad claw. Column minute, about 1 mm. high; foot curved, 2–3 mm. long. Rostellum small, bifid, the lobes obtuse. Anther peaked. Capsule small, oblique, ovate, attenuated at the base. [Adapted from A. W. Dockrill in *Orchadian* 1:28 (1963).

In his comprehensive review of this species A. W. Dockrill states: 'It is undoubtedly one of Australia's most controversial and complex orchids and has been the subject of treatment and question by numerous authors, most of whom were not the least familiar with the plant in its natural habitat'. See *Orchadian* 1:28 (1963).

To say the least, the plant is extremely variable, and although many intermediates do exist, a variety with two forms has been retained by Dockrill but not without some trepidation. The whole species-complex is probably as close to *Bulbophyllum* as it is to *Dendrobium*.—Ed.]

FLOWERING PERIOD: Very erratic, on record for every month

DISTRIBUTION: Confined to the coastal ranges of northern Qld, where often locally abundant

D. lichenastrum var. prenticei

D. lichenastrum var. *prenticei* (F. Muell.) A. W. Dockrill in *N. Qd Nat.* 24:21 (1956)

SYNONYMY: *Bulbophyllum prenticei* F. Muell. in *Sth. Sci. Rec.* 1:173 (1891); *Dendrobium prenticei* (F. Muell.) W. H. Nicholls in *N. Qd Nat.* 7:1 (1938); *Dendrobium variabile* W. H. Nicholls in *N. Qd Nat.* 7:2 (1938)

A variety of two forms, both of which are illustrated.

(a) forma **prenticei** (Plate 375)

An extremely variable plant with terete or subcylindrical leaves, and flowers similar to those of var. *lichenastrum*. Distribution and flowering as for var. *lichenastrum*.

(b) forma **aurantiaco-purpureum** (Plate 374)

D. lichenastrum var. *prenticei* forma *aurantiaco-purpureum* (W. H. Nicholls) A. W. Dockrill in *N. Qd Nat.* 24:21 (1956)

SYNONYMY: *D. aurantiaco-purpureum* W. H. Nicholls in *N. Qd Nat.* 10:2 (1942)

Differs from the preceding form in having a fairly robust flower with a broad mentum, the labellum claw more or less slightly channelled and the sepals usually recurved with prominent red stripes.

FLOWERING PERIOD and DISTRIBUTION: As in var. *lichenastrum*, but it is apparently confined to higher elevations

D. toressae (Plate 376)

D. toressae (F. M. Bailey) A. W. Dockrill in *Orchadian* 1:64 (1964)

SYNONYMY: *Bulbophyllum toressae* F. M. Bailey *Synops. Qd Flor.* Suppl. 3:72 (1890)

A diminutive plant with creeping rhizomes closely adhering to the bark of trees or rocks by roots from the under side, extending 5–8 cm. in length, often forming radiating patches. The upper surface is closely covered by distichous, sessile, ovate-lanceolate, very rugose leaves, which are so concave on the upper face as to be somewhat cymbiform, about 5 mm. long, with a solitary, nearly sessile flower at the base. Flowers yellowish-white, slightly marked with red, subtended by a prominent scarious bract; sepals broad, about 5 mm. long, the lateral ones very broad, their bases adnate to the column foot, forming a short, blunt, almost truncate spur. Petals white, delicate, shorter and narrower than the dorsal sepal. Labellum yellow, sessile on a broad base, as long as or longer than the lateral sepals, trilobed, but not markedly so, a wide channel between the lateral lobes; lateral lobes dotted with red on a yellow ground, very short; mid-lobe blunt and much thickened at the apex, wholly yellow. Column very short, yellow, wings prominent; column foot long, broad at the end, dotted with red. Anther green, attached by a long slender filament. Pollinia four, subfalcate.

Concerning this very remarkable species Dr Flecker writes, 7 February 1941: 'This tiny chap is by no means common. I have

never seen it anywhere in considerable quantity. Once I found it on the vertical trunk of a standing tree at Campbell's Creek, but could not find it elsewhere in the neighbourhood despite repeated hunts at several subsequent visits. The only other locality I have met it was at Upper Mossman River, over 1200 m. (4,000 ft.) and only last week at Mount Lewis 900 m. (3,000 ft.). It only grows in the rain forest.'

FLOWERING PERIOD: Erratic, but usually June–July and Jan.

DISTRIBUTION: Coastal gorges and tablelands of northern Qld, between the Annan and Tully Rivers

D. rigidum (Plate 377)

D. rigidum R.Br. *Prodr. Flor. Nov. Holl.* 333 (1810)

Stems slender and numerous, the young growth covered with membranous scarious sheathing-scales. Leaves 2·5–4 cm. long, numerous, oblong, occasionally falcate, broader beyond the middle; the apex shortly acute, sessile on a broad base as in *D. linguiforme*, very thick and fleshy. Racemes short, few-flowered; flowers rather small, about 1 cm. in diameter, pale yellowish, tinged with red. Dorsal sepal broadly lanceolate, acute; lateral sepals oblong, broad at the base and adnate to the column foot. Petals narrow, oblong, shorter than the dorsal sepal. Labellum deeply channelled, trilobed, about the same length as the dorsal sepal, deeply marked with crimson; lateral lobes about the same length as the mid-lobe, pointed at the end, and bordered with deep red; mid-lobe oblong, and bordered by the same deep red colour except at the apex where it is yellowish. Callus ridges three, yellowish, not crested, rather distant from each other and not prominent. Column broad, red on the edge ending in points on either side of the anther. Anther lid ovate, greenish, with a line of white tomentum in front. Pollinia amber in colour. Stigma deeply sunk in the column.

This species often grows in nearly inaccessible mangrove swamps along the coast, where it sometimes occurs in large numbers. However it has also been found inland on such trees as Ironbarks. It is a remarkably drought-tolerant plant.

FLOWERING PERIOD: Erratic, throughout the year

DISTRIBUTION: Northern Qld, from the Russell River to Cape York, mainly coastal and often locally abundant

D. cucumerinum (Plate 378)

D. cucumerinum MacLeay ex Lindl. in *Edwards' bot. Reg.* 28: Misc. 58 (1842); H. M. R. Rupp *Orchids N.S.W.* 122 (1943)

Stems rigid, creeping on the bark of trees and rocks, with prominent ribs and furrows and annular scars of the sheathing scales. Leaves terminal, ovoid-oblong, fleshy, 2–5·5 cm. long, marked with raised tuberculate ribs, similar in appearance to small cucumbers. Flowers about 2·5 cm. in diameter, one to four on very short racemes, the pedicels about 1·3 cm. long. Sepals and petals yellowish or greenish-white, streaked with reddish-purple; lateral sepals twisted; dorsal sepal similar to the petals, flat and recurved. Spur short and conical. Labellum shorter than the sepals, the lateral lobes prominent, almost acute; mid-lobe ovate, shortly acuminate, recurved with undulate crisped margins, white, streaked with reddish-purple; three to five longitudinal raised plates between the lateral lobes, and extending towards the tip, where they are undulate, and red-brown in colour. Column streaked with reddish-purple. Stigma prominent. Anther pink, marked with purple.

The species was once locally common along many northern NSW rivers, favouring Casuarina as the host tree.

FLOWERING PERIOD: Erratic, between Nov. and May

COMMON NAME: Cucumber Orchid

DISTRIBUTION: Southern Qld, and NSW as far south as the Burragorang Valley, near Sydney, often extending into drier areas

D. linguiforme (Plate 379)

D. linguiforme Swartz in *K. svenska VetenskAkad. Handl.* 21:247 (1800); H. M. R. Rupp *Orchids N.S.W.* 122 (1943)

Roots closely creeping on rocks or trees; stems prostrate, branching. Leaves numerous, very thick and tough, ovate or ovate-lanceolate, conspicuously ribbed longitudinally. Flowers in numerous rather dense racemes 6–13 cm. long, white or rarely yellowish, with faint red or purplish markings on the labellum and column. Sepals and petals about 2 cm. long, narrow-linear. Labellum very short, the lateral lobes prominent, more or less obtuse; mid-lobe narrow-ovate, recurved, obtuse; lamina with three raised longitudinal callus plates, becoming undulate towards the end. Column short with a broad foot.

This exceptionally hardy species often grows in full sunlight, the leaves becoming deeply ribbed and leathery and a deep purple. It is extremely floriferous, a large plant making a spectacular display.

FLOWERING PERIOD: July to Nov.

COMMON NAME: Tongue Orchid

DISTRIBUTION: Qld, south of the Burdekin River; NSW at least as far south as Narooma; often locally common

D. linguiforme var. nugentii (Plate 380)

D. linguiforme var. *nugentii* F. M. Bailey *Qd Flor.* 5:1533 (1902)

This outstanding form differs from the typical in the following particulars: leaves thicker and shorter, the surface very rugose; flowers smaller, pedicels shorter; petals longer than the sepals; labellum small, less than half the length of the other segments, the lateral lobes red-purple.

FLOWERING PERIOD: June to Aug.

DISTRIBUTION: Confined to northern Qld, from the Endeavour River to the Burdekin River, often locally common

D. pugioniforme (Plate 381)

D. pugioniforme A. Cunn. in *Edwards' bot. Reg.* 25: Misc. 33 (1839); H. M. R. Rupp *Orchids N.S.W.* 120 (1943)

SYNONYMY: *D. pungentifolium* F. Muell. *Fragm. Phyt. Aust.* 1:189 (1859)

Epiphytic on trees; roots slender, creeping or often aerial, developing freely at the nodes of the branches. Stems slender but woody, up to 180 cm. long, intricately branching, the plants often forming large pendulous masses on the trunks and branches of trees. Leaves very numerous, ovate to lanceolate, coriaceous and shining, thick and rigid, tapering to a sharp dagger-like point, 2–8 cm. long. Flowers solitary or two or three together, light green with bright mauve and red markings on the labellum. Perianth segments light-green, broad-linear with longitudinal brown lines towards the base, on both sides. Sepals about 1·5 cm. long, the lateral ones much wider and with the column foot forming a short blunt spur 5–6 mm. long. Petals as long as, or a little shorter than the sepals, narrower. Labellum nearly as long as the sepals, rather narrow to about the middle, then expanded into a broadly ovate, triangular, acute, recurved lamina, very undulate, but scarcely trilobed; three raised lines or plates extending to the claw, undulate on the lamina.

A very common species within its range, often forming tangled masses, parts of which break off easily and litter the ground.

FLOWERING PERIOD: Sept. to Nov.

COMMON NAME: Dagger Orchid

DISTRIBUTION: A widespread species, extending from southern Qld to the south coast of NSW, coastal and somewhat inland

D. striolatum (Plate 382)

D. striolatum Reichenb.f. in *Hamb. Gtn-Blumen Z.* 13:313 (1857); A. J. Ewart *Flor. Vict.* 310 (1931); H. M. R. Rupp *Orchids N.S.W.* 119 (1943); J. H. Willis *Handb. Pls Vict.* 1:419 (1962); M. J. Firth *Native Orchids Tasm.* 11 (1965)

SYNONYMY: *D. teretifolium* Lindl. in *Edwards' bot. Reg.* 25: Misc. 32 (1839), non R.Br. (1810); *D. milliganii* F. Muell. *Fragm. Phyt. Aust.* 1:88, t. 6 (1859)

Stems slender, the rhizome extensively creeping and branched, often forming extensive mats on rocks and cliff faces. Leaves abundant, narrow-cylindrical, falcate, pointed. Peduncles with one to three flowers, usually solitary. Pedicels 1·2–2 cm. long, including ovary. Flowers about 2 cm. in diameter, yellow to yellow-green with prominent brown longitudinal parallel stripes on the sepals and petals. Sepals about 1 cm. long, broad-lanceolate; petals shorter and narrower than the sepals. Spur thick and blunt. Labellum white, about as long as the sepals, the apex acute; margins crisped in the upper part and extending a little distance from the apex. Column comparatively long, the wings represented by laciniate lobes. Flowers fragrant.

D. striolatum grows luxuriantly on the granite boulders in East Gippsland, Vic., along water-courses. The habit of this small lithophyte is upright on the crest of the boulders, while on the sloping faces and sides, where the plants are thickly massed, it hangs in mats. On the under sides, the foliage and succulent root-growths descend from the ceilings of caves, the latter like strings of shining beads, to be reflected from the pools of clear water beneath. In the spring the abundant golden flowers stand out conspicuously from the dark-hued background of foliage. In Tasmania it grows on granite boulders near the sea.

FLOWERING PERIOD: Sept. to Nov.

COMMON NAME: Streaked Rock-orchid

DISTRIBUTION: Extending from the Hunter River in eastern NSW, through far eastern Vic., to the north-eastern coast of Tas., often locally plentiful

D. mortii (Plate 383)

D. mortii F. Muell. *Fragm. Phyt. Aust.* 1:214 (1859); H. M. R. Rupp *Orchids N.S.W.* 120 (1943)

SYNONYMY: *D. bowmanii* Benth. *Flor. aust.* 6: 286 (1873)

Epiphytic on trees and rocks. Stems elongated, very slender, rigid and branched. Leaves slender, 5–15 cm. long, obscurely angular, and sharply pointed. Peduncles short, bearing one or two pedicellate flowers, 2–2·5 cm. in diameter. Pedicels slender, about 1·3 cm. long. Flowers pale yellowish-green with a white labellum; the sepals and petals inconspicuously marked with brown longitudinal stripes. Sepals broad and blunt, somewhat lanceolate. Petals shorter and narrower than the sepals, pointed. Spur blunt, slightly curved. Labellum about as long as the sepals, the upper half with frilled margins; mid-lobe broad and acuminate, with three raised green plates very frilled in the upper half; lateral lobes small, broad, erect. Column short, white. Capsule oblong, prominently ribbed. Flowers lemon-scented.

This species prefers open dry areas where it may be found growing on rocks or trees, generally near ephemeral creeks. It does not favour the sheltered rain-forest areas and is often found well inland, although it has also been collected at least once from a Mangrove swamp.

FLOWERING PERIOD: Irregular bursts of flowering at intervals from Jan. to May

DISTRIBUTION: Extending from the Burdekin River in northern Qld as far south as Lismore, NSW; often locally common

D. tenuissimum (Plate 384)

D. tenuissimum H. M. R. Rupp in *Proc. Linn. Soc. N.S.W.* 52:570 (1927); H. M. R. Rupp *Orchids N.S.W.* 119 (1943)

An extremely slender, pendulous species found on trees in dense brush forests. Stems very fine and wire-like, flexible, branched. Leaves terete, obscurely ribbed, short and very slender, but occasionally 15 cm. long. Flowers solitary or in racemes of two or three. Sepals equal, about 1·5 cm. long, rather broad, purplish-brown or dark green on the inner surface. Petals shorter and narrower than the sepals, green. Labellum almost as long as the sepals, recurved, white with a yellowish-green median line on either side of which are four to six closely-packed oval bright purple blotches; sometimes the markings are absent; margins undulate-crisped, white. Column slender, its apex and the stigmatic plate purplish. Ovary rather long. Pedicel long and exceedingly slender. Flowers fragrant.

This species prefers highland areas where dews and fogs are frequent.

FLOWERING PERIOD: Sept. to Nov.

DISTRIBUTION: Extending from the mountains of south-eastern Qld to the southern approaches of the Barrington Tops, NSW

D. racemosum (Plate 385)

D. racemosum (W. H. Nicholls) S. C. Clemesha & A. W. Dockrill in *Orchadian* 1:52 (1964)

SYNONYMY: *D. beckleri* F. Muell. var. *racemosum* W. H. Nicholls in *N. Qd Nat.* 4:35 (1936)

A large epiphyte. Stems up to 90 cm. long, erect, branched, with masses of thin branched roots at the base. Leaves erect, decreasing in size with distance from the base of the plant, 3–20 cm. long. Racemes up to 8 cm. long with six to fifteen flowers on slender pedicels about 15 mm. long. Flowers 2–3 cm. in diameter, cream, the perianth segments spreading. Dorsal sepal shorter than the lateral sepals, oblong-lanceolate. Lateral sepals 2–2·4 cm. long, joined at the base with the column foot to form a truncate spur. Petals about 1·5 cm. long, narrower than the sepals. Labellum about 2 cm. long, trilobed, the lateral lobes erect and embracing the column; mid-lobe decurved, ovate with undulate margins, the apex filiform and often curled. Callus with three slender longitudinal ridges ending about halfway along the mid-lobe. Column erect, about 3 mm. high, foot about one and one-half times its length. Flowers fragrant.

[This species was originally included as a variety of *D. beckleri*; however comparison of the plates will show it is closer to *D. teretifolium* and deserving of specific rank. The text for this species is adapted from the article by S. C. Clemesha and A. W. Dockrill in *Orchadian* 1: 52–54 (1964).—Ed.]

FLOWERING PERIOD: Sept. and Oct.

DISTRIBUTION: Confined to the Atherton Tableland and Russell River areas of northern Qld

D. beckleri (Plate 386)

D. beckleri F. Muell. *Fragm. Phyt. Aust.* 7:59 (1869); H. M. R. Rupp *Orchids N.S.W.* 120 (1943)

SYNONYMY: *D. mortii* Benth. *Flor. aust.* 6:286 (1873), non F. Muell. (1858)

Epiphytic on trees. Stems slender, up to 90 cm. long; at first erect, but bending over and often becoming almost pendulous as they lengthen; more or less constricted at the joints. Leaves towards the base of the plant rigidly erect and often very robust, up to 16 cm. long and over 1 cm. in diameter, terete, and conspicuously ribbed, those on the branches becoming smaller and less prominently ribbed. Flowers usually solitary but numerous, white, pale green, or light mauve, with dark stripes on the perianth, fragrant. Sepals and petals nearly equal in length, 15–24 mm. long, broad-linear. Labellum shorter; lateral lobes small, the mid-lobe long and recurved, with crisped, crenulate margins, which are often purple; lamina with three parallel, undulate, narrow longitudinal ridges. Column slender at the base, the wings marked with purple-mauve.

D. beckleri is a common species in northern scrubs, occurring on trees and rocks; among the hosts are *Casuarina glauca*, *Callicoma serratifolia* and *Ehretia acuminata*. It frequently grows on small branches which break and drop to the ground.

FLOWERING PERIOD: Sept. to Nov.

COMMON NAME: Pencil Orchid

DISTRIBUTION: From south-eastern Qld to north-eastern NSW, as far south as the Hunter River; common throughout its range

D. teretifolium

D. teretifolium R.Br. *Prodr. Flor. Nov. Holl.* 333 (1810); H. M. R. Rupp *Orchids N.S.W.* 118 (1943)

SYNONYMY: *D. calamiforme* Lodd. in *Edwards' bot. Reg.* 27: Misc. 9 (1841)

A variable species. Stems clustered on a creeping rhizome, elongated, pendulous, divaricately branched; epiphytes or lithophytes, up to 270 cm. long. Leaves numerous, from 7 cm. to over 50 cm. long and 3–7 mm. in diameter, terete, pendulous, coriaceous. Racemes numerous, slender, often branched, arising from the nodes at the leaf bases; flowers few to numerous, white, cream or yellowish, on slender pedicels 1·3–2·5 cm. long. Perianth segments variable, 2–6 cm. long. Sepals linear-subulate; lateral sepals dilated at the base into a conical obtuse spur 5–7 mm. long. Petals linear-filiform, as long as or slightly longer than the sepals. Labellum about half as long as the sepals, lanceolate, canaliculate, acuminate and recurved, trilobed; lateral lobes very small, sometimes spotted with red; callus with three undulate raised plates; mid-lobe with crisped margins, long-acute to filiform, recurved or revolute. Column short and stout, spotted with red.

A widespread and variable species of three varieties, one variety being of two forms. In NSW the species favours the Swamp Oak (*Casuarina glauca*) but has also been recorded from River Oak (*C. cunninghamiana*) and paper barks (*Melaleuca* spp.).

FLOWERING PERIOD: July to Nov.

COMMON NAME: Rat's-tail Orchid

DISTRIBUTION: Extending, as various forms, from north of the Endeavour River in northern Qld, as far south as Bega, NSW; coastal and often locally common

D. teretifolium var. **fasciculatum** (Plate 387)

D. teretifolium var. *fasciculatum* H. M. R. Rupp in *Proc. Linn. Soc. N.S.W. 60*:157, t. 4 fig. 4 (1935)

SYNONYMY: *D. baseyanum* St Cloud in *N. Qd Nat. 23*:1 (1955)

Differs from the typical form in being more robust with stouter leaves. The flowers are similar to the typical form with less recurved segments; the labellum mid-lobe is all white, sometimes with a few markings near the base, and the three convoluted callus ridges are small.

FLOWERING PERIOD: Aug. to Nov.

DISTRIBUTION: Confined to northern Qld, where it is found between the Endeavour and Burdekin Rivers

D. teretifolium var. **fairfaxii**

D. teretifolium var. *fairfaxii* (R. D. FitzG. & F. Muell.) R. D. FitzG. ex C. Moore & Betche *Handb. Flor. N.S.W.* 385 (1893); H. M. R. Rupp *Orchids N.S.W.* 119 (1943)

SYNONYMY: *D. fairfaxii* R. D. FitzG. & F. Muell. in *Sydney Mail* (21 September 1872)

A variety of two forms, both illustrated.

D. teretifolium var. **fairfaxii** forma **fairfaxii** (Plate 388)

Differs from the typical in having longer, more slender stems and leaves, the latter to 70 cm. long. The racemes are smaller, generally with one to three flowers but occasionally up to seven. Flowers yellowish on dark red-brown pedicels, the sepals and petals having dark red-brown striations at the base. The labellum is unmarked on either side of the dark red-brown callus ridges.

FLOWERING PERIOD: Aug. and Sept.

DISTRIBUTION: The common form that is found in the ranges and coastal areas of NSW, from the Clarence River to the Blue Mountains

D. teretifolium var. **fairfaxii** forma **aureum** (Plate 389)

D. teretifolium var. *fairfaxii* forma *aureum* (F. M. Bailey) S. C. Clemesha in *Orchadian 2*:12 (1965); H. M. R. Rupp *Orchids N.S.W.* 119 (1943), as *D. teretifolium* var. *aureum*

SYNONYMY: *D. teretifolium* var. *aureum* F. M. Bailey *Qd Flor. 5*:1543 (1902)

Very similar to the former but with yellow-green to golden yellow flowers which are often heavily striated and commonly borne in racemes of up to seven flowers.

FLOWERING PERIOD: Aug. to Nov.

DISTRIBUTION: A rain-forest plant, ranging from near Nambour, Qld, as far south as the Richmond River, NSW

D. monophyllum (Plate 390)

D. monophyllum F. Muell. *Fragm. Phyt. Aust. 1*:189 (1859); H. M. R. Rupp *Orchids N.S.W.* 118 (1943)

Pseudobulbs arising from a creeping rhizome, often numerous, erect, thick, narrow-conical, 2·5–10 cm. long; the old growth with very persistent ribs and furrows. Leaf solitary, rarely two, terminal, oblong or lanceolate, flat, 5–10 cm. long. Raceme solitary, terminal, about as long as the leaf. Flowers small, not very numerous, yellow, on slender, often drooping pedicels. Bracts minute. Sepals broad-lanceolate, acute, 5–6 mm. long. Spur broad and obtuse,

about 3 mm. long, slightly curved upward. Petals about as long as the sepals, but narrower, especially at the base. Labellum deep yellow, nearly as long as the sepals, the lateral lobes small; mid-lobe broad-triangular or almost rhomboidal and obtuse; callus without ridges below the lobes, but one to three raised calli between the laberal lobes, sometimes produced into short undulating ridges. Column short and broad, the projecting foot about the same length. Flowers very fragrant.

The species often grows massed on rocks and trees exposed to full sunlight, the leaves and pseudobulbs being then bleached yellow.

FLOWERING PERIOD: Very irregular, but mainly during Sept. and Oct.

COMMON NAME: Lily-of-the-valley Orchid

DISTRIBUTION: Qld and northern NSW, both coastal and on the ranges, often locally common

D. schneiderae (Plates 391 and 392)

D. schneiderae F. M. Bailey *Occ. Pap. Qd Flor. 1*:7 (1886); H. M. R. Rupp *Orchids N.S.W.* 118 (1943)

SYNONYMY: *D. schneiderae* var. *major* H. M. R. Rupp in *Qd Nat. 11*:3 (1939)

Allied to *D. monophyllum*. Epiphytic on the limbs of trees but also found on rock surfaces. Pseudobulbs often densely matted, arising from a slender creeping rhizome, short, conical, about 1·5 cm. long, the flowering ones clothed with sheathing brown scales, the older leafless ones naked, stouter, prominently ribbed, green, marked with brown. Leaves 3–6 cm. long, terminal, usually two, often twisted, linear-oblong, pointed, sometimes unevenly emarginate. Racemes filiform, pendent, 5–15 cm. long; flowers four to twenty-five, pale greenish-yellow, 7–10 mm. in diameter. Bracts minute, lanceolate. Pedicel, including ovary, 5–10 mm. long. Sepals broad-ovate, incurved. Petals smaller. Perianth segments often edged with red. Spur curved inward, rather large for the size of the flower. Labellum 4–5 mm. long; the lateral lobes tipped and margined with red-brown; mid-lobe inconspicuous, very short, truncate, the callus thick, forming with the abbreviated mid-lobe a cushion-like patch, which is sometimes depressed in the centre. Column short, the upper part around the stigma marked with a horse-shoe-like red line. Flowers fragrant.

[This species is closely allied to *D. monophyllum*; however, it is smaller and frequently produces two leaves from the pseudobulb. It is a widespread species but generally uncommon. Rupp named a specimen, from the Eungella Range near Mackay, Qld, var. *major* (see Plate 392). The plant produced a raceme about 24 cm. long with thirty flowers; however this was the only departure from the typical form and the differences seem minor. A. W. Dockrill in the *Checklist orchid. Pls trop. Qd* 9 (1966) includes it as a synonym.—Ed.]

FLOWERING PERIOD: Jan. to Mar.

DISTRIBUTION: Coastal Qld and northern NSW, of scattered occurrence and uncommon

D. kingianum (Plates 393 and 394)

D. kingianum Bidw. ex Lindl. in *Edwards' bot. Reg. 30*: Misc. 11 (1844); H. M. R. Rupp *Orchids N.S.W.* 116 (1943)

Pseudobulbs clustered, 1–33 cm. high, comparatively stout in dwarf forms, slender in others, thickened towards the base, green to purplish and more or less furrowed. Leaves two to seven, comparatively thin, lanceolate or oblong-lanceolate, usually acute, 2–13 cm. long. Racemes with two to fourteen flowers, arising from between the leaves or from the summit; flowers variable, purple, mauve, pink, cream or white, or a combination of these colours, often fragrant, 2·5–3 cm. in diameter. Peduncle usually long, up to 20 cm.; pedicels, including the ovary, up to 2·7 cm. long; bracts acute. Sepals broad-lanceolate, the lateral ones falcate. Petals almost as long as the sepals but much narrower. Spur conical, slightly incurved. Labellum a little shorter than the sepals, the lateral lobes prominent, almost oblong, more or less obtuse; mid-lobe longer but very broad, almost reniform. Callus with three raised lines extending to the base of the mid-lobe. Column short and stout, the foot broad.

D. kingianum grows exclusively, and usually in extensive mats, on cliff faces, or in rock crevices, and is often remarkably abundant in the vicinity of waterfalls. This orchid forms young plants from the buds at the apex of the pseudobulb which, when mature, fall to the ground and establish themselves independently. The Scented Sun-orchid (*Thelymitra aristata*) is sometimes found in association, and flowering at the same time.

[This whole species complex is extremely variable in habit of growth and flower colour. This has resulted in a large number of varieties being named and, because the species is a popular horticultural plant, perpetuated in cultivation. Plate 394 illustrates the variation that occurs. The var. *pallidum* F. M. Bailey with weak slender stems and pale lilac stained flowers, and the var. *silcockii* F. M. Bailey (Plate 394, Figs **a**, **b**) having white flowers with a purple labellum, are but two. The species-complex is undergoing a detailed cytological study at present. See *Aust. Orchid Rev.* 32:25 (1967), l.c. 32:139 (1967), and l.c. 33:37 (1968).—Ed.]

FLOWERING PERIOD: Aug. to·Nov.

COMMON NAME: Pink Rock-orchid

DISTRIBUTION: South-eastern Qld; northern NSW

D. × **delicatum** (Plates 395 and 396)

D. × delicatum (F. M. Bailey) F. M. Bailey *Qd Flor.* 5:1527 (1902); H. M. R. Rupp *Orchids N.S.W.* 114 (1943), as *D. kestevenii*

SYNONYMY: *D. speciosum* var. *delicatum* F. M. Bailey in *Proc. roy. Soc. Qd* 1:11 (1884); *D. kestevenii* H. M. R. Rupp in *Proc. Linn. Soc. N.S.W.* 56:137 (1931); *D. kestevenii* var. *coloratum* H. M. R. Rupp *Orchids N.S.W.* 114 (1943)

Pseudobulbs numerous, arising from a shortly creeping rhizome, comparatively slender, thickened towards the base, grooved; roots densely matted. Leaves broad-lanceolate, coriaceous, three or four, at the apices of the pseudobulbs, recurved, 7–17 cm. long and 2–3 cm. wide; the apices obtuse or emarginate. Racemes erect, arching, on long peduncles, with eight to twelve flowers. Flowers white or cream, often tinted at the apices of segments with pink or mauve, often fragrant. Dorsal sepal broad, hooded, 1·8 cm. long and 1·1 cm. wide; lateral sepals broad, falcate, 1·4 cm. long and 1·2 cm. wide at the base. Spur prominent, broad, obtuse; petals thin, about 1·3 cm. long and 4 mm. wide; labellum white, often generously marked with purple, about 1·3 cm. long; lateral lobes prominent, about 1 cm. long; mid-lobe broad, with a short point; callus suffused with yellow, three fused longitudinal lines along the centre, suddenly narrowing beyond the lateral lobes. Column white, 1·3 cm. high, the foot marked with pink. Stigma narrowed upward.

[This is a natural hybrid between *D. kingianum* and *D. speciosum*. It was first discovered at Spring Bluff, near Toowoomba, Qld, in 1884. *D. kestevenii* was named by Rupp from a plant collected at Alum Mountain, Bulahdelah, NSW, in 1931. There has been much controversy about the relationship between *D. delicatum* and *D.*

kestevenii. At present it is thought that only one natural hybrid exists, and that the variation in the forms of the parents, between Qld and NSW, has possibly given rise to the differences. However, the variation seems no greater than in any other hybrid, and the problem one of misidentification. Plate 396 was painted by W. H. Nicholls as *D. kestevenii*.—Ed.]

FLOWERING PERIOD: Aug. to Oct.

DISTRIBUTION: South-eastern Qld and north-eastern NSW, of sporadic occurrence

D. **ruppianum** (Plate 398)

D. ruppianum A. D. Hawkes in *Orchid Weekly* 2:129 (1960)

SYNONYMY: *D. speciosum* var. *fusiforme* F. M. Bailey *Synops. Qd Flor.* 509 (1883); *D. fusiforme* (F. M. Bailey.) F. M. Bailey *Qd Flor.* 5:1527 (1902), non Thouars (1822)

A robust epiphytic or lithophytic plant, forming large clumps. Pseudobulbs rarely exceeding 30 cm. high, distinctly fusiform in shape, dark-coloured and deeply corrugated, thickened at the base. Leaves two to seven, near the top of the pseudobulb, ovate-oblong to oblong-lanceolate, the margins often undulate, thin and coriaceous, the apex pointed. Flowers numerous in erect racemes, white or cream, strongly fragrant. Sepals and petals about equal, 1·7–2·3 cm. long; the petals narrower than the sepals. Labellum small, about 7 mm. long, conspicuously marked with transverse purple lines; mid-lobe very short, twice as broad as long, shortly pointed, spotted with purple near the margins; callus orange, speckled with purple. Column short; pollinia waxy, in two pairs.

[A common orchid of northern Qld, found most frequently in the highlands, but occasionally extending to lowland areas. It grows on trees and rocks in rain-forests but reaches its best development on the jungle fringes where massed displays in springtime make an unforgettable sight. For a discussion of this see *Aust. Orchid Rev.* 29:40 (1964); and for its varieties see *Aust. Pls* 3:223–225 (1965).—Ed.]

FLOWERING PERIOD: Aug. to Oct.

DISTRIBUTION: Northern Qld, from the tip of Cape York Peninsula to the Burdekin River

D. **ruppianum** var. **blackburnii** (Plate 397)

D. ruppianum var. *blackburnii* (W. H. Nicholls) A. W. Dockrill in *Aust. Pls* 3:224 (1965)

SYNONYMY: *D. fusiforme* var. *blackburnii* W. H. Nicholls in *Vict. Nat.* 66:225 (1950)

[The text for this variety is based on W. H. Nicholls' original description, and the article by A. W. Dockrill.—Ed.]

A compact variety differing from the typical form chiefly in its more robust pseudobulbs which are 12–22 cm. long and 2·5–3 cm. in diameter. The pendulous racemes have shortly segmented pale primrose-yellow flowers, whereas in the typical form the creamy-white flowers have somewhat filiform spidery segments and are borne erect. Fragrance of the flowers persists for some time.

[A. W. Dockrill in his paper on *D. ruppianum* comments on this variety: 'From the measurements and illustration given by Nicholls, l.c., this plant hardly seems to be a very significant variety'. See *Aust. Pls* 3:224 (1965).—Ed.]

FLOWERING PERIOD AND DISTRIBUTION: The variety comes from Font Hill Station, northern Qld, and the flowering period is the same as for the typical form

D. speciosum (Plates 399 and 400)

D. speciosum Sm. *Exot. Bot.* 1:17, t. 10 (1804–5); A. J. Ewart *Flor. Vict.* 309 (1931); H. M. R. Rupp *Orchids N.S.W.* 113 (1943); J. H. Willis *Handb. Pls Vict.* 1:419 (1962)

Plant extremely variable, often very large, the pseudobulbs thick and fleshy, 15–80 cm. high, numerous and strongly ribbed. Leaves two to five, distichous towards the apex of the pseudobulb, broadly ovate or oblong, 8–24 cm. long, thick and leathery, flat or slightly undulate. Racemes terminal or from the bases of the leaves, often over 40 cm. long, the sheathing scales at the base of the peduncle 2·5–4 cm. long, the bracts very small, ovate or lanceolate. Flowers numerous, large, to 2·5 cm. in diameter, white, cream or yellow, fragrant, on pedicels 2·5–5 cm. long. Sepals and petals nearly equal, erect, usually incurved, 2–2·5 cm. long, lanceolate, but varying in width, lateral sepals incurved, forming a short broad pouch with the column foot. Labellum much shorter than the sepals, nearly white, or pale yellow, streaked or dotted with purple, the lateral lobes short and broad, incurved. Mid-lobe broader than long, obtuse or retuse. Column white, often spotted with purple.

[A widespread and variable species that grows on rocky outcrops, sheer rock faces or high on the trunks of rain-forest trees. It produces its best displays when massed on cliffs exposed to the full sun, with the leaves and bulbs bleached and leathery. Because of its wide distribution and great variability a number of forms have been described, however in many cases these are not distinctive and a full range of intermediates may be found.—Ed.]

FLOWERING PERIOD: July to Oct.

COMMON NAME: Rock Orchid

DISTRIBUTION: Extending from the Cooktown area of northern Qld, through eastern NSW to far eastern Vic., occupying a wide range of habitats and often locally common

D. speciosum var. hillii

D. speciosum var. *hillii* (Hook.f.) F. M. Bailey *Qd Flor.* 5:1526 (1902); H. M. R. Rupp *Orchids N.S.W.* 114 (1943)

SYNONYMY: *D. hillii* Hook.f. in *Curtis's bot. Mag.* 87: t. 5261 (1861)

Pseudobulbs very long and slender, up to 100 cm. tall. Leaves long; racemes numerous, up to 60 cm. long. Flowers numerous, small, usually white, turning yellow. Labellum short, about 8 mm. long, bordered with purple inside and out, especially on the mid-lobe. Column base and callus plate orange-yellow.

It has two forms, one of which is illustrated.

DISTRIBUTION: This showy variety is found in NSW and Qld (where it is often common)

D. speciosum var. hillii forma grandiflorum (Plate 399)

D. speciosum var. *hillii* forma *grandiflorum* (F. M. Bailey) F. M. Bailey *Qd Flor.* 5:1526 (1902)

SYNONYMY: *D. speciosum* var. *grandiflorum* F. M. Bailey *Bot. Bull.* 14:12 (1896)

Differs from var. *hillii* in having larger deep yellow flowers, which have an obtuse labellum barred with purple. The plant may often be more vigorous than in var. *hillii*, with leaves up to 30 cm. (12 in.) long.

FLOWERING PERIOD AND DISTRIBUTION: It is confined to south-eastern Qld, flowering Aug. and Sept.

D. speciosum var. nitidum (Plate 401)

D. speciosum var. *nitidum* F. M. Bailey in *Proc. roy. Soc. Qd* 1:10 (1885)

Pseudobulbs slender and numerous, almost even in diameter throughout, about 1 cm. broad, usually smooth and shining, fluted. Leaves broad, 15–18 cm. long and 4–5 cm. broad, coriaceous and shining. Racemes 15–20 cm. long, bearing up to thirty flowers, yellowish-green, becoming pure white. Sepals 1·3–1·5 cm. long and about 5 mm. broad; petals about the same length but narrower. Labellum short, the lateral lobes marked with transverse purple lines, the mid-lobe apiculate, yellowish-white; callus plates yellow.

[The taxonomic position of this variety is not clear. H. M. R. Rupp and T. E. Hunt in their review of the genus *Dendrobium* suggest that it is merely a white form of *D.* × *gracillimum* and that material apart from the type does not exist. See *Proc. Linn. Soc. N.S.W.* 72:233 (1947). The type was from Cairns in northern Qld, and W. H. Nicholls apparently obtained his material from Mount Tambourine in south-eastern Qld.—Ed.]

D. × gracillimum (Plate 402)

D. × *gracillimum* (H. M. R. Rupp) H. M. R. Rupp in *Vict. Nat.* 61:200 (1945); H. M. R. Rupp *Orchids N.S.W.* 114 (1943), as *D. speciosum* var. *gracillimum*

SYNONYMY: *D. speciosum* var. *gracillimum* H. M. R. Rupp in *Proc. Linn. Soc. N.S.W.* 54:550, fig. 1 (1929)

Epiphytic on trees and rocks. Pseudobulbs 22–60 cm. long, rarely exceeding 12 mm. in diameter at the broadest part, fairly uniform in width. Leaves three to five, 8–18 cm. long, oblong to broad-lanceolate, thin, not rigid, recurved. Racemes one to three, arising from between or below the leaves, 10–15 cm. long. Flowers dense in the shorter racemes, scattered in the longer ones, white or yellow, rather small, fragrant, the segments 15–20 mm. long; shorter than in *D. speciosum*, but conforming otherwise in structure and in the labellum markings.

[This is a natural hybrid between *D. speciosum* and *D. gracilicaule*.—Ed.]

FLOWERING PERIOD: Sept. and Oct.

DISTRIBUTION: Extending from south-eastern Qld to the Hawkesbury River in NSW, localised and generally uncommon in coastal districts.

D. gracilicaule (Plate 403)

D. gracilicaule F. Muell. *Fragm. Phyt. Aust.* 1:179 (1859); H. M. R. Rupp *Orchids N.S.W.* 116 (1943)

SYNONYMY: *D. elongatum* A. Cunn. in *Edwards' bot. Reg.* 25: Misc. 33 (1839), non Lindl. (1830); *D. brisbanense* Reichenb.f. in *Walp Ann. Bot. syst* 6:299 (1861); *D. fellowsii* F. Muell. *Fragm. Phyt. Aust.* 7:63 (1870); *D. jonesii* Rendle in *J. Bot., Lond.* 39:197 (1901)

A very slender species, the pseudobulbs numerous, cylindrical, sometimes slightly thickened at the base, more or less clothed with membranous sheaths, 30–90 cm. long. Leaves three to six, up to 13 cm. long, thin, coriaceous, lanceolate, terminal, the tip often obscurely bifid. Racemes short, up to 10 cm. long, with three to fifteen smallish, dull yellow flowers, irregularly blotched outside with red-brown, occasionally brighter yellow and not blotched. Flowers very fragrant. Bracts minute. Perianth segments thick, 10–11 mm. long; dorsal sepal oblong, incurved; lateral sepals falcate, oblong-lanceolate; petals linear-oblong, shorter and narrower than the sepals; spur curved and very blunt. Labellum shorter than the sepals, the lateral lobes rounded, erect; the mid-lobe small, short and curved, somewhat reniform, three longitudinal raised callus plates between the lateral lobes. Column stout.

FLOWERING PERIOD: July to Oct.

DISTRIBUTION: A widespread and often locally common species, near the coast from the Atherton Tableland in northern Qld to Kiama in southern NSW

D. gracilicaule var. howeanum (Plate 404)

D. gracilicaule var. *howeanum* Maiden in *Proc. Linn. Soc. N.S.W.* 24:382 (1899); H. M. R. Rupp *Orchids N.S.W.* 116 (1943)

[Plant similar to the typical but pseudobulbs often more robust with five or six rather large leaves. The flowers are a rich creamy yellow without any blotches; the labellum is marked with purplish lines for its whole length and the flowers are fragrant.

FLOWERING PERIOD: Sept. and Oct.

DISTRIBUTION: This variety is plentiful on trees amongst the lower shrubs of Lord Howe Island, where it is endemic. A plant, apparently nearly identical, has been collected from Mangrove Mountain, near Gosford, NSW.—Ed.]

D. bairdianum (Plate 405)

D. bairdianum F. M. Bailey *Synops. Qd Flor.* Suppl. 1:53 (1886)

SYNONYMY: *D. giddinsii* T. E. Hunt in *N. Qd Nat.* 15:25 (1948)

Pseudobulbs arising from a shortly creeping rhizome, 8–18 cm. high, fusiform, slightly constricted at the nodes, attenuated towards the base, the sheathing scales on the upper parts of the stem whitish, sometimes highly coloured, often prominently ribbed and otherwise adorned. Leaves linear-lanceolate, 4–9 cm. long and 1·5–2 cm. broad, prominently keeled, the margins somewhat revolute; apex obtuse or obliquely emarginate. Racemes erect, up to 8 cm. long, often abundant along the stem. Flowers two to eight in the raceme, about 2 cm. in diameter; bracts small, lanceolate; pedicels 1·5–2 cm. long. Sepals and petals a uniform pale green to yellowish-green, changing to a pale buff shade; dorsal sepal lanceolate, projecting over the column; lateral sepals triangular, spreading; spur broad and obtuse; petals broad-linear, acute. Labellum longer than the sepals, thick, deeply marked with purplish veins, oblong, the mid-lobe somewhat reniform; callus white with two prominent raised plates which terminate abruptly near the base of the mid-lobe. Column about 4 mm. high, purplish in front, the wings represented by several small tooth-like appendages on each side of, and behind the anther. Anther yellowish or green. Stigma prominent. Column-foot about 6 mm. long, stained with purple.

A distinctive species, which is hardy and with a long flowering period.

FLOWERING PERIOD: Oct. to Jan.

DISTRIBUTION: Confined to northern Qld where it is scattered between the Burdekin and the Bloomfield Rivers from 600 to 1100 m. (2,000 to 3,500 ft.) altitude

D. adae (Plate 406)

D. adae F. M. Bailey in *Proc. roy. Soc. Qd* 1:149 (1885)

SYNONYMY: *D. ancorarium* H. M. R. Rupp in *Qd Nat.* 12:115, t. 7 (1945)

Pseudobulbs 25–38 cm. long, very slender, furrowed, bearing at the apex two or three lanceolate to broadly lanceolate leaves, 6–7·5 cm. long, and 2·3–3·5 cm. broad, keeled, the texture rather thin. Flowers one to six in short racemes, white, turning cream, then apricot before withering; sometimes the sepals pale yellowish and the petals white; highly fragrant. Bracts small, acute. Sepals 1·3–2 cm. long, broadly ovate, the lateral ones falcate. Petals about as long as the sepals but narrower; the spur short and curved. Labellum about 1 cm. long, the lateral lobes tomentose on the margins, faintly marked with reddish bands; mid-lobe cordate, densely tomentose, three close ridges extending from the base to a little beyond the lateral lobes; in some flowers these ridges terminate with five apices, which are also tomentose. Column white to greenish-white, the foot prominent, and in some flowers marked at the apex with an anchor-shaped blotch, and speckled with orange-red dots.

Rupp, in his description of *D. ancorarium*, describes the labellum mid-lobe as glabrous, and the lamina with a flat plate abruptly terminating in a curious cup-like fold. In the numerous flowers examined by the author, these features have never been observed although in some flowers the mid-lobe was tomentose at the apex only. In a letter dated 14 September 1945, Rupp writes: 'My plant of *D. ancorarium* produced five flowers this year, three on one stem and two on another. The three came first, absolutely true to my description and plate, i.e. anchor very clear. Judge then of my astonishment when the other two flowers opened up perfectly typical white *adae*.' Figs **b** and **d** are from Rupp, sent as *D. ancorarium*.

The species apparently has the ability to produce flowers of different sexes, as in *Catasetum*.

FLOWERING PERIOD: July to Sept.

DISTRIBUTION: Confined to northern Qld, between the Burdekin and Annan Rivers, mostly above 750 m. (2,500 ft.) altitude

D. fleckeri (Plate 407)

D. fleckeri H. M. R. Rupp & C. T. White in *Qd Nat.* 10:25, t.1 (1937)

Epiphytic, with very slender pseudobulbs which are furrowed, 15–40 cm. long. Leaves two or three, terminal, broad-lanceolate, 7–10 cm. long. Flowers one or two, rather large, about 2·8 cm. in diameter, terminal. Perianth segments acute, a rich apricot colour; dorsal sepal broad-lanceolate, the lateral sepals broader at the base where they are adnate to the column foot; petals shorter and narrower than the sepals. Labellum 12–16 mm. long, trilobed, the lateral lobes erect, acuminate, prominently streaked with purplish-red; mid-lobe yellow, spotted and streaked with red, broader than long, with incurved densely ciliate margins; lamina more or less red-spotted, with three raised parallel longitudinal callus ridges arising from the base and extending to a short distance beyond the lateral lobes, yellow-tipped. Column incurved, with a prominent foot marked with red blotches and suffused with orange at the tip. Anther small. Ovary slender.

This species is closely related to *D. adae* with which it is associated in the field. In fact when not in flower the two species are very difficult to separate, although the flowers are quite distinct.

FLOWERING PERIOD: Aug. to Jan.

DISTRIBUTION: Confined to northern Qld, between the Johnston and Annan Rivers, where it is found above 900 m. (3,000 ft.) altitude

D. falcorostrum (Plate 408)

D. falcorostrum R. D. FitzG. in *Sydney Morning Herald* (18 November 1876); H. M. R. Rupp *Orchids N.S.W.* 116 (1943)

Pseudobulbs thick, grooved, up to 30 cm. long, gradually tapering towards each end. Leaves four or five, distichous, terminal, rather thick, ovate, 10–13 cm. long. Racemes rather short, few flowered, but produced in great abundance on a well-established plant. Flowers white or cream, slightly veined, rather large on fairly long and slender pedicels, fragrant. Sepals broader than the petals, both about 3 cm. long, spur truncate, furrowed round the edge. Petals lanceolate. Labellum about 2 cm. long, white, spotted with purple; mid-lobe long, acuminate, the point turned up; side of labellum fashioned so as to form a lobe near the point, the whole resembling the bill of a falcon; a yellow cruciform gland on the callus, lamina under gland hollow and concave to the mid-lobe. The longest arm of the gland is composed mostly of three ridges. Column short and thick; yellow from below the stigma, and spotted with purple, base rather thick. Pollinia elongated.

A truly beautiful species, found only in the highland Antarctic Beech forests (*Nothofagus moorei*). While these are favoured hosts it also grows on acacias and tree-ferns, although always in proximity to the Beech. It was discovered by FitzGerald on Mount Banda Banda near the Macleay River, NSW.

FLOWERING PERIOD: Aug. to Oct.

COMMON NAME: Beech Orchid

DISTRIBUTION: Highland beech forests of north-eastern NSW and south-eastern Qld, often locally abundant, rarely extending below 900 m. (3,000 ft.) altitude

D. moorei (Plate 409)

D. moorei F. Muell. *Fragm. Phyt. Aust.* 7:29 (1869)

Pseudobulbs 8–20 cm. high, strongly marked with prominent angles and furrows, sometimes equally thick throughout, sometimes attenuate or thickened at the base. Leaves usually four or five, rather large, 5–10 cm. long, ovate-lanceolate, rather thin in texture. Racemes usually from between the leaves, flowers snow-white. Bracts lanceolate or subulate, about 8 mm. long. Pedicels about 1 cm. long. Sepals linear-lanceolate, varying in length and shape, up to 1·5 cm. long; petals about as long as the sepals, but narrower at the base. Spur almost straight, 5–8 mm. long, dilated at apex. Labellum attached to the end of the column foot, with a narrow claw as long as the spur, expanded below the apex of the column into two short lateral lobes; mid-lobe linear-lanceolate, complicate, not undulate, at least two-thirds as long as the sepals; callus with slightly raised longitudinal lines which may be obscure.

The species has flowers of the purest white, the segments appearing as if frosted. It is extremely variable, and on Lord Howe Island grows in abundance as a lithophyte, an epiphyte or even a terrestrial, from sea-level to about 300 m. (1,000 ft.) altitude.

FLOWERING PERIOD: Very irregular, mainly Mar. to July

DISTRIBUTION: Endemic on Lord Howe Island, where it is locally abundant

D. aemulum (Plate 410)

D. aemulum R.Br. *Prodr. Flor. Nov. Holl.* 333 (1810); H. M. R. Rupp *Orchids N.S.W.* 117 (1943)

Pseudobulbs terete, thin or robust, sometimes tapering to a long thin base with a small pseudobulb as in *D. tetragonum*. Leaves two or three, terminal, ovate or oblong. Racemes one to four, terminal, from between the leaves, or at the nodes along the stem, 5–7·6 cm. long; peduncle slender, the bracts small and lanceolate. Flowers four to ten in the raceme, fragrant, on slender pedicels of 1·2–2 cm. Sepals and petals pure white or white with yellowish tips. Sepals

narrow-lanceolate, almost linear, up to 2·5 cm. long, the basal spur short and broad, upturned. Petals narrow-linear, a little shorter than the sepals. Labellum scarcely above 6 mm. long, contracted into a claw at the base, the lateral lobes broad, short and acute, the mid-lobe recurved, ovate, very undulate, with a small acute point; callus with three raised lines, the central one only prominent, extending between the lateral lobes and merging into a single broad undulate ridge to the apex of the mid-lobe. Column short, with a prominent foot. Capsule elongate-pyriform, about 2·5 cm. long, three-furrowed, green.

The species has two more or less distinctive growth forms. In the shady, more sheltered areas it grows chiefly on Brush Box (*Tristania conferta*). Here the plants are slender with pseudobulbs up to 30 cm. long, and usually with dark green shiny leaves. In the less protected open forest situations a form with shorter, stouter, crowded pseudobulbs, crowned with thick pale green leaves, is prevalent on Ironbarks (*Eucalyptus paniculata*).

FLOWERING PERIOD: Aug. to Oct.

COMMON NAME: Ironbark Orchid

DISTRIBUTION: Extending from the southern end of the Atherton Tableland in northern Qld to the Clyde River on the south coast of NSW, coastal and often locally common

D. tetragonum (Plate 411)

D. tetragonum A. Cunn. in *Edwards' bot. Reg.* 25: Misc. 33 (1839); H. M. R. Rupp *Orchids N.S.W.* 117 (1943)

SYNONYMY: *D. tetragonum* var. *variabilis* P. A. Gilbert in *Aust. Orchid Rev.* 2:20 (1937)

Pseudobulbs arising from a creeping or tufted rhizome, numerous, 2·5–60 cm. long, very prominently four-angled, rather slender in the lower portion, thickened above the middle or near the apex. Leaves two or three at the apex of the pseudobulb, oblong or broadly lanceolate, acute, 5–10 cm. long. Racemes from among the leaves and the nodes along the bare angular stem, short, the flowers few in the raceme, varying much in size and markings; the typical form being rather small, and yellowish-green bordered with brownish-red, on pedicels up to 2·5 cm. long. Bracts small and narrow. Dorsal sepal linear-lanceolate; lateral sepals from a broad triangular base, suddenly contracted into a linear almost filiform point of 2·5–4 cm.; basal spur ascending, thick and very obtuse. Petals yellow, much shorter and narrower than the sepals, linear-filiform with a slightly dilated lanceolate base. Labellum about 1·2 cm. long, pale yellow streaked with narrow bands of crimson, the lateral lobes broad and prominent, mid-lobe larger, almost rhomboidal, shortly and acutely acuminate. Callus with three raised narrow plates, scarcely undulate, the central one higher and continuing to the base of the mid-lobe. Flowers fragrant.

[A very attractive and graceful species that is common in many coastal scrubs. It is also extremely variable both in flower size and colour, and as a result many forms have been named, mostly based on individual plants rather than distinct populations from the field.—Ed.]

FLOWERING PERIOD: May to Sept., depending on latitude and altitude

COMMON NAME: Tree Spider-orchid

DISTRIBUTION: A widespread species, extending from the Endeavour River in northern Qld to the Cambewarra Mountains, north of Nowra, NSW, chiefly coastal but extending to 1200 m. (4,000 ft.) altitude

D. tetragonum var. giganteum (Plate 411)

D. tetragonum var. *giganteum* P. A. Gilbert in *Aust. Orchid Rev.* 2:20 (1937)

SYNONYMY: *D. tetragonum* var. *tomentosum* W. H. Nicholls in *Aust. Orchid Rev.* 8:40 (1942)

Differing from the typical form in having large pale flowers margined or variously ornamented with reddish-brown. Sepals up to 6 cm. long. Labellum lamina tomentose or ciliate, especially on the mid-lobe and callus ridges

FLOWERING PERIOD AND DISTRIBUTION: This large flowered variety is only found in northern Qld between the Fitzroy and Endeavour Rivers. Flowering period as in the typical form

D. canaliculatum (Plate 412)

D. canaliculatum R.Br. *Prodr. Flor. Nov. Holl.* 333 (1810)

SYNONYMY: *D. tattonianum* Bateman ex Reichenb.f. in *Gdnrs' Chron.* 1865:890 (1865)

Pseudobulbs usually rather thick, 2·5–10 cm. high. Leaves at the apex, two to six, linear, thick, almost semi-cylindrical, grooved on the upper side, 7–20 cm. long, often 4 mm. broad at the base, but tapering to the end. Racemes in the upper axils often 30–36 cm. long; peduncle slender; the sheathing scales small and the bracts still smaller. Pedicels slender, 2–4 cm. long. Sepals and petals linear, white, tipped with yellow; sepals 1·5–1·8 cm. long, the lateral ones slightly falcate, and united at the base with the column foot into a conical spur; petals rather longer than the sepals and contracted at the base. Labellum about two-thirds the length of the sepals, with three lobes of a rich mauve colour, the lateral ones prominent and obtuse, the mid-lobe nearly orbicular or rather broader than long, with a short point; callus with three prominently raised plates, undulate, between the lateral lobes and ending on the mid-lobe in richly coloured, nearly orbicular laminae.

FLOWERING PERIOD: Aug. to Nov.

COMMON NAME: Antelope Orchid

DISTRIBUTION: Confined to northern Qld, between the Fitzroy and Endeavour Rivers, often locally common

D. canaliculatum var. nigrescens (Plate 412)

D. canaliculatum var. *nigrescens* W. H. Nicholls in *Aust. Orchid Rev.* 7:40 (1942)

Flowers as in the typical form but with a different colour scheme, the perianth segments greenish towards the base, with deep sepia-brown broad lanceolate laminae, appearing black.

FLOWERING PERIOD AND DISTRIBUTION: This variety is widespread on Cape York Peninsula, north of the Mitchell River. Flowering period as in the typical form

D. smilliae (Plate 413)

D. smilliae F. Muell. *Fragm. Phyt. Aust.* 6:94 (1867)

SYNONYMY: *Coelandria smilliae* (F. Muell.) R. D. FitzG. *Aust. Orchids* 1⁷:+t. (1882)

A robust species, the pseudobulbs 30–70 cm. long, prominently angled and furrowed in the mature growths, the new stems leafy throughout. Leaves ovate or oblong-lanceolate, clasping at the base, 3–15 cm. long, those towards the base small. Racemes erect, short, the flowers crowded, numerous, about 1·3 cm. in diameter; greenish-white, flushed with pink, the segments tipped with green,

and the labellum deep green; subtending bracteoles very small. Sepals ovate-lanceolate. Spur 5–7 mm. long, straight, dilated towards the obtuse end, pink. Petals similar, but smaller than the sepals. Labellum with a long broad claw, expanded at the apex into a concave, complicate, almost hood-shaped lamina; shorter than the sepals, broader than long, entire, or broadly and obtusely trilobed. Pollinia as in the genus. Capsule waxy-white, about 2·5 cm. long, prominently corrugated.

FLOWERING PERIOD: Aug. to Nov.

COMMON NAME: Bottlebrush Orchid

DISTRIBUTION: Widely distributed, from at least as far north as the Iron Range on Cape York Peninsula to the Burdekin River in northern Qld, chiefly coastal and often locally common

D. tofftii (Plate 414)

D. tofftii F. M. Bailey *Synops. Qd Flor.* Suppl. 3:71 (1890)

A stout species resembling *D. discolor*, the stems attaining 150–300 cm. (5–10 ft.) in height, swollen above the base, all more or less compressed and usually prominently marked with purplish ribs. Leaves broadly ovate and emarginate, similar to those of *D. discolor*. Racemes several, from the upper part of the stem, about 40 cm. long; peduncle bearing about three distant, obtuse, closely sheathing scarious bracts, besides those which are crowded at the base. Pedicels attaining 4·5 cm. Sepals often over 3 cm. long, white, more or less recurved above the middle, obtuse, the dorsal one rather broad at the base, the lateral ones broader, extending down and covering the rather pointed, straight spur; petals about as long as the sepals, obtuse, narrower and tapering towards the base, faintly lined with violet and frequently but not always curled. Labellum about the same length as the sepals but much broader, the lateral lobes erect, embracing the column, stained with violet, and marked by violet, forked veins; mid-lobe small and scarcely conspicuous, obtuse, emarginate or sometimes apiculate, the margins undulate; callus of three strong dark violet plates with entire margins ending abruptly at the base of the mid-lobe. Column of medium length, violet-stained, more or less arched, with thick wings. Anther flat, not prominent. Pollinia coherent.

A superb, uncommon species which favours the very humid environs of mangrove swamps along the coast. It is very floriferous and a large specimen in flower is a sight to behold.

FLOWERING PERIOD: July to Sept.

DISTRIBUTION: Confined to northern Qld, where it is found north of the Johnstone River, chiefly coastal

D. dicuphum (Plate 415)

D. dicuphum F. Muell. *Fragm. Phyt. Aust.* 8:28 (1873)

SYNONYMY: *D. dicuphum* var. *grandiflorum* H. M. R. Rupp & T. E. Hunt in *Proc. Linn. Soc. N.S.W.* 72:241 (1948)

Pseudobulbs strongly ribbed and furrowed, usually 8–15 cm. long, but sometimes reaching over 30 cm., rather thick, fusiform, equal or scarcely contracted towards the base, sometimes shortened into a conical pseudobulb, the white sheathing scales persisting even in the old stems. Leaves four to ten, green, margined with red, lanceolate to linear-lanceolate, 3–15 cm. long. Racemes erect or gracefully arched; flowers three to fifteen, about 3·3 cm. in diameter. Perianth segments white, stained at the base with deep purple. Pedicels slender, about 1·5 cm. long. Sepals lanceolate, acutely acuminate; as in other species the lateral sepals form at their base, with the column foot, a spur, but also from the under side emerges an obtuse hollow projection, giving a distinct double-lobed spur to the flower. Petals obovate, acute, rather longer and broader than the sepals. Labellum nearly as long as the sepals, attached at the junction of the two lobes of the spur, scarcely clawed, but mobile; the lateral lobes forming a truncate base 10 mm. broad; the mid-lobe oblong-lanceolate, acute or mucronate, 4 mm. broad, the callus with three raised longitudinal lines, more or less fringed or crested, and extending some way along the mid-lobe; occasionally with one or two shorter additional fringed lines.

This species is one of the two epiphytes which extend into WA.

FLOWERING PERIOD: Apr. to Sept.

DISTRIBUTION: Northern NT and north-western WA, in swampy areas on paperbarks, etc.

D. bigibbum (Plates 416 and 417)

D. bigibbum Lindl. in *Paxton's Flower Gdn* 3:25, fig. 245 (1852)

SYNONYMY: *D. sumneri* F. Muell. *Fragm. Phyt. Aust.* 6:94 (1867)

Pseudobulbs slender, up to 45 cm. long, pencil-like, hardly tapering. Leaves four to ten, lanceolate, 8–12 cm. long, on the upper part of the stem, dark green, margined with purple. Racemes terminal on arching peduncles, 15–20 cm. long, usually abundant. Flowers three to fifteen, varying considerably in size, but usually about 5·3 cm. in diameter, brilliantly coloured, ranging from rose-purple to a very deep magenta-purple, rarely white. Sepals oblong-ovate, recurved, the spur slender, about 1 cm. long, compressed, with a cuneate base, the shortly deflexed column foot forming a second but shorter spur; the whole greenish-purple or green. Petals twice as wide as the sepals, sometimes 3·5 cm., rhomboid or broadly ovate, recurved, the base tapering to a broad claw. Labellum deep rose-purple, the lateral lobes meeting over the column; mid-lobe narrower, but longer than the lateral lobes, the tip broad and apiculate; lamina more or less conspicuously veined, the veins in the intensely-coloured throat thickened and covered with inconspicuous papillae. Callus with a more or less prominent central plate, formed by several rows of ridges. Column short and broad, the wings short. Anther comparatively small. Stigma prominent.

[This species is probably Australia's showiest and best-known orchid, and is the floral emblem of Qld. It is notoriously variable in growth habit, and flower structure and colour.

For a detailed and comprehensive review of the species and its many varieties, also allied species, see S. T. Blake in *Proc. roy Soc. Qd* 74:29–44 (1964) and in *Aust. Orchid Rev.* 31:29–32 (1966). *D. bigibbum* has often been referred to as *D. phalaenopsis* R. D. FitzG.; however, Blake has found that the latter is native to Tanimbar Island, Indonesia, although widely cultivated in Australia.—Ed.]

FLOWERING PERIOD: Almost continuous, from Jan. to Nov.

COMMON NAME: Cooktown Orchid

DISTRIBUTION: On trees or rocks, often in exposed places, from the Archer River near Cooktown in northern Qld, to the tip of the Cape York Peninsula, also the neighbouring Torres Strait Islands

D. ×superbiens (Plates 418 to 420)

D. ×*superbiens* Reichenb.f. in *Gdnrs' Chron.* new ser. 6:516 (1876)

SYNONYMY: *D. fitzgeraldii* F. Muell. in *The Leader, Melbourne* (February 1884); *D. bigibbum* var. *superbiens* (Reichenb.f.) F. M. Bailey *Synops. Qd Flor.* 509 (1883)

Pseudobulbs 30–120 cm. high, tapering towards the summit and contracted at the base. Leaves broad-lanceolate, 8–14 cm. long,

comparatively thin, coriaceous, often numerous. Peduncles slender, erect, bearing long racemes of nine to twenty-five showy rose-purple flowers, 4·5–5 cm. in diameter. Bracts lanceolate, setaceous. Sepals reflexed and undulate, reticulate-veined, the margin lighter in colour. Petals reflexed, cuneate, obovate, of deeper colouring than the sepals. Labellum trilobed, usually with five raised longitudinal toothed ridges on the lamina; the lateral lobes enclosing the column, blunt, rhomboid, minutely toothed on the margin; mid-lobe blunt-triangular, longer than broad, slightly undulate. Column purplish on the back and wings, lighter in front, marked with a few purplish spots at the base of the projecting foot. Anther white. Pollinia four in two pairs.

[A very beautiful floriferous Australian orchid, which grows on rocks and low trees, often in very exposed places. It is very hardy and free flowering, the racemes often lasting three months on the plant. It is a natural hybrid between *D. discolor* and *D. bigibbum* and as a result is extremely variable. Three forms are distinctive—the straight cross (Plate 418); the back-cross of this hybrid to *D. discolor* (Plate 420), formerly known as *D. goldei* Reichenb.f.; and the back-cross to *D. bigibbum* (Plate 419), formerly known as *D. bigibbum* var. *venosum* F. M. Bailey and *D. bigibbum* var. *georgei* C. T. White. For a comprehensive review of this hybrid and its forms see S. T. Blake in *Proc. roy. Soc. Qd* 74:29–44 (1964).—Ed.]

FLOWERING PERIOD: Very erratic, but mainly Feb. to June

DISTRIBUTION: In Australia confined to the northern tip of Cape York Peninsula, and extending through the Torres Strait Islands to New Guinea

D. discolor (Plate 421)

D. discolor Lindl. in *Edwards' bot. Reg.* 27: t. 52, Misc. 21 (1841)

SYNONYMY: *D. undulatum* R.Br. *Prodr. Flor. Nov. Holl.* 332 (1810), non Persoon (1807)

A stout species growing in large tufts, 50–500 cm. tall, the pseudobulbs more or less swollen in the middle. Leaves ovate or elliptical, obtuse or emarginate, 5–13 cm. long, flat, but thick and somewhat undulate, or the margins recurved. Racemes from the upper part of the stem, often above 45 cm. long, the flowers numerous, rather large, on pedicels often exceeding 2·5 cm. Bracts lanceolate or linear-lanceolate. Sepals and petals similar, spreading, linear-oblong, obtuse, very undulate, of a dingy brown usually bordered with yellow, 2·5–4 cm. long, the short broad basal pouch ending in a curved obtuse spur. Labellum shorter than the sepals; lateral lobes large, erect, nearly flat; mid-lobe small, broadly lanceolate or oblong, recurved and undulate; the callus with five raised lines of a light colour, of which two are prominent, especially near the base, and sometimes seven immediately below the mid-lobe. Column short and stout.

[A very large conspicuous species, forming thick congested growths on rocks, trees or even in soil. It is an extremely variable species with many named forms. For a comprehensive treatment of the species see A. W. Dockrill in *Aust. Pls* 3:28–30 (1964).—Ed.]

FLOWERING PERIOD: Apr. to Dec., but erratic

DISTRIBUTION: From Gladstone in northern Qld, extending up the Cape York Peninsula to the Torres Strait Islands, southern New Guinea and the Solomon Islands; chiefly coastal, and often locally common

D. discolor var. discolor forma broomfieldii (Plate 421)

D. discolor var. *discolor* forma *broomfieldii* (R. D. FitzG.) A. W. Dockrill in *Aust. Pls* 3:30 (1964)

SYNONYMY: *D. undulatum* var. *broomfieldii* R. D. FitzG. *Aust. Orchids* 2³:+t. (1888)

Differs from the typical forma *discolor* by having canary-yellow flowers, which may be bright and shining, with white callus ridges on the labellum.

FLOWERING PERIOD AND DISTRIBUTION: As for the typical form

D. discolor var. **fuscum** (Plate 422)

D. discolor var. *fuscum* (R. D. FitzG.) A. W. Dockrill in *Aust. Pls* 3:30 (1964)

SYNONYMY: *D. fuscum* R. D. FitzG. in *Sydney Morning Herald* (24 September 1867), and *Gdnrs' Chron.* new ser. *12*:680 (1879)

Similar to var. *discolor* but racemes fewer flowered and the individual flowers smaller, seldom exceeding 4 cm. in diameter. Sepals and petals reddish-brown with pale entire margins, the petals sometimes undulate near the apex and not tightly twisted.

FLOWERING PERIOD AND DISTRIBUTION: As for the typical form

D. johannis (Plate 423)

D. johannis Reichenb.f. in *Gdnrs' Chron.* *1865*:890 (1865)

SYNONYMY: *D. johannis* var. *semifuscum* Reichenb.f. in *Gdnrs' Chron.* new ser. *19*:368 (1883)

Pseudobulbs tufted from a shortly creeping rhizome, always more or less fusiform above the bulbous base, 17–35 cm. long. Leaves narrow, thick, 10–15 cm. long, seldom more than 1·3 cm. broad, tapering from the base to a sharp point, two to eight to each stem, often distant. Peduncle with raceme up to 45 cm. long, very slender, purplish. Bracts minute, membranous, the lower ones closely clasping the peduncle, those within the raceme spreading and more acuminate. Pedicels very slender, about 3 cm. long. Perianth segments all more or less twisted. Sepals brown with a yellowish tint, about 2·5 cm. long and 5 mm. broad, linear, marked with longitudinal dark red lines. Petals similar to the sepals but darker, shorter and narrower. Labellum trilobed, scarcely more than half the length of the sepals; lateral lobes oblong, deep red with very oblique deeper red lines; mid-lobe triangular, acute, sulphur-coloured. Callus plate with three prominent lines of calli, continued between the lateral lobes in thin plates. Column rather short, the wings ending in a broad tooth on either side of and more or less above the anther. Anther-lid patelliform, the front margin densely ciliate. Flowers very fragrant.

FLOWERING PERIOD: Sept. to Nov.

DISTRIBUTION: Confined to northern Qld, where it is widespread over the Cape York Peninsula, extending as far south as the Endeavour River

D. baileyi (Plate 424)

D. baileyi F. Muell. *Fragm. Phyt. Aust.* 8:173 (1874)

SYNONYMY: *D. keffordii* F. M. Bailey in *Proc. roy. Soc. Qd* 1:11 (1884)

Pseudobulbs slender and numerous in large masses, 30–120 cm. high, often leafy throughout. Leaves linear-lanceolate, the apex more or less obtuse, 5–8 cm. long and 6–8 mm. wide near the base, texture thin, the sheathing base striate. Racemes lateral, numerous, shorter than the leaves and mostly two-flowered. Flowers yellowish, speckled with purple, on pedicels about 1 cm. long. Sepals tapering from a broad base with filiform points, about 2·5 cm. long; the petals similar but shorter and much narrower; spur short. Labellum 1–3 cm. long, the mid-lobe bordered with a dark purple fringe, the point elongated and recurved; lateral lobes prominent, incurved in front of the column. Callus plate yellowish, with a prominently raised ridge and anterior calli. Column stout.

FLOWERING PERIOD: Dec. to Feb., but erratic

DISTRIBUTION: Confined to northern Qld, where it is scattered between the Burdekin and Endeavour Rivers, chiefly coastal

47   *Cadetia*

Cadetia Gaudich. in Freyc. *Voy. aut. Monde (Bot.)* 422, t. 33 (1829)

[Epiphytic herbs. Stems clustered, unbranched, sheathed, the apex with one leaf and several flowers. Leaves fleshy, nerveless, flat, articulate with the sheath. Flowers several, pedicellate, clustered. Capsule obovate, spiny-tuberculate. Sepals unequal; the dorsal sepal obovate-oblong, cucullate; lateral sepals subrotund-ovate, spreading above, adnate to the column foot below, forming a spur; spur emarginate. Petals linear-subulate, arching, free. Labellum concave, trilobed; lateral lobes minute. Column free, wingless, channelled on the inside; provided with a subulate appendage on each side; broad on both sides of the apex, and produced into bidentate tips below the anther. Anther terminal, operculate, unilocular, deciduous. Pollinia four, waxy. Having affinities with *Dendrobium* in its habit, but distinguished by the structure of the flowers.

A fairly large genus of about fifty species, distributed through the islands of the south-western Pacific, the Solomons, the Moluccas, New Guinea, and also Australia where there are two species.—Ed.]

C. taylori (Plate 425)

C. taylori (F. Muell.) Schlechter in *Beih. Repert. Spec. nov. Regn. veg.* *1*:424 (1912)

SYNONYMY: *Bulbophyllum taylori* F. Muell. *Fragm. Phyt. Aust.* 8:150 (1873); *Dendrobium uniflos* F. M. Bailey in *Proc. roy. Soc. Qd* 1:12 (1884)

Rhizome creeping, matted and clothed with torn old stem sheaths. Stems numerous, erect, 5–10 cm. high and 2–6 mm. broad, bluntly ribbed and bearing at the summit a single leaf and one or more flowers. Leaf 5–6 cm. long and 5–10 mm. broad, prominently keeled beneath, oblong, emarginate. Pedicel 6–7 mm. long, curved and supported by a scarious ribbed bract about 6 mm. long. Perianth segments white, about 6 mm. long, the petals a little shorter than the sepals and much narrower; dorsal sepal narrower than the lateral sepals, the spur short and broad. Labellum thick; mid-lobe cordate, about 2·1 mm. broad, glandular, transversely furrowed, white or marked with light purple. Column prominent, the narrow wings ending at the top in sharp incurved points. Anther-lid purplish.

FLOWERING PERIOD: Very erratic, but flowering almost continuously

DISTRIBUTION: Apparently confined to northern Qld, where it is widespread between the Burdekin River and the Iron Range, up to 1,100 m. (3,500 ft.) altitude

48   *Eria*

Eria Lindl. in *Edwards' bot. Reg.* 11: t. 904 (1825)

[Epiphytic plants of varying habit. Pseudobulbs fleshy (at least in the Australian species), terminated by one to four long, rather thin leaves. Flowers variable, small and pale coloured in the Australian species, but often brightly coloured in species from other countries, borne in racemose inflorescences emerging from a bract near the apex of the pseudobulb. Sepals free, rarely connate, adnate to the basal foot of the column, forming a spur. Labellum sessile, attached to the apex of the column foot, sometimes mobile, incumbent. Anther imperfectly four- or eight-celled; pollinia eight, pyriform or broad-obovoid, attached in fours to a viscous gland.

A very large genus of about three hundred and seventy-five species, distributed over tropical Asia, Polynesia and Australia, the latter having six species, all endemic.

For a comprehensive review of the genus in Australia see A. W. Dockrill in *Aust. Pls* 3:119–128 (1965).—Ed.]

E. inornata (Plate 426)

E. inornata T. E. Hunt in *Orchid J. Am.* 1⁴:190, fig. 142 (1952)

SYNONYMY: *E. linariiflora* H. M. R. Rupp in *Aust. Orchid Rev.* 18:67 (1953); *E. liparoides* T. E. Hunt in *Qd Nat.* 15:33 (1954)

Pseudobulbs sometimes stout and up to 20 cm. long, but usually shorter and ovate-conical, several to a plant, brownish. Leaves over 20 cm. long and 4–5 cm. broad, lanceolate, with about 9 nerves. Peduncles erect, stout, 20–23 cm. long. Racemes furfuraceous, flowers small, numerous, pale yellow to whitish. Bracts ovate-lanceolate, pedicel with ovary longer than the flower. Dorsal sepal lanceolate; lateral sepals deltoid. Petals nearly linear, cream inside. Labellum as long as the sepals, membranous, glabrous, narrowing towards the base, marked with two thin raised lines, the summit somewhat quadrate-ovate, yellow. Pollinia lenticular, attached in two bundles.

FLOWERING PERIOD: Aug. to Oct.

DISTRIBUTION: Confined to northern Qld, between the Tully and Annan Rivers, usually between 450 and 750 m. (1,500 and 2,500 ft.) altitude

E. queenslandica (Plate 427)

E. queenslandica T. E. Hunt in *N. Qd Nat.* 15:14 (1947)

Pseudobulbs 4–4·5 cm. long and 1–1·3 cm. broad, more or less erect, covered with sheathing scales and arising from a shortly creeping rhizome. Roots fibrous, numerous, forming large masses on the limbs of trees. Leaves two or three, lanceolate, often slightly spirally twisted, 9–14 cm. long, and 2–2·3 cm. broad at the widest part, petioles long, apex deeply emarginate or shortly acute. Racemes 5–8 cm. long, hoary, erect or pendulous, arising from between the scales, and bearing numerous, small, hoary, dingy yellow flowers with reddish markings, very shortly pedicellate, the floral bracts small, broad, scarious. Perianth segments lanceolate, somewhat spreading; dorsal sepal erect, concave, as long as but narrower than the lateral sepals; lateral sepals spreading, wide at the base; petals shorter than the sepals, and about half as wide as the lateral sepals. Labellum small, trilobed, deeply coloured internally, channelled; a divided ridge traversing the centre, but not extending beyond the lateral lobes; lateral lobes oblique, somewhat quadrate; mid-lobe oblong-cuneate, the apex emarginate. Column short; anther depressed. Pollinia eight, somewhat pyriform in shape, attached to a viscid disc.

FLOWERING PERIOD: Aug. to Oct.

DISTRIBUTION: Confined to northern Qld, between the Tully and Annan Rivers, usually between 600 and 900 m. (2,000 and 3,000 ft.) altitude

49 *Phreatia*

Phreatia Lindl. *Gen. & Spec. orchid. Pls* 63 (1830)

Epiphytic herbs, with short leafy stems sometimes thickened into pseudobulbs. Leaves thick, terete or canaliculate, distichous, their persistent bases loosely imbricate. Flowers usually minute, on exceedingly short pedicels, in axillary racemes. Sepals nearly equal, erect or connivent, the lateral ones dilated at the base and adnate to the basal projection of the column, forming a short pouch. Petals usually smaller than the sepals. Labellum articulate on the basal projection of the column, contracted and concave at the base, the lamina spreading and entire. Column very short, basal foot short, the membranous margin of the apex entire. Anther lid-like, two-celled. Pollinia eight, waxy, slightly cohering by means of a viscid substance.

A fairly large genus of about forty species, distributed over India and south-eastern Asia with three species being found in Australia.

P. baileyana (Plate 428)

P. baileyana Schlechter in *Repert. Spec. nov. Regn. veg.* 9:433 (1911)

A diminutive, rather delicate, light green epiphyte. Leaves slightly distichous, four or five to each stem, semi-cylindrical, curved, slightly grooved, fleshy, 1–2·4 cm. long, including the short base, obtuse or shortly acute. Racemes longer than the leaves, 3 cm. long, bearing about twelve minute greenish-white shortly pedicellate flowers, each subtended by a minute acuminate bracteole. Perianth widely expanding. Sepals equal in length, ovate, more or less obtuse; dorsal sepal cucullate; lateral sepals free or united at the immediate base. Petals similar to the sepals but much smaller. Labellum oval-rhomboidal, the margins entire, less than half the size of the sepals; no glands on the concave lamina. Column short and broad, the wings erect in front of column, angular and tooth-like. Pollinia eight, waxy. Capsule ovoid.

FLOWERING PERIOD: Sept. to Apr.

DISTRIBUTION: Apparently confined to northern Qld, between the Burdekin and Annan Rivers, between 600 and 1,200 m. (2,000 and 4,000 ft.) altitude

P. crassiuscula (Plate 429)

P. crassiuscula F. Muell. ex W. H. Nicholls in *Vict. Nat.* 61:151 (1945)

SYNONYMY: *P. limenophylax* Benth. *Flor. aust.* 6:290 (1873), non Reichenb.f. (1857)

A dwarf plant, epiphytic on the stems of forest trees and palms. The very short stem is covered at the base with persistent remains of fallen leaves. Leaves several, 2·5–5·5 cm. long, fleshy, crassula-like, glabrous, semi-terete, equitant, erect or somewhat spreading, channelled on the upper side. Inflorescence erect, flowers in axillary racemes, shorter than the leaves, 2–5 cm. long. Bracts longer than ovary, the margins briefly and somewhat irregularly serrate. Flowers minute, white or cream, rather crowded, almost sessile. Perianth segments spreading, with entire margins; dorsal sepal erect, ovate, obtuse, about 1 mm. long; lateral sepals free, about same length as dorsal sepal and wider at base. Petals oblong obtuse, shorter than sepals; labellum nearly as long as sepals, very concave at base, the lamina spreading, ovate-rhomboidal, entire; callus with a longitudinal raised line not extending along the lamina. Pollinia eight, minute. Column short and broad, produced forward into a foot. Capsule shortly pedicellate or nearly sessile, ovate-oblong.

FLOWERING PERIOD: Jan. and Feb.

DISTRIBUTION: Confined to northern Qld, between the Burdekin and Annan Rivers, between 600 and 1,200 m. (2,000 and 4,000 ft.) altitude

50 *Bulbophyllum*

Bulbophyllum Thouars *Hist. Pl. Orchid.* tabl. spec. 3 (1822)

Epiphytic herbs with a creeping rhizome usually covered with thin scarious sheathing scales. Leaves solitary or two together on small pseudobulbs. Racemes or one-flowered pedicels issuing, like the pseudobulbs, from the axils of the sheathing scales on the rhizome. Flowers usually small. Sepals erect, free, acuminate, nearly equal, the lateral ones obliquely dilated at the base and connate with the basal projection of the column to form a pouch or spur. Petals usually much smaller than the sepals. Labellum articulate at the end of the basal projection of the column, usually entire and contracted into a claw. Column very short, produced below its insertion, the apex with two teeth or horns in front. Anther terminal, operculate. Pollinia four, waxy, connate, or cohering in pairs, without any gland or caudicle.

A genus of about 1,000 species found in tropical and southern temperate regions of America, Africa, and Asia, and extending through Malaysia to New Guinea, Australia, and NZ. There are about twenty species in Australia, where they are most numerous in the eastern tropical region.

B. baileyi (Plate 430)

B. baileyi F. Muell. *Fragm. Phyt. Aust.* 9:5 (1875)

SYNONYMY: *B. punctatum* R. D. FitzG. in *J. Bot., Lond.* 21:205 (1883)

Rhizome creeping, often forming extensive masses on the stems and branches of tropical trees. Pseudobulbs short and angular. Leaves 5–20 cm. long, rather thick, channelled, the apex obliquely emarginate. Pedicel 5–6 cm. long. Flowers pale yellow, about 4 cm. in diameter, spotted with a purplish colour on both sides. Dorsal sepal lanceolate; lateral sepals falco-lanceolate. Petals shorter and narrower than the sepals. Labellum linguiform, thick, obtuse, arched, spotted, channelled below. Column thick, the lateral wings toothed at the top, the column foot arched, about as long as the column itself.

FLOWERING PERIOD: Oct. to Jan.

DISTRIBUTION: Northern Qld, from the Endeavour River to Burdekin River, generally near the coast between 300 and 900 m. (1,000 and 3,000 ft.) altitude

B. weinthalii (Plate 431)

B. weinthalii R. S. Rogers in *Trans. roy. Soc. S. Aust.* 57:95 (1933); H. M. R. Rupp *Orchids N.S.W.* 124 (1943)

A diminutive plant with a short creeping rhizome and fibrous roots. Pseudobulbs numerous, flask-shaped, wrinkled, scarcely compressed laterally, about six in a row, 9 mm. high. Leaf solitary, apical on pseudobulb, rather flat, coriaceous, oblong-elliptical, sub-sessile, glabrous, margins entire, 1·5–2·5 cm. long, 4–6 mm. wide, obtuse at apex, with very conspicuous midrib. Flower solitary, relatively large for size of plant; ovary-pedicel slender, 1·0–1·1 cm. long; peduncle short. Perianth segments white or pale greenish, dotted or splashed with reddish-brown or magenta markings. Dorsal sepal widely lanceolate, erect-incurved over the column, concave,

apex acute or slightly apiculate, about 9 mm. long, 5 mm. wide; lateral sepals semi-patent, acutely falcate at the apex, obliquely falco-triangular, equal to or a little shorter than the dorsal sepal; anterior margin crescentic; adnate throughout their entire base to the foot of the column for a distance of about 1 cm., forming with it a shallow pouch or trough. Petals erect or slightly divergent, oblong-oval, apices very blunt, three-nerved, about 6 mm. long, 3 mm. wide. Labellum movable, articulate to the apex of the column foot, large, linguiform, conspicuous, fleshy, dark purple, the lower part reflexed against the column foot, then markedly recurved upward and forward; trilobed; the lateral lobes dentate, very minute; mid-lobe very obtuse, with revolute margins; lamina dotted, concave in the middle, traversed by two wide parallel longitudinal calli coalescing near the apex. Column short and stout, with quadrate membranous wings; produced at the base into an elongated slender linear foot about 1 cm. long, adnate to the bases of the lateral sepals. Anther operculate, pollinia four.

Dr Rogers writes: '*B. weinthalii* would appear to be most closely related to *B. baileyi*. The latter however, is enormously larger in all its parts and with very differently shaped leaves'. It is found high up on the trunk and branches of *Araucaria cunninghamii*.

FLOWERING PERIOD: Mar. to May

DISTRIBUTION: South-eastern Qld and north coast of NSW

B. aurantiacum (Plate 432)

B. aurantiacum F. Muell. *Fragm. Phyt. Aust.* 3:39 (1862); H. M. R. Rupp *Orchids N.S.W.* 124 (1943)

Creeping but the rhizomes often hanging loose from the bark of trees. Allied to *B. crassulifolium*, but a stouter plant. Pseudobulbs small and ovoid. Leaves oblong or oblong-linear, thick but flat, sometimes almost cylindrical, contracted at the base, 3·5–5 cm. long, sometimes up to 9 cm., and often 2 cm. broad. Pedicels one-flowered, very short, covered by the scarious sheathing bracts which, although only two or three, overlap each other. Flowers about 5 mm. long, often numerous, similar in structure to those in *B. crassulifolium*, showing however a more decided angle or spur at the end of the basal projection of the column. Sepals bluntly conical at the apex, waxy, orange. Petals ovate, obtuse, colourless. Labellum reddish-brown, prominently recurved, the lateral margins with short cilia.

[This species usually grows in the sun, on rocks and on trees. It is very variable. For a discussion of its relationship with *B. crassulifolium* see S. C. Clemesha and W. T. Upton in *Orchadian* 1:91–94 (1964).—Ed.]

FLOWERING PERIOD: Mainly summer, but flowers may be found at any time of the year

DISTRIBUTION: Coast and coastal ranges from northern Qld as far south as the Hunter River in central NSW

B. radicans (Plate 433)

B. radicans F. M. Bailey in *Qd agric. J.* 1:81 (1897)

SYNONYMY: *B. cilioglossum* R. S. Rogers & W. H. Nicholls in *Trans. roy. Soc. S. Aust.* 59:204, t. 1 (1935)

A small plant with creeping rhizome and numerous fibrous roots. Pseudobulbs obliquely obconical, sessile, truncate at apex, slightly concave on one side, 5–6 mm. high. Leaves sessile, rather narrowly elliptical or falco-elliptical, arising singly from the apex of the pseudobulb, acute at the apex, attenuating towards the base, 6–7 cm. long, about 1·3 cm. wide in the middle, upper surface channelled, convex below, pendulous. Scape single, one-flowered, arising behind the leaf at the base of the concave side of the pseudobulb, slender, glabrous, about 1·5 cm. long; an acute sheathing bract near the base of the pedicel, the floral bract similar below the ovary. Flower minute, about 5 mm. long, white or pinkish with darker reddish longitudinal stripes, yellow, and red-brown. Dorsal sepal erect, oblong-ovate, three-nerved, slightly concave, about 4 mm. long; lateral sepals about the same length, wider, falco-ovate, three-nerved, slightly concave, attached to the foot of the column so as to form an obtuse mentum; petals narrowly oblong, obtuse, erect, one-nerved, about 2 mm. long. Labellum pink, ovate, entire, rather fleshy, obtuse at the apex; recurved, concave above, longitudinally sulcate below; mobile, delicately articulate at the apex of the foot of the column; margins reddish, raised, ciliate. Column erect, very short, obliquely produced at the base into a long foot and provided above on each side with a linear subulate appendage greatly exceeding the anther in height.

[*B. radicans* has been confused with *B. nematopodum* in the past. For a discussion of their differences see S. C. Clemesha in *Orchadian* 1:76 (1964). Plate 433 was originally intended to illustrate *B. cilioglossum*, but this is now considered to be synonymous with *B. radicans*.—Ed.]

FLOWERING PERIOD: Throughout the year

DISTRIBUTION: Along the coast of northern Qld, from the Endeavour River to Burdekin River, usually in the lowlands below 750 m. (2,500 ft.) altitude

B. bowkettae (Plate 434)

B. bowkettae F. M. Bailey in *Proc. roy. Soc. Qd* 1:89 (1885)

SYNONYMY: *B. waughense* H. M. R. Rupp in *Contr. N.S.W. Herb.* 1:318 (1951)

Rhizomes creeping, forming dense patches. Pseudobulbs oval-oblong, compressed, bluntly ribbed, 1–2 cm. long and 1–2 cm. broad. Leaves solitary on the pseudobulb, thick, dark green, ovate to suborbicular, 2–6 cm. long and 1–2·3 cm. broad. Flowers solitary on scapes 2–4 cm. long, articulate about the middle, just above a minute more or less obtuse sheathing bract. Sepals 5–7 mm. long, greenish-yellow; dorsal sepal oblong with an obtuse point, or narrowing to an acute apex, bordered by a reddish-purple line and having three reddish-purple lines down the centre; lateral sepals ovate-oblong, united at the base and forming a short spur, indistinctly marked with lines as in the dorsal sepal, apiculate at the tips. Petals about half the length of the dorsal sepal, with only one central purple stripe, but otherwise more or less lined, or blotched with the same colour; broadly ovate, pale yellowish-white. Labellum oblong-linear, thick, longer than the petals, golden-yellow towards the tip, the posterior portion more or less marked with red or reddish-purple blotchings; a narrow groove on the upper surface of the posterior portion, also along the under side of the anterior part, apex emarginate. Column short, the front teeth erect, as high as or higher than the anther; column foot broad with an horizontal apex. Pollinia four, in two pairs.

FLOWERING PERIOD: Apr. to Sept.

DISTRIBUTION: Coastal northern Qld, from the Annan River to Tully River, and generally above 600 m. (2,000 ft.) altitude

B. lageniforme (Plate 435)

B. lageniforme F. M. Bailey in *Qd agric. J.* 15:494 (1904)

Rhizome creeping, rather slender, nearly glabrous, corrugated when dry; pseudobulbs numerous but not crowded, flask-shaped, smooth, becoming corrugated when dry, 4–7 mm. high. Leaves solitary,

linear-lanceolate, 2·3–6·5 cm. long, 4–5 mm. at their widest part, upper surface foveolar dotted; mid-rib sharp and prominent, with numerous parallel veins on either side. Peduncles filiform, about as long as the leaves or longer, bearing a linear bract about the centre, and a similar but shorter one close under the flower. Flowers one or two, open and somewhat bell-shaped, pale greenish with pale brownish longitudinal nerves. Pedicels about 5 mm. long, slightly enlarging upward, and prominently tuberculose in the upper part. Sepals 5–6 mm. long, three-nerved; dorsal one lanceolate, cucullate; lateral ones much broader at the base, the apex recurved. Petals ovate-lanceolate, shorter than the sepals, transparent, three-nerved, the lateral nerves not reaching the apex of the petal. Labellum coriaceous, articulate at the base of the column, shorter than the other segments, ovate, the margins recurved, dusky brown, the callus plate with three prominent ribs, the outer ones raised anteriorly. Column short, wings prominent, widely toothed at the summit. Anther depressed.

FLOWERING PERIOD: Nov. to Feb.

DISTRIBUTION: Northern Qld, from the Big Tableland to the Johnston River on the east coast, usually above 750 m. (2,500 ft.) altitude

B. exiguum (Plate 436)

B. exiguum F. Muell. *Fragm. Phyt. Aust.* 2:72 (1860); H. M. R. Rupp *Orchids N.S.W.* 125 (1943)

SYNONYMY: *B. exiguum* var. *dallachyi* Benth. *Flor. aust.* 6:289 (1873)

Growing on trees and on rock surfaces. Creeping rhizomes sometimes forming dense masses, sometimes elongated in single threads with distant pseudobulbs. Pseudobulbs ovoid or nearly globular, fleshy, angular and furrowed when fresh, very deeply rugose when dry, 5–10 mm. in diameter. Leaves solitary on the pseudobulbs, oblong-linear or lanceolate, contracted at the base, 0·8–4 cm. long, the margins recurved, the mid-rib prominent underneath. Peduncles filiform, 2·5–5 cm. long, bearing two to four flowers on short filiform pedicels. Sepals lanceolate, 5–7 mm. long, the lateral ones dilated at the base into a short broad pouch. Petals scarcely half as long as the sepals. Labellum nearly as long as the sepals, linear, thick and channelled, tapering and slightly recurved towards the end. Column very short.

[This species is described in some detail and discussed by A. W. Dockrill in *Orchadian* 2:104, cum icon. (1967). In this article he reduces the var. *dallachyi* to synonymy, as he considers that it does not differ in any significant way from the typical.—Ed.]

FLOWERING PERIOD: Feb. to June

DISTRIBUTION: From Rockingham Bay in northern Qld to south-eastern NSW, on both the coast and the coastal ranges

B. minutissimum (Plate 437)

B. minutissimum F. Muell. in *Fragm. Phyt. Aust.* 11:53 (1878); H. M. R. Rupp *Orchids N.S.W.* 124 (1943)

Stems creeping, very dense. Pseudobulbs orbicular, flattened, 1–1·5 mm. in diameter, bearing at the apex a solitary minute lanceolate leaf about 1 mm. long. Flowers very small, diameter less than that of pseudobulb, more or less rosy red, pedicels short and more or less tuberculose. Ovary oval, densely hairy. Dorsal sepal ovate, cucullate. Lateral sepals very broad, the bases dilated and forming a prominent wide and blunt spur, three red lines traversing each sepal. Petals white with one red line, narrow-lanceolate. Labellum red, oval-oblong, curved, tip rounded, margins entire; callus somewhat raised, extending from the base upward and thickened towards the tip. Column short, the base elongated, the wings erect and tooth-like. Anther incumbent with a short mucro. Pollinia in two pairs.

This diminutive species grows on the branches and trunks of trees, and on rocks. It was discovered by Archdeacon King in 1849 at a spot which is now near the centre of the city of Sydney.

FLOWERING PERIOD: Oct. and Nov.

DISTRIBUTION: South-eastern Qld; eastern NSW as far south as Kiama, on the coast and near-coastal ranges

B. globuliforme (Plate 438)

B. globuliforme W. H. Nicholls in *Orchidol. zeylan.* 5:123 (1938); H. M. R. Rupp *Orchids N.S.W.* 124 (1943)

Rhizome creeping on the bark of trees. Pseudobulbs very small, globular, green, 1–1·5 mm. in diameter. Leaf solitary at the apex of the pseudobulb, linear-subulate, fugacious, about 2·5 mm. long. Flowers small, solitary, 3–5 mm. in diameter, white, suffused with pale yellow, and in some flowers with crimson on the spur and sepals. Perianth segments widely expanding; dorsal sepal lanceolate; lateral sepals broad. Spur short and obtuse. Petals lanceolate. Ovary short, rough-glandular, the upper part of pedicel also marked with glands. Pedicel rather long, the subtending bract long, loosely sheathing. Labellum with entire margins, oblong, curved, channelled towards the base, cream or pale yellow, the apex hardly acute. Column very short and broad, the base produced into a slender, curved foot, about two and a half times the height of the column, two prominent upward curved subulate lobes in front.

B. globuliforme is closely allied to F. Mueller's *B. minutissimum*, also to *B. moniliforme* Reichenb.f., a Burma species. It is specifically distinct from Mueller's species in its still more diminutive size, in its globuliform pseudobulbs (as opposed to the flat, shield-like pseudobulbs of *B. minutissimum*), in the different nature and the colour of the flowers, and in the differences of the labellum and column.

From *B. moniliforme* it differs in the different size, structure, and the colour of the flowers. The author's specimens of *B. globuliforme* were collected on the NSW side of the Macpherson Range, the border between Qld and NSW. It grows in small colonies, often strung out on high branches of the Hoop pine (*Araucaria cunninghamii*). A. W. Dockrill found it on a number of trees in a limited area. The only other orchid in association was *B. weinthalii*.

FLOWERING PERIOD: Oct. and Nov., but also recorded for May and Aug.

DISTRIBUTION: Apparently confined to the area around the eastern end of the Qld–NSW border, mainly in the Macpherson Range and Lamington Plateau

B. macphersonii (Plate 439)

B. macphersonii H. M. R. Rupp in *Vict. Nat.* 51:81, cum icon. (1934)

SYNONYMY: *B. purpurascens* F. M. Bailey in *Proc. roy. Soc. Qd* 1:88 (1885), non Teys. & Binn. (1862); *Osyricera purpurascens* (F. M. Bailey) H. Deane in R. D. FitzG. *Aust. Orchids* 2⁵:+t. (1894)

Rhizome creeping, forming dense matted patches. Pseudobulbs about 1·5–2 mm. long, often so close together as to give a moniliform appearance to the rhizome, the scarious scales prominent. Leaves 5–10 mm., occasionally up to 15 mm., green, thick and channelled above, the back convex, linear-lanceolate or broadly ovate, attached to the pseudobulb by a short stalk. Pedicels erect, filiform, 1·5–2 cm. long, with one or more scarious bracts at the base and one close under the flower. Flower solitary, purplish or

deep red. Sepals about 5 mm. long, all about equal in length; the lateral ones sometimes united, broad, lanceolate, somewhat obtuse, or the dorsal one sometimes emarginate, pouch or spur very short. Petals about 4 mm. long, one-nerved, narrow-lanceolate, with elongated points and irregular margins. Labellum clawed, articulate at the basal extension of the column, shorter than the sepals, dark purple or purplish-red, lanceolate with fringed margins, minutely two-lobed at the base, and a raised rib along the centre; lamina with reflexed margins or very convex, both sides glandulose. Column white, the prominent wings ending in elongated points; either bifid or trifid. Anther terminal, shorter than the wings, operculate, incumbent, convex, two-celled, the anterior surface suborbicular, glandulose, with appendage. Pollinia two, in two pairs, waxy, ovoid, without appendage, free. Capsule oblong-ribbed.

FLOWERING PERIOD: Mainly Mar. and Apr., but flowering may take place at almost any time of the year

DISTRIBUTION: Northern Qld, from the Annan River to Fitzroy River and generally near the coast from 450 to 1,200 m. (1,500 to 4,000 ft.) altitude

B. bracteatum (Plate 440)

B. bracteatum F. M. Bailey in *Qd Dep. Agric. Bot. Bull.* 4:17 (1891); H. M. R. Rupp in *Orchids N.S.W.* 125 (1943)

SYNONYMY: *Adelopetalum bracteatum* R. D. FitzG. in *J. Bot., Lond.* 29:152 (1891)

On rocks and trees, the rhizome shortly creeping. Pseudobulbs glossy, depressed-globular, 6–15 mm. in diameter, crowded upon the rhizome, wrinkled and ribbed with six to eight prominent angles. Leaves solitary, oblong to lanceolate, recurved, 1–3 cm. long, coriaceous, deep green, mid-rib prominent. Flowers racemose, numerous, closely packed, mottled purple or red; the raceme 3–9 cm. long; the peduncle as long or a little longer. Bracts numerous on the peduncle, cordate-acuminate, 5–8 mm. long, the one subtending the pedicels smaller; the rhachis and the bracts glaucous or hoary white. Flowers very small, 6–8 mm. in diameter; sepals mottled with light coloured margins, broad-lanceolate, three-nerved; petals one-nerved, very small, linear, softly coloured, erect on each side of the column. Labellum very short, thick and linguiform, buff on the upper, purplish on the under surface and glossy; claw elastic and as long as the lamina, three-nerved below the articulation. Column very short; anther-lid rotund, off-white. Pollinia golden-yellow, almost globular, in two pairs, and attached to a small gland.

F. M. Bailey writes: 'In the flower I dissected, I found only two globular pollinia'. In the several flowers examined by the author, the pollinia were almost globular in two pairs, and attached to a small gland; the size of the pollinia unequal in the extreme.

FLOWERING PERIOD: Oct. to Dec.

DISTRIBUTION: South-eastern Qld and north-eastern NSW, mainly on the ranges between the Bunya Mountains and the Clarence River

B. elisae (Plate 441)

B. elisae (F. Muell.) Benth. *Flor. aust.* 6:289 (1873); H. M. R. Rupp *Orchids N.S.W.* 125 (1943)

SYNONYMY: *Cirrhopetalum elisae* F. Muell. *Fragm. Phyt. Aust.* 6:120, t. 57 (1868)

Pseudobulbs hardly crowded, though rather close together on a shortly creeping rhizome, 1·5–1·75 cm. high and 1·1–1·3 cm. wide, more or less ovoid, and covered with shortly pointed tubercles arranged in about seven somewhat irregular vertical rows with furrows between them. Leaf solitary, occasionally two, smooth, rather rigid, blunt, moderately thick, frequently flat, oblong or oblong-elliptical, 5–10 cm. long; the mid-rib prominent. Flowers inverted, usually secund, in very slender arching racemes, green or yellowish, with a dark red or purplish labellum or occasionally wholly reddish-purple, or white tinged with pink. Pedicels 1–2 cm. long, including ovary. Bracts small and narrow. Lateral sepals lanceolate, 1·3–2 cm. long, their oblique bases adnate to the basal projection of the column thus forming a short pouch; dorsal sepal about half as long as the lateral sepals. Petals still shorter, ovate-lanceolate. Labellum oblong, clawed, as long as the petals, erect at the base, then almost horizontal, very conspicuous by reason of its dark hue: deep prune, red and purple, or dark reddish-brown; lamina spreading, grooved above. Column short, with two prominent teeth.

FLOWERING PERIOD: May to Nov.

DISTRIBUTION: South-eastern Qld to the north coast of NSW, extending as far south as the Hunter River

51   *Dipodium*

Dipodium R. Br. *Prodr. Flor. Nov. Holl.* 330 (1810)

Terrestrial glabrous herbs, with imbricate sheaths at base of the scape, the upper ones passing into more distant bracts. Flowers often spotted. Perianth segments free, nearly equal, spreading. Labellum sessile, erect, trilobed; lateral lobes much shorter than mid-lobe; lamina with a hairy track along the mid-line. Column erect, semi-cylindrical. Anther terminal, lid-like, deciduous. Pollinia two, waxy, bilobed, attached when mature to the rostellum by a large disc and double stipes produced backward from the latter.

A small genus of about twelve species distributed from China through Malaysia and the Philippines to New Guinea, New Caledonia, NZ, and Australia, where there are three endemic species.

D. ensifolium (Plate 442)

D. ensifolium F. Muell. *Fragm. Phyt. Aust.* 5:42 (1865)

Stems leafy, from 8–24 cm. high, without the racemes. Leaves 8–20 cm. long, distichous, complicate or canaliculate, linear-lanceolate, acute, strongly keeled and prominently ribbed on each side; the persistent truncate base usually rather long. Racemes with the peduncle often above 30 cm. long, sometimes appearing at first terminal, but really always axillary, usually only one or two racemes on the same stem. Sheathing scales small, distant, with a few imbricate ones at the base of the peduncle. Pedicels with the ovary 1·5–2 cm. long. Sepals and petals rose coloured or purplish, spotted, 15–18 mm. long, the sepals oblong-lanceolate; petals similar, but more contracted at the base. Labellum about as long as the other segments, scarcely gibbous at the base, but shortly connate with the column as in other species, the lateral lobes placed much below the middle, linear or linear-spathulate, incurved; mid-lobe about twice as long, broadly rhomboidal; the callus with two pubescent lines between the lateral lobes, becoming confluent into one at the base of the mid-lobe, a dense patch of scaly hairs at the end. Column not half the length of the sepals, pubescent in front. Pollinia two, lobed, the two caudicles long and slender.

This is one of Australia's most beautiful orchids.

FLOWERING PERIOD: Oct. to Jan.

DISTRIBUTION: Confined to northern Qld between the Herbert and Endeavour Rivers, extending to 1,200 m. (4,000 ft.) altitude

D. punctatum (Plates 443 to 445)

D. punctatum (Sm.) R. Br. *Prodr. Flor. Nov. Holl.* 331 (1810); A. J. Ewart *Flor. Vict.* 322 (1931); J. M. Black *Flor. S. Aust.* ed. 2:210 (1943); H. M. R. Rupp *Orchids N.S.W.* 126 (1943); J. H. Willis *Handb. Pls Vict.* 1:420 (1962); M. J. Firth *Native Orchids Tasm.* 29 (1965)

SYNONYMY: *Dendrobium punctatum* Sm. *Exot. Bot.* 1:21, t. 12 (1804-5)

A tall leafless plant 30–90 cm. high, with a thick, elongated, tuberous, much-branched root system. Leaves reduced to a varying number of small, loosely imbricate, protective bracts at the base of the peduncle. Stem-bracts above reduced to sheathing scales, distant, acute or obtuse. Flowers often numerous, up to sixty in vigorous specimens, in an extended terminal raceme, usually pink with dark spots, sometimes wholly pink or white. Ovary narrow-oblong on a slender pedicel, the subtending bracteole small, acute. Perianth segments free, similar, oblong-lanceolate, spreading, often recurved, sepals 15–17 mm. long; petals slightly shorter. Labellum 13–15 mm. long, sessile, rigid, erect, trilobed; lateral lobes 5–7 mm. long, narrow, petaloid, much shorter than the mid-lobe; mid-lobe oblong or oblong-ovate, traversed by a double raised pubescent central ridge narrowing upward to a single broad hairy keel, with inturned hairs, which extends to an acute apex, and occasionally also along the margins at the tip. Column 8–9 mm. high, erect, inconspicuously winged, semi-cylindrical, the inner face pubescent with numerous minute glands. Anther hemispherical, lid-like, two-celled. Stigma deeply excavated, transversely oval, immediately below the rostellum. Rostellum small, its apex projecting. Pollinia two, waxy, bilobed.

A widespread and well known species, which is a common sight in most scrubs of coastal and inland areas. It tolerates a wide range of soils but is invariably found in close association with large trees, chiefly eucalypts, on which it was once thought to be parasitic. The orchid, however, is not a parasite but a saprophyte living on dead organic material in symbiosis with a fungus in its root-system. The fungus supplies certain food materials to the orchid, thus dispensing with the need for leaves, and in return is able to use some compounds from the orchid.

FLOWERING PERIOD: Very irregular, from Nov. to Apr., reaching a peak in Dec. and Jan.

COMMON NAME: Hyacinth Orchid

DISTRIBIUTON: All states, including NT, but absent from WA; from the coast to the ranges, up to 1,200 m. (4,000 ft.) altitude, but not in the drier inland; often locally common

52   *Cymbidium*

Cymbidium Swartz in *Nova Acta Soc. Sci. upsal.* 6:70 (1799)

Plants often large, growing in decayed timber or on trees. Stems often short and swollen into pseudobulbs at the base. Leaves elongated, keeled, striate. Flowers numerous, in large racemes arising from the lower leaf axils, small in the Australian species, the peduncle often long with sheathing rigid scales at the base. Bracts usually small. Flowers in all Australian species pleasantly fragrant.

Sepals and petals nearly equal, free, spreading. Labellum sessile, free, articulate on the base of the column, or very shortly adnate to it, concave, entire or trilobed. Column erect or slightly incurved, semi-terete, sometimes narrowly winged. Anther lid-like, very concave, more or less two-celled. Pollinia two, usually bilobed, sessile on a somewhat triangular gland.

A fairly large genus of about forty species, distributed over Africa, eastern Asia, and extending through south-eastern Asia to Australia, where there are three species, all endemic.

C. suave (Plate 446)

C. suave R. Br. *Prodr. Flor. Nov. Holl.* 331 (1810); H. M. R. Rupp *Orchids N.S.W.* 128 (1943)

SYNONYMY: *C. gomphocarpum* R. D. FitzG. in *J. Bot., Lond.* 21:203 (1883)

Stems up to 35 cm. long, usually slender, not pseudobulbous, densely covered with the imbricate, strongly striate remains of leaves and fibres. Leaves 15–45 cm. long and 1–2 cm. broad, narrow, keeled and strongly striate. Racemes 10–25 cm. long, rather dense, the sheathing scales at the base of the peduncle rigid and leaf-like, flowers 2–3 cm. in diameter, green blotched with red. Sepals and petals scarcely 11 mm. long, rather acute. Labellum narrow, almost as long as the petals, undivided or obscurely tri-lobed; lamina without longitudinal plates but thickened along the centre. Column with two narrow wings. Capsule ovoid-globular, scarcely 2·5 cm. long.

This species is the smallest Australian member of the genus, and is typically found on hardwood trees of open forest country, occasionally entering rain-forests. It grows in hollows of branches or trunks, the roots penetrating deep into the decaying heartwood.

FLOWERING PERIOD: Aug. to Oct. in the tropics, but extending to Jan. in southern NSW

DISTRIBUTION: From the Annan River of northern Qld to the southern coast of NSW, chiefly coastal but extending to 1,100 m. (3,500 ft.) altitude

C. canaliculatum (Plate 447)

C. canaliculatum R. Br. *Prodr. Flor. Nov. Holl.* 331 (1810); H. M. R. Rupp *Orchids N.S.W.* 127 (1943)

SYNONYMY: *C. canaliculatum* var. *sparkesii* (Rendle) F. M. Bailey *Compreh. Cat. Qd Pls* 845 (1913); *C. sparkesii* Rendle in *J. Bot., Lond.* 36:221 (1898)

Plants epiphytic on trees in open forests. Pseudobulbs short, 5–14 cm. long, densely clustered together and covered with the bases of both withered and living leaves. Leaves two to six, elongated, up to 60 cm. long, thick, rigid, narrow, keeled, very deeply channelled, the lower ones short and bract-like. Racemes arising from the lower axils, sometimes 35–40 cm. long. Sheathing scales at base of peduncle rigid. Flowers about 3 cm. in diameter, numerous, brownish-green in varying tints; inside of perianth usually blotched red-brown or purplish. Pedicels 2–5 cm. long; subtending bracteoles very small, often acuminate. Sepals and petals oblong-lanceolate, acute or obtuse. Petals shorter than the sepals. Labellum somewhat shorter than the petals, trilobed, white, marked with purple; lateral lobes decurrent along the claw; mid-lobe broadly ovate or almost rhomboidal, papillose on the upper surface, the callus between the lateral lobes with two longitudinal raised plates, slightly pubescent or shortly fringed; apex acute or obtuse. Column about as long as the lateral lobes of the labellum, slightly incurved, with two narrow longitudinal wings.

[A very variable species, particularly in regard to flower colour. Many varieties and forms have been named on the basis of this character, which on its own is of little importance taxonomically. It is very hardy, favouring the dry interior regions, and rarely extending to the coast or the moist mountains. It is one of the only two epiphytes to be found in WA.—Ed.]

FLOWERING PERIOD: Sept. to Nov.

DISTRIBUTION: Across the north of Australia, from Roebuck Bay in WA to the tip of Cape York Peninsula in Qld, then south as far as the Hunter River in NSW, usually in the drier inland parts

C. madidum (Plate 448)

C. madidum Lindl. in *Edwards' bot. Reg.* 26: Misc. 9 (1840); H. M. R. Rupp *Orchids N.S.W.* 128 (1943), as *C. iridifolium*

SYNONYMY: *C. iridifolium* A. Cunn. in *Edwards' bot. Reg.* 25: Misc. 34 (1839), non Roxb. (1814); *C. albuciflorum* F. Muell. *Fragm. Phyt. Aust.* 1:188 (1859)

[Pseudobulbs large, 6–25 cm. long and 2–6 cm. broad, bright green. Leaves up to nine, 20–90 cm. long and 3 cm. broad, thin, decurved, not deeply channelled. Racemes arising from the axils of lower bracts, pendulous, up to 60 cm. long and bearing up to seventy scattered flowers. Flowers 2–3 cm. in diameter, greenish-brown, perianth segments not widely spreading, thick, 9–15 cm. long; petals directed forward, slightly shorter than the sepals, more or less obliquely obovate. Labellum 9–15 mm. long and 5 cm. broad, trilobed; lateral lobes crescentic, green, the anterior part triangular; mid-lobe yellow, sub-obovate, obtuse, the lateral margins and apex decurved; lamina with a very broad keel, contracted near the middle, glandular and slightly viscid. Column 1 cm. high, slightly decurved and dilated near the apex.

This species favours moist open forests and rain-forests, where it frequently forms large masses on its supporting hosts.

FLOWERING PERIOD: Aug. to Oct. in tropical areas, but later in the south

DISTRIBUTION: Extending from the tip of Cape York Peninsula to NSW, at least as far south as the Clarence River; from sea-level to 1,200 m. (4,000 ft.) altitude, usually near the coast.—Ed.]

53 *Phalaenopsis*

Phalaenopsis Blume *Bijdr. Flor. Ned. Indie* 294 (1825)

Large epiphytes with short to moderately elongated stems and large pendulous flattened leaves, broadest near the apex. Inflorescences usually short racemes, sometimes branching panicles, peduncles long. Flowers large and showy. Sepals subequal, petals often broader. Labellum spurless, adnate to column foot, lateral lobes erect; disc with one or two large calli, usually bifid. Column long, anther two-celled, pollinia round or ovoid, caudicle linear to spathulate with a disc.

A genus of about forty species extending from Indo-Malaysia through the Philippines, Indonesia and New Guinea to Australia, with only one species being found in Australia.

P. amabilis

P. amabilis (L.) Blume *Bijdr. Flor. Ned. Indie* 294 (1825)

SYNONYMY: *Epidendrum amabile* L. *Spec. Plant.* 2:953 (1753)

A species of several varieties, only one being found in Australia.

P. amabilis var **rosenstromii** (Plate 449)

P. amabilis var. *rosenstromii* (F. M. Bailey) W. H. Nicholls in *Aust. Orchid Rev. 14*:104 (1949); A. W. Dockrill *Australas. Sarcanth.* 5 (1967)

SYNONYMY: *P. rosenstromii* F. M. Bailey in *Qd agric. J. 17*:231 (1906)

Leaves four or five, deep green, distichous, about 25 cm. long and 5 cm. wide, oblong, of comparatively thin texture with an obliquely emarginate apex; mid-rib not prominent, longitudinal and transverse nerves numerous and prominent in the dried specimen; lamina obliquely spreading above the sheath, which is hard, coriaceous, about 5 cm. long and more or less flattened. Panicle composed of racemose branches up to 10 cm. long, each bearing five to ten showy white flowers on slender pedicels, about 4 cm. long. Sepals ovate-lanceolate, 3–3·8 cm. long, the base cuneate; dorsal sepal broader than the lateral sepals. Petals round-ovate, 3·5–4 cm. broad, scarcely clawed. Labellum about 3·5 cm. long, white with yellow stains and red markings, trilobed, with a two-horned callosity at the base; lateral lobes incurved; mid-lobe strap-shaped, with two twisted filiform appendages at the apex. Column short, incurved, angular. Rostellum prominent.

Bushmen find this orchid by means of the long flat roots which often grow right down the trunks of jungle trees. The flowers of this variety resemble those of the species but are not quite so large. It is a particularly free flowering orchid and one of the most beautiful species in Australia. It grows from the rivers to the summits of nearby ranges in dense jungle.

Mr. Glindeman who sent my material writes: 'This elegant orchid grows on almost any tree that has a fairly rough bark, or even on vines, and also on granite boulders. Seldom does one find a plant with sound leaves, they are nearly always more or less damaged by a green caterpillar. There are insects which eat the leaves and then the crown of the plant, eventually killing it.'

FLOWERING PERIOD: Dec. to Feb.

DISTRIBUTION: Confined to north-eastern Qld where it is distributed over the Seaview Range and along the Mossman and Daintree Rivers, generally uncommon

54 *Robiquetia*

Robiquetia Gaudich. in Freyc. *Voy. aut. Monde (Bot.)* 426 (1829)

Epiphytes with pendulous stems; leaves oblique, oblong or narrowly elliptic. Inflorescence moderately long, unbranched, usually pendulous, many flowered. Flowers radiating in all directions but more or less facing the apex of the inflorescence, small, sepals and petals free. Dorsal sepal distinctly cucullate over the column, the other segments flatter. Labellum immovably joined to the base of the column, trilobed, spurred; lateral lobes small, sometimes with a fleshy thickening inside, the posterior margins usually partly joined to the column; mid-lobe small, conical or linear, fleshy or concave, straight or decurved, sometimes with a ridge or thickening at the base; spur rather long, more or less cylindrical, rarely conical, often bent in various ways and flattened, no septum or appendages present, the posterior wall sometimes thickened, but the orifice never closed by a prominent callus. Column short, with no foot, the top more or less bent backward. Anther large with a narrow

rostrum. Pollinia two, round, more or less cleft; stipe long, slender near the base but dilated, often considerably, near the apex; retinaculum small.

[Adapted from A. W. Dockrill *Australas. Sarcanth.* 6 (1967). Dockrill considers that this genus is morphologically identical with *Malleola* J. J. Smith and Schlechter. See *Australas. Sarcanth.* 6 (1967).—Ed.]

A small genus, ranging from tropical Asia, through Malaysia, Indonesia and New Guinea to Australia, where the three species are all endemic in far north-eastern Qld.

R. tierneyana (Plate 450)

R. tierneyana (H. M. R. Rupp) A. W. Dockrill *Australas. Sarcanth.* 7, t. 18 (1967)

SYNONYMY: *Saccolabium tierneyanum* H. M. R. Rupp in *Qd Nat. 12*:18 (1942)

A rather large epiphyte with a stem not greater than 30 cm. in length. Roots creeping or aerial, thick. Leaves 7–14 cm. long, oblong, with bifid or emarginate tips. Racemes shorter than the leaves, bearing six to twelve small pale green and brown mottled flowers. Sepals and petals concave, the former about 3–5 mm. long, the petals shorter and a little narrower. Labellum 2–3 mm. long, trilobed; mid-lobe long and narrow, yellow; lateral lobes short and broad. Spur about 4 mm. long, slightly curved, channelled above and dilated towards the blunt apex. Column very short and stout. Pollinia four.

This species was discovered in the Pine Creek area of Cairns in April 1934, and named after its discoverer, W. F. Tierney.

FLOWERING PERIOD: Mar. to May

DISTRIBUTION: Lowland rain-forests and low coastal ranges of north-eastern Qld, from Rockingham Bay to the Bloomfield River

55 *Rhinerrhiza*

Rhinerrhiza H. M. R. Rupp in *Vict. Nat. 67*:206 (1951)

A monotypic genus confined to eastern Australia. It is botanically close to *Sarcochilus* but differs in the thick tuberculate roots, the filiform perianth segments and the fugacious flowers.

R. divitiflora (Plate 451)

R. divitiflora (F. Muell. ex Benth.) H. M. R. Rupp in *Vict. Nat. 67*:206 (1951); H. M. R. Rupp *Orchids N.S.W.* 132 (1943), as *Sarcochilus divitiflorus*; A. W. Dockrill *Australas. Sarcanth.* 13 (1967)

SYNONYMY: *Sarcochilus divitiflorus* F. Muell. ex Benth. *Flor. aust. 6*:292 (1873)

Stems 6–8 cm. long, flat, clothed with the brown bases of old leaves. Roots flattened upon the branches or stems of the supporting plants, of a dark colour and rough as a rasp. Leaves oblong, two to five, and 7–18 cm. long, coarse, rigid and leathery, dark green, prominently corrugated. Scapes 15–45 cm. long, a few empty bracts below the inflorescence. Flowers fugacious, usually numerous, on short pedicels; subtending bracteoles ovate. Sepals and petals very narrow, tapering into a filiform point, often 4–5 cm. or more long, yellow or orange, marked at the base with red-brown; base of perianth segments white; lateral sepals narrow-lanceolate towards the base, without any prominent spur. Labellum small, white, on a narrow claw; trilobed, lamina with an erect central saccate spur in front, the lateral lobes large, erect, 3–4 mm. long, incurved, oblong, obtuse, clasping the very short column; mid-lobe small, situated on top of the spur. Column short with a long foot set at an acute angle to it. Rostellum consisting of two, widely separated, decurved tooth-like arms. Anther peaked and rostrate. Pollinia four, in two closely appressed pairs; stipe very short, lorate; retinaculum rather small, appearing to be a continuation of the stipe.

The racemes of flowers are normally straight in nature, but are shown curved in the plate for lack of space. Among the *Sarcanthinae* species found in Australia, this orchid has earned the title of unique. It is an outstanding species with very harsh foliage and rich golden-hued, spider-like flowers, which resemble those of several *Dendrobium* species, more especially *D. teretifolium* and *D. aemulum*. The attractive flowers are short-lived, rarely lasting over a few days.

There are two forms of *R. divitiflora*, one with smooth leathery leaves, the other possessing extremely rigid, deeply corrugated rough foliage. The former bears large, pale yellow flowers; the latter has flowers of a normal size and a deeper hue.

FLOWERING PERIOD: Aug. to Nov.

COMMON NAME: Raspy-root Orchid

DISTRIBUTION: Extending from the Atherton Tableland in Qld, south to Berowra in NSW, in coastal ranges

56 *Sarcochilus*

Sarcochilus R. Br. *Prodr. Flor. Nov. Holl.* 332 (1810)

Epiphytes or lithophytes with short or elongated stems, the bases covered with persistent scarious leaf-bases. Roots smooth, thick and fleshy. Leaves few, lanceolate to linear or falcate, flat or thick and channelled. Flowers few or many, showy, sometimes fragrant, borne on axillary racemes. Sepals and petals free, more or less equal, lateral sepals joined in part to the column foot. Labellum articulate at the apex of the column foot, saccate, trilobed, spurred in front; lateral lobes large, more or less erect; mid-lobe attached to the spur, very small, fleshy; spur short, often poorly developed, fleshy or hollow; the disc with callus thickenings. Column short and erect with a well-developed foot. Rostellum small. Anther two-celled, rostrate. Pollinia four in two closely appressed pairs, each member unequal, stipe not broad nor elongate, retinaculum of moderate size, usually attached to the ventral surface of the rostellum. [Adapted from A. W. Dockrill *Australas. Sarcanth.* 14 (1967).—Ed.]

A small genus of eleven species, almost exclusively Australian, with one species extending to New Guinea and the Solomon Islands.

S. falcatus (Plates 452 and 453)

S. falcatus R. Br. *Prodr. Flor. Nov. Holl.* 332 (1810); A. J. Ewart *Flor. Vict.* 310 (1931); H. M. R. Rupp *Orchids N.S.W.* 132 (1943); J. H. Willis *Handb. Pls Vict.* 1:422 (1962); A. W. Dockrill *Australas. Sarcanth.* 18 (1967)

SYNONYMY: *S. montanus* R. D. FitzG. *Aust. Orchids* 1⁵:+t. (1879); *S. falcatus* var. *montanus* (R. D. FitzG.) F. M. Bailey *Qd Flor.* 5:1552 (1902)

Stems short, covered with the imbricate sheathing remains of fallen leaves. Leaves five to eight, oblong-falcate, 6–14 cm. long and 1·5–2·3 cm. broad, rather thick, channelled. Racemes usually one to three, hanging downward from under the leaves, the peduncles flexuose. Flowers three to ten per raceme, 3–5 cm. in diameter, white or cream, with various colour markings restricted to the labellum and column, and in some instances to the mid-rib of the perianth segments. Pedicels, including the ovary, 1·5–3 cm. long, the bracteole at the base ovate. Sepals and petals about equal, oblong-obtuse; the lateral sepals adnate to the column foot. Labellum small, the lateral lobes erect, ovate and often incurved at the apices, flushed with orange and streaked with red; mid-lobe very short and broad, the spur thick and fleshy, often marked with deep mauve; the bifid callus on the disc large and spotted. Column short, the foot 5–7 mm. long, streaked with red. Capsule large, terete and prominently ribbed, usually 6–7·5 cm. long. Flowers fragrant.

S. falcatus was at one time plentiful along the streams in eastern Vic., especially the Cann River and tributaries. It is now rarely seen, being confined to a few spots in the district; thus it appears doomed to vanish from this, its only Victorian habitat, unless drastic steps are taken to preserve it. The hosts of *S. falcatus* are numerous throughout its range, but here the author noted it on several *Acacia* species, also on the Tree Violet (*Hymenanthera dentata*) and *Pittosporum undulatum*. The Rock Felt-fern (*Pyrrosia rupestris*) is usually in association, the long roots of the orchid finding an ideal home in the matted wealth of fern growth.

FLOWERING PERIOD: Extending from July in the north to Nov. in the south

COMMON NAME: Orange-blossom Orchid

DISTRIBUTION: Extending from the Bloomfield River in northern Qld, south through NSW to far-eastern Vic.; usually in coastal ranges and often locally common

S. fitzgeraldii (Plate 454)

S. fitzgeraldii F. Muell. *Fragm. Phyt. Aust.* 7:115 (1870); H. M. R. Rupp *Orchids N.S.W.* 136 (1943); A. W. Dockrill *Australas. Sarcanth.* 18 (1967)

SYNONYMY: *S. fitzgeraldii* var. *aemulus* H. M. R. Rupp in *Proc. Linn. Soc. N.S.W.* 69:73 (1944)

Plant somewhat prostrate, branching, growing chiefly on rocks in deep shady ravines. Stems rather long, the bases scaly with the brownish clasping remains of fallen leaves. Roots often very long. Leaves long and clasping, falcate, narrowed upward, channelled, of moderately firm texture, yet not flaccid, 10–18 cm. long. Racemes arising from between the leaves, and below them on the old stem. Peduncle deep crimson; flowers often numerous, up to sixteen per raceme; perianth widely expanding, white or diffused with pale purple on the sepals and petals, spotted or otherwise marked at the base of the segments with crimson, rose or pink, 2·5–3 cm., occasionally 3·5 cm. in diameter. Pedicels pale green, 2·5–3 cm. long, the subtending bracteoles small, crimson. Sepals and petals about equal in length, but varying much in width; contracted at the base. Labellum small, orange marked with red, the lateral lobes erect, ovate, falcate, white marked finely with red; mid-lobe small, the spur short and blunt; disc with a large, very prominent channelled callus between the lobes, and a smaller one behind. Column short, marked with red. Pollinia four, in two pairs, attached by a short, broad stipe to a prominent gland. Flowers fragrant.

S. fitzgeraldii is an exceedingly graceful, free-flowering orchid. Fortunate indeed are those who have been able to visit its haunts, where it scrambles over the rocks to a length of as much as 120 cm. (4 ft.), often in great profusion. Its habit is pendulous; the racemes of showy flowers are thus seen to full advantage. The Ravine Orchid's home is a secluded one, well-sheltered by giant trees, palms, vines, ferns and other vegetation.

FLOWERING PERIOD: Oct. and Nov.

COMMON NAME: Ravine Orchid

DISTRIBUTION: Scattered over rocks and in ravines of south-eastern Qld and north-eastern NSW, once locally common but becoming rare due to extensive collecting

S. hartmannii (Plate 455)

S. hartmannii F. Muell. *Fragm. Phyt. Aust.* 8:248 (1874); H. M. R. Rupp *Orchids N.S.W.* 137 (1943); A. W. Dockrill *Australas. Sarcanth.* 19 (1967)

SYNONYMY: *S. rubicentrum* R. D. FitzG. *Aust. Orchids.* 2¹:+t. (1884)

Stems numerous, rather stout, erect, 5–10 cm. high, the base clothed with the strongly ribbed bases of fallen leaves. Leaves six to eight, thick and fleshy, 10–18 cm. long, oblong-lanceolate, prominently falcate, deeply channelled, the apex acute or obliquely emarginate. Peduncles erect, stout, darkly coloured, exceeding the leaves; flowers up to sixteen, about 3·5 cm. in diameter, white with crimson spots or blotches restricted to the centre of the perianth, sometimes the base of the perianth wholly crimson, blotched with deep maroon, or the flowers wholly crimson or wholly pure white; pedicels up to 2 cm. long, finely spotted with red; bracteoles acute, green. Perianth segments oblong, the sepals usually wider than the petals; labellum small with a large blunt spur, white suffused with yellow; the lateral lobes prominently marked with red lines, etc.; mid-lobe erect, obtuse, a large bifid yellow gland on the disc, with two smaller conjoined ovate white ones at the rear. Column stout, blotched with red, pollinia four.

S. hartmannii grows in full sunshine on cliffs and rock ledges, or occasionally on the bark at the butts of trees, with its roots penetrating the top layer of leaves and soil.

FLOWERING PERIOD: Sept. to Nov.

DISTRIBUTION: Extending from south-eastern Qld to the Hunter River in NSW; usually near the coast and now becoming uncommon because of extensive collecting

S. ceciliae (Plates 456 and 457)

S. ceciliae F. Muell. *Fragm. Phyt. Aust.* 5:42, t. 42 (1865); H. M. R. Rupp *Orchids N.S.W.* 137 (1943); A. W. Dockrill *Australas. Sarcanth.* 19 (1967)

SYNONYMY: *Thrixspermum ceciliae* (F. Muell.) Reichenb.f. *Beitr. syst. Pflk.* 71 (1871); *S. eriochilus* R. D. FitzG. in *J. Bot., Lond.* 29:153 (1891)

Stems erect, slender, leafy, rather short, often forming large clumps on rocks or trees. Leaves linear, linear-lanceolate or lanceolate, rather thick, 6–12 cm. long, green, often marked and spotted with brown, or becoming deep reddish-brown. Peduncles slender, erect, 10–18 cm. long, bearing above the middle a loose raceme of from six to fifteen flowers, pale pink, mauve-pink or purple. Pedicels short, rarely long. Bracteoles minute. Lateral sepals almost ovate, 8–12 mm. long, adnate to the long foot of the column. Dorsal sepal about the same length as the lateral sepals, but narrower. Petals narrower still. Labellum small, the lateral lobes oblong-falcate, the mid-lobe shorter than the lateral ones, thick and prominently tomentose on the surface; the dorsal spur broadly obtuse; disc with several golden-hued calli more or less adnate to the lateral lobes. Column small, the foot prominent. Pollinia four in two pairs.

A variable species in growth habit and flower form; two subspecies are recognised, one of them of two varieties.

FLOWERING PERIOD: Nov. to Jan., but sometimes as late as Mar.

DISTRIBUTION: Extending from the Atherton Tableland in northern Qld, south as far as the Hastings River in NSW, seldom below 450 m. (1,500 ft.)

S. hillii (Plate 458)

S. hillii (F. Muell.) F. Muell. *Fragm. Phyt. Aust.* 2:94 (1860); H. M. R. Rupp *Orchids N.S.W.* 138 (1943); A. W. Dockrill *Australas. Sarcanth.* 20 (1967)

SYNONYMY: *Dendrobium hillii* F. Muell. *Fragm. Phyt. Aust.* 1:88 (1859); *Thrixspermum hillii* (F. Muell.) Reichenb.f. *Beitr. syst. Pflk.* 71 (1871); *S. minutiflos* F. M. Bailey *Compreh. Cat. Qd Pls* 845, t. 974 (1913)

A small epiphyte, the stems short. Leaves narrow-linear, often spotted, channelled, fleshy, 2·5–15 cm. long. Racemes slender, usually shorter than the leaves; flowers few, one to six, pale pink or white, 1–1·3 cm. in diameter, very fragrant. Pedicels short. Sepals ovate or ovate-oblong. Petals about same length as sepals but usually narrower. Labellum shorter than the other segments, sessile or almost so, on the short foot of the column; lateral lobes oblong; mid-lobe broader than long but variable, retuse, thickly covered on the upper surface with short white glandular hairs; spur narrow-conical, longer than the lateral lobes, the disc with very prominent orange coloured calli. Column short, the upper margins toothed in some flowers. Anther mauve.

S. hillii grows on the trunks and twigs of small trees (*Melaleuca styphelioides* and *Backhousia myrtifolia* chiefly). It is a common plant in many brushes, but nevertheless the dainty blooms are little gems.

FLOWERING PERIOD: Nov. to Feb.

DISTRIBUTION: From central eastern Qld, south to Bega in NSW, often locally common, but inconspicuous

S. olivaceus (Plate 459)

S. olivaceus Lindl. in *Edwards' bot. Reg.* 25: Misc. 32 (1839); H. M. R. Rupp *Orchids N.S.W.* 134 (1943); A. W. Dockrill *Australas. Sarcanth.* 20 (1967)

SYNONYMY: *Thrixspermum olivaceum* (Lindl.) Reichenb.f. *Xenia orchid.* 2:122 (1865)

A plant of similar habit to *S. falcatus* but stems shorter. Leaves oblong, usually broad, falcate, dark green, often purplish, flat and undulate, texture thin, 8–12 cm. long and 2·3–3 cm. wide. Racemes several, axillary, not exceeding the leaves; peduncle flexuose, the bracts small; flowers usually not exceeding twelve, olive-green or golden-green, 2·5–3 cm. in diameter. Sepals and petals linear-oblong, widely dilated, contracted below the middle; lateral sepals dilated at the base and adnate to the foot of the column. Labellum about half as long as the sepals, whitish, marked with red-brown, its base attached on a short wide claw, trilobed, the lateral lobes oblong-falcate; mid-lobe very short and orbicular; spur short, fleshy, blunt; disc with several very prominent calli between the lobes. Column short, with a long foot. Pollinia four. Capsule slender.

In Qld this fragrant orchid is known as the Lawyer-orchid, because it is found, abundantly, on the so-called 'Lawyer vines'. It has other varied hosts, viz. Myrtle (*Backhousia* sp.), *Araucaria cunninghamii*, *Trochocarpa laurina*, *Pseudomorus brunoniana*, *Pittosporum undulatum* and *Citriobatus multiflorus*. It also grows on rocks, where the roots penetrate deep into the surrounding soil; the plants themselves are healthy and in many instances exceedingly robust.

FLOWERING PERIOD: From July to Sept. in northern Qld, Oct. to Nov. in southern NSW

DISTRIBUTION: Extending from the upper Bloomfield River in northern Qld, south as far as Bega, NSW; sometimes locally abundant

S. olivaceus var. **borealis** (Plate 460)

S. olivaceus var. *borealis* W. H. Nicholls in *N. Qd Nat.* *860*:1, fig. A, B (1939); A. W. Dockrill *Australas. Sarcanth.* 20 (1967)

Plant similar in all respects to the typical form. Inflorescence exceeding the leaves in length. Flowers 2 cm. in diameter, in a loose raceme. Sepals and petals green (darker than in the typical form), suffused with yellow towards the centre, and markedly blotched towards the base with deep red-brown—the blotchings more intense on the reverse side. Sepals wider than in typical flowers; the dorsal sepal similar in shape to that in *S. dilatatus*. Petals only half as wide as sepals. Labellum with a white ground, generously blotched and marked with dark red-brown. Flowers very fragrant.

The whole appearance of this variety is strongly suggestive of *S. dilatatus*, and it may have been confused with that species.

FLOWERING PERIOD: Oct. and Nov.

DISTRIBUTION: Northern Qld, from the upper Johnston River to the upper Bloomfield River

S. **dilatatus** (Plate 461)

S. dilatatus F. Muell. *Fragm. Phyt. Aust.* 1:191 (1859); H. M. R. Rupp *Orchids N.S.W.* 136 (1943), in note; A. W. Dockrill *Australas. Sarcanth.* 20 (1967)

SYNONYMY: *S. bancroftii* F. M. Bailey *Compreh. Cat. Qd Pls* 532 (1913)

Stems short, covered with the scarious sheathing bases of fallen leaves. Roots long and numerous. Leaves lanceolate, often falcate, 6–9 cm. long. Racemes longer than the leaves, flowers four to seven, distant, 1·2–1·5 cm. in diameter; peduncle flexuose, the pedicels (including ovary) about 1 cm. long; subtending bracteoles small. Sepals and petals widely spreading, dilated at the base, green, blotched with red-brown; sepals bluntly spathulate, rhomboidal; lateral sepals adnate to the column foot; petals somewhat similar in shape to the sepals, but shorter and much narrower. Labellum white, trilobed; lateral lobes erect, broadly oblong, oblique, about 4 mm. long, exceeding the column and clasping it with the posterior margins, the apex white; basal portion prominently marked with red stripes, orange-brown on the inside, and on the outer margins; mid-lobe thick and blunt, mottled with orange-brown; spur short and blunt; disc with a conical callus on each side, arising from the base of the lateral lobes and with a bluntly recurved process at the rear. Column short with a prominent foot, marked with red-brown. Flowers fragrant.

My material of this species came from Mount French, south-eastern Qld—a solitary plant which flowered in the open, under tree ferns in Melbourne. This plant was recorded as growing on an *Acacia* sp. near the summit.

Bentham includes *S. dilatatus* under *S. olivaceus*, and Bailey in *Qd Flor.* follows him. The two species are however quite distinct.

FLOWERING PERIOD: Aug. to Nov.

DISTRIBUTION: Extending from the Eidsvold district of south-eastern Qld, at least as far south as Casino, north-eastern NSW

S. **australis** (Plate 462)

S. australis (Lindl.) Reichenb.f. in Walp. *Ann. Bot. syst.* 6:501 (1863); A. J. Ewart *Flor. Vict.* 310 (1931), as *S. parviflorus*; H. M. R. Rupp *Orchids N.S.W.* 134 (1943); J. H. Willis *Handb. Pls Vict.* 1:422 (1962); M. J. Firth *Native Orchids Tasm.* 9 (1965); A. W. Dockrill *Australas. Sarcanth.* 21 (1967)

SYNONYMY: *Gunnia australis* Lindl. in *Edwards' bot. Reg.* 20: sub t. 1699 (1834); *S. parviflorus* Lindl. in *Edwards' bot. Reg.* 24: Misc. 34 (1838)

Habit similar to *S. falcatus*, but sometimes much larger (especially those from the Dandenong Ranges, Vic.). Stem short, about 2 cm. long, the base covered with the imbricate remains of fallen leaves. Leaves five to fifteen, narrower and usually of a deeper green than in *S. falcatus*, narrow-oblong falcate, 5–15 cm. long. Scapes much longer than the leaves, bearing from five to seventeen pale yellowish-green or green flowers with brown markings; the labellum comparatively large, white with various colour markings. Pedicels 1–1·3 cm. long. Sepals narrow-oblong, 1–1·4 cm. long, the lateral ones adnate to the foot of the column. Petals rather shorter than the sepals. Labellum almost sessile on the column foot, the lateral lobes ovate-oblong, often nearly as long as the sepals; mid-lobe very small, the spur conical or obovoid, at least as long as the lateral lobes; lamina with several prominent calli. Column spotted in its lower portion. Capsule linear, 2–3 cm. long.

S. australis is a very charming epiphyte, a gem of the forest and deep mountain gullies. To see this orchid at its best one must see it *in situ*. In the Dandenongs at Fern Tree Gully, Vic., where there are two forms, the majority of the plants are high in the branches, far from the reach of wanton hands. There is the typical form, which is depicted here, and the robust plant which produces larger dark-hued flowers. The lateral sepals and petals in the latter form are more rigidly dilated than in the typical form. *S. australis* has many hosts, the Musk, Hazel, Pomaderris, Sassafras, Pittosporum and the Blackwood are a few.

The flowers are delicately and sweetly fragrant.

FLOWERING PERIOD: Oct. to Jan., but sometimes as late as Mar.

COMMON NAME: Butterfly Orchid

DISTRIBUTION: Extending from north-eastern NSW, south to eastern Vic. and the Otway Ranges; also western and north-western Tas. and several Bass Strait islands; often locally abundant. Doubtfully recorded from Qld

57   *Parasarcochilus*

Parasarcochilus A. W. Dockrill *Australas. Sarcanth.* 22 (1967)

Small epiphytes, with short stems and leaves. Inflorescences racemose. Flowers widely expanding. Sepals more or less similar, the lateral ones joined, at least in part, to the column foot. Petals slightly smaller than the sepals. Labellum articulate at the apex of the column foot, trilobed, spurred, no calli present but a slight swelling at the base of the disc; lateral lobes erect, long and slender and more or less oblong but broadest at the apex; mid-lobe on top of the base of the spur, very small or even vestigial; spur projected forward as in *Sarcochilus*, well developed or reduced to a small sac and either hollow or fleshy. Column short, with a foot at least twice its length, almost at right angles to it. Pollinia four in two closely appressed pairs, the members of each pair unequal; stipe about the same length as the pollinia, slightly dilated at the apex; retinaculum about half the length of the pollinia. [Adapted from A. W. Dockrill *Australas. Sarcanth.* 22 (1967).—Ed.]

A small genus of three species, all confined to eastern Australia.

P. spathulatus (Plate 463)

P. spathulatus (R. S. Rogers) A. W. Dockrill *Australas. Sarcanth.* 22, t. 8 (1967); H. M. R. Rupp *Orchids N.S.W.* 136 (1943), as *Sarcochilus spathulatus*

SYNONYMY: *Sarcochilus spathulatus* R. S. Rogers in *Trans. roy. Soc. S. Aust.* 51:1 (1927)

A small epiphyte. Roots elongated, filiform, flexuose. Stems very short and covered with the dry, persistent remains of fallen leaves. Leaves two to five, erect and spreading, falcate or elliptic-falcate, acute, 1–8 cm. long, gradually narrowing towards the base. Inflorescence small, flowers one to four, small, 1–1·4 cm. in diameter, greenish-yellow with purplish and brown markings, fragrant. Pedicel with ovary about 6 mm. long. Dorsal sepal oblong-elliptical, concave, blunt; lateral sepals bluntly oblong, joined in part to the column foot. Petals bluntly falcate; labellum cream, attached by a short movable claw to tip of the column foot, trilobed; lateral lobes large, erect, narrow-oblong or linear-spathulate, 4–5 mm. long, much longer than the mid-lobe, and exceeding the anther in height, abruptly dilated at the apices; mid-lobe short, cushion-like, with an inturned tooth, its anterior margins convex, purple and pubescent, with two purple vertical tooth-like markings immediately below it, the spur flat, blunt, oblong, hollow, glabrous inside. Column very short, the foot slender, elongated. Pollinia four.

[Superficially this species is close to *S. olivaceus* but it lacks the large callus on the disc, and the calli at the base of the lateral lobes. These features actually distinguish this genus from *Sarcochilus*.—Ed.]

FLOWERING PERIOD: July to Oct.

DISTRIBUTION: Extending from the Bunya Mountains of south-eastern Qld, south as far as the Hunter River, NSW; generally near the coast

P. weinthalii (Plates 464 and 465)

P. weinthalii (F. M. Bailey) A. W. Dockrill *Australas. Sarcanth.* 23, t. 9 (1967); H. M. R. Rupp *Orchids N.S.W.* 134 (1943), as *Sarcochilus weinthalii*

SYNONYMY: *Sarcochilus weinthalii* F. M. Bailey in *Qd agric. J.* 13:346 (1903); *S. longmanii* F. M. Bailey in *Qd agric. J.* 23:261 (1909)

Stems short. Roots white and fleshy. Leaves about five, somewhat curled and spreading, 7–9 cm. long and 2–2·3 cm. broad, obtuse or somewhat acute. Racemes longer than the leaves, bearing four to fifteen white or cream, prominently spotted, fragrant flowers. Bracts narrow-lanceolate, 5–7 mm. long, sometimes with a dark spot near the middle. Pedicel, including the ovary, 1 cm. long, dotted. Sepals and petals similar, the latter shorter, oblong, obtuse, marked along the back with one to several, sometimes large, dark spots, which show through to the front; each segment also marked at the base with a cluster of smaller spots. Labellum sessile, at the end of the column foot; lateral lobes linear, falcate, incurved and meeting at or above the anther, dotted purple inside; mid-lobe almost globular, velvety-glandular on the back with a large purple spot at the centre; disc with a few short purple lines and two yellow

spots at the base; sides woolly-glandulose. Column yellowish-green, about 2–5 mm. high. Anther pale yellow, rostrate. Pollinia ovoid, yellow.

[Of the two plates depicting this species, Plate 465 depicts an atypical form from Toowoomba, Qld, unusual in the hairy labellum and long, slender perianth segments. W. H. Nicholls painted this form as *Sarcochilus longmanii*, the plants coming from the type locality near Toowoomba.—Ed.]

FLOWERING PERIOD: Aug. to Oct.

DISTRIBUTION: Limited to a small area of south-eastern Qld and north-eastern NSW, generally uncommon

58   *Mobilabium*

Mobilabium H. M. R. Rupp in *N. Qd Nat.* 13[78]:2, fig. 1–5 (1946)

[A monotypic genus confined to tropical Qld. Its main distinction is the large fleshy callus, adnate to the lateral lobes of the labellum and completely filling the disc.—Ed.]

M. hamatum (Plate 466)

M. hamatum H. M. R. Rupp in *N. Qd Nat.* 13[78]:4, fig. 1–5 (1946); A. W. Dockrill *Australas. Sarcanth.* 24 (1967)

A small epiphyte, with long stems up to 35 cm. Leaves small, well spaced, persistent, 4–7 cm. long, rigid, their apices hooked or even revolute. Inflorescence short, racemose. Flowers small, pale yellowish-green with brown blotches and other markings on labellum and column. Sepals about 3 mm. long, similar; the dorsal sepal slightly concave. Petals slightly shorter and narrower. Labellum hinged to the upturned point of the column foot by a short very mobile claw, bilobed; lateral lobes large, erect; spur broad-cylindrical, fleshy; disc with a very large callus which appears to be an extension of the fleshy spur and which is adnate to the proximal half of the lateral lobes. Column spotted, short with a well-developed foot; foot more or less vertical with a short hook at the apex. Pollinia four in two pairs. [Adapted from A. W. Dockrill *Australas. Sarcanth.* 24 (1967).—Ed.]

FLOWERING PERIOD: June to Sept.

DISTRIBUTION: Restricted to the highland areas of northern Qld, in the vicinity of the Atherton Tableland

59   *Peristeranthus*

Peristeranthus T. E. Hunt in *Qd Nat.* 15:17, fig. A–I (1954)

[A monotypic genus confined to eastern Australia. Its chief distinction is the hollow spur at the rear of the labellum, which has an erect finger-like callus projecting from the thickened anterior wall.—Ed.]

P. hillii (Plate 467)

P. hillii (F. Muell.) T. E. Hunt in *Qd Nat.* 15:17, fig. A–I (1954); H. M. R. Rupp *Orchids N.S.W.* 130 (1943), as *Ornithochilus hillii*; A. W. Dockrill *Australas. Sarcanth.* 24 (1967)

SYNONYMY: *Saccolabium hillii* F. Muell. *Fragm. Phyt. Aust. 1*:192 (1859); *Ornithochilus hillii* (F. Muell.) Benth. in *J. Linn. Soc. (Bot.) 18*:334 (1881)

Semi-pendulous epiphytes. Stems rigid, flexuose, often long; covered with the prominent, deeply ribbed bases of fallen leaves. Roots often long, fairly thick and numerous. Leaves distichous, rigid in some plants, nerves prominent; 6–20 cm. long and 2–5 cm. broad. Racemes pendent, often as long as the leaves; flowers small, numerous on very short pedicels, greenish with brown markings; sepals and petals oblong-linear, all about 3 mm. long, falcate, incurved; lateral sepals adnate to the column foot; labellum bilobed, yellowish with brown markings, nearly as long as the sepals; spur short and broad, with an erect finger-like callus from the base of the anterior wall; lamina concave and embracing the column, much broader than long, truncate, without any mid-lobe; lateral lobes shortly acuminate, incurved. Column short, foot long. Pollinia waxy, globular, four in two pairs.

Schlechter had considered creating the genus *Fitzgeraldiella* for this species but he died before doing so.

FLOWERING PERIOD: Mainly Sept. and Oct., but erratic

DISTRIBUTION: A fairly widespread species, extending from the Bloomfield River in northern Qld, as far south as Port Macquarie, NSW; coastal and often locally abundant

60 *Thrixspermum*

Thrixspermum Lour. *Flor. cochinch. 2*:519 (1790)

Epiphytes with either short stems and a few leaves close together, or elongated stems and many well spaced leaves. Inflorescences racemose, either short or long. Floral bracts variable. Flowers large or medium, fugacious, borne in succession, one or a few at a time. Sepals and petals more or less equal, short or long and narrow. Labellum immovably joined to the column foot, saccate, trilobed, the sac produced posteriorly so that it is almost a spur, with a short thick callus on the anterior wall near the opening and directed towards the front of the labellum; lateral lobes erect; mid-lobe short or long, usually fleshy. Column short, more or less enclosed within the lateral lobes of the labellum, the foot short and broad. Pollinia four, unequal, in two pairs. [Adapted from A. W. Dockrill *Australas. Sarcanth. 25* (1967).—Ed.]

A widespread genus of at least fifty species, extending from India through Malaysia, Indonesia and New Guinea to Australia, where there are two endemic species.

T. congestum (Plate 468)

T. congestum (F. M. Bailey) A. W. Dockrill *Australas. Sarcanth. 27*, t. 35 (1967)

SYNONYMY: *Cleisostoma congestum* F. M. Bailey in *Proc. roy. Soc. Qd 11*:17 (1895); *Thrixspermum album* H. M. R. Rupp in *N. Qd Nat. 9*:1 (1940), non (Ridley) Schlechter (1911)

Stems short, the longest seen under 5 cm., the lower part covered by scarious bases of fallen leaves. Leaves two to twelve, alternate, linear-oblong, obtuse-acuminate, base more or less cuneate, the longest about 4 cm. long and 7–9 mm. broad; veins in the live leaf obscure, but both the longitudinal ribs and cross veins plainly visible in dried specimens. Peduncle usually longer than the leaves, 6–9 cm., with one or two scarious sheathing bracts at the base,

and one or two or none between these and the bracteoles subtending the flowers. Bracts broad, fleshy, pointed. Flowers white, crowded at the apex, forming a head, but opening one or two at a time, very fragrant, on pedicels about 1 cm. long. Perianth segments all incurved, resembling some small-flowered *Dendrobiums*. Sepals broad-lanceolate, 7–8 mm. long. Petals narrow-linear, slightly shorter than sepals. (In one flower examined the dorsal sepal and petals were united to the middle—see plate.) Labellum about as long as the sepals, the lateral lobes long and broad, the mid-lobe reduced to a truncate end; margins and upper surface of labellum covered with short glandular cilia, the central appendage broad with ciliate margins and a recurved coloured point. Labellum lamina marked on both sides with dark spots. Sac broad, obtuse, stained with yellow, a transverse plate at the orifice. Column short and broad, the foot as long as the column. Pollinia oval, yellow, stipe short and broad. Capsule about 6·4 cm. long.

FLOWERING PERIOD: Mainly Aug. to Dec.

DISTRIBUTION: Confined to north-eastern Qld, where found between the Bloomfield and Tully Rivers

61 *Plectorrhiza*

Plectorrhiza A. W. Dockrill *Australas. Sarcanth. 27* (1967)

Small epiphytes with long wiry stems, relatively persistent leaves and numerous and often tangled roots. Flowers small, sepals and petals free, more or less of equal length. Labellum immovably joined to the very short column foot, saccate, trilobed, spurred; spur either in line with the column or at right angles to it, a hirsute finger-like callus attached to the anterior wall near the orifice and projecting towards the apex of the spur; lateral lobes small, not touching the column; mid-lobe rather small, either hollow like the toe of a shoe or fleshy. Column erect, not winged. Rostellum long, projected forward. Anther with a long recurved or reflexed rostrum. Pollinia four in two closely appressed, even pairs; stipe two to three times the length of the pollinia, slightly dilated near the apex, retinaculum attached to the ventral surface of the rostellum, small, more or less ovate. [Adapted from A. W. Dockrill *Australas. Sarcanth. 27* (1967).—Ed.]

A small genus of three species, two of which are confined to eastern Australia and the third to Lord Howe Island.

P. tridentata (Plate 469)

P. tridentata (Lindl.) A. W. Dockrill *Australas. Sarcanth. 27*, t. 14 (1967); H. M. R. Rupp *Orchids N.S.W.* 129 (1943), as *Sarcanthus tridentatus*; J. H. Willis *Handb. Pls Vict. 1*:421 (1962), as *Thrixspermum tridentatum*

SYNONYMY: *Cleisostoma tridentata* Lindl. *Edwards' bot. Reg. 24*: Misc. 33 (1838); *Sarcanthus tridentatus* (Lindl.) H. M. R. Rupp in *Vict. Nat. 57*:218 (1941); *Thrixspermum tridentatum* (Lindl.) T. E. Hunt in *Qd Nat. 16*:27 (1958)

Stems leafy, slender, often long, rarely branched. Roots numerous, arising from between the leaves, very long and curled, often in a tangled mass. Leaves 4–10 cm. long, usually linear-oblong, falcate. Racemes slender, flexuose, sometimes longer than the leaves. Bracts small. Flowers three to twelve, very small, fragrant, shortly pedicellate, 7 mm. to 1 cm. in diameter, green or green with red-brown markings. Sepals and petals oblong-lanceolate, the petals narrower than the sepals; lateral sepals and petals falcate; dorsal sepal hooded, broader than the lateral sepals; lateral sepals adnate to the short foot of the column. Labellum fleshy, varying in size but shorter than the sepals, the spur prominent and deflexed with a ciliate membrane inside; labellum lobes prominent, falcate, more or less acute, the mid-lobe short. Column short with two anterior narrow lobes in front. Pollinia four, attached to a long, very slender stipe. Capsule slender, falcate, $1 \cdot 5 - 3 \cdot 5$ cm. long.

P. tridentata grows in jungle country, always close to well-clad streams. It is a true air-plant, hanging from the twigs, both the green and the dead, of the host trees at various places in its range. In some northern plants the stipe of the pollinia may be short and broad (see plate). It is a common plant throughout its distribution.

FLOWERING PERIOD: Mainly Aug. to Jan., but erratic

COMMON NAME: Tangle Orchid

DISTRIBUTION: Extending from the Atherton Tableland in northern Qld, through NSW to far eastern Vic.; often locally abundant

P. erecta (Plate 470)

P. erecta (R. D. FitzG.) A. W. Dockrill *Australas. Sarcanth.* 28, t. 13 (1967)

SYNONYMY: *Cleisostoma erectum* R. D. FitzG. *Aust. Orchids* 1^4:+t. (1878); *Sarcanthus erectus* (R. D. FitzG.) H. M. R. Rupp in *Vict. Nat.* 57:218 (1941)

Stems erect, 24–30 cm. high. Leaves thick, sessile or shortly petiolate, distichous along the stem, oblong, channelled, $2 \cdot 5 - 4 \cdot 5$ cm. long, the apex thickened and deflexed. Roots long, thick, arising from below the leaves and descending to support the plant. Racemes very short, few-flowered; flowers small, ochraceous yellow, about 8 mm. in diameter, on moderately long pedicellate ovaries. Sepals and petals about equal in length, not spreading widely, oblong-lanceolate. Labellum large, white with a short, broad, truncate spur; mid-lobe obtuse; lateral lobes oblong-lanceolate, the gland within the spur ciliate. Column short and broad, purplish. Rostellum and anther points short. Pollinia four, attached to a moderately long stipe.

This interesting species was found by FitzGerald in 1869 and again in 1877. It is confined to Lord Howe Island, where it grows on rocks and the limbs of trees in the coastal areas, almost to the water mark.

FLOWERING PERIOD: Oct. to Dec.

DISTRIBUTION: Confined to the open scrubby areas of Lord Howe Island, where often locally plentiful

P. brevilabris (Plate 471)

P. brevilabris (F. Muell.) A. W. Dockrill *Australas. Sarcanth.* 28, t. 12 (1967)

SYNONYMY: *Cleisostoma brevilabre* F. Muell. *Fragm. Phyt. Aust.* 11:87 (1880); *Saccolabium brevilabre* (F. Muell.) H. M. R. Rupp in *Vict. Nat.* 57:219 (1941)

Stems often elongated, up to 50 cm., clothed with the brown sheaths of fallen leaves, the filiform roots numerous and long. Leaves from ovate to narrow-lanceolate, $5 \cdot 8$ cm. long, numerous on large plants. Racemes filiform, longer than the leaves, 8–13 cm. long, arising from between the leaves, chiefly towards the summit. Bracts deltoid or lanceolate, small. Pedicel, including ovary, 5 mm.–1 cm. long. Flowers small, about 1 cm. in diameter, eight to fourteen to a raceme, green marked with brown; sepals oblong, falcate; petals oblong, shorter than the sepals; labellum fleshy, the lateral lobes very small, semi-orbicular; mid-lobe almost conical;

spur about 5 mm. long, green. Column short. Capsule slender, 6–8 cm. long. Flowers strongly fragrant.

FLOWERING PERIOD: Nov. to Feb.

DISTRIBUTION: Eastern Qld generally, from the Bloomfield River in the north to the vicinity of the Noosa River in the south

62   *Pomatocalpa*

Pomatocalpa Breda *Gen. & Spec. Orchid. & Asclepiad.* t. 15 (1828–29)

Epiphytes with short or long stems which are sometimes climbing and have oblong or narrow leaves. Inflorescences short or long, erect or decurved, sometimes branched, usually densely many-flowered. Flowers small, facing the apex of the inflorescence. Sepals and petals subequal, free and more or less spreading. Labellum immovably attached to the base of the column or apex of the short column foot, trilobed, spurred near the base; lateral lobes small, posterior margins usually adnate, for a short distance, to the base of the column, broadly triangular, the anterior margins incurved; mid-lobe straight or decurved, fleshy, usually round or ovate-triangular; spur rounded, widening somewhat from the orifice, the anterior wall with a fleshy thickening, the posterior wall with a valvate callus arising from the middle, or lower, and extending to the orifice; the callus often with toothed upper margins, sometimes with its lateral margins adnate to the walls of the spur. Column short, with or without a foot. Rostellum small, bifid. Anther with a short rostrum. Pollinia four in two rounded bodies on a slender thin stipe, the margins of which curve backward; retinaculum small. [Adapted from A. W. Dockrill *Australas. Sarcanth.* 29 (1967).—Ed.]

A fairly large genus of about thirty species, extending from Burma, through Malaysia, Indonesia and some Pacific Islands to New Guinea and Australia, the latter with a single species endemic in the eastern tropical region.

P. macphersonii (Plate 472)

P. macphersonii (F. Muell.) T. E. Hunt in *Qd Nat.* 16:27, fig. A–H (1958); A. W. Dockrill *Australas. Sarcanth.* 29 (1967)

SYNONYMY: *Saccolabium macphersonii* F. Muell. *Fragm. Phyt. Aust.* 7:96 (1870); *Sarcanthus macphersonii* (F. Muell.) H. M. R. Rupp in *Vict. Nat.* 57:219 (1941)

Stems comparatively short, covered with the prominent bases of fallen leaves. Leaves 10–20 cm. long and $3 - 3 \cdot 5$ cm. broad, the veins inconspicuous, except the mid-rib, which forms an acute keel underneath; texture coarse, coriaceous, unevenly emarginate at the tip. Racemes short, rigid, the flowers rather numerous, shortly pedicellate, yellow, spotted with red. Sepals and petals rather thick, about 6 mm. long; petals a little shorter than the sepals, oblong-spathulate, obtuse. Column very short and broad, about 2 mm. high, not produced into a foot at the base. Labellum sessile, white, marked with red and yellow, the spur oblong, obtuse, rather dilated beyond the middle, about 5 mm. long, closed at the orifice by a large ovate plate close under the column; lamina short and broad, the mid-lobe orbicular, somewhat papillose, about 3 mm. in diameter, the lateral lobes short, falcate and narrow. Capsule oblong, strongly ribbed, $2 \cdot 5 - 3 \cdot 5$ cm. long.

Common in northern rain-forest areas, this species grows in shady, moist situations on almost any jungle tree that has a rough bark. Some of the *Ficus* species are favourite hosts.

FLOWERING PERIOD: July to Nov.

DISTRIBUTION: Northern Qld, from the Endeavour River to the Fitzroy River

63 Schistotylus

Schistotylus A. W. Dockrill *Australas. Sarcanth.* 29, t. 43 (1967)

A monotypic genus confined to north-eastern NSW. It is very closely related to *Saccolabiopsis*, differing chiefly in the callus within or overhanging the orifice of the spur, and the members of each pair of pollinia being equal.

S. purpuratus (Plate 473)

S. purpuratus (H. M. Rupp) A. W. Dockrill *Australas. Sarcanth.* 30, t. 43 (1967); H. M. R. Rupp *Orchids N.S.W.* 130 (1943), as *Sarcanthus purpuratus*

SYNONYMY: *Cleisostoma purpuratum* H. M. R. Rupp in *Vict. Nat.* 54:190 (1938); *Sarcanthus gemmatus* H. M. R. Rupp in *Vict. Nat.* 57:219 (1941); *S. purpuratus* (H. M. R. Rupp) H. M. R. Rupp in *Vict. Nat.* 58:41 (1941)

A small epiphyte similar to *Papillilabium beckleri*. Leaves three to six, linear-falcate, 2–4 cm. long. Flowers four to eight in the raceme; racemes more numerous than in *P. beckleri*. Sepals ovate-acute, nearly 3 mm. long, pale green with purplish-brown margins, and often a purple median line on the back. Petals hardly 2 mm. long, with conspicuously purplish-brown margins. Labellum white; lateral lobes broad and falcate; mid-lobe obtuse, thick, with orange spots; lamina very short. Spur as long as the sepals, with a ciliate callus inside the orifice. Column short; except for the white stigma, bright reddish-purple. Pollinia four in two pairs, stipe long.

On external appearance this species is very similar to *Papillilabium beckleri*, and probably has been confused with it in the field. Because of this it is possible that the distribution of *Schistotylus* is greater than indicated.

FLOWERING PERIOD: Sept. and Oct.

DISTRIBUTION: Apparently confined to north-eastern NSW, on the Dorrigo Plateau

64 Saccolabiopsis

Saccolabiopsis J. J. Smith in *Bull. Jard. bot. Buitenz.* sér. 2, 26:93 (1918)

Small epiphytic plants. Stems short. Leaves few, small, more or less flat. Inflorescence racemose, containing many small flowers which face the apex of the inflorescence; flowers green and lasting several days. Sepals and petals free, sub-similar, more or less oblong; lateral sepals oblique. Labellum immovably joined to the base of the column, spurred near the base, sub-trilobed, concave, lacking calli; lateral lobes very short but broad and barely distinguishable from the extension of the mid-lobe which is saccate and separated from the spur by a transverse keel. Column short; foot absent. Stigma large. Anther cucullate, its rostrum triangular. Pollinia four in two pairs, closely appressed, members of a pair unequal; stipe slightly dilated near the apex; retinaculum medium sized. [Adapted from A. W. Dockrill *Australas. Sarcanth.* 30 (1967).—Ed.]

A small genus of about seven species, one occurring in Java, five in New Guinea and one endemic in tropical eastern Australia.

S. armitii (Plate 474)

S. armitii (F. Muell.) A. W. Dockrill *Australas. Sarcanth.* 30, t. 20 (1967)

SYNONYMY: *Sarcochilus armitii* F. Muell. *Phragm. Phyt. Aust.* 9:49 (1875); *Saccolabium orbiculare* (H. M. R. Rupp) H. M. R. Rupp in *Vict. Nat.* 57:220 (1941); *S. armitii* (F. Muell.) H. M. R. Rupp in *Proc. Linn. Soc. N.S.W.* 76:56 (1951)

A small epiphyte, stem rather short. Leaves three to five, with a prominent keel, 5–6 cm. long. Racemes 3–6 cm. long, straight, spreading or slightly deflexed under the leaves. Flowers small, often very numerous, almost sessile, with narrow bracteoles, yellowish-green, marked with red, the labellum white. Dorsal sepal about 2 mm. long and 1 mm. broad, narrowed basally. Lateral sepals similar but longer and narrower, adnate to the very short column foot. Petals orbicular, about 1 mm. long. Labellum with a prominent basal spur, trilobed above; mid-lobe rounded with inturned margins; lateral lobes small, erect and rather sharply angular. Column about 1·5 mm. long. Anther prominent, red. Pollinia four, with a long slender stipe.

This species is not frequent in rain-forest, but prefers drier, open scrub areas.

FLOWERING PERIOD: Sept. to Dec.

DISTRIBUTION: Northern Qld from the coast to the inland ranges, between Princess Charlotte Bay and the Fitzroy River

65 Papillilabium

Papillilabium A. W. Dockrill *Australas. Sarcanth.* 31, t. 7 (1967)

A monotypic genus confined to central eastern Australia. Its chief distinction is in the column foot, which forms the back of the spur.

P. beckleri (Plate 475)

P. beckleri (F. Muell. ex Benth.) A. W. Dockrill *Australas. Sarcanth.* 31, t. 7 (1967); H. M. R. Rupp *Orchids N.S.W.* 130 (1943), as *Sarcanthus beckleri*

SYNONYMY: *Cleisostoma beckleri* F. Muell. ex Benth. *Flor. aust.* 6:296 (1873); *Sarcanthus beckleri* (F. Muell. ex Benth.) H. M. R. Rupp in *Vict. Nat.* 57:219 (1941); *Saccolabium virgatum* T. E. Hunt in *Qd Nat.* 15:50 (1955)

Epiphytic on the slender limbs of 'brush' trees. A diminutive plant with a very short rigid stem. Roots often flexuose and long, sometimes much thickened at the tips. Leaves about three, linear to narrow-lanceolate, 1·5–4 cm. long and 2–4 mm. wide. Racemes slender, 3–4 cm. long, flowers pale-greenish, very fragrant. Sepals 4–5 mm. long, incurved, the dorsal one erect, cucullate over the column, its apex often recurved; lateral sepals often adnate to the foot of column. Petals similar to the sepals. Labellum immovably joined to the end of the column foot; spur narrow, conical, hollow, about 3·5 mm. long, the orifice half closed by a transverse plate on the basal side; lamina short and broad; the lateral lobes erect, shorter than the spur, but about as wide, a dark spot towards the summit of each, joined to the lateral margins of the apical half of the column foot to form a long mentum (as in *Dendrobium*) which is unadorned with calli; mid-lobe shortly and broadly semi-orbicular, bifid or emarginate. Column erect, not winged, the foot about 3·5 mm. long. Pollinia four in two pairs.

E. Nubling, who sent my material, writes: '*P. beckleri* grows in brush forests on Water Gum (*Tristania laurina*), attached to slender twigs right over Narara Creek; mostly found thus, or close to water in moist gullies. Other host trees I have found this orchid on are *Trochocarpa laurina*, *Backhousia myrtifolia*, also less freely on *Eugenia smithii*, and *Doryphora sassafras*.'

FLOWERING PERIOD: Sept. to Dec.

DISTRIBUTION: Coastal areas of south-eastern Qld and north-eastern NSW

66 *Drymoanthus*

Drymoanthus W. H. Nicholls in *Vict. Nat.* 59:173, fig. A–L (1943)

A small genus of two species, one confined to the eastern tropics of Australia and the other to NZ. Its chief distinctions are that the labellum has no spur or free calli, and the mid-lobe is fleshy.

D. minutus (Plate 476)

D. minutus W. H. Nicholls in *Vict. Nat.* 59:175, fig. A–L (1943); A. W. Dockrill *Australas. Sarcanth.* 32 (1967)

A diminutive epiphyte. Stem very short, about 1 cm. long. Leaves flat, oblong-elliptic, 4–5 cm. long. Racemes shorter than leaves. Flowers very small, greenish, fragrant, labellum white. Sepals and petals free, spreading, linear-spathulate, falcate, concave, obtuse, more or less equal. Labellum sessile at the base of column, immobile, obovate, white, fleshy, margins entire; no basal spur; lamina traversed by a wide longitudinal channel, no callosities or glands on disc, anterior part pubescent; mid-lobe almost obsolete; an almost globular eminence below anterior margin of lamina. Column short, with two almost horizontal subulate teeth in front; no foot. Pollinia four in two pairs, sessile.

FLOWERING PERIOD: Dec. to Feb.

DISTRIBUTION: Endemic in northern Qld, where it is apparently confined to thick scrub on the Seaview and Bellenden Ker Ranges

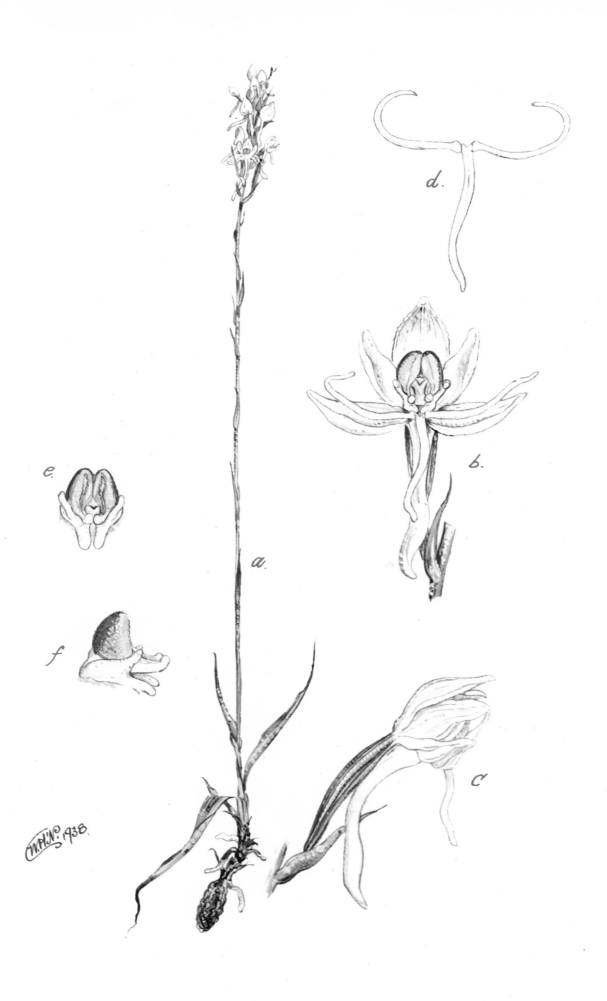

1 *Habenaria ferdinandii* (see also p. 1)

a flowering specimen from northern Qld **b** flower, from front **c** flower, from side **d** labellum lobes **e** column, from front **f** column, from side
Fig. **a** natural size

2 *Monadenia micrantha* (see also p. 1)

a specimen from Upper King River area, WA   **b** column and petals   **c** column and petals from side   **d** column and petals, showing anther (left)   **e** column, showing anther—pollinia removed   **f** pollinia   **g** column, showing stigma   **h** column wing, also rostellum and column wings   **i** flower and bract, from side   **j** labellum   **k** flower, from front
Fig. **a** natural size

3 *Thelymitra circumsepta* (see also p. 2)

a **b** two Mount Irvine, NSW, specimens—the smaller one without leaf **c** column, from front **d** **e** column heads, from above **f** anther-case **g** column, from side
h types of third column-lobe
Figs **a, b** natural size

4 *Thelymitra retecta* (see also p. 2)

a typical specimen **b** column, from rear **c** cross-section of leaf **d** column, from front **e** column, from side
Fig. **a** natural size

5 *Thelymitra ixioides* (see also p. 2)

a an outsize specimen of the typical form, from Wandin, Vic.   **b** a diminutive specimen (probably a young seedling) common on lightly-clad hillslopes   **c** stigma, with disc in place   **d** cross-section of leaf   **e** pollinia   **f** column, from side   **g** column, from above—hair-tufts removed
Figs **a, b, d** natural size

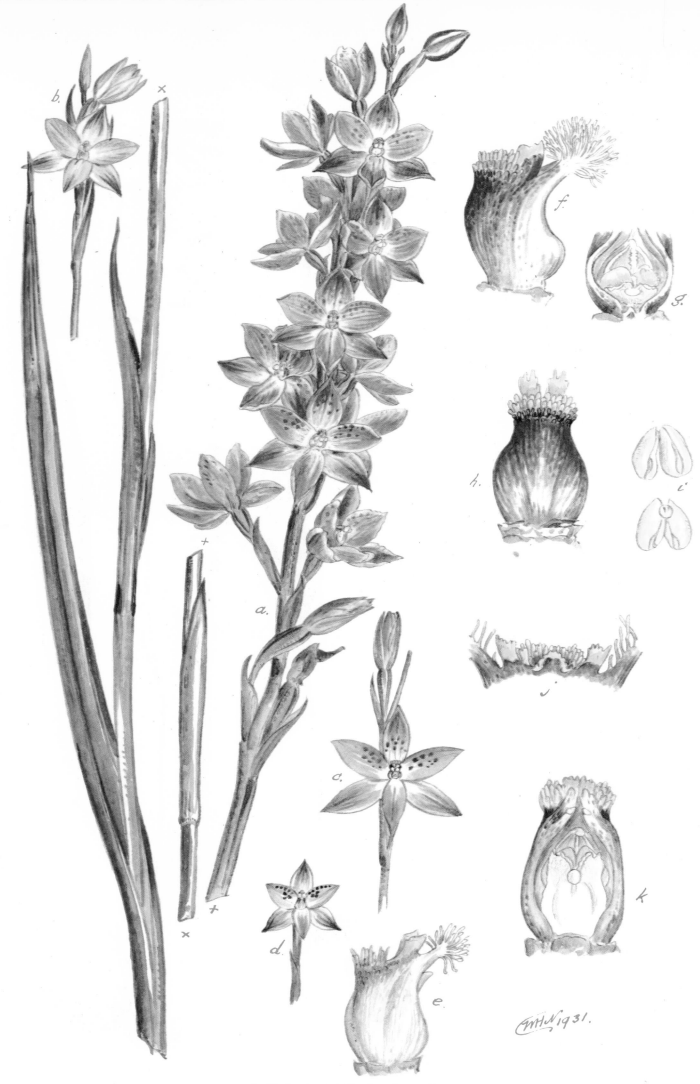

6 *Thelymitra ixioides* (see also p. 2)

a robust many-flowered form   **b** unspotted form   **c d** two flower types   **e** column, (from flower of Fig. **d**—a form not uncommon in the Hume Vale district, near Whittlesea, Vic.)   **f** column, from side (of a robust form such as Fig. **a**)   **g** column showing pollinia ready for removal   **h** column, from rear—hair-tufts removed   **i** pollinia, two positions   **j** head of column—spread out   **k** column, from front—hair-tufts removed

Figs **a–d** natural size

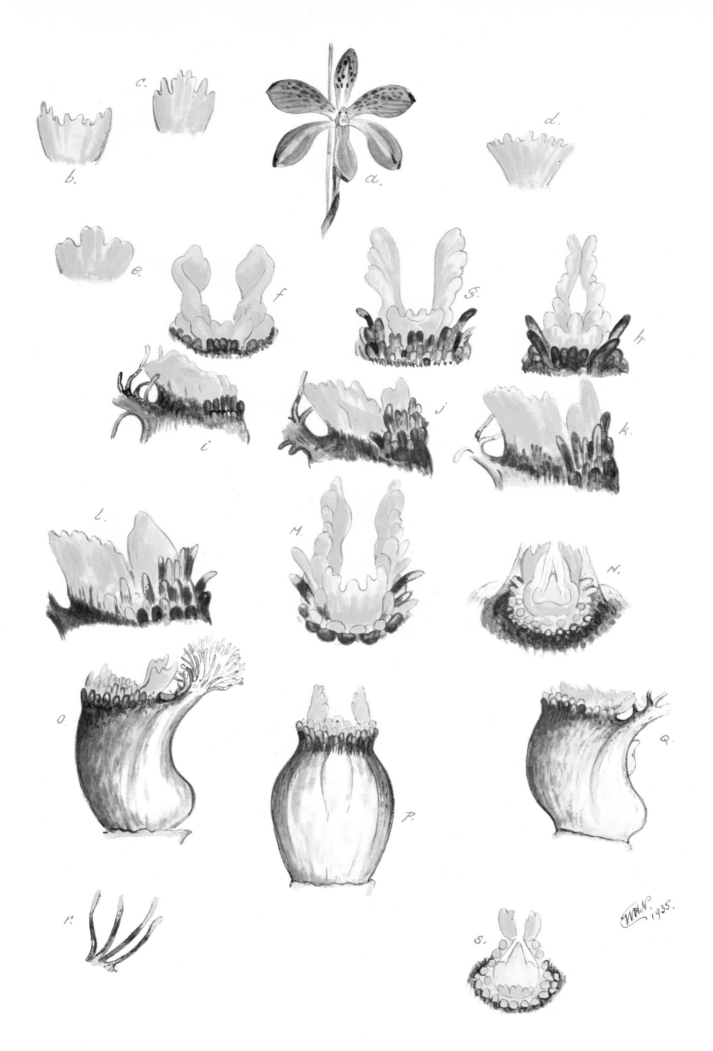

7 *Thelymitra ixioides* (see also p. 2)

a flower with very narrow segments **b c d e** figures depicting the considerable variation in form to which the mid-lobe region of the column is subject **f g h** some remarkable shapes of the mid-lobe, from above **i j k l** forms of the mid-lobe **m** mid-lobe, from above **n** fusion of sections of the mid-lobe, from above **o** typical column, from side **p** column, from rear—hair-tufts removed **q** column, from side—hair-tufts removed—same column as Fig. **n**, from side **r** hairs from lateral lobes **s** another column, from above

Fig. **a** natural size

8 *Thelymitra ixioides* var. *subdifformis* (see also p. 2)

a specimen from Portland, Vic. (type locality)   **b** column, from side   **c** column, from front—hair-tufts removed
Fig. **a** natural size

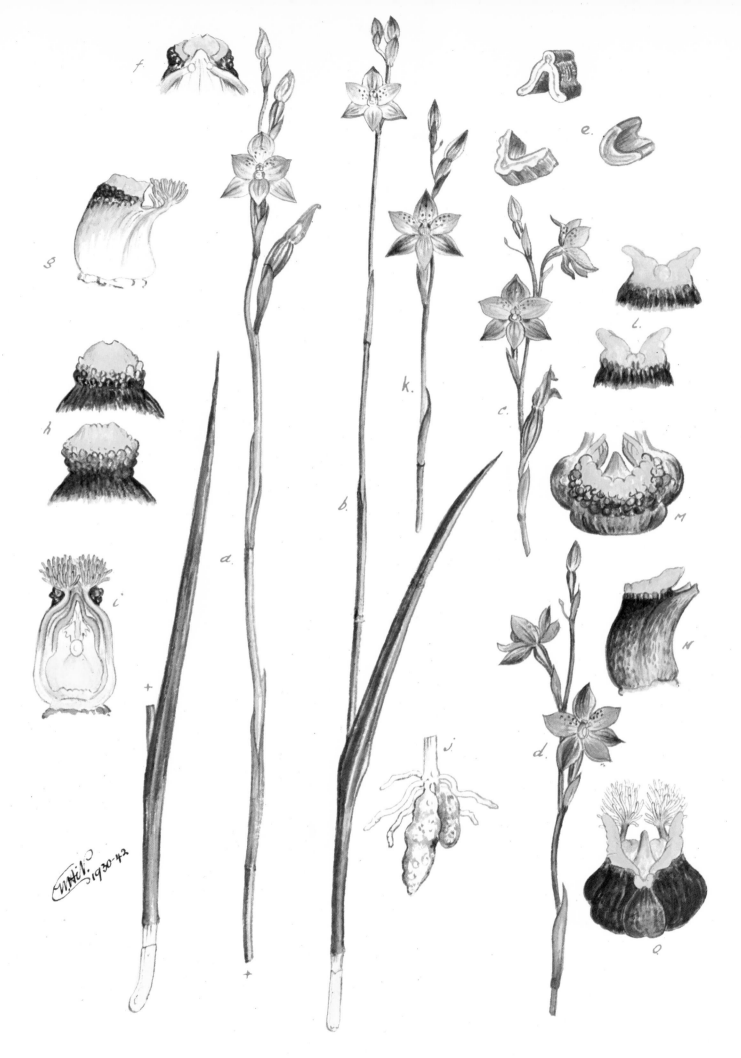

9 *Thelymitra ixioides* var. *truncata*: Figs **a–j** (see also p. 2)
T. ixioides forma *merranae*: Figs **k–o** (see also p. 2)

a specimen from Wonthaggi, Vic. **b** specimen from Ringwood, Vic. **c** one from Pyrete Ranges, near Gisborne, Vic. **d** one from Staughton Vale at the eastern foot of the Brisbane Ranges, Vic. **e** cross-sections of leaves (variable in both forms) **f** column mid-lobe, from front—hair-tufts removed **g** typical column, from side **h** column mid-lobes, from rear **i** column, from front **j** tubers **k** a specimen from Airey's Inlet, Vic. **l** column mid-lobes, from rear **m** another column, from above (intermediate) **n** column, from side, with hair-tufts removed **o** column, from above
Figs **a–d, j, k** natural size

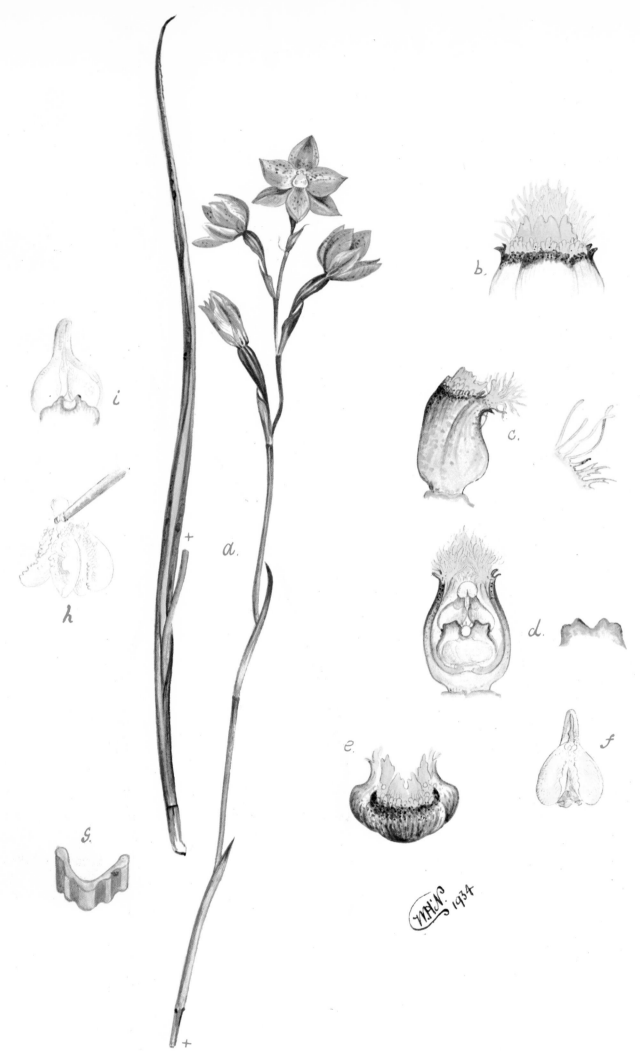

10 *Thelymitra irregularis* (see also p. 3)

a the type specimen   **b** column mid-lobe, from rear   **c** column, from side, also characteristic cilia from the lateral lobes   **d** column, from front, also upper margin of stigma
e column, from above—lateral lobes removed   **f** pollinia and anther—from a bud   **g** cross-section of leaf   **h** pollinia   **i** pollinia in position, upper margin of stigma also showing
Fig. **a** natural size

11 *Thelymitra media* (see also p. 3)

a a superior specimen from Heathmont, Vic.   **b** column, from front—hair-tufts removed   **c** cross-section of leaf   **d** column, from side   **e** column, from above—hair-tufts removed

Fig. **a** natural size

12

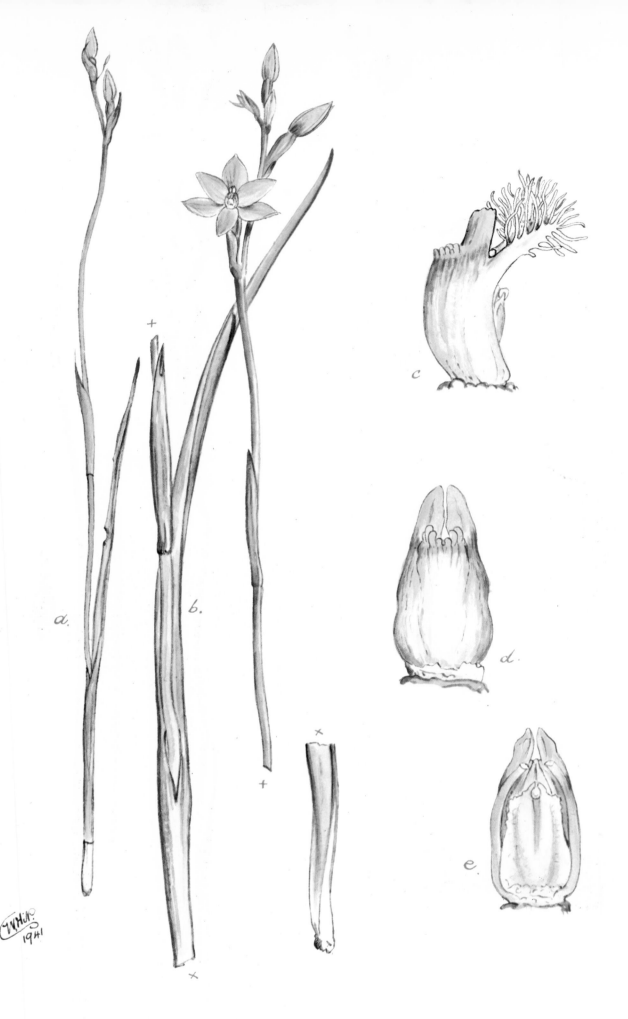

13 *Thelymitra media* var. *carneo-lutea* (see also p. 3)

a specimen in bud **b** robust specimen **c** column, from side **d** column, from rear **e** column, from front—hair-tufts removed
Figs **a, b** natural size

12 *Thelymitra media* (see also p. 3)

a an excellent example from Silvan, Vic. **b c** two plants from Foster, Vic. **d** a flower with bright colour markings, from rear **e** a column, from side **f** head of column,
from above—hair-tufts removed **g** column, from front—hair-tufts removed **h** cross-section of leaf **i** pollinia **j** column, from side **k** same, from front **l** head of
column, from above—hair-tufts removed
Figs **a–c** natural size

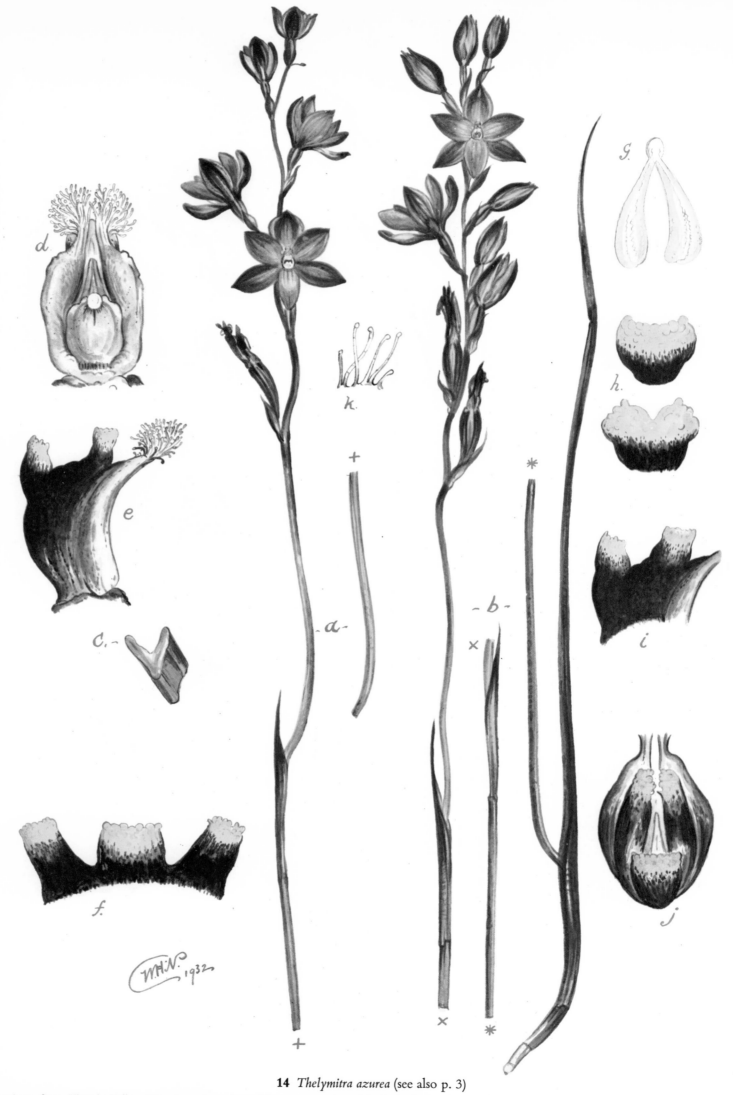

14 *Thelymitra azurea* (see also p. 3)

a specimen from Victoria Valley, Vic. **b** specimen from SA **c** cross-section of leaf **d** column, from front **e** column, from side **f** lobes of column **g** pollinia
h variation in the mid-lobe **i** upper part of column—hair-tufts not shown **j** column, from above—hair-tufts removed **k** cilia from the lateral lobes
Figs **a, b** natural size

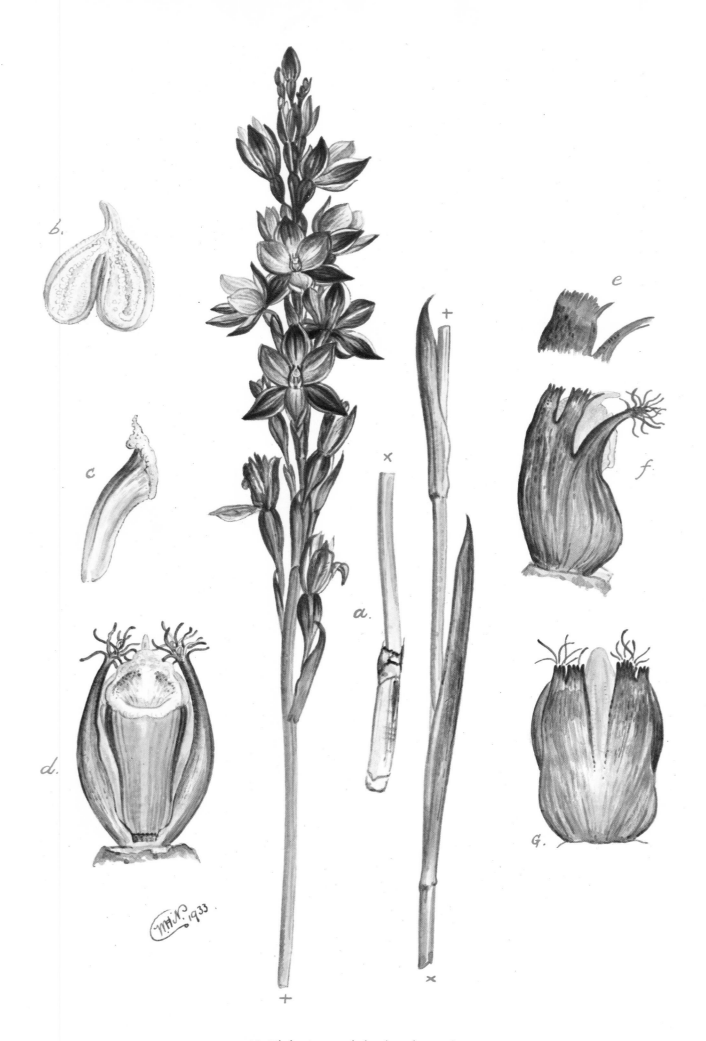

15 *Thelymitra murdochae* (see also p. 4)

a type specimen **b** pollinia in position in anther-case **c** stigma, from side **d** column, from front **e** head of column, from side **f** column, from side **g** column, from rear
Fig. **a** natural size

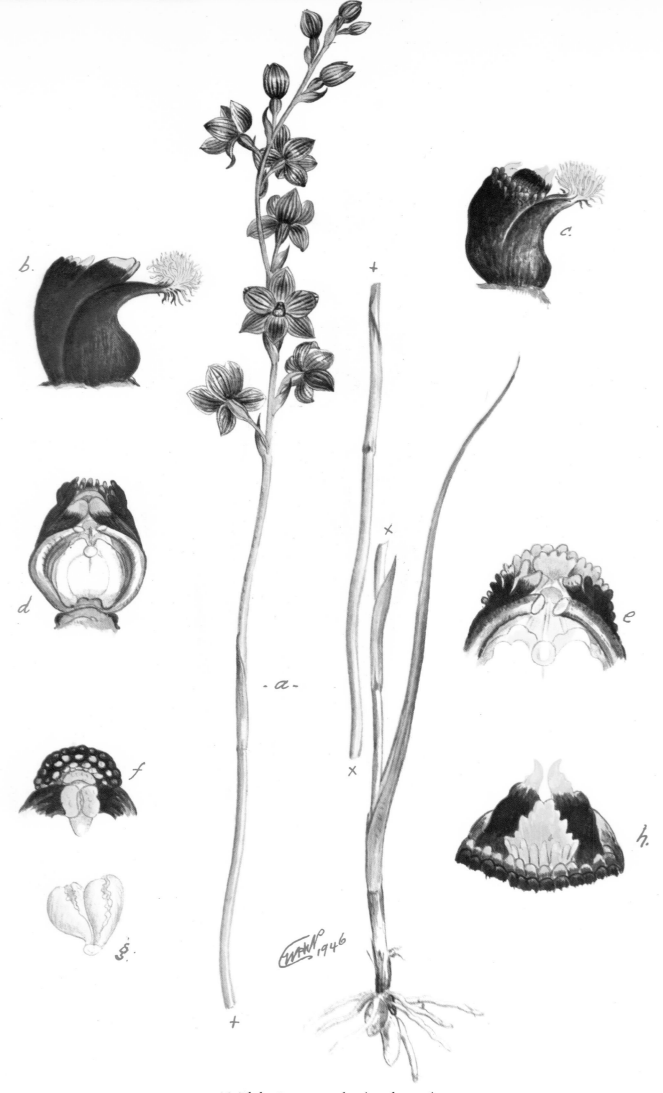

16 *Thelymitra campanulata* (see also p. 4)

a specimen from Applecross, Perth district, WA **b** column, from side **c** another column, from side **d** column, from front—hair-tufts removed **e** head of column, from front **f** head of column, from above **g** pollinia **h** head of column, from rear
Fig. **a** natural size

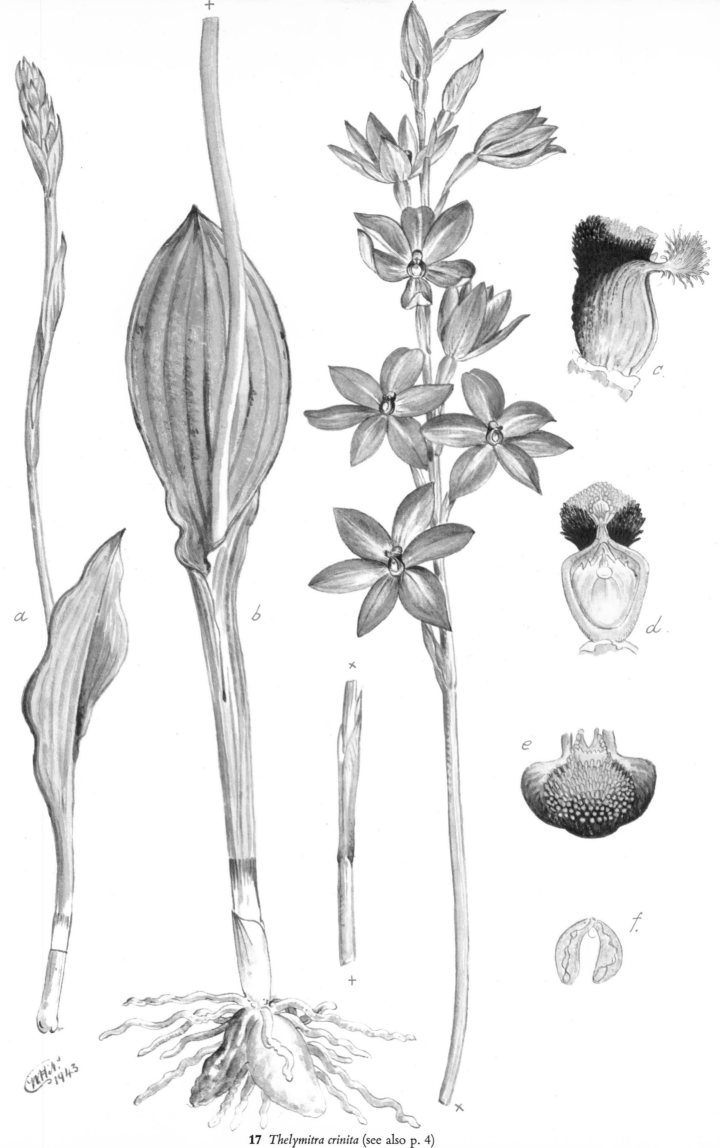

17 *Thelymitra crinita* (see also p. 4)

a an immature specimen **b** an attractive example **c** column, from side **d** column, from front—hair-tufts removed **e** column, from above—hair-tufts removed **f** pollinia
Figs **a, b** natural size

18 *Thelymitra fasciculata* (see also p. 4)

a a superior specimen from Walpole district, WA **b** flowers from near Manjimup, WA **c** column, from front **d** column, from side **e** column mid-lobe, from above
f head of column, from side
Figs **a, b** natural size

19 *Thelymitra luteocilium* (see also p. 4)

a typical specimen, Ararat district, Vic. **b** column, from front from a bud **c** column, from side **d** column mid-lobe—portion only of lateral lobes shown **e** column, from front—one lobe removed **f** column mid-lobe, from above **g h i** mid-lobe (hood), variations from rear **j** raceme from Langwarrin district, Vic.
Figs **a, j** natural size

20 *Thelymitra chasmogama* (see also p. 5)

a two typical specimens from Ararat, Vic. **b** column, from side **c** column, from front—hair-tufts removed **d** column mid-lobe, from above **e** pollinia **f** portion of lateral lobe of column

Fig. **a** natural size

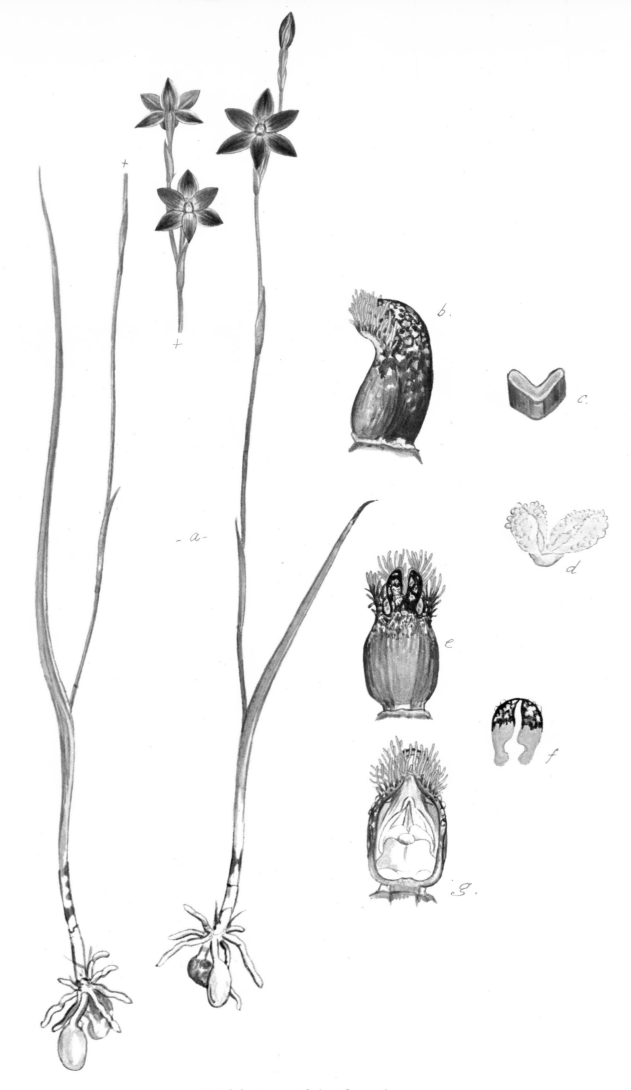

21 *Thelymitra mucida* (see also p. 5)

a two specimens from Nanarup, WA   **b** column, from side   **c** cross-section of leaf   **d** pollinia   **e** column, from rear   **f** column mid-lobe, from above   **g** column, from front

Fig. **a** natural size

22 *Thelymitra pauciflora*: Figs **a–l** (see also p. 5)
T. pauciflora var. *holmesii*: Figs **m, n** (see also p. 5)

a specimen from Wattle Glen, Vic. **b c** colour forms **d** column, from side—lobes removed to show stigma and anthers **e** a column, from side **f** a pink-flowering form, Middleton's Gap, Serra Range, Vic. **g** cross-sections of leaves **h** column, from rear **i** column, from rear **j** abnormal flower, showing parts of an additional column distributed around the perianth, the dorsal sepal evenly divided and labellum represented by a filiform lobe which is clavate at the tip (note the pollinia on margins of the dorsal sepal) **k** head of column, from rear **l** same, from directly above **m** portion of inflorescence **n** column, from side
Figs **a–c, f, j, m** natural size

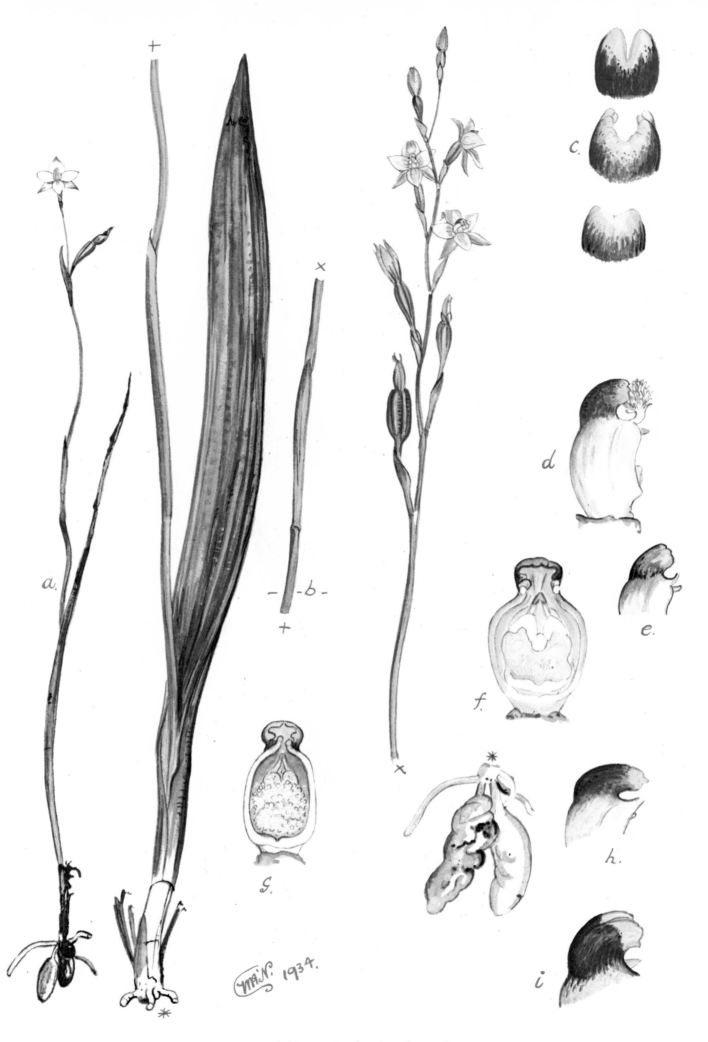

23 *Thelymitra pauciflora* (see also p. 5)

a   b specimens from Hurstbridge, Vic.   **c** variations in the column mid-lobe   **d** typical column, from side   **e** head of column, from side   **f** column of a bud, from front—
lateral lobes removed   **g** column, from front—upper lobes removed   **h   i** column mid-lobe variations, from side
Figs **a, b** natural size

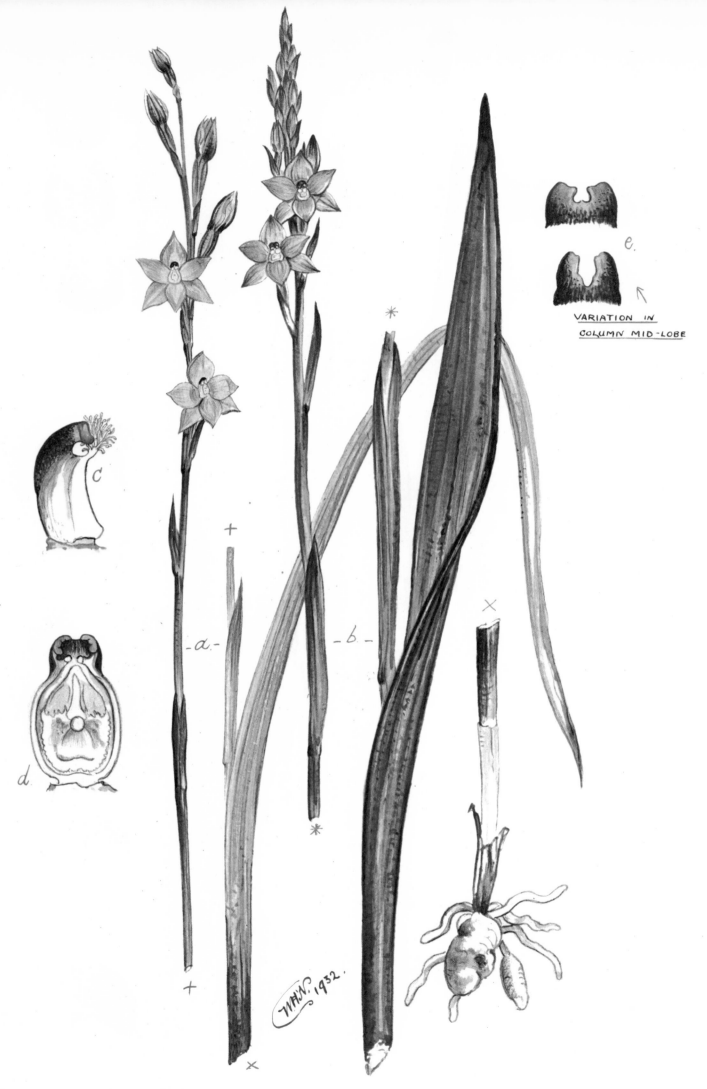

VARIATION IN
COLUMN MID-LOBE

24 *Thelymitra pauciflora* (see also p. 5)

a   b typical specimens, from Hurstbridge, Vic. **c** column, from side—note dilated apex of mid-lobe (an inconsistent character) **d** column, from front—lateral lobes
removed **e** apices of column mid-lobe, showing variation
Figs **a, b** natural size

25 *Thelymitra pauciflora* (see also p. 5)

a large-flowered form, from railway enclosure near Boronia, Vic.—four specimens were seen of approximately the same height, but bearing from ten to fifteen flower buds
b an unusually brilliant form from same locality **c** flower (of Fig. **b**) **d** pale-toned flower from Portland, Vic.(approximately same diameter as Fig. **a**) **e** column mid-lobe
of an intensely-coloured flower from Boronia, Vic. **f** column of a flower (shown at Fig. **a**), from front—lateral lobes removed **g** column of a flower (shown at Fig. **d**),
from front—lateral lobes removed **h** the same column, from side
Figs **a, b** natural size

26 *Thelymitra pauciflora* (see also p. 5)

a   b typical specimens   **c** column mid-lobe, from side   **d** column, from side   **e** flower, fully expanded   **f** mid-lobe of column, from above   **g** column mid-lobe, from front
h column, from front   **i** stigma with pollinia in position and pollen grains dehisced over surface (depicted at an advanced stage in Fig. **h**)   **j** column, from side   **k** tubers, etc.
l cross-section of leaf
Figs **a, b, e, k** natural size

27 *Thelymitra aristata* (see also p. 6)

a specimen from Bendigo, Vic.   **b** typical examples from railway enclosure near Riddell, Vic.   **c** expansion of the perianth on a warm day   **d** another specimen from near Riddell

Figs **a–d** natural size

28 *Thelymitra aristata* (see also p. 6)

A splendid mountain form (from the Dart-Diggings Track, beyond Cravensville, north-eastern Vic.)
Fig. natural size

29 *Thelymitra aristata* (see also p. 6)

a stigma and pollinia (note frilled upper margins of stigma) **b c** pollinia **d** column, from side, also mid-lobe from above **e** same views of column and mid-lobe, from another flower **f** column mid-lobe, from above **g** portion of column, from side, also view of mid-lobe from above **h** column, from side, also mid-lobe from above **i** stigma with pollinia **j k** views of the mid-lobe, from rear **l** column, from front—hair-tufts removed **m** mid-lobe, from rear, also the column from front—hair-tufts removed. (Note that Figs **h** and **m** show a somewhat undeveloped form of mid-lobe)

30 *Thelymitra aristata* var. *megcalyptra* (see also p. 6)

a a typical pink-flowered specimen from Pomonal, Vic.—the flowers may vary from pale violet-blue to bright pink   **b** extreme tip of column   **c** mid-lobe, from above
d column, from side   **e** extreme tip of column
Fig. **a** natural size

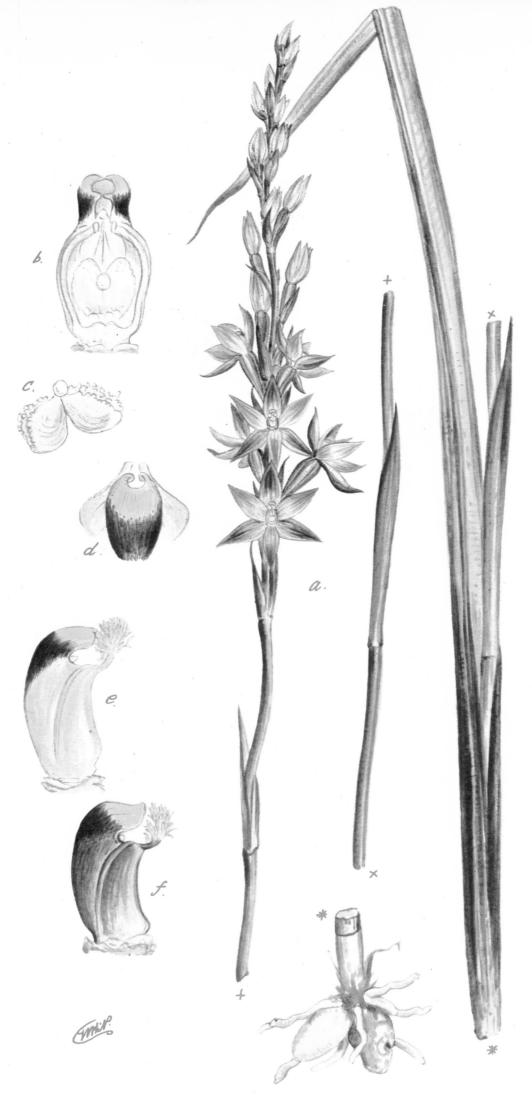

31 *Thelymitra nuda* (see also p. 6)

a a Burleigh Heads, Qld, specimen **b** column, from front—hair-tufts removed **c** pollinia **d** column mid-lobe, from above **e** column, from side **f** a sturdy column, from side
Fig. **a** natural size

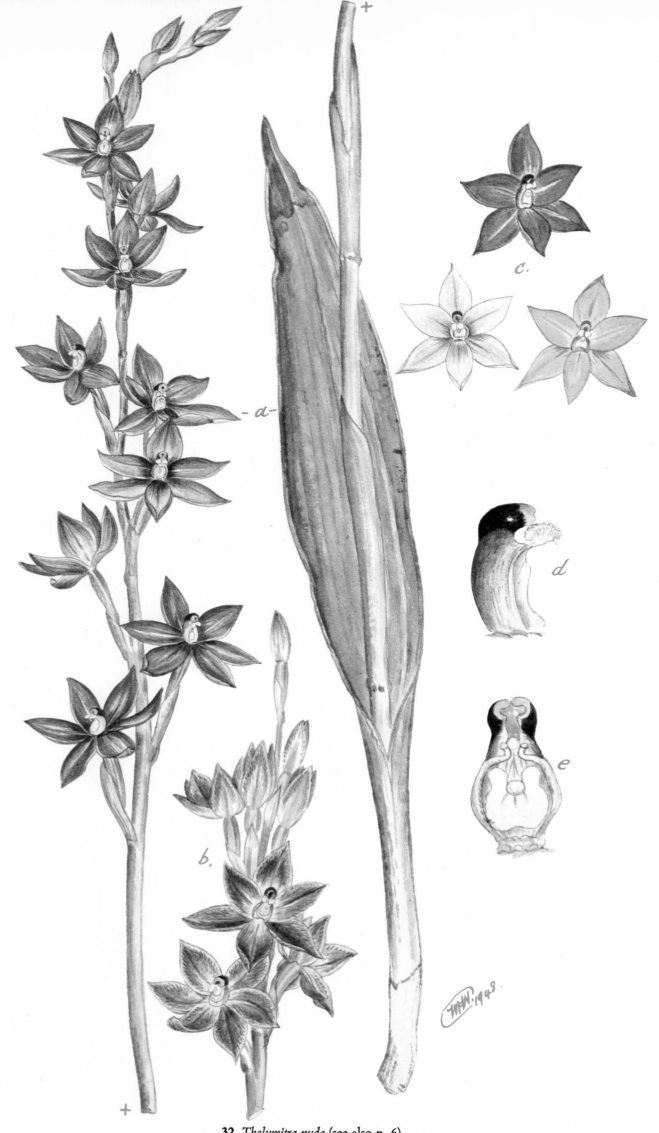

32 *Thelymitra nuda* (see also p. 6)

a a purple-flowered form from Waterloo, WA, where the following other colour forms were also collected: **b** a 'gilt-edged' perianth **c** three unusual colour shades **d** column
from side **e** column, from front—lateral lobes removed
Figs **a–c** natural size

33 *Thelymitra grandiflora* (see also p. 6)

a typical specimen **b** a rare flower from Pomonal, Vic. **c** small form (flowers numerous) from Portland, Vic. **d** pollinia **e** mid-lobes of column, from rear **f** column, from side **g** head of column, from side **h** cilia from lateral lobes

Figs **a–c** natural size

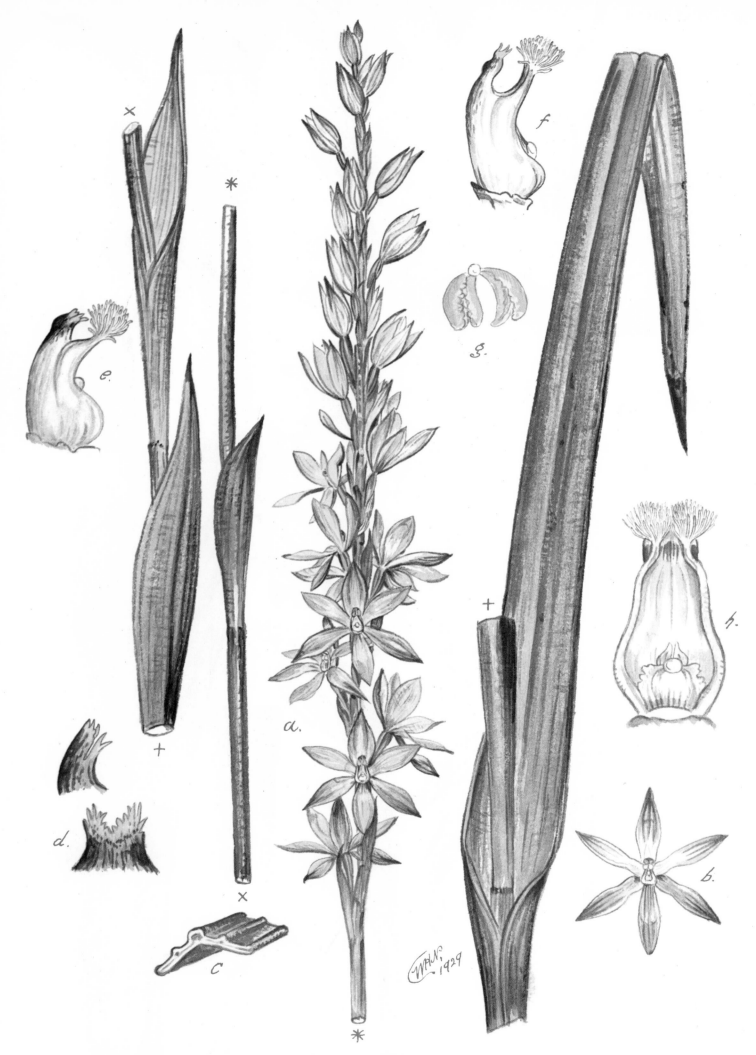

34 *Thelymitra grandiflora* (see also p. 6)

a a slender form from Heathmont, Vic.   **b** flower with narrow segments   **c** cross-section of leaf   **d** column mid-lobe, from rear and side   **e f** columns, from side   **g** pollinia
h column, from front
Fig. **a** natural size

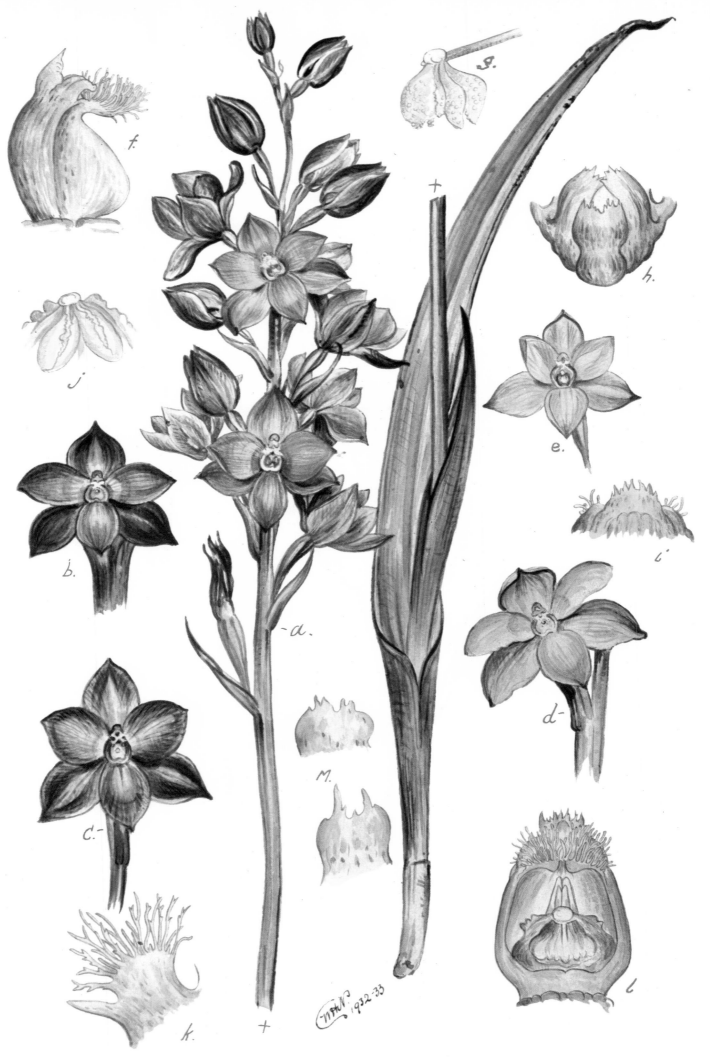

35 *Thelymitra epipactoides* (see also p. 7)

a an attractively-coloured specimen **b c d e** remarkable colour forms **f** column, from side **g** pollinia **h** upper part of column, from above **i** head of column, from rear **j** pollinia in position **k** lateral lobes of column **l** column, from front **m** lateral portions of column mid-lobe
Figs **a, e** natural size

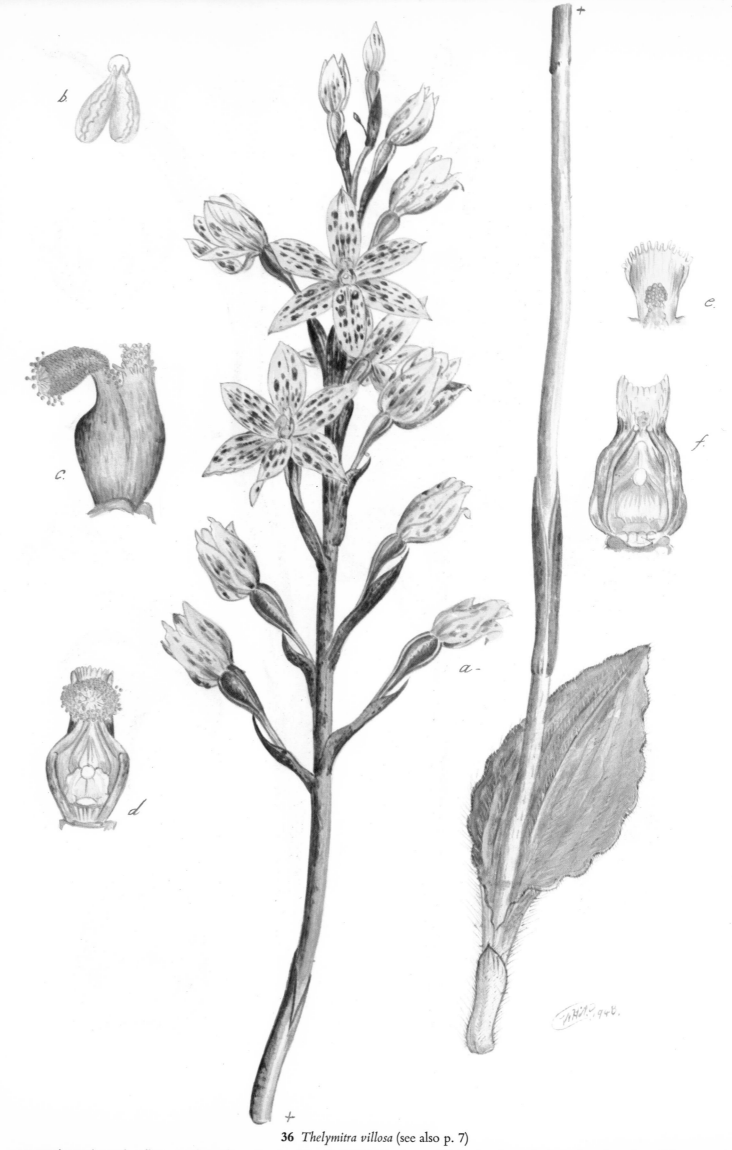

36 *Thelymitra villosa* (see also p. 7)

a a superior specimen **b** pollinia **c** column, from side **d** column, from front **e** column mid-lobe, from front **f** column, from front—lateral lobes removed
Fig. **a** natural size

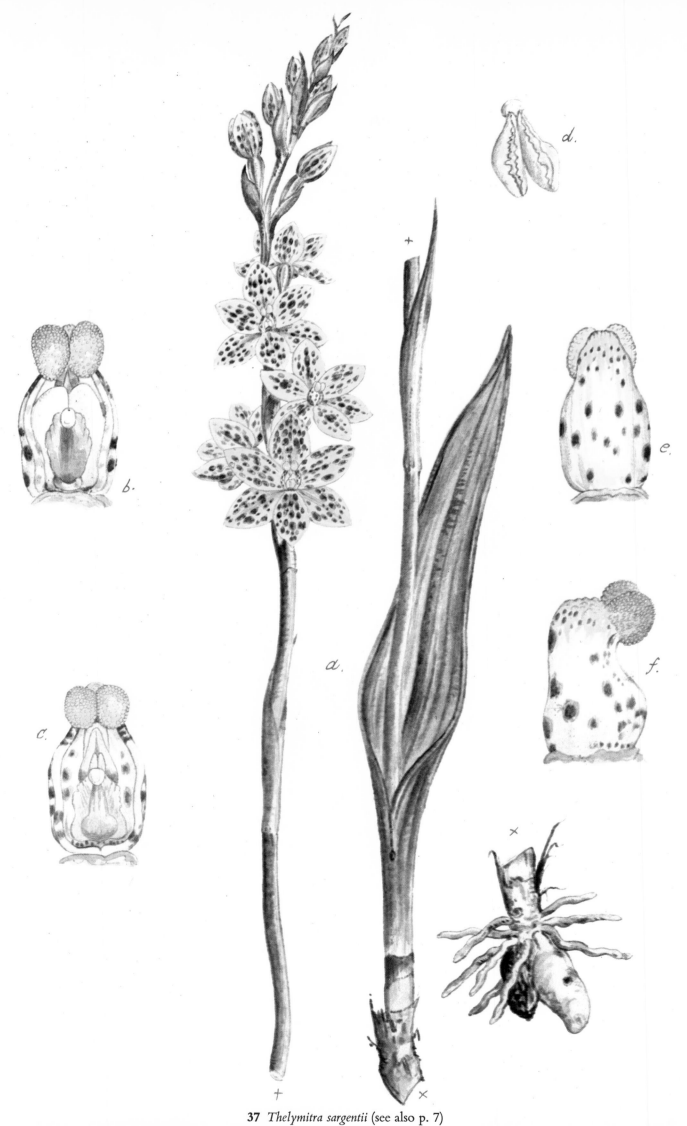

37 *Thelymitra sargentii* (see also p. 7)

a a superior specimen from near Mount Tampia, WA **b** column, from a well-developed bud **c** column, from front **d** pollinia **e** column, from rear **f** column, from side
Fig. **a** natural size

38 *Thelymitra fusco-lutea* (see also p. 7)

a a superior example from the Grampians, Vic.   **b** column, from front   **c** column, from side   **d** rostellum   **e** cilia from upper margin of lateral lobes   **f** anther   **g** head of column, from side   **h** flower from WA   **i** petal, showing markings   **j** head of column, from above, showing dorsal appendage, lateral lobes and anther (below) Figs **a, h** natural size

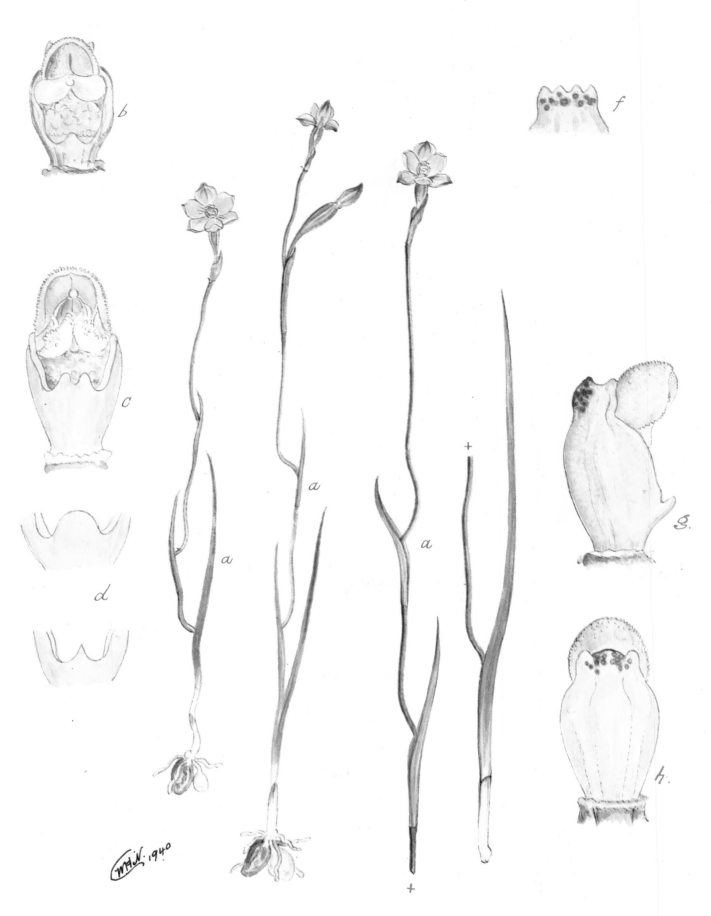

39 *Thelymitra flexuosa* (see also p. 8)

a typical specimens b column, from front, from a bud c column, from front d variation in the frontal margin of wings (see also Fig. c) e cross-section of leaf
f head of column, from rear g column, from side h column, from rear
Fig. **a** natural size

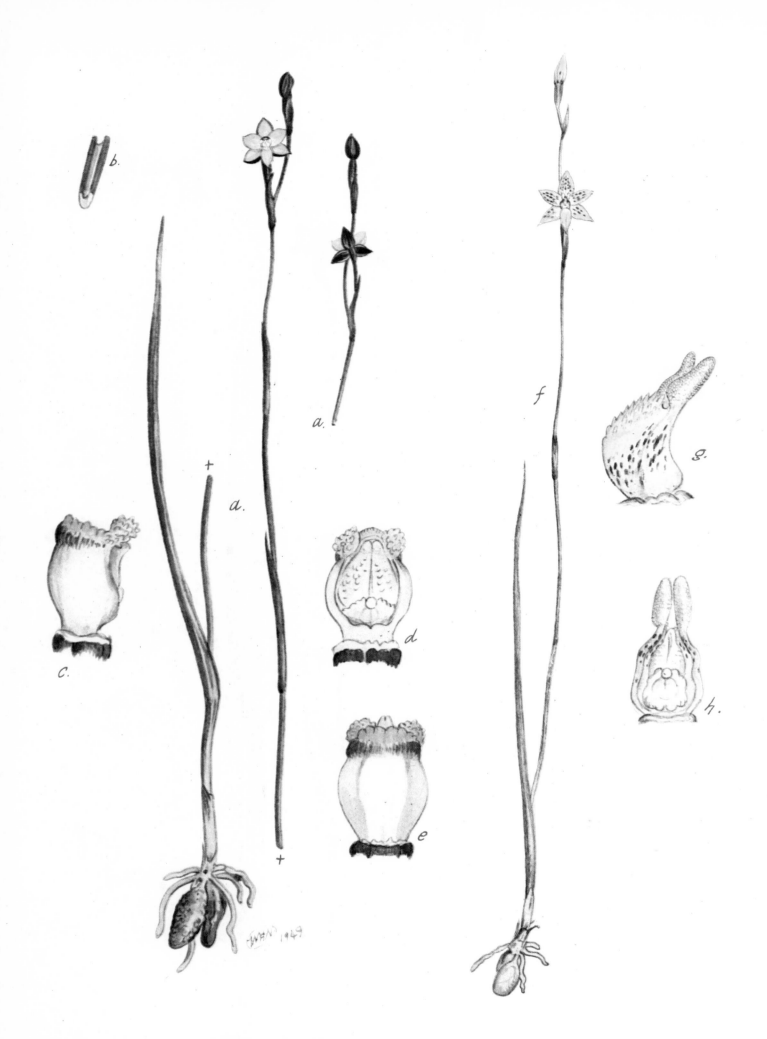

40 *Thelymitra urnalis*: Figs **a–e** (see also p. 8)
T. tigrina: Figs **f–h** (also see p. 8)

a two specimens collected by the author **b** cross-section of leaf **c** column, from side **d** column, from front **e** column, from rear **f** specimen from Yarloop, WA
g column, from side **h** column, from front
Figs **a, f** natural size

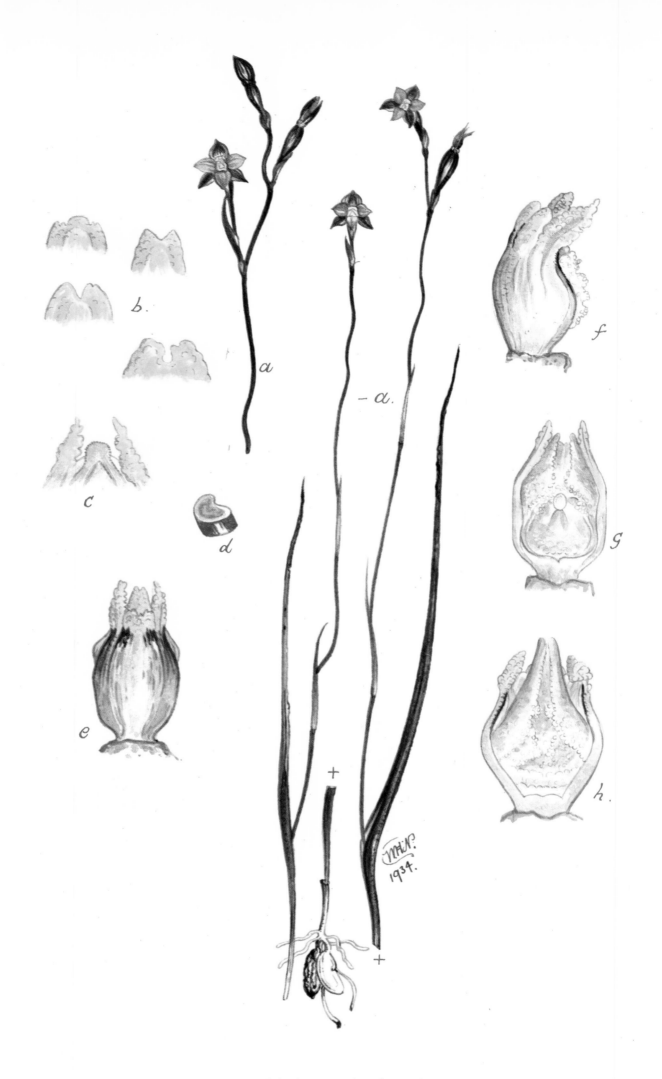

41 *Thelymitra carnea* (see also p. 8)

a typical specimens from Sandringham, Vic. **b** variations in mid-lobe of column **c** head of column, from front **d** cross-section of leaf **e** column, from rear **f** column, from side **g** column, from front, from a bud **h** column, from front (stigma hidden by pollen grains)
Fig. **a** natural size

42 *Thelymitra rubra* (see also p. 9)

(see also p. 9)

a b two specimens from Ocean Grove, Vic.   **c** column, from side, showing an abnormal development at base—vestige of one of the inner row of stamens   **d** column, from side   **e** column, from rear   **f** head of column, from above   **g** head of column, from front   **h** column, from side, from an undeveloped bud   **i** same, from front   **j** head of column from side   **k** cross-section of leaf   **l** a delicately-tinted form from Bayswater, Vic.   **m** a flower of the form occurring in Ironbark country
Figs **a, b, l, m** natural size

43 *Thelymitra macmillanii* (see also p. 9)

a a Bannockburn, Vic., specimen **b** specimen from Maldon, Vic. **c** specimen from Rushworth Vic. **d** mottled form from Airey's Inlet, Vic. **e f g** types of lateral
lobes **h** column, from front **i** column, from side **j** head of column, from rear **k** head of column, from above—lobes not shown **l** pollinia
Figs **a–d** natural size

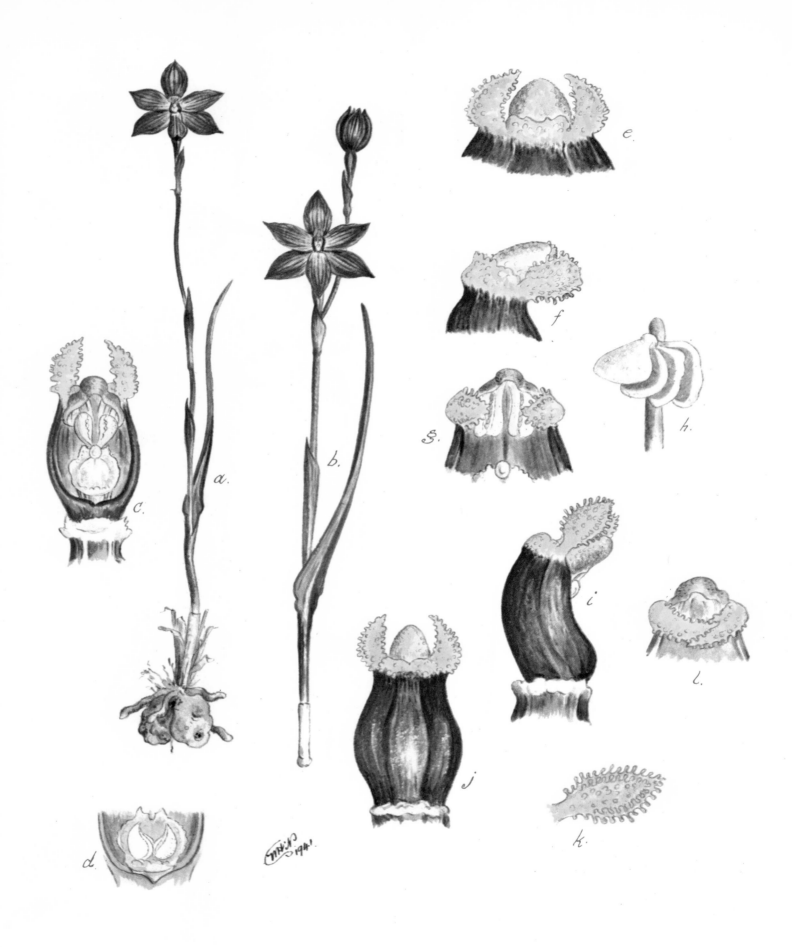

44 *Thelymitra mackibbinii* (see also p. 9)

a b typical violet-flowered specimens **c** column, from front **d** pollinia which have been deposited intact on the stigma **e** summit of column, from above **f** same, from side **g** same, from front—note pollinia below anther **h** pollinia **i** column, from side **j** column, from rear **k** lateral lobe of column **l** head of column, from front—appendages covering the empty anther case

Figs **a, b** natural size

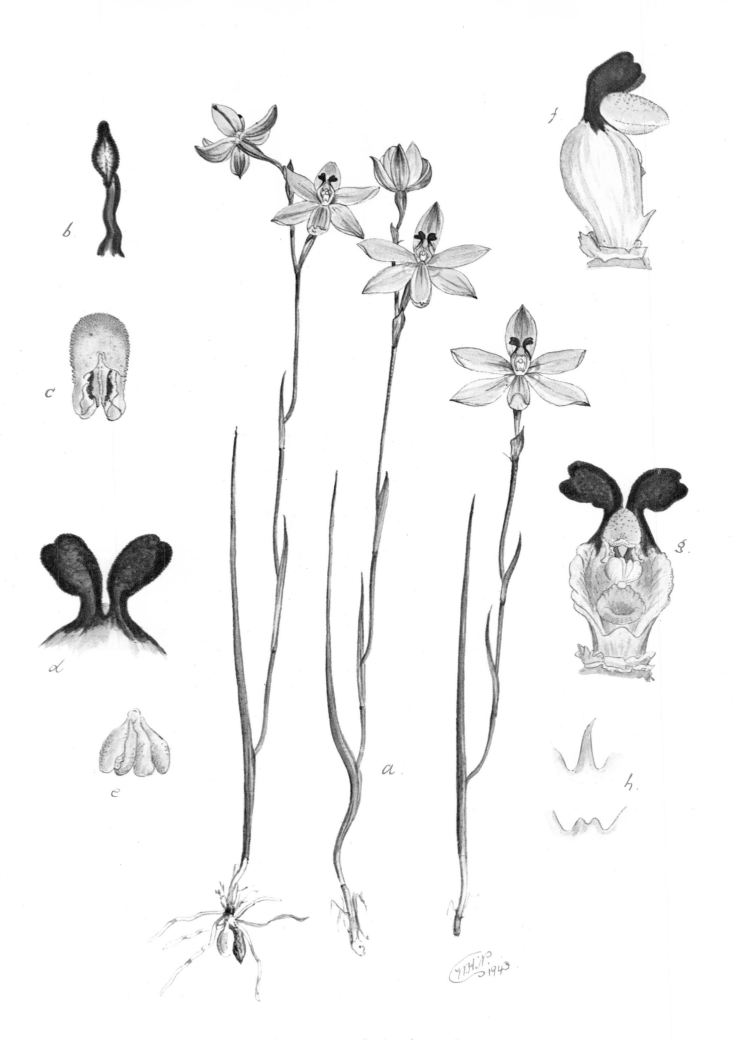

45 *Thelymitra antennifera* (see also p. 10)

a three typical specimens, from open Ironbark country at Steiglitz, Vic.   **b** column appendage, lobe dissected   **c** anther, from front   **d** head of column, from rear   **e** pollinia
f column, from side   **g** column, from front   **h** appendages from base of column, showing variation (also see Figs **f** and **g**)
Fig. **a** natural size

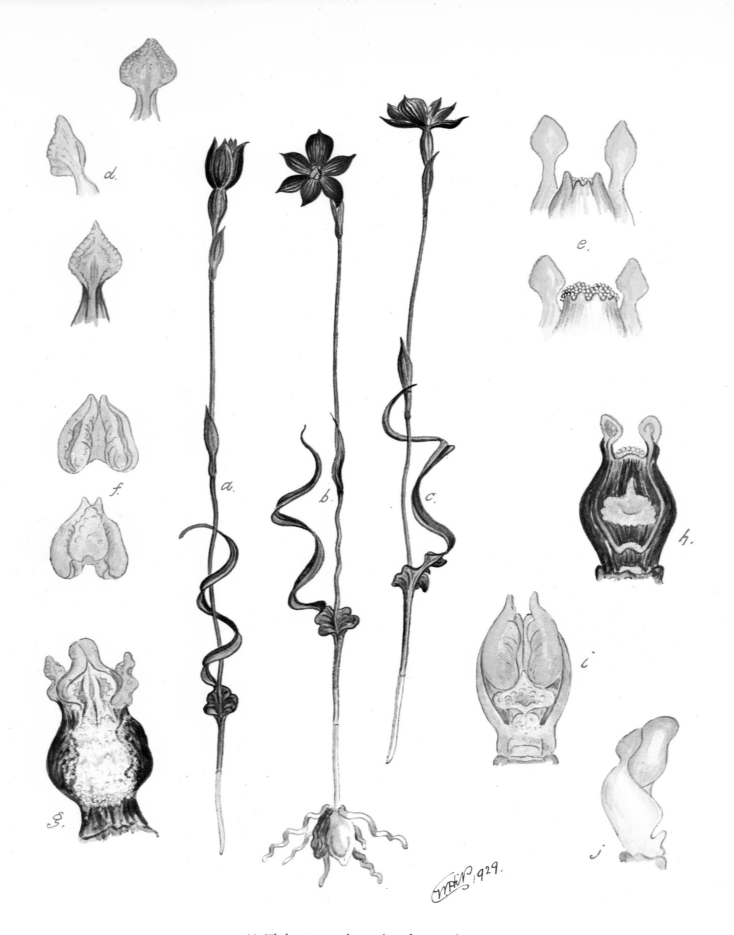

46 *Thelymitra matthewsii* (see also p. 10)

a b c typical specimens from Vic. localities **d** column appendages **e** column appendages and mid-lobe, from rear **f** anther-case—two aspects **g** column, from front—note pollen grains dispersed over stigma **h** column, from front—anther removed **i** column, from front, from a bud **j** same as Fig. **i**, from side
Figs **a–c** natural size

47 *Thelymitra spiralis*: Figs **e, f, h–k** (see also p. 10)
T. spiralis var. *punctata*: Fig. **a** (see also p. 11)
T. spiralis var. *scoulerae*: Fig. **b** (see also p. 11)
T. spiralis var. *pulchella*: Figs **c, g** (see also p. 11)
T. spiralis var. *pallida*: Fig. **d** (see also p. 11)

a flowering specimen **b** flowering specimen **c** single flower **d** two flowering specimens **e** flowers **f** pollinia **g** column, from side **h i** columns, from front—pollinia removed **j** column, from side **k** column, from rear
Figs **a–e** natural size

f.

g.

h.

a.

b.

c.

d.

e.

i.

j.

k.

x

x

x

+

+

MW. 1949

47

48 *Thelymitra variegata* (see also p. 11)

a specimen collected near Yarloop, WA **b** lower portion of plant, showing spiral form of leaf **c** flower **d** column, from front **e** column, from side **f** head of column, from rear, showing crest behind the anther **g** flower, from the underside **h** spiral form of a leaf lamina
Figs **a–c, g** natural size

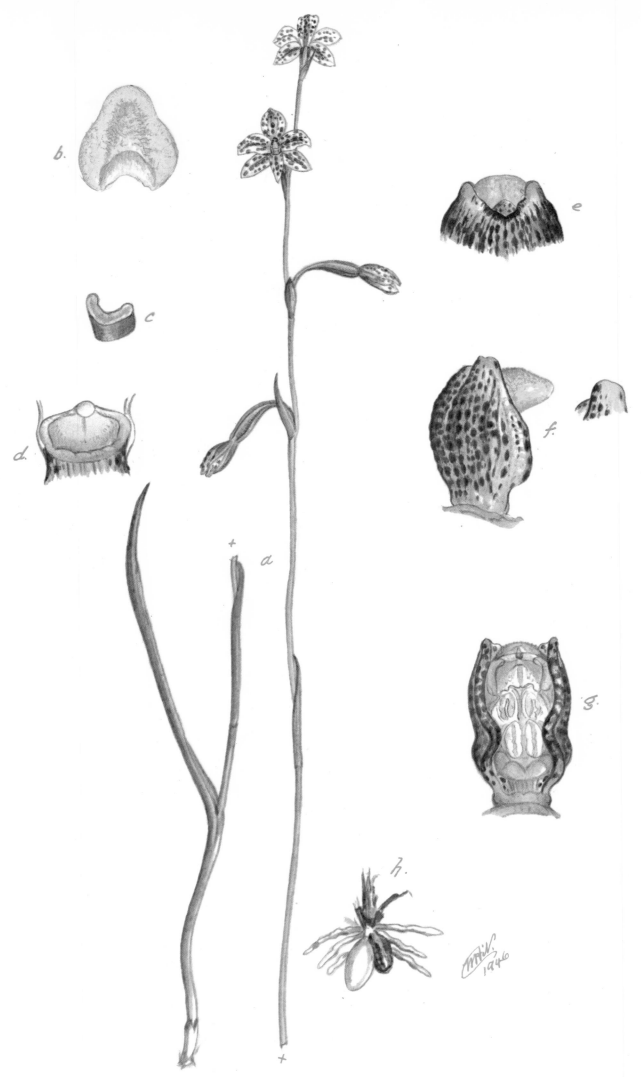

49 *Thelymitra cucullata* (see also p. 11)

a specimen from Upper King River, WA **b** anther, from below **c** cross-section of leaf **d** stigma **e** summit of column, from above **f** column, from side, also figure showing some variation of the lateral lobe **g** column, from front—pollinia deposited on stigma **h** tubers
Figs **a, h** natural size

50 *Thelymitra venosa*: Figs **b–i** (see also p. 11)
T. venosa var. *magnifica*: Fig. **a** (see also p. 12)

a specimen from Woodford, NSW **b** specimen from Lake Mountain, Vic. **c** two specimens from Mt Cobbler Hut, Vic. **d** cross-section of leaf **e** two columns, from side
f column, from front **g** two columns, from front, at varying stages **h** column appendages **i** pollinia
Figs **a–c** natural size

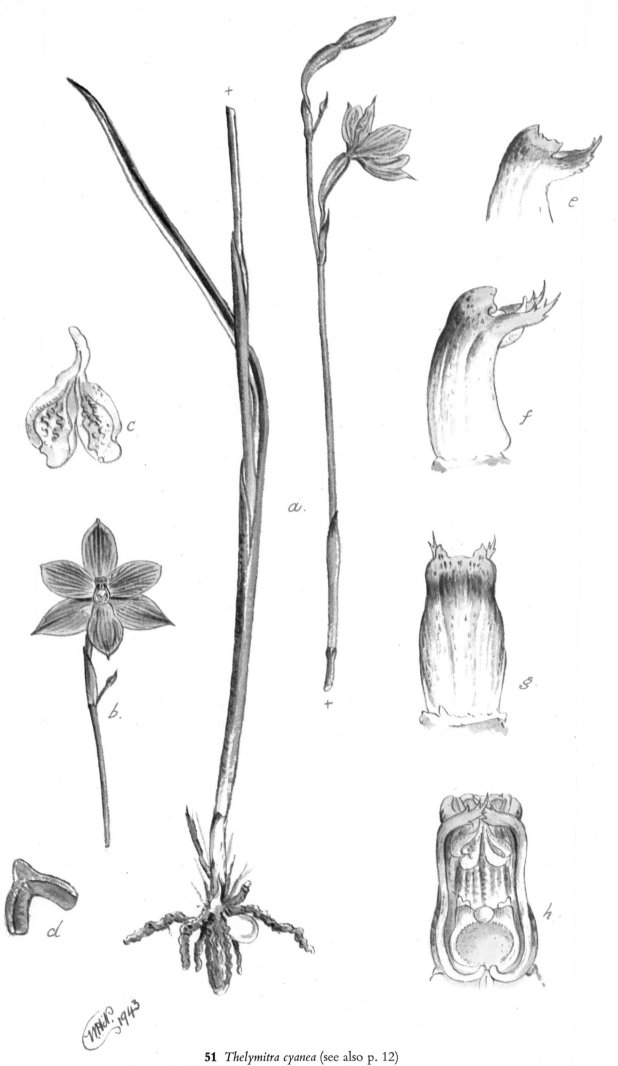

51 *Thelymitra cyanea* (see also p. 12)

a typical specimen from Bidwell, Vic.   **b** flower from same area   **c** anther   **d** cross-section of leaf-lamina   **e** upper part of column, from side   **f** column, from side
g column, from rear   **h** column, from front—pollinia removed
Fig. **a** natural size

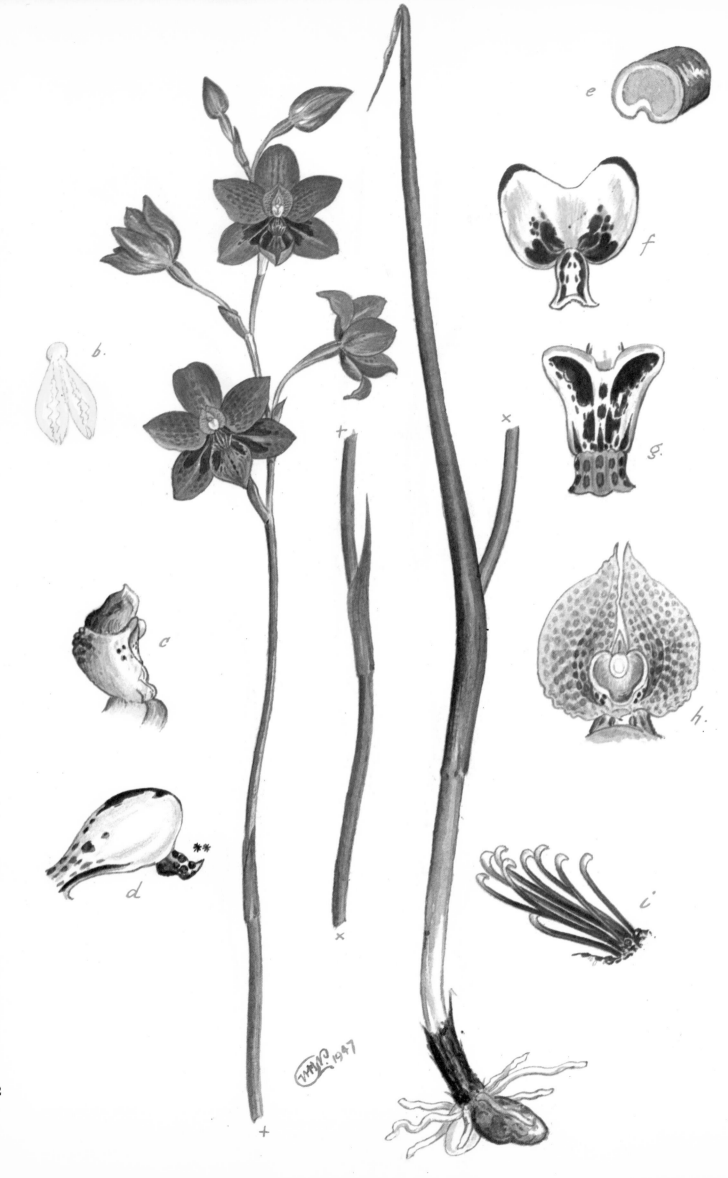

52

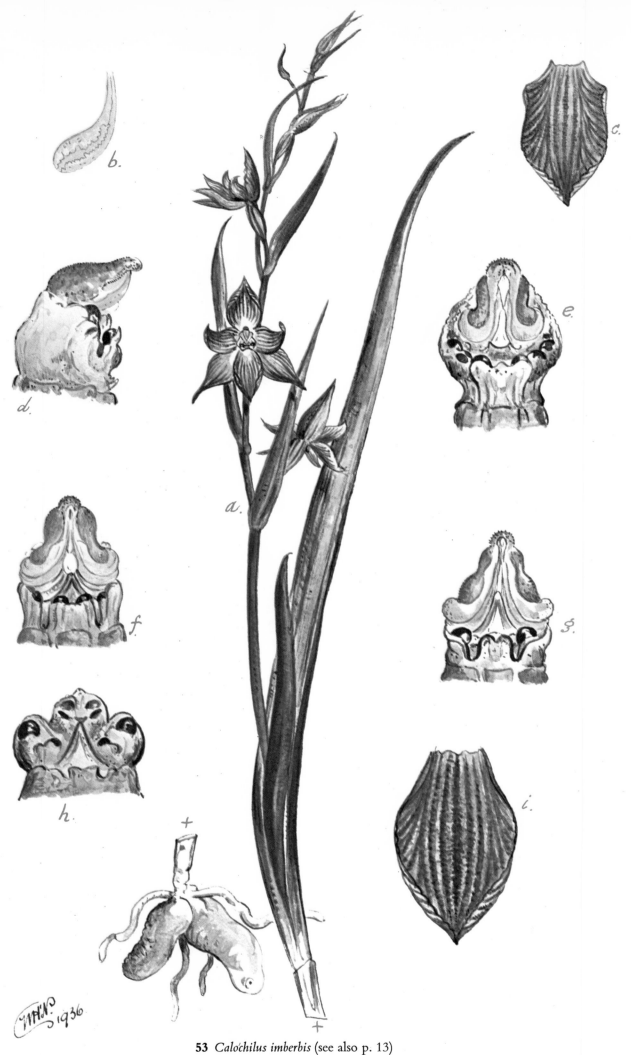

53 *Calochilus imberbis* (see also p. 13)

a a superior specimen from Rushworth, Vic.   **b** pollinia   **c** labellum, from above   **d** column, from side   **e f g** column types, from front   **h** column, anther, etc., removed to show glands, from rear   **i** labellum, from above

Fig. **a** natural size

52 *Epiblema grandiflorum* (see also p. 12)

a typical specimens   **b** pollinia   **c** column, from side   **d** labellum appendage, from side (the basal processes have been removed from lamina where marked **)   **e** cross-section of leaf   **f** labellum appendage   **g** same, from above   **h** column and lateral wings   **i** basal processes, from labellum

Fig. **a** natural size

54 *Calochilus richae* (see also p. 13)

a type specimens **b** column, from side **c** faded flower **d** labellum, from above **e** labellum, from below **f** labellum apex **g** column, from front **h** dorsal sepal **i** lateral sepal **j** petal **k** glands from labellum lamina
Fig. **a** natural size

55 *Calochilus paludosus* (see also p. 13)

a b typical specimens from Kinglake district, Vic. **c** column, from front **d** column, from side (also figures of two wings—one abnormal, above) **e** column, from side, with imperfect wings **f** same column, from front **g** pollinia **h** cross-section of leaf **i** labellum base, from above, also the immediate base of another labellum **j** individual hairs and glands of labellum **k** tubers, etc. **l** petal
Figs **a, b, k** natural size

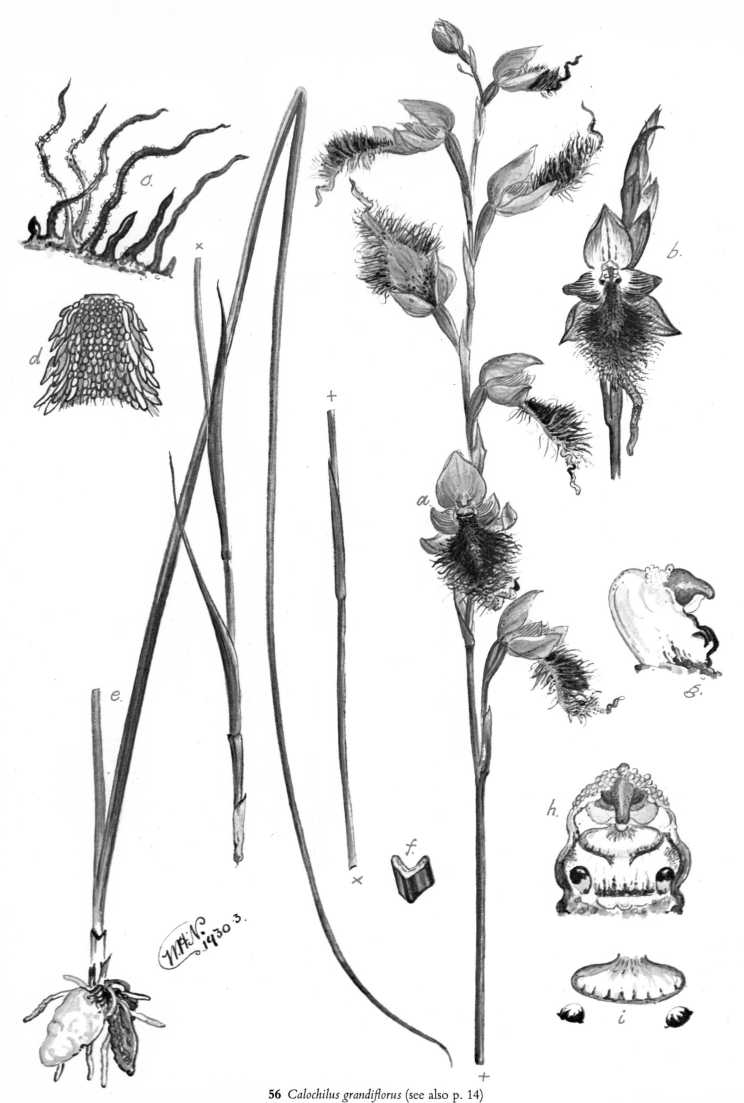

56 *Calochilus grandiflorus* (see also p. 14)

a typical specimen from Stradbroke Island, Qld (leaf missing)   **b** flower and buds of a brightly coloured form   **c** hairs from labellum lamina   **d** figure, showing formation of glands at the labellum base (tinted only)   **e** leaf and tubers   **f** cross-section of leaf   **g** column, from side   **h** column, from front   **i** stigma and glands

Figs **a, e** natural size

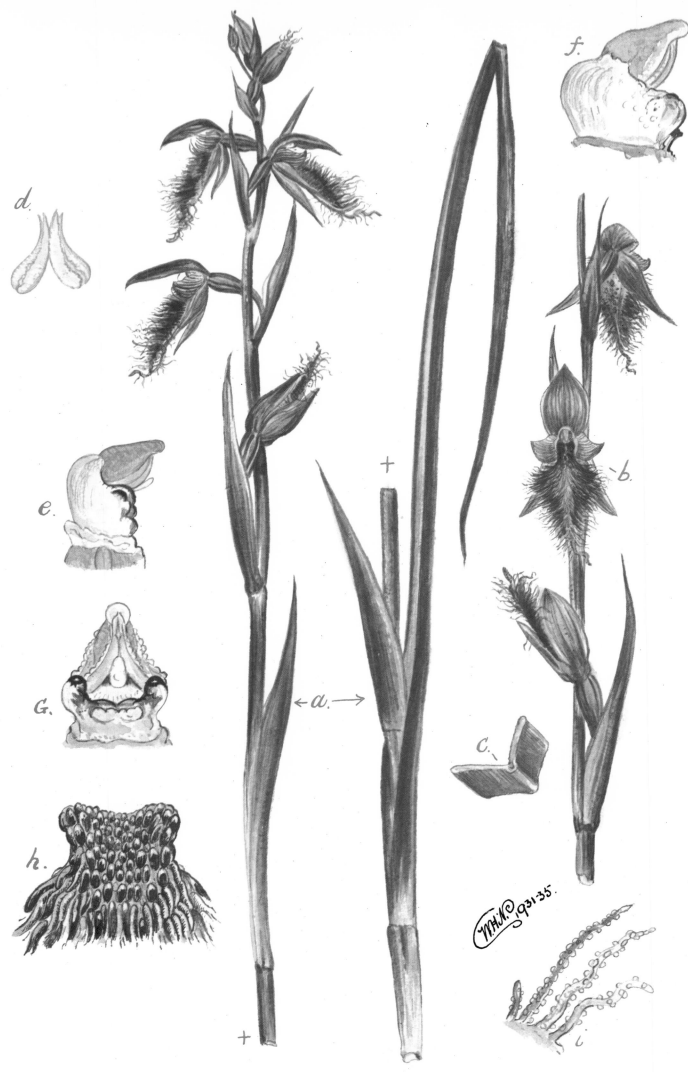

57 *Calochilus robertsonii* (see also p. 14)

a b specimens from Rushworth, Vic. **c** figure to show triangular section of leaf **d** pollinia **e f** column, from side **g** column, from front **h** gland–covered base of labellum **i** hairs from labellum lamina

Figs **a, b** natural size

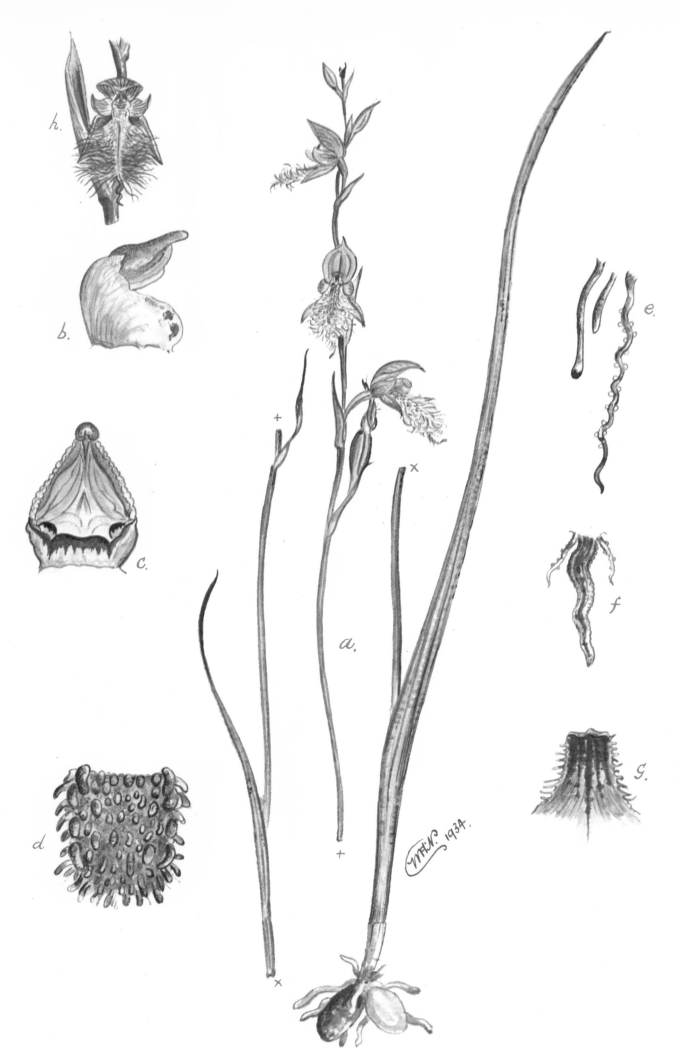

58 *Calochilus robertsonii* (see also p. 14)

a a pale-flowered form from the Pyrete Range near Gisborne, Vic. **b** column, from side **c** column, from front **d** base of labellum, from above **e** hairs from labellum lamina **f** labellum apex, showing ligule and two hairs **g** base of labellum, from below **h** a green flower of the typical form, from near Hagley, Tas.
Figs **a, h** natural size

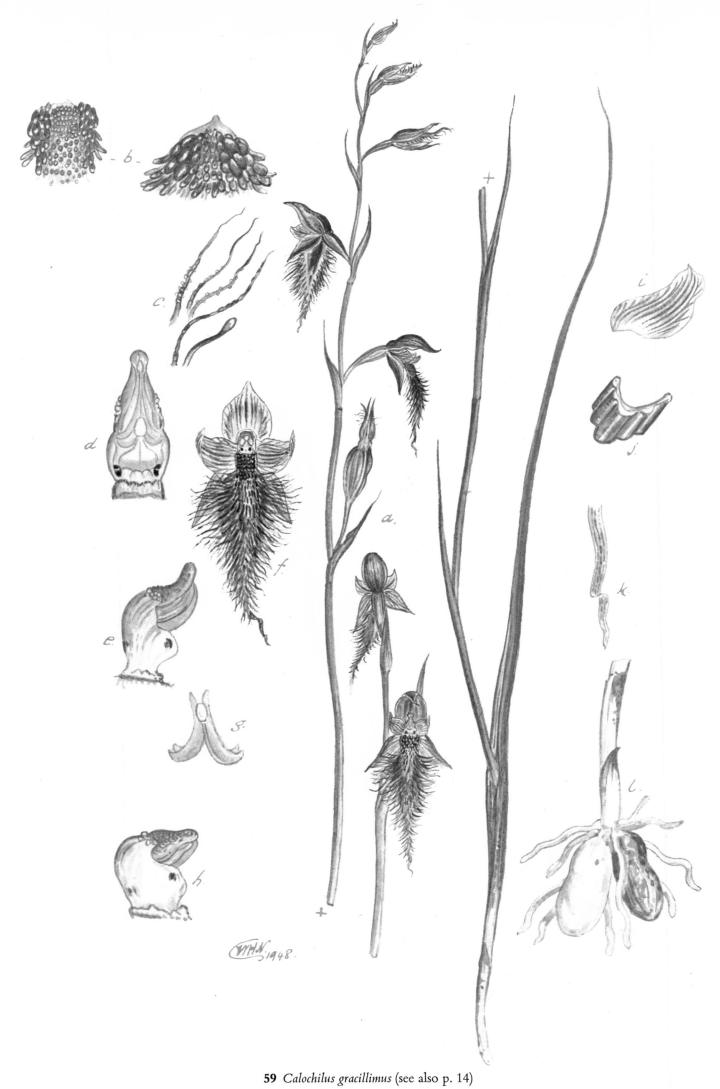

59 *Calochilus gracillimus* (see also p. 14)

a a typically slender specimen, also two flowers from Glen Aplin, Qld **b** figures to show labellum base (the arrangement of papillae vary considerably) **c** typical hairs of the labellum **d** column, from front **e** column, from side **f** flower **g** pollinia **h** column, from side (note differences between this and Fig. **e**) **i** a petal **j** cross-section of a leaf **k** ribbon-like apex of labellum **l** tubers, etc.
Figs **a, l** natural size

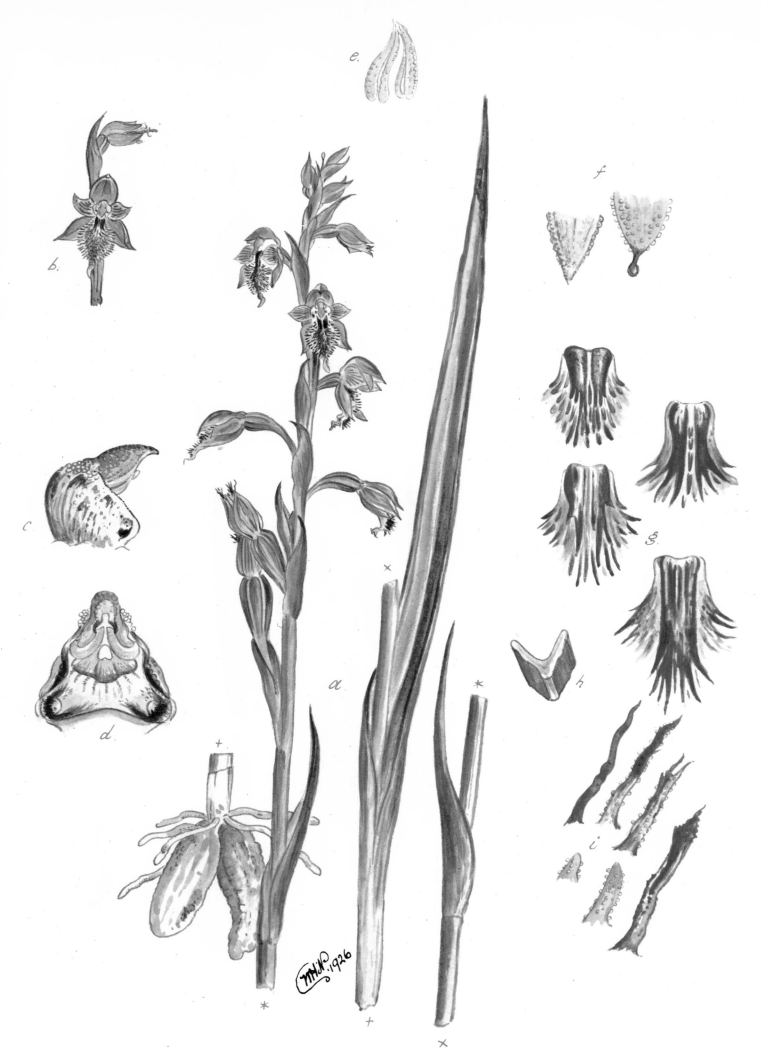

60 *Calochilus campestris* (see also p. 14)

a typical specimen, Healesville district, Vic. **b** flower from Gypsum, Vic. **c** column, from side, of flower from Smithton, Tas. **d** column, from front, of flower from Bayswater, Vic. **e** pollinia **f** apices of two labella **g** figures to show variation in basal plate of labellum **h** cross-section of leaf **i** cilia from labellum lamina
Figs **a, b** natural size

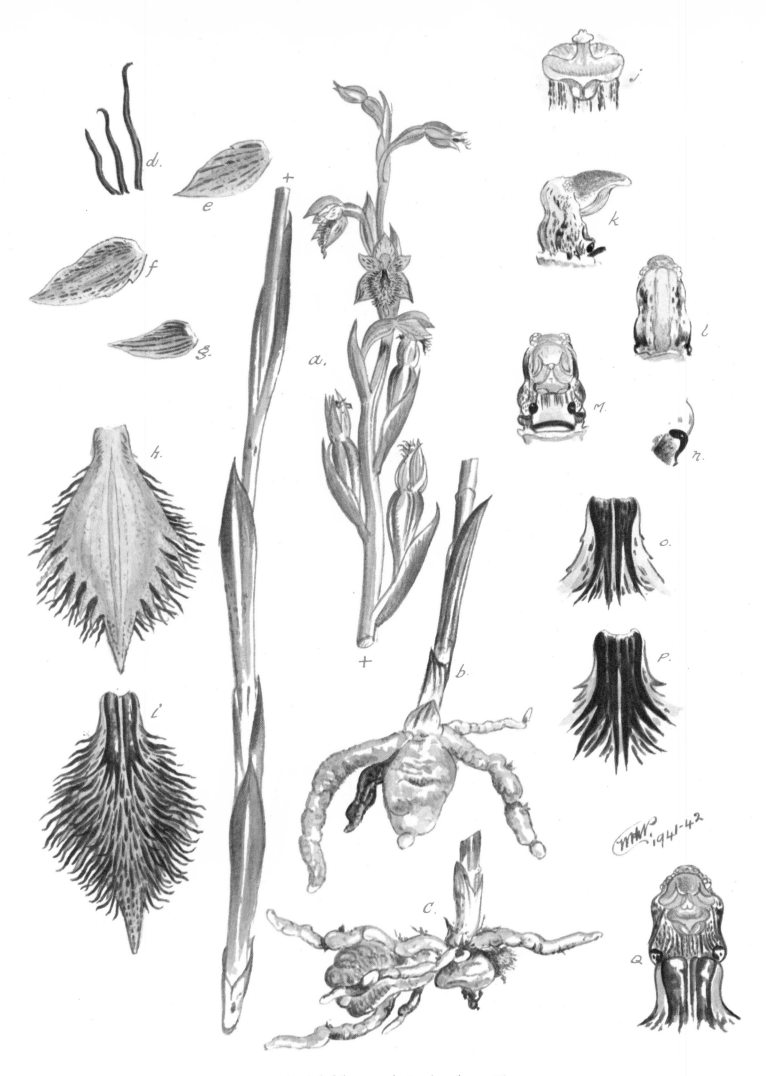

61 *Calochilus saprophyticus* (see also p. 15)

a Portland, Vic., specimen **b** **c** the underground system (note fleshly ribbed bract, representing an abortive leaf lamina in Fig. b) **d** hairs from the labellum lamina
e **f** lateral sepals **g** petal **h** labellum, from below **i** labellum, from above **j** stigma **k** column, from side **l** column, from rear **m** column, from front **n** gland
on column wing **o** **p** base of labellum lamina **q** column and labellum base, from front
Figs **a–c** natural size

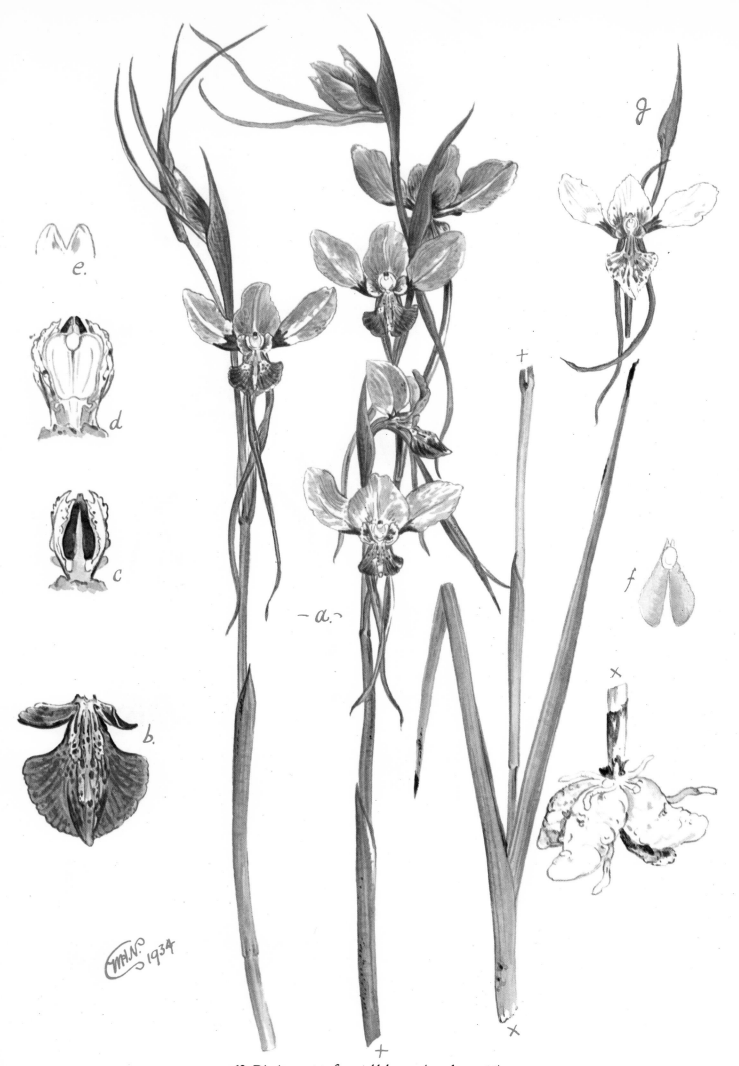

62 *Diuris punctata* forma *blakneyae* (see also p. 16)

a specimens from Beaconsfield, Vic. **b** labellum, from above, one lateral lobe spread out **c** column, showing anther, etc. **d** column, showing stigma, etc. **e** rostellum **f** pollinia **g** [pale form—origin unknown—Ed.]
Figs **a, g** natural size

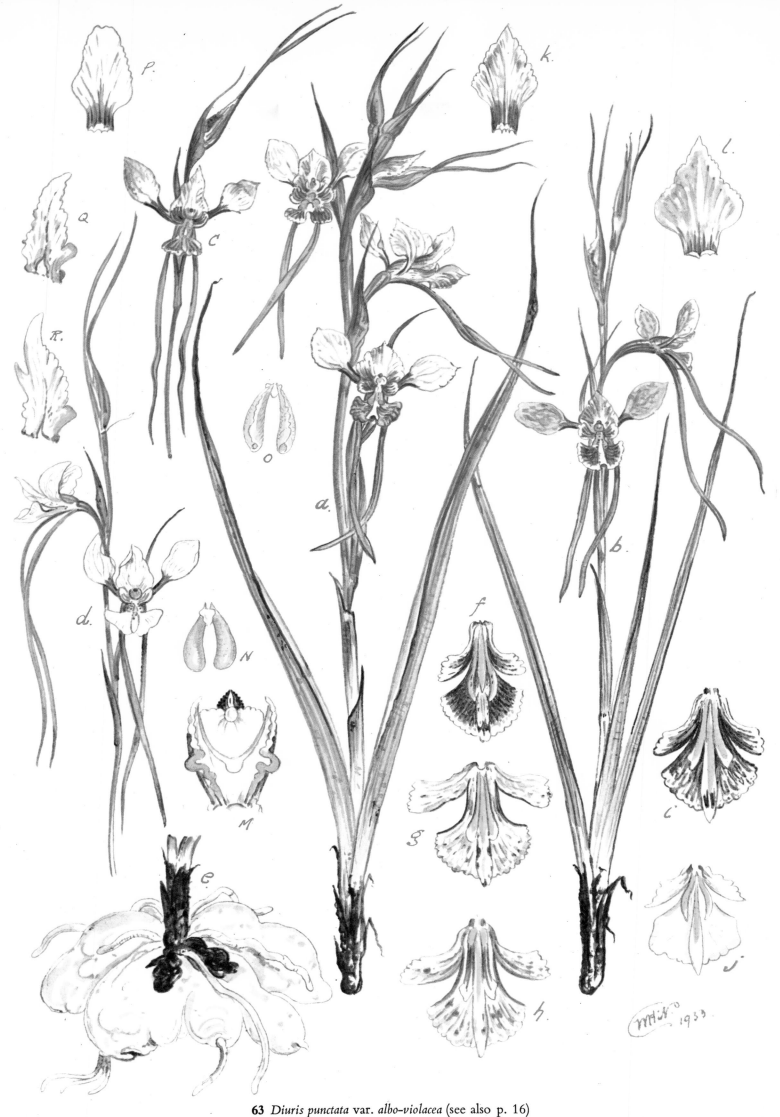

63 *Diuris punctata* var. *albo-violacea* (see also p. 16)

a b c typical specimens **d** a rare form **e** tubers **f g h i j** labella, showing much variation in markings, etc. **k l** dorsal sepals **m** column, showing stigma, etc.
n o pollinia **p** dorsal sepal **q r** column appendages
Figs **a–e** natural size

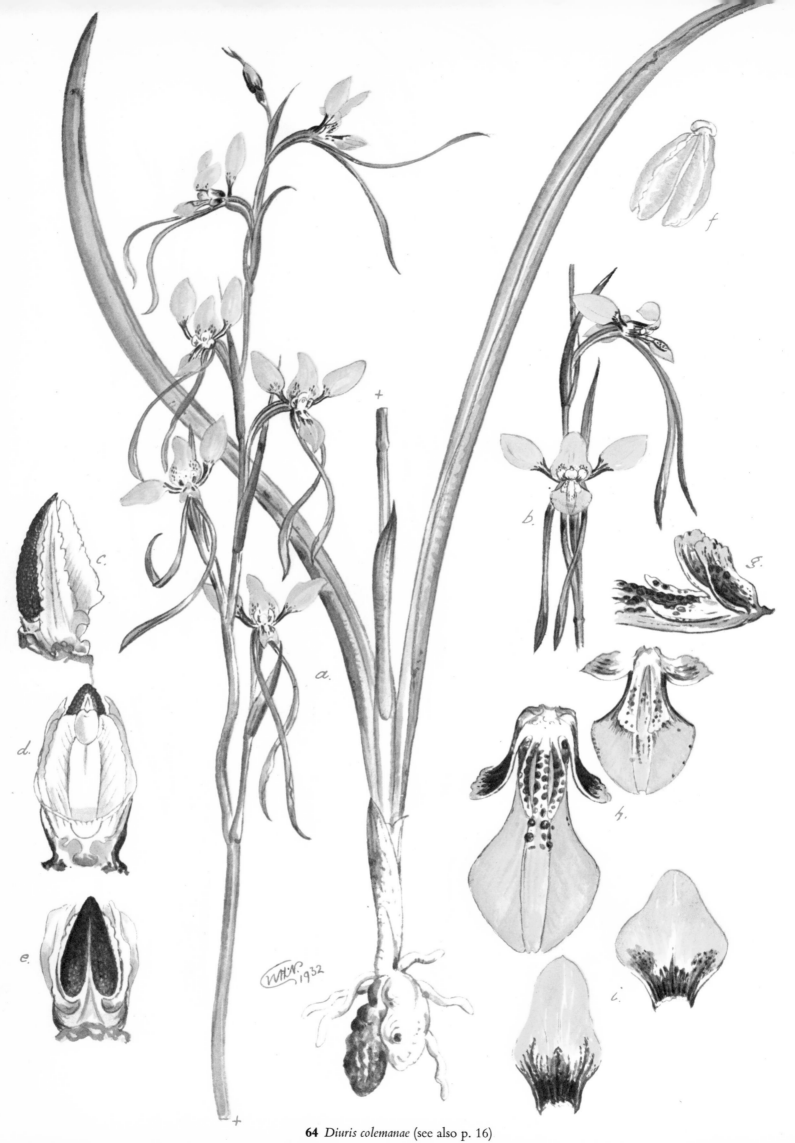

64 *Diuris colemanae* (see also p. 16)

a plant with raceme of flowers from Ganmain, NSW   **b** pale-coloured flowers   **c** column, from side   **d** column, showing stigma, etc.   **e** column, showing anther, etc.
f pollinia   **g** base of labellum, showing callus plates and lateral lobes   **h** two labella, showing the different character of the twin callus plates   **i** two dorsal sepals
Figs **a, b** natural size

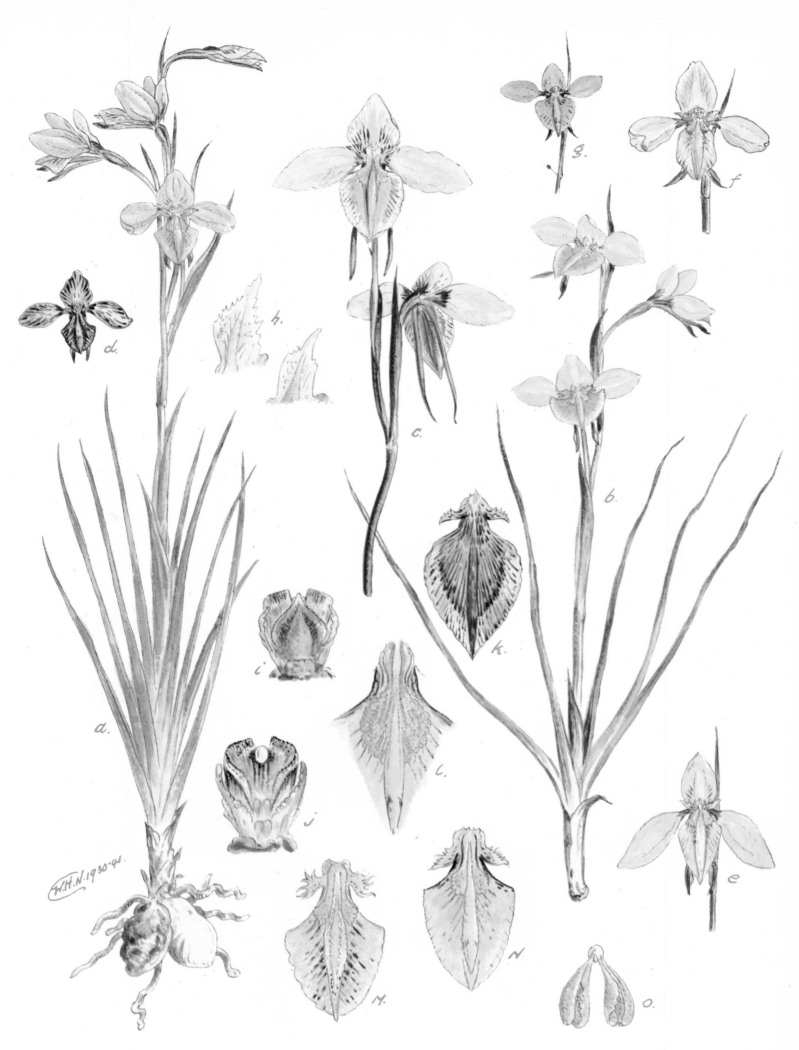

65 *Diuris pedunculata*: Figs **a, b, d–j, m–o** (see also p. 16)
D. pedunculata var. *gigantea*: Figs **c, k, l** (see also p. 16)

a typical specimen **b** showy form from Sydenham, Vic. **c** specimen from Riddell, Vic. **d** striated flower from Mt Buffalo, Vic., also collected at Cravensville, Vic.
e f flower types from Cravensville, Vic. **g** a Keilor Plains, Vic., form **h** column appendages **i** column, showing anther, etc. **j** column, showing stigma, etc. **k** labellum,
from below **l** portion of labellum, showing pubescent lines **m n** labella from Cravensville specimens **o** pollinia
Figs **a–g** natural size

66 *Diuris pallens* (see also p. 16)

a two specimens with filiform leaves **b** two specimens with narrow-linear leaves **c** labellum, from below **d** labellum, from above—also an additional base showing variation of callus plates **e** pollinia **f** lateral sepals **g** dorsal sepal **h** column, showing anther, etc. **i** column, showing stigma, etc. **j** column appendage **k** cross-section of leaf

Figs **a, b** natural size

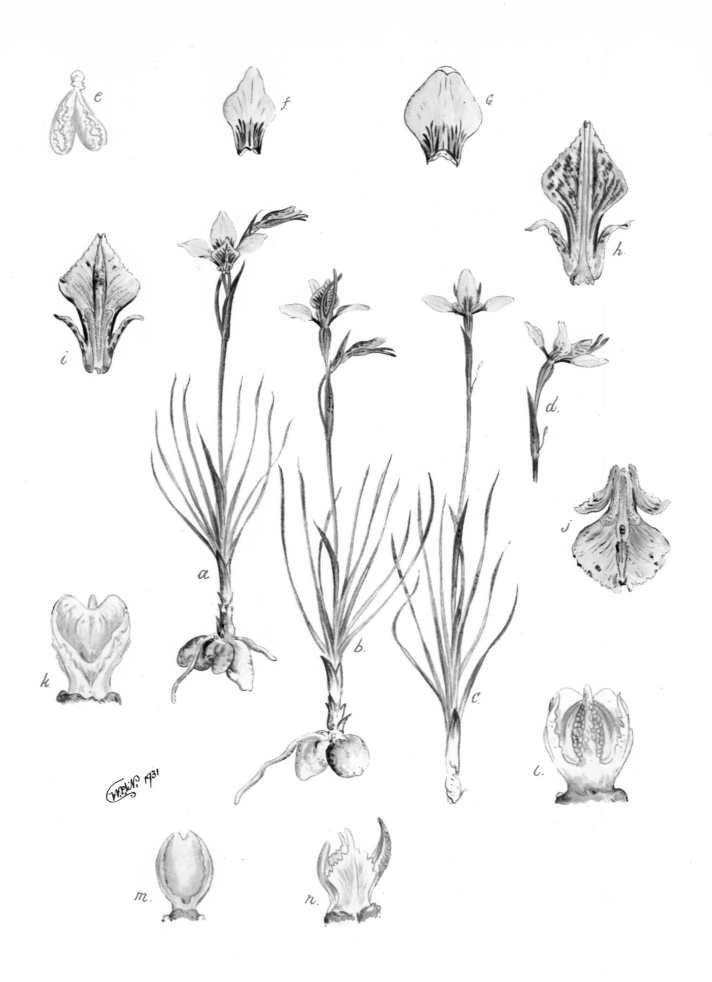

67 *Diuris fastidiosa* (see also p. 17)

(see also p. 17)

a b c d typical specimens **e** pollinia **f g** dorsal sepals **h** labellum, from below **i** labellum, from above **j** labellum, from above **k** column, showing stigma, etc.
l column, showing anther, etc. **m** stigma, showing rostellum (above) **n** column, from side—pollinia removed
Figs **a–d** natural size

68 *Diuris palachila* (see also p. 17)

a b c the most common forms (also the flower above Fig. **a**) **d** specimen from the swampy area near Tottenham, Vic. **e** flowers from Moe, Vic. **f** dorsal sepal **g** a robust, well-marked flower, from rear **h** labella, from above and below (from the Tottenham specimen in Fig. **d**) **i** mid-lobe of a Moe specimen **j** pollinia **k** column appendage **l** column, showing stigma, etc. **m** column, showing anther, etc. **n** base of mid-lobe of labellum, showing plates

Figs **a–e** natural size

69 *Diuris aurea* (see also p. 18)

a typical specimen **b** a well-marked form **c** specimen from Qld **d** pollinia, front and reverse **e f** mid-lobes of labella **g** two labella **h** column, showing stigma, etc.
i column, showing anther, etc. **j** an outsize flower **k** column, showing stigma, etc. (from a flower of Fig. **c**)
Figs **a–c, j** natural size

70 *Diuris abbreviata* (see also p. 18)

a b typical plants from Byron Bay, NSW **c** column, showing stigma covered with pollen **d** labellum, from side **e** labellum and lateral sepals, from above **f** petal
g column, from front, showing stigma, etc. **h** column, from side **i j** variation in the dorsal sepal
Figs **a, b** natural size

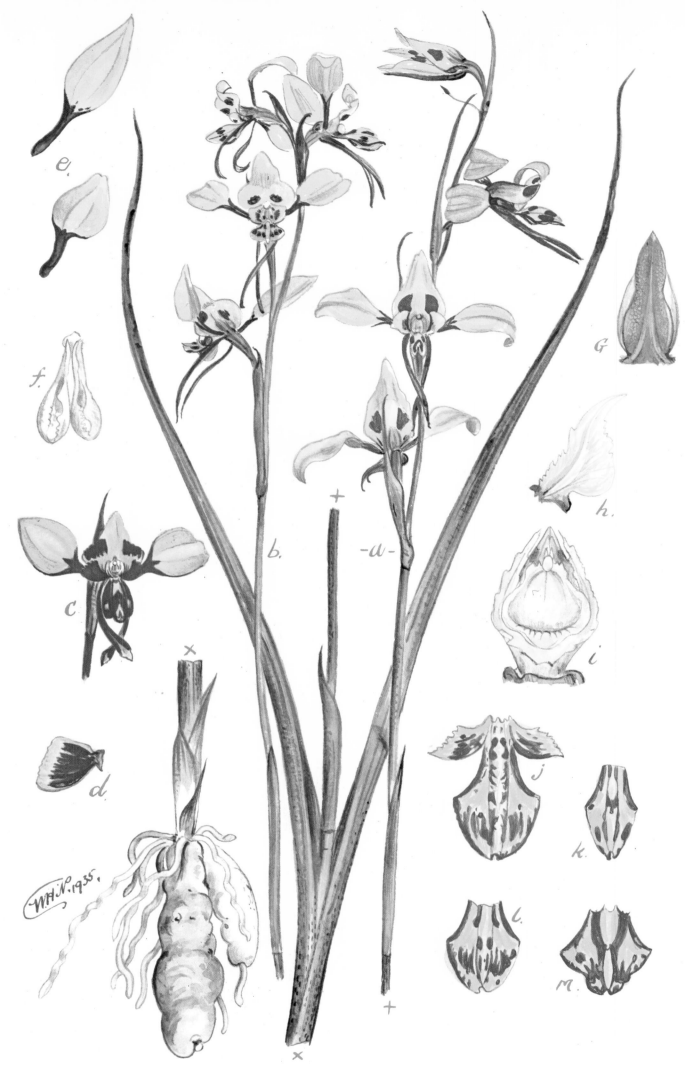

71 *Diuris sulphurea* (see also p. 18)

71 *Diuris sulphurea* (see also p. 18)

a specimen from Coimadai West, Vic.   **b** flowers from Langwarrin South, Vic.   **c** an unusual colour-form from Coimadai, Vic.   **d** lateral lobe from the labellum (Coimadai)
e petal types   **f** pollinia   **g** anther, from rear   **h** column appendage   **i** column, showing stigma, etc.   **j** labellum, from above   **k l m** variation of labellum mid-lobe
Figs **a–c** natural size

72 *Diuris sulphurea*—pelorial form (see also p. 18)

All Figs natural size

73 *Diuris brevifolia* (see also p. 18)

a   b   c   d typical specimen, also racemes of flowers and portion of plant showing tubers   **e** labellum, from above—one lateral lobe removed   **f** pollinia   **g** upper margin of stigma, the disc removed   **h** column, from side   **i** column, showing anther, etc.   **j** column, showing stigma, etc.

Figs **a–d** natural size

74 *Diuris emarginata* (see also p. 19)

a specimen from Manjimup, WA b column, showing stigma, rostellum, etc. c labellum, from above—the lateral lobes spread out d column, showing anther, etc.
e cross-section of leaf f pollinia g column appendage h dorsal sepal
Fig. a natural size

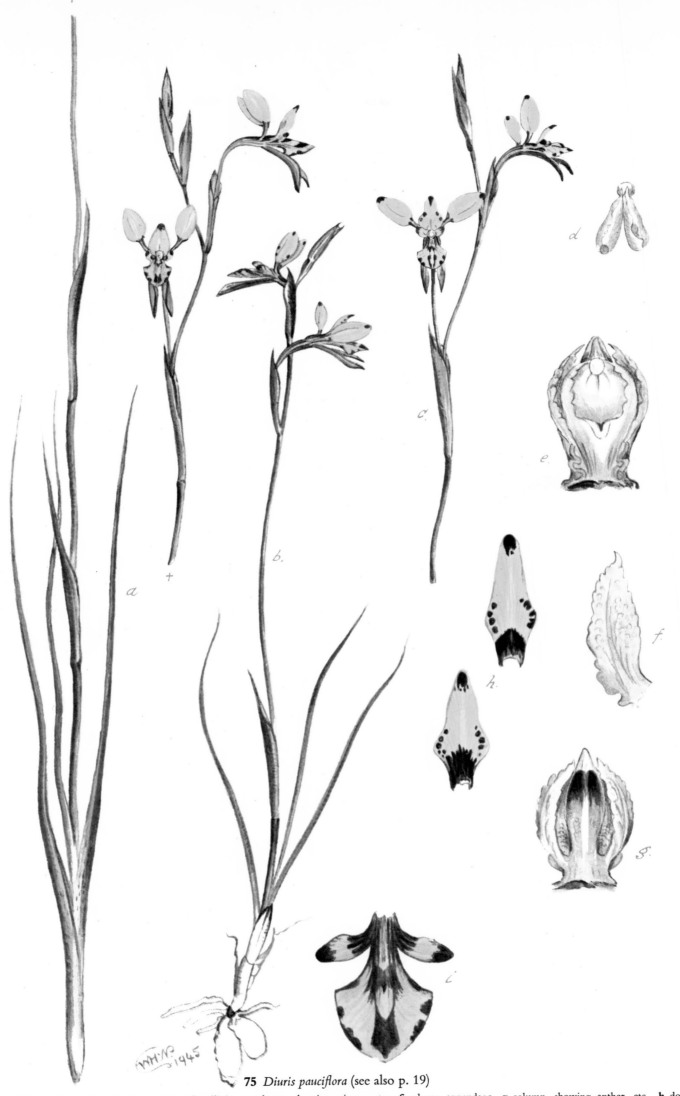

75 *Diuris pauciflora* (see also p. 19)

a b c typical specimens from Yarloop, WA **d** pollinia **e** column, showing stigma, etc. **f** column appendage **g** column, showing anther, etc. **h** dorsal sepals
i labellum, lobes spread out
Figs **a–c** natural size

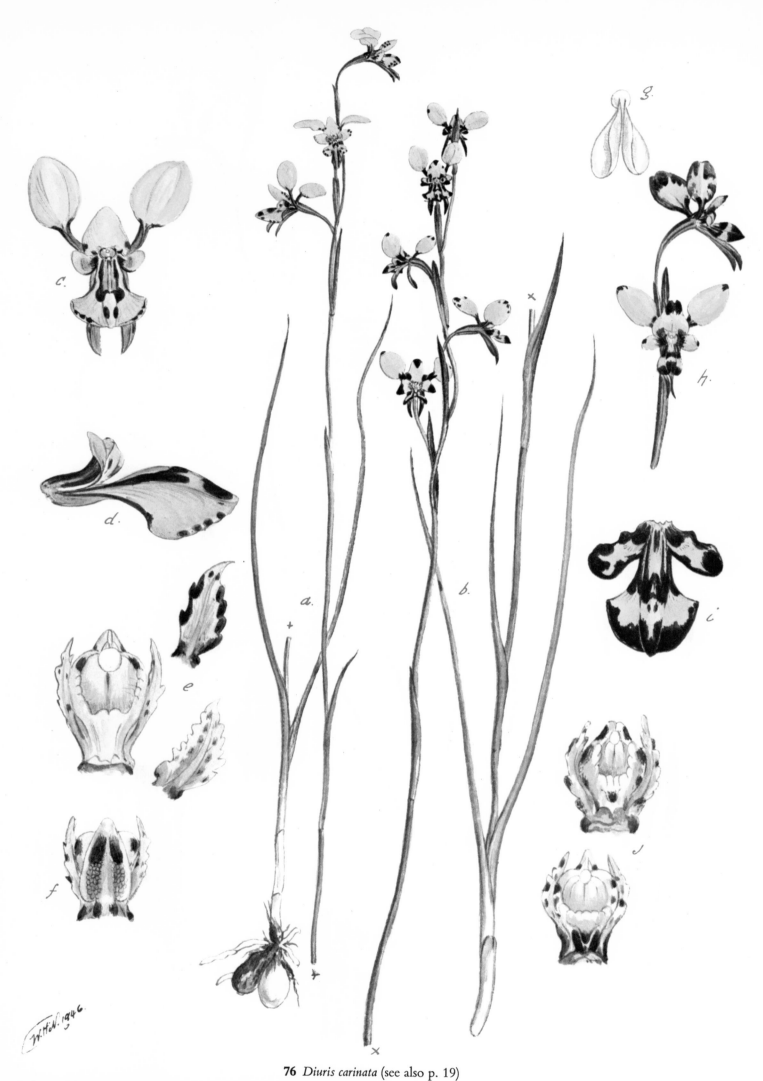

76 *Diuris carinata* (see also p. 19)

a a pale-flowered form from Busselton, WA **b** a well-marked form from the Yarloop district, WA **c** flower from front of form (illustrated in Fig. **a**) **d** labellum, from side (pale form) **e** column, showing stigma, etc., also two column appendage types **f** column, showing anther, etc. **g** pollinia **h** flowers of the larger form found near Perth **i** labellum of same, lamina spread out **j** two more columns, showing stigma, etc.
Figs **a, b, h** natural size

77 *Diuris setacea* (see also p. 19)

a two typical specimens **b** dorsal sepal **c** column, showing anther, etc. **d** column, showing stigma, etc. **e** column appendages **f** pollinia **g** labellum, from above
h labellum, from side
Fig. **a** natural size

78 *Diuris purdiei* (see also p. 19)

a typical Busselton, WA specimen, also single flower and a raceme from the same district   **b** pollinia **c** column appendage **d** a well-marked labellum, from above **e** column, showing stigma, etc. **f** column appendages, showing additional (abnormal) lobes **g** normal column appendage and an abnormal one, from side **h** petal
Fig. **a** natural size

79 *Diuris laevis* (see also p. 20)

a specimen from Upper King River, WA   **b** raceme of flowers from same area   **c**   **d** dorsal sepal types   **e** petals, two types   **f** typical labellum   **g** a broad labellum   **h** column, showing anther, etc.   **i** column appendage   **j** column, showing stigma, etc.
Figs **a, b** natural size

80 *Diuris venosa* (see also p. 20)

a flowering specimen **b** dorsal sepal **c** pollinia **d** column appendage **e** column, showing stigma, etc. **f** column, showing anther, etc. **g** labellum, from side **h** labellum, from above **i** petal

Fig. **a** natural size

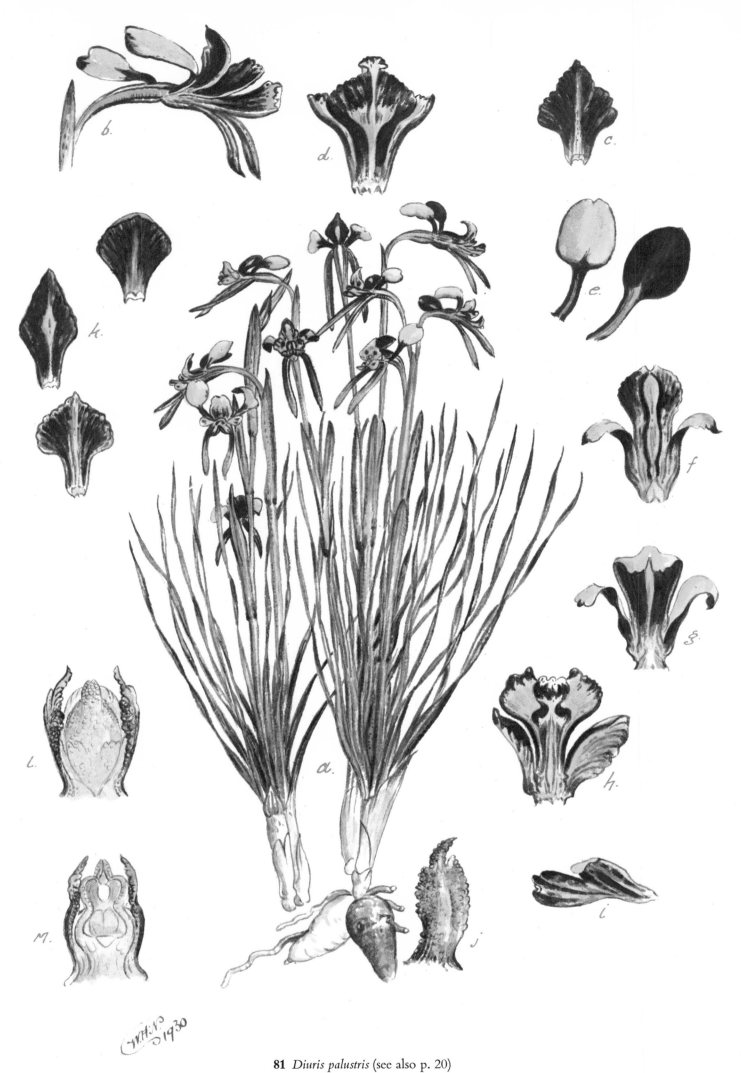

81 *Diuris palustris* (see also p. 20)

a four plants which formed one tuft (tubers on one plant) **b** flower, from side **c** dorsal sepal **d** a labellum, from below **e** petals, from rear and front **f g** labella, from below **h** labellum from above, one lobe spread out **i** labellum, from side **j** column appendage **k** three dorsal sepals **l** column, showing anther, etc. **m** column, showing stigma, etc.

Fig. **a** natural size

82 *Diuris longifolia*: Figs **a–i, k** (see also p. 20)
D. longifolia var. *parviflora*: Figs **j, l, m** (also see p. 20)

a specimen from Staughton Vale, Vic. **b c** flower forms from Croydon, Vic. **d e** two pale-coloured forms **f** labellum, from above **g** column, showing anther, etc.
h column, showing stigma, etc. **i** pollinia **j** flowers **k** a flower from Upper King River, WA **l** column **m** column appendage
Figs **a–e, j, k**, natural size

83 *Diuris maculata* (see also p. 21)

a robust specimen **b** a very rare colour form from Rushworth, Vic. **c** a form resembling the var. *concolor* **d** labellum, from side **e** labellum, from front, one lobe spread
out **f** dorsal sepals **g** column appendage **h** pollinia **i** column, showing stigma, viscid disc, etc.
Figs **a–c** natural size

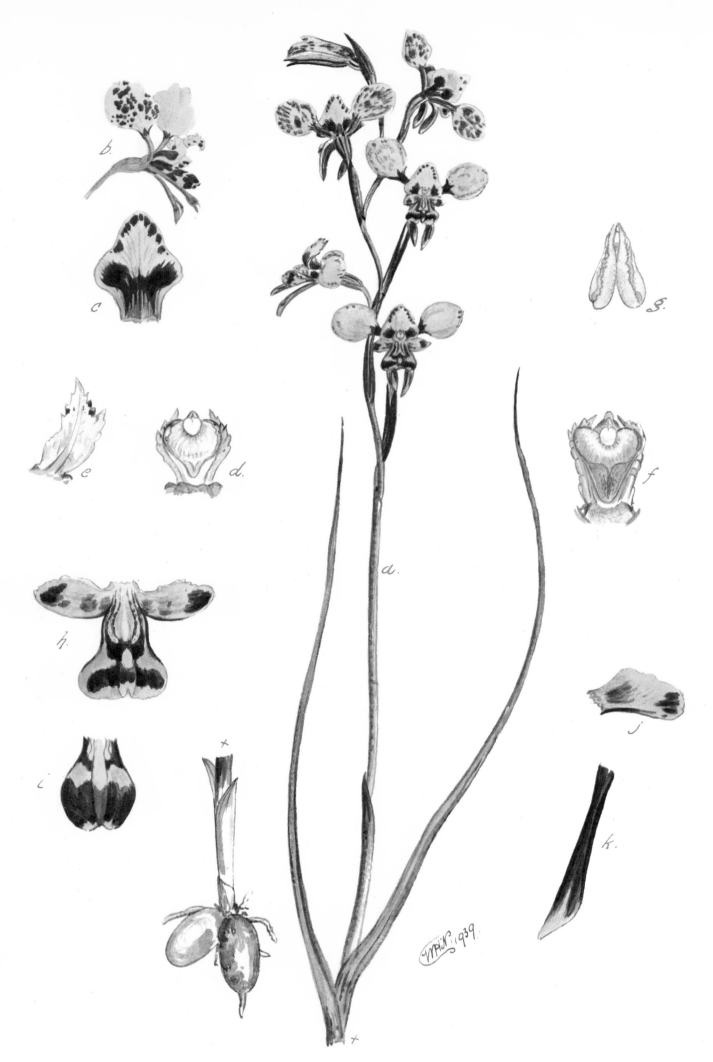

84 *Diuris brevissima* (see also p. 21)

a specimen from near Ararat, Vic. **b** a large-flowered form **c** dorsal sepal **d** column, showing stigma, etc. **e** column appendage **f** another column **g** pollinia
h labellum, the lobes spread out **i** mid-lobe of labellum (not typical) **j** lateral lobe of labellum **k** lateral sepal
Figs **a, b** natural size

85 *Diuris flavopurpurea* (see also p. 21)

a flowering specimen b labellum, from above c dorsal sepal d petal e column, showing stigma, etc. f column appendage g another flowering specimen h labellum, from above i dorsal sepal j column, showing stigma, etc. k column appendage

Figs **a, g** natural size

86 *Diuris citrina* (see also p. 21)

a typical plant   **b** labellum and lateral sepals   **c** dorsal sepal   **d** column, showing stigma, etc.   **e** column appendage
Fig. **a** natural size

87 *Diuris althoferi* (see also p. 22)

a flowering specimen **b** another flowering specimen **c** flower **d** labellum, from above, also lateral sepals **e** column, showing stigma, etc. **f** lateral lobe of column
g labellum, from above **h** column, showing stigma, etc.
Figs **a–c** natural size

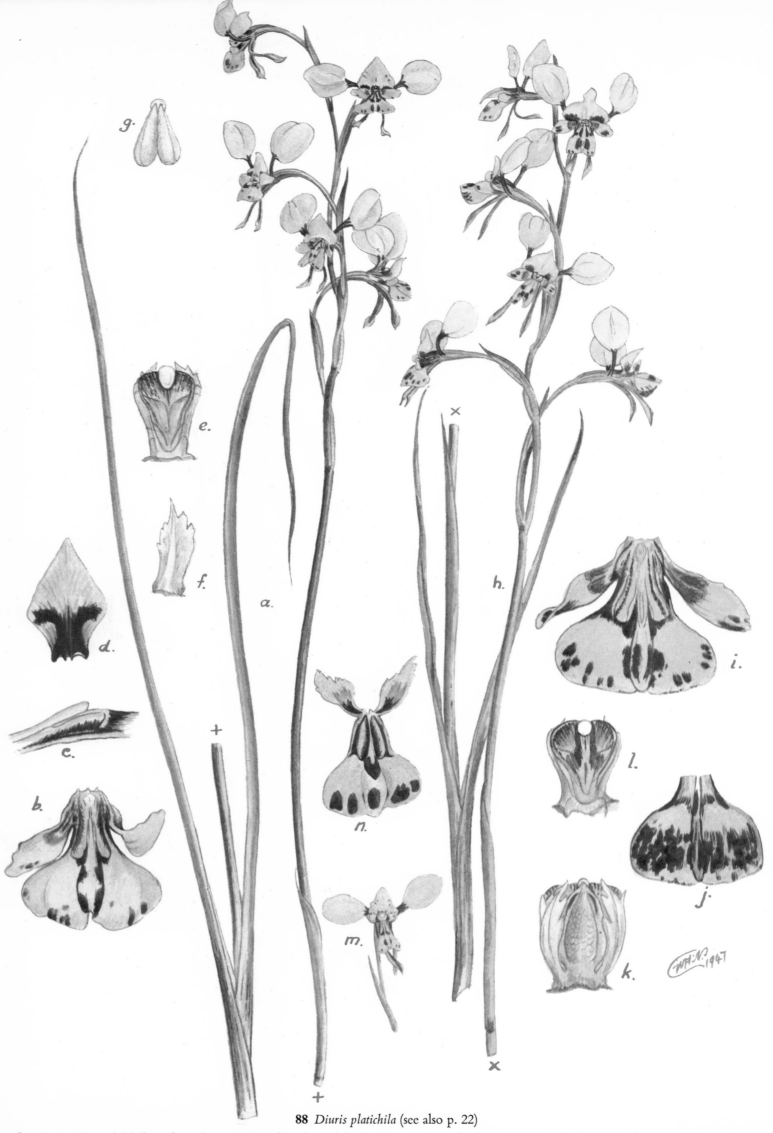

88 *Diuris platichila* (see also p. 22)

a flowering specimen b labellum, from above c ridge of labellum d dorsal sepal e column, showing stigma, etc. f column appendage g pollinia h flowering
specimen i labellum, from above j labellum mid-lobe k column, showing anther, etc. l column, showing stigma, etc. m flower n labellum, lateral lobes spread out
Figs a, h, m natural size

89 *Diuris lineata* (see also p. 22)

a specimen from Kerr's Creek, NSW **b** labellum, one lobe spread out **c** mid-lobe **d** column, showing stigma, etc. **e** column appendage **f** pollinia
Fig. **a** natural size

90 *Orthoceras strictum* (see also p. 22)

a b two specimens from Boronia, Vic. **c** column, from front **d** golden-green flowers from Sassafras, Vic. **e** pollinia **f** apices of petals **g** column and petals, from side
h labellum, from above **i** labellum, from side
Figs **a, b, d** natural size

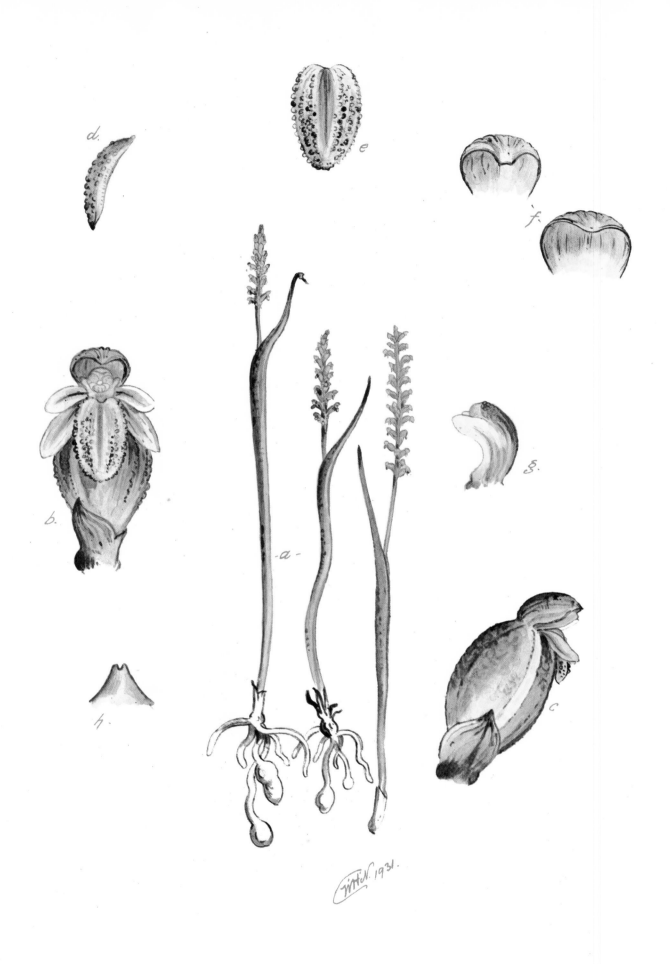

91 *Microtis atrata* (see also p. 23)

a robust specimens **b** flower, from front **c** flower, from side **d** labellum, from side **e** labellum, from front **f** upper parts of dorsal sepals **g** column, from side **h** rostellum
Fig. **a** natural size

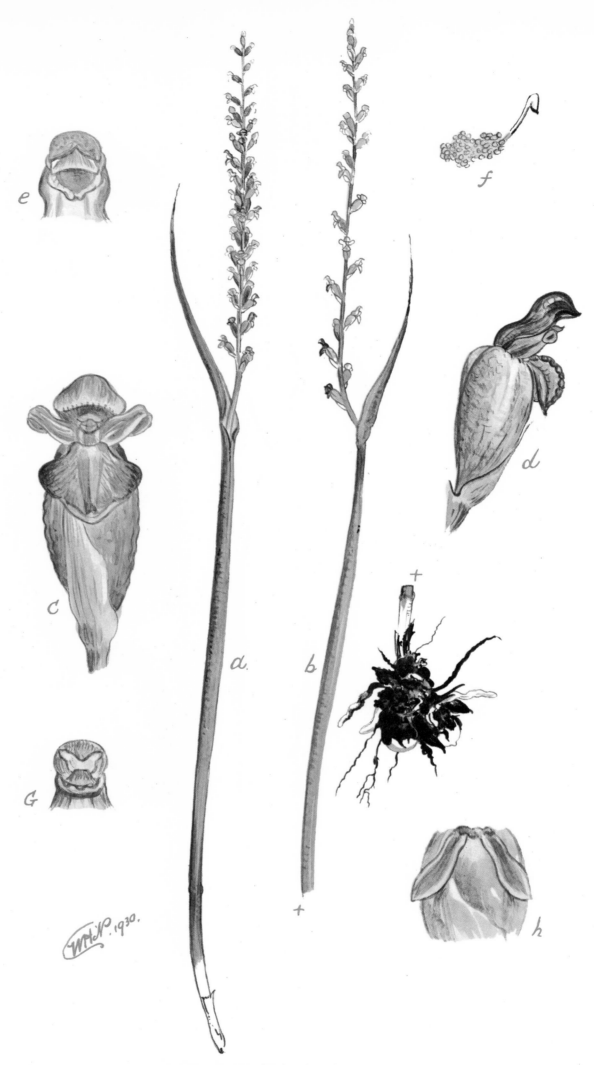

92 *Microtis orbicularis* (see also p. 23)

a b typical specimens from Wonthaggi, Vic. **c** flower, from front **d** flower, from side **e** column, from front—pollinia removed **f** pollinia **g** column, from front—from a bud **h** lateral sepals

Figs **a, b** natural size

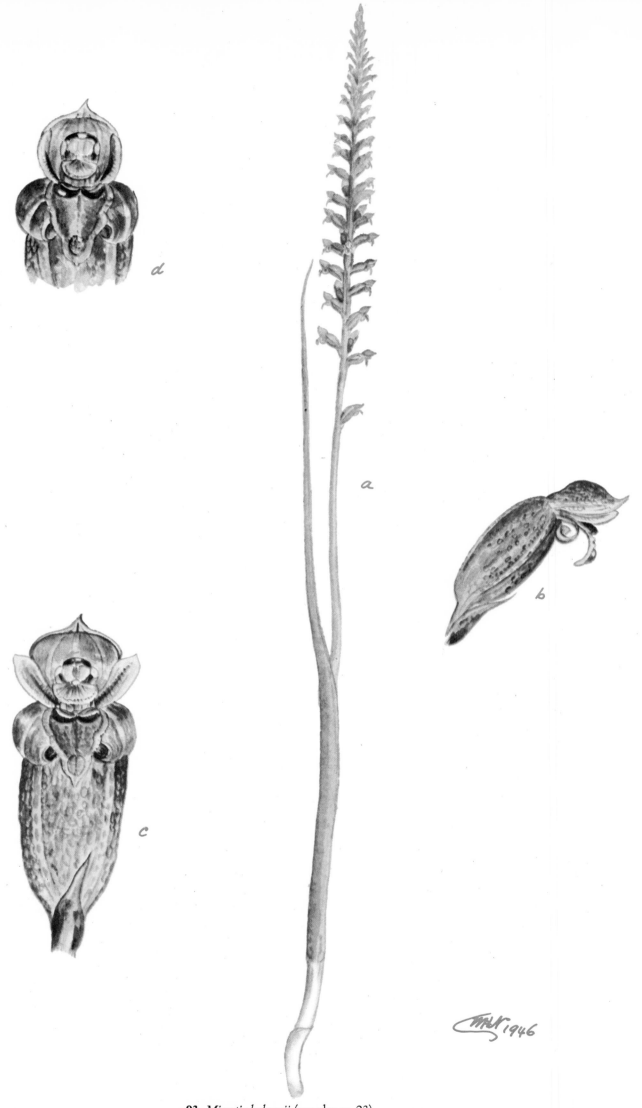

93 *Microtis holmesii* (see also p. 23)

a typical specimen   **b** flower, from side   **c** flower, from front   **d** upper part of another flower
Fig. **a** natural size

94 *Microtis parviflora* (see also p. 23)

a typical specimen   **b** pollinia, from two aspects   **c** upper portion of flower   **d** apex of labellum   **e** flower, from side   **f** labellum, from side   **g** basal callosities of labellum
h two labella   **i** flower, from side   **j** two columns   **k** column, from front   **l** flower, from side
Fig. **a** natural size

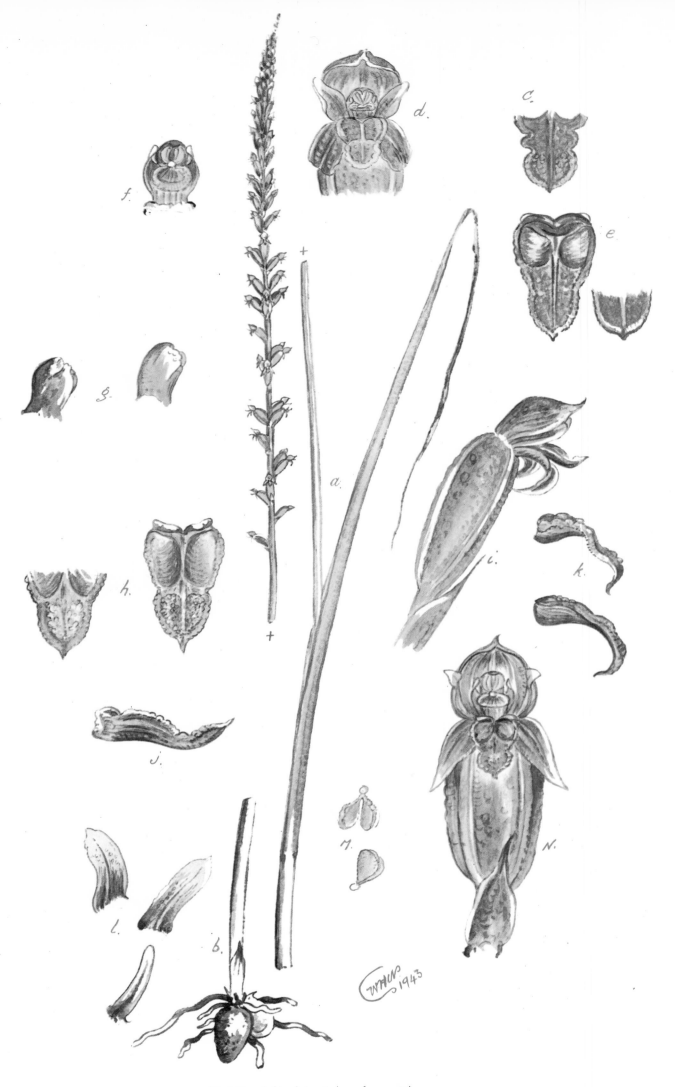

95 *Microtis bipulvinaris* (see also p. 24)

a typical specimen b tubers, etc. c an unusual labellum tip d a flower type e labellum and apex f column, from front g columns, from side h typical labellum and another apex i flower, from side j typical labellum, from side k two labella, from side l petals m two pairs of pollinia n flower, from front
Figs **a, b** natural size

96 *Microtis unifolia* (see also p. 24)

a a specimen collected near Bordertown, SA **b** three flowers, from side **c** flower, from front **d** pollinia **e** two columns, from side **f** column, from front **g** flower, from side

Fig. **a** natural size

97 *Microtis biloba* (see also p. 24)

a typical specimen   **b** flower, from front   **c** flower, from side   **d** labellum
Fig. **a** natural size

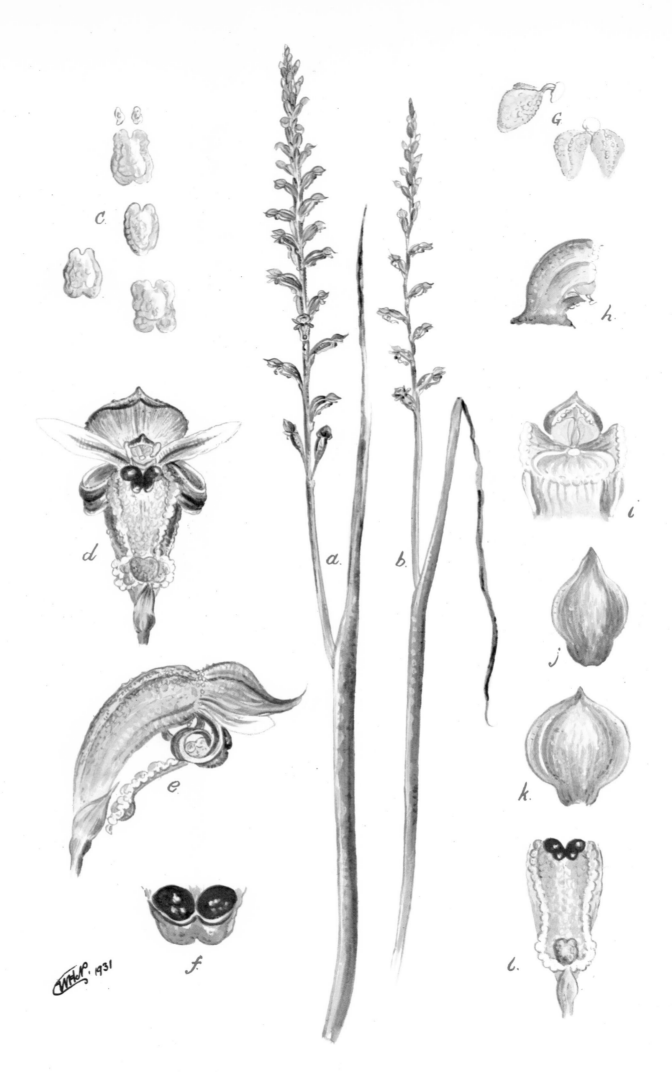

98 *Microtis oblonga* (see also p. 24)

a b typical specimens **c** variable character of callosities near apex of labellum lamina **d** flower with widely-spread petals **e** flower, from side **f** callosities at base of lamina
g pollinia **h** column, from side **i** column, from front **j k** dorsal sepals **l** labellum, etc.
Figs **a, b** natural size

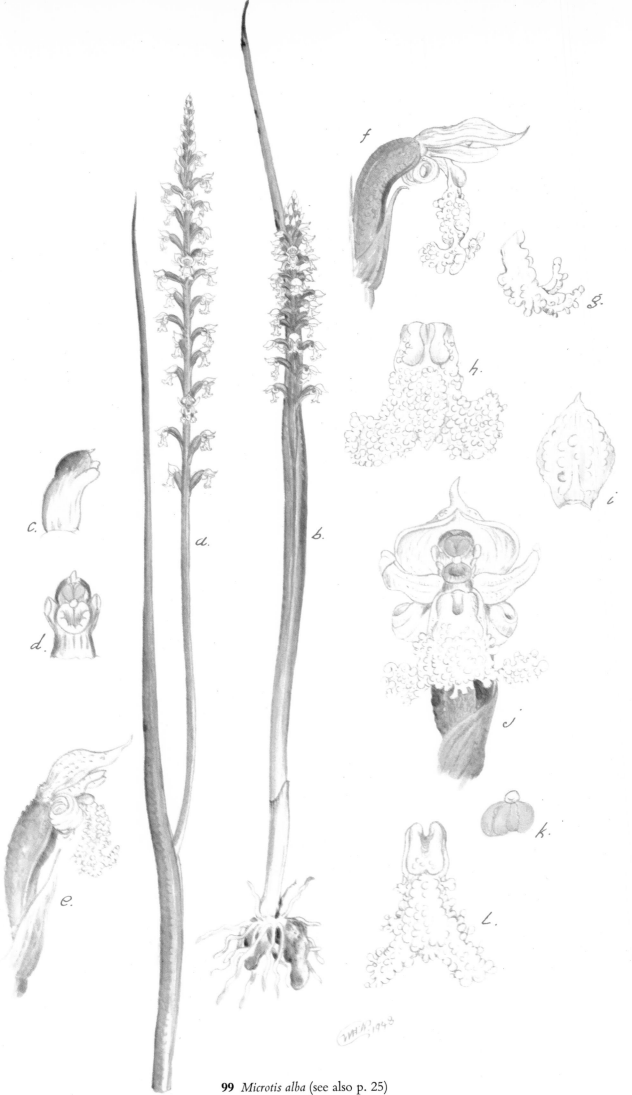

99 *Microtis alba* (see also p. 25)

a a specimen (lower part removed) from the Darling Range area, WA **b** specimen typical of the sandy slopes near Albany, WA **c** column, from side **d** column, from front
e flower, from side **f** another flower, from side **g** tip of a labellum, from side **h** labellum, from front **i** a dorsal sepal **j** flower, from front **k** pollinia **l** another labellum,
from front
Figs **a, b** natural size

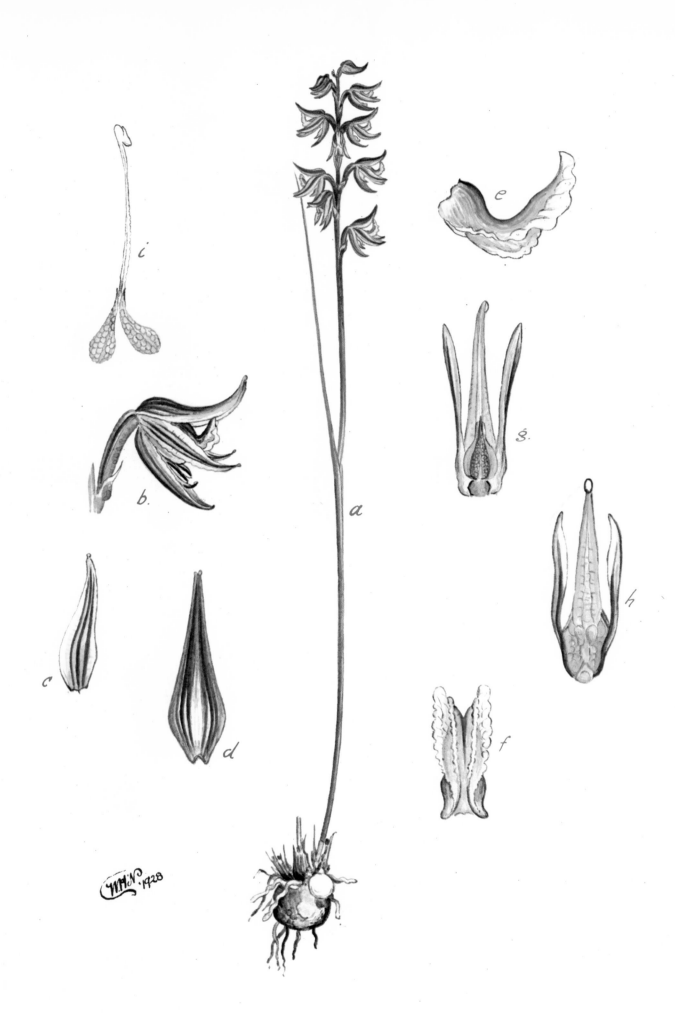

100 *Prasophyllum striatum* (see also p. 25)

a typical specimen **b** flower, from side **c** petal **d** conjoined sepals **e** labellum, from side **f** labellum, from below **g** column, showing anther, etc. **h** column, showing stigma, etc. **i** pollinia
Fig. **a** natural size

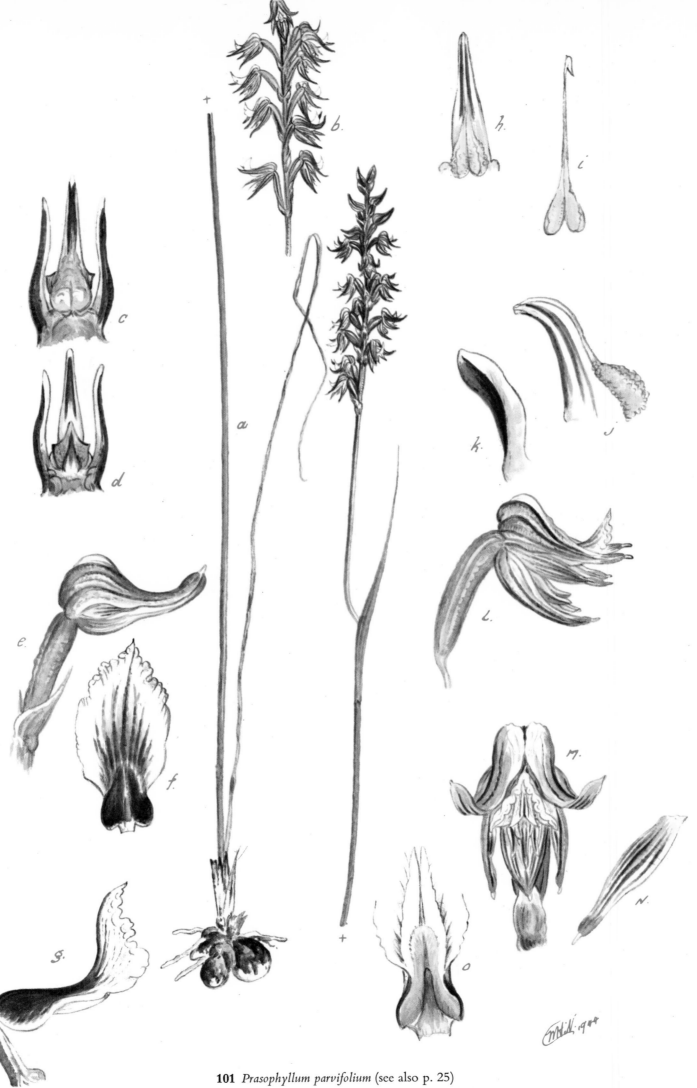

101 *Prasophyllum parvifolium* (see also p. 25)

a b two Yarloop, WA, specimens (note withered remains of previous season's leaf in Fig. **a**) **c** column, showing stigma, etc. **d** column, showing anther, etc. **e** characteristic bud—note the reptilian-like appearance **f** labellum, from below **g** labellum attached to the basal projection of column, from side **h** rostellum with pollinia in position **i** pollinia **j** rostellum and pollinia, from side **k** appendage of column, from side **l** flower, from side **m** flower, from front **n** petal **o** base of labellum, from front
Figs **a, b** natural size

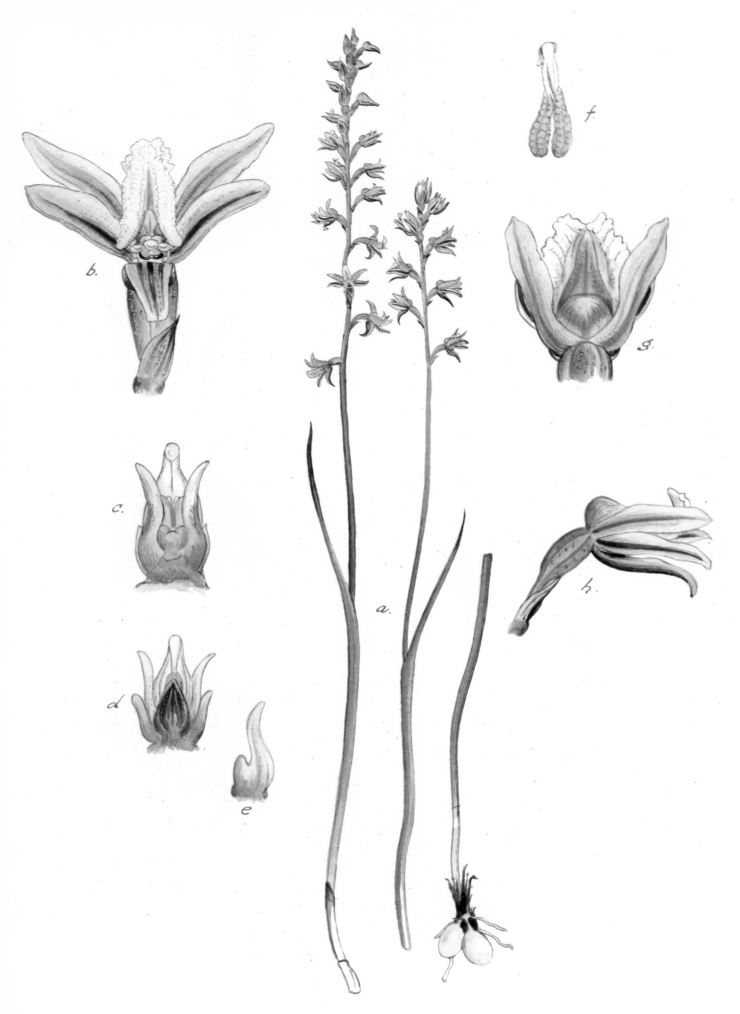

102 *Prasophyllum cyphochilum* (see also p. 26)

a two typical specimens **b** flower, from front **c** column, showing stigma, etc. **d** column, showing anther, etc. **e** column appendage **f** pollinia **g** flower, from above
h flower, from side
Fig. **a** natural size

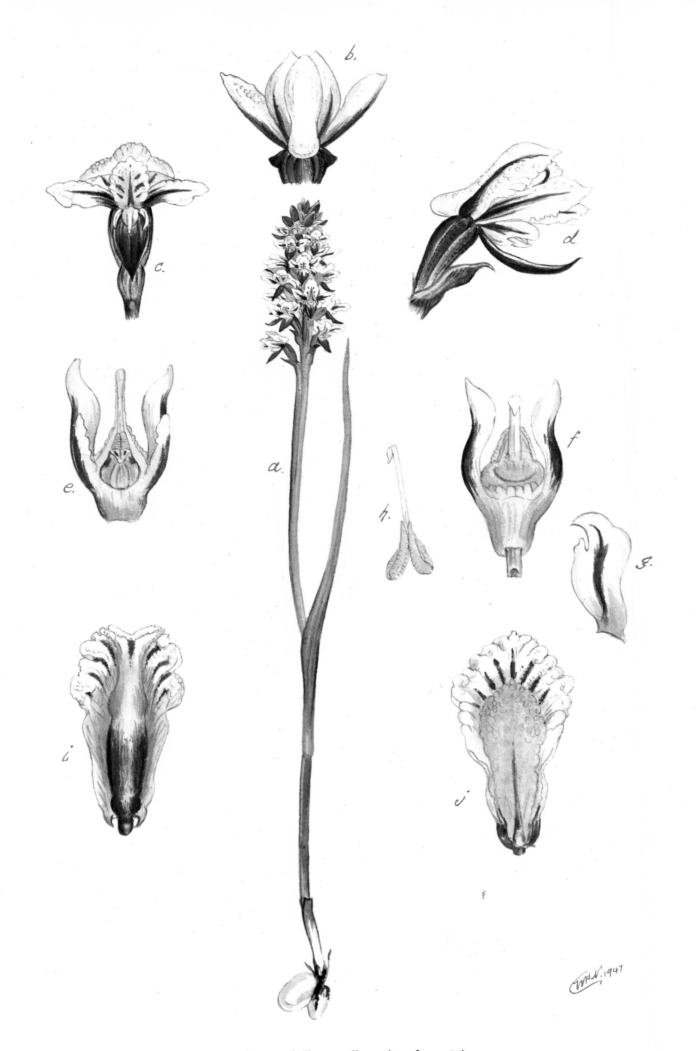

103 *Prasophyllum cucullatum* (see also p. 26)

a typical specimen   b flower, from above   c flower, from front   d flower, from side   e column, showing anther, etc.   f column, showing stigma, etc.   g column appendage
h pollinia   i labellum, from above   j labellum, from front
Fig. **a** natural size

104 *Prasophyllum fimbria* (see also p. 26)

a a specimen collected from the wet swamp areas of the Upper King River, WA **b** the fimbriated callus plate of the labellum **c** pollinia **d** flower, from side **e** column, showing stigma, rostellum, etc.—pollinia removed **f** column, showing anther, etc. **g** flower, from front—also fimbria, from the labellum **h** column appendage
Fig. **a** natural size

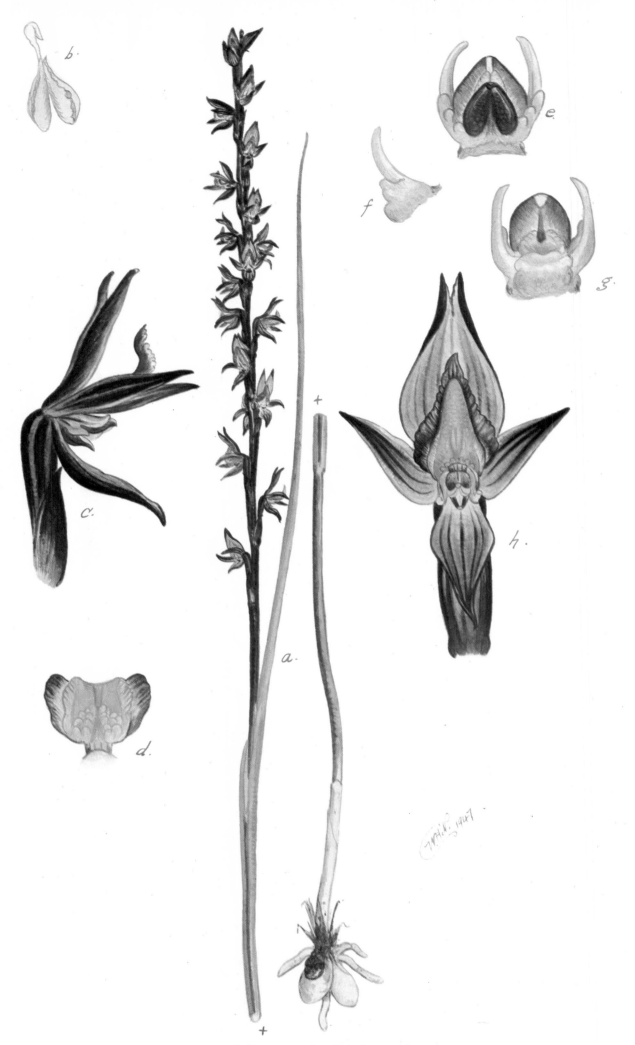

105 *Prasophyllum triangulare* (see also p. 26)

a a specimen from the Upper King River district, WA   **b** pollinia   **c** flower, from side   **d** labellum, from rear   **e** column, showing anther, etc.   **f** column appendage
g column, showing stigma, etc.   **h** flower, from front
Fig. **a** natural size

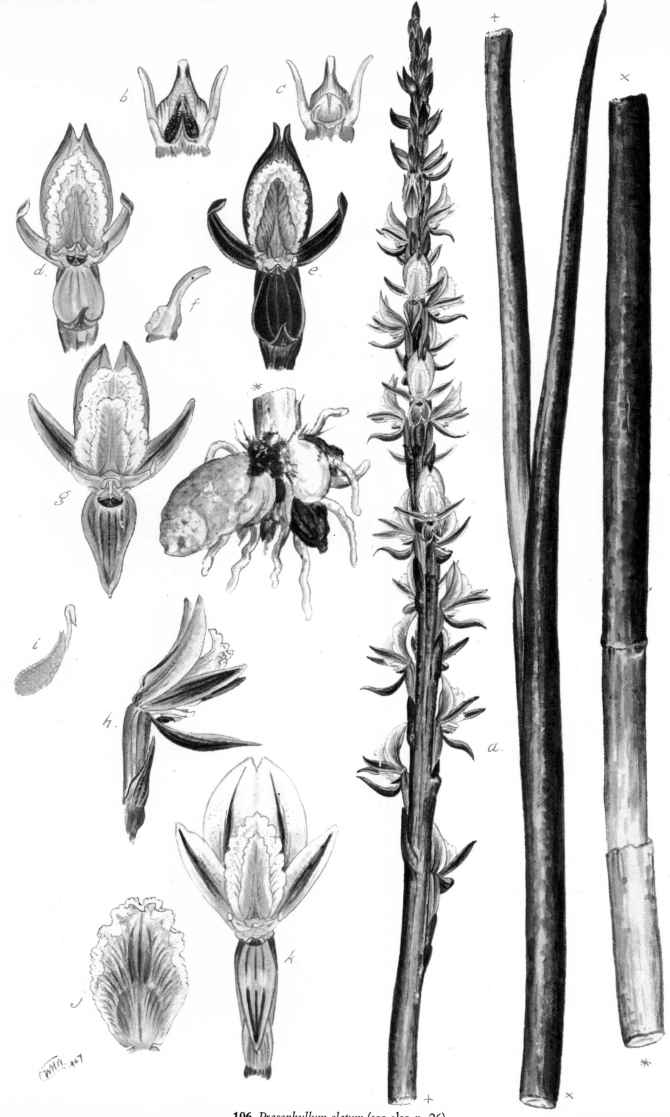

106 *Prasophyllum elatum* (see also p. 26)

a a specimen from Yarloop, WA **b** column, showing anther, etc. **c** column, showing stigma, etc. **d** yellowish form from Cheltenham, Vic. **e** dusky form from Cheltenham, Vic. **f** column appendage **g** another Yarloop flower **h** same, from side **i** pollinia **j** labellum, from above **k** a fine flower from Busselton, WA
Fig. **a** natural size

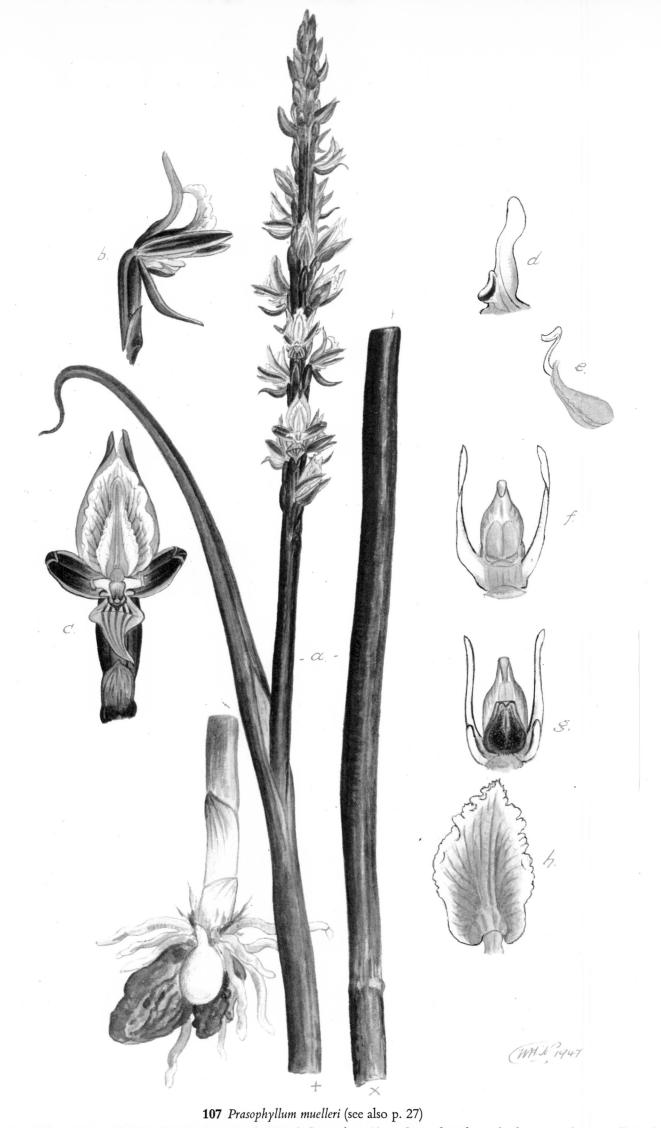

107 *Prasophyllum muelleri* (see also p. 27)

a a typical, though smallish, specimen, collected at City Beach near Perth, WA   **b** flower, from side   **c** flower, from front   **d** column appendage   **e** pollinia   **f** column, showing stigma, etc.   **g** column, showing anther, etc.   **h** labellum, from above
Fig. **a** natural size

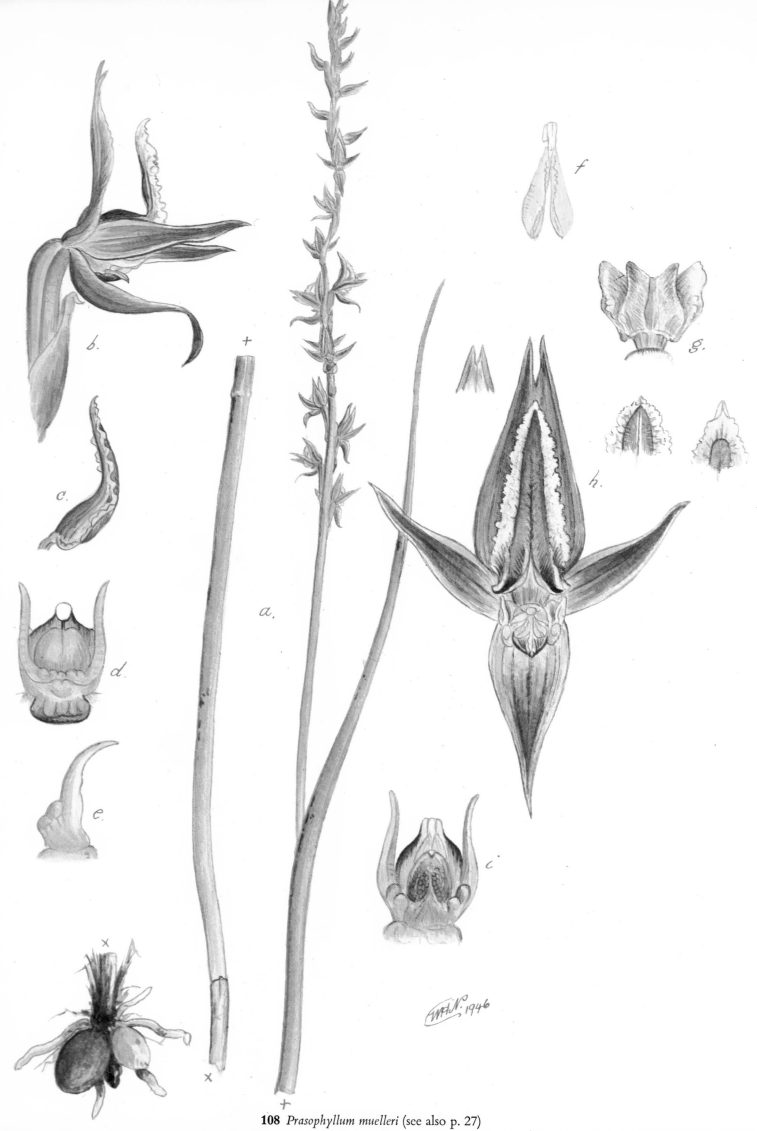

108 *Prasophyllum muelleri* (see also p. 27)

a a typical specimen **b** flower, from side **c** labellum, from side **d** column, showing stigma, etc. **e** column appendage **f** pollinia **g** labellum, from rear **h** flower, from front, also variation at apex of lateral sepals and tip of labellum **i** column, showing anther, etc.

Fig. **a** natural size

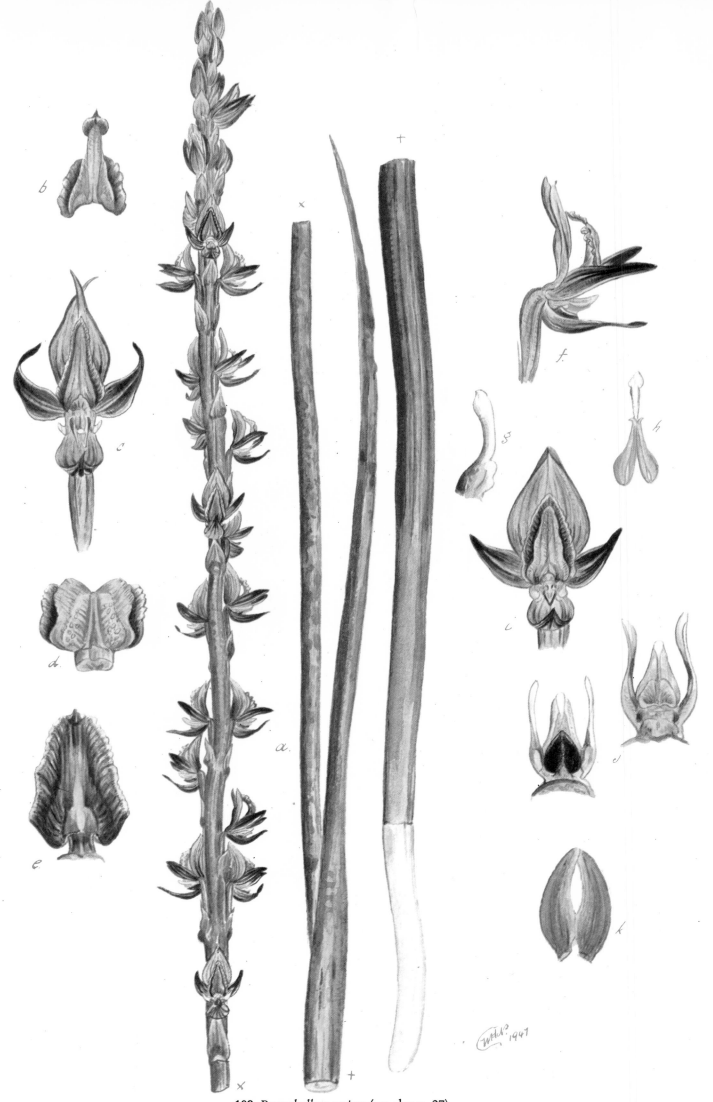

109 *Prasophyllum regium* (see also p. 27)

a a comparatively small example   **b** labellum, from front of an Oyster Cove specimen   **c** flower, Upper Kalgan district, WA   **d** labellum, from below   **e** labellum, from above   **f** flower, from side, from the Oyster Cove specimen   **g** column appendage   **h** pollinia   **i** flower, from front, from a Manjimup, WA, specimen   **j** column, from rear and front   **k** conjoined sepals, connate towards base only

Fig. **a** natural size

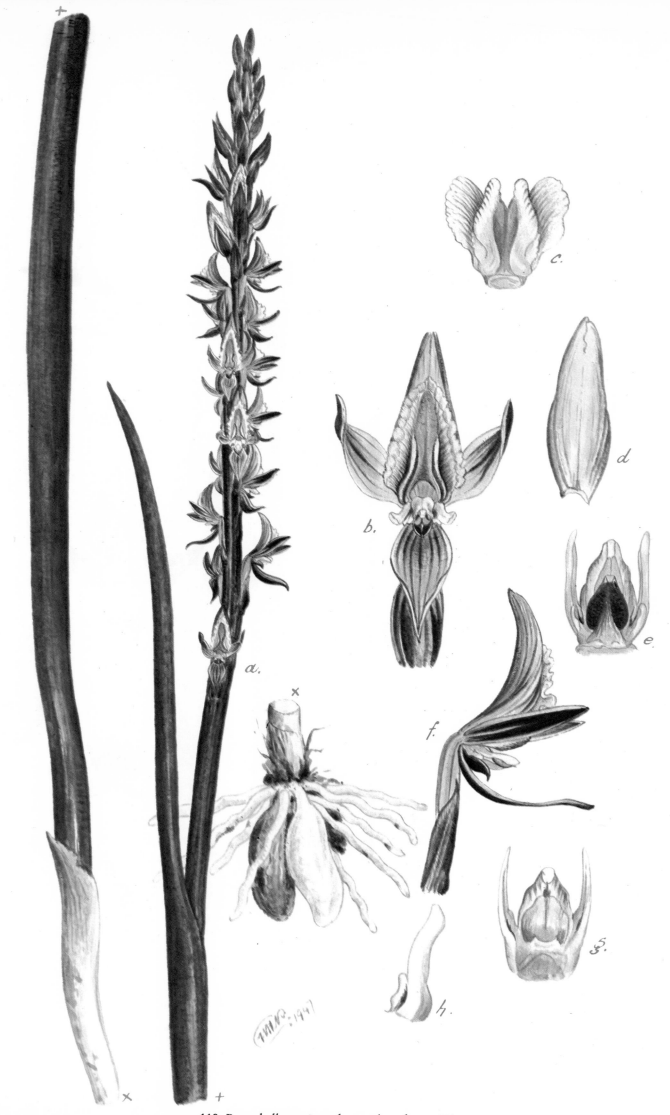

110 *Prasophyllum grimwadeanum* (see also p. 27)

a the type specimen **b** flower, from front **c** labellum, from rear **d** lateral sepals, from above **e** column, showing anther, etc. **f** flower, from side **g** column, showing stigma, etc. **h** column appendage
Fig. **a** natural size

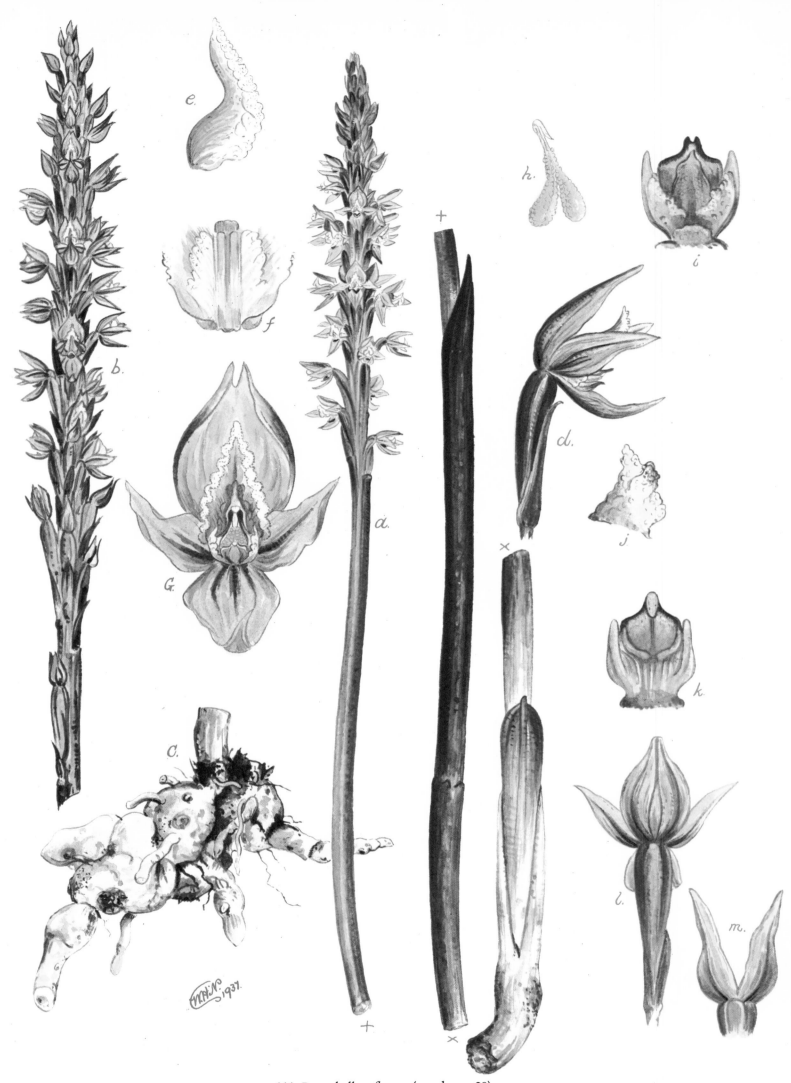

111 *Prasophyllum flavum* (see also p. 28)

a a mountain form, typical of specimens found growing in the Dandenong Ranges and near Mt Wellington, Vic. **b** flowers from the foothills of the Baw Baws, Vic. **c** tuber **d** flower, from side **e** labellum, from side **f** base of labellum lamina **g** flower, from front **h** pollinia **i** column, showing anther, etc. **j** appendage of column **k** column, showing stigma, etc. **l** flower, from above **m** lateral sepals—free

Figs **a, b, c** natural size

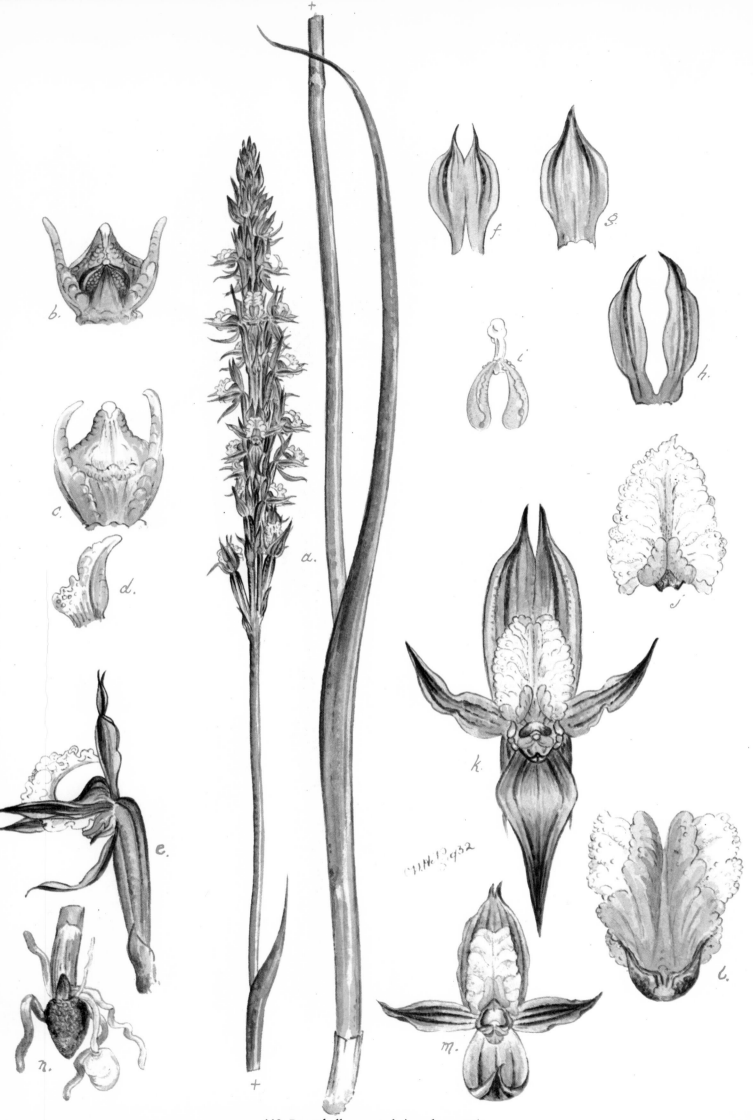

112 *Prasophyllum australe* (see also p. 28)

a typical specimen **b** column, showing anther, etc. **c** column, showing stigma, etc. **d** column appendage **e** flower, from side **f g h** lateral sepals, united and otherwise
i pollinia **j** labellum, from front **k** flower, from front **l** labellum, from base, showing prominent callus plate **m** flower from Smithton, Tas. **n** tubers
Figs **a, n** natural size

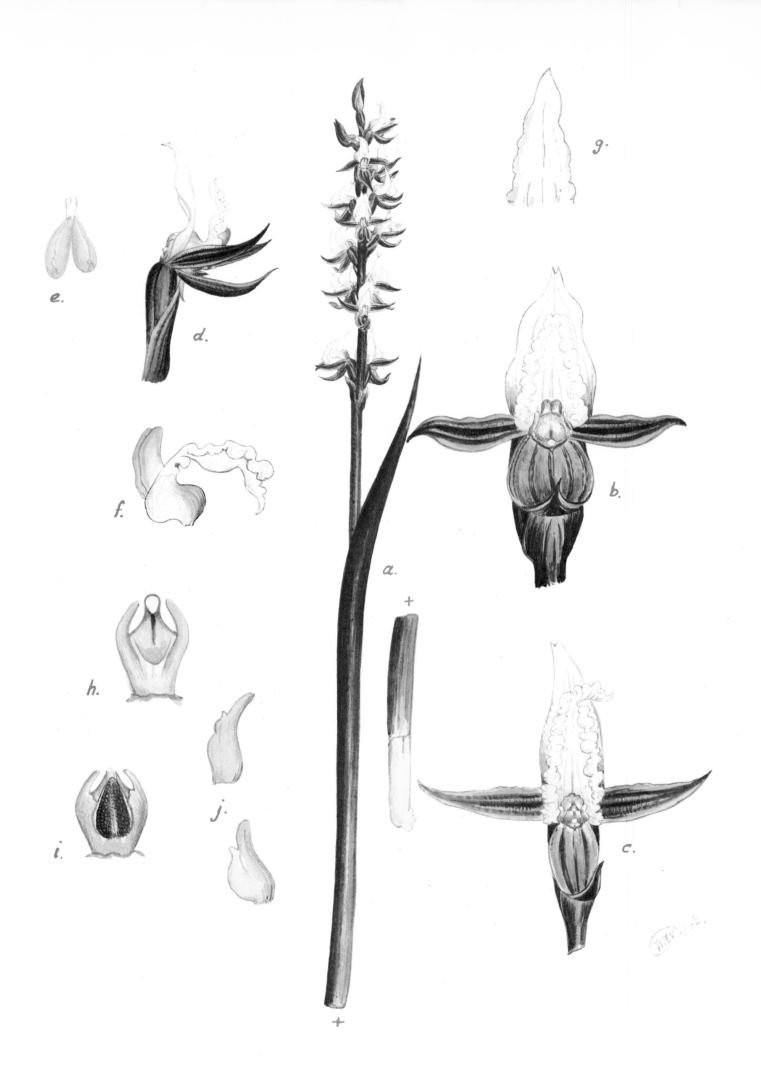

113 *Prasophyllum australe* var. *sargentii* (see also p. 29)

a flowering specimen **b c** flowers, from front **d** flower, from side **e** pollinia **f** labellum, from side **g** labellum lamina **h** column, showing stigma, etc. **i** column, showing anther, etc. **j** column appendages

Fig. **a** natural size

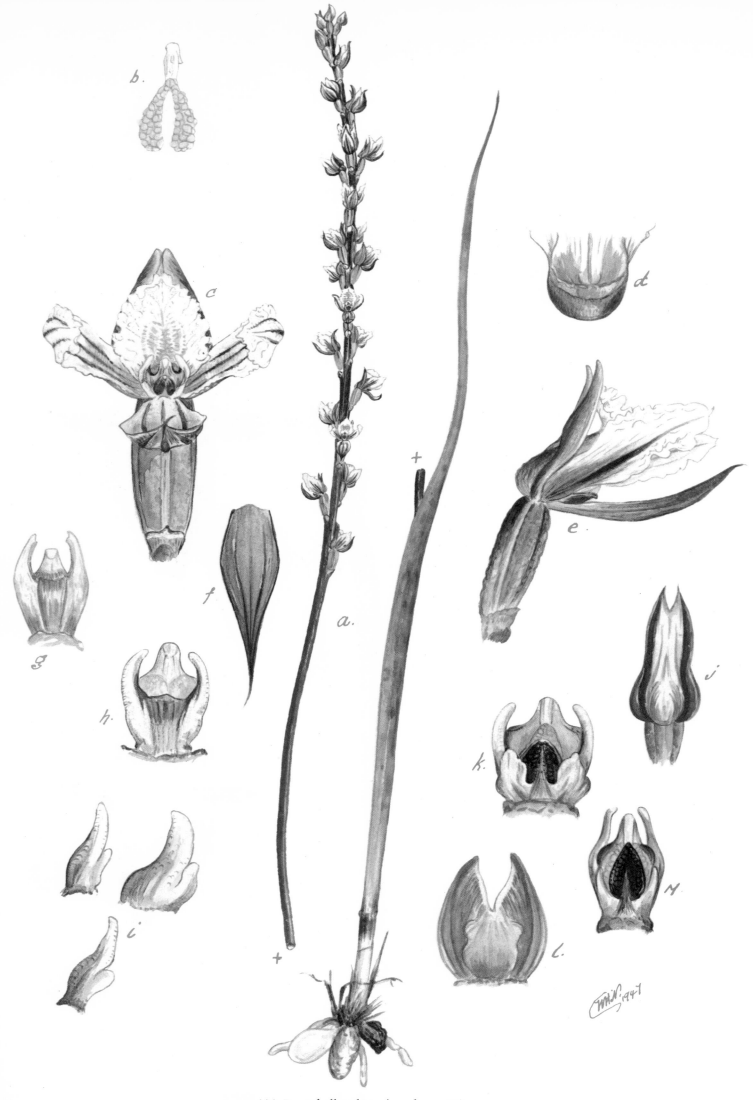

114 *Prasophyllum hians* (see also p. 29)

a specimen from the Nanarup district, WA   **b** pollinia   **c** flower, from front   **d** cup-like depression at base of labellum   **e** flower, from side   **f** dorsal sepal   **g h** columns, showing stigma, etc.   **i** column appendages   **j** conjoined sepals, from above   **k** column, showing anther, etc.   **l** lateral sepals, showing sac at base, formed by the protruding base of the labellum   **m** another column, showing anther, etc.

Fig. **a** natural size

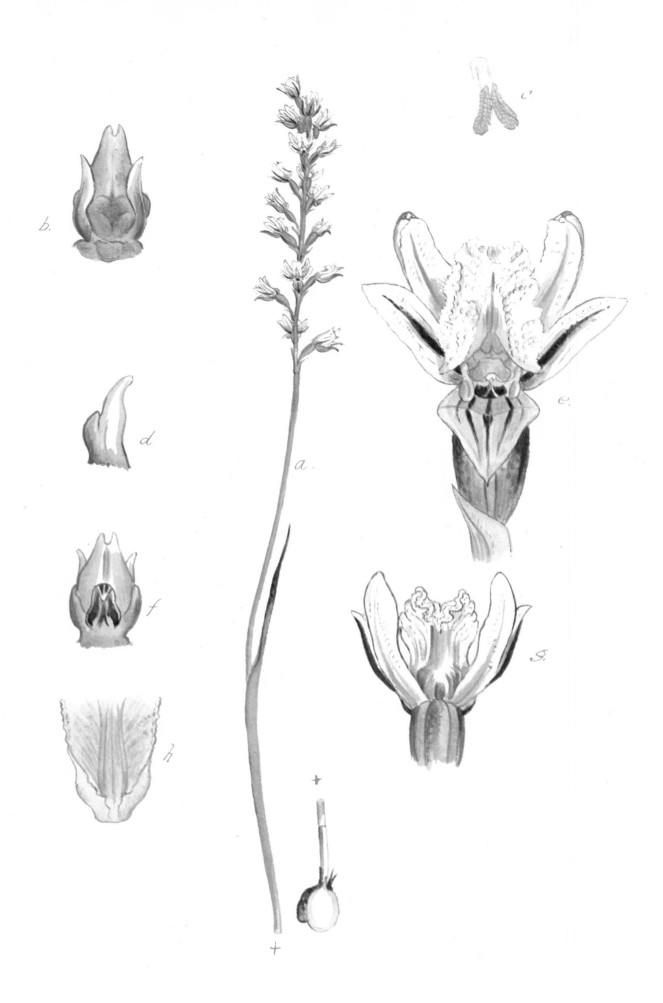

115 *Prasophyllum plumaeforme* (see also p. 29)

a specimen from the Arrowsmith district, WA b column, showing stigma, etc.—pollinia removed c pollinia d column appendage e flower, from front f column, showing anther, etc.—pollinia removed g flower, from above h base of labellum, from below

Fig. **a** natural size

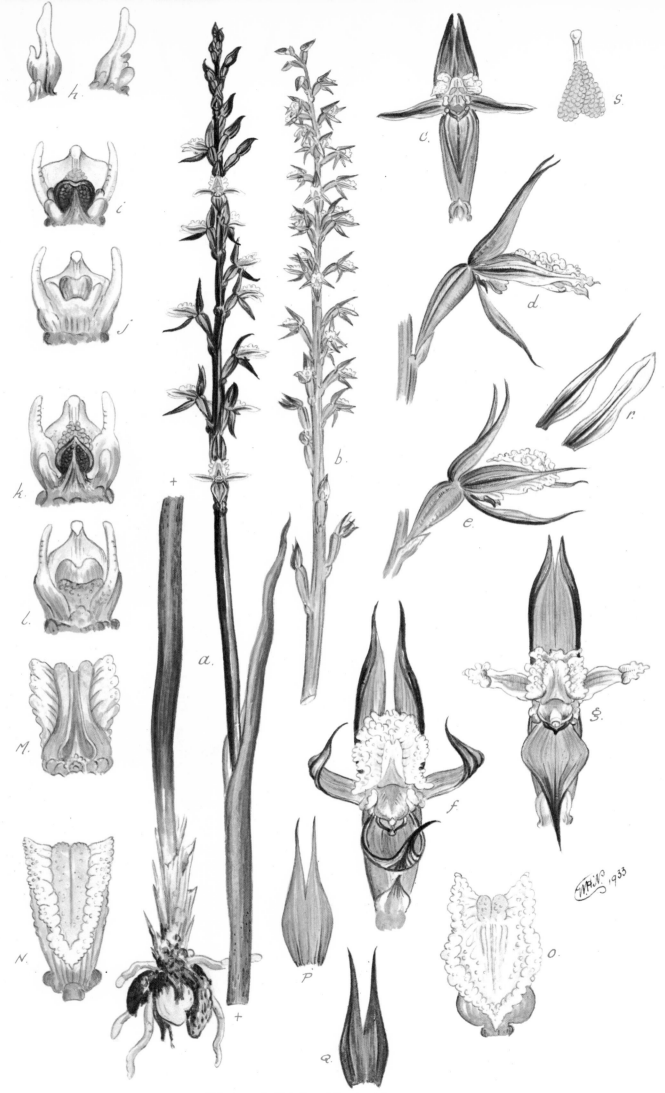

116 *Prasophyllum brevilabre* (see also p. 29)

a typical specimen from Cravensville, Vic.   b a specimen from Kinglake, Vic.   c f g flowers, from front   d e flowers, from side   h column appendages   i k columns, showing anther, etc.   j l columns showing stigma, etc.   m labellum, showing base   n o labella, from above   p q lateral sepals   r petal types   s pollinia
Figs a, b natural size

117 *Prasophyllum odoratum* (see also p. 29)

a an excellent sample from Boronia, Vic. **b** a specimen from Silvan, Vic. **c** a Lara, Vic., specimen **d** flower, from front, of the common form **e f** a flower collected at Bayswater, Vic., from front and side **g** a Lara flower (var. *album*) **h i** columns, showing anthers, etc. **j** flower, of the common form, from side **k l** remarkable examples of teratologic forms from Gorae, Vic. **m** column appendages **n** pollinia

Figs **a–c** natural size

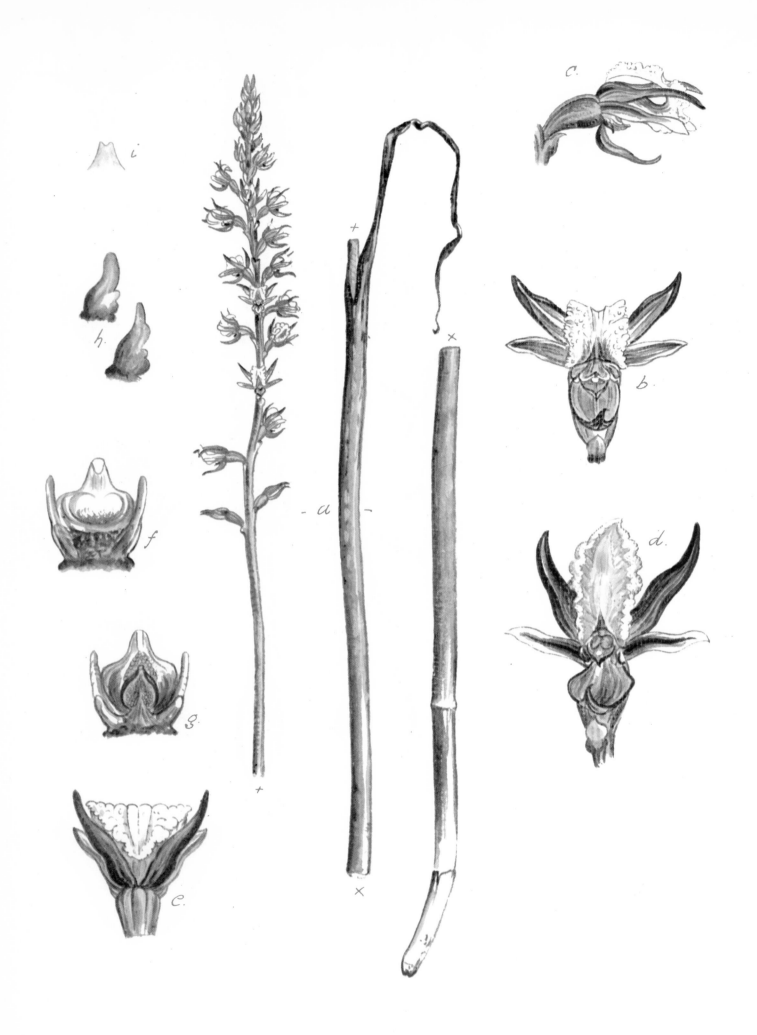

118 *Prasophyllum odoratum* var. *album* (see also Plate 117, Fig. **g,** and p. 30)

a typical form collected at Hurstbridge, Vic.   **b** flower, from front   **c** a flower from a specimen collected near Boronia, Vic., from side   **d** also from Boronia, from front
e flower, from above   **f** column, from front   **g** column, from rear   **h** column appendages   **i** rostellum
Fig. **a** natural size

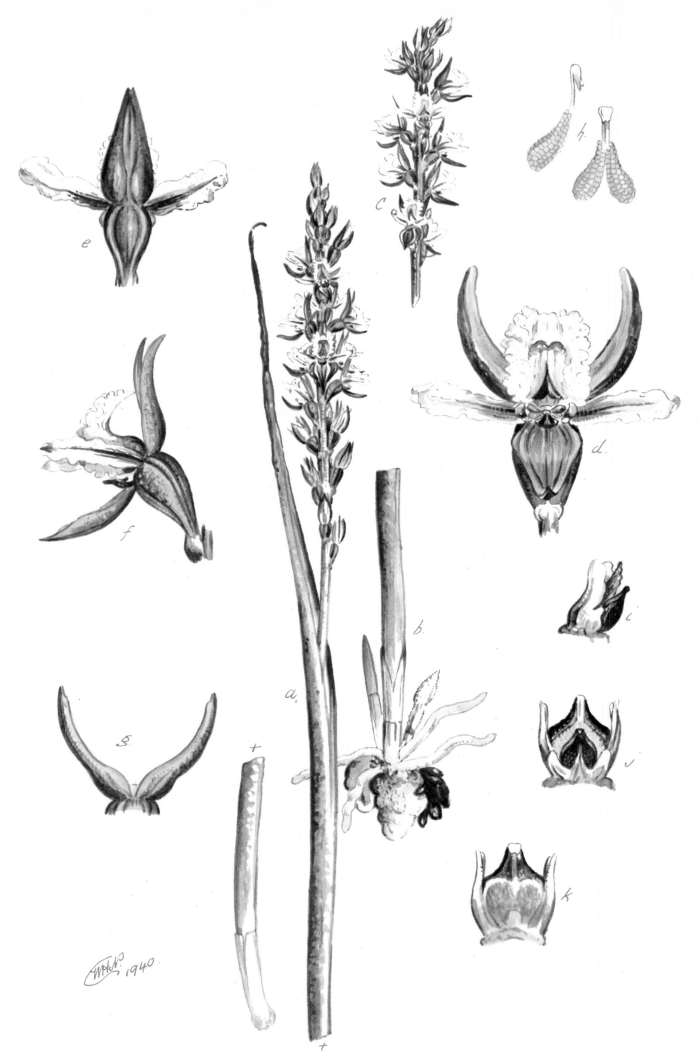

119 *Prasophyllum suttonii* (see also p. 30)

a a very fine specimen from Mt Wellington (Gable End), Vic.   **b** root system of plant collected on Mt Erica (Talbot Peak Morass), Vic.   **c** spike of flowers with red markings
d flower, from front, lateral sepals free   **e** flower, from above, lateral sepals united   **f** flower, from side   **g** lateral sepals, from above   **h** pollinia   **i** column, from side
j column, showing anther, etc.   **k** column, showing stigma, etc.
Figs **a–c** natural size

120 *Prasophyllum colemanae* (see also p. 30)

a typical specimen from Bayswater, Vic.   **b** flower, from front   **c** flower, from side   **d** column, showing anther, etc.   **e** column, showing stigma, etc.   **f** pollinia
Fig. **a** natural size

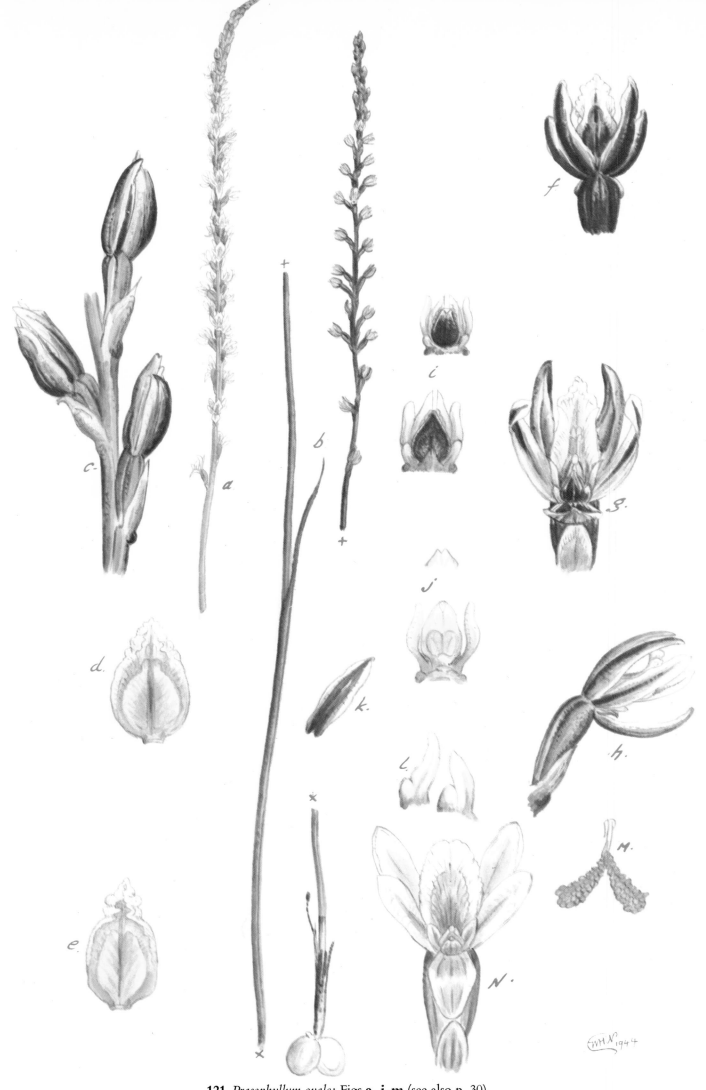

121 *Prasophyllum ovale*: Figs **a, i–m** (see also p. 30)
P. ovale var. *triglochin*: Figs **b–h** (see also p. 31)

a flower spike   **b** specimen from Lesmurdie, W A   **c** enlarged study of buds   **d e**   labella, from two unopened flowers   **f** flower, from above   **g** flower, from above   **h** flower, from side   **i** two columns, showing anther, etc.   **j** column, showing stigma and rostellum, etc.   **k** petal   **l** two column appendages   **m** pollinia   **n** flower, from front
Figs **a, b** natural size

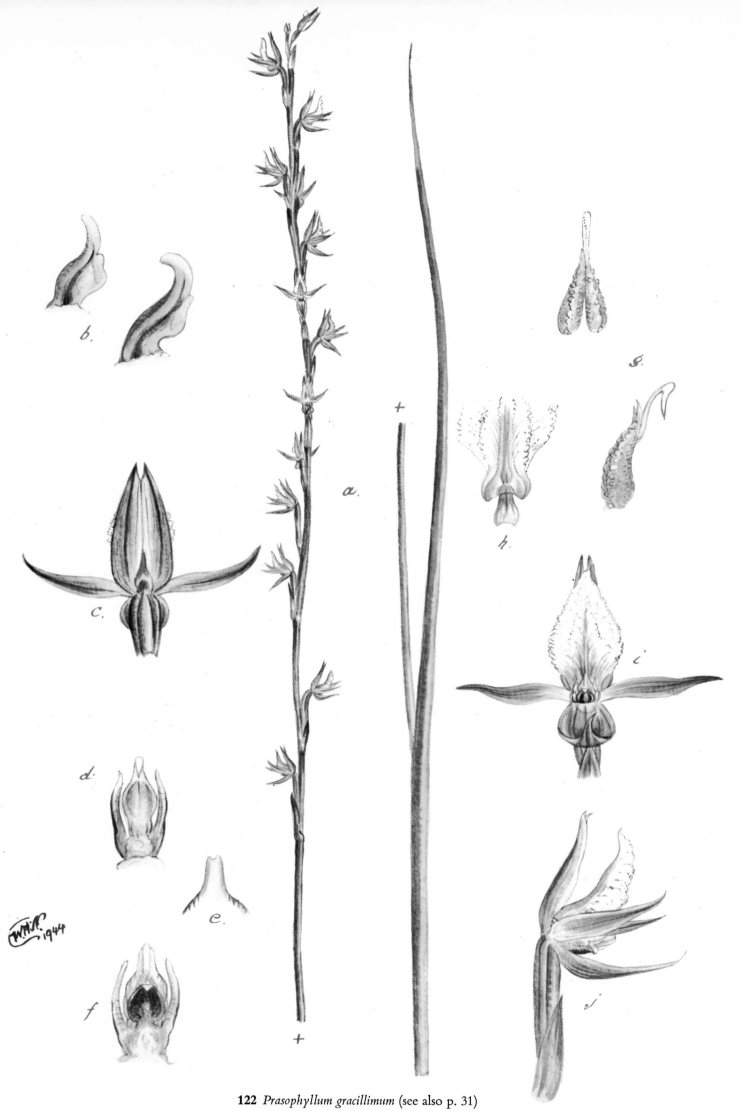

122 *Prasophyllum gracillimum* (see also p. 31)

a typical specimen **b** column appendages **c** flower, from above **d** column, showing stigma, etc. **e** rostellum **f** column, showing anther, etc. **g** pollinia **h** labellum base **i** flower, from front **j** flower, from side

Fig. **a** natural size

123 *Prasophyllum patens* (see also p. 31)

a b specimens from Mt Lofty Range, SA **c** flower, from front **d** column, showing anther, etc. **e** column appendages **f** pollinia **g** labellum **h** flower, from front
i column, showing stigma, etc. **j** flower, from side **k** labellum, from above
Figs **a, b** natural size

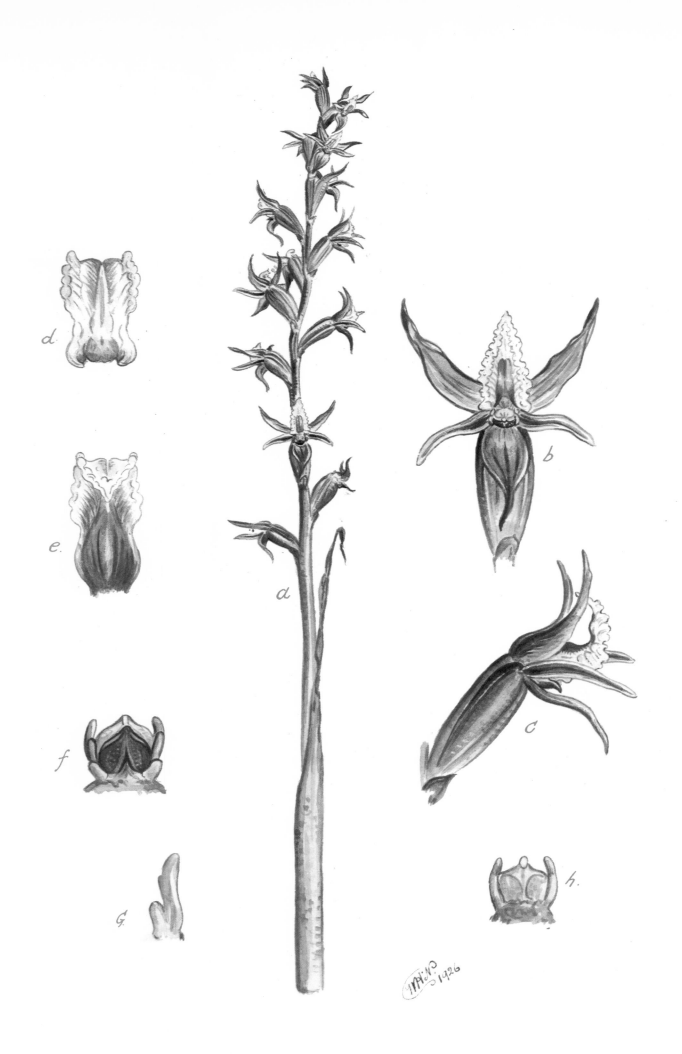

124 *Prasophyllum patens* var. *robustum* (see also p. 31)

a the type specimen **b** flower, from front **c** flower, from side **d** labellum, from below **e** labellum, from above **f** column, showing anther, etc. **g** column appendage
h column, showing stigma, etc.
Fig. **a** natural size

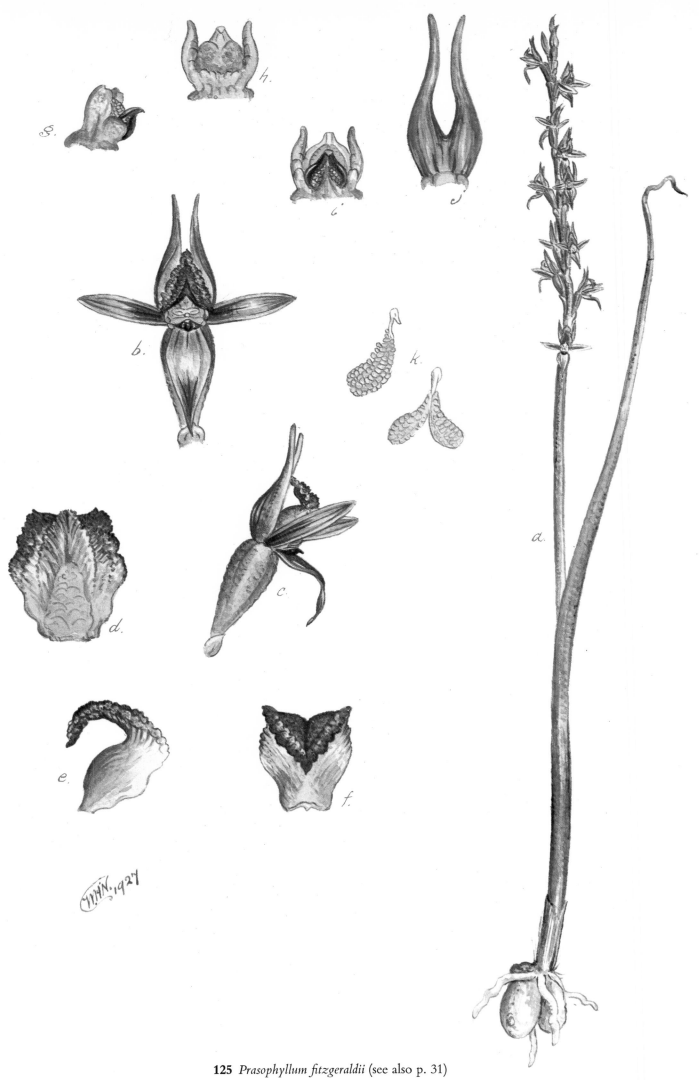

125 *Prasophyllum fitzgeraldii* (see also p. 31)

a typical specimen, National Park, SA   **b** flower, from front   **c** flower, from side   **d** labellum, from front   **e** labellum, from side   **f** labellum, from rear   **g** column, from side   **h** column, showing stigma, etc.   **i** column, showing anther, etc.   **j** lateral sepals, connate at base   **k** pollinia

Fig. **a** natural size

126 *Prasophyllum rogersii* (see also p. 32)

a specimen from Tas. b flower, from front c flower, from side d labellum, from front e pollinia f column, showing anther, etc. g column, showing stigma, etc.
h tip of rostellum i column, from side
Fig. **a** natural size

127 *Prasophyllum diversiflorum* (see also p. 32)

a typical specimen **b c d** labella, from front **e f** labella, from side **g h** apices of labella **i** flower, from front, also variation of apex of lateral sepal **j** flower, from side, also variation in position of dorsal sepal **k** pollinia **l** column, showing stigma, etc. **m** rostellum, after removal of disc **n** column, from side **o** column, from front, showing anther, etc. **p** column appendage (see also Fig. **n**) **q** tubers, etc. **r** portion of stem showing withered leaf **s** petal

Figs **a, q, r** natural size

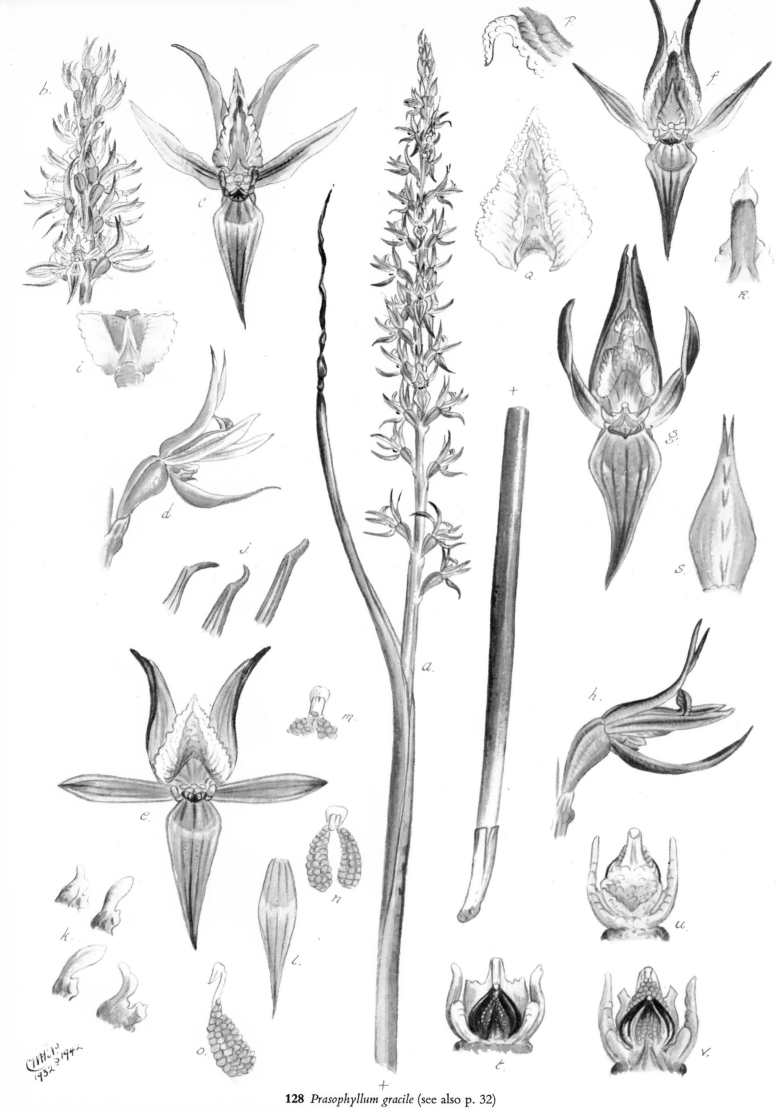

128 *Prasophyllum gracile* (see also p. 32)

a specimen from Gorae West, Vic. b flowers of a mountain plant, Cobungra district, Vic. c d flowers, typical of eastern Vic. specimens, from Bairnsdale e a Cobungra flower, petals and dorsal sepal spread out f flower from Airey's Inlet, Vic. g flower from Portland, Vic. h flower, from side, from Ararat, Vic. i labellum, from base j tips of lateral sepals k column appendages l a narrow form of dorsal sepal m a short caudicle to pollinia n a still shorter one o normal attachment p abnormal callus-plate (apex) q labellum from an alpine flower, from Dondangadale Ck, Vic. r callus-plate from constricted labellum s lateral sepal, showing degrees of union t column, showing anther, etc. u a column, showing stigma, etc. v column, showing anther (note abnormal upper margin of stigma in Figs t and v)
Figs **a, b** natural size

129 *Prasophyllum gracile* (see also p. 32)

a specimen from The Terraces, Ararat, Vic.   **b** labellum, from side   **c** lateral sepals (free), from above   **d** flower, from above, lateral sepals connate at base   **e** column, showing
anther, etc.   **f** column, from side   **g** pollinia   **h** column, showing stigma, etc.   **i** flower, from front   **j** flower, from side
Fig. **a** natural size

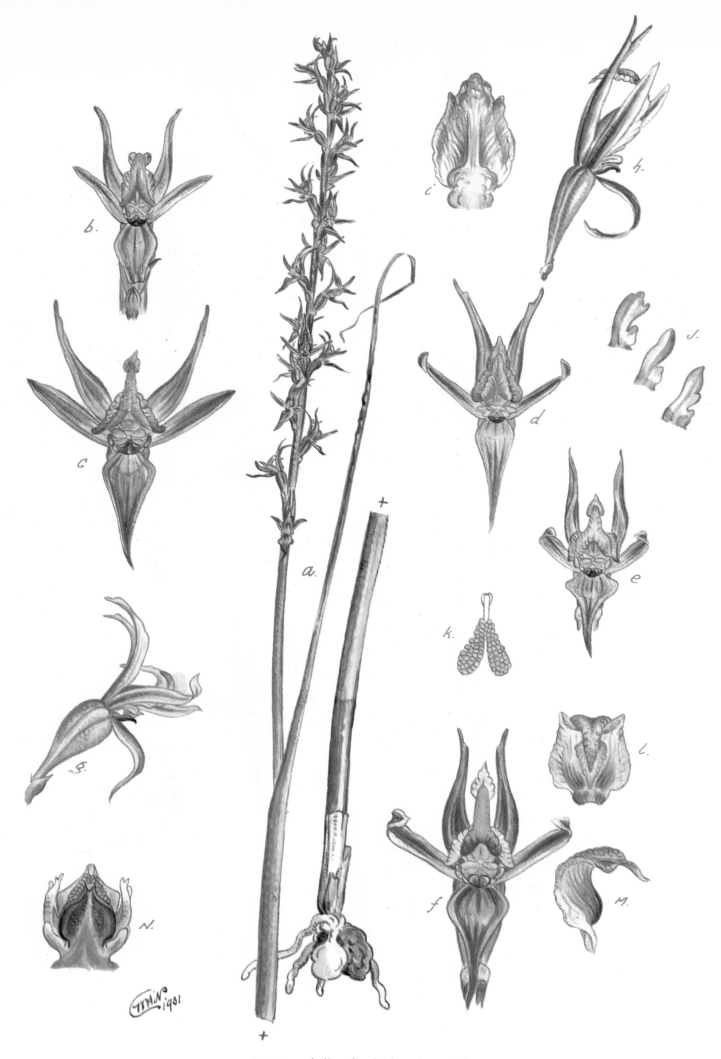

130 *Prasophyllum frenchii* (see also p. 33)

a a sturdy specimen **b c d e f** flowers, from front (Fig. **f** an unusual colour form from Airey's Inlet, Vic.) **g** flower, from side—green form **h** an abnormal flower form, often plentiful **i** labellum, from front **j** column appendages **k** pollinia **l** labellum, from above **m** labellum, from side **n** column, showing anther

Fig. **a** natural size

131 *Prasophyllum validum* (see also p. 33)

a typical specimen **b** labellum, from front **c** conjoined lateral sepals showing degrees of union, from above **d** flower, from front **e** flower, from side **f** column, showing anther, etc. **g** column, showing stigma, etc. **h** pollinia **i** column appendage

Fig. **a** natural size

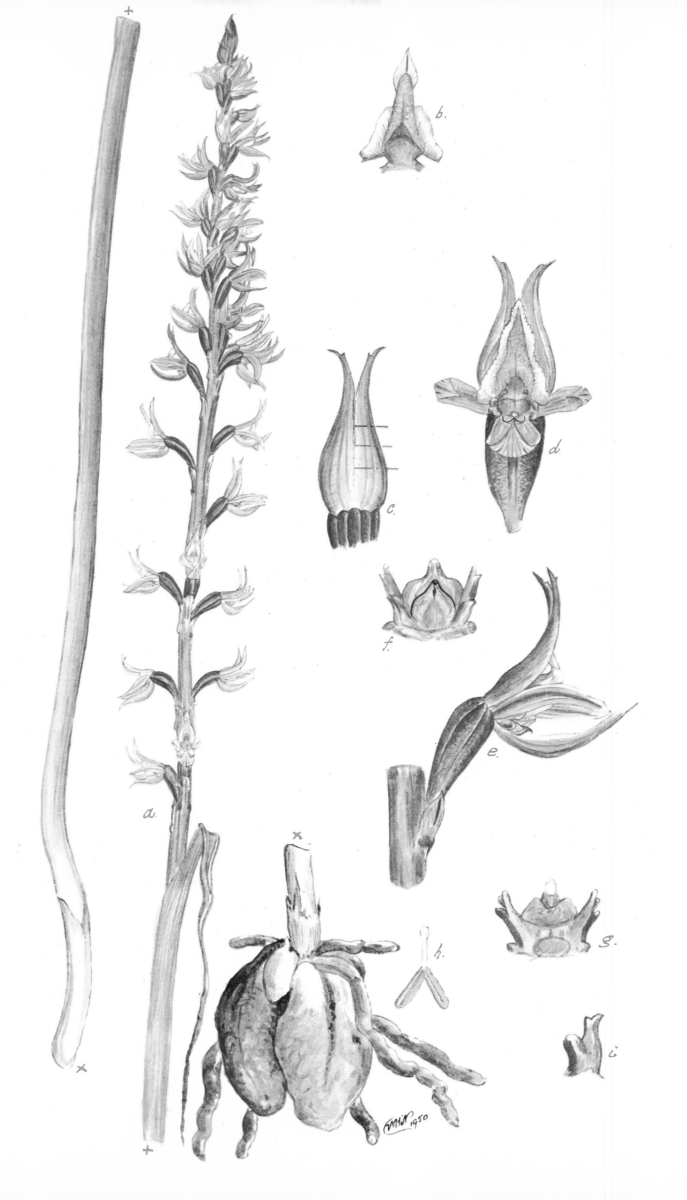

132 *Prasophyllum occidentale* (see also p. 33)

a typical specimen **b** lateral sepals, from above **c** pollinia **d** flower, from side **e** flower, from front **f** column appendages **g** column, from front, showing stigma, etc.
h column, showing anther, etc. **i** labellum, from front
Fig. **a** natural size

133 *Prasophyllum pallidum* (see also p. 34)

a typical specimen **b** flower, from side **c** flower, from front **d** labellum base **e** pollinia **f** column, showing anther, etc. **g** column appendage **h** column, showing sitgma and the erect appendage, etc. **i** rostellum **j** lateral sepals, connate at base **k** margin of labellum
Fig. **a** natural size

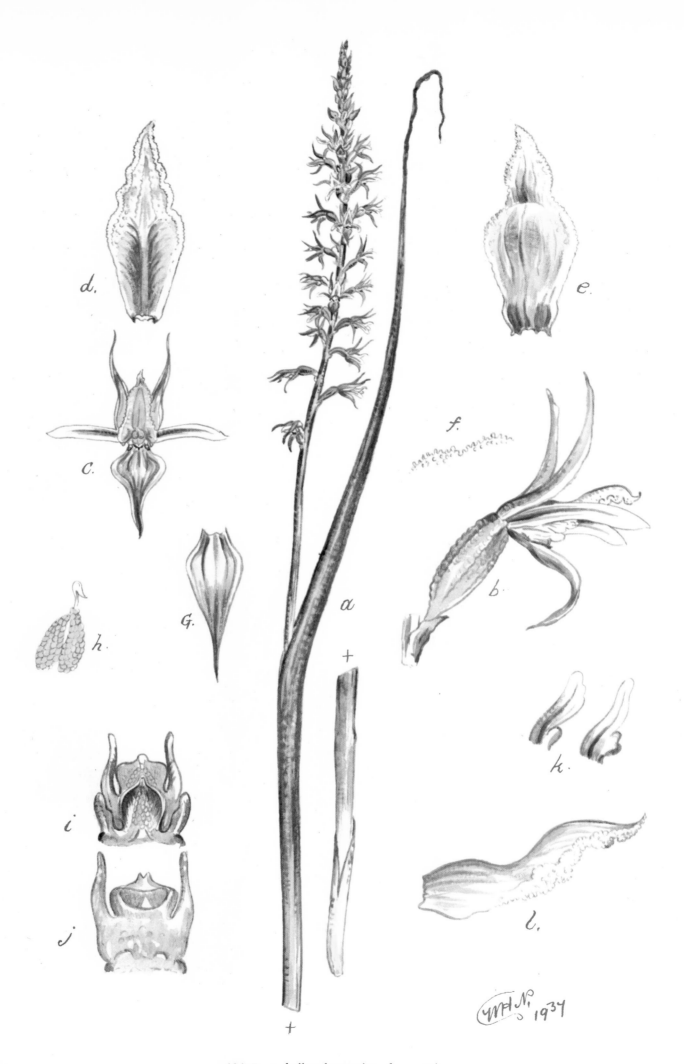

134 *Prasophyllum brainei* (see also p. 34)

a typical specimen **b** flower, from side **c** flower, from front **d** labellum, from front **e** labellum, from rear **f** formation of labellum surface **g** dorsal sepal **h** pollinia
i column, showing anther, etc. **j** column, showing stigma, etc. **k** column appendages **l** labellum, from side
Fig. **a** natural size

135 *Prasophyllum parviflorum* (see also p. 34)

a typical specimen **b** flower, from front **c** flower, from side **d** variation in curvature of labellum **e** lateral sepals, showing degrees of union **f** tips of lateral sepals
g labellum, from front **h** callus plate, from front **i** labellum, from rear **j** types of column appendages **k** column (two views), and rostellum **l** pollinia
Fig. **a** natural size

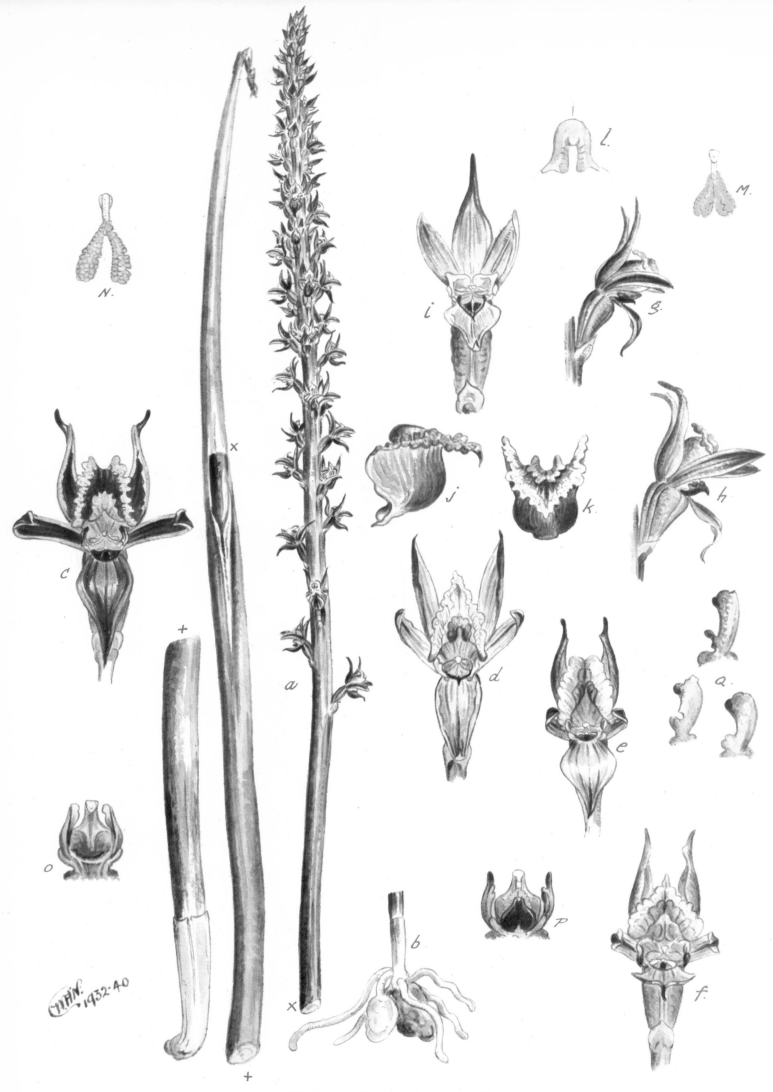

136 *Prasophyllum hartii* (see also p. 35)

a robust specimen **b** root system **c d e f** flowers, from front **g h** flowers, from side **i** a teratological mutant—no labellum segment (note abnormally developed column appendages, etc.) **j** labellum, from side **k** labellum, from above **l** callus plate, from front **m n** pollinia **o** column, showing stigma, etc. **p** column, showing anther, etc. **q** column appendages

Figs **a, b** natural size

137 *Prasophyllum subbisectum* (see also p. 35)

a typical specimen **b** column, from side **c** flower, from side **d** pollinia **e** flower, from front **f** rostellum **g** labellum, from below—also tip of a labellum
Fig. **a** natural size

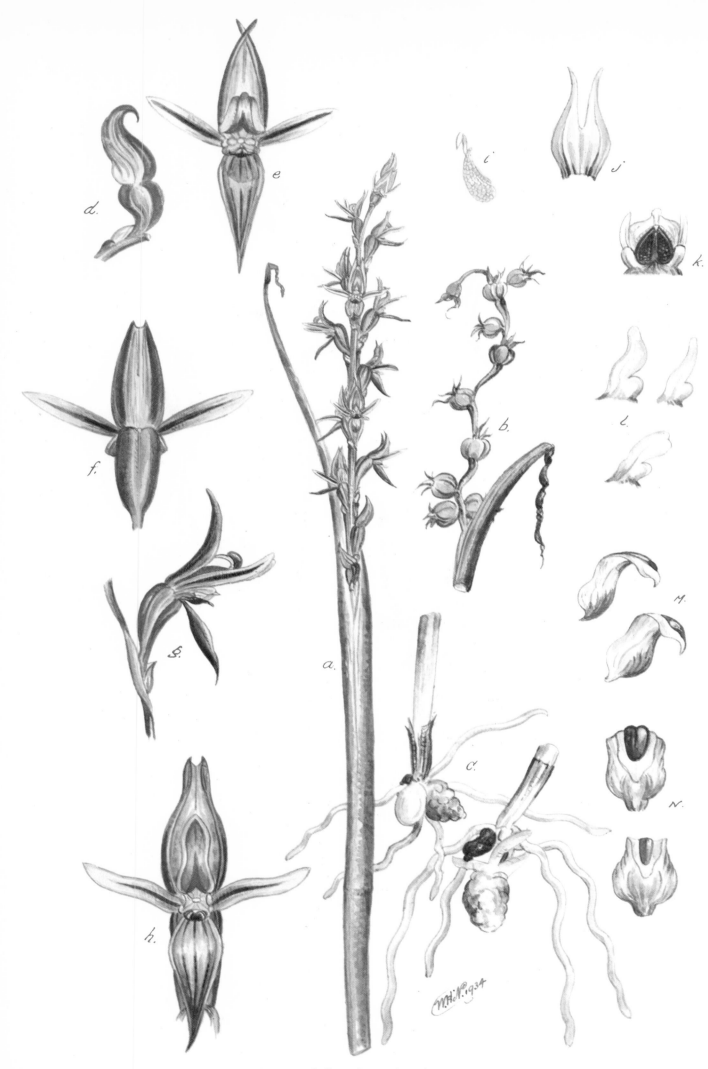

138 *Prasophyllum alpinum* (see also p. 35)

a specimen, slightly enlarged, from Talbot Peak, Vic. **b** turgid capsules **c** tubers, etc., from specimens growing in the peaty soil of the morass **d** characteristic bud **e** flower, from front **f** flower, from above **g** flower, from side **h** flower, from front **i** pollinia **j** lateral sepals, from above **k** column, showing anther, etc. **l** column appendages **m** labella, from side **n** labella, from above

Figs **b, c** natural size

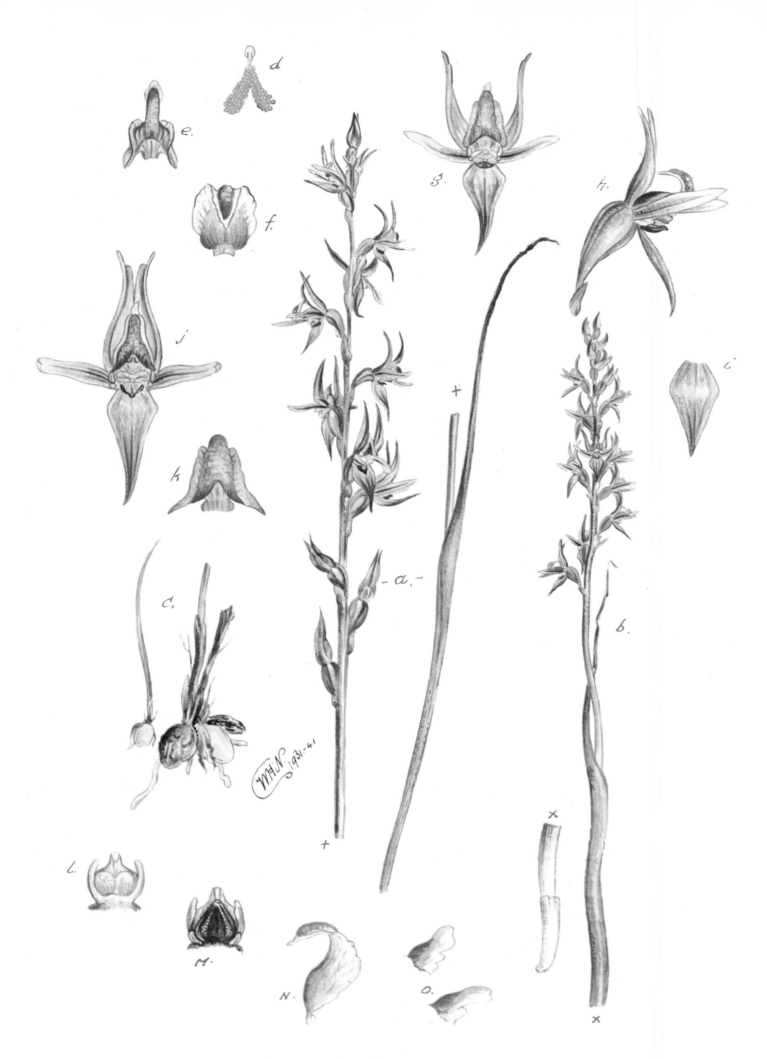

139 *Prasophyllum fuscum* (see also p. 36)

a specimen enlarged **b** another specimen **c** tubers, juvenile plant, etc. **d** pollinia **e** labellum, from front, margins revolute **f** labellum, from above **g** flower, from front
h flower, from side **i** dorsal sepal **j** flower, from front, sepals united for a brief period only **k** labellum, from front **l** column, showing stigma, etc. **m** column, showing
anther, etc. **n** labellum, from side **o** column appendages
Figs **b, c** natural size

140 *Prasophyllum concinnum* (see also p. 36)

a typical specimen **b** labellum, from below **c** flower **d** flower, from side **e** pollinia **f** lateral sepals **g** column appendage **h** column, showing anther, etc.—pollinia removed **i** column, showing stigma, etc.—pollinia removed
Fig. **a** natural size

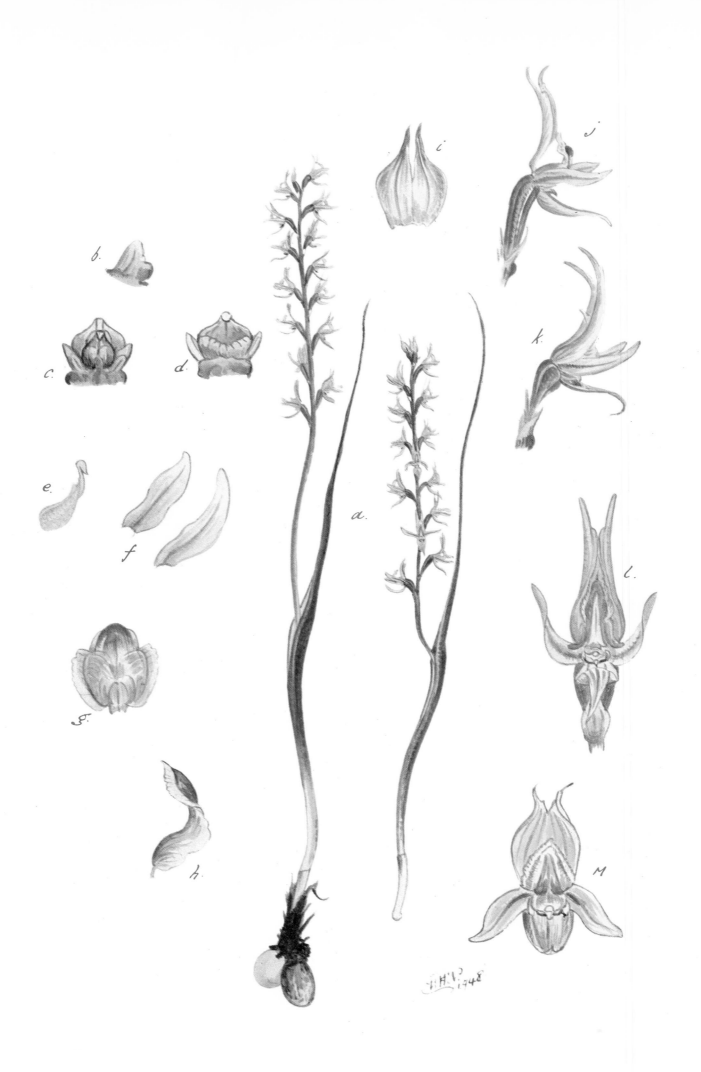

141 *Prasophyllum macrostachyum* (see also p. 36)

a two specimens collected near Arrowsmith State School, WA   b column appendage   c column, showing anther, etc.   d column, showing stigma, etc.   e pollinia   f petals
g labellum, from the base   h labellum, from side   i lateral sepals (stout form)   j flower, from side   k another flower, from side—note the very different ovary   l flower, from front   m flower of a stout form, from front
Fig. a natural size

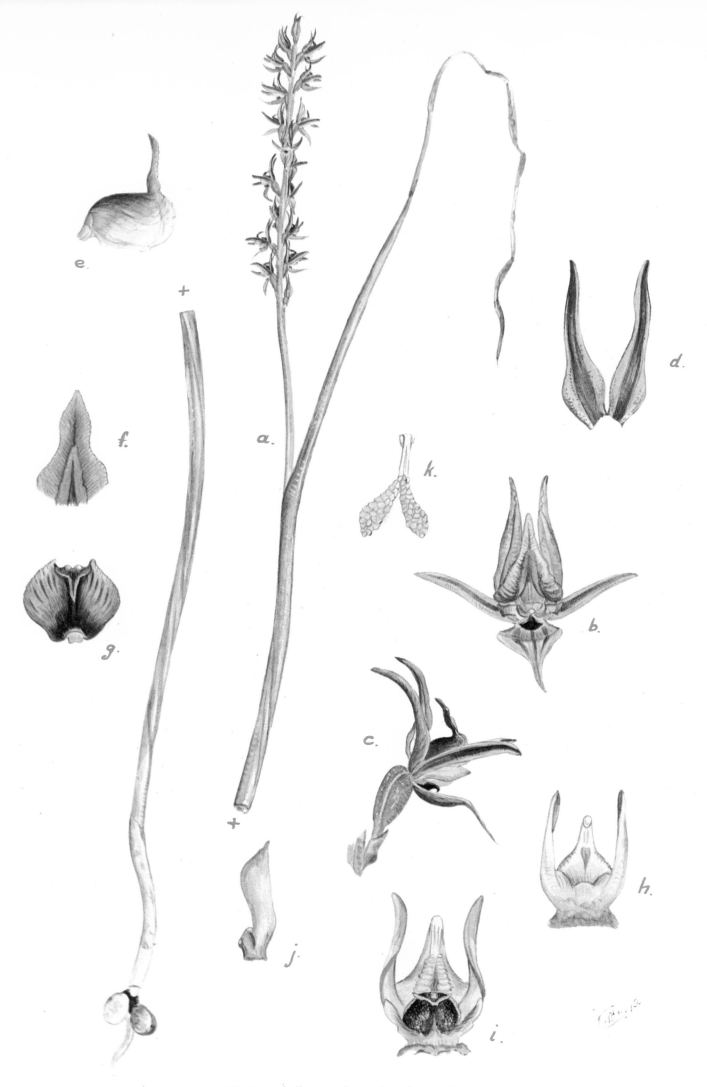

142 *Prasophyllum uroglossum* (see also p. 36)

a flowering specimen from Burrawang, NSW **b** flower, from front **c** flower, from side **d** lateral sepals **e** labellum, from side **f** labellum lamina, from front **g** labellum, from above **h** column, showing stigma, etc. **i** column, showing anther, etc. **j** column appendage **k** pollinia
Fig. **a** natural size

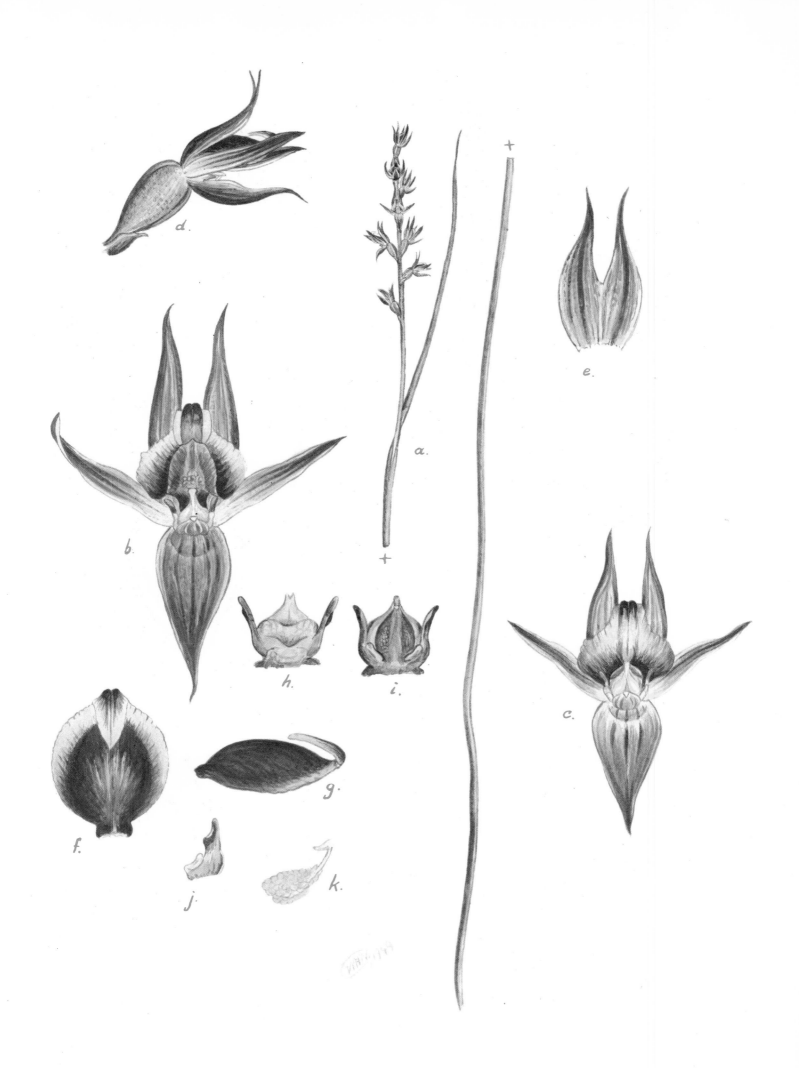

143 *Prasophyllum appendiculatum* (see also p. 37)

a flowering specimen **b c** flowers, from front **d** flower, from side **e** lateral sepals **f** labellum, from above **g** labellum, from side **h** column, showing stigma, etc.
i column, showing anther, etc. **j** labellum appendage **k** pollinia
Fig. **a** natural size

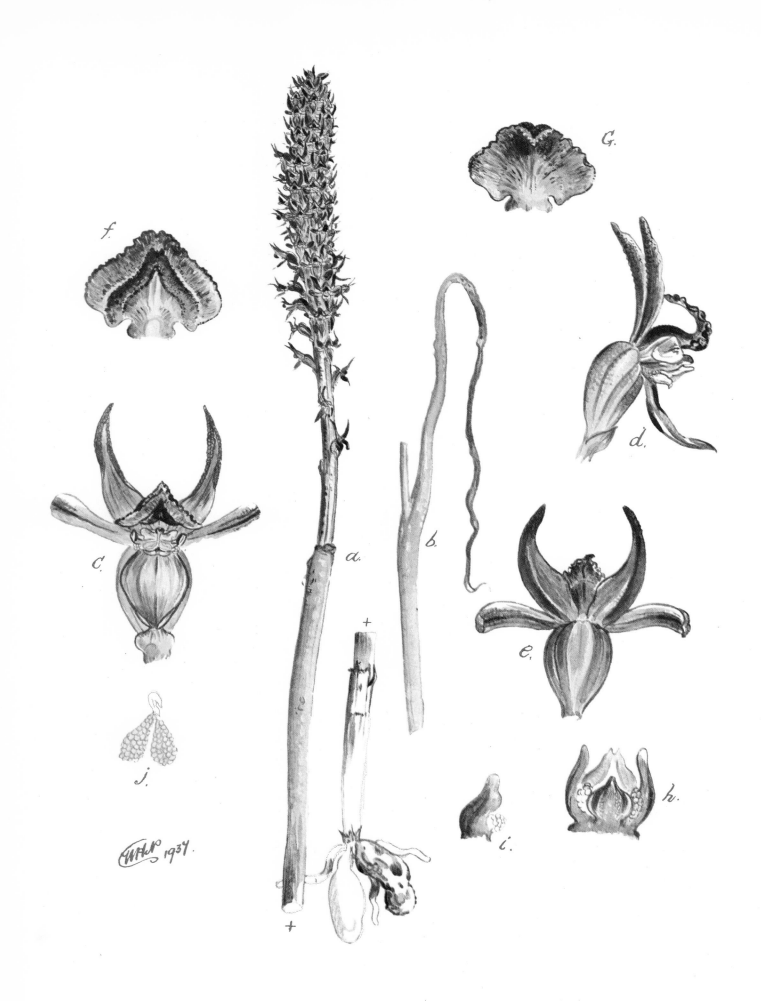

144 *Prasophyllum morganii* (see also p. 37)

a type specimen (leaf missing) **b** leaf **c** flower, from front **d** flower, from side **e** flower, from above **f** labellum, from front **g** labellum, from above **h** column, showing anther, etc. **i** column appendage **j** pollinia

Figs **a, b** natural size

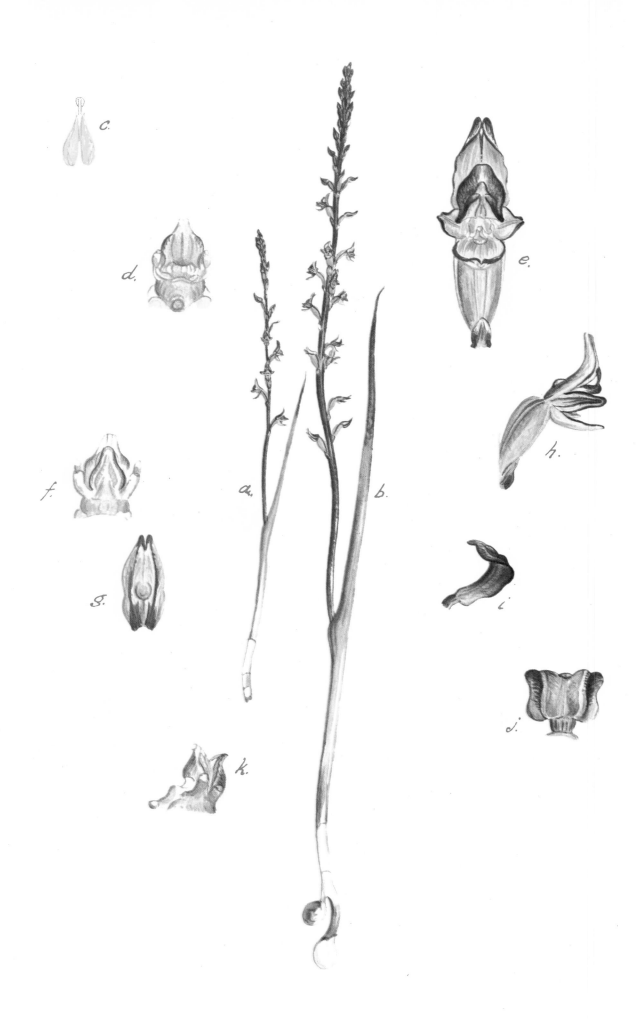

145 *Prasophyllum attenuatum* (see also p. 37)

a   b two specimens from Nanarup, WA   c pollinia   d column, showing stigma, etc.   e flower, from front   f column, showing anther, etc.   g lateral sepals, from above
h flower, from side   i labellum, from side   j labellum, from below   k column, from side
Figs a, b natural size

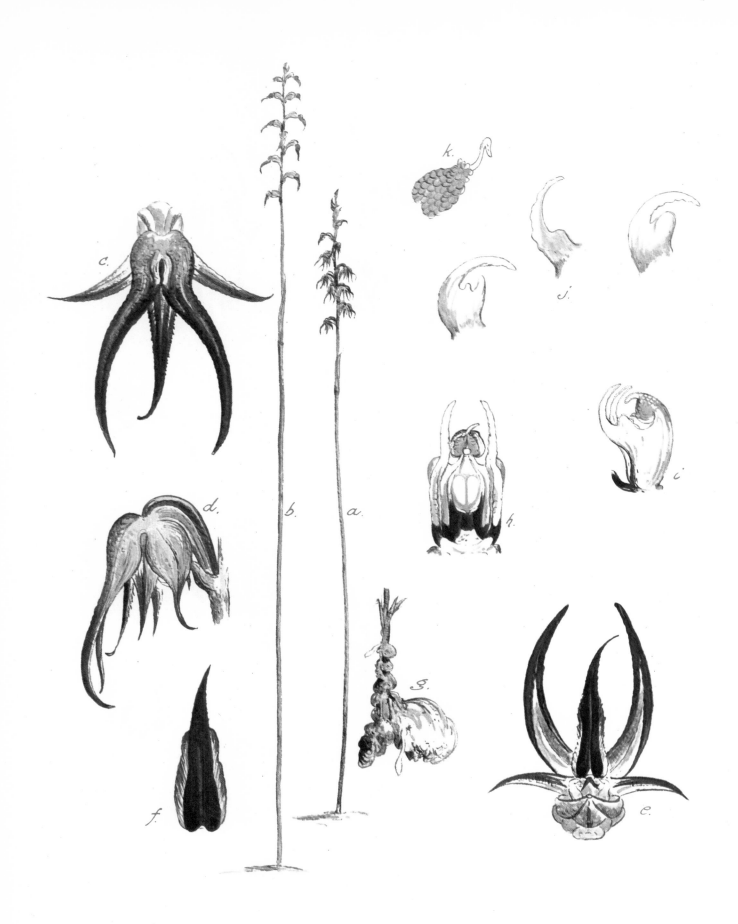

146 *Prasophyllum despectans* (see also p. 37)

a a robust specimen **b** a fruiting specimen **c** flower, from above **d** flower, from side **e** flower, from below **f** labellum, from below **g** root system **h** column, from front **i** column, from side **j** column appendages **k** pollinia

Figs **a, b** natural size

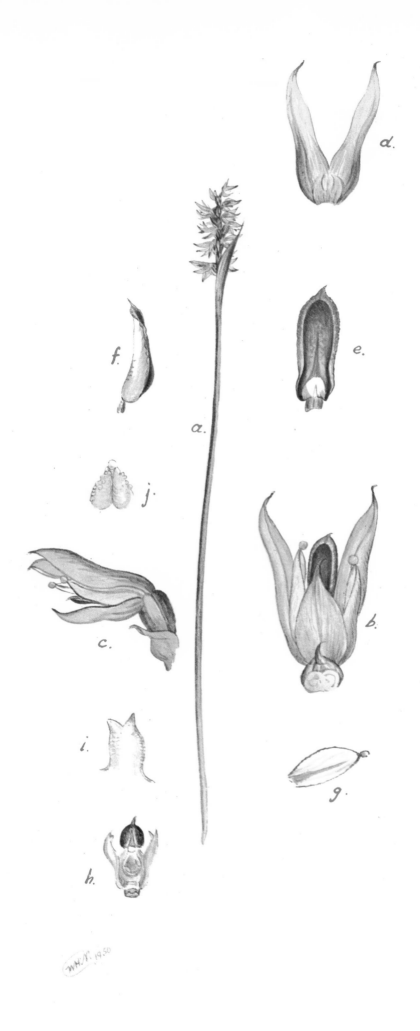

147 *Prasophyllum nichollsianum* (see also p. 38)

a flowering specimen from Woodford, NSW **b** flower, from below **c** flower, from side **d** lateral sepals, from above **e** labellum, from below **f** labellum, from side
g petal **h** column, from front **i** column appendage **j** pollinia
Fig. **a** natural size

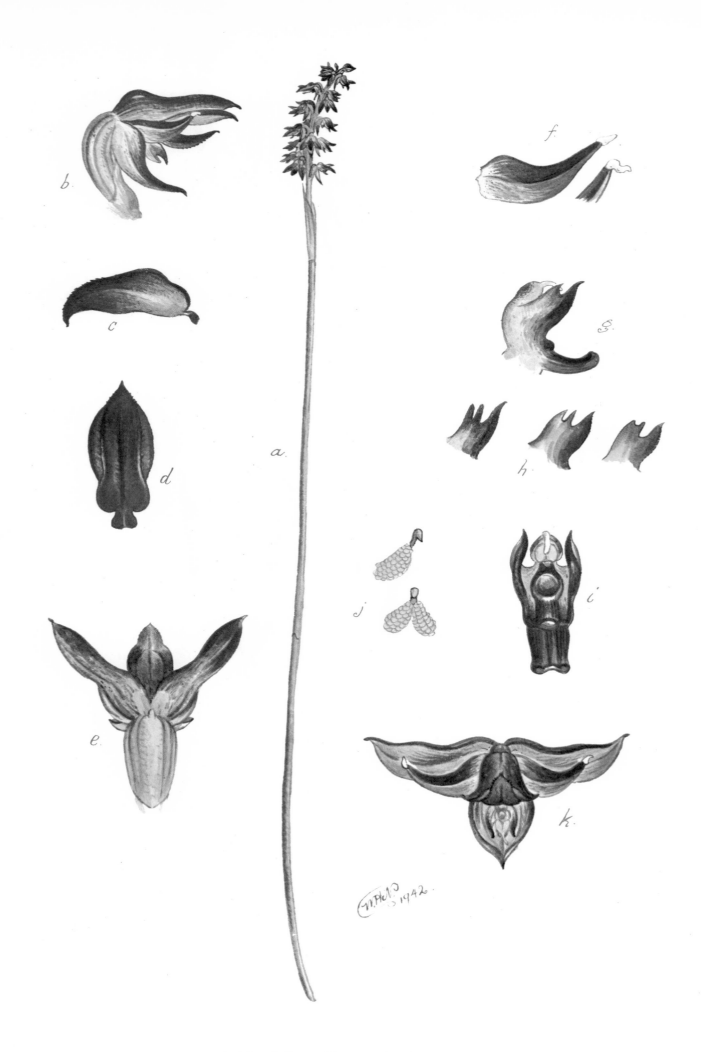

148 *Prasophyllum trifidum* (see also p. 38)

a typical specimen   **b** flower, from side, with bifid appendages   **c** labellum, from side   **d** labellum, from below   **e** flower, from above   **f** petal, from side, also a twisted gland
g column, from side, with bifid appendages   **h** trifid appendages   **i** column, from front   **j** pollinia   **k** flower, from front
Fig. **a** natural size

153 *Prasophyllum fusco-viride* (see also p. 39)

a flowering plant with tubers **b** column, from side **c** column, from front, with appendages spread out **d** flower, from side **e** flower, from above, ovary not shown
f flower, from front **g** petal **h** labellum, from side **i** labellum, from front
Fig. **a** natural size

154 *Prasophyllum brachystachyum* (see also p. 39)

a typical specimens from Stanley, Tas. **b** pollinia **c** flower, from above, a dark–coloured specimen **d** column, from front (note slight variation at apex of appendage)
e column, from side **f** unexpanded flower with glands—also some variation of lateral sepals **g** labellum, from side **h** flower, from side (note that the sepals are not gibbous at
base) **i** a golden–hued flower, from above **j** apex of petal **k** petal **l** a typical flower, from front
Fig. **a** natural size

155 *Prasophyllum densum* (see also p. 40)

a two specimens from Normanhurst, NSW **b** specimen from Mt Wellington, Vic. **c** flower, from above, Vic. **d** column, from front **e** rostellum **f** flower, from side, NSW **g** pollinia **h** flower, from above, NSW **i** flower, from front, the segments spread out, NSW **j** a gland-tipped petal **k** column appendages **l** labellum, from front **m** labellum, from side

Figs **a**, **b** natural size

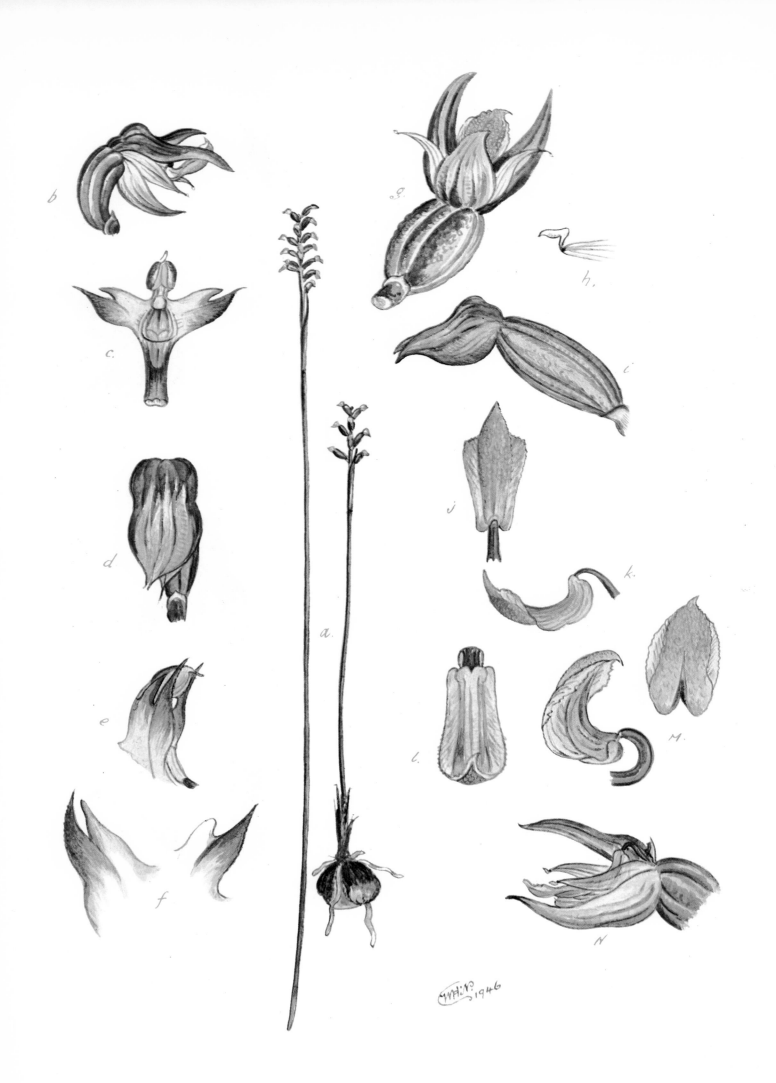

156 *Prasophyllum viride* (see also p. 40)

a two typical specimens, National Park, NSW   **b** flower, from side   **c** column with appendages spread out   **d** an unopened bud   **e** column, from side   **f** types of column appendages   **g** flower, from below   **h** apical gland of petal   **i** an unopened bud, from side   **j** labellum, from front   **k** labellum, from side   **l** labellum, from rear   **m** labellum, from side, and front   **n** flower, from side—lateral sepal removed
Fig. **a** natural size

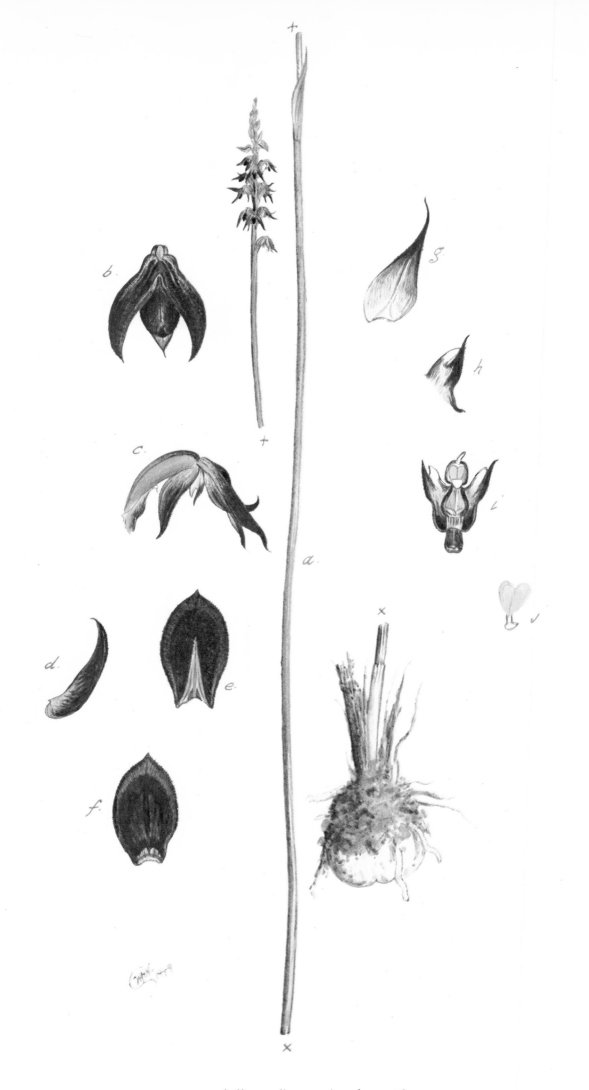

157 *Prasophyllum mollissimum* (see also p. 40)

a a robust specimen **b** flower, from above **c** flower, from side **d** labellum, from side **e** labellum, from front **f** labellum, from rear **g** petal **h** column appendage
i column, from front—appendages spread out **j** pollinia
Fig. **a** natural size

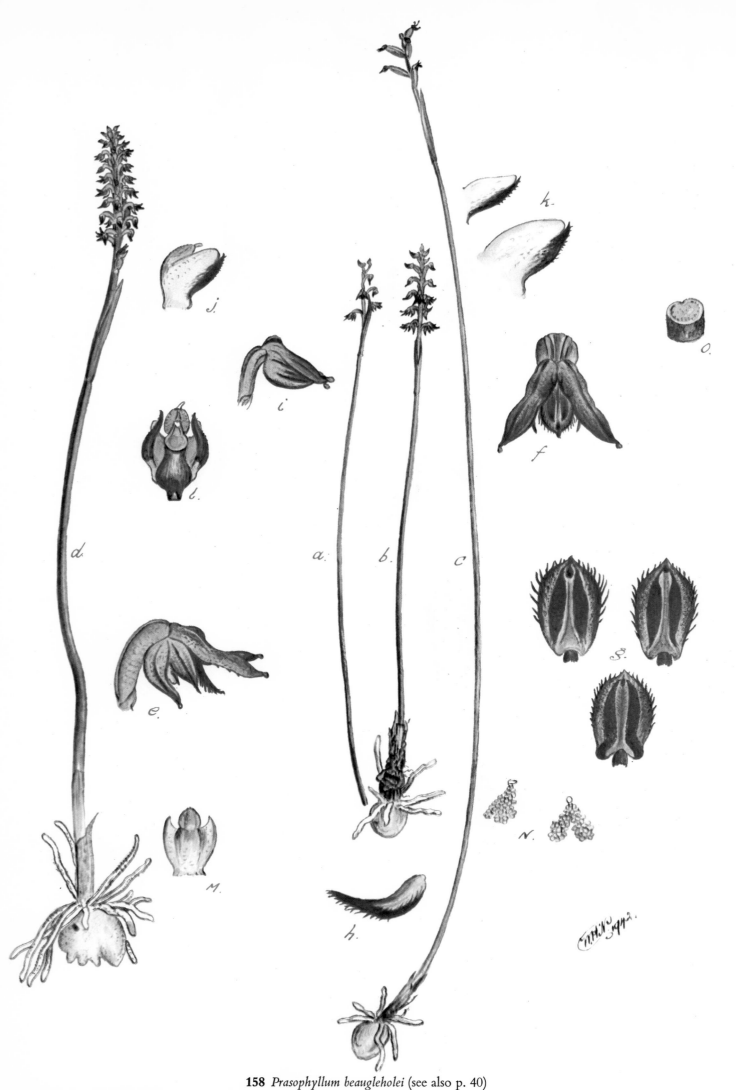

158 *Prasophyllum beaugleholei* (see also p. 40)

a b typical specimens from Portland, Vic. **c** fruiting specimen **d** robust specimen **e** flower, from side **f** flower, from above **g** labella, showing variation **h** labellum, from side **i** unexpanded flower **j** column, from side **k** column appendages **l** column, from front **m** column, from above **n** pollinia **o** cross-section of stem
Figs **a–d** natural size

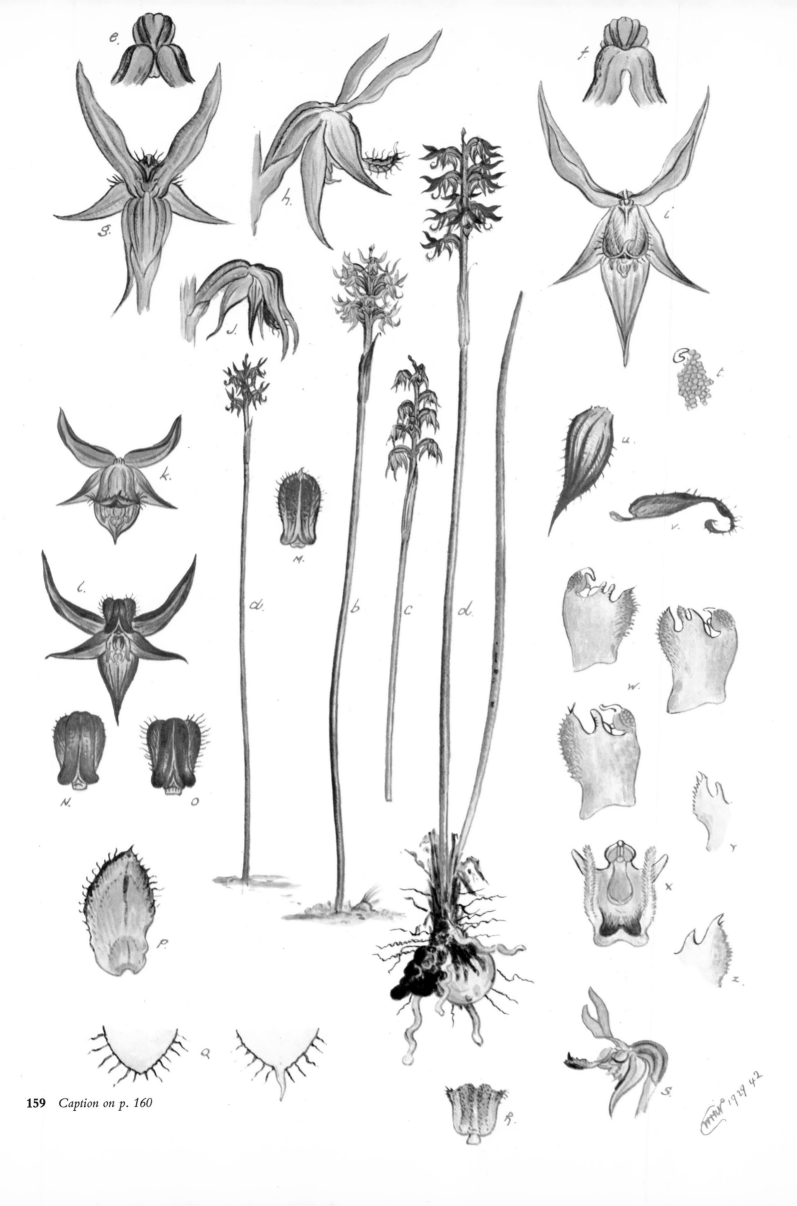

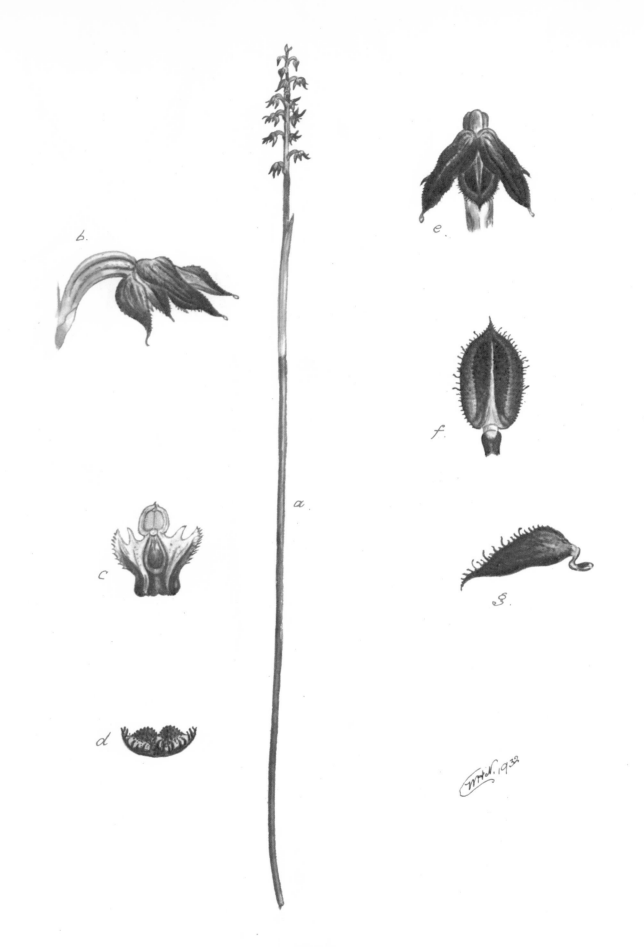

160 *Prasophyllum wilsoniense* (see also p. 41)

a typical specimen **b** flower, from side **c** column, from front, appendages spread out **d** labellum, from apex end **e** flower, from above **f** labellum, from front **g** labellum, from side

Fig. **a** natural size

159 *Prasophyllum archeri*: Figs **a–b, d–i, k, l, n–z** (see also p. 41)
P. archeri var. *deirdrae*: Figs **c, j, m** (see also p. 41)

a a specimen from Oakleigh, Vic. **b** a fine Burleigh Heads, Qld, specimen **c** specimen from Maryborough, Vic. **d** a specimen from Dodangadale, Vic. **e f** base of lateral sepals **g** a flower, from above **h** same, from side **i** flower, from front **j** flower, from side **k** flower, from front, from Black Rock, Vic. **l** flower from front, from Oakleigh, Vic. **m** labellum, from front **n o** labella, from front, specimens from Black Rock and Cheltenham, Vic. **p** labellum, from rear, Ararat, Vic., specimen **q** variation in tip of labella **r** labellum, from front, Ararat specimen **s** flower, from side, Ararat specimen **t** pollinia **u** abnormal petal, specimen from Mt Cobbler, Vic. **v** labellum, from side, Oakleigh specimen **w** abnormal columns, from side **x** column, from front **y** column appendage, Ararat specimen **z** column appendage

Figs **a–d** natural size

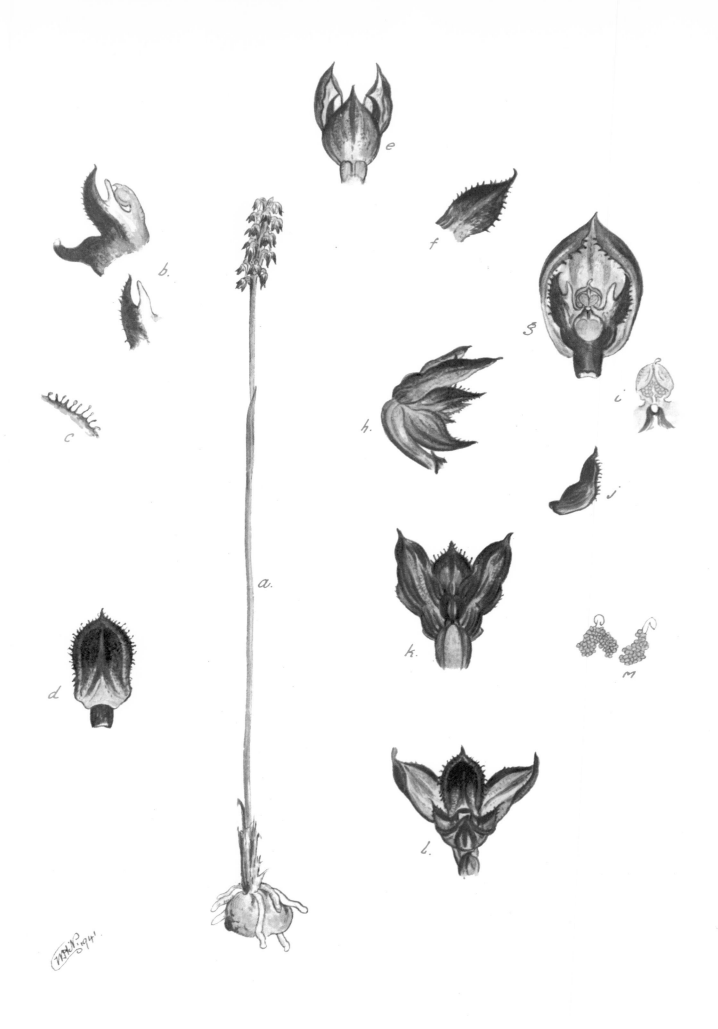

161 *Prasophyllum woollsii* (see also p. 41)

a a Mt Irvine, NSW, specimen **b** column, from side, also a column appendage **c** cilia, from labellum **d** labellum, showing prominent callus-plate **e** flower, from below
f petal **g** dorsal sepal and column **h** flower, from side **i** anther and rostellum, with pollinia in position **j** labellum, from side **k** flower, from above **l** flower, from
front **m** pollinia
Fig. **a** natural size

162 *Prasophyllum nublingii* (see also p. 42)

a typical specimen **b** pollinia **c** column, from front **d** column, from side **e** labella, from front and side **f** petal **g** flower, from above **h** flower, from side **i** conjoined base of lateral sepals
Fig. **a** natural size

163 *Prasophyllum ruppii* (see also p. 42)

a typical specimen   b labellum types, the two upper, from front, the lower figure, from rear   c labellum, from side   d cilia, from the labellum margin   e two flowers, from above   f pollinia   g flower, from side   h petal   i dorsal sepal   j column with appendages spread out
Fig. **a** natural size

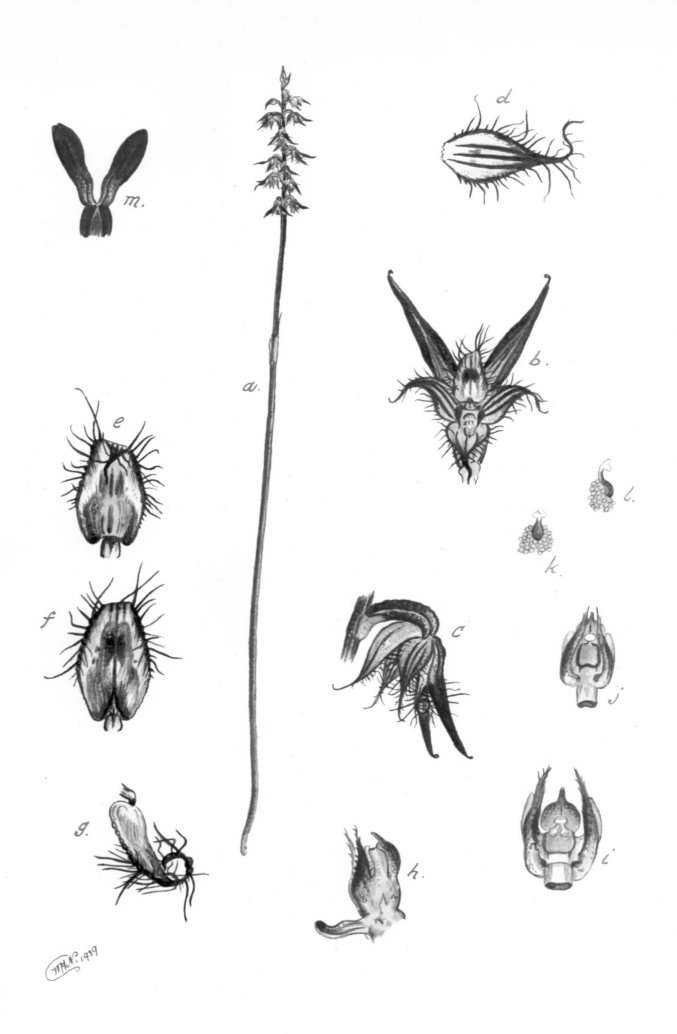

164 *Prasophyllum acuminatum* (see also p. 42)

a typical specimen **b** flower, from front **c** flower, from side **d** petal **e** labellum, from rear **f** labellum, from front **g** labellum, from side **h** column, from side
i column, from front **j** another column, from front **k l** pollinia **m** lateral sepals, from above
Fig. **a** natural size

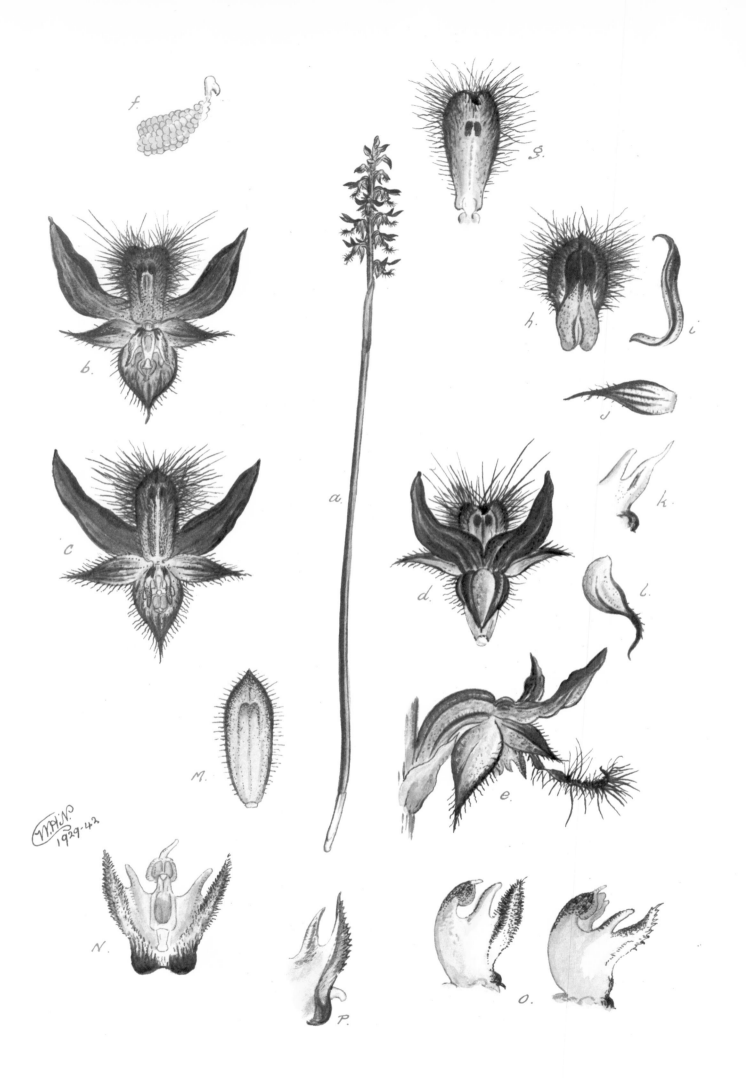

165 *Prasophyllum morrisii* (see also p. 42)

a typical specimen b c flowers, from front d flower, from above e flower, from side f pollinia g labellum, from rear h labellum, from front i labellum, from side—hairs removed j k l petal, column appendage and side view of dorsal sepal, specimens from Mt Irvine, NSW m labellum, from a bud n column, from front o columns, from side p column appendage
Fig. **a** natural size

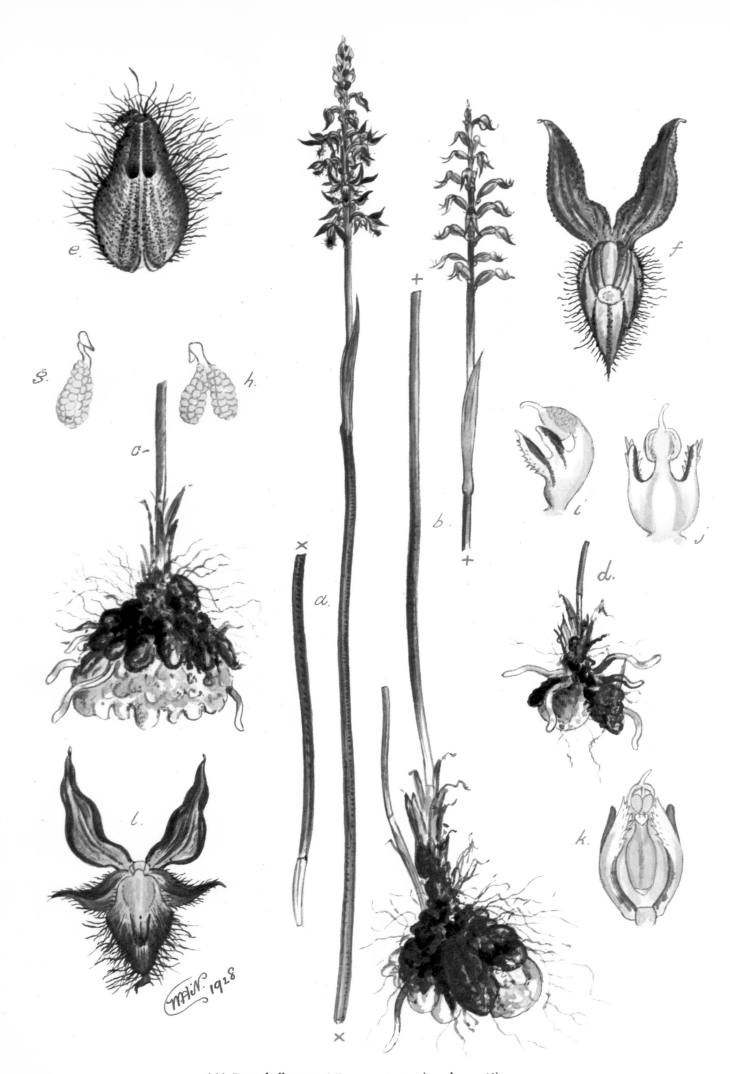

166 *Prasophyllum morrisii* var. *contortum* (see also p. 43)

a typical specimen **b** fruiting specimen with tubers **c** lower portion of plant with tubers **d** tubers of normal form **e** labellum, from front **f** ovary, lateral sepals and dorsal sepal, from above **g h** pollinia **i** column, from side **j** column, from rear **k** column, from front **l** flower, from front
Figs **a–d** natural size

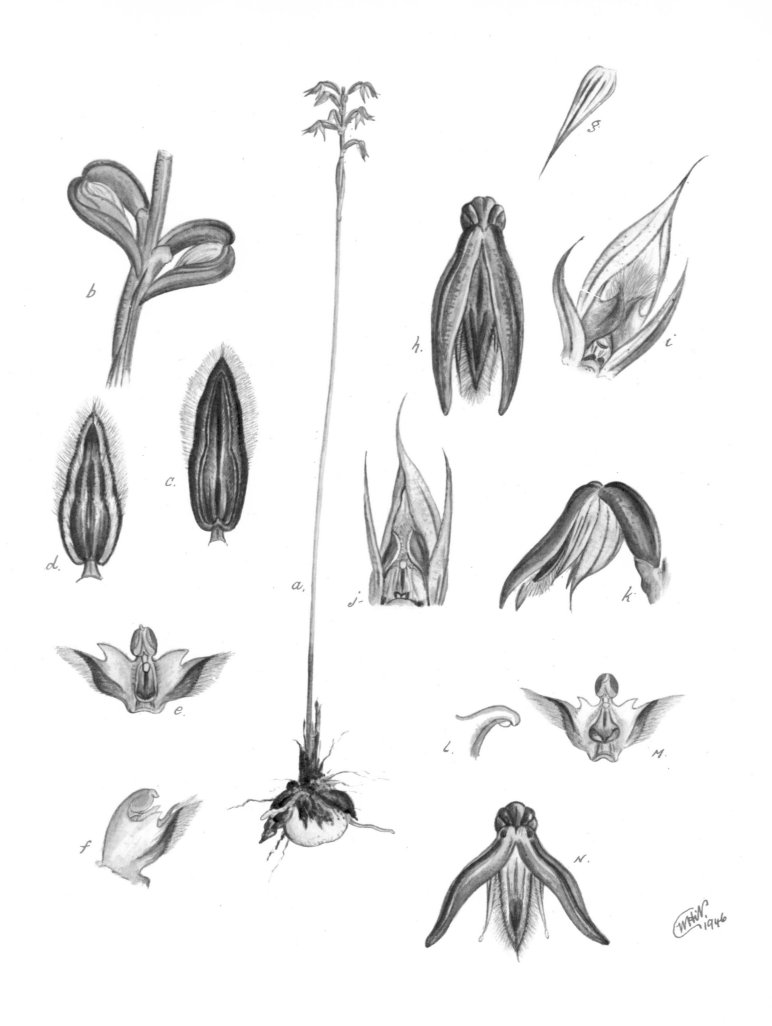

167 *Prasophyllum plumosum* (see also p. 43)

a typical plant **b** unopened buds **c d** labella, from front **e f** column, from front, and side **g** petal **h** flower, from above **i** lower portion of flower, showing column appendages covering the column **j** lower portion of flower, the column appendages separated **k** flower, from side **l** rostellum **m** column, from front, appendages spread
n flower, from above, with well-spread lateral sepals
Fig. **a** natural size

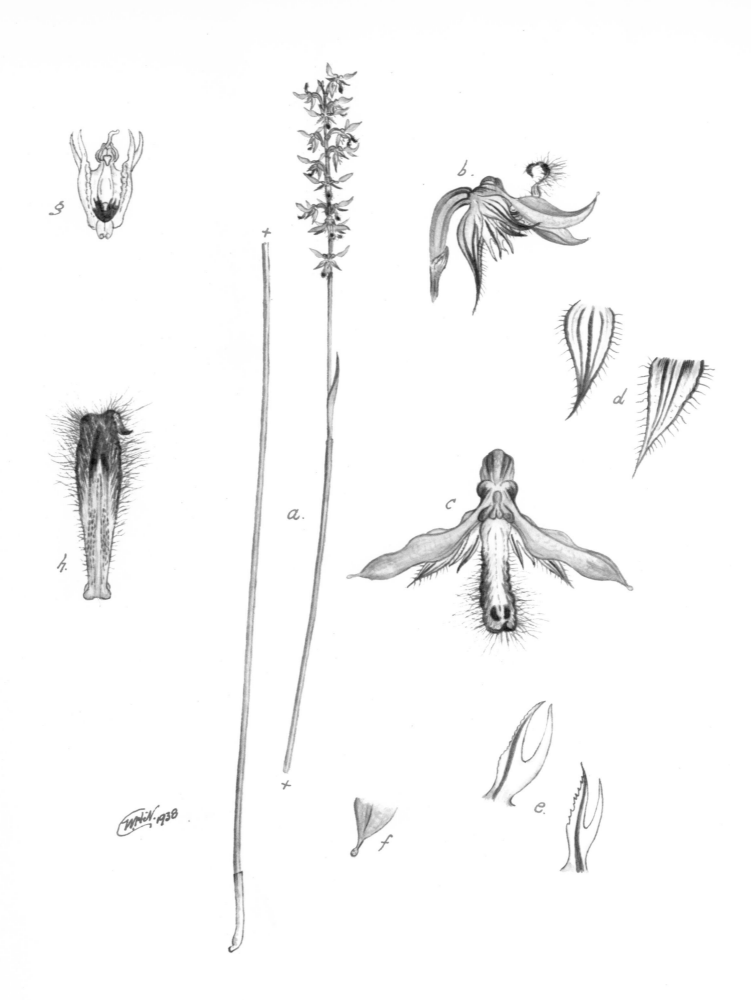

168 *Prasophyllum fimbriatum* (see also p. 43)

a typical specimen **b** flower, from side **c** flower, from above **d** petals **e** column appendages **f** tip of lateral sepal **g** column, from front **h** labellum, from front
Fig. **a** natural size

169 *Prasophyllum bowdenae* (see also p. 43)

a typical specimen **b** labellum, from side **c** flower **d** column, showing prominent labellum claw, dorsal sepal, petals and column appendages **e** column, showing dorsal sepal, petals and labellum claw **f** a well-developed column

Fig. **a** natural size

170 *Prasophyllum anomalum* (see also p. 44)

a typical specimen **b** flower, from above **c** unexpanded flower **d** column, from side, showing abnormal characteristics **e** abortive anther **f** stigma with obsolete rostellum and abortive pollinia **g** trilobed base of a column, showing the claws of the petals, and labellum claw **h** stigma and obsolete rostellum **i** flower, from front **j** dorsal sepal **k** hinged petals **l** a fixed petal **m** labellum, from rear
Fig. **a** natural size

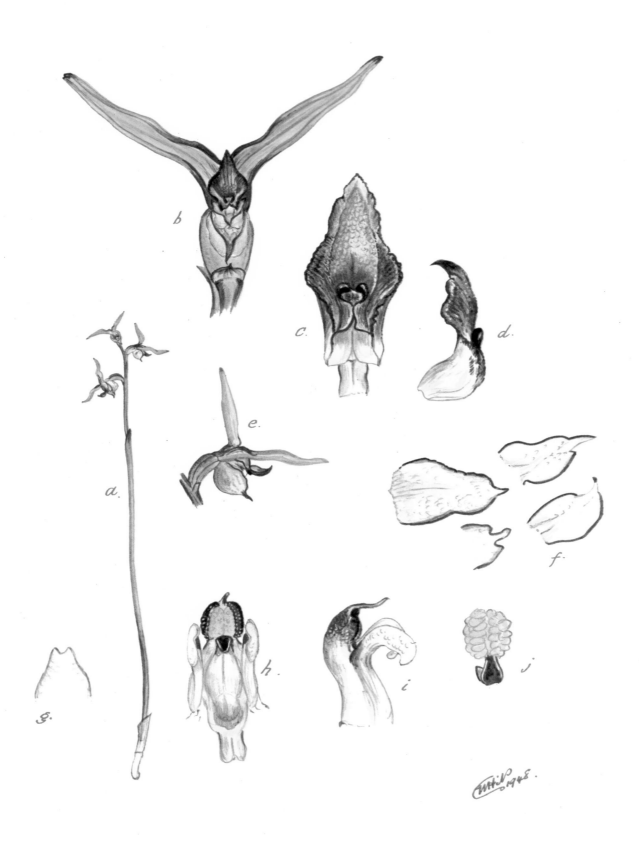

171 *Genoplesium baueri* (see also p. 44)

a a Woodford, NSW, specimen   **b** flower, from front   **c** labellum, from front   **d** labellum, from side   **e** flower, from side   **f** variation in the shape of the petals   **g** rostellum
h column, from front   **i** column, from side   **j** pollinia
Fig. **a** natural size

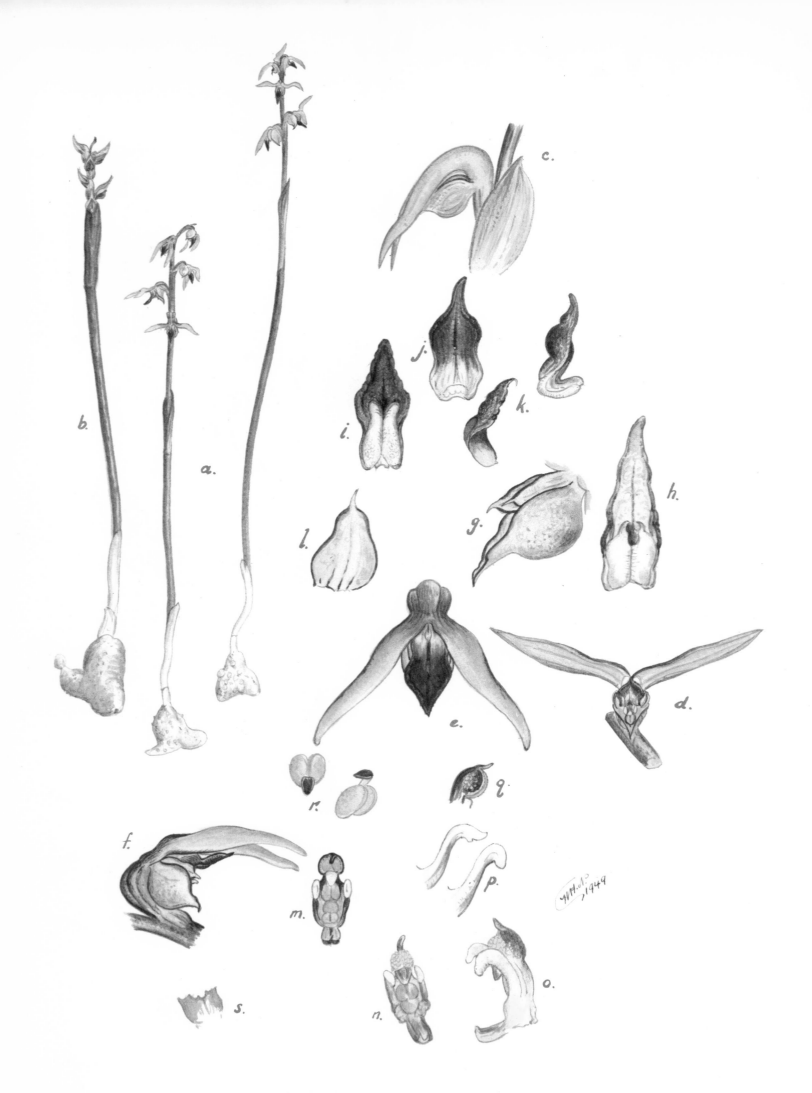

172 *Genoplesium baueri* (see also p. 44)

a flowering specimens **b** specimen in bud **c** opened flower **d** flower, from front **e** flower, from above **f** flower, from side **g** dorsal sepal and petals, from side **h** labellum with unusual callus formation, from front **i** labellum, from front **j** labellum, from rear **k** labella, from side **l** petal **m n** columns, from front **o** column, from side **p** column appendages **q** anther, from side **r** pollinia **s** floral bract

Figs **a**, **b** natural size

173 *Caleana major* (see also p. 45)

a b c specimens from Coimadai, Vic. **d** a rufous flower **e** a very fine example from near Mt Erica, Vic. **f** flower, from front **g** flower, from side **h** leaves—a familiar sight during autumn and winter **i** a pale-coloured flower (lateral sepals not shown) **j** strap-like claw to labellum **k** labellum, from rear **l** pollinia **m** stigma **n** capsule Figs **a–e, h, n** natural size

174 *Caleana nigrita* (see also p. 45)

a b c typical specimens **d** column, from side **e** column, from front **f** pollinia **g** labellum lamina, from above **h** same, from below **i** labellum, from side
Figs **a–c** natural size

175 *Caleana minor* (see also p. 45)

a   b typical specimens   **c** flower, from side   **d** bud   **e** labellum, from side   **f** pollinia   **g** lateral sepal   **h** column, from front   **i** labellum lamina, from below   **j** labellum, from above

Figs **a, b** natural size

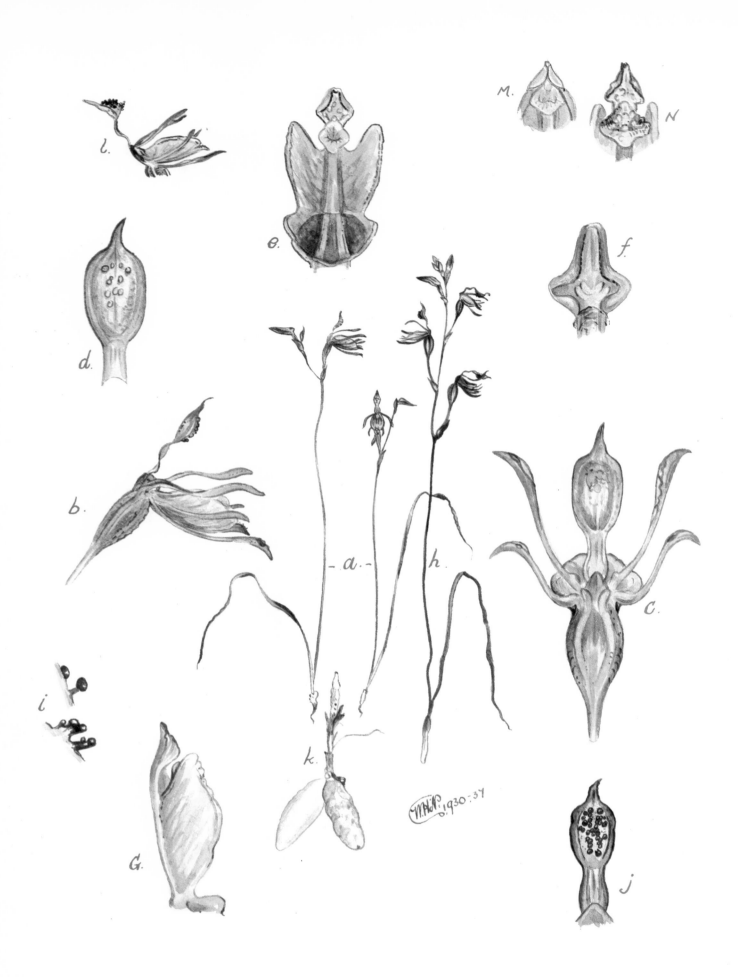

176 *Caleana sullivanii* (see also p. 45)

a specimens from the Wonderland Range, Vic. **b** flower, from side, **c** flower from above **d** labellum lamina, from front **e** column, from front **f** undeveloped anther case **g** column, from side **h** specimen from Mt Byron, Black Range, Vic. **i** glands from labellum lamina **j** labellum, from front **k** tubers **l** flower, from side **m n** heads of column, from front

Figs **a**, **h** natural size

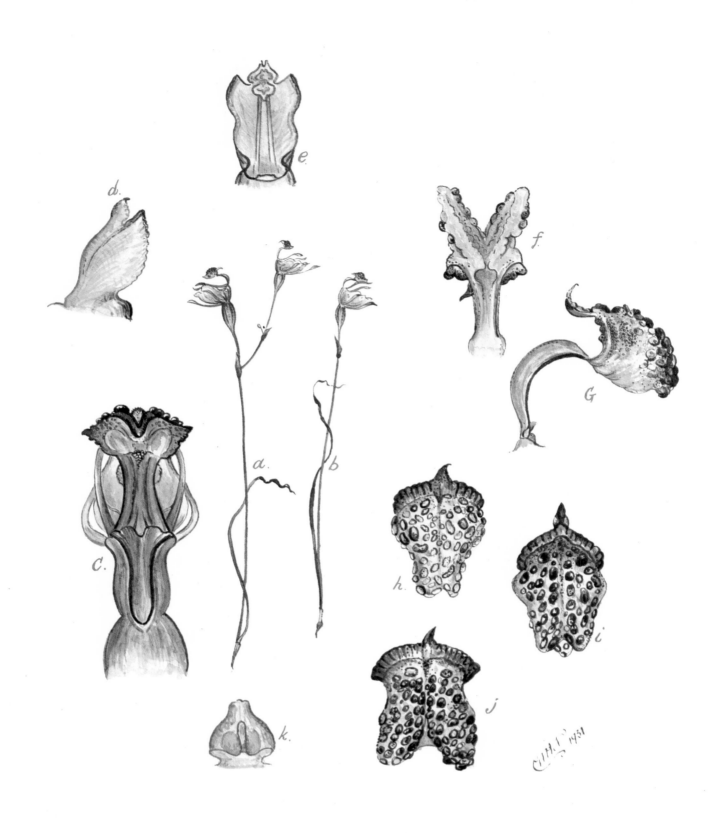

177 *Caleana nublingii* (see also p. 46)

a b the type material **c** flower, from above **d** column, from side **e** column, from front **f** labellum, from below, the lamina pressed down **g** labellum, from side
h i j labella, showing glands **k** anther-case
Figs **a, b** natural size

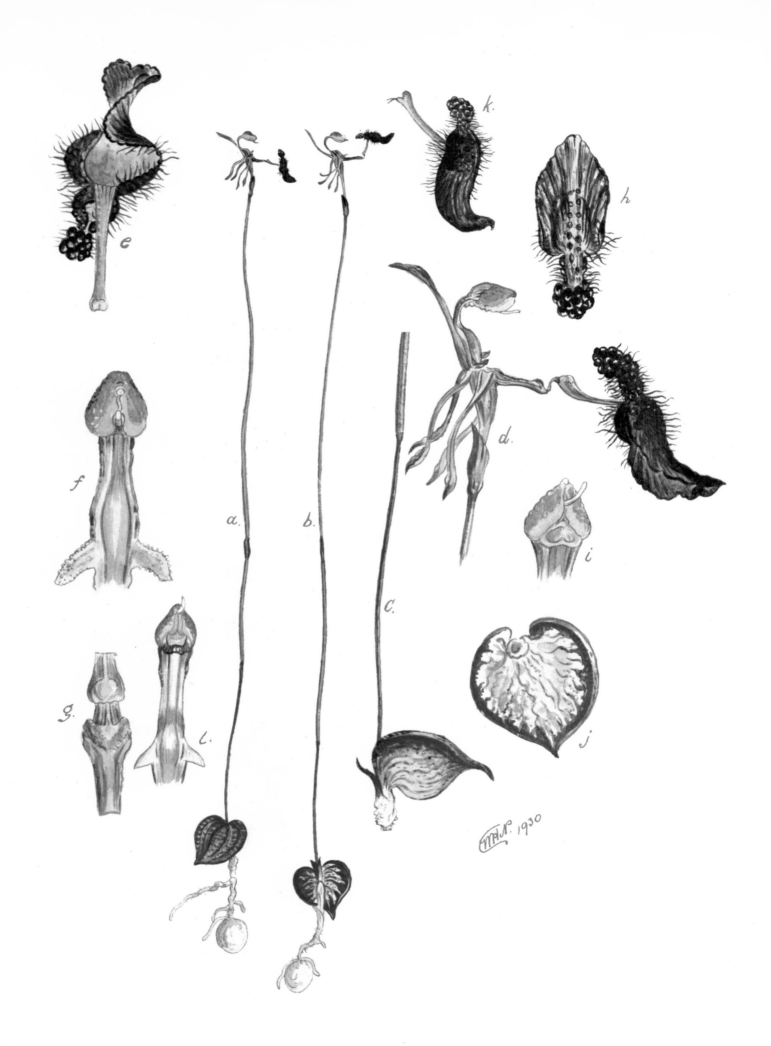

178 *Drakaea elastica* (see also p. 46)

a b typical specimens **c** lower part of stem with leaf **d** flower, from side **e** labellum, from below **f** column, from front **g** labellum hinge **h** labellum, from a bud, from above **i** anther and stigma, from below **j** leaf, from below **k** labellum from a freshly-opened flower **l** column, from front

Figs **a, b** natural size

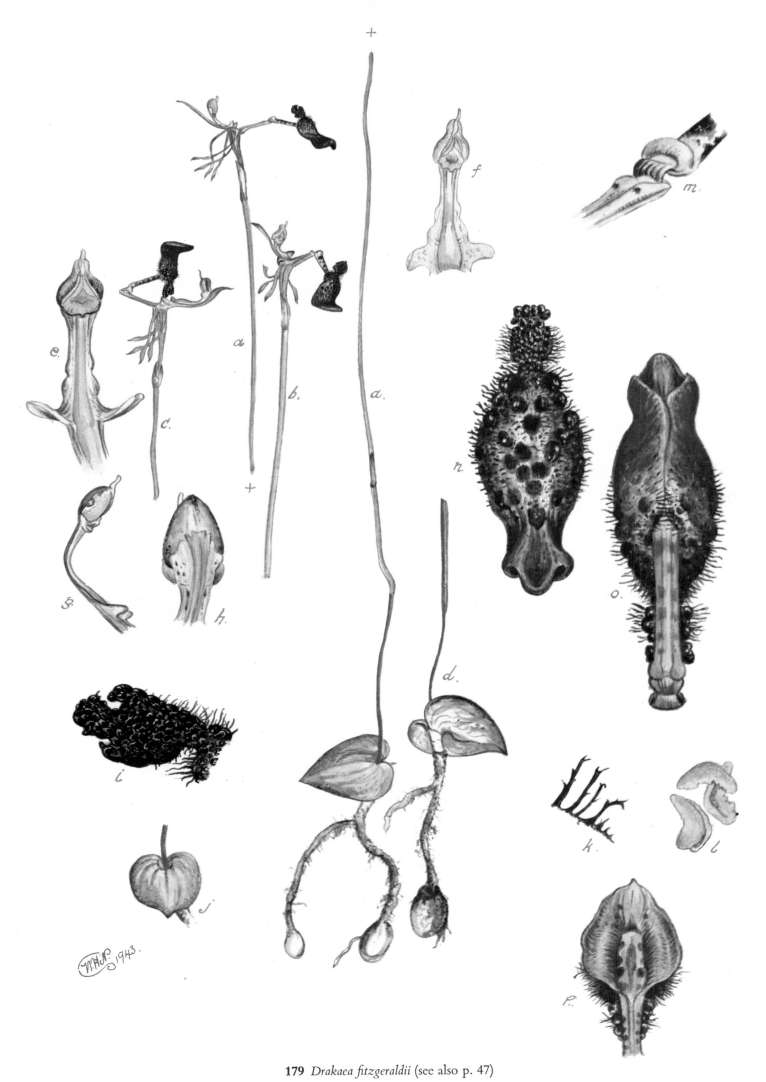

179 *Drakaea fitzgeraldii* (see also p. 47)

a b c typical specimens from Yarloop, WA **d** leaf and lower portion of stem with tubers **e f** columns, from front **g** column, from side **h** anther, from above
i labellum head, from side **j** leaf **k** hairs from labellum **l** pollinia **m** hinge of labellum **n** labellum, from above **o** labellum, from below **p** labellum, from below,
from a bud
Figs **a–d, j** natural size

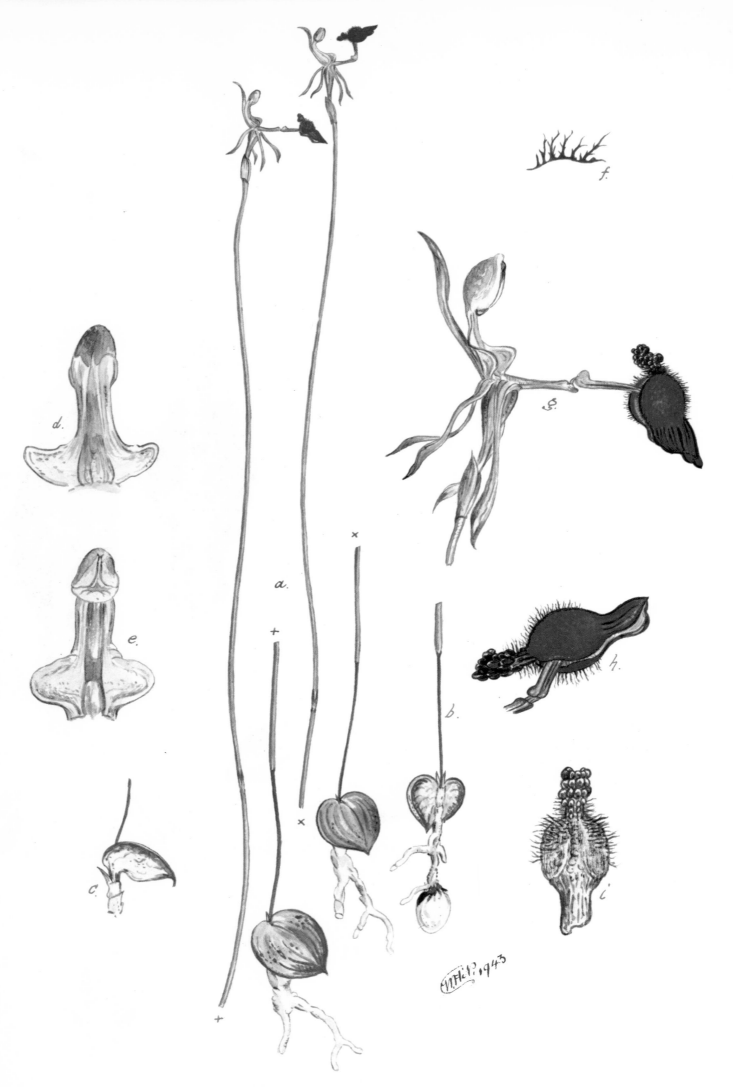

180 *Drakaea glyptodon* (see also p. 47)

a two specimens collected at Yarloop, WA **b** leaf, from below, tubers, etc. **c** leaf, from side, **d** column, from rear **e** column, from front **f** hairs from the labellum
g flower, from side **h** labellum, from side **i** labellum, from above (not coloured)
Figs **a–c** natural size

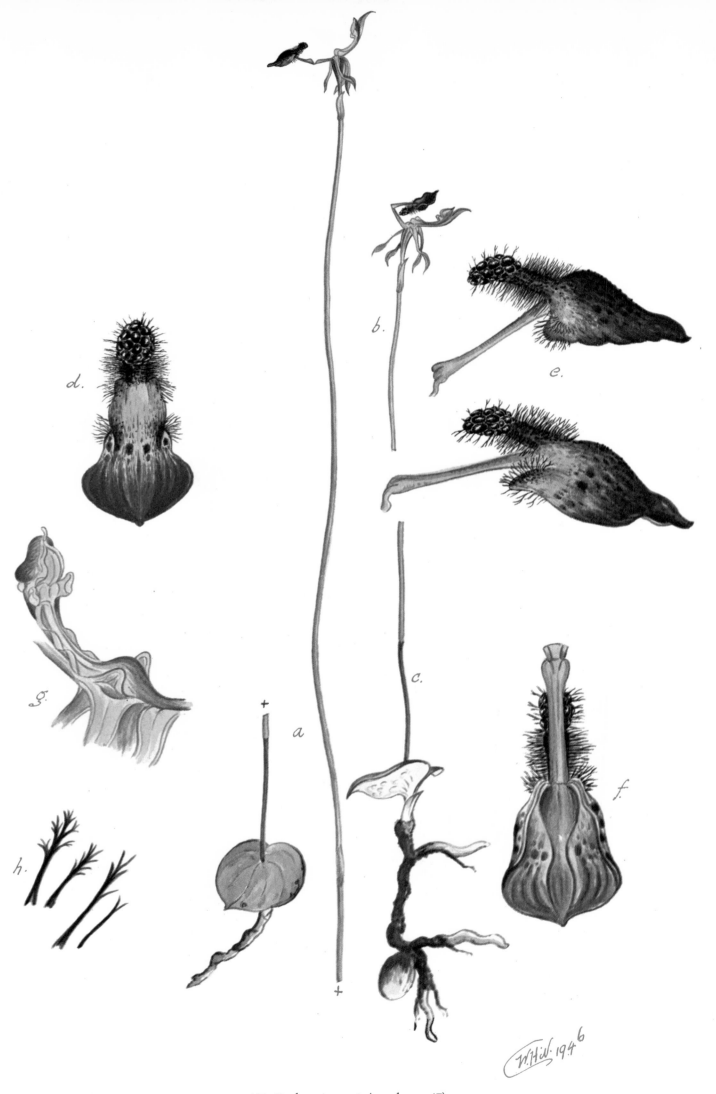

181 *Drakaea jeanensis* (see also p. 47)

a specimen from Yarloop, WA   **b** flower, from side   **c** leaf, lower portion of stem and tubers   **d** labellum, from above   **e** two labella, from side   **f** labellum, from below
g column   **h** bifurcated hairs
Figs **a–c** natural size

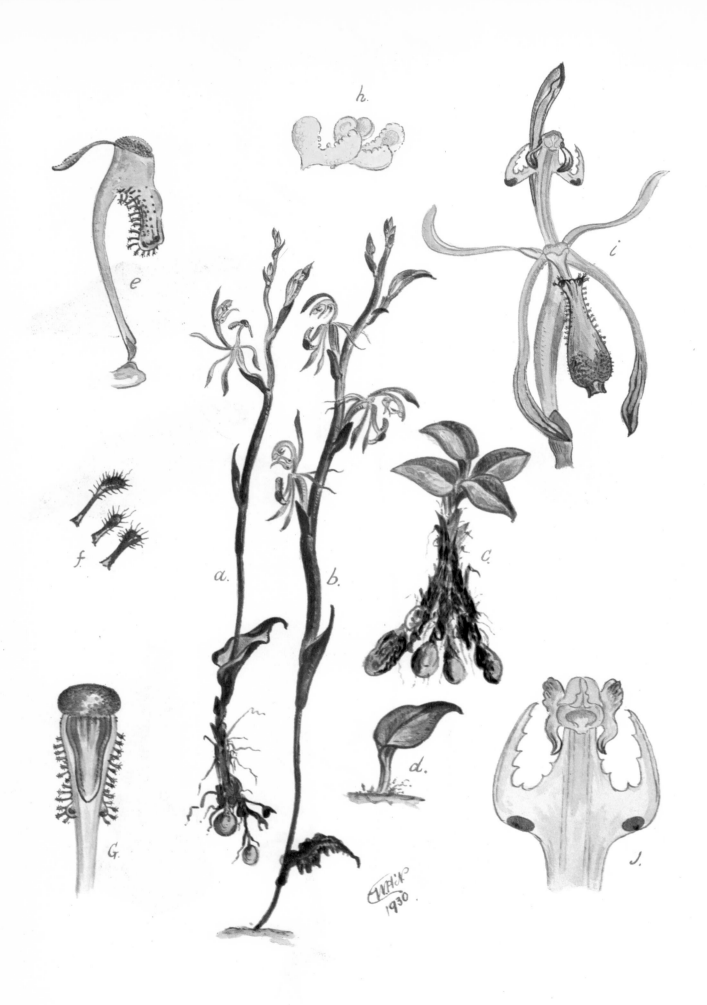

182 *Spiculaea ciliata* (see also p. 48)

a b typical specimens **c d** radical leaves **e** labellum, from side **f** glands from the labellum lamina **g** labellum, from above **h** pollinia **i** flower **j** head of column, from front

Figs **a–d** natural size

183 *Spiculaea irritabilis* (see also p. 48)

a typical plants from Bulahdelah, NSW   **b** flower, from side   **c** head of column, from front   **d** labellum lamina, from above   **e** labellum hinge
Fig. **a** natural size

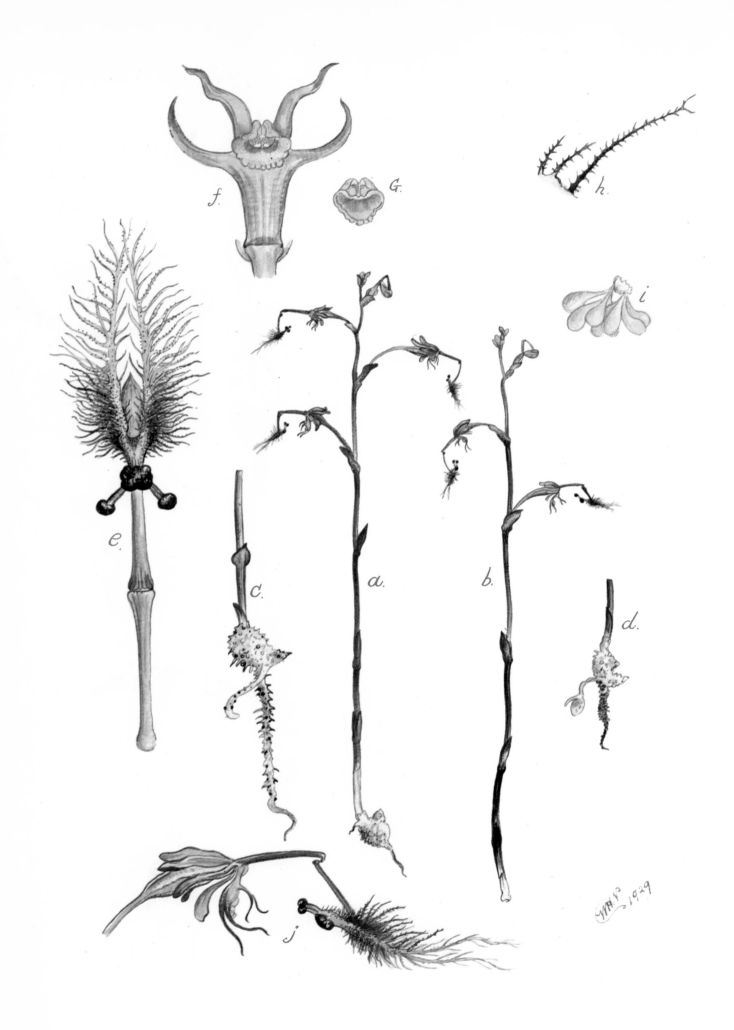

184 *Spiculaea huntiana* (see also p. 48)

a b specimens collected in the Pyrete Range, Gisborne, Vic. **c d** root systems **e** labellum, from above **f** column **g** stigma, anther, etc. **h** cilia from the labellum
i pollinia **j** flower, from side
Figs **a–d** natural size

185 *Chiloglottis cornuta* (see also p. 49)

a specimen from Acheron Valley, Vic. **b** specimen from Sherbrooke Forest, Vic. **c** one of two specimens found among the dense undergrowth off the main highway, Kinglake, Vic. **d** specimen from the morass on Talbot Peak, Baw Baws, Vic. **e** fruiting specimen from Acheron Valley, Vic. **f** dormant tubers—uncovered in Mar. **g** pollinia **h i j k** labella, from above **l** column, from front **m** column, from side
Figs **a–f** natural size

186 *Chiloglottis gunnii* (see also p. 49)

a a specimen from Cobungra, Vic. **b** a lowland specimen from Ballarat, Vic. **c** specimen from the summit of Mt Macedon, Vic. **d** a pale-coloured specimen **e** a fruiting plant from Baw Baws, Vic. **f** calli from the labellum lamina **g** labellum types **h** labellum, from side **i** pollinia **j** column, from front **k** column and ovary, from side **l** labellum from a Grampians, Vic., flower
Figs **a–e** natural size

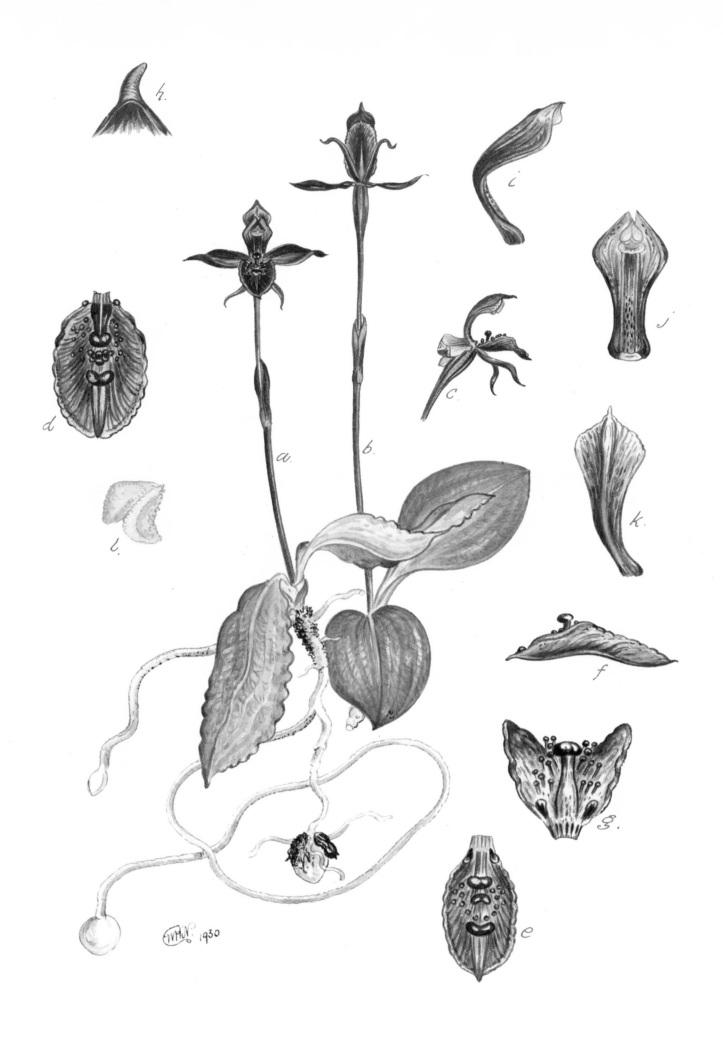

187 *Chiloglottis pescottiana* (see also p. 50)

a b specimens from Cravensville, Vic. **c** flower, from side **d e** labella, from above **f** labellum, from side **g** labellum, from rear **h** apex of dorsal sepal **i** column, from side **j** column, from front **k** dorsal sepal, from rear **l** pollinia
Figs **a–c** natural size

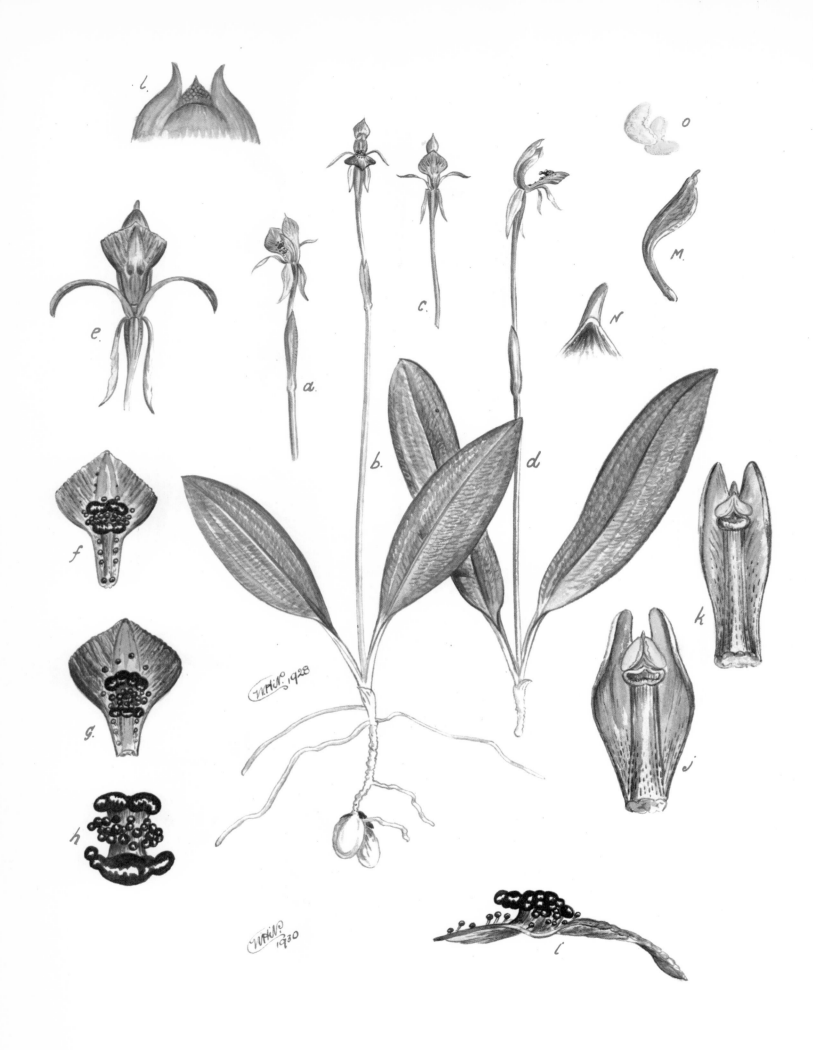

188 *Chiloglottis trapeziformis* (see also p. 50)

a b c d specimens gathered in the Cravensville district, Vic.   **e** flower, from below   **f g** labella, from above   **h** glands from the labellum lamina   **i** labellum, from side
j k columns, from front   **l** head of a column, from rear   **m** dorsal sepal, from side   **n** apex of dorsal sepal, from front   **o** pollinia
Figs **a–d** natural size

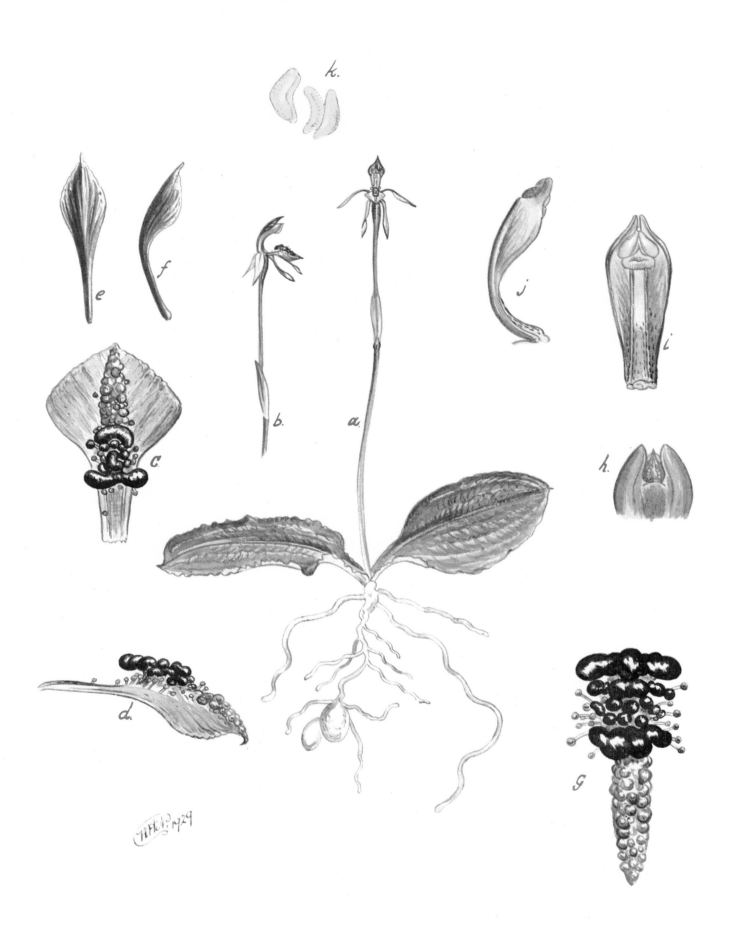

189 *Chiloglottis formicifera* (see also p. 50)

a b specimens from Glenbrook, NSW **c** labellum, from above **d** labellum, from side **e** dorsal sepal, from above **f** dorsal sepal, from side **g** glands from the labellum lamina **h** head of column, from above **i** column, from front **j** column, from side **k** pollinia

Figs **a, b** natural size

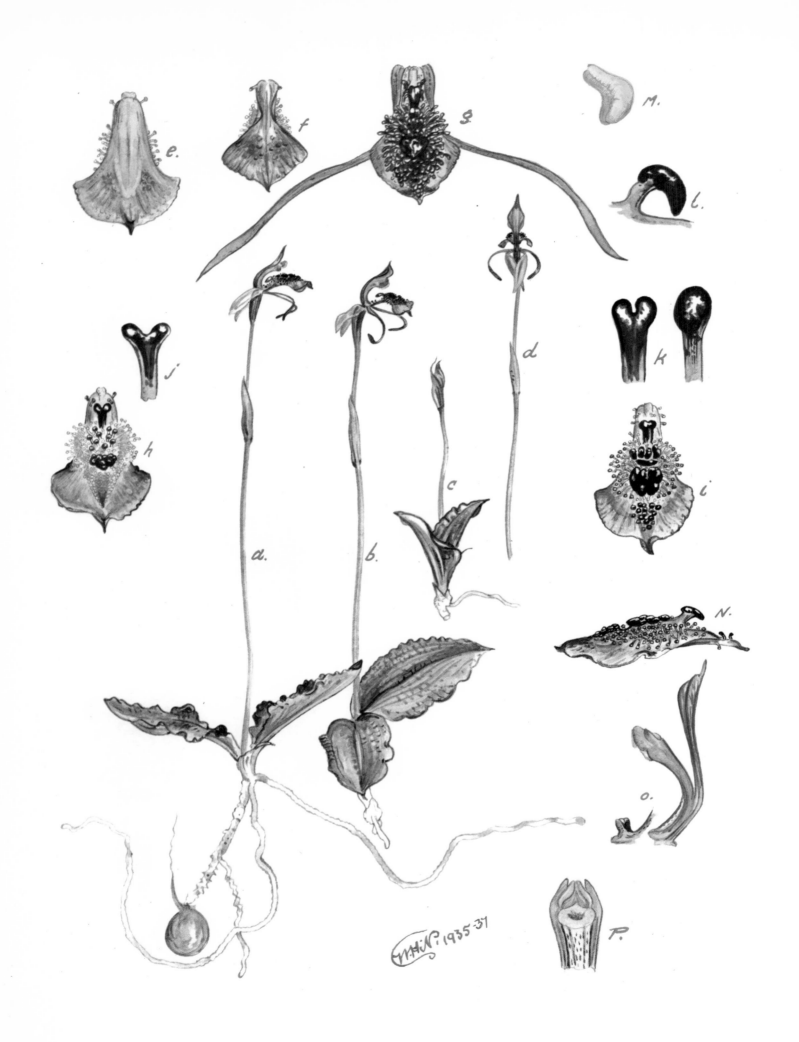

190 *Chiloglottis reflexa* (see also p. 50)

a b typical specimens from bracken fern lands, Cranbourne, Vic. **c** plant in bud **d** flower, from rear **e** labellum, from below **f** another labellum, from below **g** labellum and sepals, from above, Qld specimen (note compact arrangement of glands) **h** labellum, from above, Vic. specimen **i** another labellum, from above **j k l** variation in form of the stalked gland from labellum lamina **m** pollinia **n** labellum, from side **o** column and dorsal sepal, from side, also short column foot **p** head of column, from front
Figs **a–d** natural size

191 *Acianthus caudatus* (see also p. 51)

a b c typical specimens **d** flower, filiform points of the sepals not shown **e** head of column, from front **f** glands at the base of the labellum **g** column, from side
h labellum, from side **i** base of dorsal sepal, from rear **j** pollinia
Figs **a–c** natural size

192 *Acianthus exsertus* (see also p. 51)

a b very fine examples collected near Airey's Inlet, Vic. **c** specimen from Cheltenham Park, Vic. **d** juvenile plant **e** labellum, from above **f** column, from side **g** head of column, showing stigma, etc. **h i** flowers, from front **j** flower, from side **k** pollinia

Figs **a–d** natural size

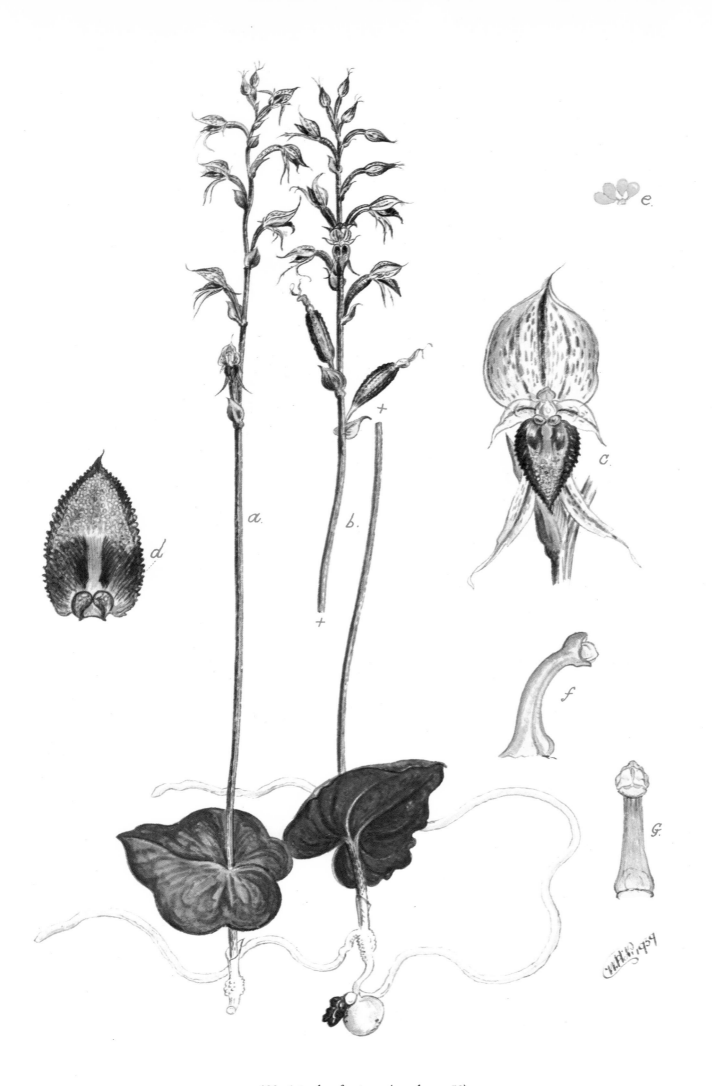

193 *Acianthus fornicatus* (see also p. 52)

a   b large specimens from Kurri Kurri, NSW   **c** flower, from front   **d** labellum, from above   **e** pollinia   **f** column, from side   **g** column, from front
Figs **a, b** natural size

194 *Acianthus ledwardii* (see also p. 52)

a typical specimen **b** flower, from front **c** flower, from side **d** labellum, from front (note that part only of marginal fringe is incurved—a novel instance of variation)
Fig. **a** natural size

195 *Acianthus reniformis* (see also p. 52)

a typical specimen **b** a fine example from the You Yangs, Vic. **c** fruiting specimen **d** head of column, from side **e** callus plates from the labellum lamina **f** head of column, from above—pollinia removed **g** head of column, from side, more prominently winged than that figured above **h** head of column, from front **i** pollinia **j** basal calli and plates of the labellum lamina **k** labellum, from above **l** variation of the labellum tip **m** flower
Figs **a–c** natural size

196 *Acianthus huegelii* (see also p. 53)

a typical specimens **b** flower, from side **c** dorsal sepal, from front **d** labellum, from above **e** head of column **f** pollinia—one pair **g** glands from the labellum **h** lateral sepal **i** petal

Fig. **a** natural size

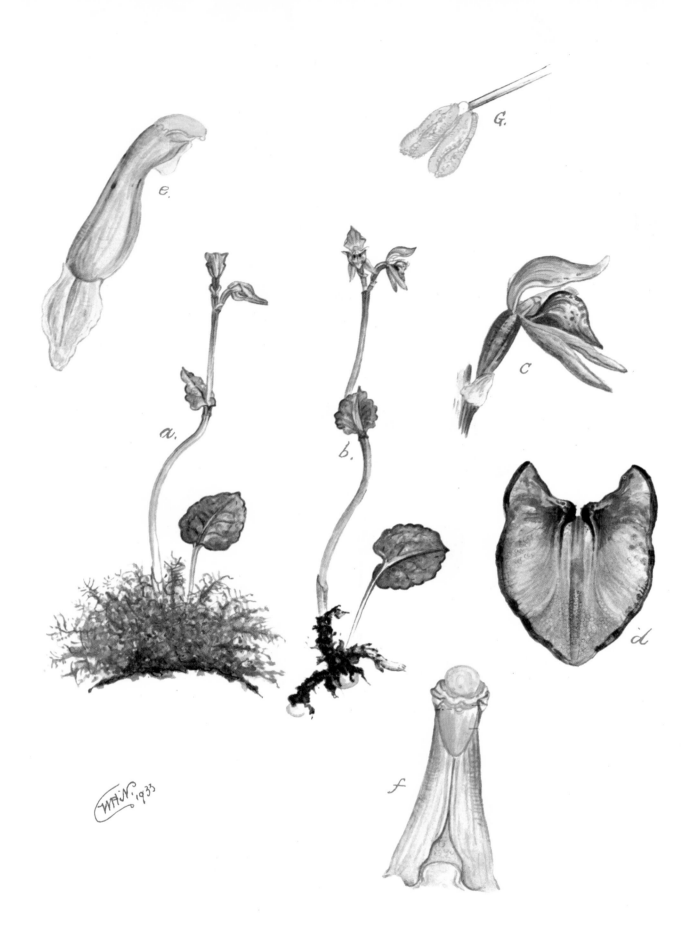

197 *Townsonia viridis* (see also p. 53)

a plant in bud **b** flowering plant with root system **c** flower, from side **d** labellum, from front **e** column, from side **f** column, from front, with petal attached **g** pollinia
Figs **a, b** natural size

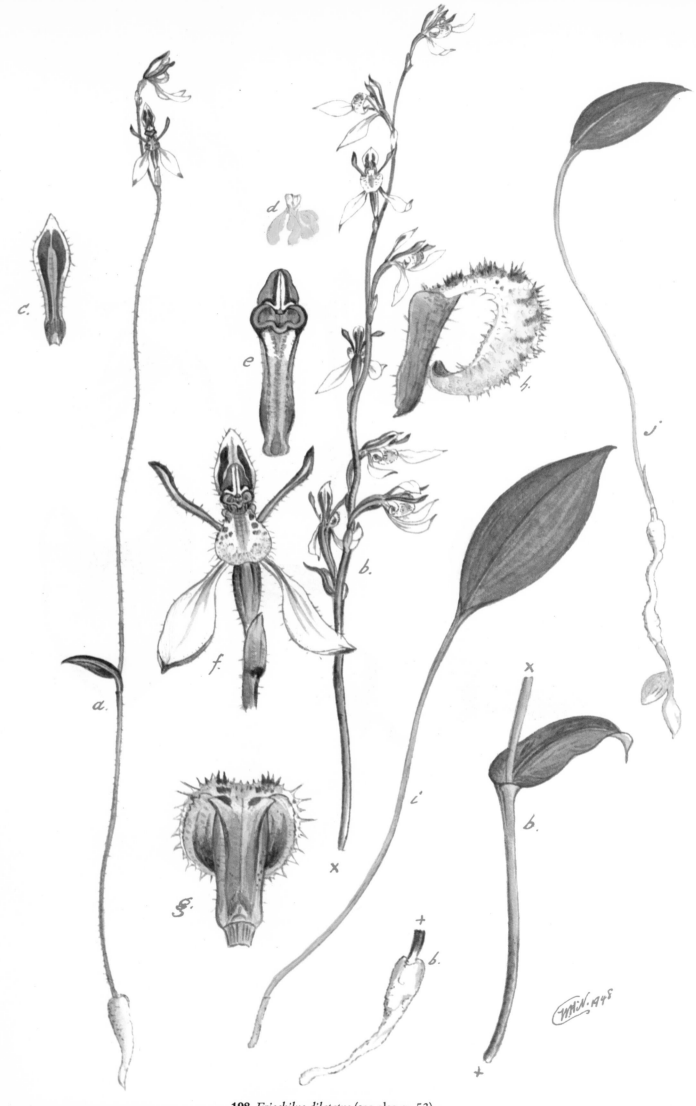

198 *Eriochilus dilatatus* (see also p. 53)

a typical specimen **b** a broad-leafed form **c** dorsal sepal **d** pollinia **e** column, from front **f** flower, from front **g** labellum, from above **h** labellum, from side **i** radical leaf **j** radical leaf with tubers, etc.

Figs **a, b, i, j** natural size

199 *Eriochilus cucullatus* (see also p. 54)

a typical specimen **b c d** NSW specimens **e** from the Keilor plains, Vic., occasionally growing in congested tufts **f** plant found at Sunshine, Vic., in Aug. (note lines of hairs along the nerves of leaf) **g** hairs from the labellum lamina **h** petal **i** labellum, from above **j** labellum, from side **k** three plants collected during July **l** column, from front **m** upper margin of stigma, etc. **n** pollinia **o** dorsal sepal, from side **p** congested tuft of plants, Keilor plains, Vic.
Figs **a–f, k, p** natural size

200 *Eriochilus scaber* (see also p. 54)

a b c two flowering and one fruiting specimen **d** column, from side **e** column, from front **f** pollinia **g** flower, from side **h** labellum, from above (lamina not coloured) **i** labellum lamina (not coloured), showing glabrous tip, the extreme apex not shown **j** flowers from Young's Siding, WA

Figs **a–c, j** natural size

201 *Rimacola elliptica* (see also p. 54)

a   b racemes of flowers   **c** portion of plant with rhizomes   **d** plant taken from a fissure   **e** flower, from side   **f** labellum, from above   **g** column, from front   **h** column, from side   **i** dorsal sepal   **j** pollinia

Figs **a–d** natural size

202 *Lyperanthus forrestii* (see also p. 55)

a b two specimens from Young's Siding, WA   **c** column, from side   **d** column, from front   **e** pollinia   **f** labellum, from above   **g** labellum, from side   **h** leaves *in situ* at Upper King River, WA

Figs **a, b, h** natural size

203 *Lyperanthus nigricans* (see also p. 55)

a b c typical plants from Pomonal, Vic. **d** dried herbarium specimen **e** capsules **f** flower, from side **g** labellum mid-lobe **h** labellum, from above **i** column, from side **j** head of column, from front **k** head of column, from rear **l** pollinia
Figs **a–e** natural size

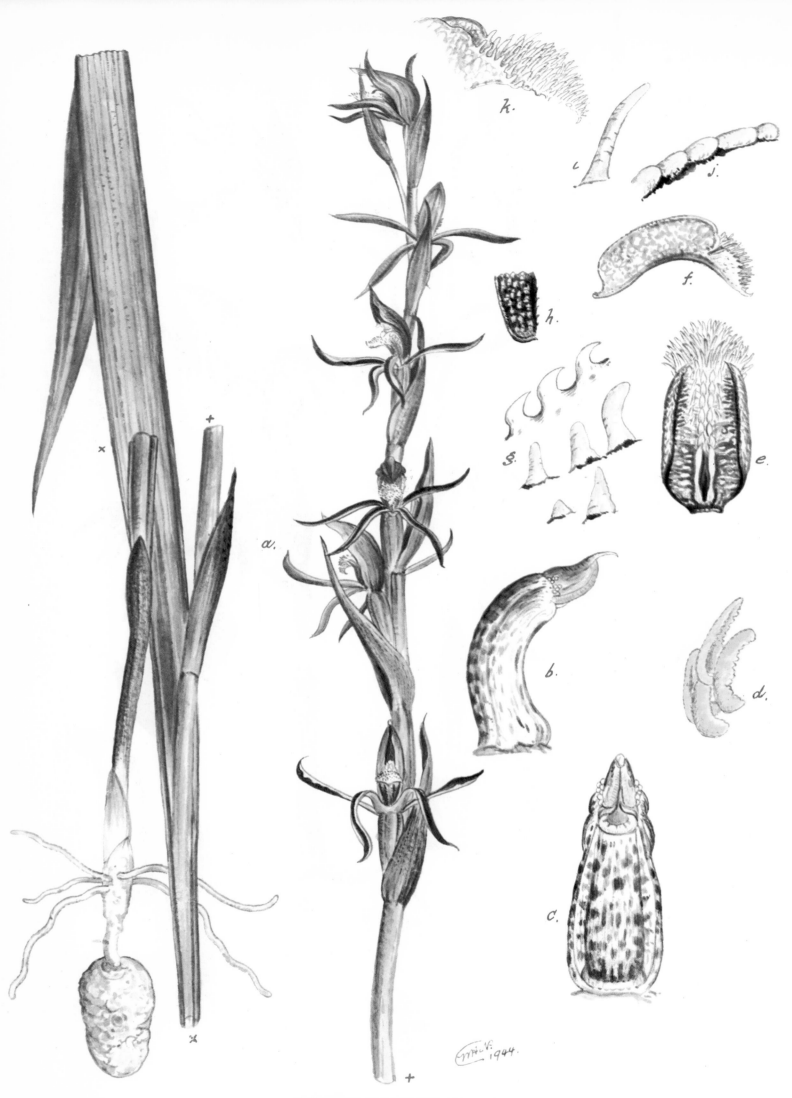

204 *Lyperanthus serratus* (see also p. 55)

a specimen from Yarloop, WA **b** column, from side **c** column, from front **d** pollinia **e** labellum, from above **f** labellum, from side **g** calli from the labellum **h** inner surface of labellum **i** callus from the mid-lobe **j** row of calli from the lamina **k** tip of labellum, showing brush-like mass of calli
Fig. **a** natural size

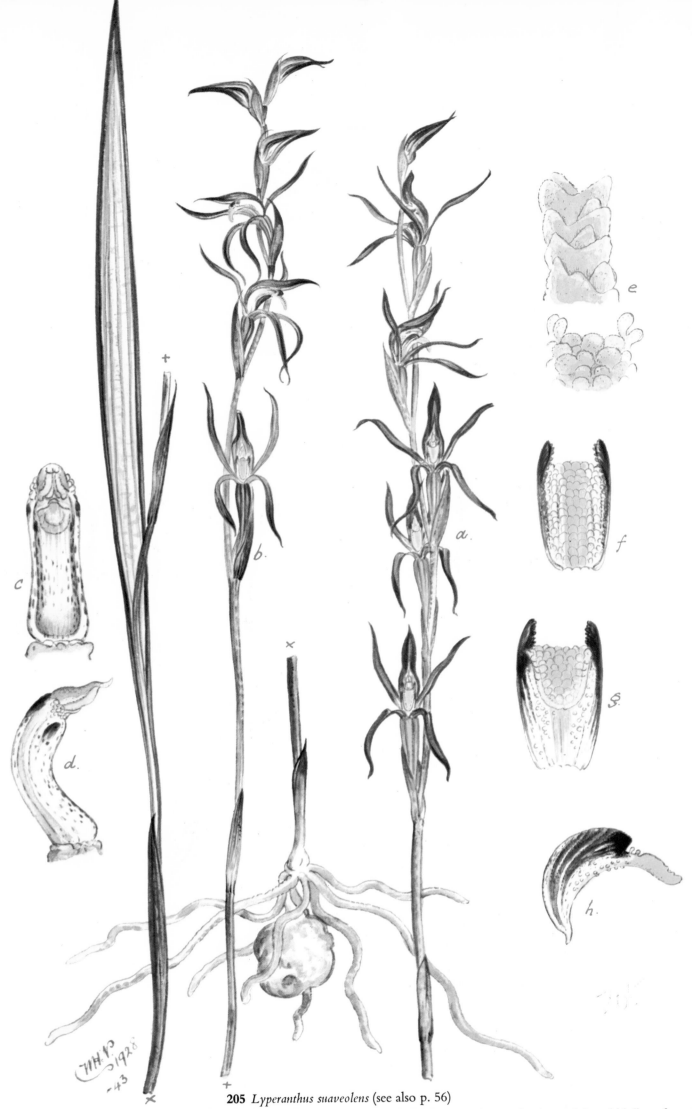

205 *Lyperanthus suaveolens* (see also p. 56)

a raceme of flowers **b** typical specimen **c** column, from front **d** column, from side **e** glands from labellum lamina, showing variation **f** labellum, from above
g labellum, from front **h** labellum, from side
Figs **a, b** natural size

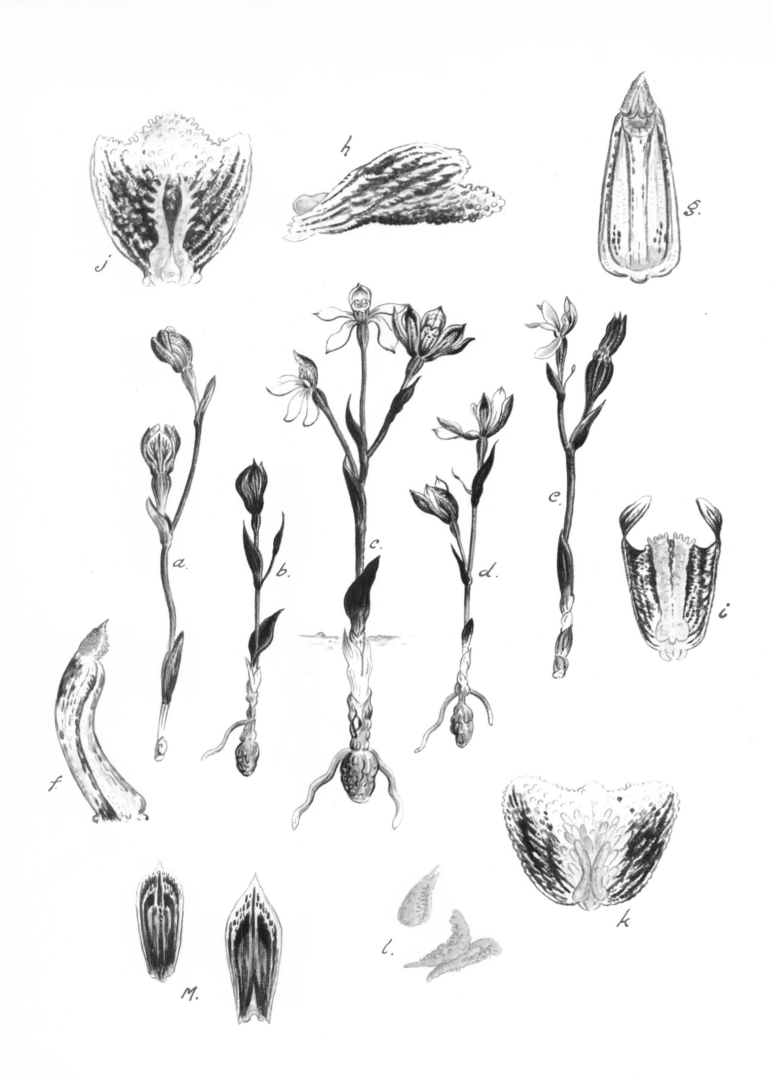

206 *Burnettia cuneata* (see also p. 56)

a b c d e typical plants **f** column, from side **g** column, from front **h** labellum, from side **i** labellum, from above **j** labellum, from above, spread out **k** labellum, from above, spread out **l** pollinia **m** dorsal sepals, from rear

Figs **a–e** natural size

207 *Leptoceras fimbriatum* (see also p. 56)

a b c d specimens from Cheltenham, Vic. **e** leaf, tuber, etc. **f** petal **g** labellum, from below **h** column, from front **i** pollinia **j** dorsal sepal, from above **k** lateral sepal **l** labellum, from front **m** column, from side

Figs **a–e** natural size

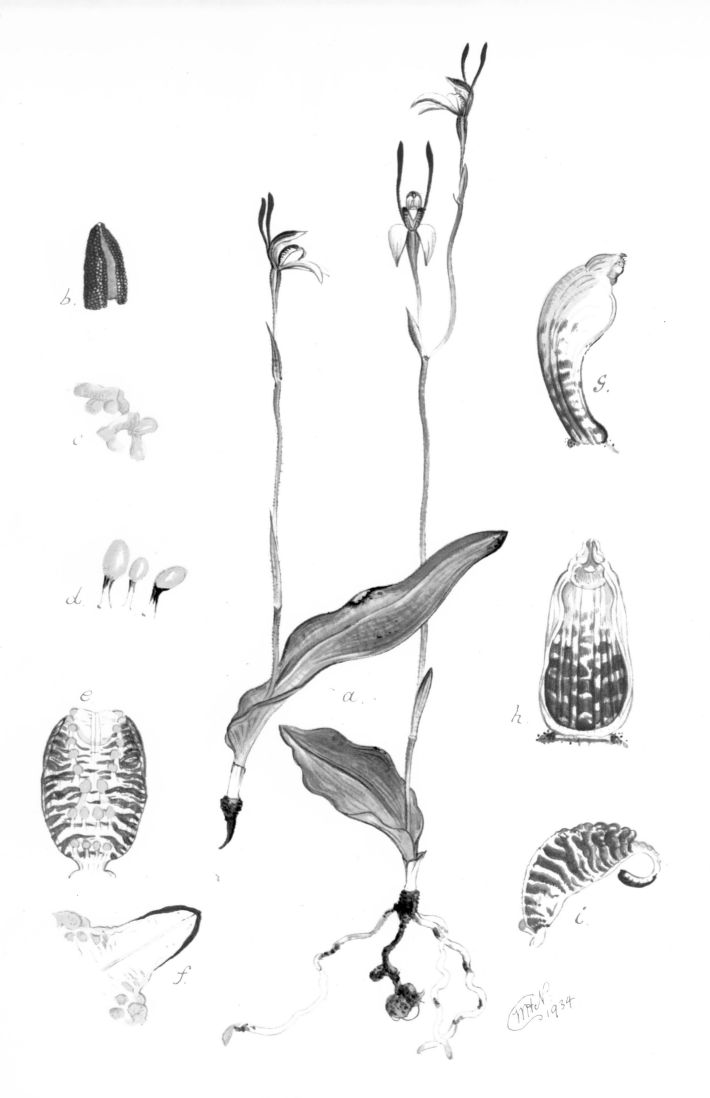

208 *Caladenia menziesii* (see also p. 57)

a typical specimens **b** tip of petal **c** pollinia **d** calli from labellum lamina **e** labellum, from above **f** tip of labellum **g** column, from side **h** column, from front
i labellum, from side
Fig. **a** natural size

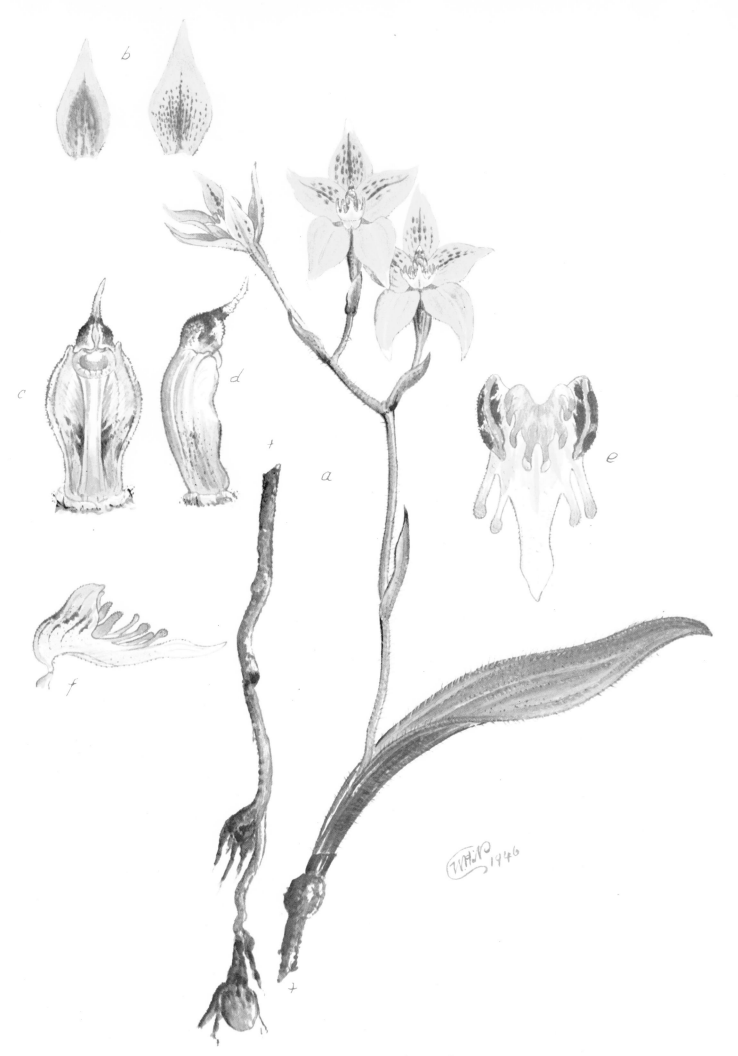

209 *Caladenia flava* (see also p. 57)

a typical specimen **b** variation in the colouring of the dorsal sepal **c** column, from front **d** column, from side **e** labellum, from above **f** labellum, from side
Fig. **a** natural size

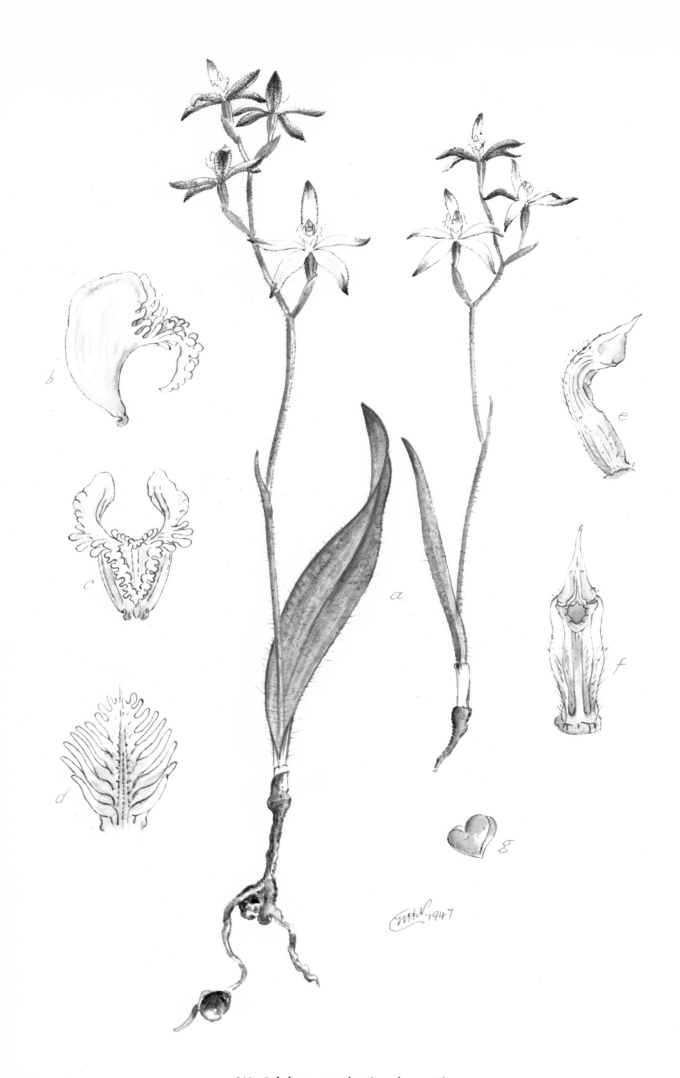

210 *Caladenia paniculata* (see also p. 57)

a two Upper King River, WA, specimens **b** labellum, from side **c** labellum, from front **d** callus-plate **e** column, from side **f** column, from front **g** pollinia
Fig. **a** natural size

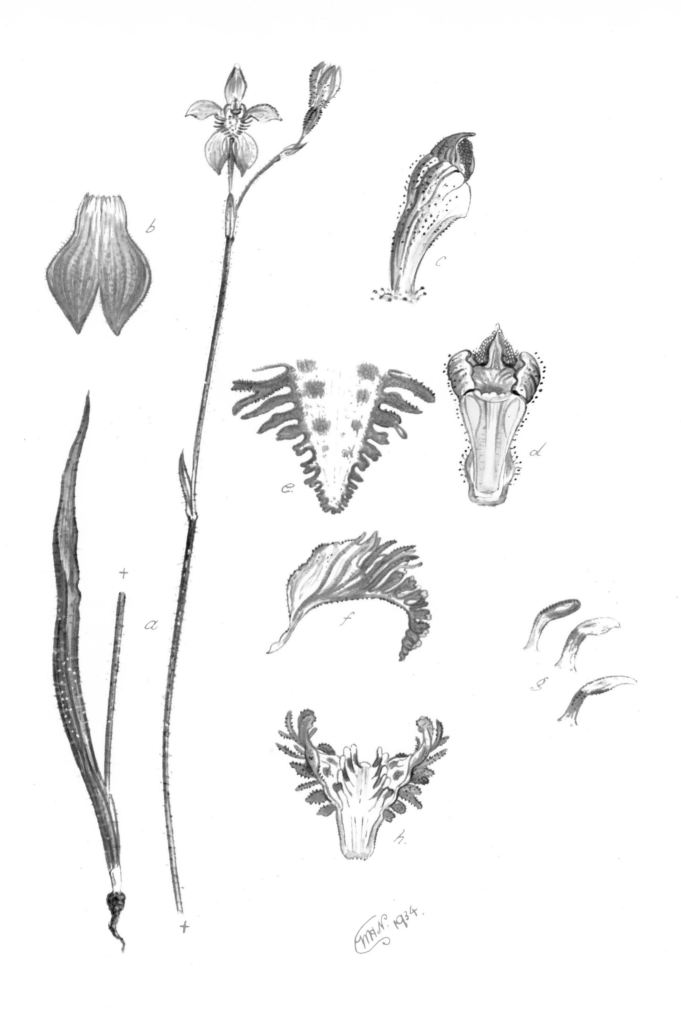

211 *Caladenia unita* (see also p. 58)

a typical specimen **b** united lateral sepals **c** column, from side **d** column, from front **e** tip of labellum **f** labellum, from side **g** calli from the labellum lamina
h labellum, from above
Fig. **a** natural size

212 *Caladenia latifolia* (see also p. 58)

a b c typical specimens from Mornington, Vic. **d** a seedling plant, raised by the author **e** column, from front **f** column, from side **g** labellum, from front **h** labellum, from side **i** pollinia **j** calli from labellum lamina

Figs **a–c** natural size

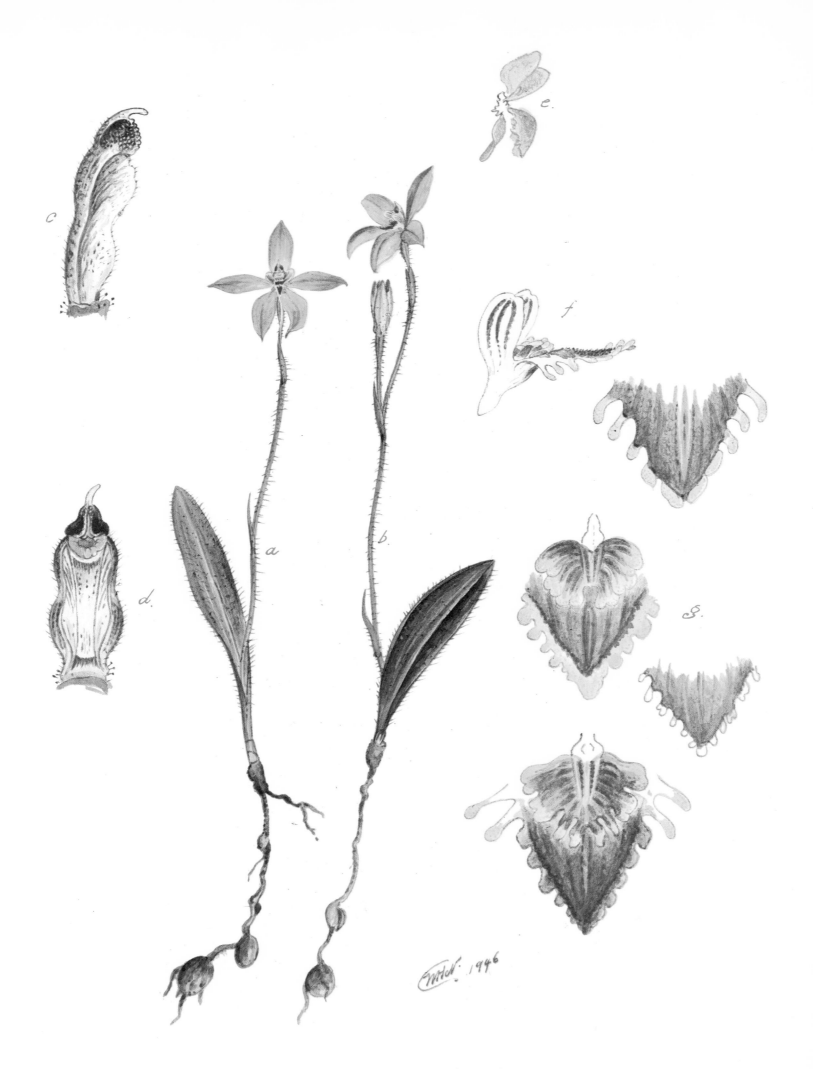

213 *Caladenia reptans* (see also p. 58)

a typical specimen from Yarloop, WA **b** specimen from Orchid Valley, WA **c** column, from side **d** column, from front **e** pollinia **f** labellum, from side **g** mid-lobes and apices, showing variation to marginal fringe
Figs **a, b** natural size

214 *Caladenia sericea* (see also p. 58)

a b typical plants from the Darling Range, WA **c** labellum, from front **d** calli **e** column, from front **f** labellum, from above
Figs **a, b** natural size

215 *Caladenia gemmata*: Figs **a, c–j** (see also p. 58)
C. gemmata forma *lutea*: Fig. **b** (see also p. 59)

a specimen from York district, WA   **b** another specimen   **c   d** flower types   **e** specimen from Narembeen district, WA   **f** labellum, from side   **g** labellum, from rear
h pollinia   **i** column, from side   **j** column from front
Figs **a–e** natural size

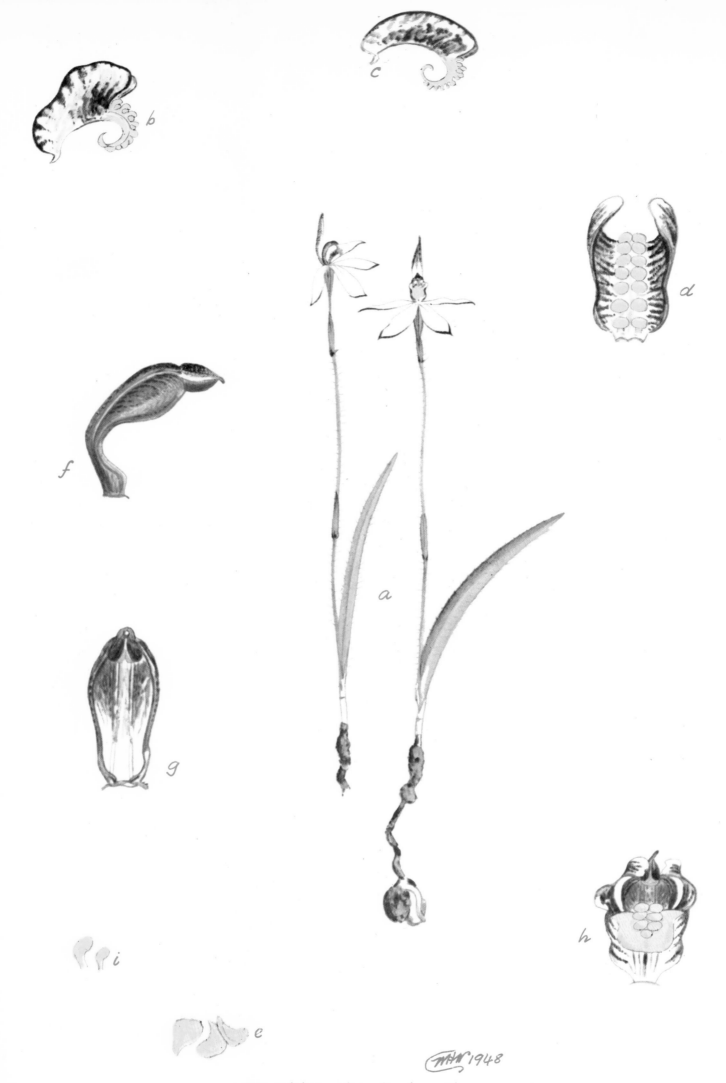

216 *Caladenia saccharata* (see also p. 59)

a typical specimens b labellum, from side c labellum (somewhat different in shape), from side d labellum, from above e pollinia f column, from side g column, from front h labellum and column, from front i calli from the labellum lamina
Fig. **a** natural size

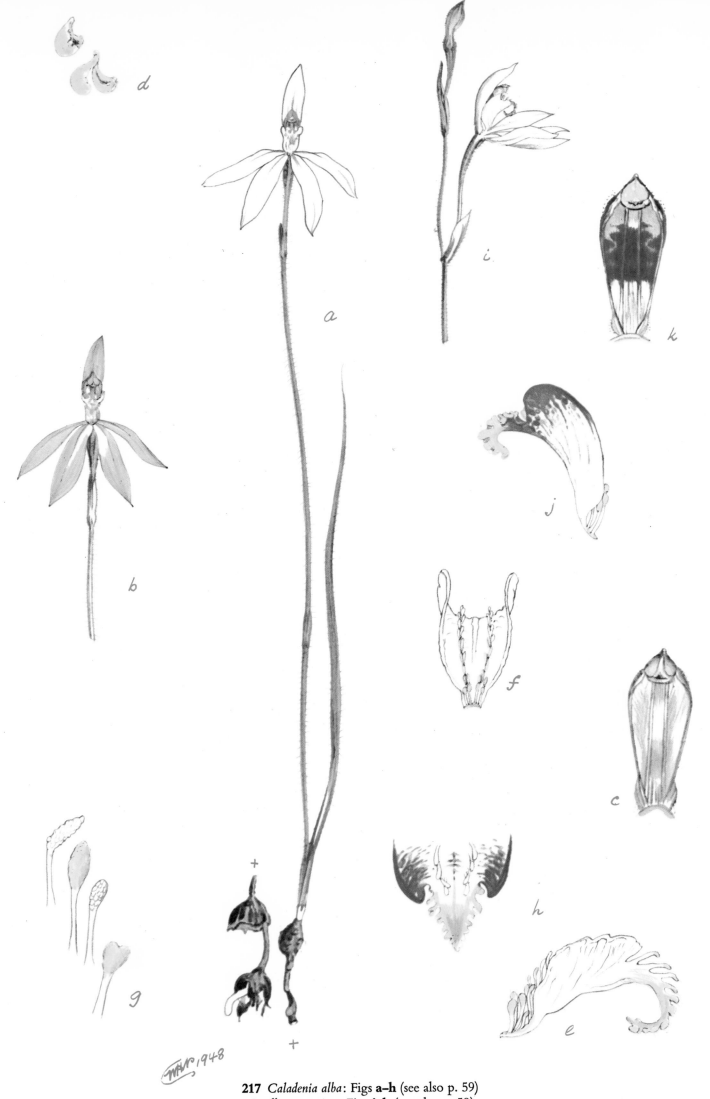

217 *Caladenia alba*: Figs **a–h** (see also p. 59)
C. alba var. *picta*: Figs **i–k** (see also p. 59)

a flowering specimen **b** pink form **c** column, from front **d** pollinia **e** labellum, from side **f** labellum, from above **g** calli from labellum lamina **h** tip of labellum
i flowers **j** labellum, from side **k** column, from front
Figs **a, b, i** natural size

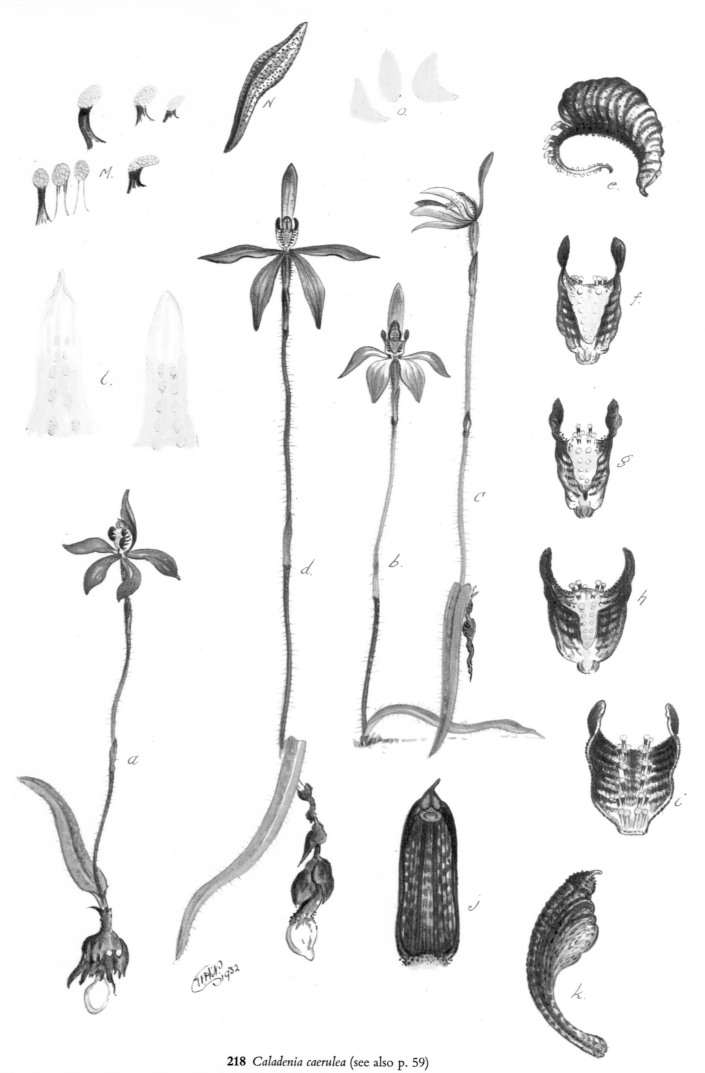

218 *Caladenia caerulea* (see also p. 59)

a b c typical specimens **d** a very fine example from Weston, NSW **e** labellum, from side **f g h** labella, from front **i** labellum, from above **j** column, from front **k** column, from side **l** labellum apices **m** calli from labellum lamina **n** dorsal sepal **o** pollinia

Figs **a–d** natural size

219 *Caladenia carnea*: Figs **a–d, l–n** (see also p. 59)
C. carnea var. *pygmaea*: Figs **e–k** (see also p. 60)

a a form from Airey's Inlet, Vic.   **b c d** typical forms from localities in Vic.   **e** a small-flowered form from rocky places in the Grampians, Vic.   **f** flower, from side, from Grampians, Vic.   **g h i** specimens from Wonthaggi, Vic.   **j k** conjoined sepals, often found in this variety   **l** flower, showing barred sepals, labellum and column removed
m a rare form from Kinglake, Vic.   **n** a richly coloured labellum
Figs **a–e, g–i, l, m** natural size

220 *Caladenia carnea* var. *gigantea* (see also p. 60)

a flowers   **b** flowers of a small form   **c** labellum   **d** calli from labellum lamina   **e** lateral lobe of labellum   **f g** variation in the apex of the labellum   **h** labellum, from rear   **i** labellum, from side   **j** column, from side   **k** column, from front

Figs **a, b** natural size

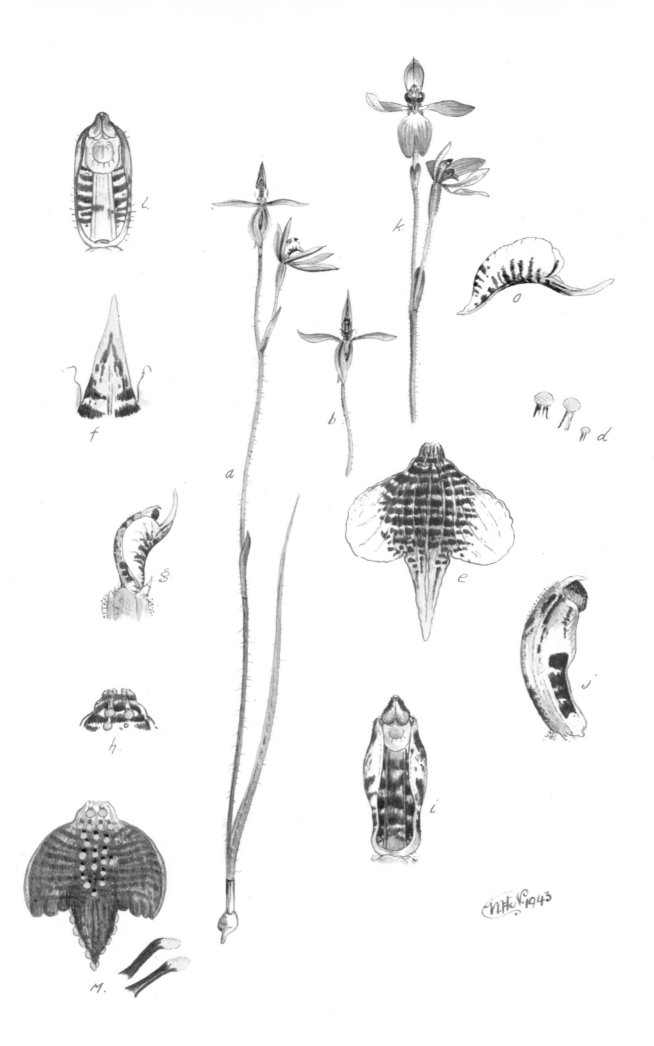

221 *Caladenia carnea* var. *subulata*: Figs **a–j** (see also p. 60)
C. carnea var. *ornata*: Figs **k–m** (see also p. 60)

a flowering specimen **b** flower **c** labellum, from side **d** calli from labellum lamina **e** labellum, from above, lobes spread out **f** mid-lobe of labellum **g** column and labellum, from side **h** calli at base of labellum **i** column, from front **j** column, from side **k** flowers **l** column, from front **m** labellum, from above, lobes spread out, also calli from labellum lamina

Figs **a, b, k** natural size

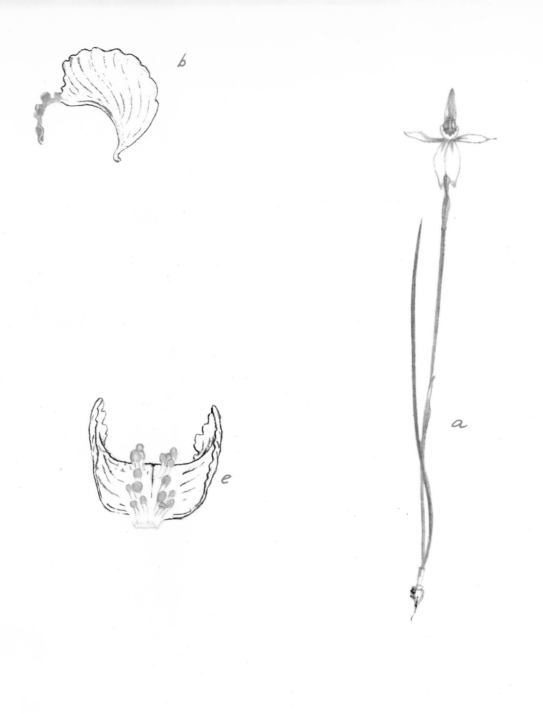

222 *Caladenia aurantiaca* (see also p. 60)

a flowering specimen **b** labellum, from side **c** calli from labellum lamina **d** column, from front **e** labellum, from rear **f** labellum tip
Fig. **a** natural size

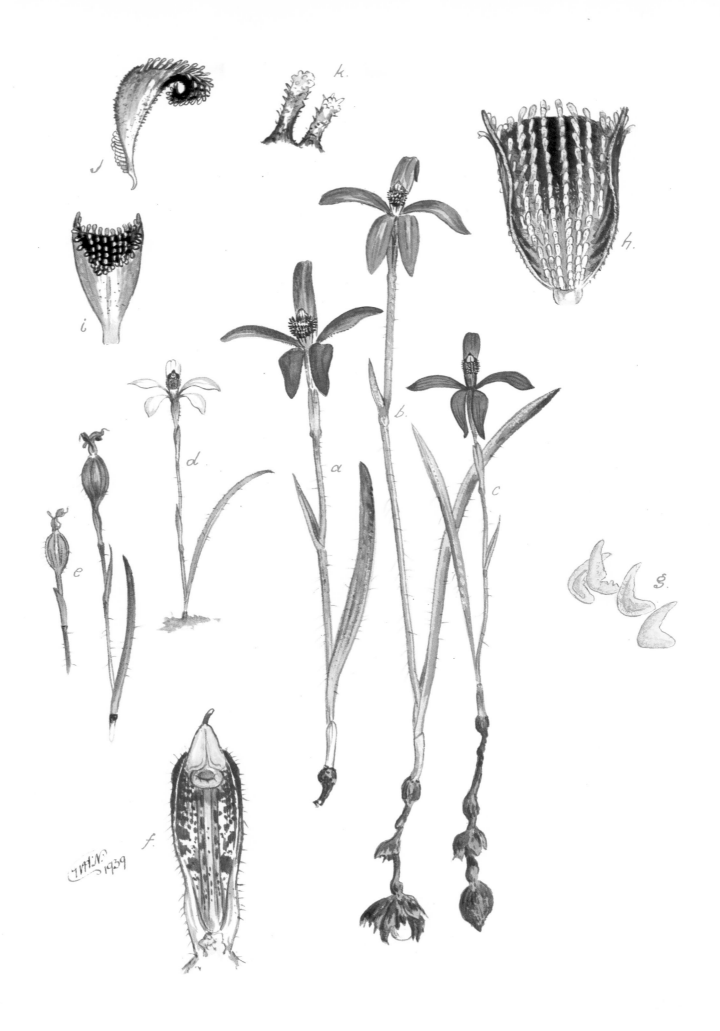

223 *Caladenia deformis* (see also p. 60)

a b specimens from Ringwood, Vic. **c** specimen from Ararat, Vic. **d** specimen from Point Lonsdale, Vic. **e** fruiting specimens **f** column, from front **g** pollinia
h labellum, from above **i** labellum, from below **j** labellum, from side **k** calli from the labellum lamina
Figs **a–e** natural size

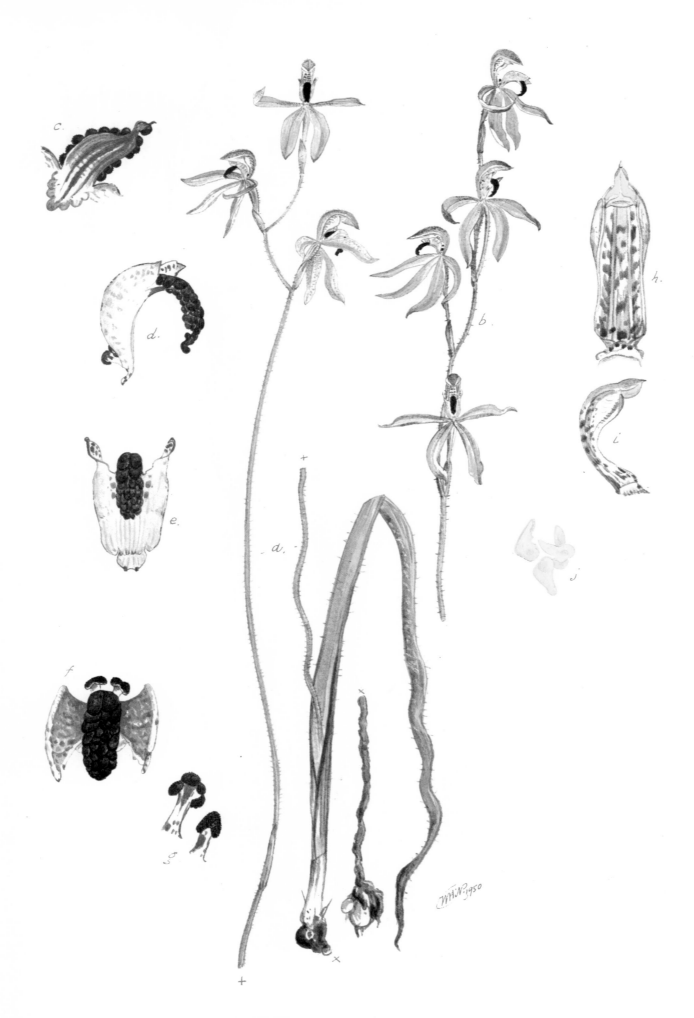

224 *Caladenia congesta* (see also p. 61)

a flowering plant b inflorescence c labellum mid-lobe, from below d labellum, from side e labellum, from below f labellum, from above g calli from base of labellum h column, from front i column, from side j pollinia

Figs **a, b** natural size

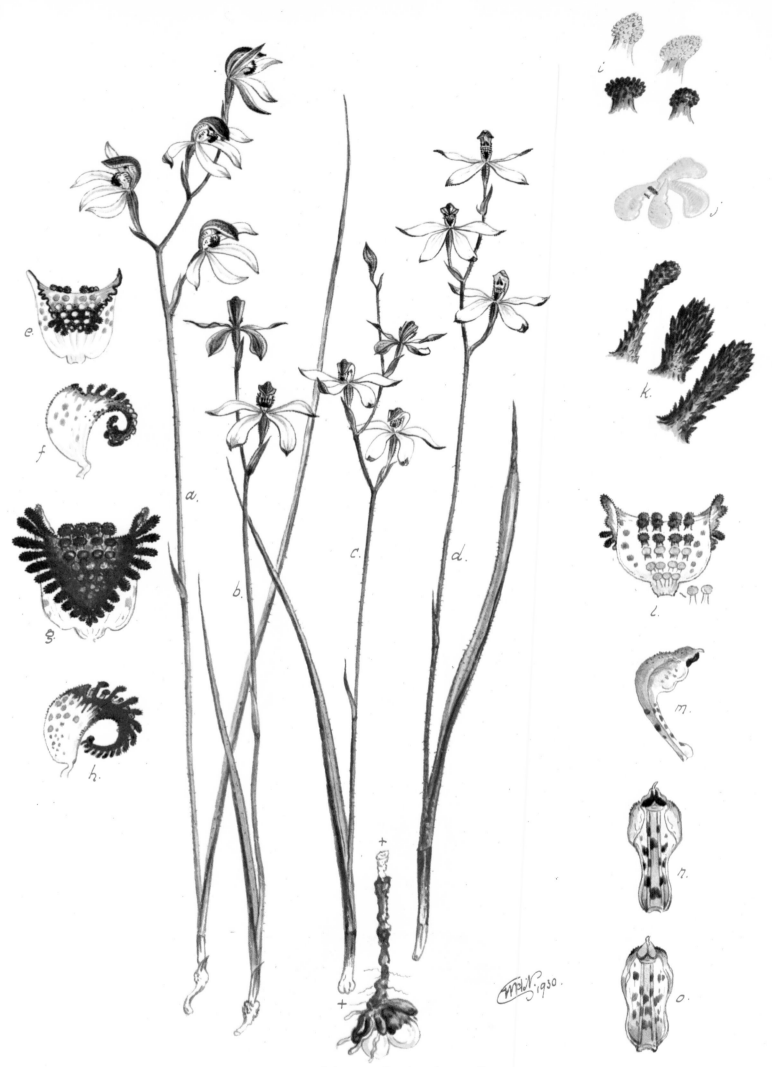

225 *Caladenia cucullata* (see also p. 61)

a b specimens from Rushworth, Vic. **c d** specimens from Staughton Vale, Vic. **e** labellum, from front **f** labellum, from side **g** a well-combed labellum, from front **h** a similar labellum, from side **i** calli from labellum lamina **j** pollinia **k** character of labellum fringe **l** labellum, from above (sometimes two calli only at base) **m** column, from side **n** column, from front **o** column, from front, widely-winged throughout

Figs **a–d** natural size

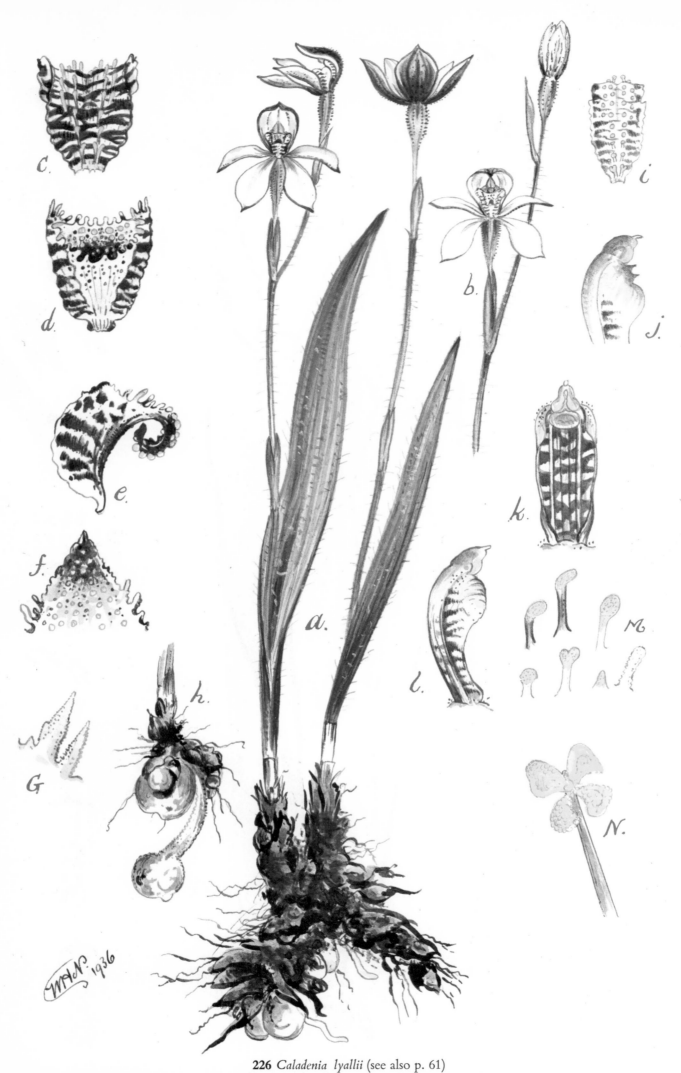

226 *Caladenia lyallii* (see also p. 61)

a b specimens collected at Middleton's Gap, Grampians, Vic. **c** labellum, from above **d** labellum, from front **e** labellum, from side **f** tip of labellum **g** character of labellum fringe **h** uncovered tubers **i** labellum, from above, specimen from Mt Erica, Vic. **j** abnormal wing to column **k** column, from front **l** column, from side **m** calli from labellum lamina **n** pollinia
Figs **a, b, h** natural size

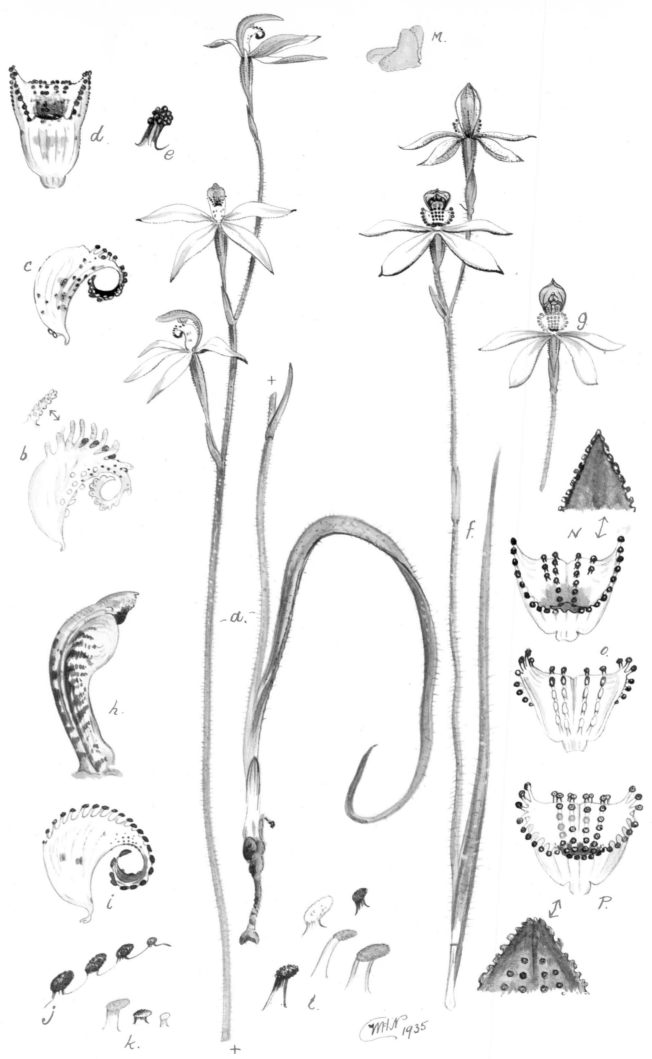

227 *Caladenia angustata*: Figs **a–e** (see also Plate 228 and p. 61)
C. dimorpha: Figs **f–p** (see also p. 61)

a specimen from Bell, NSW **b** labellum, from side **c** labellum, showing abnormal features **d** labellum, from front **e** calli from labellum fringe **f** typical specimen
g flower with pale tints **h** column, from side **i** labellum, from side **j k l** calli of labellum fringe and lamina **m** pollinia **n** labellum, from front, also extreme apex
o labellum, from rear **p** labellum, from front, also extreme apex
Figs **a, f, g** natural size

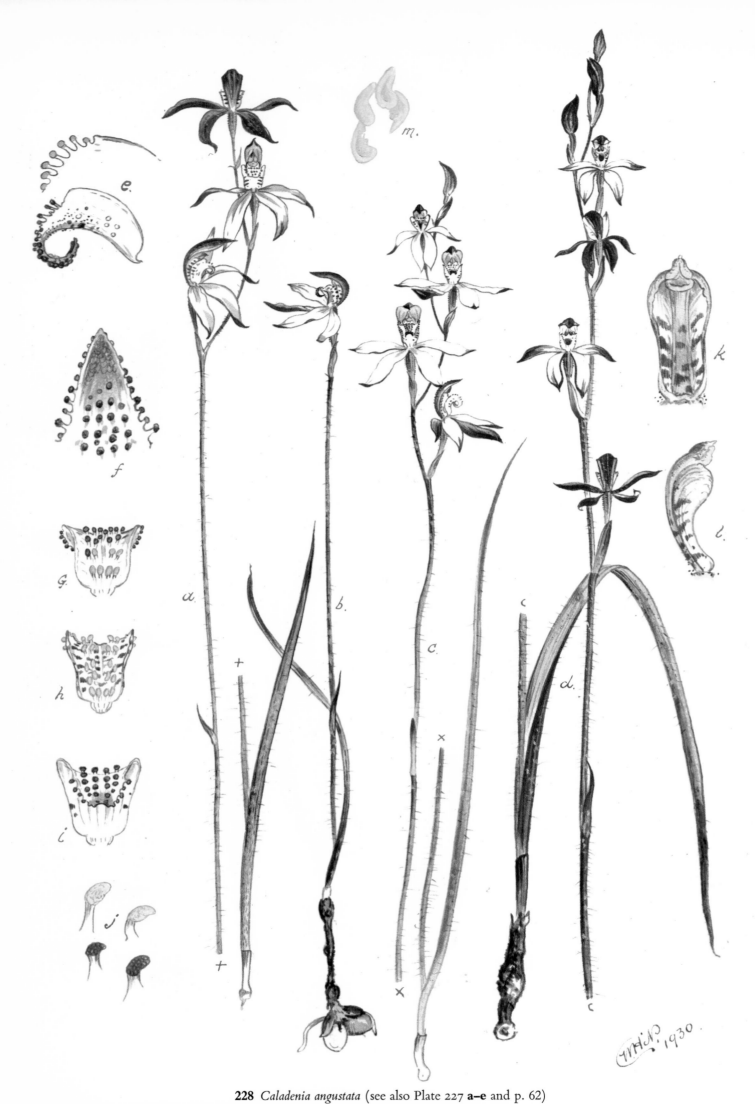

228 *Caladenia angustata* (see also Plate 227 **a–e** and p. 62)

a b c d specimens from Hurstbridge and Staughton Vale, Vic.   **e** labellum, from side (note some variation above)   **f** labellum tip   **g h** labella, from above—two types
i labellum, from front   **j** calli from the labellum lamina   **k** column, from front   **l** column, from side   **m** pollinia
Figs **a–d** natural size

229 *Caladenia praecox* (see also p. 62)

a b c d specimens from Bayswater and Beaconsfield, Vic. (Fig. **a** being an uncommon form)   **e f g** labella   **h** calli from the labellum lamina   **i** pollinia   **j** calli from the labellum fringe   **k l** columns, from side and front
Figs **a–d** natural size

230 *Caladenia testacea*: Figs **a–c, e–k, m–o** (see also p. 62)
C. testacea var. *hildae*: Figs **d, l** (see also p. 63)

a b c typical specimens from NSW habitats **d** a luxuriant form from Cobungra, Vic. **e** a rare colour-form from Cann River, Vic. **f** labellum, from above **g** labellum, from front **h i** calli from marginal fringe of labellum **j** calli from labellum lamina **k** pollinia **l** dorsal sepal **m** column, from side **n** labellum, from side **o** head of column
Figs **a–e** natural size

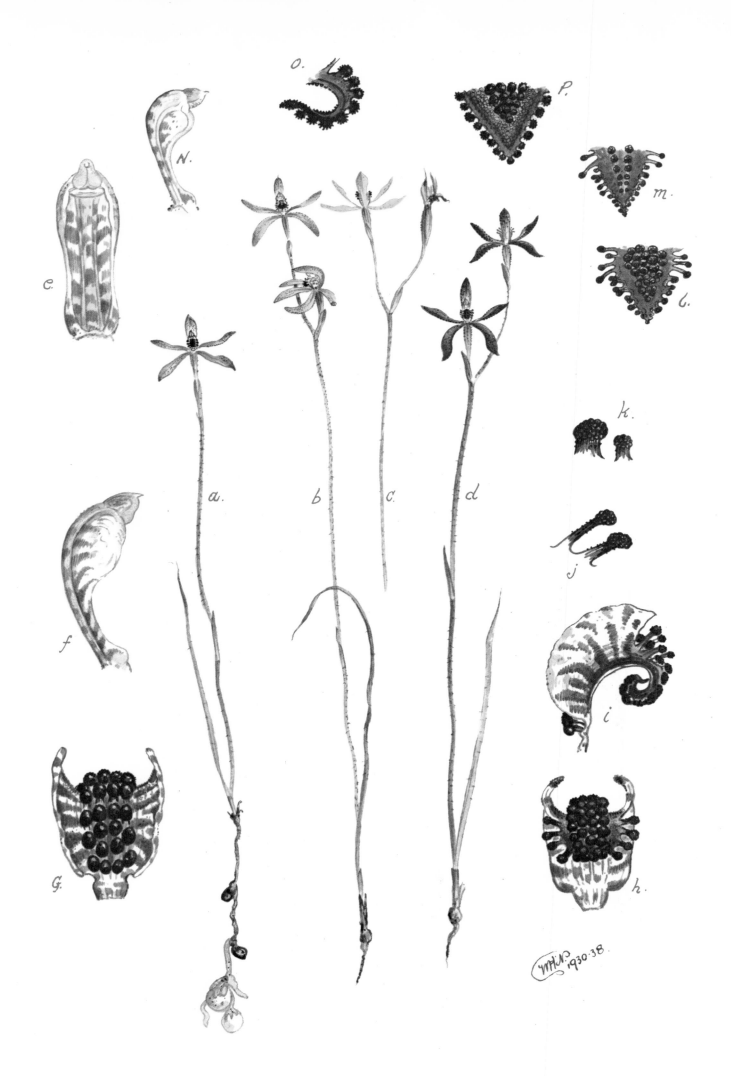

231 *Caladenia iridescens* (see also p. 63)

a b c d typical specimens from Grampians, Vic. **e** column, from front **f** column, from side **g** labellum, from above **h** labellum, from front **i** labellum, from side **j** calli from the labellum margin **k** calli from the labellum lamina **l m** variations in the labellum tip **n** column, from side **o** labellum tip, from side **p** labellum tip
Figs **a–d** natural size

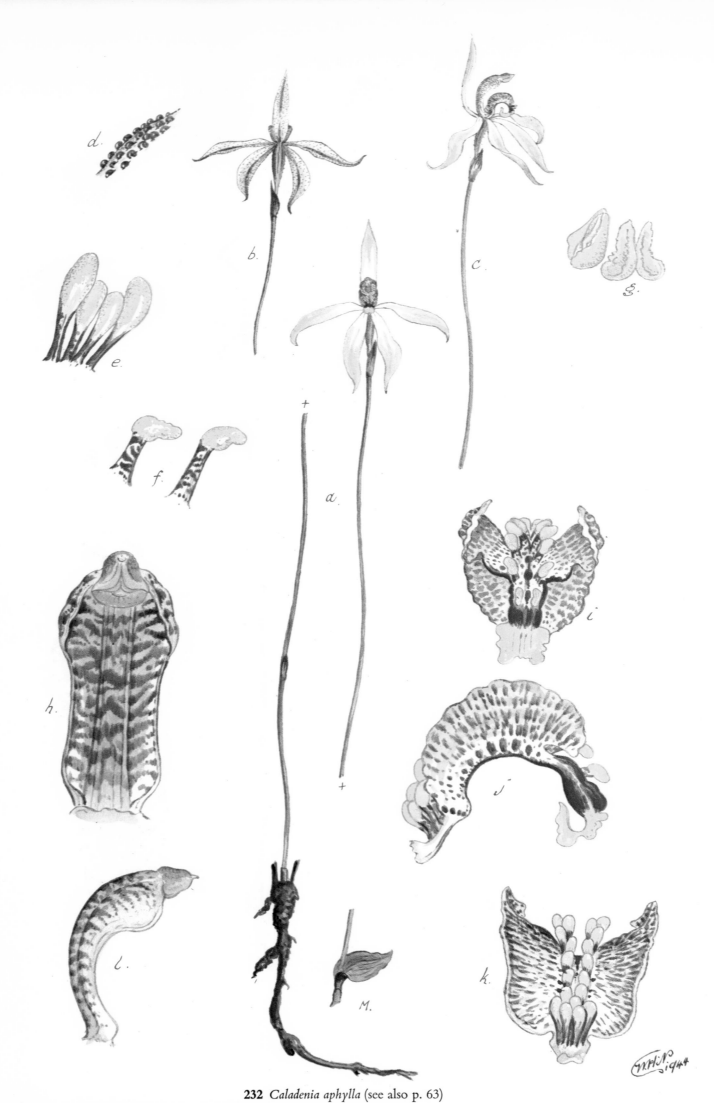

232 *Caladenia aphylla* (see also p. 63)

a typical specimen **b c** flowers, from rear and side **d** glands from the under-surface of perianth segments **e** calli from base of labellum lamina **f** calli from labellum lamina **g** pollinia **h** column, from front **i** labellum, from front **j** labellum, from side **k** labellum, from above **l** column, from side **m** dry leaf found at base of flowering stem

Figs **a–c, m** natural size

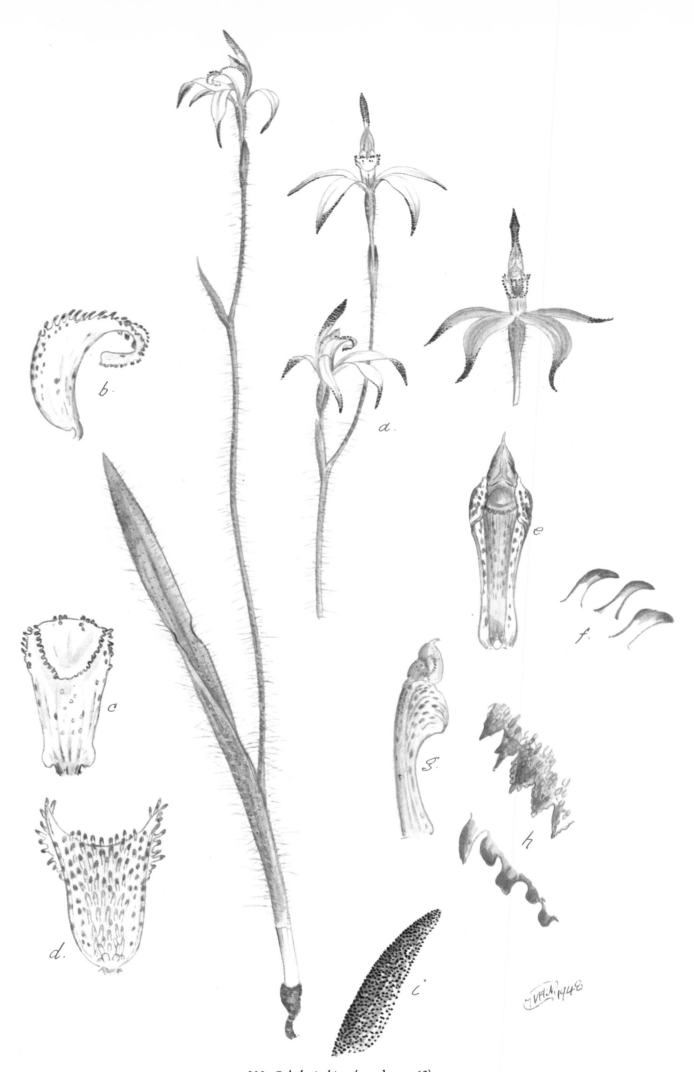

233 *Caladenia hirta* (see also p. 63)

a flowering specimen and flowers **b** labellum, from side **c** labellum, from front **d** labellum, from above **e** column, from front **f** calli from the labellum lamina
g column, from side **h** variation in the labellum margin (tip) **i** apex of sepal, showing minute glands
Fig. **a** natural size

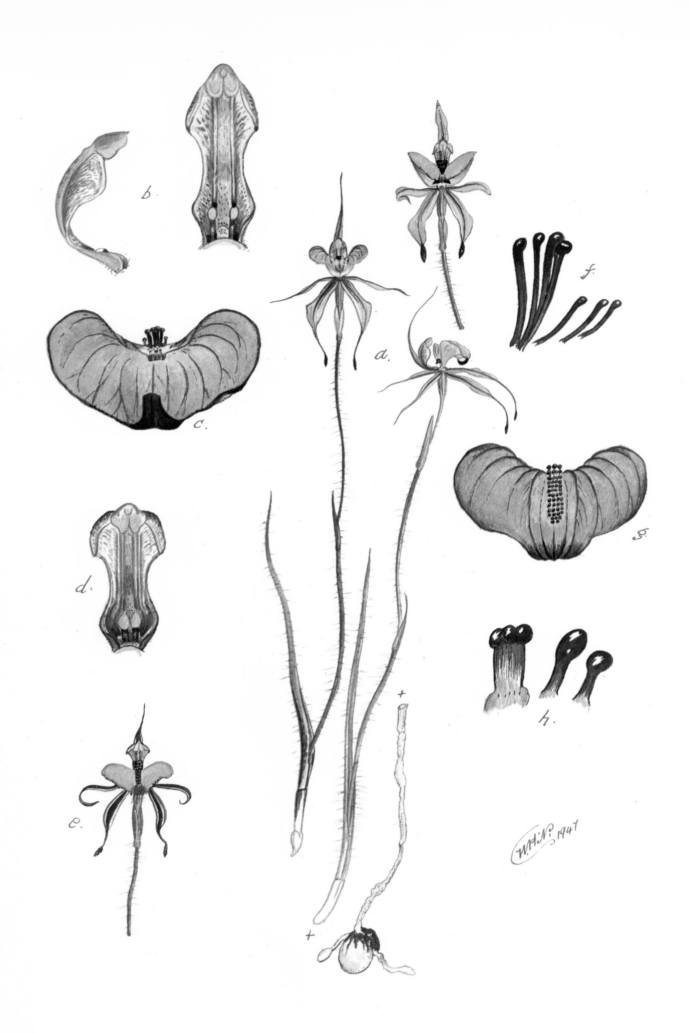

234 *Caladenia roei* (see also p. 63)

a two specimens, also a flower, collected in granite country around Arrowsmith, WA **b** column, from side and front **c** labellum, from below **d** another column, from front **e** flower from Wannon Hills district, WA **f** calli from the labellum lamina **g** labellum, from front **h** calli types from the base of labellum

Figs **a, e** natural size

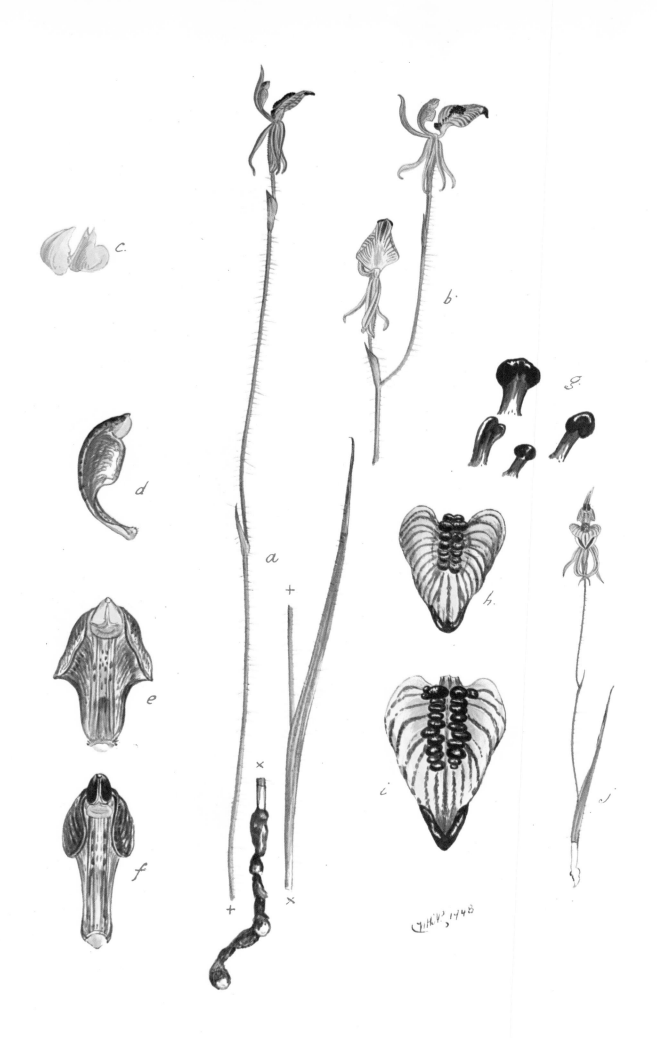

235 *Caladenia cairnsiana* (see also p. 63)

a specimen from Upper King River district, WA **b** flowers **c** pollinia **d** column, from side **e** column, from front **f** column, from front, Bolgart, WA, specimen
g calli **h** labellum, from front **i** labellum, from front **j** a Bolgart specimen
Figs **a, b, j** natural size

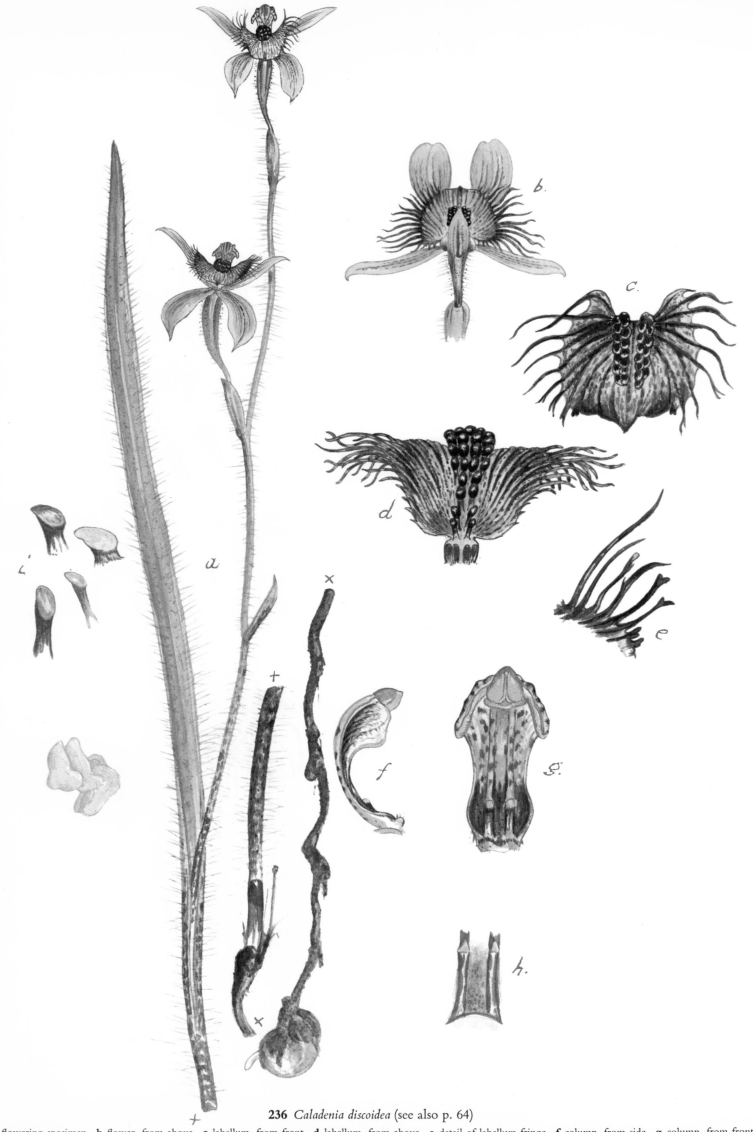

236 *Caladenia discoidea* (see also p. 64)

a flowering specimen **b** flower, from above **c** labellum, from front **d** labellum, from above **e** detail of labellum fringe **f** column, from side **g** column, from front
h glands at base of column **i** calli from labellum lamina **j** pollinia
Fig. **a** natural size

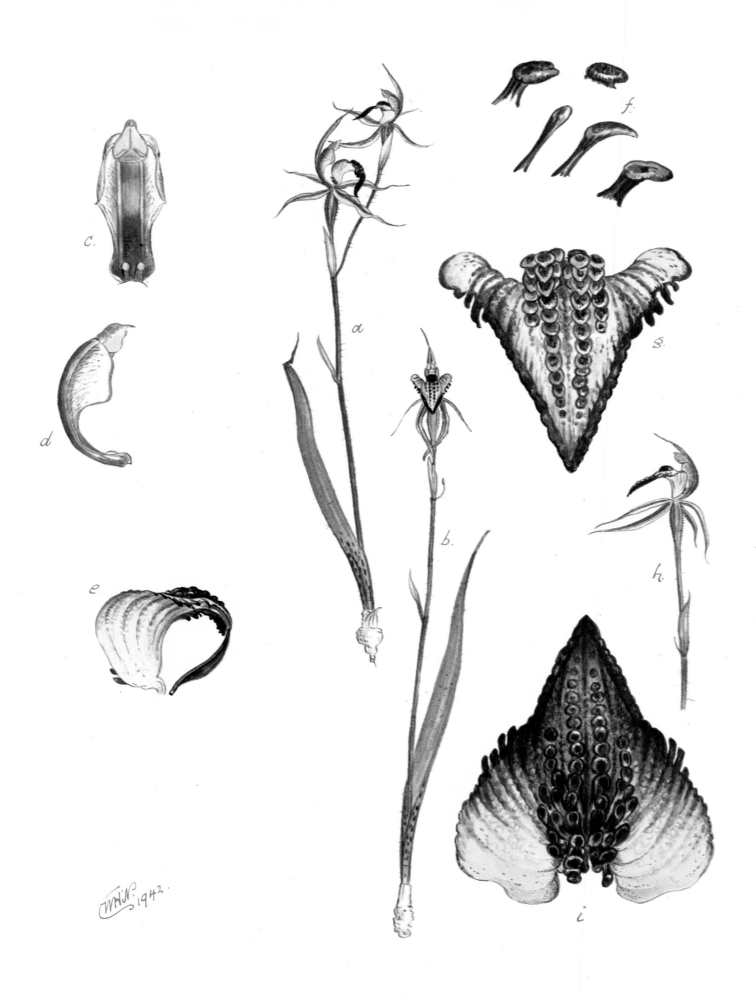

237 *Caladenia tessellata* (see also p. 64)

a b typical specimens **c** column, from front **d** column, from side **e** labellum, from side **f** calli from the labellum lamina **g** labellum, from front **h** flower, from side **i** labellum, from above

Figs **a, b, h** natural size

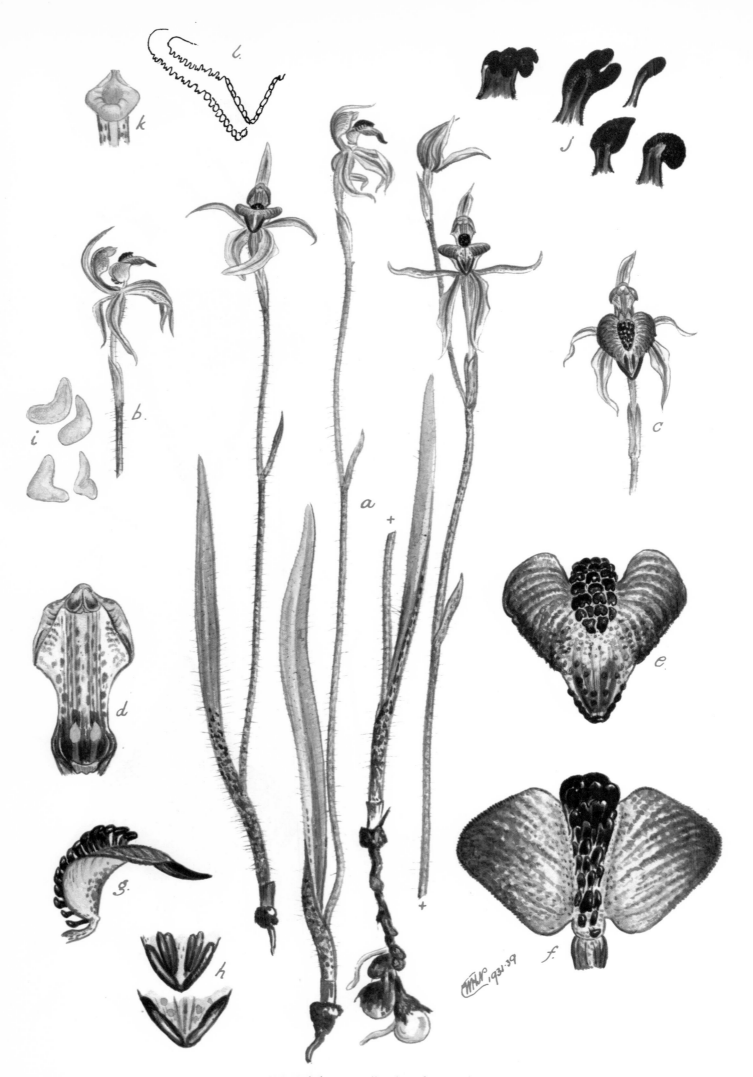

238 *Caladenia tessellata* (see also p. 64)

a typical specimens **b** flower, from side **c** flower from the Mallee scrubs, Vic. **d** column, from front **e** labellum, from front **f** labellum, and claw, from rear **g** labellum, from side **h** apices of two labella **i** pollinia **j** calli from labellum lamina **k** stigma **l** figures showing the variable nature of the labellum margin
Figs **a–c** natural size

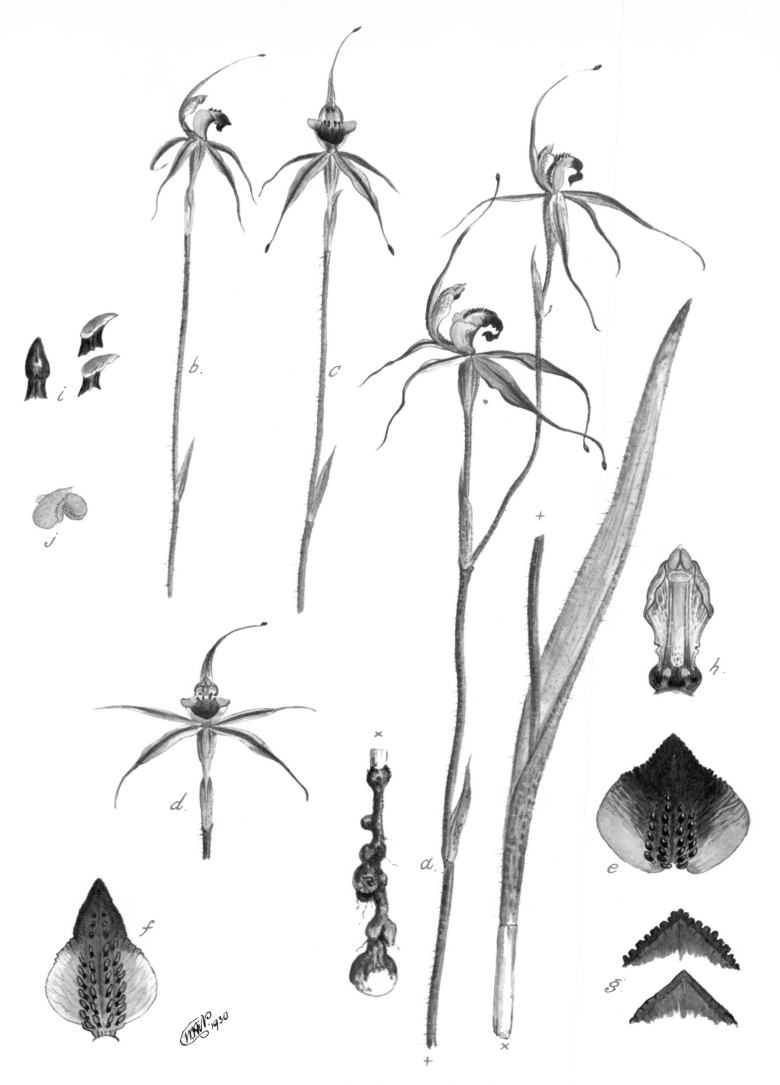

239 *Caladenia clavigera* (see also p. 64)

a a robust specimen **b c d** typical flowers **e f** labella spread out **g** marginal variation at tip of labellum **h** column, from front **i** calli from labellum lamina
j pollinia
Figs **a–d** natural size

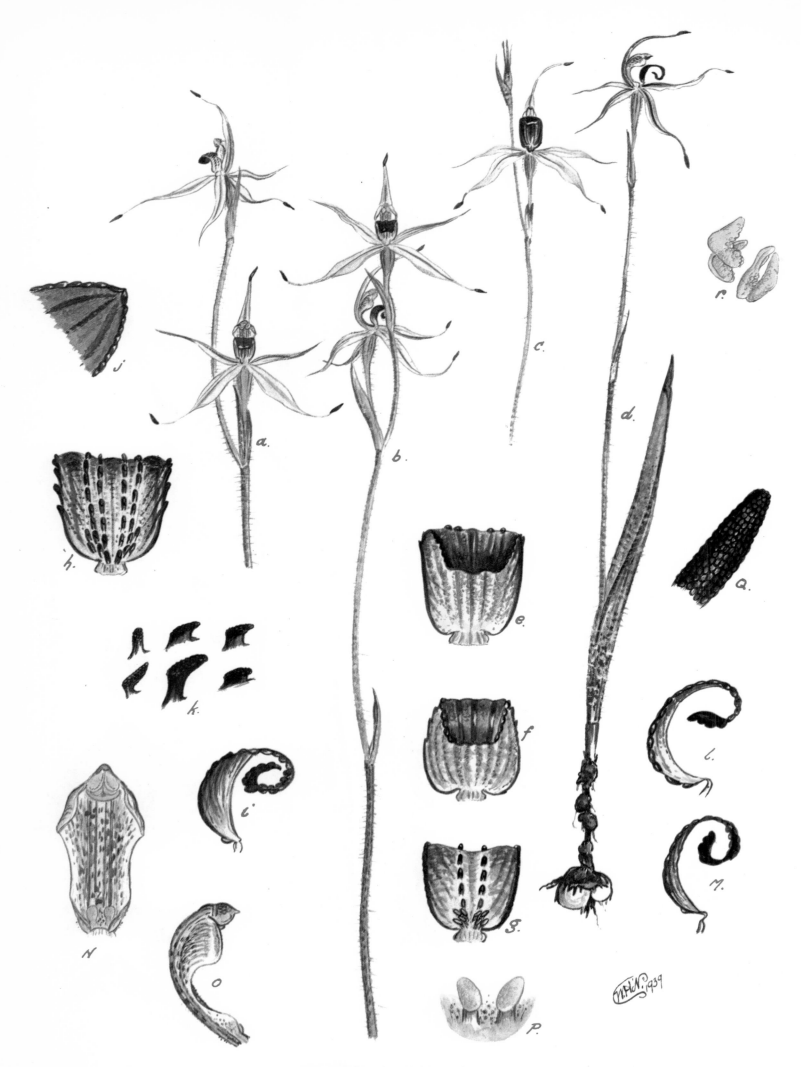

240 *Caladenia leptochila* (see also p. 65)

a b c d typical specimens from National Park, SA **e f** labella, from below **g h** labella, from above **i** labellum, from side **j** tip of labellum **k** calli from labellum lamina **l m** labella, from side **n** column, from front **o** column, from side **p** calli or glands from base of column **q** portion of clubbed sepal **r** pollinia
Figs **a–d** natural size

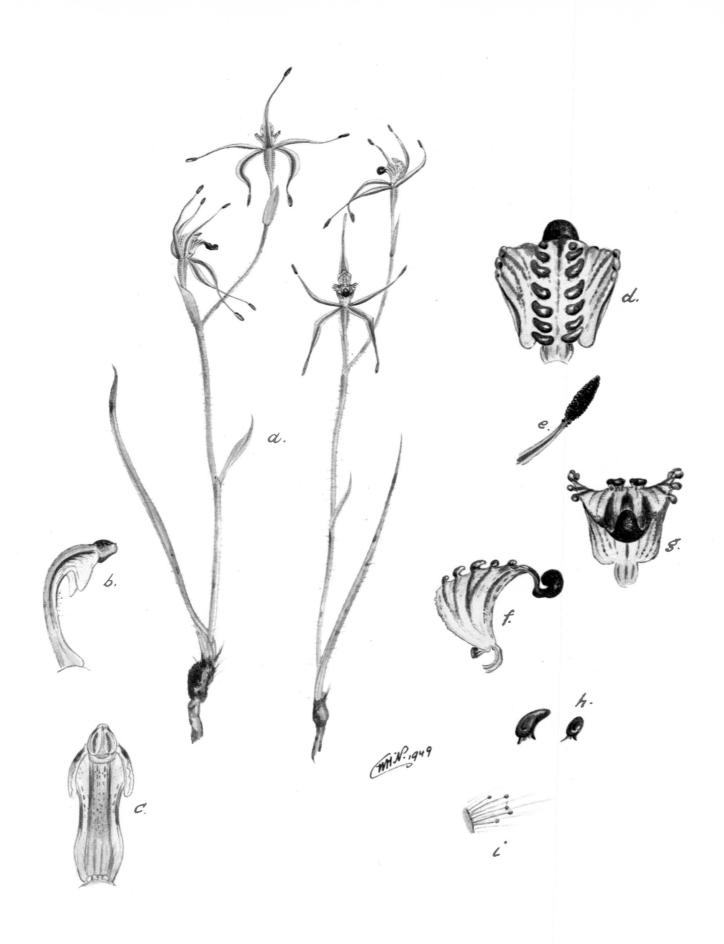

241 *Caladenia sigmoidea* (see also p. 65)

a two flowering specimens b column, from side c column, from front d labellum, from above e clavate tip of perianth segment f labellum, from side g labellum, from front h calli from labellum lamina i hairs from pedicel, peduncle and leaf
Fig. a natural size

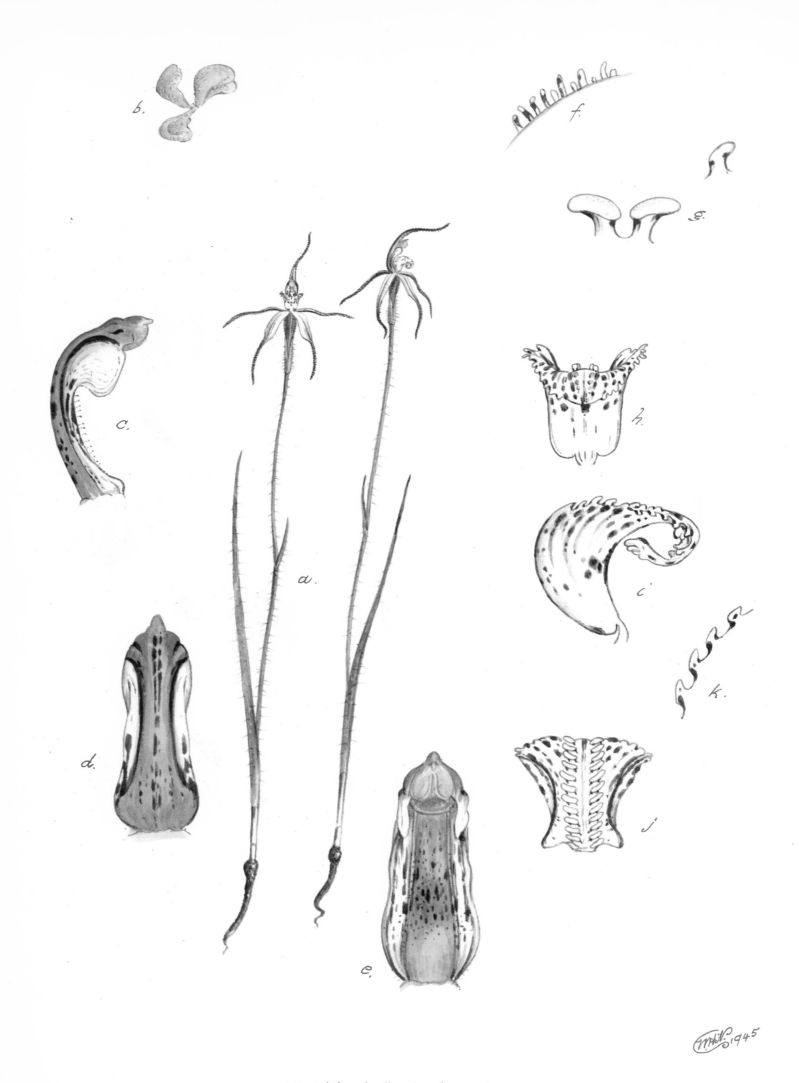

242 *Caladenia bicalliata* (see also p. 65)

a two typical specimens **b** pollinia **c** column, from side **d** column, from rear **e** column, from front **f** glands from the caudae of the sepals, etc. **g** calli from the labellum lamina **h** labellum, from front **i** labellum, from side **j** labellum, from above **k** calli from the labellum margin
Fig. **a** natural size

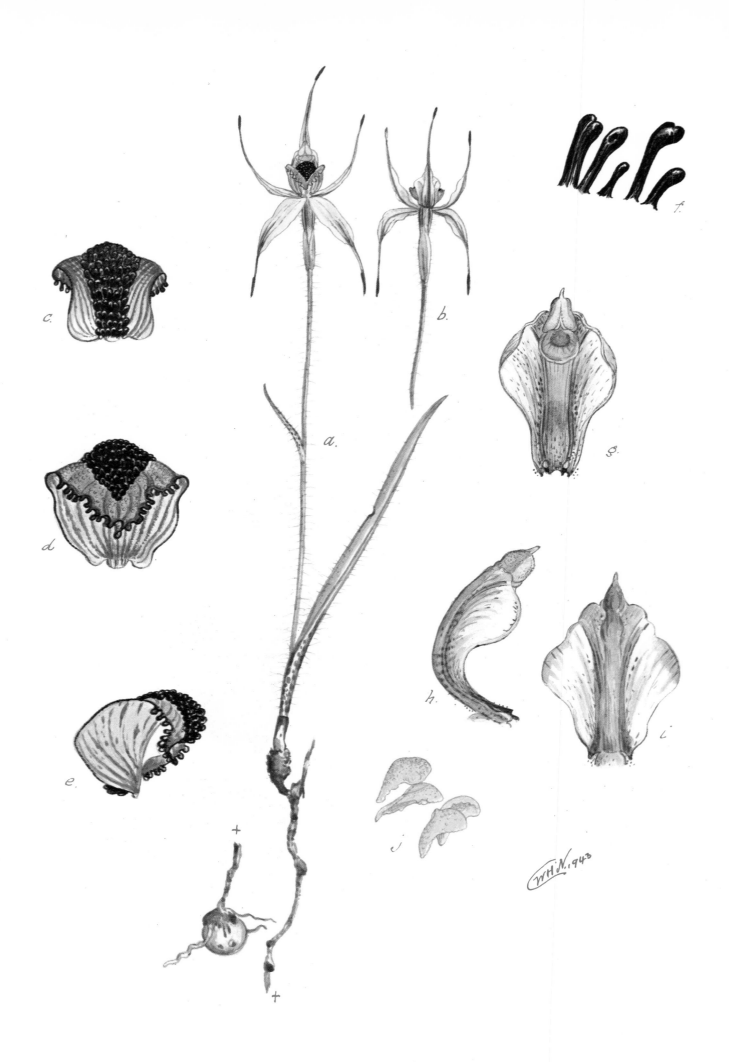

243 *Caladenia macrostylis* (see also p. 65)

a typical specimen from Yarloop, WA   b flower, from rear   c labellum, from above   d labellum, from front   e labellum, from side   f calli from the labellum lamina
g column, from front   h column, from side   i column, from rear   j pollinia
Figs **a, b** natural size

244 *Caladenia ericksonae* (see also p. 66)

a a blood-red form   **b** typical form   **c** flower of typical form, from side   **d** pollinia   **e** calli from labellum lamina   **f** column, from side, and front   **g** labellum, from front   **h** labellum, from side

Figs **a–c** natural size

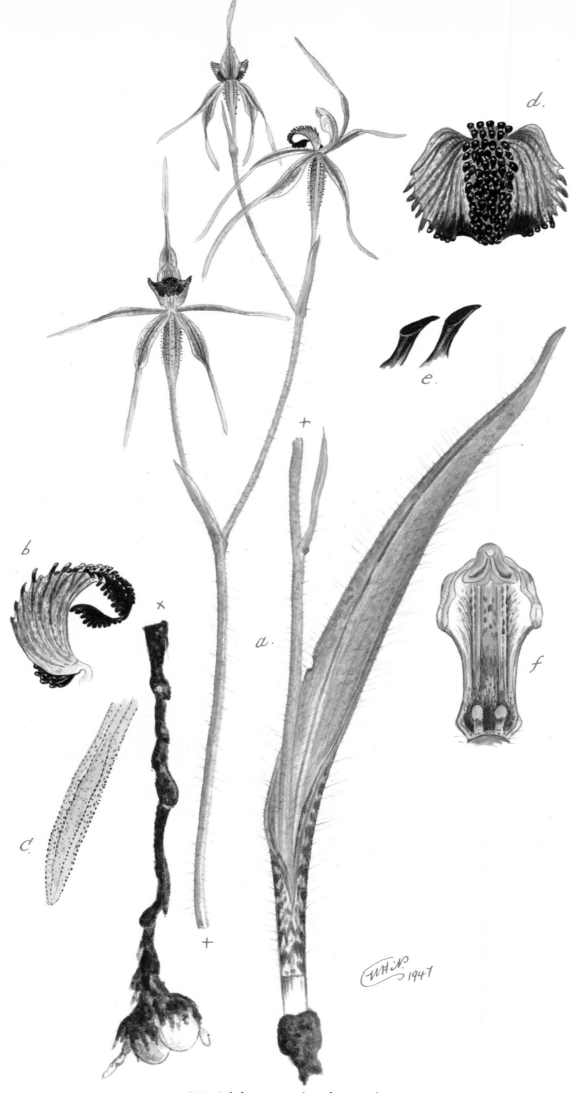

245 *Caladenia ensata* (see also p. 66)

a typical specimen **b** labellum, from side **c** apex of perianth segment **d** labellum, from above **e** calli from labellum lamina **f** column, from front
Fig. **a** natural size

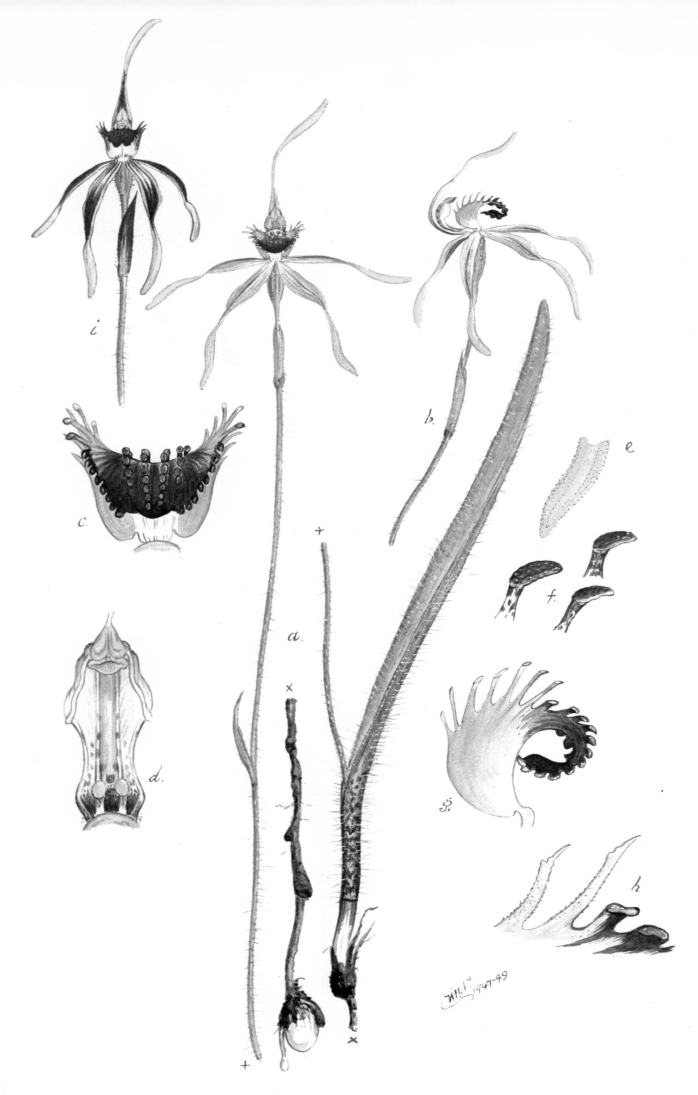

246 *Caladenia longiclavata* (see also p. 66)

a   b specimens from Karri country near Manjimup, WA   **c** labellum, from front   **d** column, from front   **e** section of perianth segment   **f** calli from the labellum lamina
g labellum, from side   **h** marginal fringe of labellum   **i** typical flower
Figs **a, b, i** natural size

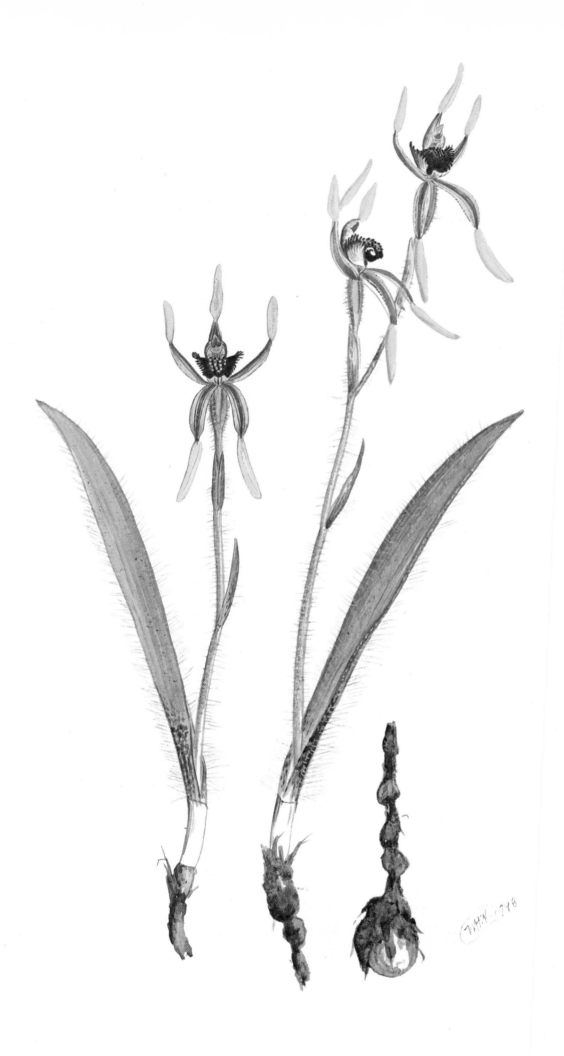

247 *Caladenia longiclavata* (see also p. 66)
A form from the deep shade of the Karri forest, WA
All Figs natural size

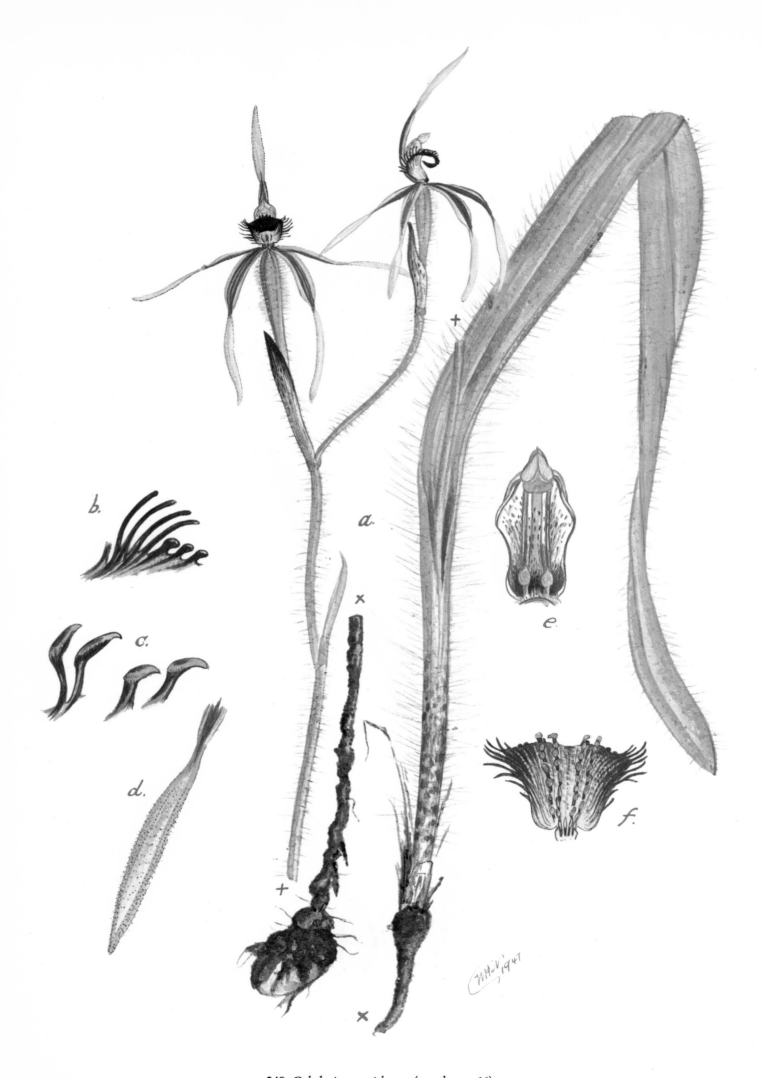

248 *Caladenia magniclavata* (see also p. 66)

a typical specimen **b** labellum fringe **c** calli from the labellum lamina **d** clubbed tip of perianth segment **e** column, from front **f** labellum, from rear
Fig. **a** natural size

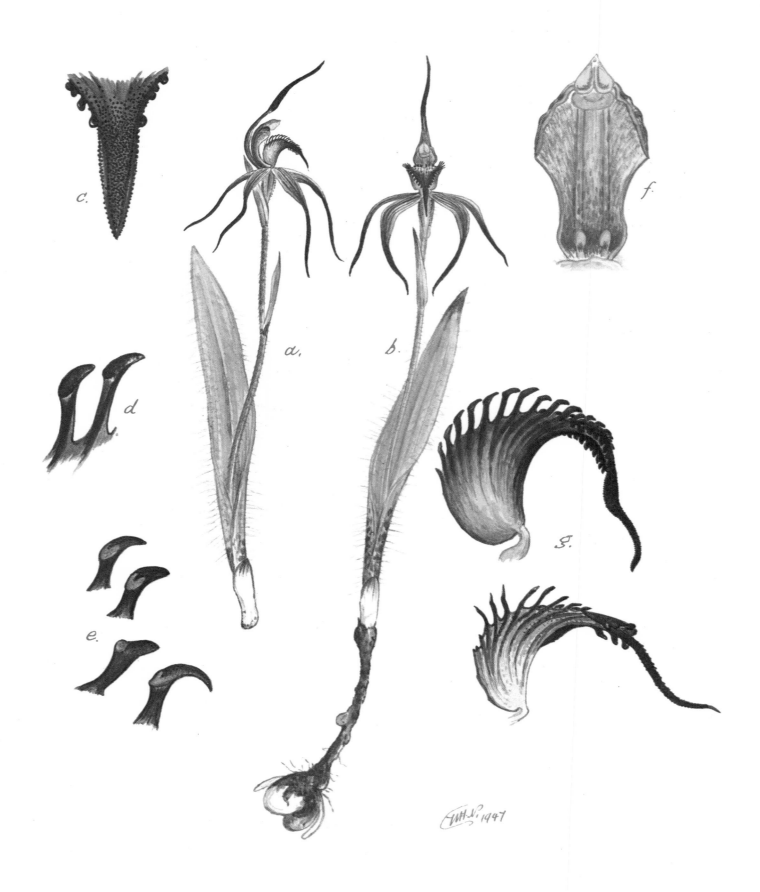

249 *Caladenia caudata* (see also p. 67)

a b typical specimens **c** apex of labellum **d** calli from the labellum fringe **e** calli from the labellum lamina **f** column, from front **g** two labella, from side
Figs **a, b** natural size

250 *Caladenia reticulata* (see also p. 67)

Specimens from Airey's Inlet, Vic.
All Figs natural size

251 *Caladenia reticulata* var. *valida* (see also p. 67)

a typical specimen **b** column, from front **c** tip of clavate point **d** calli from labellum lamina **e** calli from marginal fringe of labellum **f** pollinia
Fig. **a** natural size

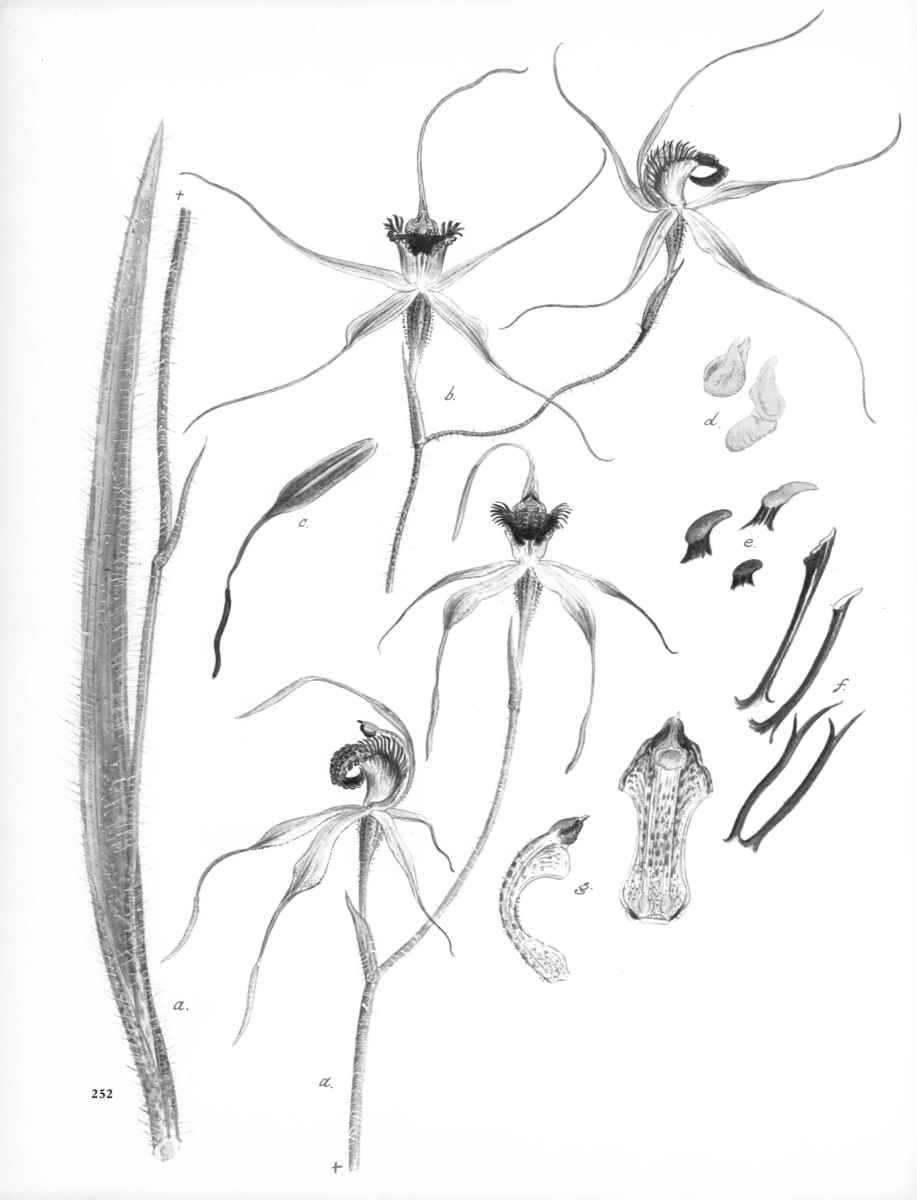

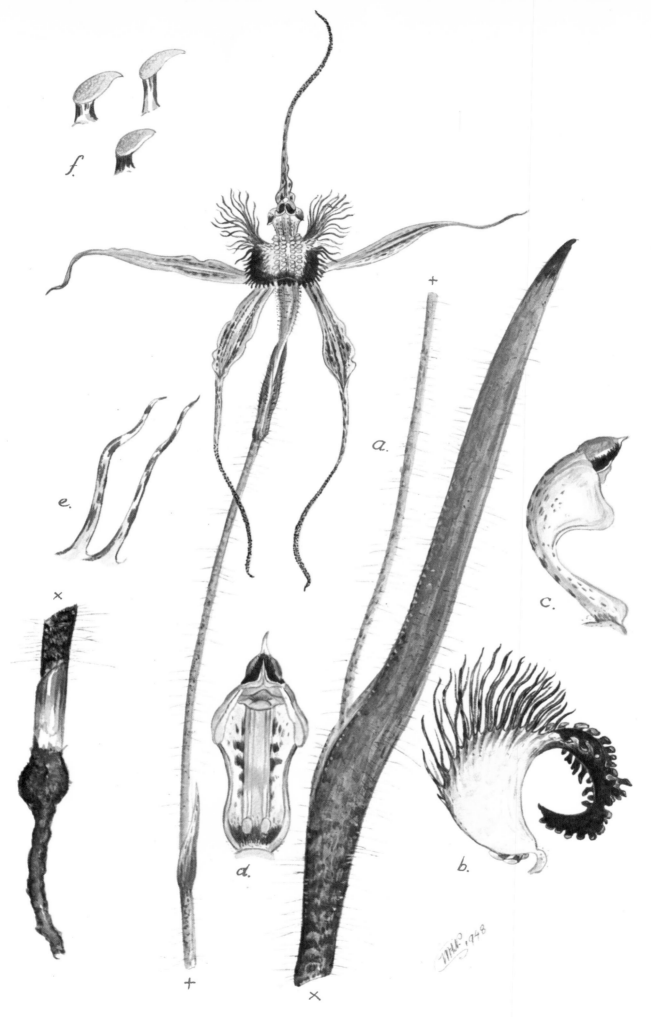

253 *Caladenia* species (see also p. 68)

a flowering plant   **b** labellum, from side   **c** column, from side   **d** column, from front   **e** teeth from labellum margin   **f** calli from labellum lamina
Fig. **a** natural size

252 *Caladenia pectinata* (see also p. 67)

a typical specimen   **b** hybrid form   **c** highly coloured lateral sepal   **d** pollinia   **e** calli from labellum lamina   **f** teeth from labellum margin   **g** column, from front and side
Figs **a–c** natural size

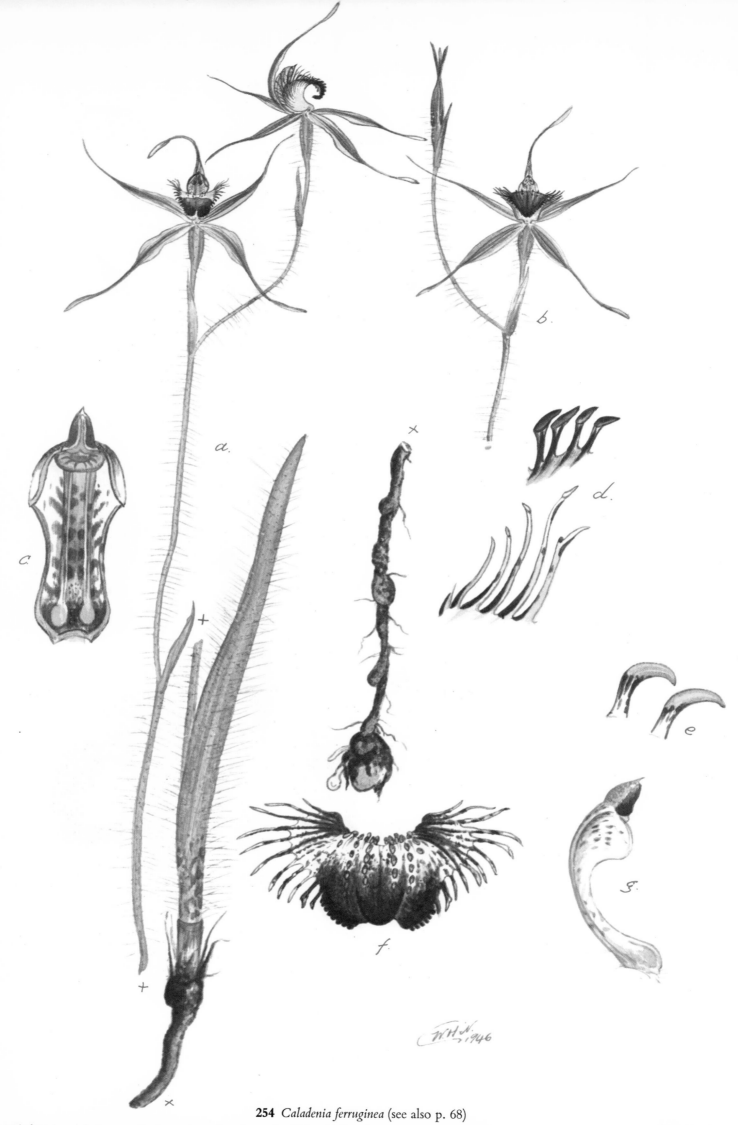

254 *Caladenia ferruginea* (see also p. 68)

a typical specimen **b** flower and bud **c** column, from front **d** calli from labellum fringe **e** calli from labellum lamina **f** labellum, from front **g** column, from side
Figs **a**, **b** natural size

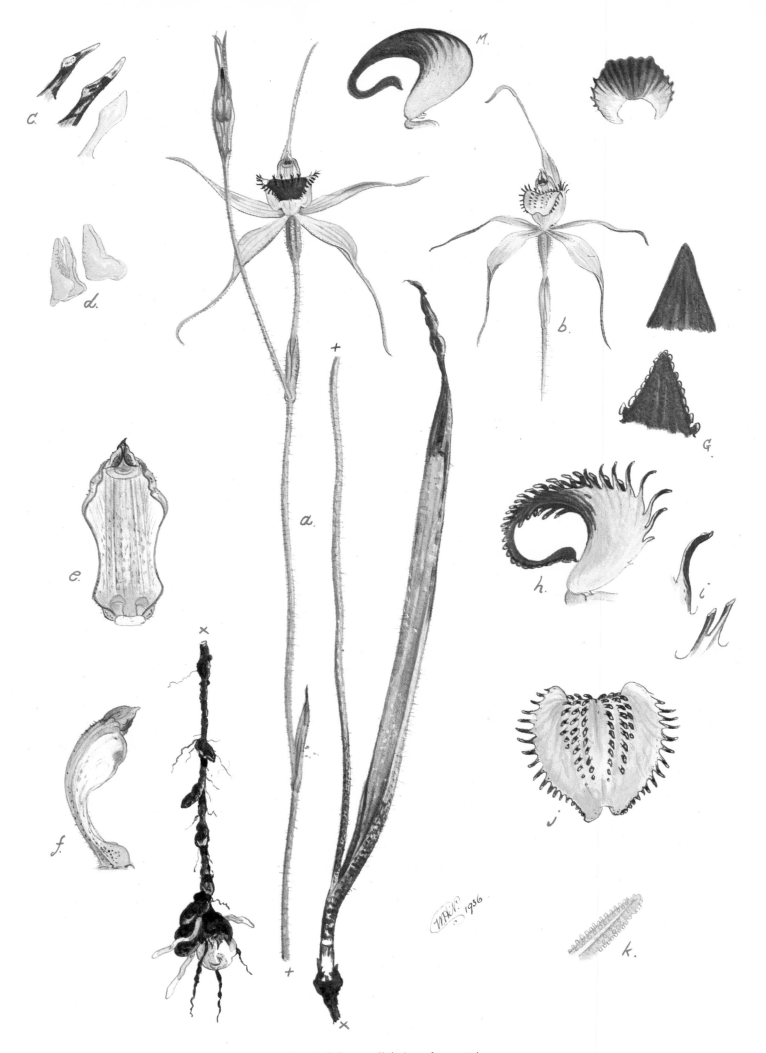

255 *Caladenia pallida* (see also p. 68)

a specimen from Portland, Vic. **b** flower from Ringwood, Vic. **c** calli from the labellum lamina **d** pollinia **e** column, from front **f** column, from side **g** variation in labellum apex **h** labellum, from side **i** marginal calli of labellum **j** labellum, from front **k** glands from the segment tips **l** labellum of a teratological form, showing a total absence of calli, from Gorae West, Vic. **m** labellum with entire margins, from Portland, Vic.

Figs **a, b** natural size

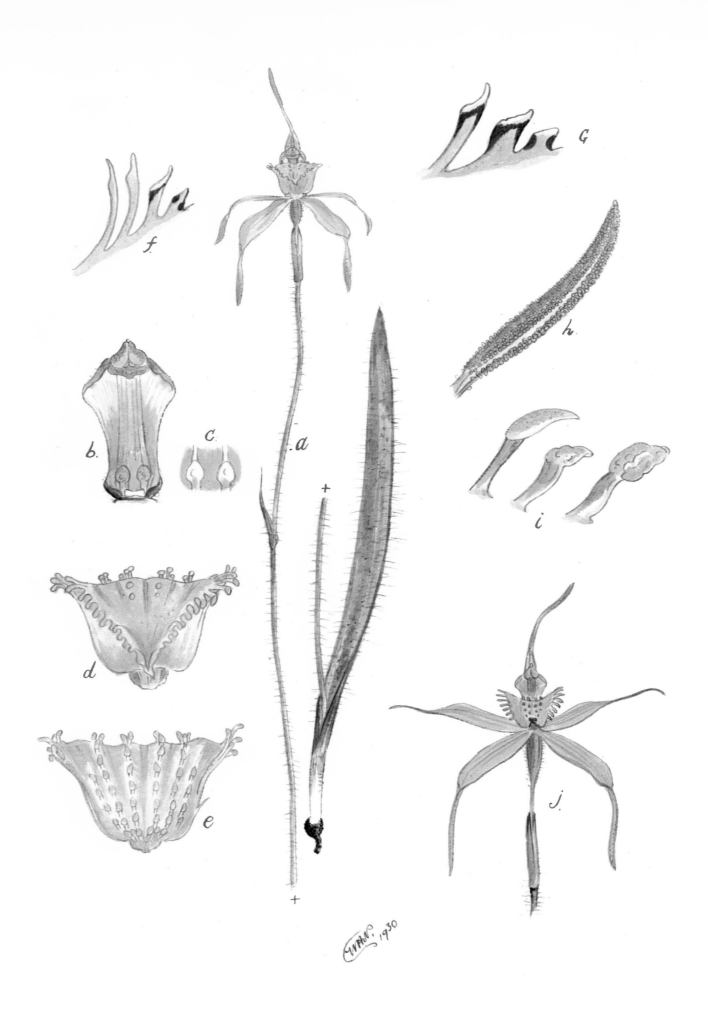

256 *Caladenia pallida* (see also p. 68)

a a very rare clubbed form, from Boronia, Vic.   **b** column, from front   **c** glands, from base of column   **d** labellum, from front   **e** labellum, from above   **f** marginal fringe of labellum   **g** marginal fringe of labellum   **h** clavate tip of perianth segment   **i** calli from the labellum lamina   **j** flower, from Healesville, Vic.
Figs **a, j** natural size

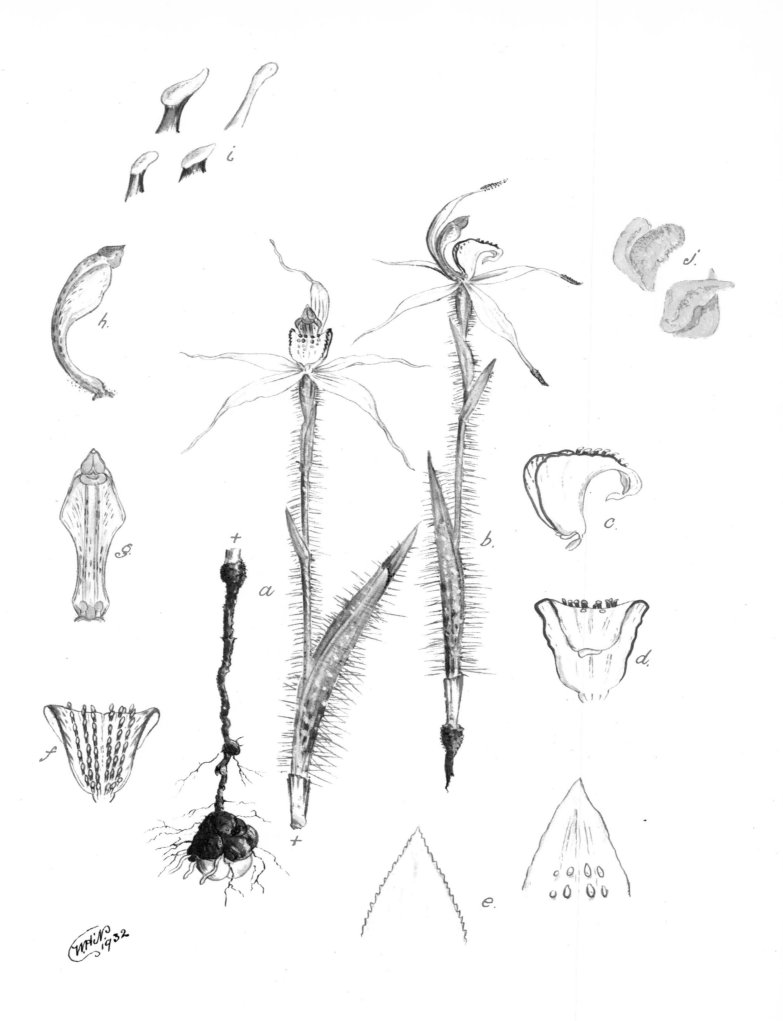

257 *Caladenia pumila* (see also p. 68)

a typical specimen **b** specimen, showing clubbed sepals **c** labellum, from side **d** labellum, from front **e** apices of labella **f** labellum, from above **g** column, from front
h column, from side **i** calli from labellum lamina **j** pollinia
Figs **a, b** natural size

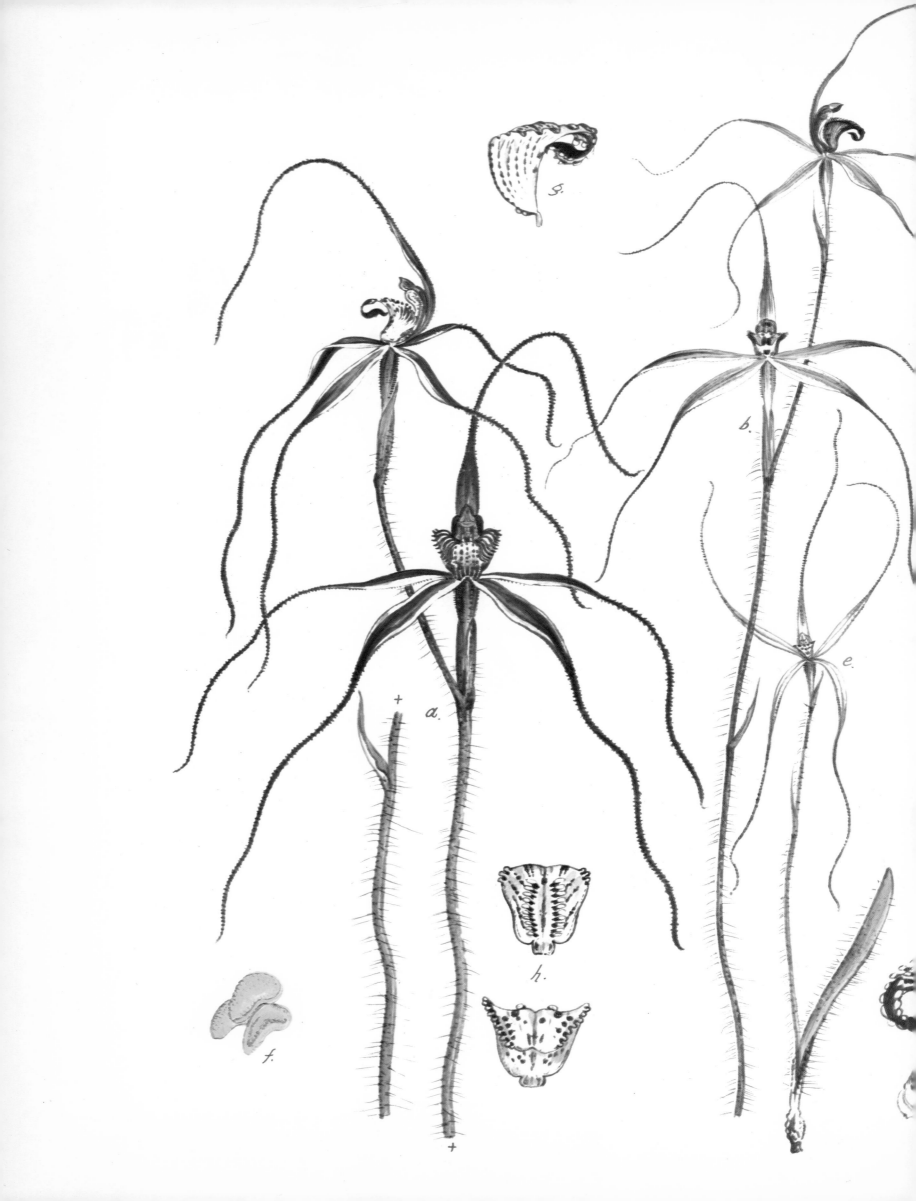

258 *Caladenia filamentosa*: Figs **a–d, f–r** (see also p. 69)
C. filamentosa var. *tentaculata*: Fig. **e** (see also p. 69)

a large-flowered specimen from WA **b** excellent form from Maldon, Vic. (note linear calli on labellum margin) **c** typical specimen from Grampians, Vic. **d** brightly-hued form from Anglesea, Vic. **e** specimen from Coimadai East, Vic. **f** pollinia **g** labellum, from side **h** labellum, from above, and from front **i** column, from front **j** stigma **k** column, from side **l** calli from base of labellum **m** glands from the filaments **n** some calli forms **o** labellum tip **p** **q** labellum, from above, and from front **r** labellum, from side
Figs **a–e** natural size

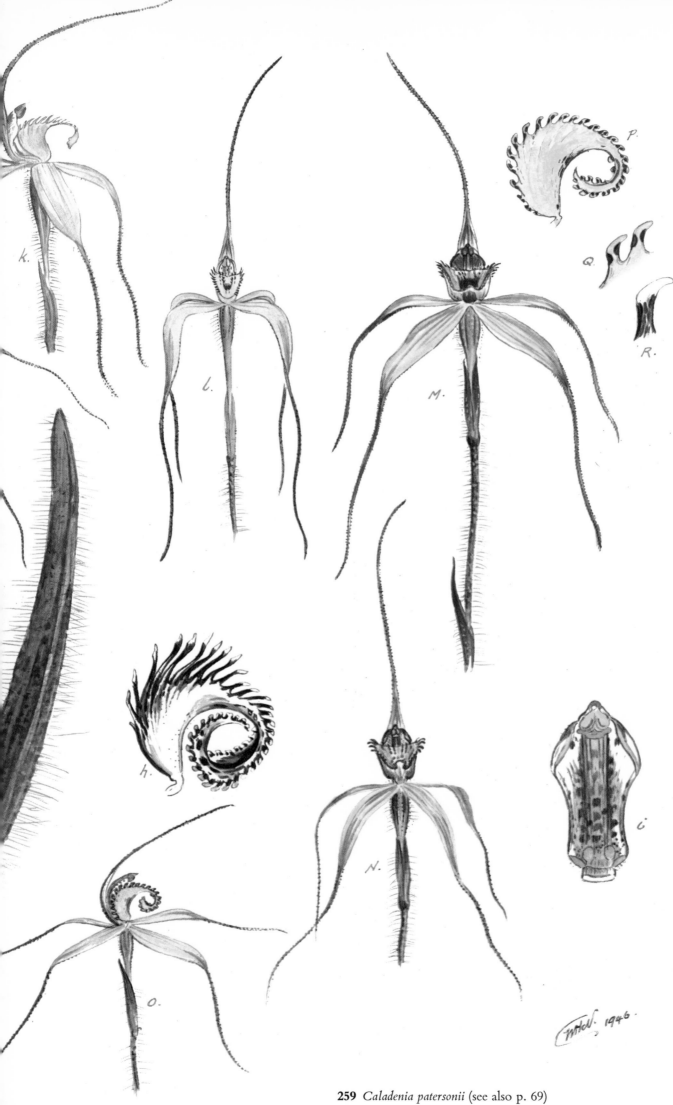

259 *Caladenia patersonii* (see also p. 69)

a large form from Portland, Vic. **b** section of a perianth segment, showing glands **c** calli from labellum fringe **d** calli from labellum lamina **e** labellum, from front
f labellum fringe **g** leaf and portion of stem (from Fig. **a**) **h** labellum, from side **i** column, from front **j** specimen from Eltham, Vic. **k l** two flowers from Yarram, Vic.
m flower from Wonthaggi, Vic. **n** an uncommon form from Wonthaggi, Vic. **o** flower from Portland, Vic. **p** labellum, from side **q** calli from labellum margin **r** single
callus from labellum lamina
Figs **a, j–o** natural size

260 *Caladenia patersonii* var. *arenaria* (see also p. 69)

a specimen from Hedley, Vic. **b** labellum, from side **c** calli from labellum margins, flowers from Hedley and Portland, Vic. **d** column, from front **e** calli from labellum laminas **f** labellum, from front, from Portland, Vic.

Fig. **a** natural size

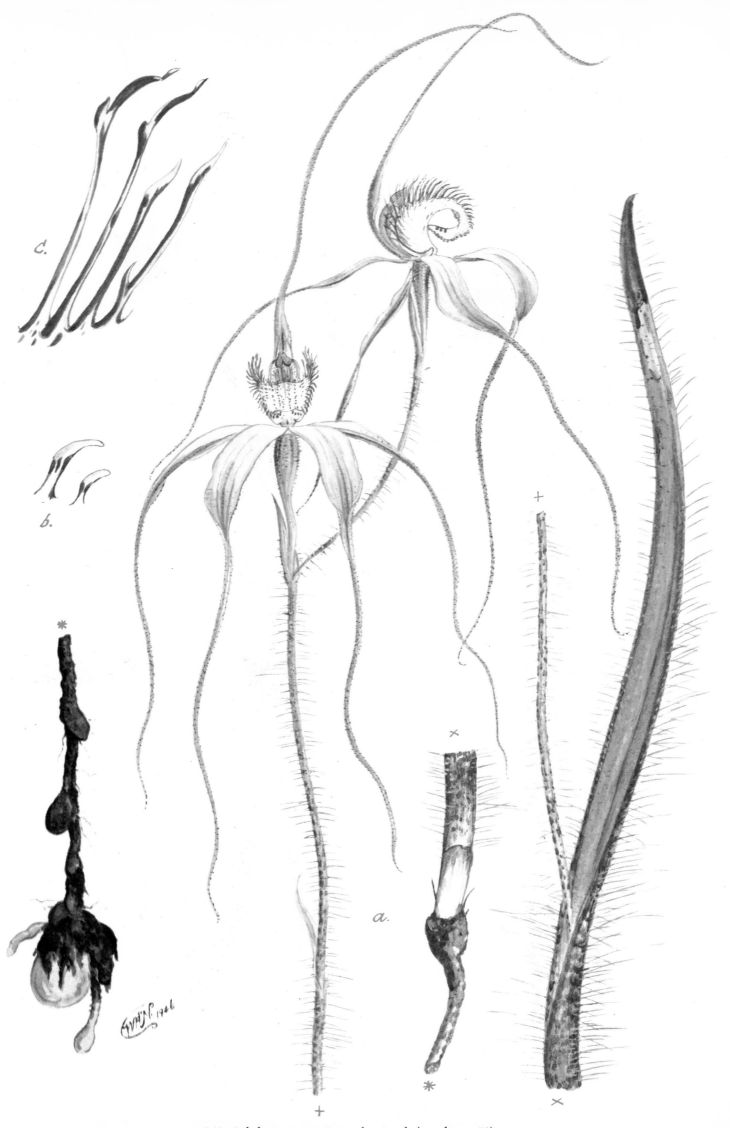

261 *Caladenia patersonii* var. *longicauda* (see also p. 70)

a very fine example from the Upper Kalgan River, WA   **b** calli from labellum lamina   **c** detail of labellum fringe
Fig. **a** natural size

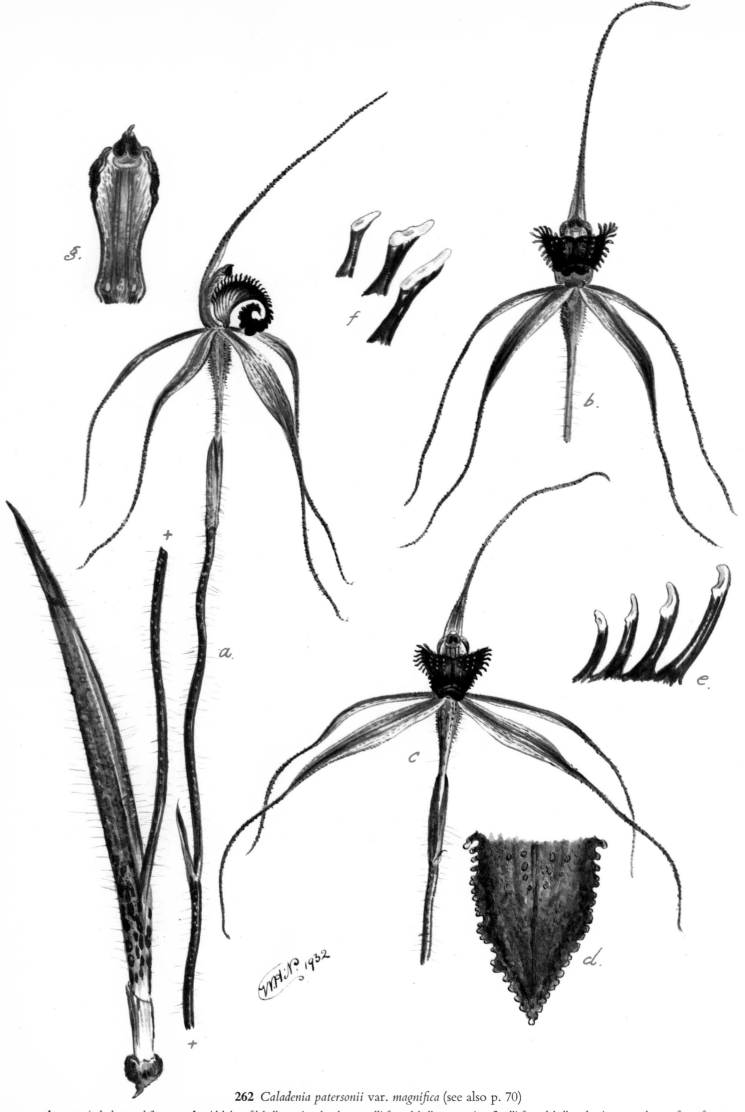

262 *Caladenia patersonii* var. *magnifica* (see also p. 70)

a b c typical plant and flowers **d** mid-lobe of labellum, tinted only **e** calli from labellum margin **f** calli from labellum lamina **g** column, from front
Figs **a–c** natural size

263 *Caladenia patersonii* var. *suaveolens* (see also p. 70)

a   b typical Portland, Vic., specimens   **c** glands from the perianth segments   **d** calli from labellum lamina   **e** calli from labellum margin
Figs **a, b** natural size

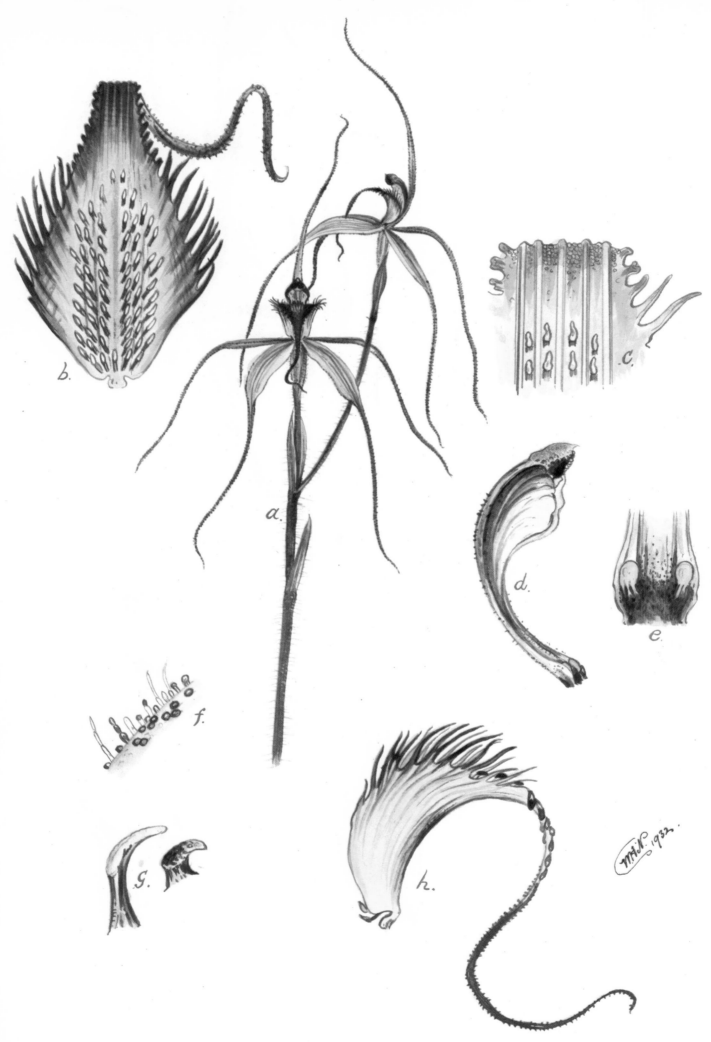

264 *Caladenia echidnachila* (see also p. 70)

a the type specimen b labellum, from above, spread out c ridges, etc. towards tip of labellum d column, from side e glands from base of column f glands from labellum
tip g calli from labellum lamina h labellum, from side
Fig. a natural size

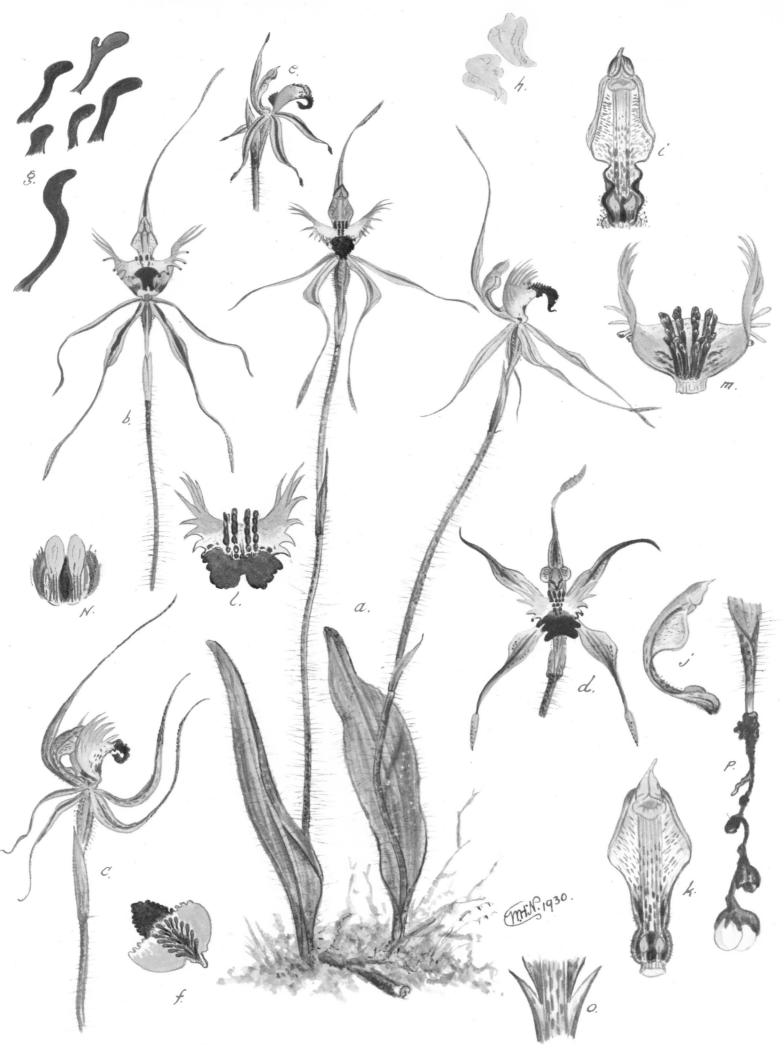

265 *Caladenia dilatata*: Figs **a–d, g–p** (see also p. 70)
C. dilatata var.? *concinna*: Figs **e, f** (see also p. 70)

a typical specimens **b c d** three flower types **e** another flower **f** labellum, spread out, flower from Greensborough, Vic. **g** calli from labellum lamina **h** pollinia
i column, from front **j** column, from side **k** column, from front **l** labellum, from front **m** labellum, from rear **n** glands from base of column **o** base of column wings, showing vestiges of the inner whorl **p** root system
Figs **a–e, p** natural size

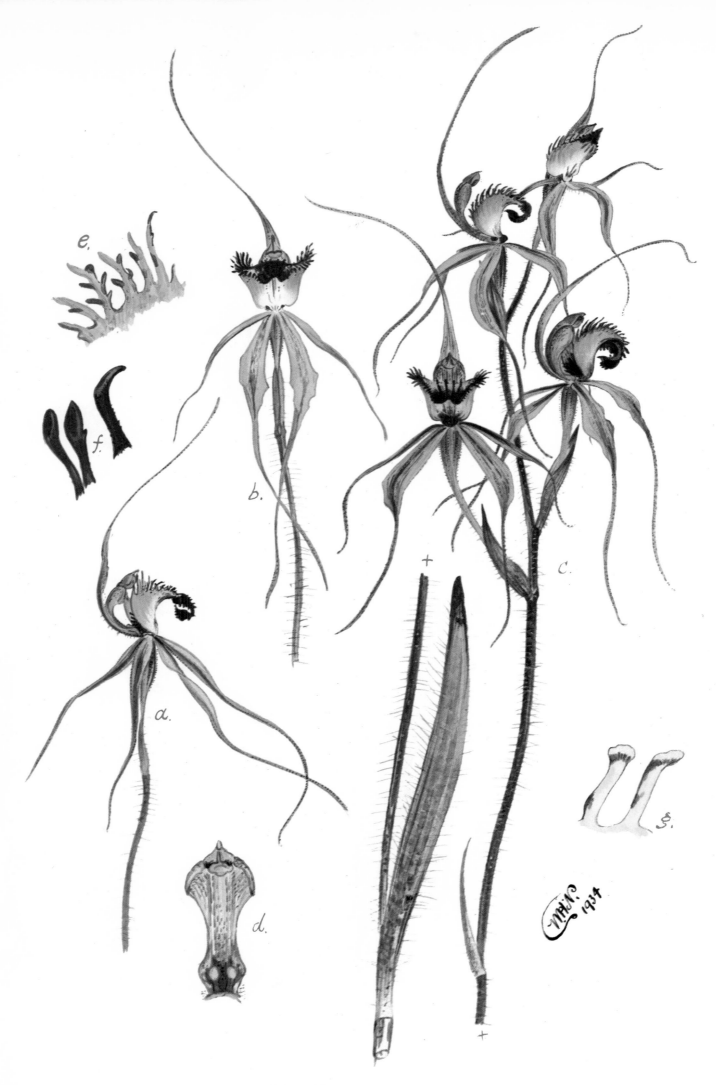

266 *Caladenia dilatata ×patersonii* (see also p. 71)

a b typical flowers **c** very fine specimen **d** column, from front **e** character of the labellum fringe **f** calli from the labellum lamina **g** another form of labellum fringe
Figs **a–c** natural size

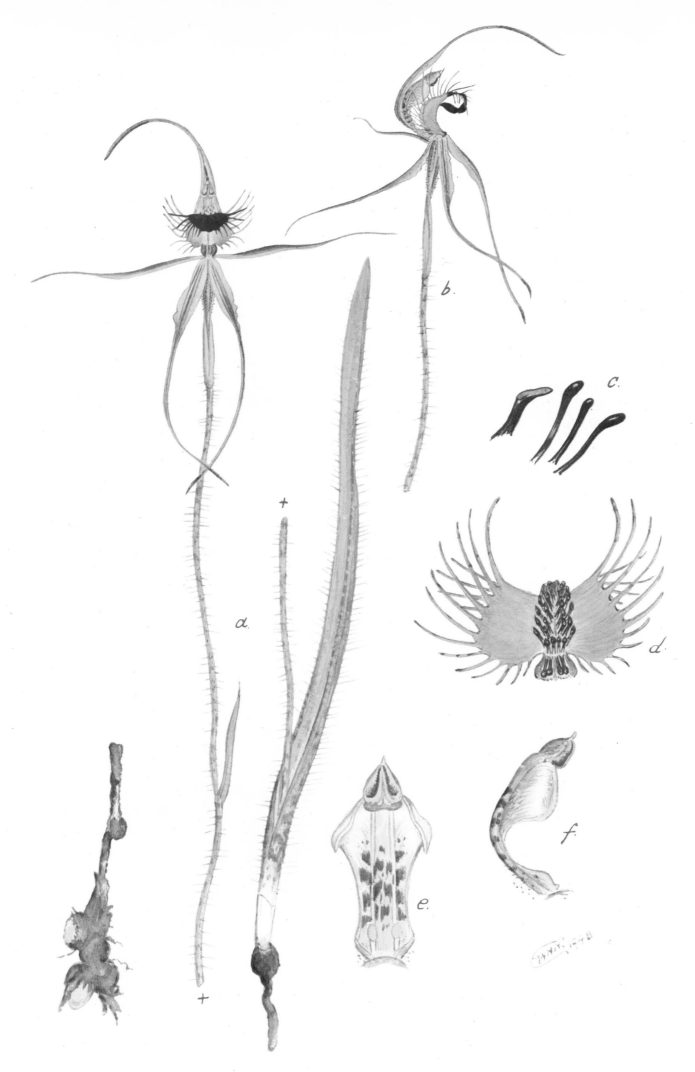

267 *Caladenia radiata* (see also p. 71)

a typical specimen   **b** flower, from side   **c** calli from the labellum lamina   **d** labellum, from above   **e** column, from front   **f** column, from side
Figs **a, b** natural size

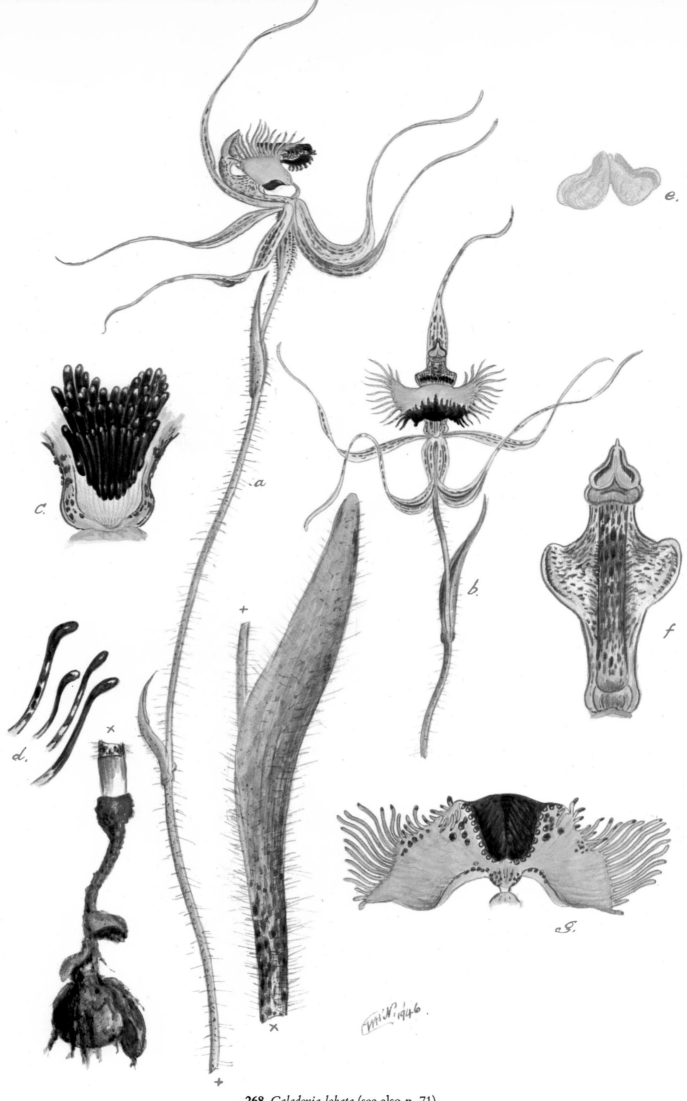

268 *Caladenia lobata* (see also p. 71)

a b specimens collected near Waterloo, WA **c** calli from base of labellum **d** calli from labellum lamina **e** pollinia **f** column, from front **g** labellum, from front
Figs **a, b** natural size

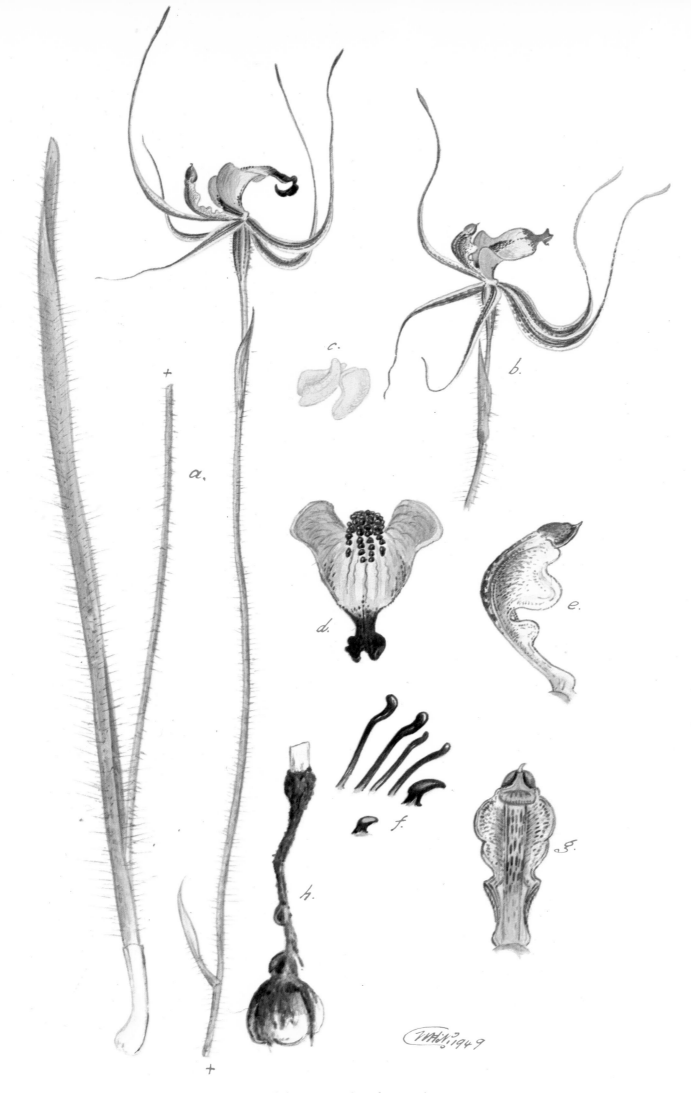

269 *Caladenia integra* (see also p. 71)

a typical Mt Bakewell, WA, specimen   b flower   c pollinia   d labellum, from front   e column, from side   f calli   g column, from front   h tubers, etc.
Figs **a, b, h** natural size

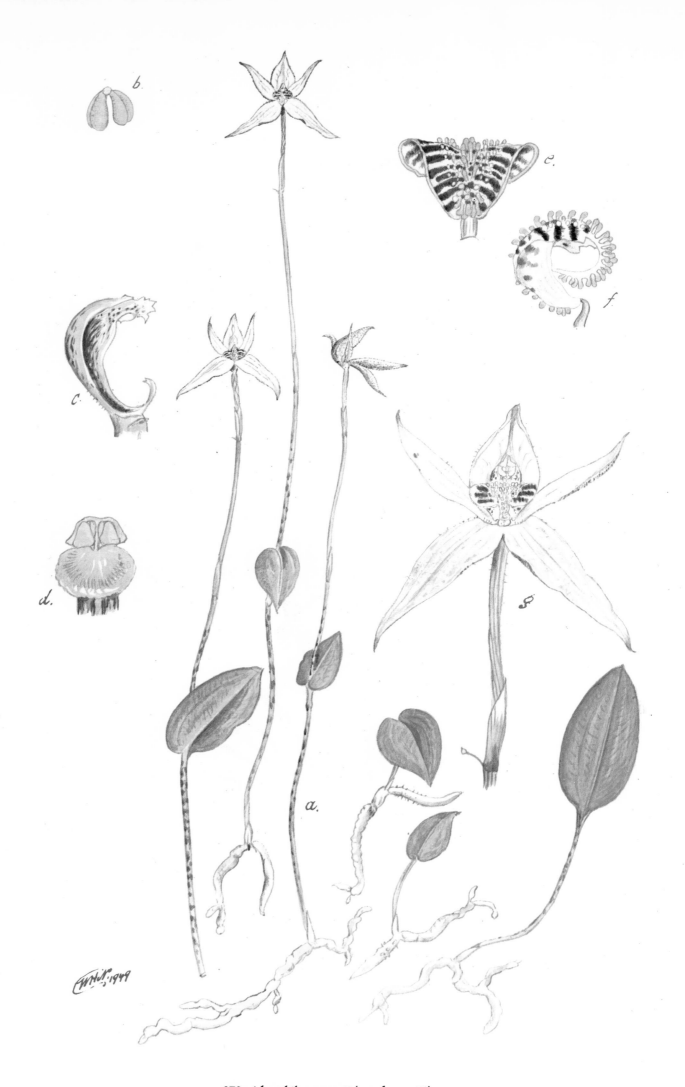

270 *Adenochilus nortonii* (see also p. 71)

a typical plants **b** pollinia **c** column, from side **d** stigma and anther **e** labellum, from above **f** labellum, from side **g** flower
Fig. **a** natural size

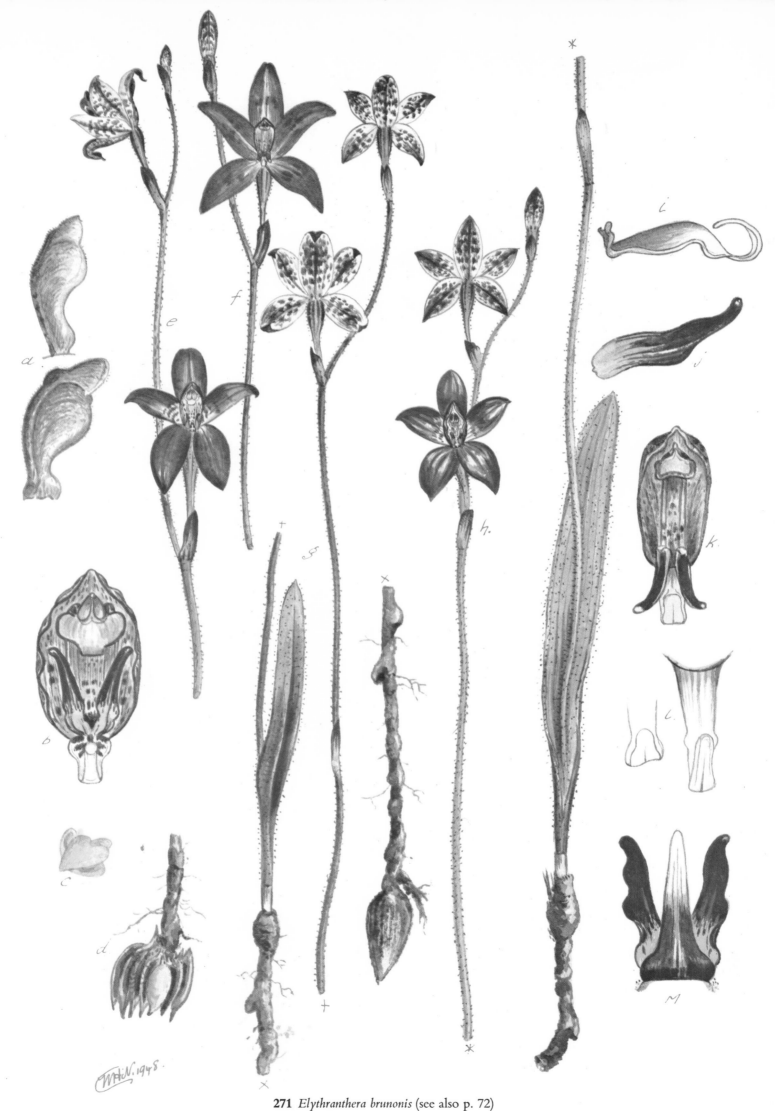

271 *Elythranthera brunonis* (see also p. 72)

a two columns, from side **b** column, from front, showing the labellum and the two prominent conjoined calli **c** pollinia **d** root system, with the covering cut open to show enclosed tuber **e** flowers of the typical form **f** flower, etc., of a specimen collected in the depths of the Karri forest at Manjimup, WA **g** typical specimen, showing flowers from the rear **h** another typical specimen **i** labellum, from side **j** single callus from the labellum base **k** column, from front, showing both the calli and the labellum **l** figures showing much variation towards the apex **m** labellum and calli, from below

Figs **d–h** natural size

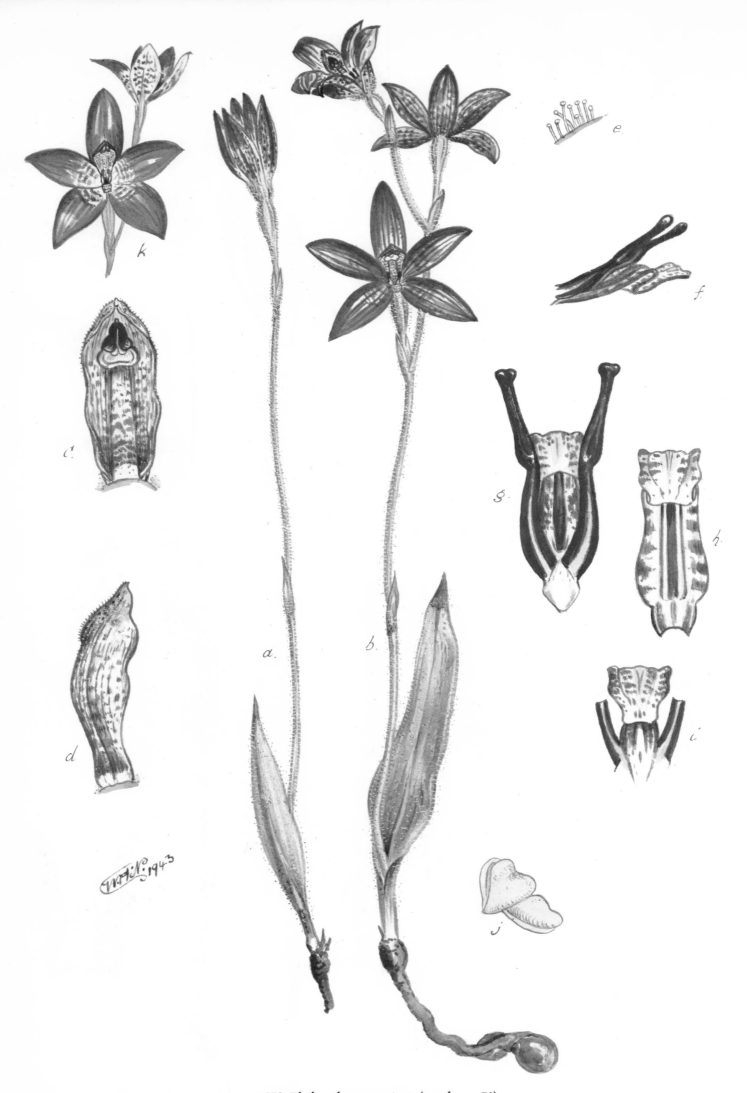

272 *Elythranthera emarginata* (see also p. 72)

a b two specimens collected at Yarloop, WA   **c** column, from front   **d** column, from side   **e** glandular-hairs from pedicel—these are characteristic of the whole plant
f labellum and calli, from side   **g** calli and labellum, from above   **h** labellum, from below   **i** apex of labellum   **j** pollinia   **k** flower from Wagerup, WA
Figs **a, b, k** natural size

273 *Elythranthera emarginata* (see also p. 72)

a a Yarloop, WA, specimen   **b** two pollinia   **c** column, from front   **d** labellum, from above   **e** calli and labellum, from above   **f** a labellum with an additional fold
Fig. **a** natural size

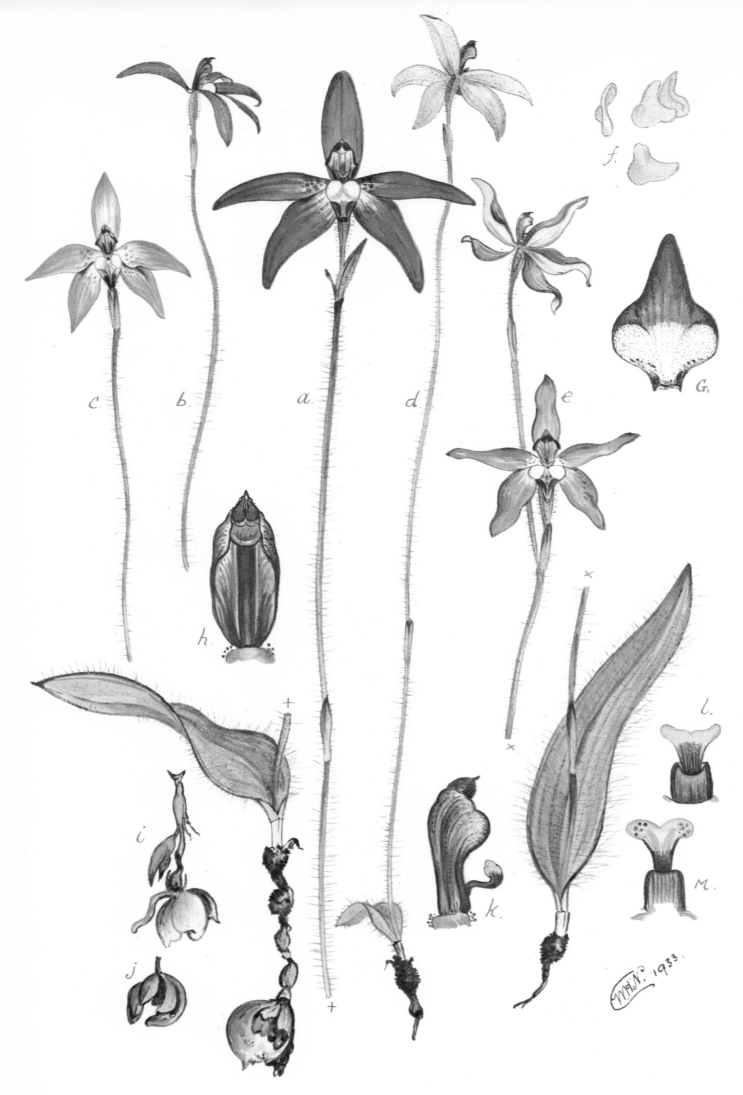

274 *Glossodia major* (see also p. 73)

a a large-flowered form **b c d** typical specimens **e** flowers with undulate perianth **f** pollinia **g** labellum, from above **h** column, from front **i** encased tubers
j the casing of the tubers **k** column and appendage, from side **l m** two forms of bilobed appendage
Figs **a–e, i, j** natural size

275 *Glossodia minor* (see also p. 73)

a typical specimens and flowers   **b** pollinia   **c** column with basal calli, from side   **d** root system: tubers and protective covering   **e** calli, from front   **f** a single callus, from side
g column, from front   **h** labellum, from above   **i** labellum, from the base   **j** labellum, from side
Figs **a, d** natural size

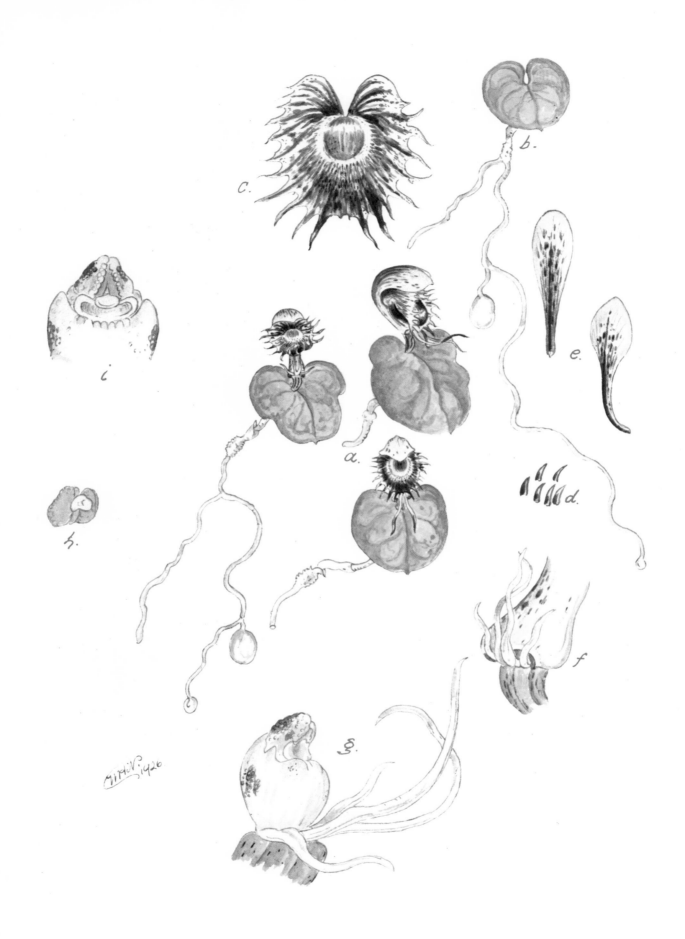

276 *Corybas pruinosus* (see also p. 73)

a typical specimens **b** non-flowering plant **c** labellum lamina **d** calli from the labellum lamina **e** dorsal sepals **f** base of labellum, showing sepals and petals **g** column,
lateral sepals and petals **h** pollinia **i** head of column
Figs **a, b** natural size

277 *Corybas fimbriatus* (see also p. 74)

a b c d typical specimens from Paterson, NSW **e** base of labellum tube, showing sepals and petals **f** ovary, column and appendages **g** labellum lamina **h** calli
i labellum, from side **j** interior of labellum tube **k** auricles at base of labellum **l** dorsal sepal
Figs **a–d** natural size

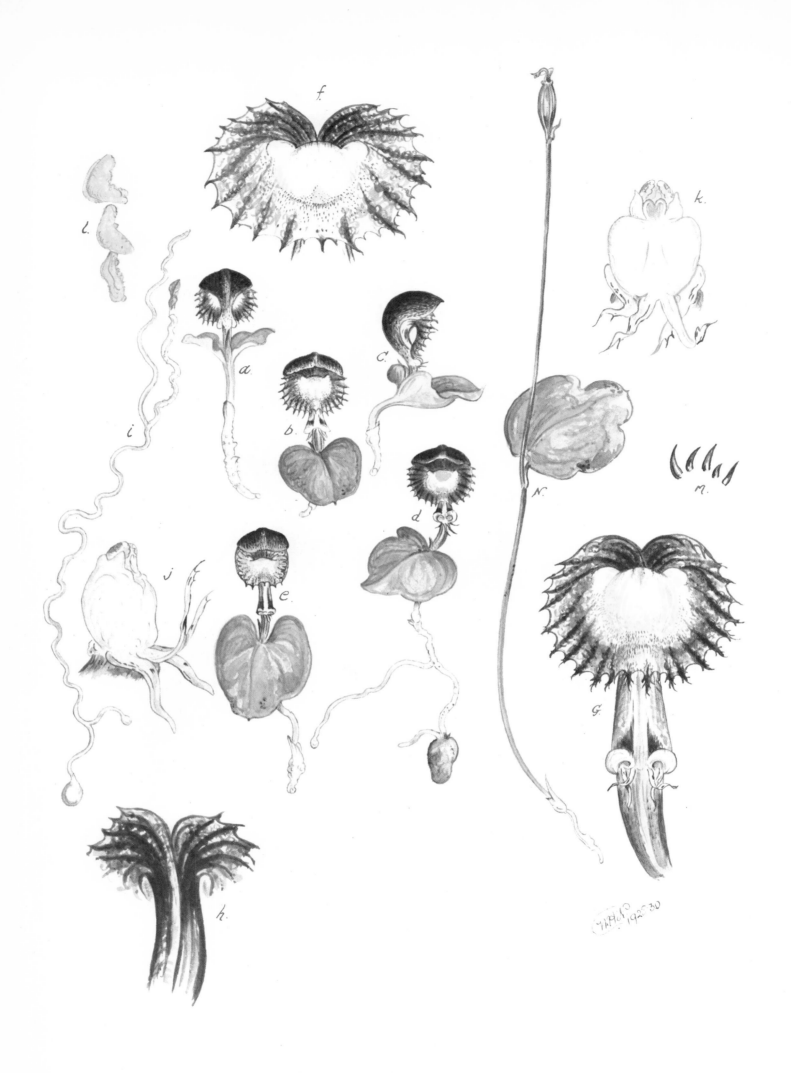

278 *Corybas dilatatus* (see also p. 74)

a b c specimens from Lockwood, Vic. **d** a Tas. specimen **e** specimen from Mount Donna Buang, Vic. **f** labellum lamina **g** labellum and ovary, from front **h** labellum tube, from above **i** juvenile plant from Mount Donna Buang, Vic. **j** column, etc., from side **k** column, etc., from front **l** pollinia **m** calli from labellum lamina **n** fruiting plant from summit of tree fern, Sherbrooke Gully, Vic.

Figs **a–e, i, n** natural size

279 *Corybas diemenicus* (see also p. 74)

a b c d e f typical specimens from Lockwood, Vic. **g** fruiting specimen **h** column, from side **i j** columns, from front, showing sepals and petals **k** sepals and petals **l** labellum lamina, Vic. specimen **m** labellum lamina, Tas. specimen **n** lower margins of the labellum **o** labellum, etc., from side **p** interior view of labellum tube **q** calli from the labellum **r** apices of dorsal sepals **s** pollinia **t** a robust specimen from Bairnsdale, Vic.

Figs **a–g, t** natural size

280 *Corybas undulatus* (see also p. 75)

a typical specimens **b** column, from side, showing long sepals and abbreviated petals **c** column, from front **d** column, from rear **e** dorsal sepal **f** base of labellum tube, showing petals and ovary **g** labellum, from rear **h** labellum lamina **i** glands from labellum lamina **j** ovary and bract **k** pollinia

Fig. **a** natural size

281 *Corybas aconitiflorus* (see also p. 75)

(see also p. 75)

a b g h large specimens from Bulahdelah, NSW   **c** specimen collected in a Healesville gully, Vic.   **d** plant showing root system   **e** specimen from Rocky Cape, Tas.
f a pale form from near Sydney   **i** flower, from front—dorsal sepal removed   **j** labellum, from front (note sepals at base)   **k l** labella, from side   **m** column, showing sepals
and petals   **n** petals   **o** sepals   **p** column, from front   **q** basal spur of labellum
Figs **a–h** natural size

282 *Corybas unguiculatus* (see also p. 75)

a b c typical plants collected near Oakleigh, Vic. **d e f** three Tas. specimens **g** juvenile plant **h** from the sand dunes at Airey's Inlet, Vic. **i** fruiting plant **j** leaf found after the flowering season **k** apex of labellum lamina, from side **l** labellum lamina, from front **m** calli from the labellum **n** column, from front **o** stigma, etc., from front **p** pollinia **q** column and appendages, from side **r s** column bases, from front **t** dorsal sepal, from side **u** column, etc., from side **v** column appendages from a specimen collected at Airey's Inlet
Figs **a–j** natural size

283 *Corybas fordhamii* (see also p. 75)

a typical specimens, one figure with dorsal sepal moved to show labellum **b** labellum, from front **c** tip of labellum lamina, showing calli **d** calli **e f** dorsal sepal, from side, and from below **g** labellum, from side **h i** column, petals and sepals, from front and side **j** head of column, showing stigma, etc., anther opened out
Fig. **a** natural size

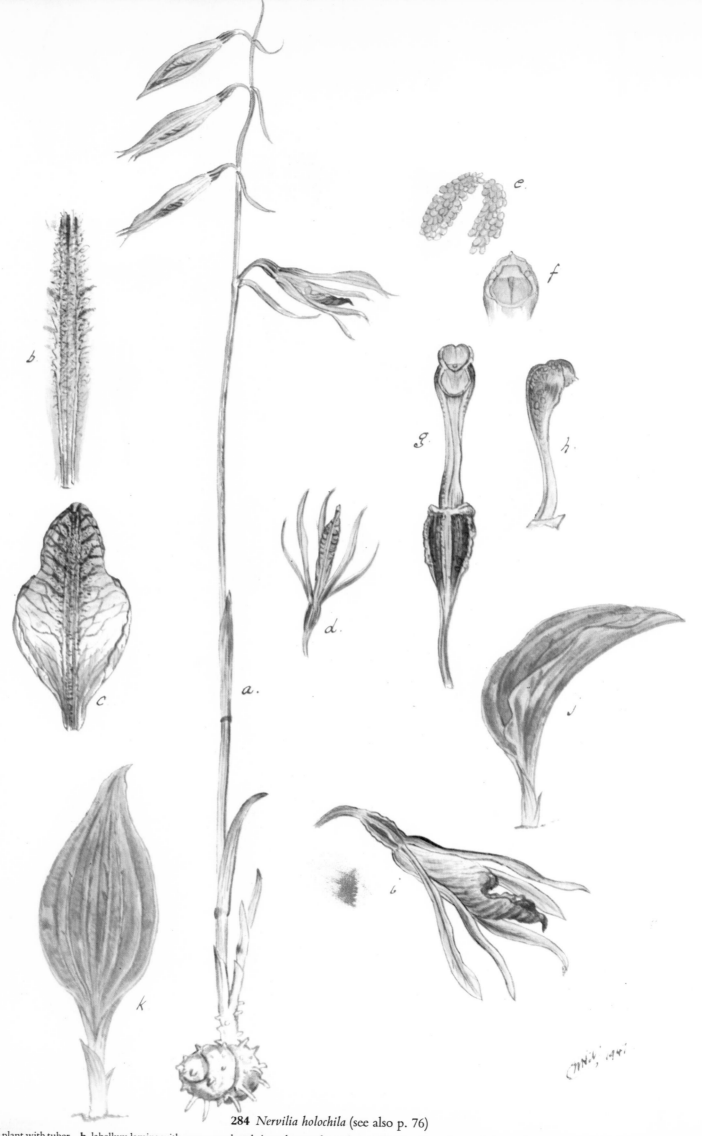

284 *Nervilia holochila* (see also p. 76)

a flowering plant with tuber   **b** labellum lamina with numerous short hairs and serrated margins   **c** labellum, from above   **d** flower, from below   **e** pollinia   **f** head of column, anther removed   **g** column and ovary, from front   **h** column, from side   **i** flower, from side   **j k** radical leaves
Figs **a, d, j, k** natural size

285 *Cryptostylis erecta* (see also p. 76)

a Vic. specimen **b** flower, from side **c** flower, from front **d** base of callus-plate **e** pollinia **f** anther with pollinia in position **g** column
Figs **a–c** natural size

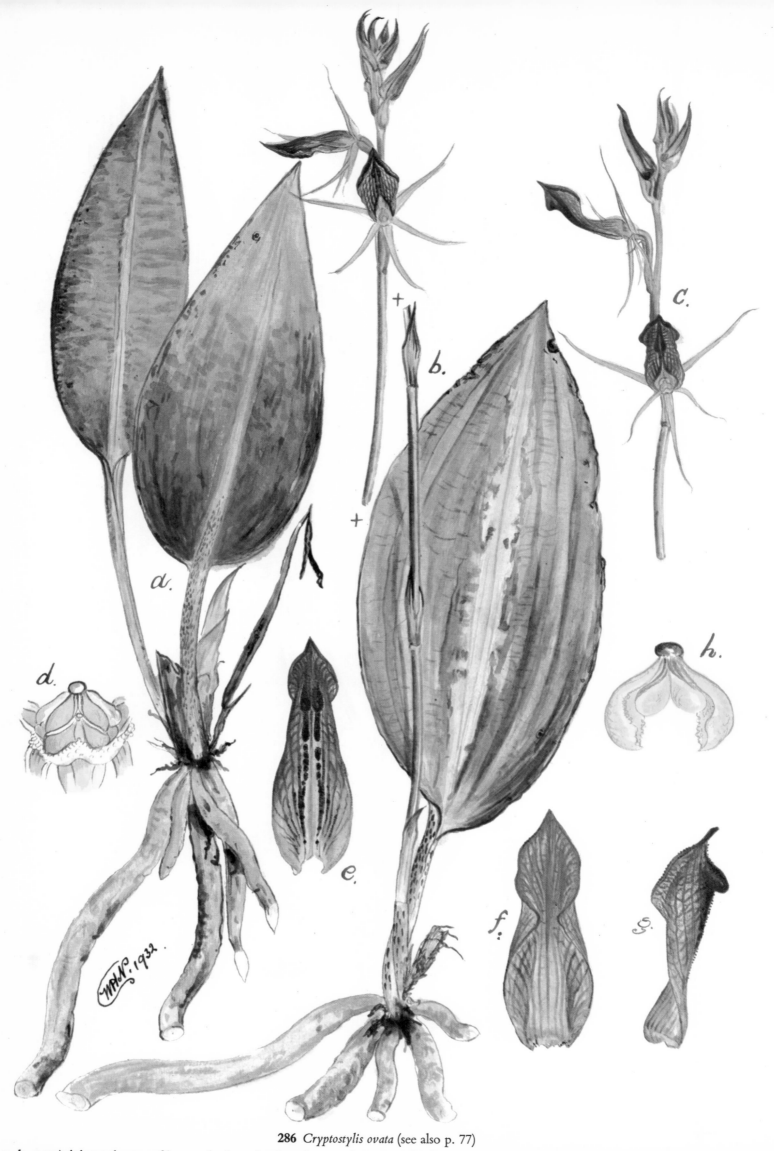

286 *Cryptostylis ovata* (see also p. 77)

a   b   c typical plants and racemes of flowers   **d** column, showing anther, appendages, etc.   **e** labellum, from front   **f** labellum, from above   **g** labellum, from side,   **h** pollinia
Figs **a–c** natural size

287 *Cryptostylis leptochila* (see also p. 77)

a b typical specimens **c** juvenile plant and root system **d** glands from labellum lamina **e** male Ichneumonid, *Lissopimpla semipunctata*, showing pollinia adhering to abdomen
f female Ichneumonid wasp **g** pollinia **h** column, showing anther, appendages, etc. **i** labellum, from front **j** base of labellum, from front **k** labellum, from front **l** callus
from labellum lamina **m** labellum, from side
Figs **a–c** natural size

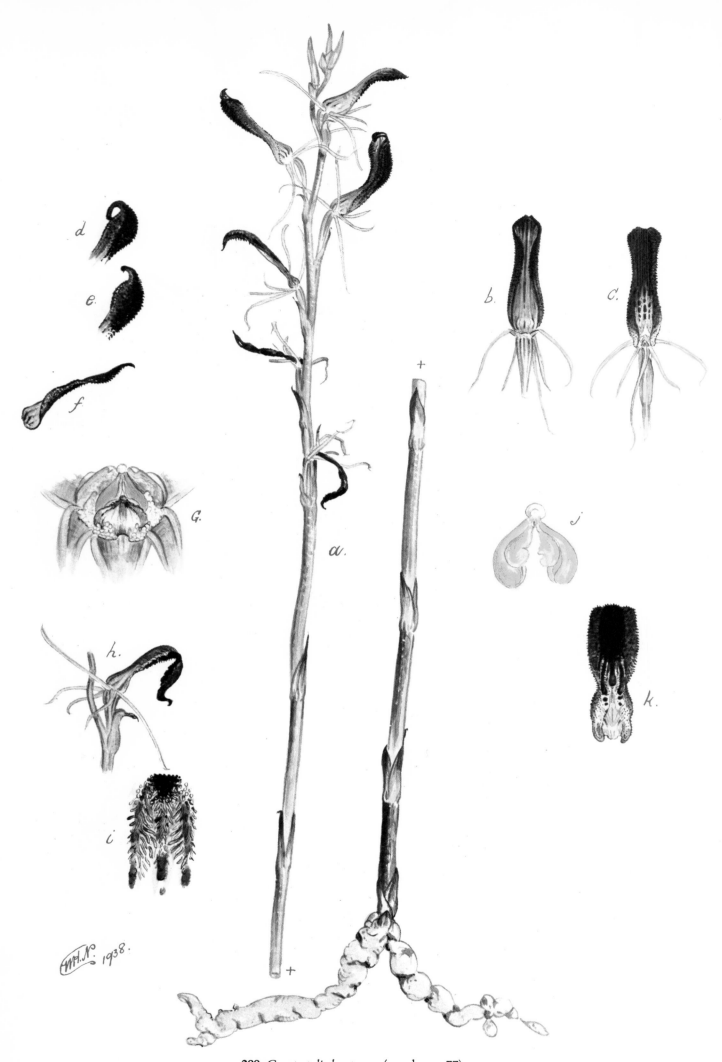

288 *Cryptostylis hunterana* (see also p. 77)

a typical specimen **b c** individual flowers, from above and below **d e** labellum apices **f** labellum, from side **g** column **h** a withered flower **i** glands from the base of labellum lamina **j** pollinia **k** labellum, from front

Figs **a–c, f, h** natural size

289 *Pterostylis falcata* (see also p. 78)

a b c d typical specimens **e f** radical leaves **g** part of conjoined sepals, also the divided apices **h** column, from side **i** stigma **j** pollinia **k** petal **l** labellum, from side **m** labellum lamina, from above **n** labellum appendage

Figs **a–f** natural size

290 *Pterostylis acuminata* (see also p. 78)

a b c d e typical specimens and flowers f column, from side g stigma h conjoined sepals, from rear i petal j abnormal upper lobes of column wings k rostellum,
with adhering pollen grains l pollinia m labellum, from side n labellum, from above, appendage removed o cross-section of labellum p radical rosette
Figs a-e, p natural size

291 *Pterostylis acuminata* var. *ingens* (see also p. 78)

a a superior specimen **b** specimen from Cravensville, Vic. **c** specimen from Bayswater, Vic. **d** basal leaves and well-developed stem-leaf **e** labellum, from above (lamina flattened to show markings and tip)
Figs **a–d** natural size

292 *Pterostylis nutans*: Figs **a–i, k, l** (see also p. 78)
P. nutans var. *hispidula*: Fig. **j** (see also p. 79)

a robust example from Greensborough, Vic. **b** flower, from front **c** a twin-flowered specimen **d** pollinia **e** capsule **f** flower, from rear **g** column and labellum
h conjoined sepals, interior view **i** stigma and rostellum on right **j** flowering specimen **k** labellum apex **l** cross-section of labellum
Figs **a–c, e, j** natural size

293 *Pterostylis pedoglossa* (see also p. 79)

a **b** two specimens from Cheltenham, Vic.   **c** specimen from Eaglehawk Neck, Tas.   **d** specimen from Springvale, Vic.   **e** anther and rostellum   **f** labellum, from above—
Vic. specimen   **g** column, from side   **h** stigma   **i** radical leaves, plant with tubers, etc.   **j** sepals, showing labellum in position   **k** labellum, conjoined from side   **l** labellum of
a Tas. flower, from above   **m** labellum, from below
Figs **a–d, i** natural size

294 *Pterostylis nana* (see also p. 79)

a fruiting specimen **b d** specimens from Everton district, Vic. **c** specimen from Werribee Gorge, Vic., on left, and one from Greensborough, Vic., for comparison **e** a WA specimen **f** radical leaves **g** inflexed lobule on the conjoined sepals (inside) **h** labellum, from above **i** labellum, from side **j** labellum, from tip **k** column, from side **l** petal **m** stigma **n** bead–like papillae at base of labellum

Figs **a–f** natural size

295 *Pterostylis pyramidalis* (see also p. 79)

a b c d e specimens from Canning River, WA **f** stigma **g** inflexed lobule of conjoined sepals **h** labellum, from above **i** petal **j** upper part of column, from side

Figs **a–e** natural size

296 *Pterostylis celans* (see also p. 80)

a b c typical examples **d e** two incomplete specimens **f** flower, from front—conjoined sepals pulled down to shown labellum which completely closes entrance to galea
g column, from side **h** column, from front **i** labellum, from above **j** vestigial appendage of labellum **k** labellum, from side **l** another labellum, from above **m** apex of
labellum **n** conjoined sepals
Figs **a–e** natural size

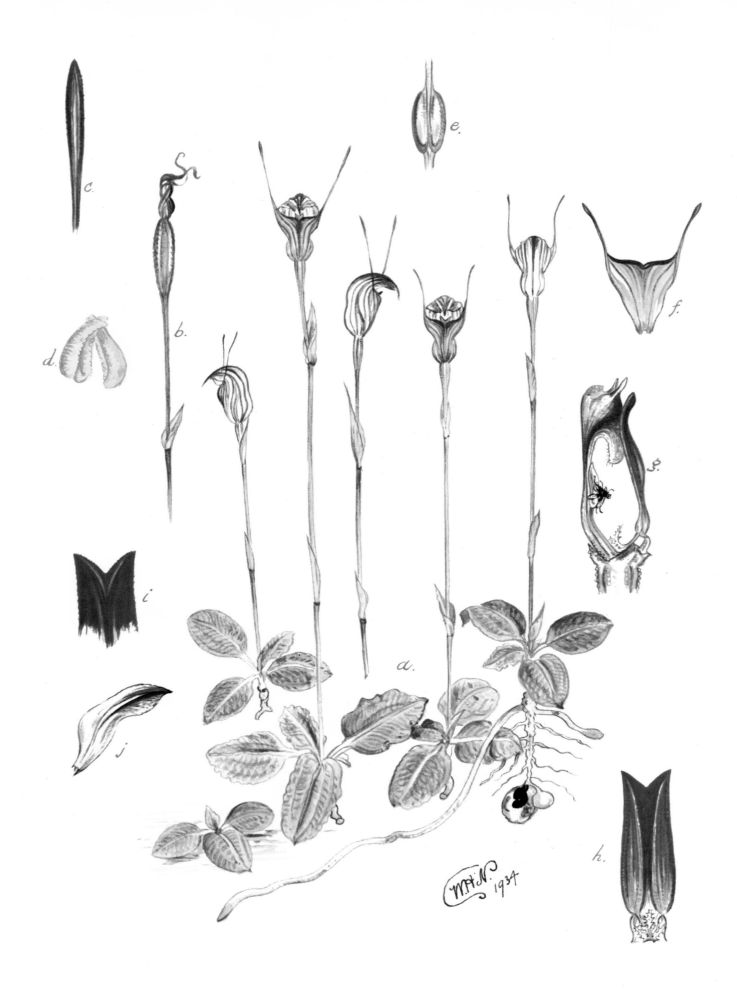

297 *Pterostylis concinna* (see also p. 80)

a typical specimens from Frankston, Vic. (note adventitious root on right, by which the colony rapidly extends) **b** fruiting capsule **c** apex of lateral sepal **d** pollinia **e** stigma
f conjoined sepals, from inside **g** column and labellum, from side (note remains of insect on stigma) **h** labellum, from above **i** apex of labellum, from below **j** petal
Figs **a, b** natural size

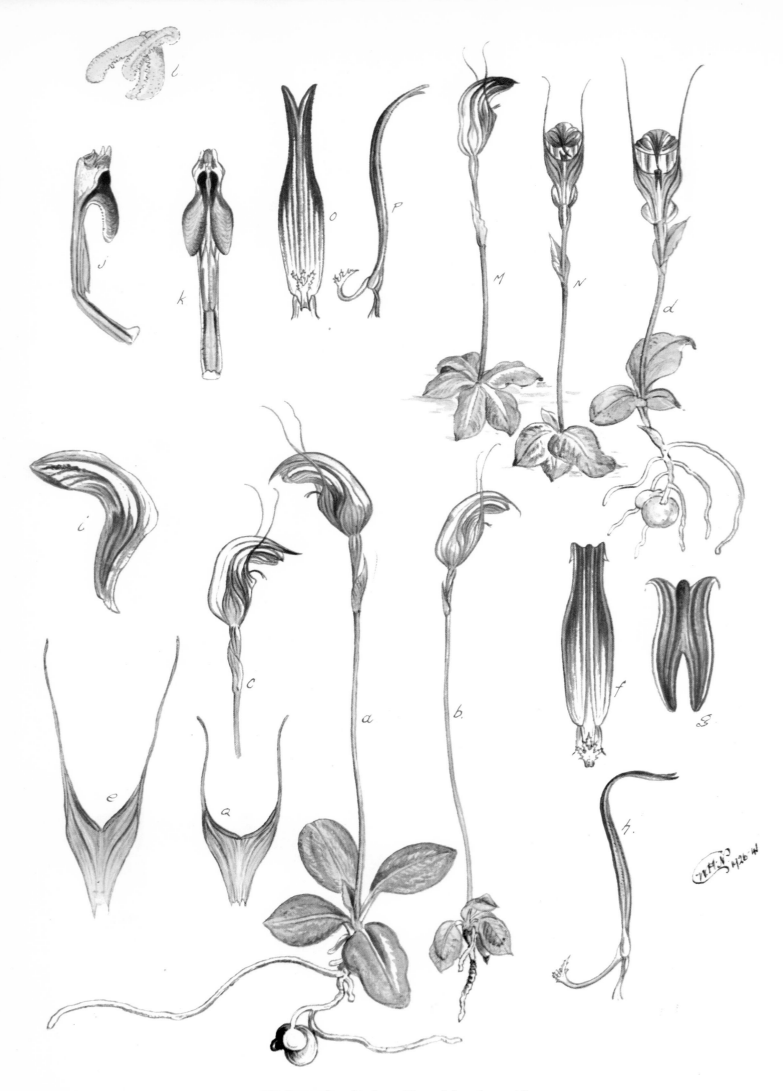

298 *Pterostylis ophioglossa*: Figs **a–l** (see also p. 80)
P. ophioglossa var. *collina*: Figs **m–q** (see also p. 80)

a b c d typical specimens **e** conjoined sepals **f** labellum, from above **g** tip of labellum **h** labellum, from side **i** petal **j** column, from side **k** column, from front
l pollinia **m n** flowering specimens **o** labellum, from above **p** labellum, from side **q** conjoined sepals
Figs **a–d, m, n** natural size

299 *Pterostylis allantoidea* (see also p. 80)

a two typical specimens **b** column, from side and front **c** labellum, from front **d** labellum, from side **e** conjoined sepals **f** stem-bract, showing marginal cilia **g** petal
Fig. **a** natural size

300 *Pterostylis baptistii* (see also p. 81)

a b two specimens from Lake Macquarie, NSW **c** head of column, from front **d** column, from side **e** labellum, from side **f** labellum, from above **g** labellum, from below **h** pollinia **i** portion of the conjoined sepals, from inside **j** petal **k** stigma

Figs **a, b** natural size

301 *Pterostylis curta* (see also p. 81)

a typical specimens **b** conjoined sepals, from inside **c** pollinia **d** stigma **e** column and labellum, from side **f** petal **g** labellum, from above **h** labellum tip, from below
Fig. **a** natural size

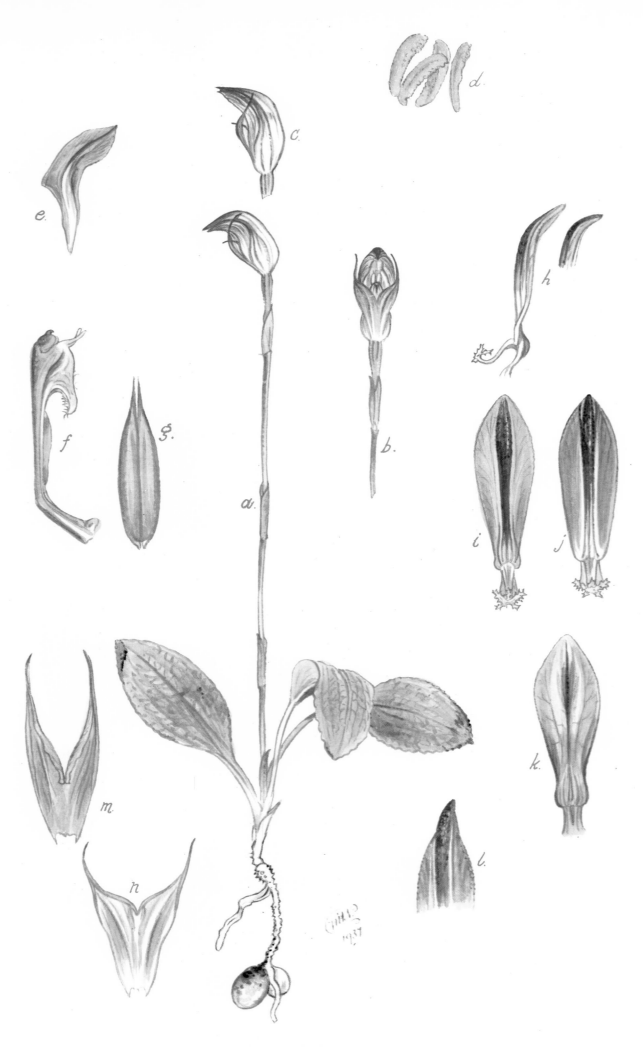

302 *Pterostylis hildae* (see also p. 81)

a typical plant **b** flower, from front **c** flower, at an advanced stage **d** pollinia **e** petal **f** column, from side **g** stigma **h** labellum, from side **i** labellum, from above
j labellum, from above **k** labellum, from below **l** labellum apex **m** conjoined sepals **n** conjoined sepals (Figs **i** and **k** represent the normally shaped labellum, while Fig. **m**
typifies the conjoined sepals)
Figs **a–c** natural size

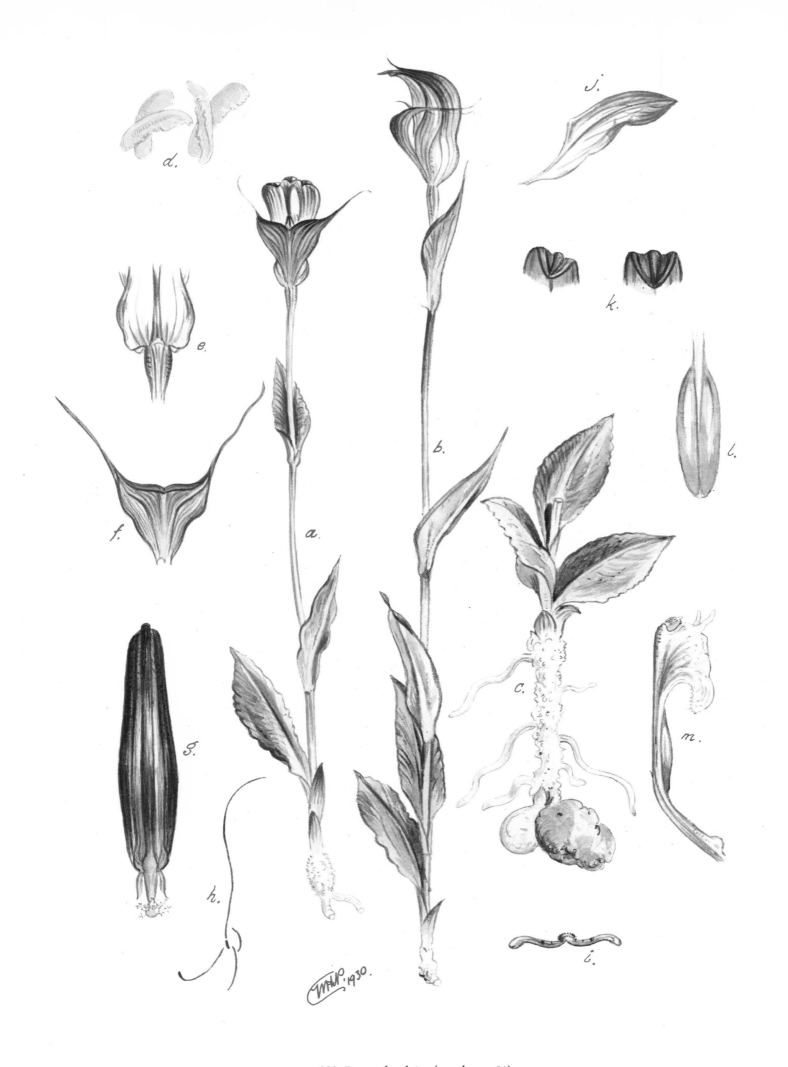

303 *Pterostylis alpina* (see also p. 81)

a b typical specimens **c** lower leaves and tubers, etc. **d** pollinia **e** lower part of galea, showing twin glands at the base (noted in some specimens) **f** conjoined sepals, from inside **g** labellum, from above—usually greenish **h** figure to show curvature of labellum **i** cross-section of labellum **j** petal **k** apices of labella **l** stigma **m** column, from side

Figs **a–c** natural size

304 *Pterostylis furcata* (see also p. 82)

a three specimens from Russell River, Tas.   **b** petal   **c** column, from side   **d** stigma   **e** pollinia   **f** column wing, showing inturned marginal cilia   **g** labellum, from below
h labellum, from above   **i** labellum, from side   **j** specimen from Lake St Clair, Tas.   **k** dorsal sepal and petals, from above (note short petal)   **l** labellum, from front   **m** stigma
n labellum, from above—appendage removed   **o** column and labellum, from side   **p** flower, from front (Figs **j**–**p**—Lake St Clair specimens)
Figs **a, j, p** natural size

305 *Pterostylis vereenae* (see also p. 82)

a b c specimens from Mount Bischoff, Tas. **d** column, from side **e** column, from front **f** labellum, from above **g** labellum, from side **h** labellum lamina, spread out
i conjoined sepals, from inside **j** petal **k** pollinia
Figs **a–c** natural size

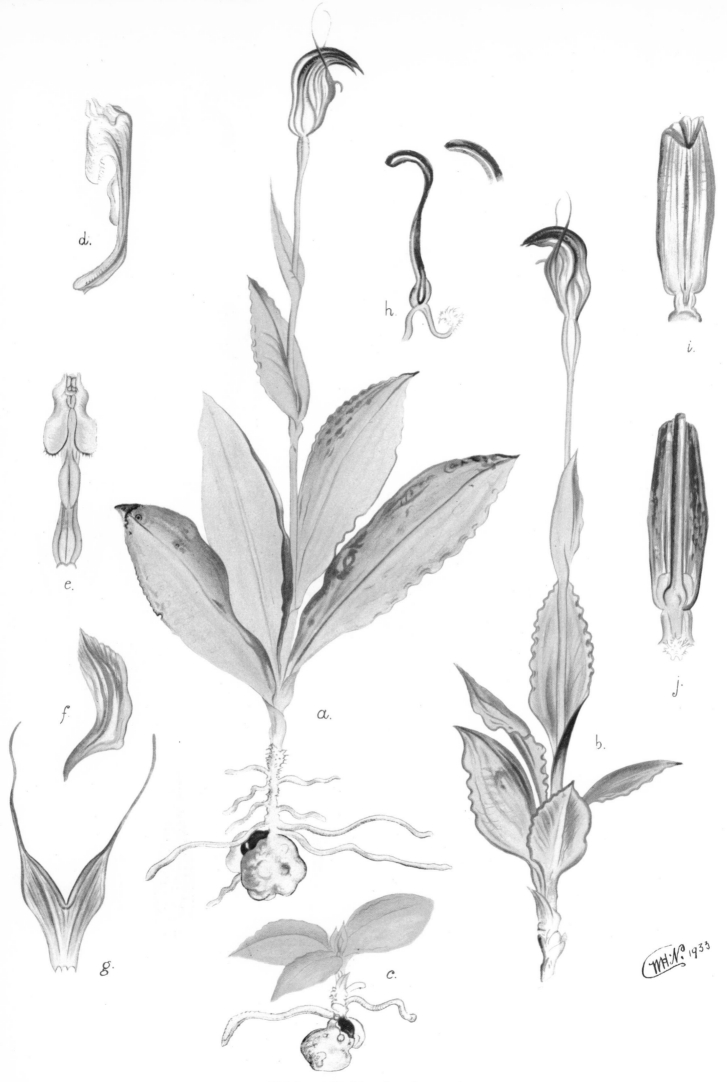

306 *Pterostylis foliata* (see also p. 82)

(see also p. 82)

a a Tas. specimen **b** specimen from Olinda, Vic. **c** juvenile plant **d** column, from side **e** column, from front **f** petal **g** conjoined sepals **h** labellum, from side
i labellum, from below **j** labellum, from above
Figs **a–c** natural size

307 *Pterostylis foliata* (see also p. 82)

a large specimen from Portland, Vic.　**b** a Cravensville, Vic., specimen with broad stem-leaves　**c** specimen from Greensborough, Vic.　**d** specimen from Wandin, Vic.
Figs **a–d** natural size

308 *Pterostylis cucullata* (see also p. 83)

a b typical examples **c** flower, with the conjoined sepals removed **d** column, from side **e** petal **f** bud—a characteristic bird-like study **g** rostellum **h** stigma **i** labellum, from above **j** one pair of pollinia **k** conjoined sepals, from inside
Figs **a, b, f** natural size

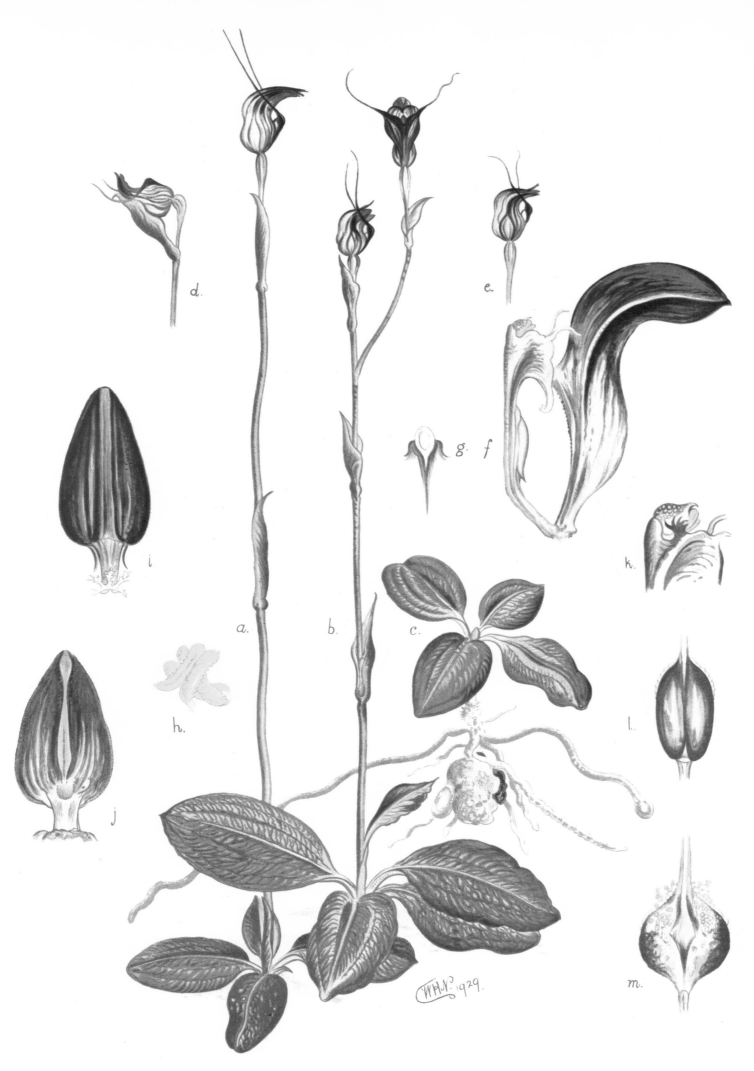

309 *Pterostylis pedunculata* (see also p. 83)

a b typical plants **c** juvenile plant **d** flower, held by uppermost bract **e** flower **f** column and petal **g** rostellum **h** pollinia **i** labellum, from above **j** labellum, from below **k** abnormal margin of column wing **l** stigma **m** stigma distorted with pollen-grains
Figs **a–e** natural size

310 *Pterostylis recurva* (see also p. 83)

a b c typical specimens **d** labellum, from above **e** labellum, from side **f** column, from side, also stigma from front

Figs **a–c** natural size

311 *Pterostylis alata* (see also p. 84)

a a Tas. specimen   **b   c** sturdy specimens from Greensborough, Vic.   **d** specimen from sandy soil at Cheltenham, Vic.   **e** two-flowered specimen   **f   g   h   i** various forms of radical rosettes, the first being observed only in dry seasons   **j** flower opened to show structure of galea   **k** labellum, from above   **l** cross-section labellum   **m** petal   **n** pollinia   **o** column and labellum, from side   **p** stigmas   **q** an unusual form of stigma, also showing rostellum (above)

Figs **a–j** natural size

312 *Pterostylis toveyana* (see also p. 84)

a specimen from Mentone, Vic. **b c d** Greensborough, Vic., specimens **e** radical leaves **f** labellum, from above, also variation of lamina shape **g** labellum, from side **h** labellum, from below **i** column, from side **j** petal **k** conjoined sepals, from inside **l** pollinia **m** upper portion of column (wings removed)

Figs **a–e** natural size

313 *Pterostylis robusta* (see also p. 84)

a b c typical specimens from Vic. habitats **d e** juvenile plants with radical rosettes **f** tuber **g** petal **h** labellum lamina, from above **i** labellum, from below **j** tip of labellum **k** cross-section of labellum **l** column and labellum, from side **m** stigma and rostellum (column wings removed) **n** pollinia

Figs **a–f** natural size

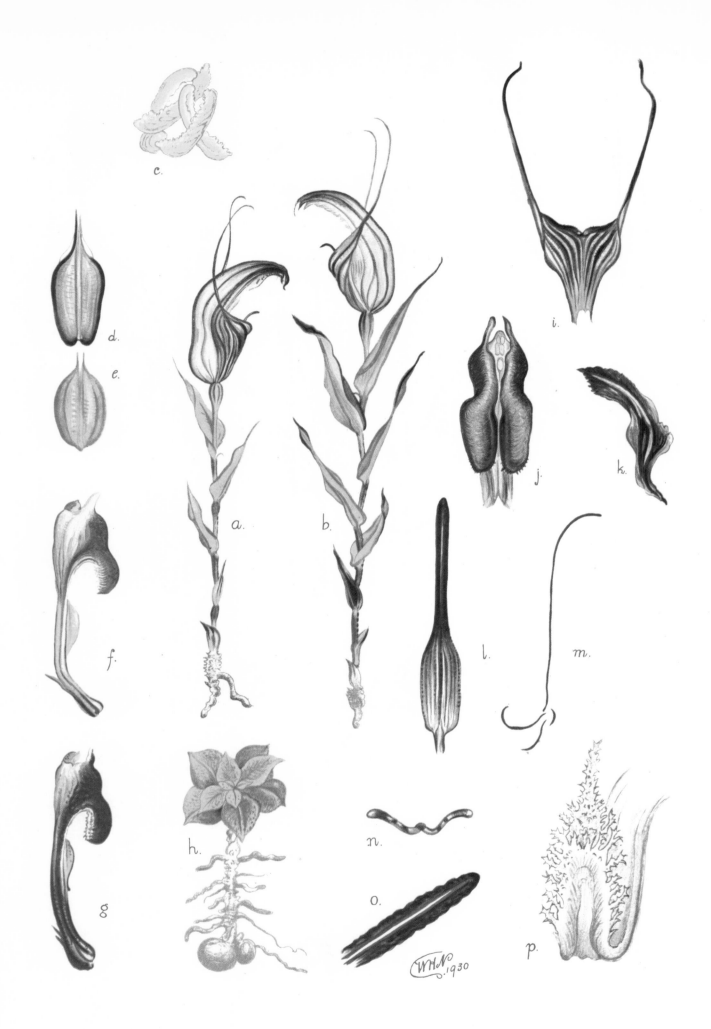

314 *Pterostylis hamiltonii* (see also p. 85)

a b typical specimens from Boyup Brook, WA **c** pollinia **d e** stigmas **f g** columns, from side **h** juvenile plant **i** conjoined sepals **j** column wings, from front
k petal **l** labellum lamina, from above **m** curvature of the labellum **n** cross-section of labellum **o** apex of labellum **p** penicillate apex of labellum appendage
Figs **a, b, h** natural size

315 *Pterostylis truncata* (see also p. 85)

(see also p. 85)

a typical specimen from You Yangs, Vic. **b** specimen with leaf-like stem-bracts **c** dark-coloured specimen from Keilor plains, Vic. **d** twin-flowered specimen from Coimadai East, Vic. **e f g h i** radical leaves **j** column, from front **k** column, from side **l** labellum, from above—tip not visible **m** labellum, from above **n** labellum, from side **o** tips of labella **p** pollinia

Figs **a–i** natural size

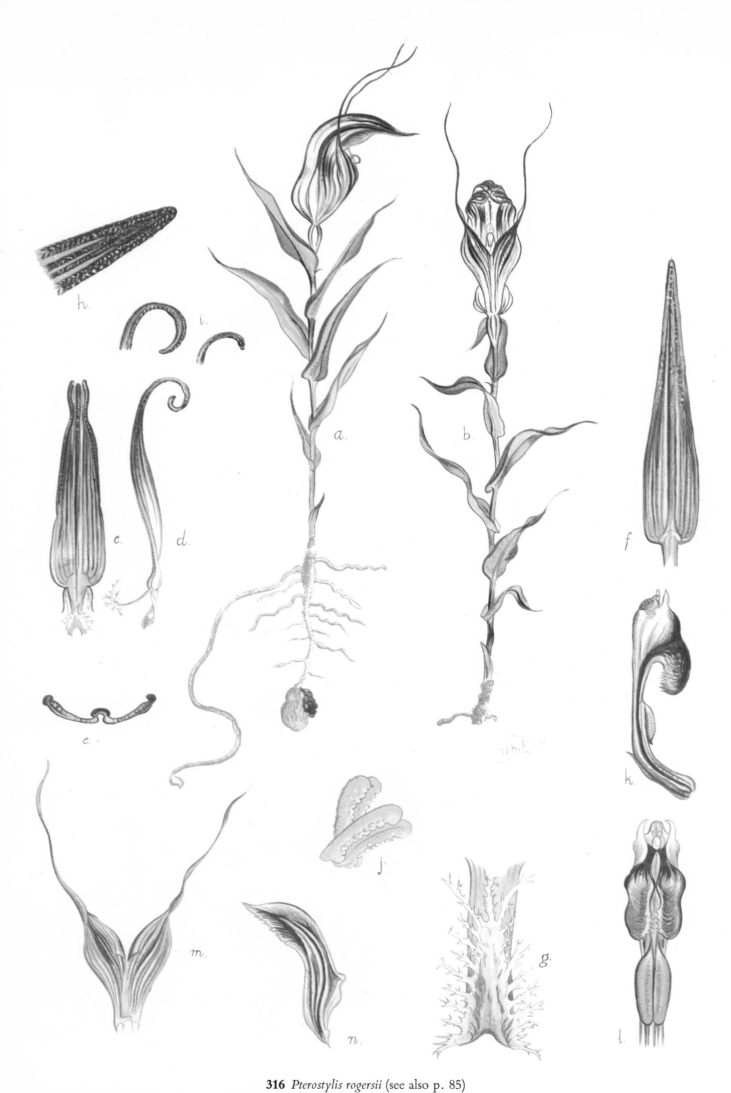

316 *Pterostylis rogersii* (see also p. 85)

a   b typical specimens   **c** labellum, from above   **d** labellum, from side   **e** cross-section of labellum   **f** labellum lamina, spread out   **g** apex of labellum appendage   **h** apex of labellum, showing cilia   **i** apex of labellum, from side   **j** pollinia   **k** column, from side   **l** upper portion of column, from front   **m** conjoined sepals, from inside   **n** petal
Figs **a, b** natural size

317 *Pterostylis constricta* (see also p. 86)

a b c typical specimens from Bruce Rock, WA **d** radical rosette of leaves **e** petal **f** column, from side **g** stigma **h** pollinia **i** labellum **j** conjoined sepals—one segment removed

Figs **a–d** natural size

318 *Pterostylis grandiflora* (see also p. 86)

a superior examples from Lockwood near Belgrave, Vic. **b** petal **c** conjoined sepals **d** column, from side **e** stigma **f g** radical leaves (two kinds) **h** labellum, from above **i** lateral growth **j** pollinia
Figs **a, f, g, i** natural size

319 *Pterostylis revoluta* (see also p. 86)

a b typical specimens **c** radical rosettes **d** flower, from rear **e** dorsal sepal, from rear **f** petal **g** galea, to show effect of wind **h** column, from side **i** stigma **j** pollinia
k labellum, from a specimen collected in the former Ashburton woods near Melbourne, Vic. **l** cross-section of labellum **m** column wing, showing cilia
Figs **a–d** natural size

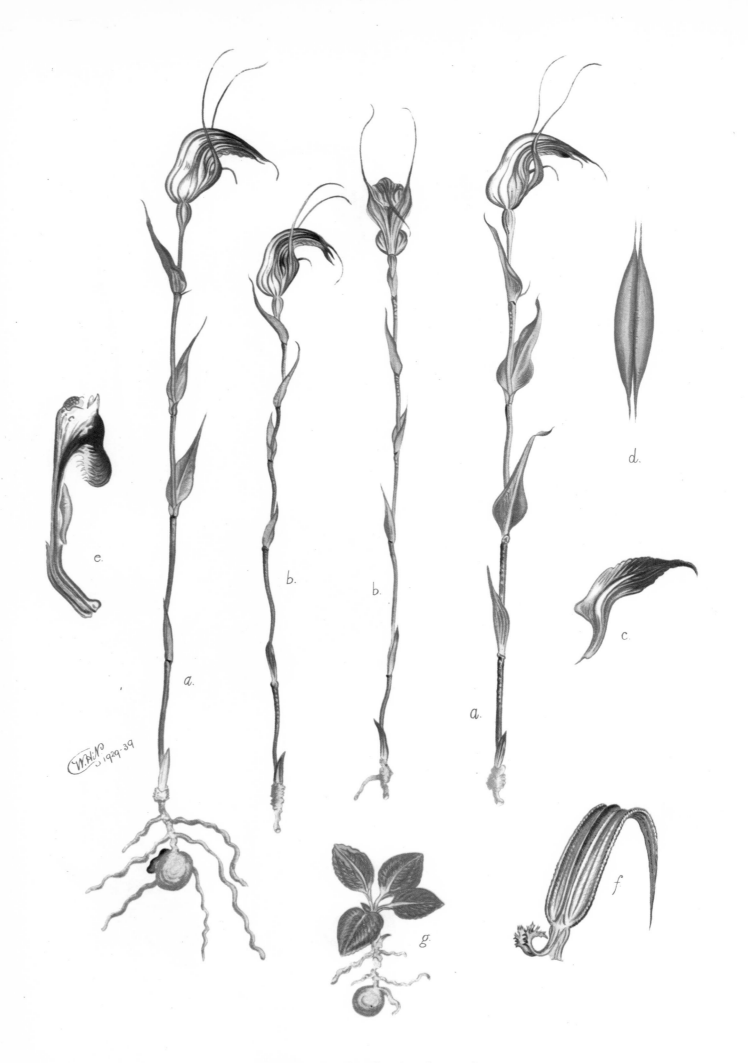

320 *Pterostylis reflexa* (see also p. 87)

a typical specimens from Glenbrook, NSW **b** specimens from Orbost district, Vic. **c** petal **d** stigma **e** column, from side **f** labellum **g** juvenile plant
Figs **a, b, g** natural size

321 *Pterostylis coccinea* (see also p. 87)

a typical specimen **b** flower, from front **c** column, from side **d** column head, also stigma, from front **e** labellum, from side **f** labellum, from above **g** conjoined
sepals, from inside **h** pollinia
Figs **a, b** natural size

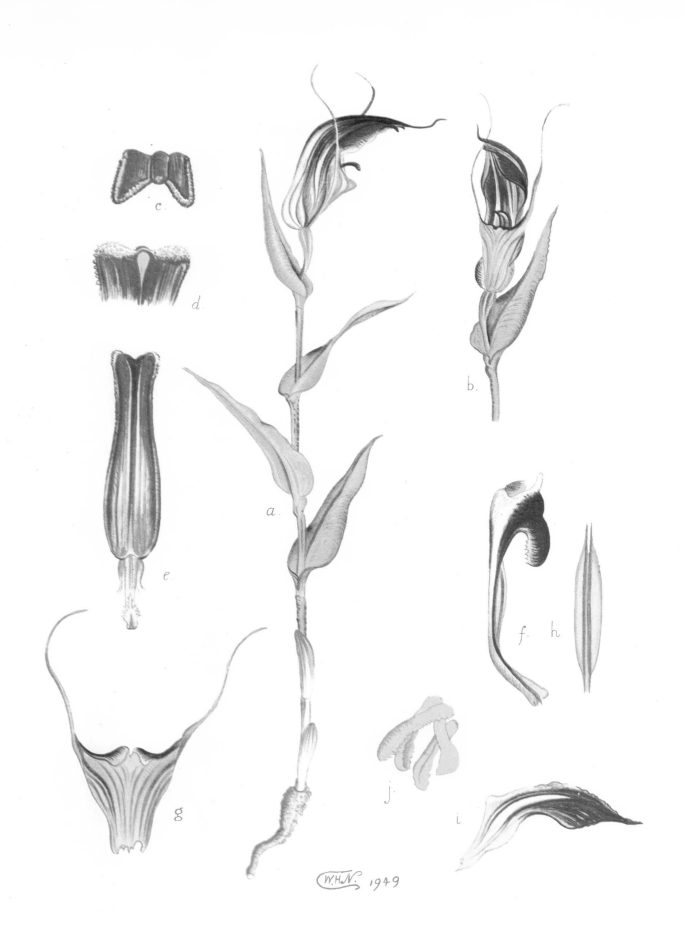

322 *Pterostylis pulchella* (see also p. 87)

a typical specimen, collected at Fitzroy Falls, NSW   **b** flower of same   **c** apex of labellum   **d** apex of labellum, from below   **e** labellum, from above   **f** column, from side
g conjoined sepals, from inside   **h** stigma   **i** petal   **j** pollinia
Figs **a, b** natural size

323 *Pterostylis obtusa*: Figs **b–h, k–p** (see also p. 87)
P. alveata: Figs **a, i, j** (see also p. 88)

a flowering specimen from coastal habitat, Vic.   **b** flower from Paterson, NSW   **c d** graceful specimens from Glenbrook, NSW   **e** a Vic. specimen with ovate leaves, from Mount Macedon   **f** typical example from Fern Tree Gully, Vic.   **g h** radical leaves—two forms   **i j** labella, from above and side   **k** labellum, from above   **l** apices of labella   **m** labellum apex, from below   **n** petal   **o** column, from side   **p** stigma
Figs **a–h** natural size

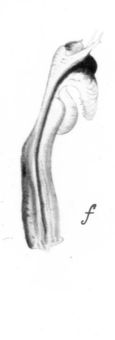

324 *Pterostylis crypta* (see also p. 88)

a b flowers, from front and side **c** typical specimen **d** labellum of same, from above **e** labellum, from side **f** column, from side
Fig. **c** natural size

325 *Pterostylis fischii* (see also p. 88)

a b c three specimens, the one on the right, from the front **d e** rosettes of leaves **f** column and labellum, from side **g** labellum, from above and side **h** cross-sections of labellum **i** labellum, from beneath **j** pollinia **k** conjoined sepals **l** column, enlarged to show insect visitor **m** column, from front, showing wings, anther and stigma **n** petal

Figs **a–e** natural size

326 *Pterostylis decurva* (see also p. 89)

a a superior example from the Barry Mountains, Vic. **b** Barry Mountains flower, from front **c** radical leaves **d** stigma **e** column, from front **f** column, from side **g** pollinia **h** petal **i** radical leaves **j** juvenile tubers from base of a parent plant **k** labellum lamina, flattened out **l** labellum, from side **m** conjoined sepals, from inside
Figs **a–c, i** natural size

327 *Pterostylis decurva* (see also p. 89)

a flowering plant from the Barrington Tops, NSW **b** flower, from side **c** petal **d** labella, from front and side **e** labellum, from above **f** labella, from front and side
g h columns, from side **i** stigma
Figs **a, b** natural size

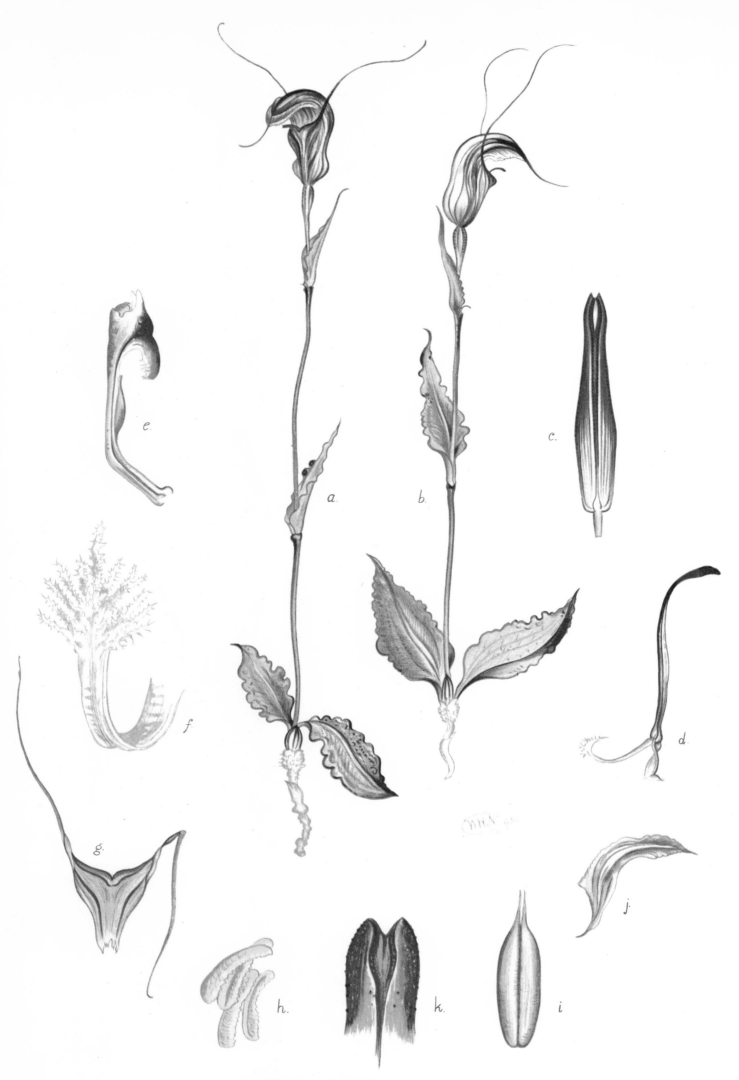

328 *Pterostylis furcillata* (see also p. 89)

a b typical specimens **c** labellum lamina, from above **d** labellum, from side **e** column, from side **f** labellum appendage **g** conjointed sepals **h** pollinia **i** stigma
j petal **k** apex of labellum, from above
Figs **a, b** natural size

329 *Pterostylis parviflora* (see also p. 89)

a b c three examples—coastal, inland and alpine **d** root system with lateral growths of leaves **e** seedlings **f** seedling **g** conjoined sepals **h** flower, from front, with dilated petals **i** petals **j** pollinia **k** columns, from front and side **l** labella, from above and side **m** flower types, from side

Figs **a–e** natural size

330 *Pterostylis daintreana* (see also p. 90)

a b typical specimens **c** juvenile plant **d e** lateral tufts of leaves **f** pollinia **g h** labella, from side **i** labellum, from above **j** labellum, from below **k** petal
l winged stigma **m** column, from side **n** conjoined sepals, from inside
Figs **a–e** natural size

331 *Pterostylis vittata* (see also p. 90)

a fine specimen from Steiglitz, Vic.   **b** clavate hairs from column wings   **c** fine example from Black Rock, Vic.   **d** specimen from Airey's Inlet, Vic., showing a lateral growth of leaves   **e f** radical leaves—juvenile plants   **g** labellum of the Black Rock specimen, from above   **h** same labellum, from side   **i** apex of the same labellum   **j** petal of Black Rock specimen   **k** conjoined sepals from an Airey's Inlet flower

Figs **a**, **c–f** natural size

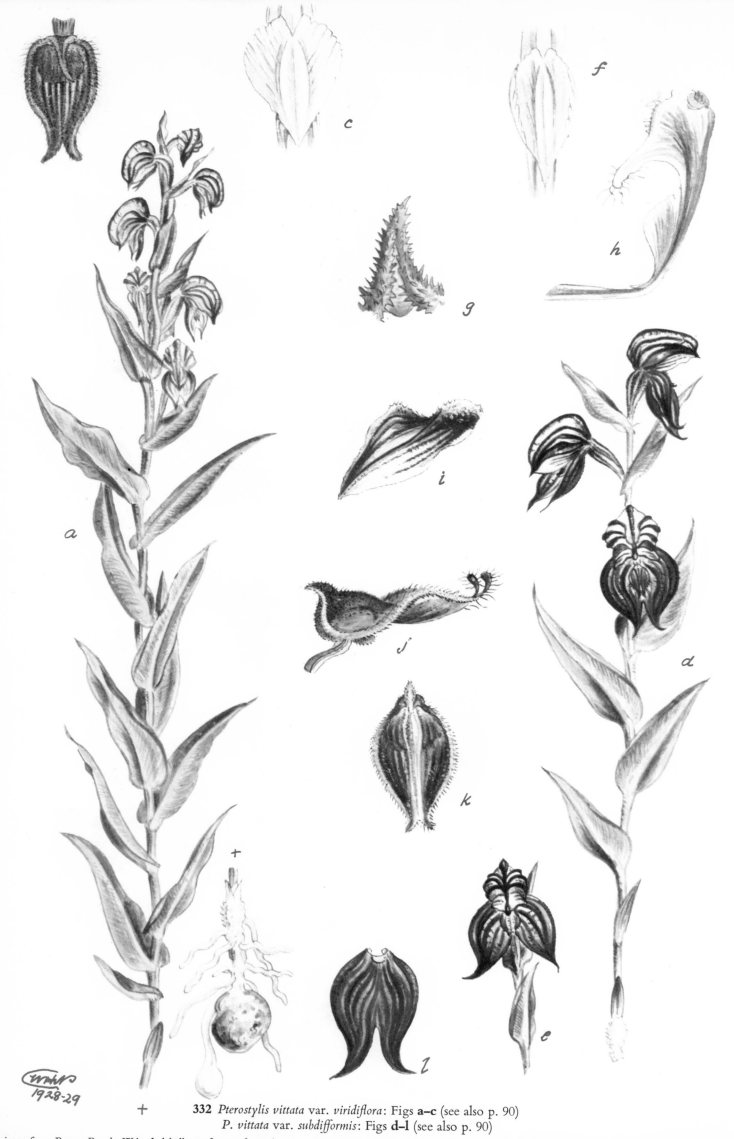

WDW 1928-29

332 *Pterostylis vittata* var. *viridiflora*: Figs **a–c** (see also p. 90)
P. vittata var. *subdifformis*: Figs **d–l** (see also p. 90)

a specimen from Boyup Brook, WA **b** labellum of same, from above **c** stigma **d e** specimens from Boyup Brook **f** stigma with incurved margins **g** appendage of
labellum **h** column, from side **i** petal **j** labellum, from side **k** labellum, from above **l** conjoined sepals
Figs **a, d, e** natural size

333 *Pterostylis longifolia* (see also p. 90)

a b two typical specimens **c** rostellum and anther, etc. **d** column, from side **e** petal **f** stigma **g** labellum, from above **h** labellum, from side
Figs **a, b** natural size

334 *Pterostylis longifolia* (see also p. 90)

a b two specimens from Were's Paddock, Greensborough, Vic. **c** capsules **d e f g h i j** juvenile plants (seedlings, etc.)

Figs **a–j** natural size

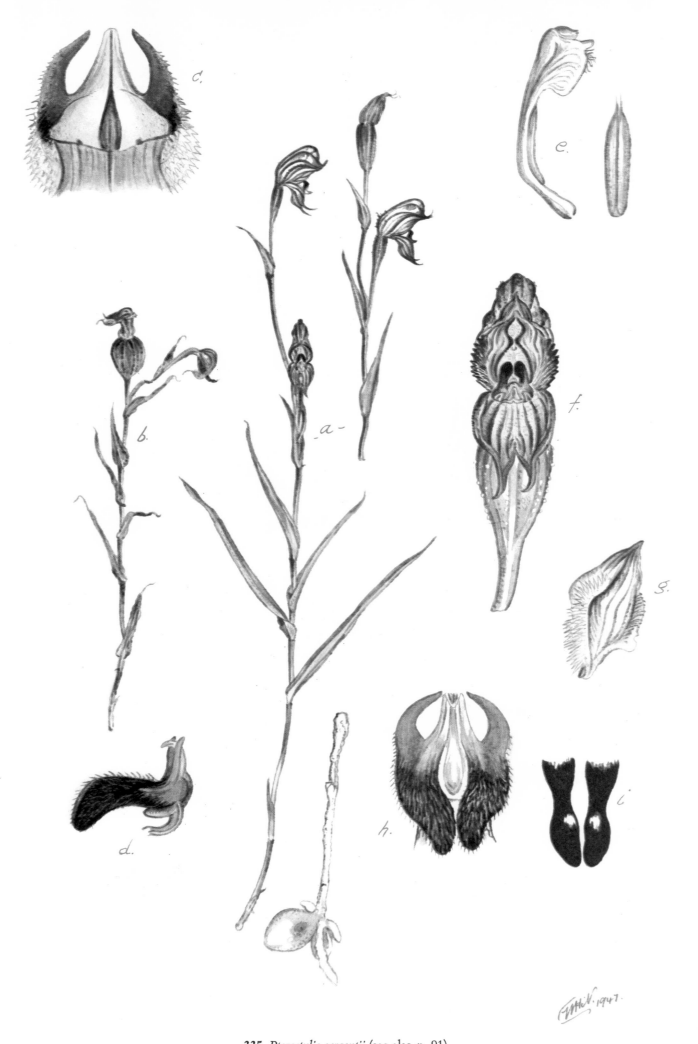

335 *Pterostylis sargentii* (see also p. 91)

a two specimens found in the Arrowsmith district, WA **b** fruiting specimen **c** labellum, from below **d** labellum, from side **e** column, from side, also stigma, from front
f flower, from front, showing serrated margins of petals, etc. **g** petal, showing rows of bristly hairs **h** labellum, from above **i** glabrous lobes of labellum
Figs **a, b** natural size

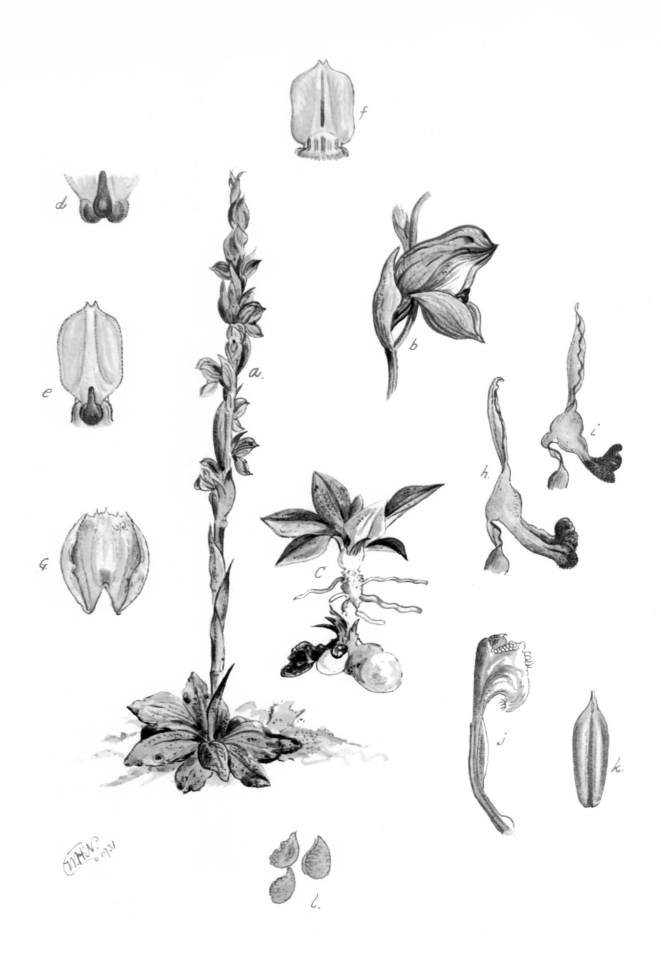

336 *Pterostylis cycnocephala* (see also p. 91)

a typical plant **b** flower from side **c** radical leaves, also tubers **d** labellum appendage **e** labellum, from above **f** labellum, from rear **g** conjoined sepals **h** **i** labella, from side (note variation and see also Figs **d** and **e**) **j** column, from side **k** stigma **l** pollinia

Figs **a**, **c** natural size

337 *Pterostylis mutica* (see also p. 91)

a b the common form of the basalt plains near Footscray, Vic.   **c** specimen from Barellan, NSW   **d** capsules   **e f** labella, from front (note variation in the appendage)
g labellum, from above   **h** labellum, from rear   **i** labellum, from side   **j** appendage of the labellum   **k** tubers   **l** flower, from side   **m n** tips of conjoined sepals   **o p** varying stigma shapes   **q** column, from side   **r** pollinia
Figs **a–d, k** natural size

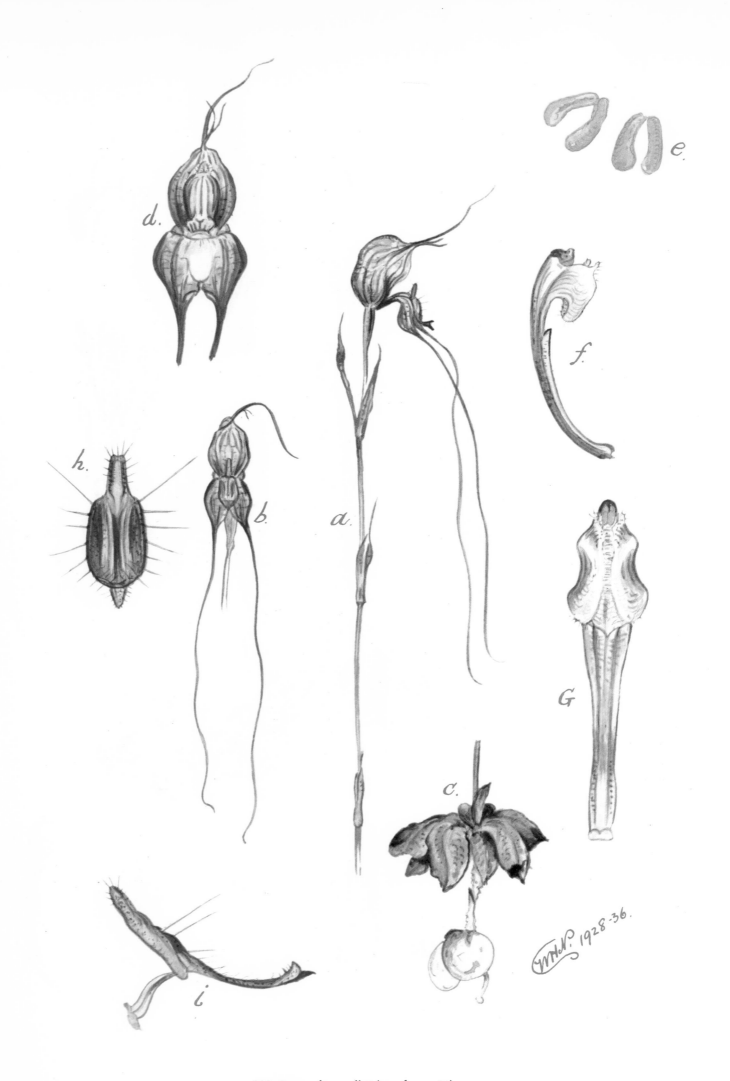

338 *Pterostylis woollsii* (see also p. 92)

a the Rushworth, Vic., specimen **b** flower, from front **c** leaves and tubers **d** flower, from front, lower sepals shortened, the labellum in the closed position **e** pollinia
f column, from side **g** same from front, showing ciliate upper lobes of the wings **h** labellum, from above **i** labellum, from side
Figs **a–c** natural size

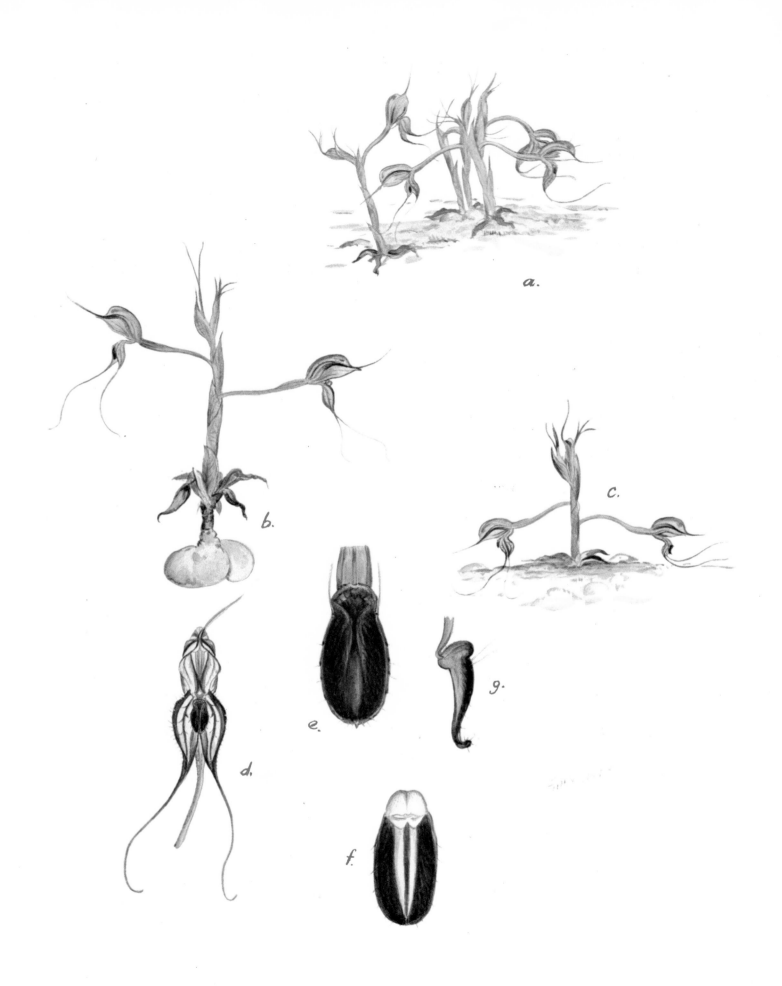

339 *Pterostylis biseta* (see also Plate **340,** Figs **a-d, f-i, l-r,** and p. 92)

a flowering plants from Maryborough, Vic. **b** single plant **c** single plant showing the habit sometimes assumed by the species **d** flower, from front **e** labellum, from above **f** labellum, from below **g** labellum, from side

Figs **a-c** natural size

340 *Pterostylis biseta*: Figs **a–d, f–i, l–r** (see also Plate **339** and p. 92)
P. gibbosa ssp. *mitchellii*: Figs **e, j, k** (see also p. 92)

a specimen from Creswick, Vic.   **b** specimen from St Arnaud, Vic.   **c d** two very fine plants from Bendigo, Vic.   **e** a Qld specimen from Burleigh Heads   **f** radical rosette
g pollinia   **h** labellum, from side, specimen from Bendigo, Vic.   **i** same, from above   **j** labellum, from side, Qld specimen   **k** same, from above   **l m** labella, from below,
of Bendigo specimens—cilia removed   **n** same, from above   **o** petal   **p** column, from front (base not shown)   **q** column, from side   **r** robust rosette showing tubers,
from Bendigo
Figs **a–f, r** natural size

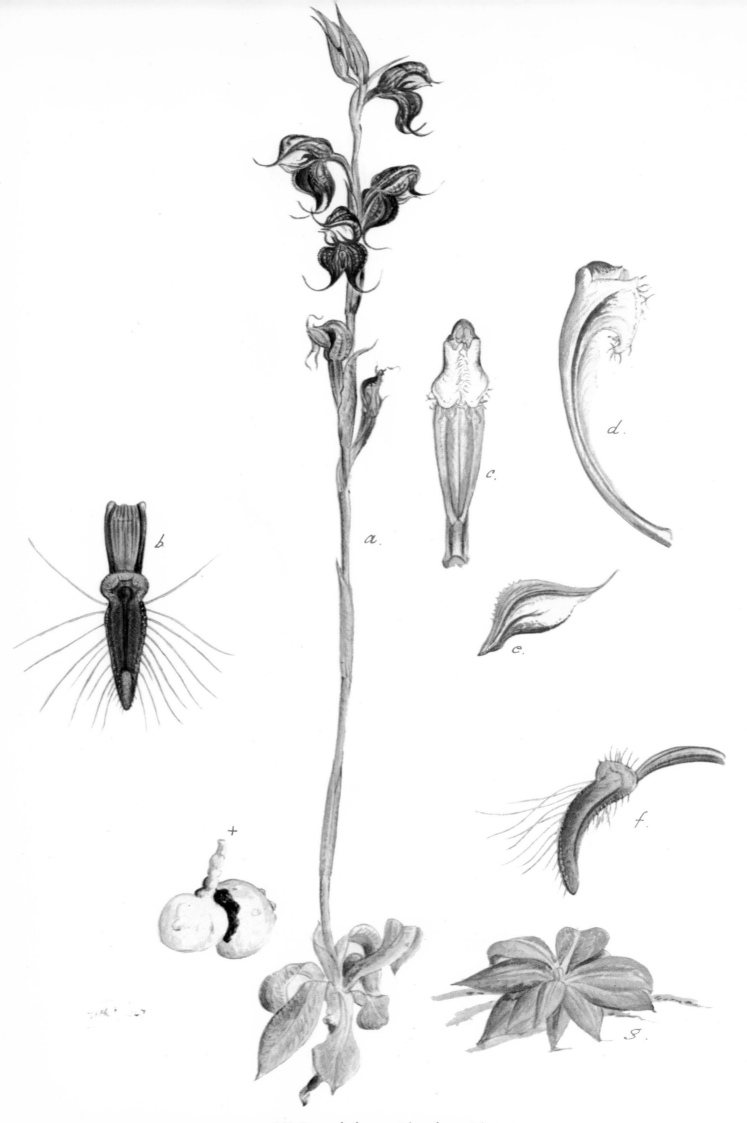

341 *Pterostylis boormanii* (see also p. 93)

a Peak Hill, NSW, specimen **b** labellum and claw, from above **c** column, from front **d** column, from side **e** petal **f** labellum and claw, from side **g** radical rosette
Figs **a**, **g** natural size

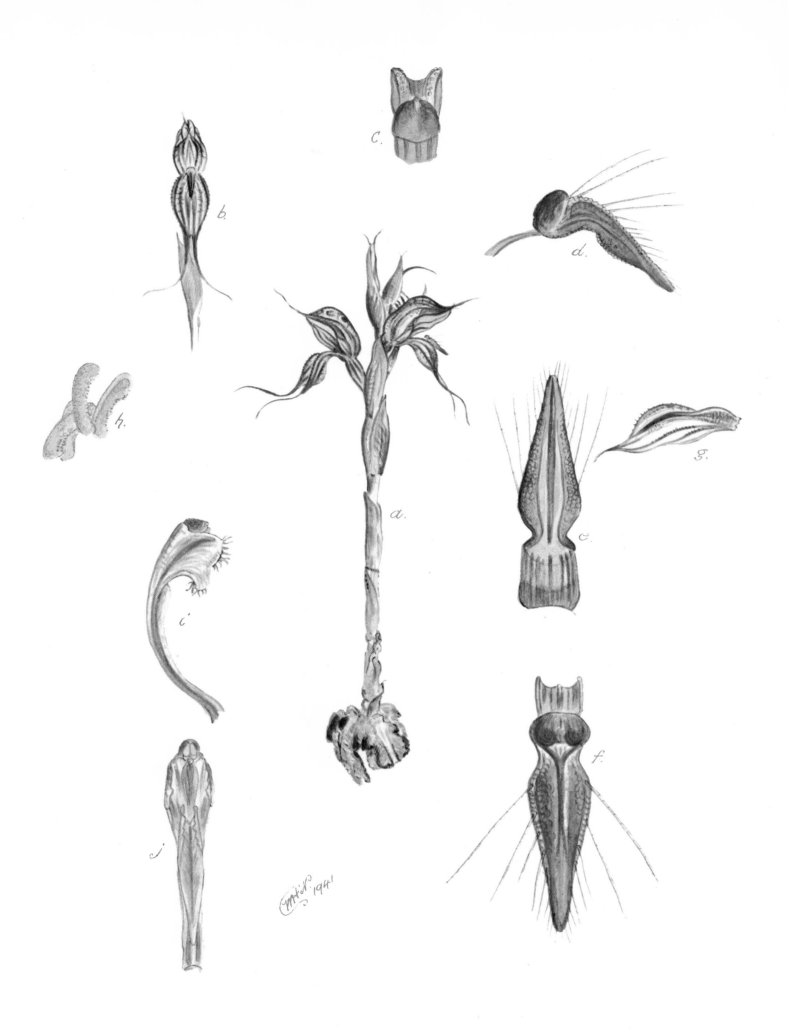

342 *Pterostylis boormanii* (see also p. 93)

(see also p. 93)

a typical specimen **b** flower, from front **c** labellum from rear, cilia not shown **d** labellum, from side **e** labellum, from below **f** labellum, from above **g** petal **h** pollinia
i column, from side **j** column, from front—wings removed
Fig. **a** natural size

343 *Pterostylis rufa* ssp. *rufa*: Figs **a–g, i–r, t, u** (see also p. 93)
P. rufa ssp. *aciculiformis*: Figs **h, s** (see also p. 93)

a specimen from Rushworth, Vic.   **b** flower, from side   **c** flower, from front   **d** labellum, from above   **e** labellum, from side   **f g** the common Vic. form   **h** flowering plant   **i** deep red form, formerly *P. pusilla* var. *prominens*   **j** column, from side   **k** labellum, from side, specimen from Vic.   **l** pollinia   **m** petal   **n** stigma   **o** labellum, from above   **p** labellum, from below   **q r** labella, from above   **s** labellum, from above   **t** labellum (as Fig. **d**) from below   **u** figures showing the variable labellum cilia
Figs **a, f–i** natural size

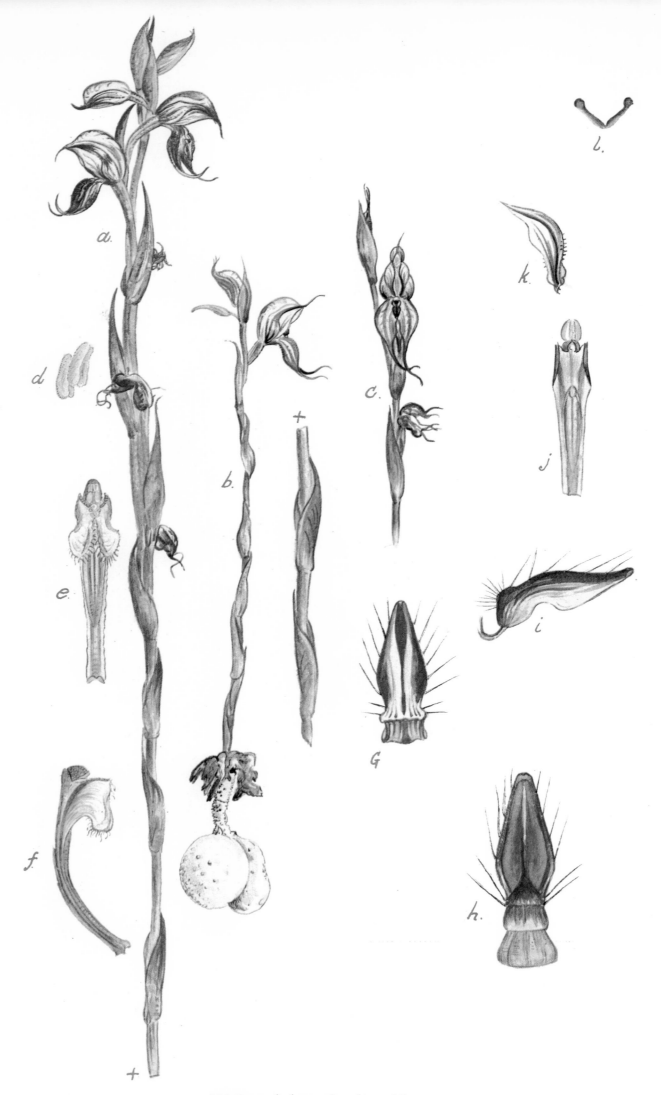

344 *Pterostylis hamata* (see also p. 93)

a sturdy specimen from Benalla, Vic. **b** another Benalla specimen **c** flower, from front **d** pollinia **e** column, from front **f** column, from side **g** labellum, from below
h labellum, from above **i** labellum, from side **j** rostellum and (above) the anther-case **k** petal **l** deep channel of the labellum lamina
Figs **a–c** natural size

345 *Pterostylis barbata* (see also p. 94)

a rare two-flowered specimen **b** leafy example **c** flower, from rear **d** flower, from side (labellum withdrawn into galea) **e** labellum **f** labellum appendage **g** pollinia
h column, from side (lower part of labellum shown) **i** head of column, from front—wings removed to show rostellum, etc.
Figs **a–d** natural size

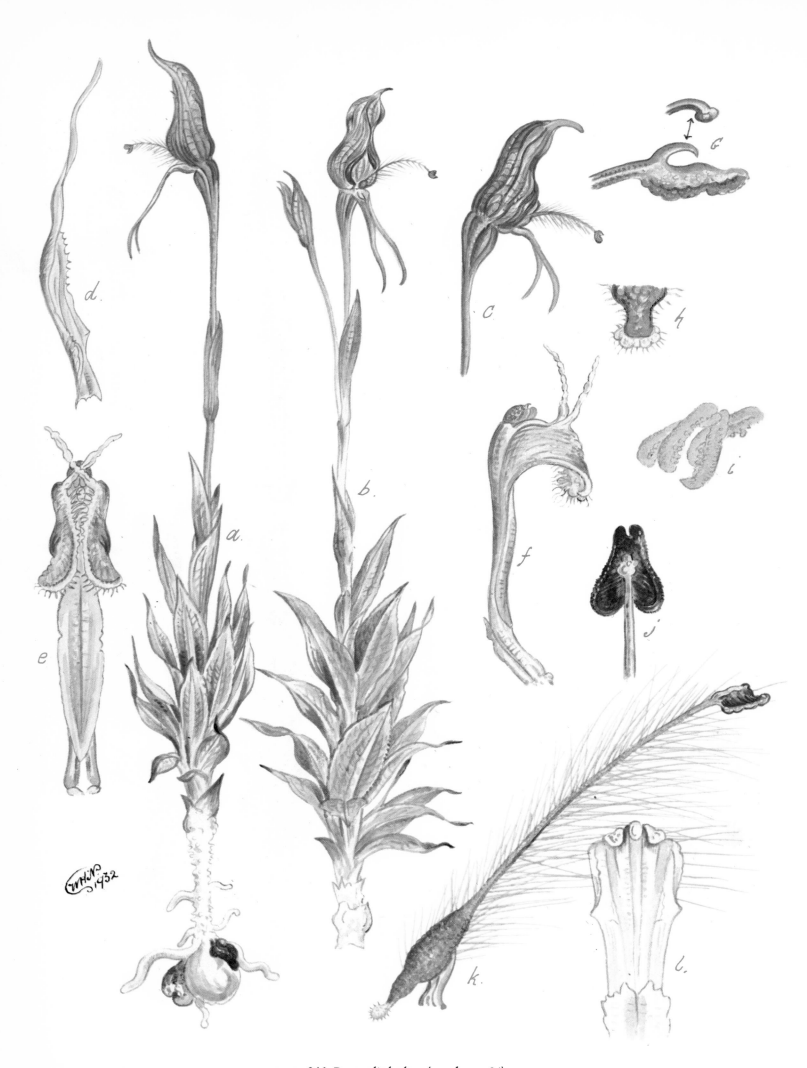

346 *Pterostylis barbata* (see also p. 94)

a b typical specimens **c** flower of a robust specimen from Airey's Inlet, Vic. **d** petal **e** column, from front **f** column, from side **g** labellum appendage (note variation)
h basal appendage of labellum **i** pollinia **j** labellum appendage, from above **k** labellum **l** upper margin of stigma, rostellum, etc.
Figs **a–c** natural size

347 *Galeola cassythoides* (see also p. 94)

a portion of plant with racemes of flowers, also buds and rootlets with portions of bark of support attached **b** flower, from front **c** labellum, from side **d** labellum, from above (spread out) **e** column, from side **f** column, from front **g** pollinia
Fig. **a** natural size

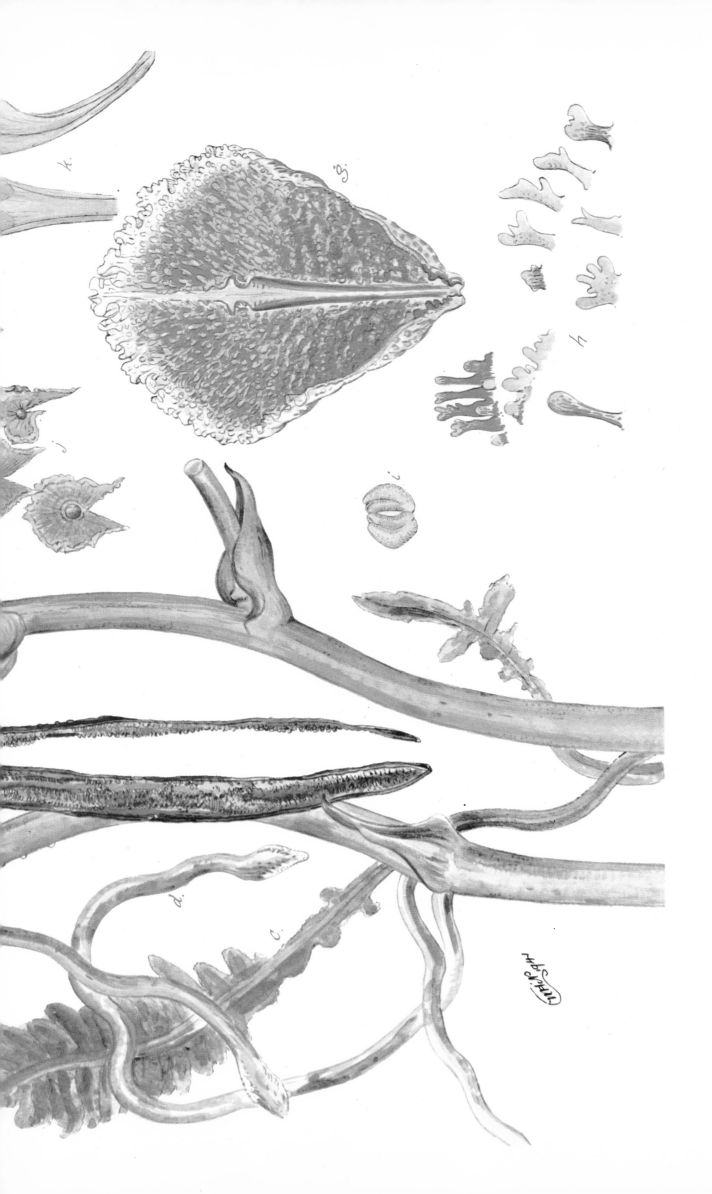

348 *Galeola foliata* (see also p. 94)

a small panicle of bloom b young shoot c climbing roots d undeveloped root tips e ripe capsule f labellum and column, from side g labellum, spread out h calli
types i pollinia j seeds k column, from front and side
Figs **a–e** natural size

349 *Epipogium roseum* (see also p. 95)

a specimen from Chuchaba, Qld **b** flower, from front **c** labellum and column, from side **d** flower, from side **e** labellum, from above, from Chuchaba, Qld **f** anther, opened out **g** column, from side **h** column, from front **i** pollinia **j** abnormal floral bract **k** turgid ovary and withered flower **l** cross-section of peduncle **m** specimen from Tambourine North, Qld **n** interior of rhizome **o** labellum, from above, Tambourine North

Figs **a, b, m, n** natural size

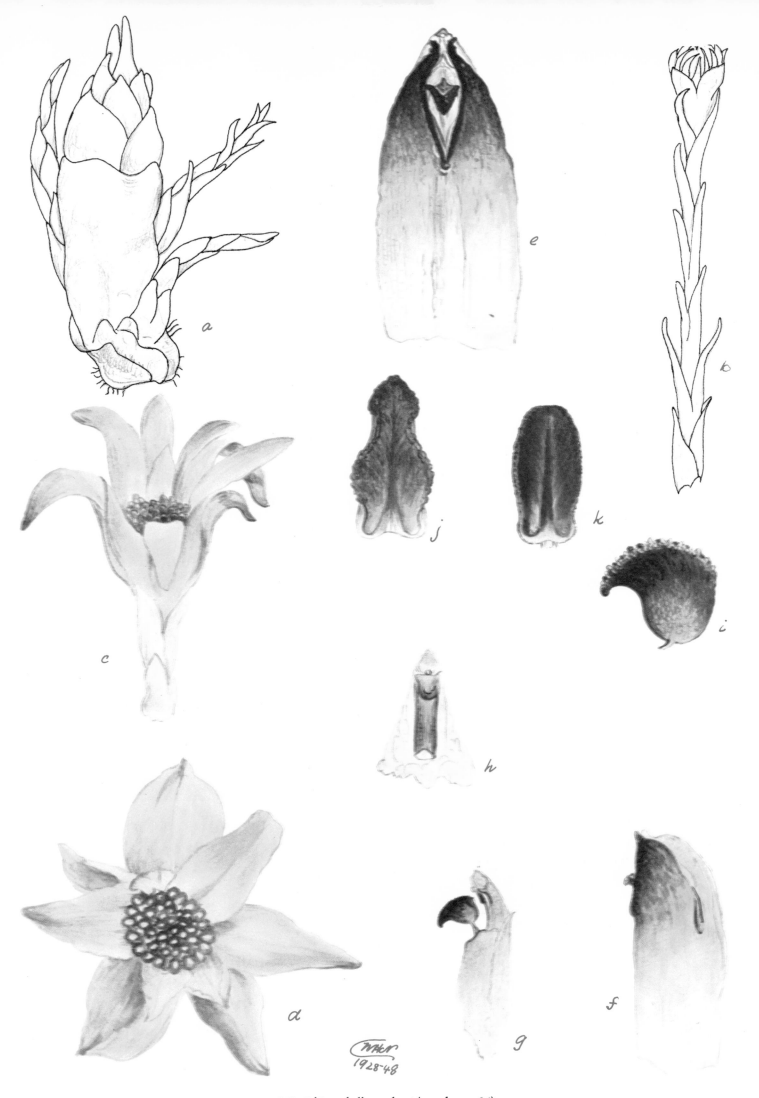

351 *Rhizanthella gardneri* (see also p. 96)

a main system, showing terminal bud and lateral branches **b** a slender scape with terminal bud from 20 cm. below ground-level **c** capitulum, from side **d** capitulum, from above **e** flower, from front **f** flower, from side **g** column, labellum, and ovary from side **h** column, from front, showing anther and stigma—remains of dorsal sepal at back **i** labellum, from side **j** labellum, from above **k** another labellum from above

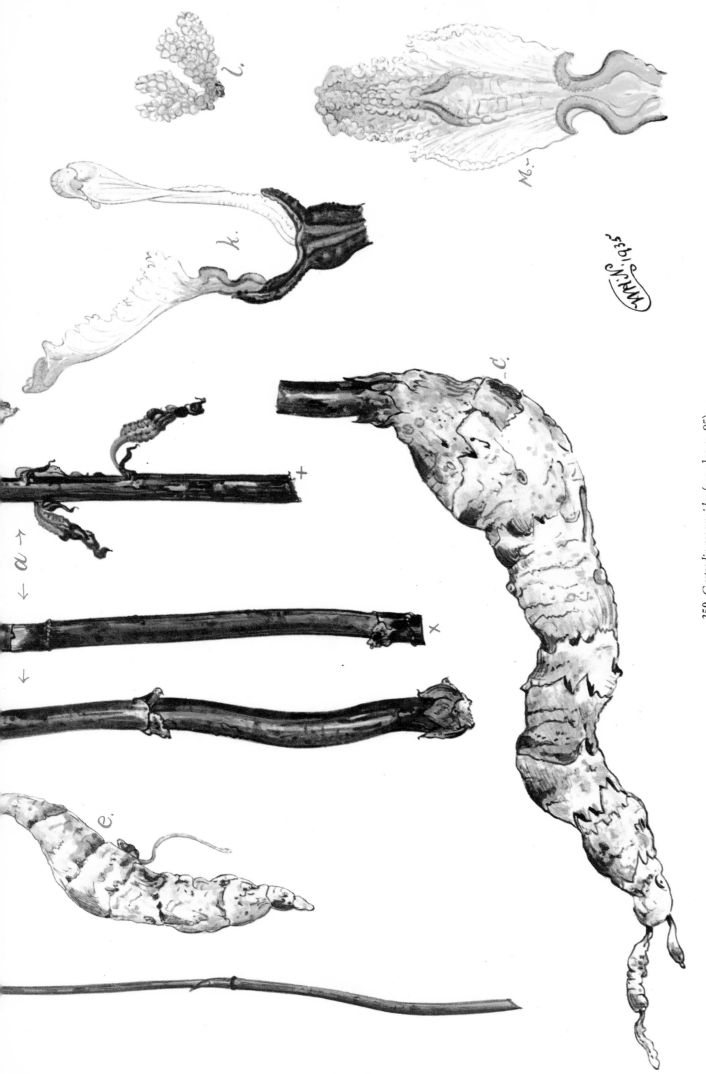

350 *Gastrodia sesamoides* (see also p. 95)

a sturdy mountain specimen from the Acheron Valley, Vic. **b** capsules **c** underground system **d** small specimen from near Mt Howitt, Vic. **e** rhizome, with rootlet **f** flower, from side **g** anther **h** perianth opened out **i** flower, from below **j** column, from front **k** labellum and column, from front **k** labellum, from below **j** column, from side **l** pollinia **m** labellum, from above **n** seeds

Figs **a–e** natural size

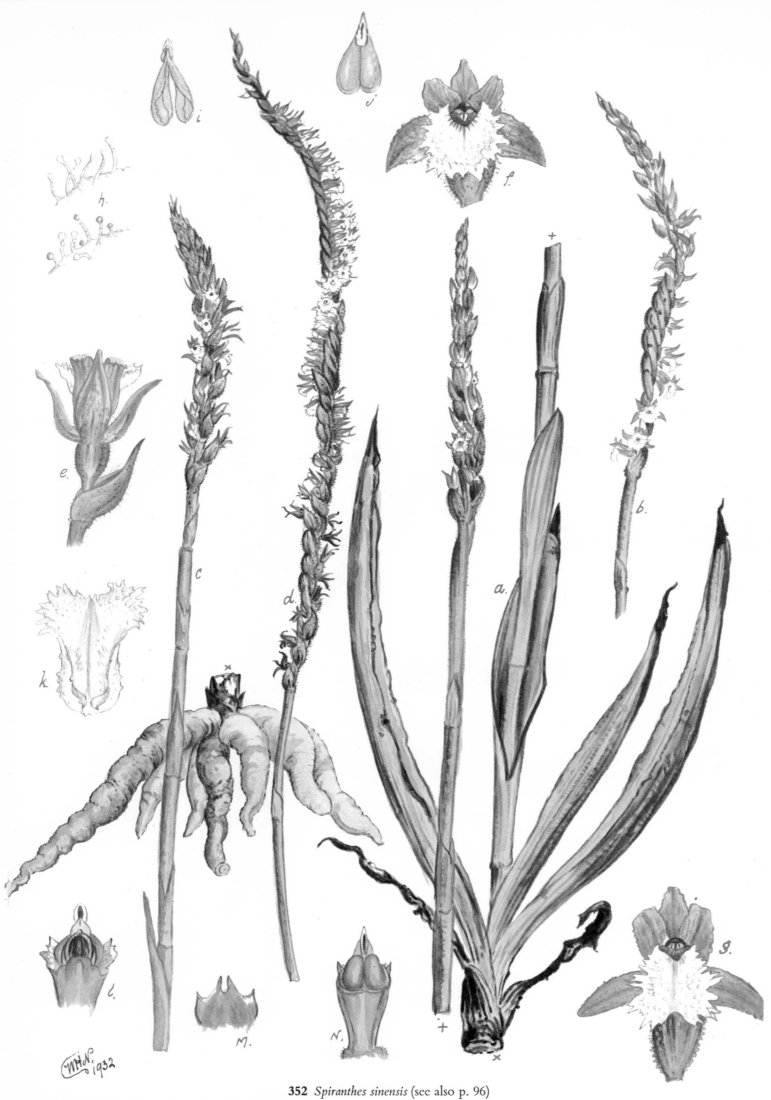

352 *Spiranthes sinensis* (see also p. 96)

a b c d typical specimens **e** flower, from above **f g** flowers, from front **h** hairs from the perianth segments **i j** pollinia **k** labellum, from above **l** column, from above **m** figure, showing rostellum **n** column, from front
Figs **a–d** natural size

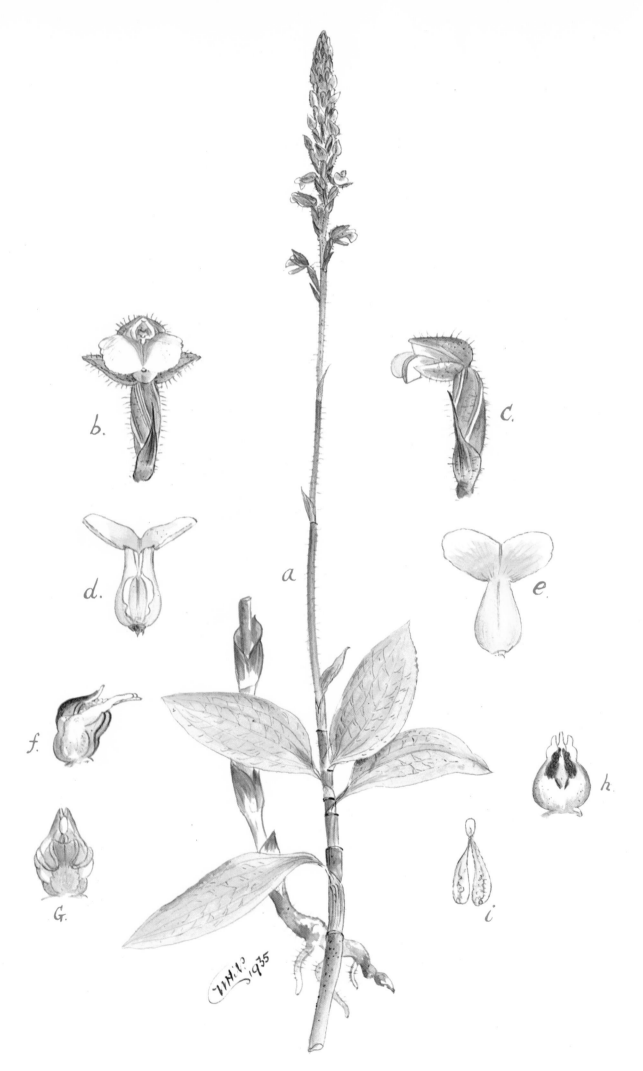

353 *Zeuxine oblonga* (see also p. 97)

a specimen from the Proserpine district, Qld **b** flower, from front **c** flower, from side **d** labellum, from above **e** labellum, from below **f** column, from side **g** column, from front **h** column, from rear **i** pollinia

Fig. **a** natural size

355 *Malaxis latifólia* (see also p. 98)

a typical specimen from Mt Fox, Qld **b** flower, from front **c** apex of labellum **d** flower, from side **e** column and labellum, from above **f** pollinia **g** lateral sepals and labellum, from below **h** **i** column, from front (appendages obsolete) **j** head of column, showing prominent appendages **k** raceme of flowers **l** flower, from below
m capsule **n** conjoined lateral sepals
Figs **a**, **k** natural size

354 *Hetaeria polygonoides* (see also p. 97)

a flowering plant **b** flower, from front **c** flower, from side **d** dorsal sepal and petals **e** same, from side, showing bract enclosing ovary **f** lateral sepal **g** column, from front **h** same, with rostellum folded back to show pollinia and stigma **i j** labella, from above

Fig. **a** natural size

356 *Pholidota pallida* (see also p. 98)

a specimen from Mt Fox, Qld **b** flower, from front **c** column appendage **d** pollinia **e** pollinia attached to upper margin of stigma
Fig. **a** natural size

357 *Liparis coelogynoides* (see also p. 99)

a small plant with racemes **b** capsules **c** flower, from front **d** column, from side **e** pollinia **f** cross-section of the winged peduncle **g** sepal **h** labellum, from above
i labellum, from side
Figs **a, b** natural size

358 *Liparis reflexa*: Figs **a–j** (see also p. 99)
L. reflexa var. *parviflora*: Figs **k, l** (see also p. 99)

a typical plant **b** flower, freshly expanded **c** flower about to unfold its segments **d** flower with its segments reflexed **e** base of labellum **f** pollinia **g** capsule **h** labellum, from side **i** head of column—anther removed **j** column, from side **k l** flowers
Figs **a, k** natural size

359 *Liparis cuneilabris* (see also p. 99)

a typical plant with racemes from Mt Fox, Qld **b** flower **c** flower with reflexed perianth **d** labellum, from side **e** column, from side **f** pollinia **g** head of column, anther removed
Fig. **a** natural size

360 *Liparis fleckeri* (see also p. 99)

a plant with raceme of bloom **b** flower, showing variation at apex of labellum **c** labellum, from rear, showing glands **d** labellum, from side, of a freshly expanded flower
e labellum glands, from front **f** column, from side **g** head of column, from front **h** pollinia **i** labellum, from side
Fig. **a** natural size

361 *Liparis bracteata* (see also p. 99)

a flowering plant **b** flower, from front **c** labellum, from above, showing basal calli
Fig. **a** natural size

362 *Liparis nugentae* (see also p. 100)

a flowering plant **b** flowers **c** flower, from above **d** column, from front **e** pollinia **f** labellum, from above
Fig. **a** natural size

363 *Liparis habenarina* (see also p. 100)

a Qld specimen **b** labellum, from above **c** flower, from side **d** conjoined lateral sepals **e** pollinia—one pair from three angles **f** dorsal sepal, from above **g** petal, from a bud **h** column, from side **i** column, from front **j** flower, from front
Fig. **a** natural size

364 *Oberonia muellerana* (see also p. 100)

a **b** typical plants, in bud and in fruit **c** raceme of flowers **d** flower, from front **e** flower and bract, from side **f** labellum, from side **g** anther—pollinia removed
h column, from front **i** pollinia **j** bracts **k** capsules
Figs **a, c** natural size

G.

h.

366 *Phaius australis* (see also p. 101)

a flowering plant from south-eastern Qld   b flower, from front   c labellum, from front   d flower, from rear, showing portion of perianth   e head of column, from front, showing stigma appendage   f head of column—anther removed to show pollinia   g pollinium   h head of column, from front, from a bud

Figs **a, b, d** natural size

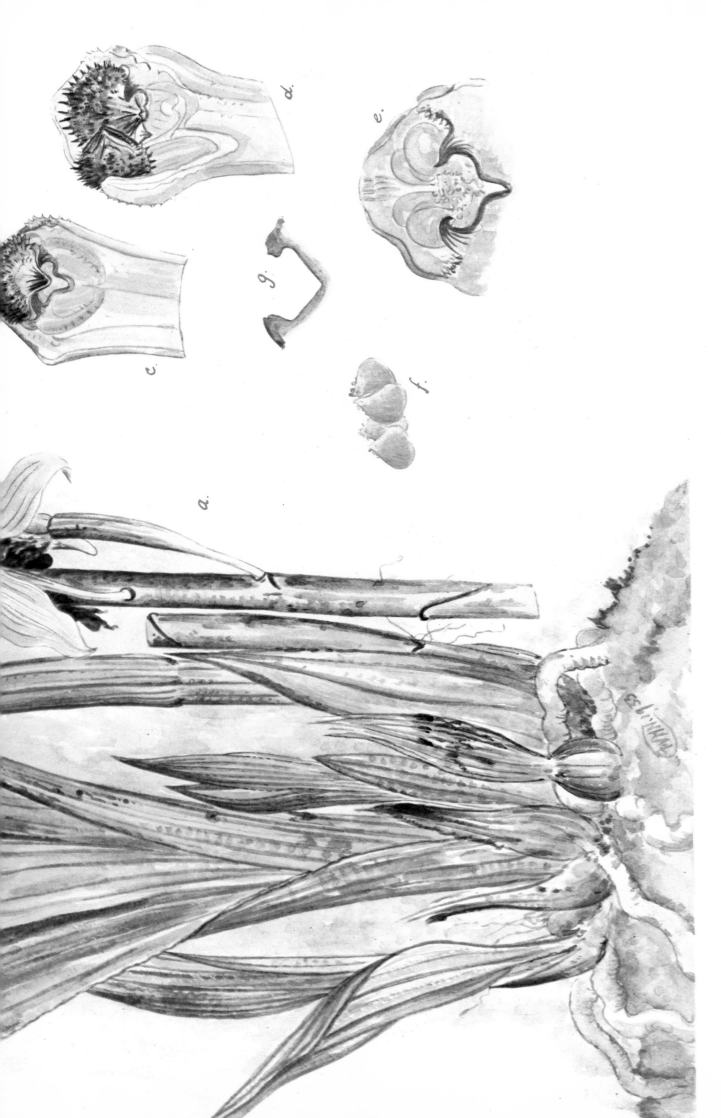

367 *Phaius australis* var. *bernaysii* (see also p. 101)

a flowering plant b labellum, from above, lobes flattened out c head of column, from front d same, showing development of a supplementary anther (staminode) e head of column—anther removed to show stigma appendage and pollinia in position f pollinia g stigma appendage

Fig. **a** natural size

368 *Phaius tankervilliae* (see also p. 101)

a flowering plant   b column, from front, showing labellum spur at base   c plate from labellum lamina   d head of column, from front, showing rostellum and anther   e pollinia
f variation in tip of spur
Fig. **a** natural size

369 *Calanthe triplicata* (see also p. 102)

a small plant, with flowers **b** flower, showing blackened segments caused by handling **c** flower, from below **d** flower, from front **e** callosities **f** pollinia

Figs **a**, **b** natural size

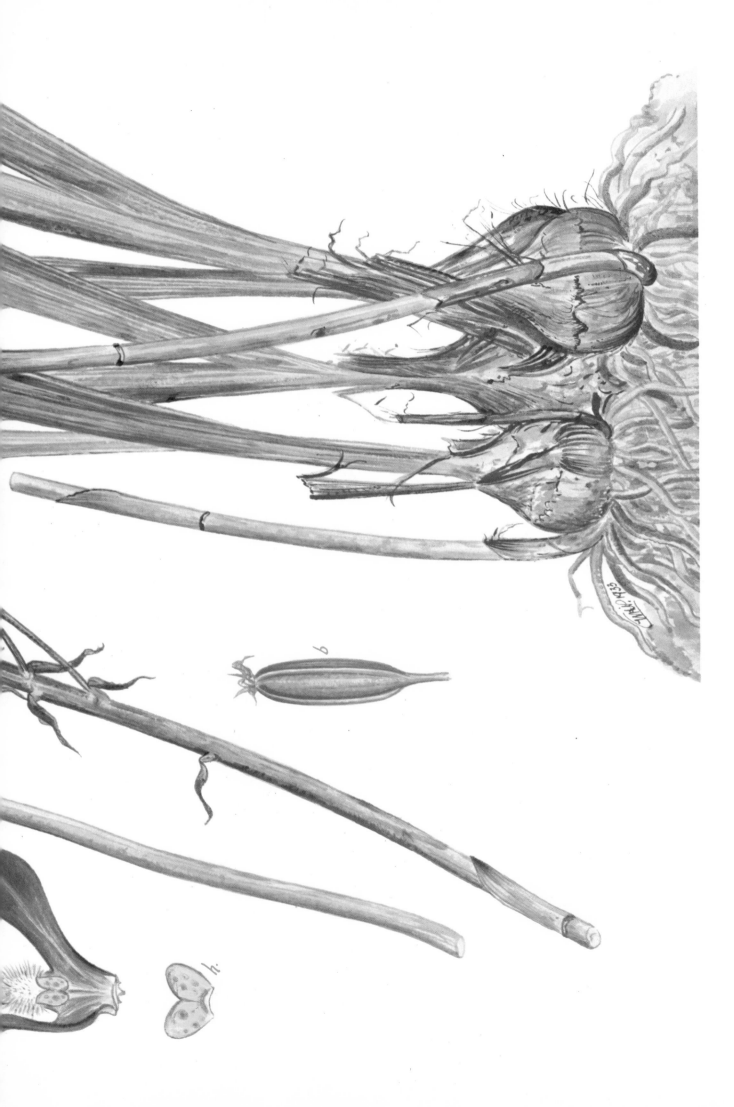

370 *Spathoglottis paulinae* (see also p. 102)

a plant with raceme of flowers, also capsules   **b** ripened capsule of seed   **c** pollinia   **d** column, from side   **e** head of column, from front   **f** rostellum   **g** labellum, from above, one lobe spread out   **h** calli from the labellum

Figs **a**, **b** natural size

365 *Oberonia palmicola* (see also p. 100)

a b typical plants **c** racemes of flowers **d** flowers **e f** flowers, from front **g** flower expanding **h** capsule **i** cross-section of a leaf **j** column, from front and side **k** pollinia

Figs **a–c** natural size

371 *Spathoglottis paulinae* (see also p. 102)

a flowering plant **b** raceme of flowers **c** labellum, from above, lobes spread out **d** column, from front **e** head of column, from side **f** pollinia
Figs **a, b** natural size

372 *Geodorum pictum* (see also p. 103)

a plant from Tambourine North, Qld b labellum, from above, also variation of tip c flower, from front, the labellum removed d labellum, from side e another labellum, from above f column, from side g anther h head of column, from front, showing stigma—anther removed i pollinia j head of column, from side, the anther raised to show pollinia

Fig. **a** natural size

373 *Epidendrum × obrienianum* (see also p. 103)

a plant with raceme of flowers **b** flower, from above **c** labellum and head of column, oblique view **d** pollinia **e** pollinia enclosed in rostellum
Fig. **a** natural size

374 *Dendrobium lichenastrum* var. *lichenastrum*: Figs **a–j** (see also p. 103)
D. lichenastrum var. *prenticei* forma *aurantiaco-purpureum*: Figs **k–q** (see also p. 104)

a typical plant **b** leaves, etc. **c** column, from front **d** column, from side—anther removed **e** pollinia **f** flower, from side **g** labellum, from above **h** flower, from front **i** base of leaf and petioles **j** leaves **k** small plant **l** flower, from front **m** flower, from side **n** labellum, from above **o** column, from front **p** column, from side—anther removed **q** pollinia

Figs **a, j, k** natural size

375 *Dendrobium lichenastrum* var. *prenticei* forma *prenticei* (see also p. 104)

a typical plant **b** leaf **c** flower, from side **d** flower, from front **e f** labella, from above and side **g** column, from front **h** pollinia **i** leaf petioles
Fig. **a** natural size

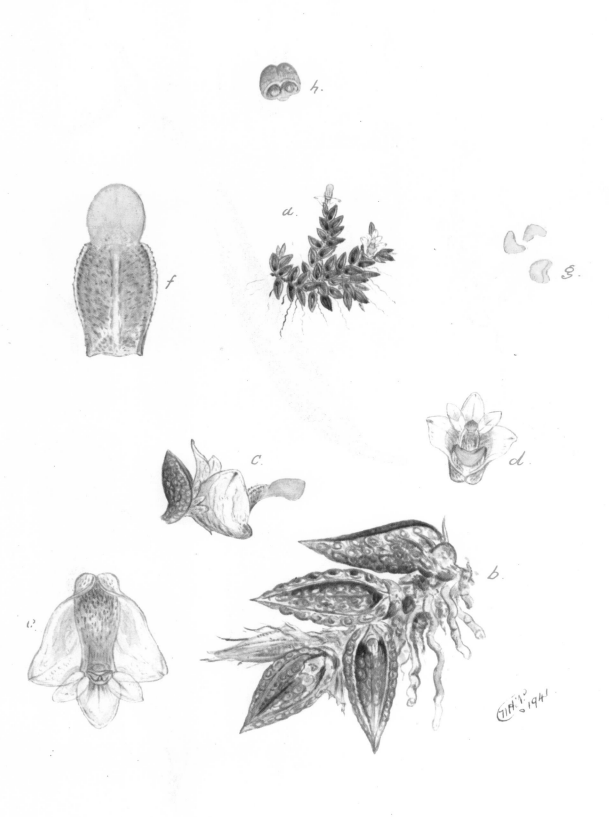

376 *Dendrobium toressae* (see also p. 104)

a a plant in bloom from Upper Mossman River, Qld   **b** leaves, etc.   **c** flower and leaf, from side   **d** flower, from front   **e** flower with labellum and anther removed
f labellum, from above   **g** pollinia   **h** anther
Fig. **a** natural size

377 *Dendrobium rigidum* (see also p. 104)

a typical plant **b** flower **c** labellum, from side **d** labellum, from above **e** column, from side **f** column from front **g** flower, from side **h** pollinia
Fig. **a** natural size

378 *Dendrobium cucumerinum* (see also p. 104)

a typical plant with flowers **b** labellum, from above, mid-lobe spread out **c** portion of flower, from rear **d** pollinia **e** column, from side—anther removed **f** flower, from above **g** column, from front
Fig. **a** natural size

379 *Dendrobium linguiforme* (see also p. 105)

a specimen plant from southern Qld **b** labellum, from front **c** labellum, from above **d** labellum, from side **e** column, from front **f** capsule **g** pollinia
Fig. **a** natural size

380 *Dendrobium linguiforme* var. *nugentii* (see also p. 105)

a typical plant, showing raceme **b** leaves **c** flower **d** column **e** pollinia **f** labellum, from side **g** labellum, from above
Fig. **a** natural size

381 *Dendrobium pugioniforme* (see also p. 105)

a portion of plant in bloom **b** pollinia **c** leaves, typical and abnormal **d** head of column, from front **e** head of column, from side—anther removed **f** labellum spread out, from above **g** flower **h** markings on perianth segments, from below

Figs **a, c** natural size

382 *Dendrobium striolatum* (see also p. 105)

a small portion of plant with flowers **b** foliage and flowers from a Tas. plant **c** column, from front **d** column, from side—anther removed **e** labellum, from side **f** labellum, from above **g** lateral sepal with broad stripes **h** pollinia **i** apex of labellum
Fig. **a** natural size

383 *Dendrobium mortii* (see also p. 105)

a typical plant with flowers **b** cross-section of leaf **c** anther with pollinia in position **d** petal **e** column, from side **f** column, from front **g** flower **h** labellum
Fig. **a** natural size

384 *Dendrobium tenuissimum* (see also p. 106)

a small plant with flowers **b** flower, from rear **c** flower, from front **d** labellum, from above, apex not visible **e** pollinia **f** head of column, from side—anther removed
g column, from front
Fig. **a** natural size

386 *Dendrobium beckleri* (see also p. 106)

a typical plant from Tambourine North, Qld   **b   c** flower types   **d** labellum, lobes spread out   **e** column, from side   **f** pollinia
Fig. **a** natural size

385 *Dendrobium racemosum* (see also p. 106)

a plant in bloom **b** flower, from front **c** labellum, from above—lateral lobes flattened **d** pollinia **e** column, from front **f** head of column, from side—anther removed

Fig. **a** natural size

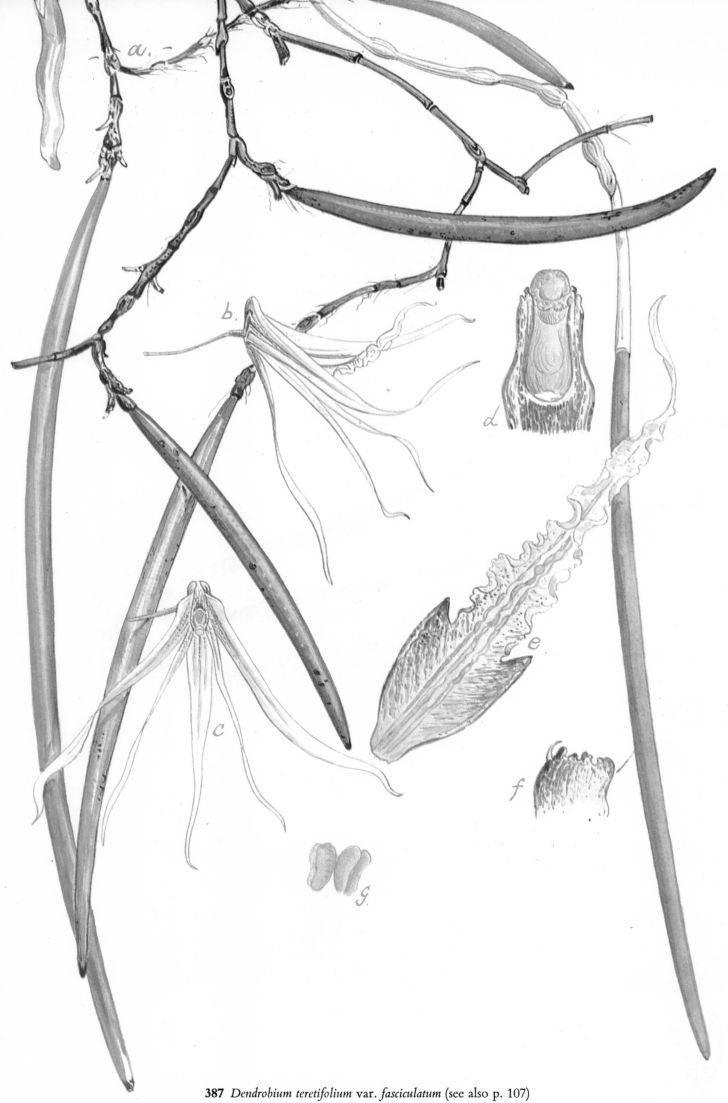

387 *Dendrobium teretifolium* var. *fasciculatum* (see also p. 107)

a small portion of plant, showing roots, leaves, etc.   b flower, from side   c flower, from front, labellum removed   d column, from front   e labellum, from above, lobes spread out   f head of column—anther removed   g pollinia

Fig. **a** natural size

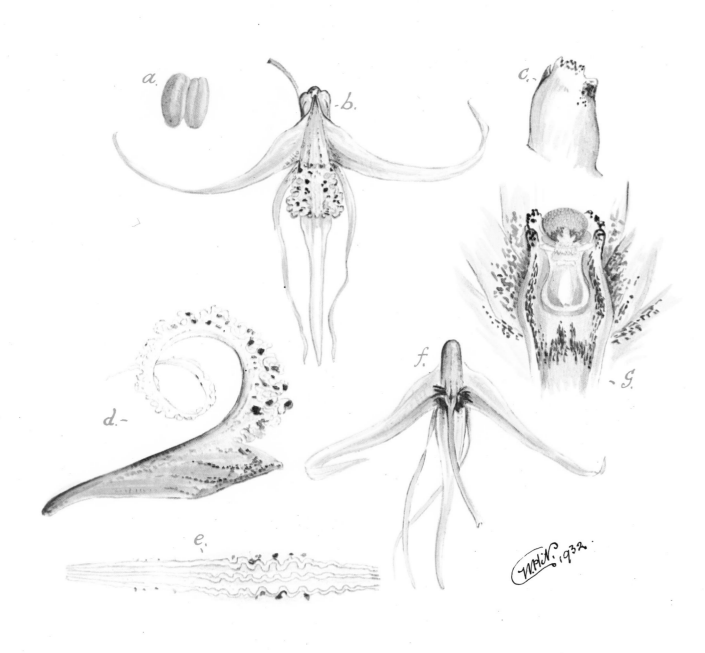

388 *Dendrobium teretifolium* var. *fairfaxii* (see also p. 107)

a pollinia   **b** flower, from front   **c** head of column, from side—anther removed   **d** labellum, from side   **e** callus ridges   **f** flower, from rear   **g** column and portion of perianth, from front

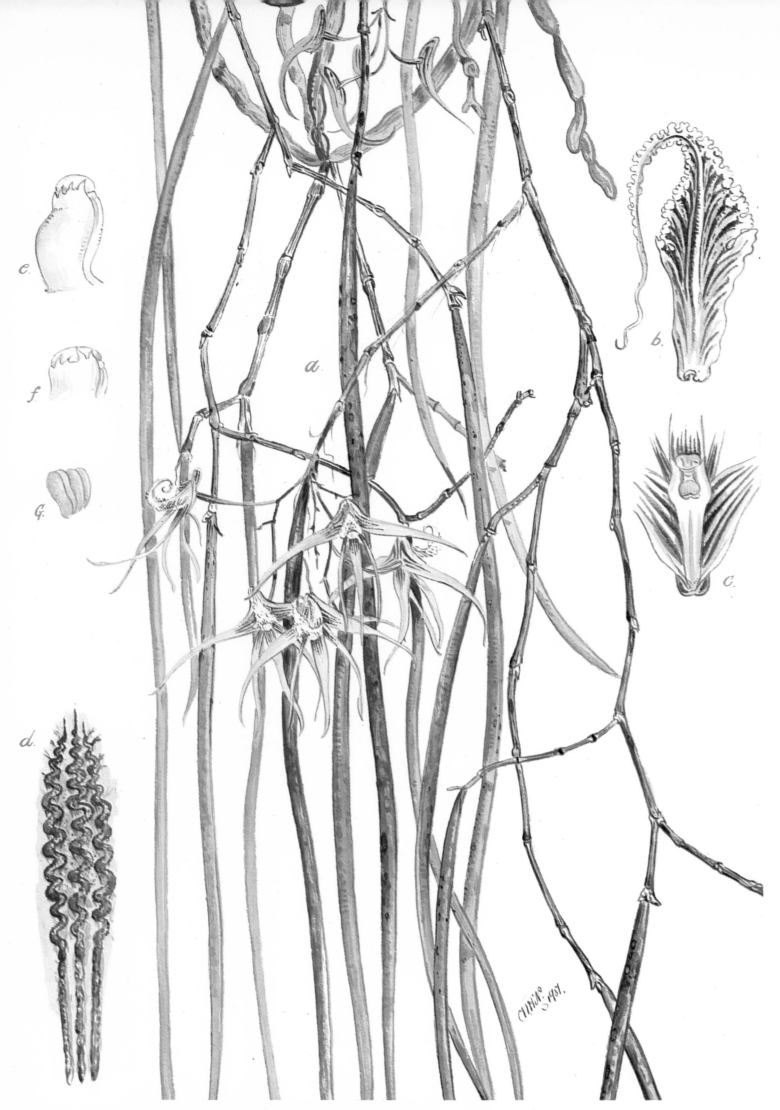

389 *Dendrobium teretifolium* var. *fairfaxii* forma *aureum* (see also p. 107)

a portion of plant, showing leaves, flowers, etc. **b** labellum, showing reverse markings **c** column and portion of perianth, from front **d** callus plates **e** column, from side
f head of column, from side **g** pollinia
Fig. **a** natural size

390 *Dendrobium monophyllum* (see also p. 107)

a portion of plant with flowers   **b** flower, from below   **c** flower, from front   **d** pollinia   **e** labellum, from above   **f** column, from front
Fig. **a** natural size

391 *Dendrobium schneiderae* (see also p. 107)

a colony of pseudobulbs with racemes **b** flower, from front **c** flower, from side **d** labellum, from above **e** column, from front
Fig. **a** natural size

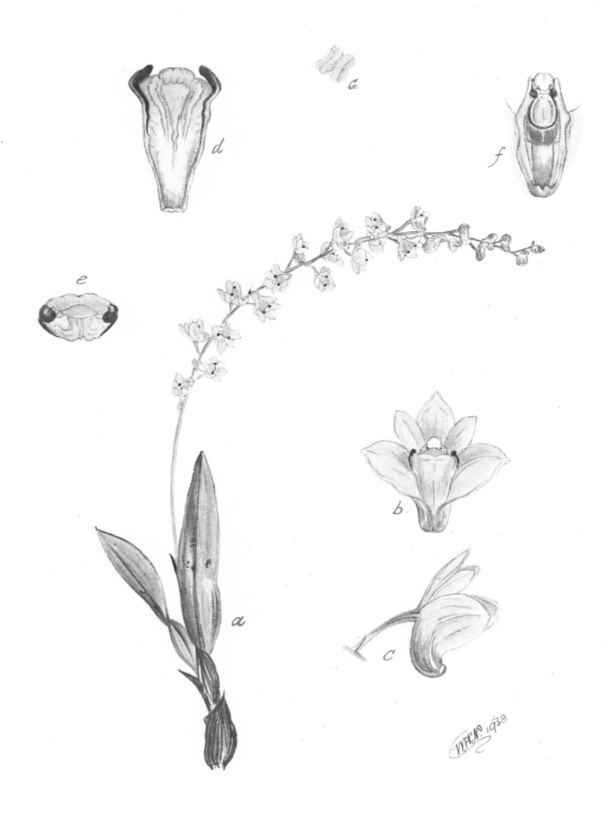

392 *Dendrobium schneiderae* (see also p. 107)

a flowering stem from Mackay, Qld **b** flower, from front **c** flower, from side **d** labellum, from above **e** labellum, end view **f** column, from front **g** pollinia
Fig. **a** natural size

393 *Dendrobium kingianum* (see also p. 107)

A specimen plant from Tambourine North, Qld
Fig. natural size

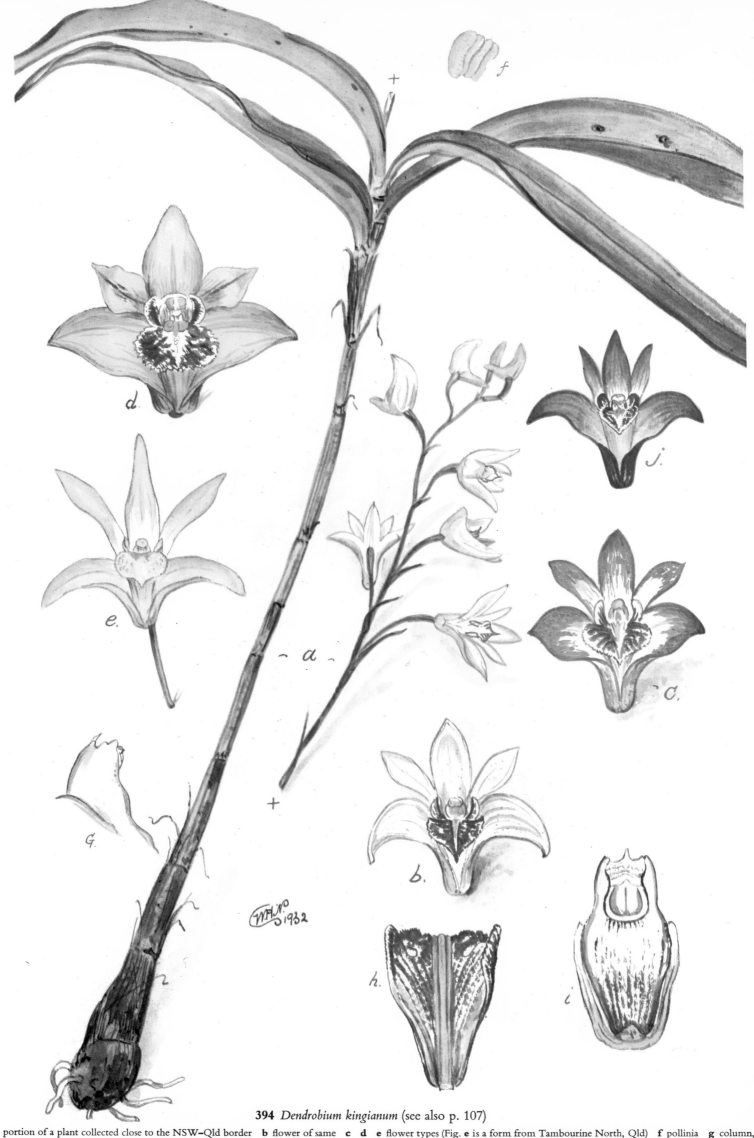

394 *Dendrobium kingianum* (see also p. 107)

a portion of a plant collected close to the NSW–Qld border   **b** flower of same   **c d e** flower types (Fig. **e** is a form from Tambourine North, Qld)   **f** pollinia   **g** column, from side—anther removed   **h** labellum, from above   **i** column, from front—anther removed   **j** flower type
Fig. **a** natural size

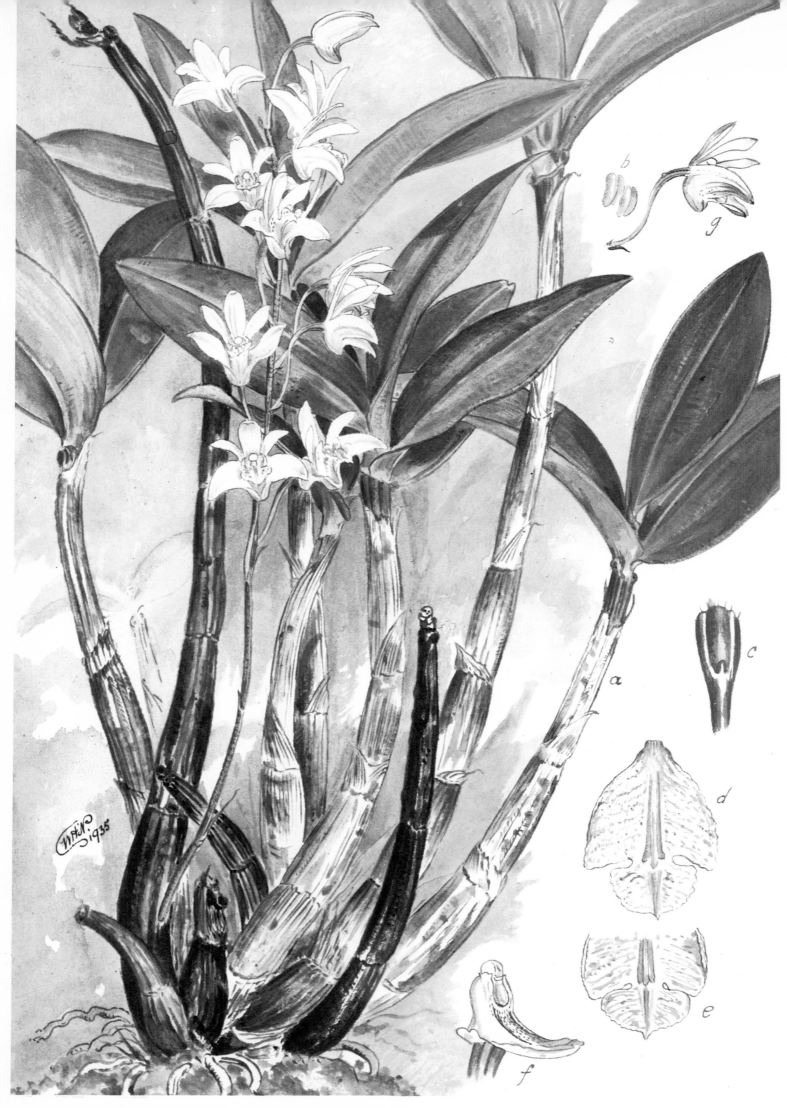

395 *Dendrobium × delicatum* (see also p. 108)

a flowering plant from the type locality **b** pollinia **c** ovary, from above (from Fig. **g**) **d** labellum, spread out **e** variation in the mid-lobe, etc. **f** column **g** flower tinged with pink, from side

Figs **a, g** natural size

396 *Dendrobium × delicatum* (see also p. 108)

a small plant from Bulahdelah, NSW **b** labellum, from side **c** column, from side **d** labellum, from front, lobes spread out
Fig. **a** natural size

398 *Dendrobium ruppianum* (see also p. 108)

a flowering plant b labellum, from side c labellum, from above, lobes spread out d column, from side—anther removed e pollinia

Fig. a natural size

399 *Dendrobium speciosum*: Figs **a–e** (see also p. 109)
D. speciosum var. *hillii* forma *grandiflorum*: Fig. **f** (see also p. 109)

a flowering plant **b** labellum, from front **c** pollinia **d** column, from front **e** labella types **f** flower, from front
Figs **a**, **f** natural size

400 *Dendrobium speciosum* (see also p. 109)

a flowering plant **b** labellum, from above **c** column, from side

Fig. **a** natural size

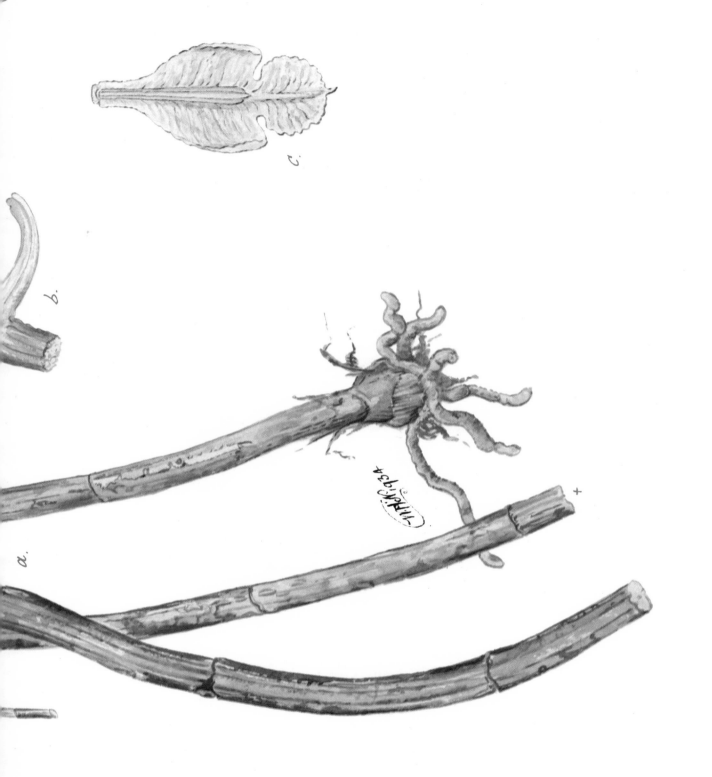

401 *Dendrobium speciosum* var. *nitidum* (see also p. 109)

a portion of a cultivated plant **b** column, from side **c** labellum, from above, the lateral lobes spread out **d** pollinia

Fig. **a** natural size

402 *Dendrobium* ×*gracillimum* (see also p. 109)

a small portion of plant with raceme of flowers **b** flower, from front **c** pollinia **d** column, etc. **e** labellum, from side **f** labellum, from above

Fig. **a** natural size

403 *Dendrobium gracilicaule* (see also p. 109)

a typical flowering plant **b** labellum, from side **c** labellum, from above **d** callus plates **e** flower, from front **f** flower, from side **g** head of column—anther removed
h pollinia
Fig. **a** natural size

397 *Dendrobium ruppianum* var. *blackburnii* (see also p. 108)

a flowering plant **b** flower, from front **c** labellum, from above **d** pollinia
Fig. **a** natural size

404 *Dendrobium gracilicaule* var. *howeanum* (see also p. 110)

a small plant with buds, also raceme of bloom **b** flower, from front **c** labellum, from side **d** flower, from side **e** labellum, from above, apex not visible
Fig. **a** natural size

405 *Dendrobium bairdianum* (see also p. 110)

(see also p. 110)

a a plant from Mt Fox district, Qld **b** labellum, from above **c** anther and head of column from front—pollinia removed **d** flower, from front **e** labellum, from front
f labellum, from above **g** pollinia **h** column, from front **i** flower in its last stages, from front **j** flower, from side
Fig. **a** natural size

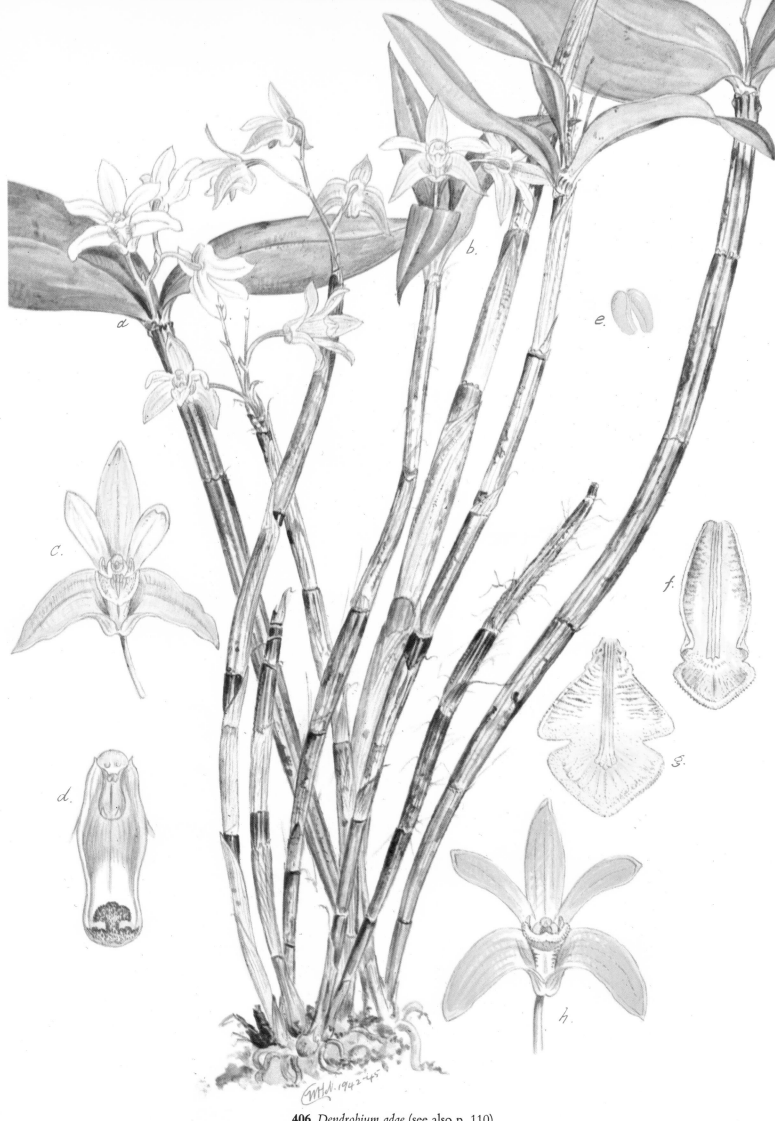

406 *Dendrobium adae* (see also p. 110)

a plant with typical white flowers **b** plant with cream and greenish-white flowers **c** flower, from front **d** column, from front **e** pollinia **f** labellum, from above
g labellum, lobes spread out **h** flower at maturity
Figs **a, b** natural size

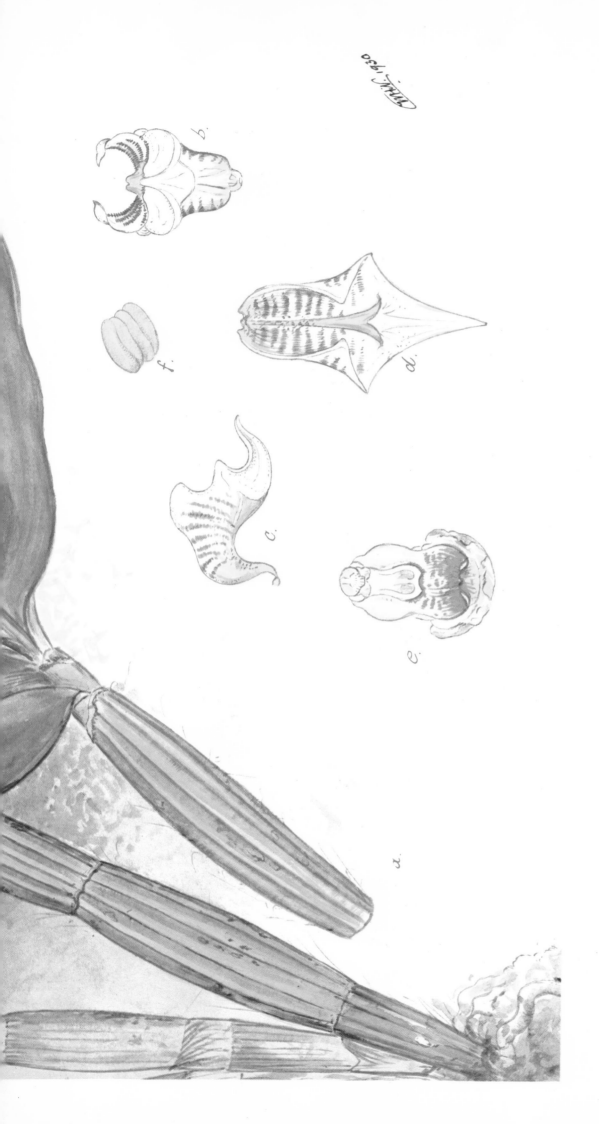

408 *Dendrobium falcorostrum* (see also p. 110)

a flowering plant **b** labellum, from front **c** labellum, from side **d** labellum, from above **e** column, from front **f** pollinia

Fig. **a** natural size

407 *Dendrobium fleckeri* (see also p. 110)

a typical plant **b** labellum, from side **c** labellum, from rear **d** labellum, from front **e** cilia, from labellum mid-lobe **f** column, from front **g** apex of column with uplifted anther **h** pollinia

Fig. **a** natural size

409 *Dendrobium moorei* (see also p. 111)

a small portion of plant with flowers **b** column, from side **c** pollinia **d** flower, from front **e** column, from front—anther removed **f** anther with pollinia *in situ* **g** flower, from side **h** labellum and spur, from side **i** labellum, from above
Fig. **a** natural size

411 *Dendrobium tetragonum*: Figs **a, c–e, k–m** (see also p. 111)
D. tetragonum var. *giganteum*: Figs **b, f–j** (see also p. 112)

a typical NSW plant in bloom   **b** flower   **c**   **d** flowers, showing various forms   **e** pseudobulb, leaves and flowers   **f** pseudobulb, leaves and flowers   **g** labellum, from side
h column, from front   **i** apex of labellum   **j** callus ridges   **k** portion of labellum, showing callus ridges   **l** pollinia   **m** flower
Fig. **a** natural size

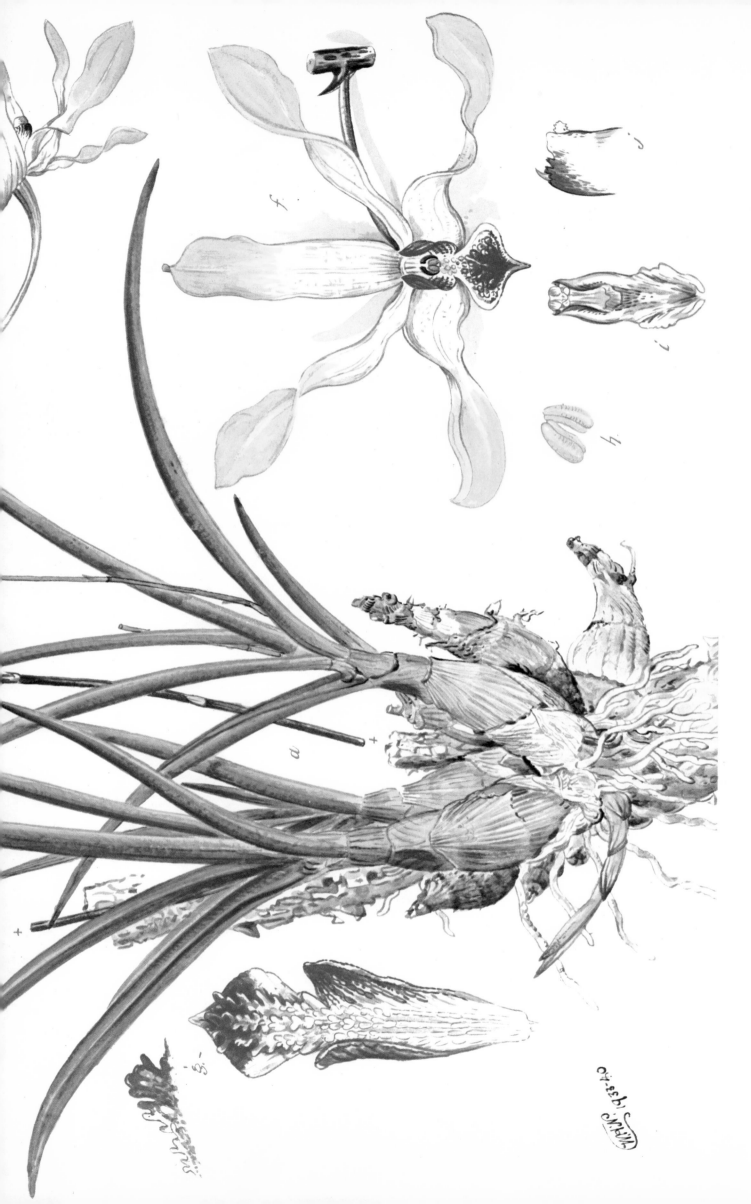

412 *Dendrobium canaliculatum*: Figs **a, d, e** (in part), **f-j** (see also p. 112)
D. canaliculatum var. nigrescens: Figs **b, c, e** (in part) (see also p. 112)

a typical flowering specimen **b** raceme of flowers **c** flower, from front **d** capsule **e** flowers of the typical form and var. *nigrescens*, from side **f** typical flower, from front
g labellum, from above, one lobe spread out; also figure showing the character of callus plates, from side **h** pollinia **i** column, from front **j** head of column, from side—
anther removed

Figs **a, b** natural size

413 *Dendrobium smilliae* (see also p. 112)

a plant from Pine Creek, Qld b flower, from front c flower, from side d labellum, from above e head of column, from side—anther removed f column, from front
g head of column, from rear h pollinia, one pair only shown
Fig. a natural size

414 *Dendrobium toffii* (see also p. 112)

a plant with raceme of flowers **b** labellum, spread out **c** column, from front **d** pollinia
Fig. **a** natural size

410 *Dendrobium aemulum* (see also p. 111)

a typical plant (portion only) of the slender-stemmed form   **b** flower, from front   **c** flower from Pittwater, NSW, from side   **d** same, from front   **e** column, from side
f labellum, from above   **g** labellum, from side   **h** labellum, from front   **i** column, from above   **j** pollinia   **k** callus plate, from side
Fig. **a** natural size

415 *Dendrobium dicuphum* (see also p. 112)

a plant and flowers, from Koolpinyah, NT   **b** labellum, from above, lobes spread out   **c** column, from front   **d** head of column, from side—anther removed   **e** pollinia
f callus ridges of the labellum lamina   **g** double spur
Fig. **a** natural size

416 *Dendrobium bigibbum* (see also p. 113)

a typical form   **b** flower   **c** labellum, spread out   **d** crest on labellum lamina   **e** spur, divided longitudinally   **f** pollinia   **g** column, from front   **h** labellum, spread out
Fig. **a** natural size

425 *Cadetia taylori* (see also p. 114)

a b plant types **c** bud **d e** flowers, from front **f** pollinia **g** flower, from rear **h** bud **i** column, from rear **j** column, from side **k** two columns, from front **l** two labella, from above

Figs **a, b** natural size

417 *Dendrobium bigibbum* (see also p. 113)

a plant and racemes of flowers **b** labellum with lobes spread out **c** column, from front **d** capsule **e** pollinia **f** flower **g** column base

Figs **a**, **d**, **f** natural size

418 *Dendrobium* ×*superbiens* (see also p. 113)

a typical plant **b** raceme of flowers **c** flowers of a pale hue **d e** labella, from above **f** keel **g** column, from front **h** callus plates, two types **i** column, from side
j pollinia
Figs **a**–**c** natural size

419 *Dendrobium × superbiens* (see also p. 113)

a plant with raceme of bloom   **b** labellum, spread out   **c** head of column, from front   **d** pollinia   **e** variation of keel   **f** callus plate

Fig. **a** natural size

420 *Dendrobium × superbiens* (see also p. 113)

a raceme of flowers **b** column and spur, from front **c** labellum, spread out **d** spur, ovary, etc. **e** callus plate **f** column, from side **g** callus ridges of labellum

Fig. **a** natural size

421 *Dendrobium discolor* var. *discolor* forma *discolor*: Figs **a**, **b**, **e** (see also p. 113)
D. discolor var. *discolor* forma *broomfieldii*: Figs **c**, **d** (see also p. 113)

a portion of plant with raceme of flowers   **b** labellum, from above   **c** labellum, from above   **d** column   **e** pollinia
Fig. **a** natural size

b.

a.

d.

+

+

422 *Dendrobium discolor* var. *fuscum* (see also p. 114)

a raceme of flowers, leaves, etc.   b head of column, from rear   c labellum, from above   d column, from front, including pollinia
Fig. a natural size

423 *Dendrobium johannis* (see also p. 114)

a small plant **b** raceme of flowers **c** column, from front **d** pollinia **e** head of column, from side **f** labellum, from side **g** labellum, from above, lobes spread out **h** labellum mid-lobe, showing callus plates **i** flower of a brown-flowered form

Figs **a**, **b**, **i** natural size

424 *Dendrobium baileyi* (see also p. 114)

a flowering plant **b** flower, from front **c** flower, from side **d** buds **e** anther **f** column—anther removed **g** labellum, from above **h** labellum, from side

Figs **a, d** natural size

a.

b.

c.

d.

e.

f.

g.

h.

i.

j.

k.

l.

426

427 *Eria queenslandica* (see also p. 115)

a typical plant **b** flower, from front **c** flower, from side **d** labellum, from above **e** pollinia **f** labellum, from side **g h** column, from side and front **i** anther-case
j labellum, spread out
Fig. **a** natural size

426 *Eria inornata* (see also p. 115)

a portion of a flowering plant **b** raceme **c** flower, from side **d** anther-case **e** petal **f** pollinia **g** flower, from front **h** apex of labellum, from above **i** apex of labellum,
from below **j** labellum, from above **k** column, from front—anther removed **l** column and labellum, from side—anther removed
Figs **a, b** natural size

428 *Phreatia baileyana* (see also p. 115)

a b plants, showing variation in foliage **c** portion of plant **d** flower and bract, from above **e** flowers **f** flower, from above, sepals united at base **g** capsule **h** labellum,
from above **i** column, from side **j** anther-case **k** pollinia **l** column and portions of lateral sepals **m** plant, showing variation in foliage

Figs **a, b, m** natural size

429 *Phreatia crassiuscula* (see also p. 115)

a flower and bract **b** flower, from above **c** labellum, from above **d** typical plants with racemes **e** labellum, from side **f** capsule **g** pollinia **h** column, from front
i cross-section of leaf **j** flower, from side **k** portion of raceme **l** unexpanded flower
Fig. **a** natural size

430 *Bulbophyllum baileyi* (see also p. 116)

a plant with flowers from Green Hill, near Cairns, Qld **b** pollinia, with a definite but irregular viscid attachment—possibly an accidental occurrence in *Bulbophyllum?* **c** column, from side **d** column and labellum, from front, the labellum raised **e** labellum, from front **f** labellum, from rear **g** labellum, from side
Fig. **a** natural size

431 *Bulbophyllum weinthalii* (see also p. 116)

a flower, from rear **b** lateral sepal **c** typical colony of flowering plants **d** column, from front **e** flower, from front **f** labellum, from above **g** margin of labellum
(lateral lobe) **h** labellum, from front
Fig. **c** natural size

432 *Bulbophyllum aurantiacum* (see also p. 116)

a typical plant in bloom **b** column, from front **c** pollinia, two views **d** cross-section of leaf **e** capsule **f** thinner type of leaf, with cross-section **g** petal types **h** flower, from side **i** column, from side **j** labellum, from side **k** labellum, from above **l** flower, from front
Figs **a, d–f** natural size

433 *Bulbophyllum radicans* (see also p. 116)

a the type specimen of *Bulbophyllum cilioglossum* **b** labellum, from side **c** petal **d** flower, from front **e** ovary **f** column, from side **g** pollinia **h** column, from front
(tips of column appendages and column foot not shown) **i** labellum, from above **j** apex of labellum, from below **k** posterior margin of labellum
Fig. **a** natural size

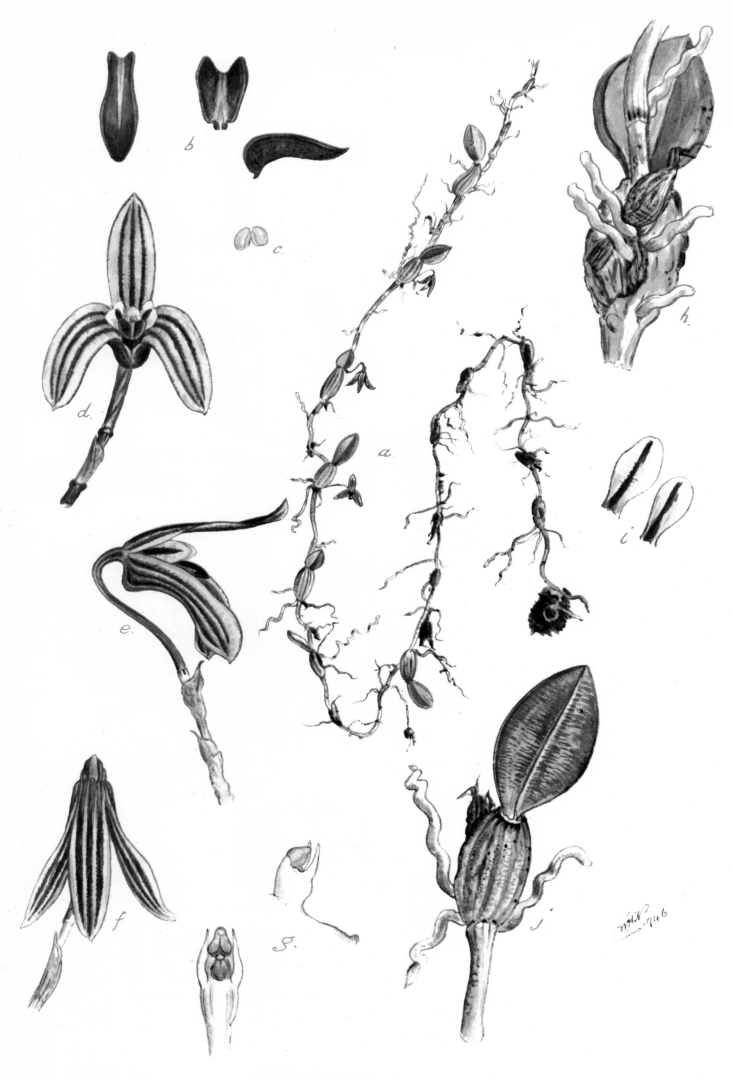

434 *Bulbophyllum bowkettae* (see also p. 117)

a specimen with flowers b labella, from three positions c pollinia d flower, from front e flower, from side f flower, from above g column, from front and side
h pseudobulb, etc., from below i petals j pseudobulb, leaf, etc.
Fig. **a** natural size

435 *Bulbophyllum lageniforme* (see also p. 117)

a Mt Islay, Qld, plant with flowers **b** lateral sepal **c** dorsal sepal **d** petal **e** flower, from above **f** flower, from front, also showing the peduncle and pedicel **g** column, from front **h** column, from side **i** pollinia **j** labellum, from below **k** labellum, from above **l** labellum, from front **m** labellum, from side
Fig. **a** natural size

436 *Bulbophyllum exiguum* (see also p. 117)

a plant in flower from Eungella Range, Qld **b** flower, from front **c** column and labellum, from side **d** labellum, from front **e** column, from front **f** small plant **g** typical small form from Tambourine North, Qld **h i** plants from Waterfall Creek, NSW **j** typical flower, from front **k** labellum, from rear **l** labellum, from front **m** labellum, from side **n** petal **o** column appendage, from side **p** column, from front
Figs **a, g–i** natural size

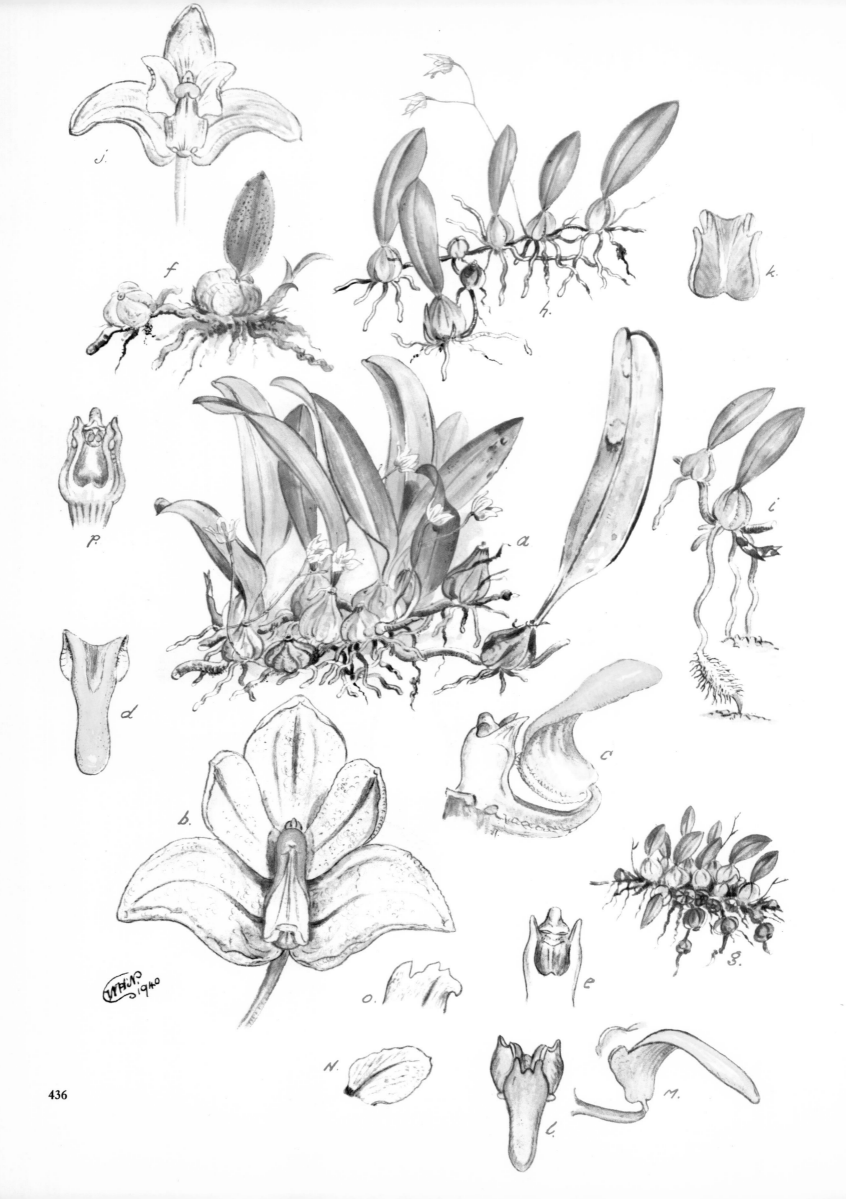

437 *Bulbophyllum minutissimum* (see also p. 117)

a flower, from front **b** colony of plants **c** capsules **d** column, from front **e** head of column, from above **f** anther–case—pollinia removed **g** flower expanding its segments, from front **h** pollinia **i** petal **j** dorsal sepal **k** pseudobulbs **l** pseudobulbs, etc. with young bud attached, from below **m** pseudobulbs and leaves **n** labellum flattened out, from above **o** labellum, from front **p** flower, from side
Fig. **b** natural size

438 *Bulbophyllum globuliforme* (see also p. 118)

a plant   **b** plant with flower   **c** column, from front   **d** column and ovary, from side   **e** pollinia   **f** flower, from front   **g** flower, from side   **h** flower from a cultivated plant, from front   **i** labellum, from above   **j** labellum, from side   **k** labellum, from below
Fig. **a** natural size

439 *Bulbophyllum macphersonii* (see also p. 118)

a b plants with flowers and capsules   c d plants, showing different types of leaf   e leaves, capsule, etc.   f flower with connate lateral sepals   g flower with free lateral sepals
h flower, from side   i petal   j column, from front, also ovary, etc.   k column, from side   l another column, from front—columnar foot not shown   m column, from rear—
anther removed   n leaf, pseudobulb and bract   o p labella   q labellum, from side   r pollinia
Figs a–d natural size

440 *Bulbophyllum bracteatum* (see also p. 118)

a typical plant with flowers and capsules b raceme c petal d pollinia e flower, from side f flower, from front g pseudobulb, etc. h pseudobulbs, leaves and raceme
Figs **a, h** natural size

441 *Bulbophyllum elisae* (see also p. 118)

a small form with yellowish flowers b typical plant c column, from side d pollinia e flower, from front f flower, from side, with lower sepals removed g labellum, from above

Figs a, b natural size

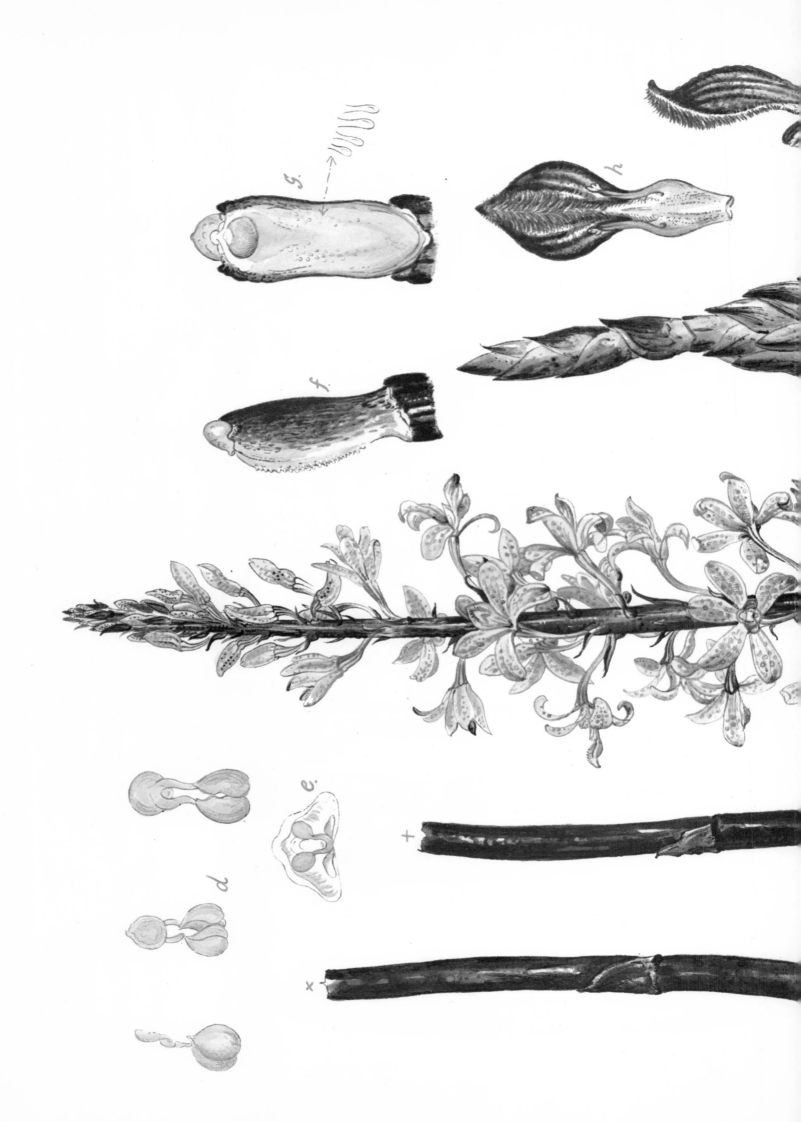

443 *Dipodium punctatum* (see also p. 119)

a sturdy specimen from the hill country, Vic.   b young plant, showing root system, from Airey's Inlet, Vic.   c flower types   d pollinia, from three positions   e pollinia in position   f column, from side   g column, from front   h labellum, from above   i labellum, from side

Figs **a–c** natural size

444 *Dipodium punctatum* (see also p. 119)

a fruiting specimen from Kinglake, Vic.   b cross-section of capsule   c seeds

Figs **a**, **b** natural size

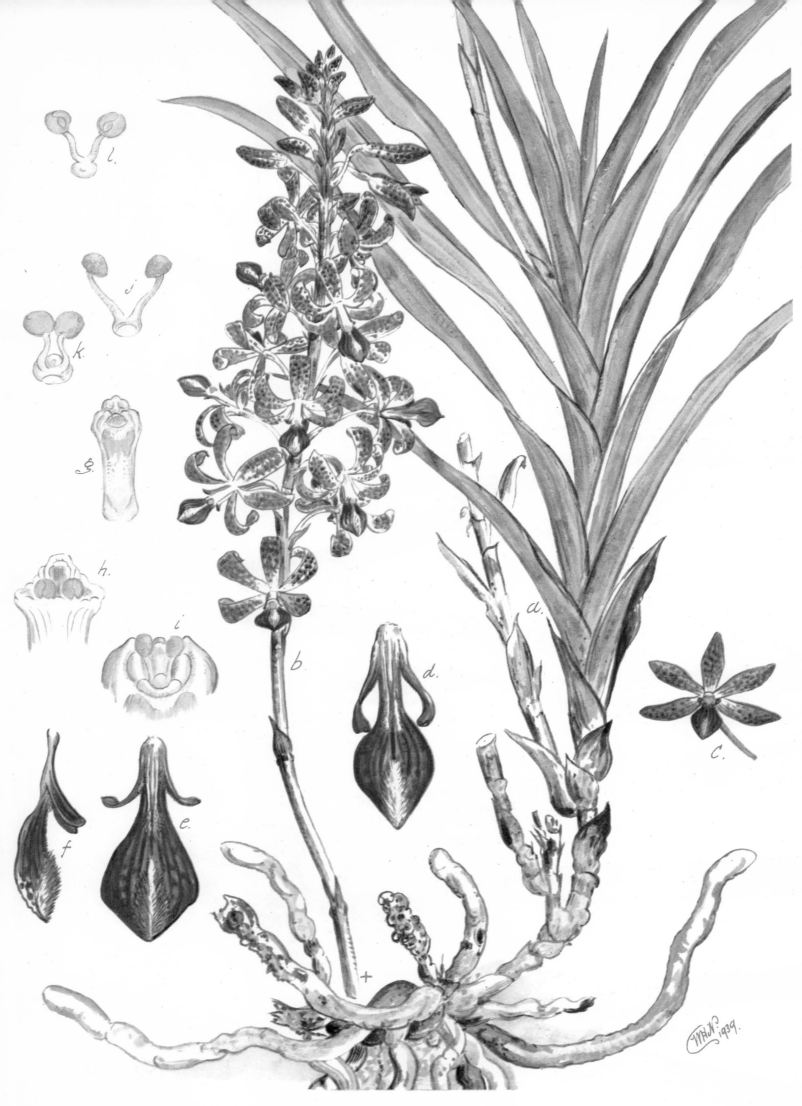

442 *Dipodium ensifolium* (see also p. 119)

a b plant and raceme of flowers **c** flower, from front **d e** labella, from above **f** labellum, from side **g** column, from front **h** head of column—anther removed to show pollinia in position **i** head of column, from rear and above **j k l** pollinia
Figs **a–c** natural size

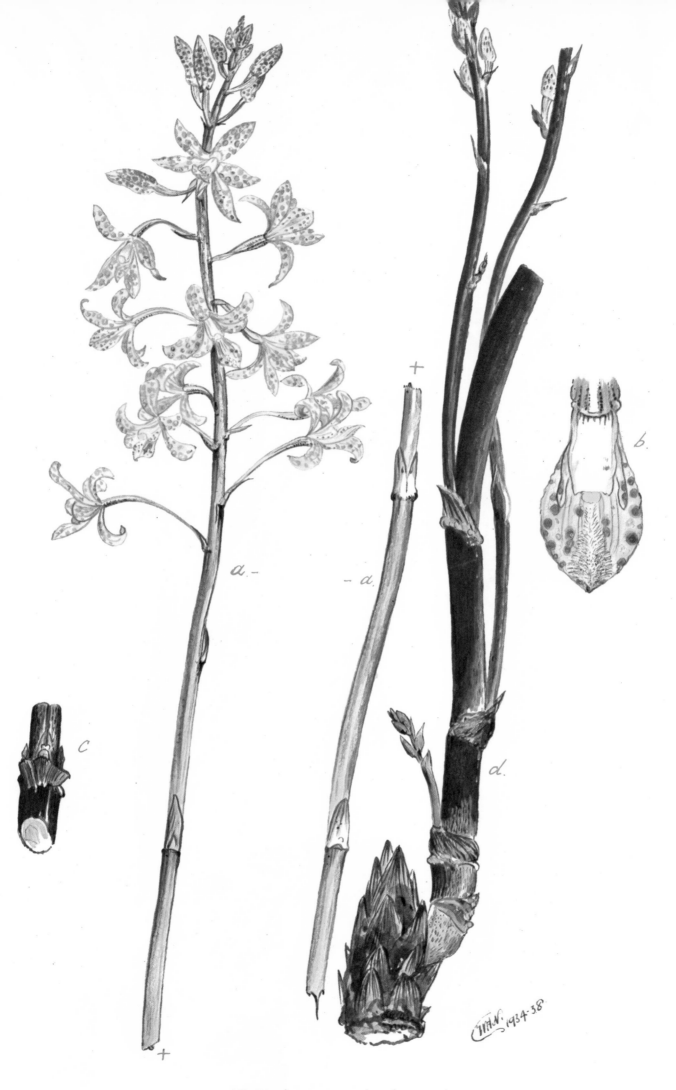

445 *Dipodium punctatum* (see also p. 119)

a specimen from Creswick, Vic., with pale flowers and green stem **b** column and labellum (from a flower in Fig. **a**) **c** stem bracts showing dormant buds beneath **d** branched specimen from Boronia, Vic.

Figs **a**, **c**, **d** natural size

446 *Cymbidium suave* (see also p. 120)

a portion of typical plant with flowers **b** a more colourful form **c** pollinia **d** column, from side **e** column, from front **f g** labella, from above, spread out **h** labellum, from side

Figs **a, b** natural size

451 *Rhinerrhiza divitiflora* (see also p. 121)

a typical plants   **b** centre of flower with labellum and column   **c** column, from front   **d** column, from side   **e** labellum, from rear   **f** pollinia
Fig. **a** natural size

447 *Cymbidium canaliculatum* (see also p. 120)

a portion of pseudobulb and foliage   b raceme of flowers   c flower of a pale form, from front   d flower of Fig. b, from front   e flower of a dark-flowered form, from front
f flowers of a green form   g column, from side and front   h labellum, from above   i pollinia

Figs **a, b, e, f** natural size

448 *Cymbidium madidum* (see also p. 120)

a plant with a raceme of flowers **b** flower, from rear **c** labellum, from above **d** column, from front **e** pollinia **f** ripe capsule **g** withered capsule **h** cross-section of ripe capsule

Fig. **a** natural size

449 *Phalaenopsis amabilis* var. *rosenstromii* (see also p. 121)

a plants with raceme of flowers **b** pollinia **c** labellum appendages **d** callus, from above **e** column, from front **f** column, from side

Fig. **a** natural size

450 *Robiquetia tierneyana* (see also p. 121)

a flowering specimen b flower, from front c flower, from side d column, from side e column, from front f labellum g pollinia h unripe capsules
Fig. a natural size

452 *Sarcochilus falcatus* (see also p. 122)

a specimen from Mt Wilson, Blue Mountains, NSW **b** flexuose peduncle, (from Fig. **a**), showing buds **c** capsule **d** flower, from front, of southern Qld plant **e** flower, from front, of Barrington Tops, NSW, plant **f** same, from rear **g** flower, from front, of Cann River, Vic., plant **h** same, from rear **i** another Cann River flower, from the front **j** column and perianth segments of Cann River flower—labellum removed

Figs **a–c** natural size

453 *Sarcochilus falcatus* (see also p. 122)

a flowering plant from Cann River, Vic., *in situ*   **b** column   **c** labellum, from rear   **d** labellum, from inside, half only shown   **e** pollinia
Fig. **a** natural size

454 *Sarcochilus fitzgeraldii* (see also p. 122)

a small plant with raceme of bloom   **b** labellum, from rear   **c** labellum, from side   **d e** flower types, from front   **f** column   **g** pollinia, two sets
Fig. **a** natural size

455 *Sarcochilus hartmannii* (see also p. 123)

a small plant with raceme of bloom **b** flowers of a lighter shade **c** labellum, from side **d** column, from front **e** column, from side **f** pollinia **g** labellum, from above—
one lobe removed
Figs **a, b** natural size

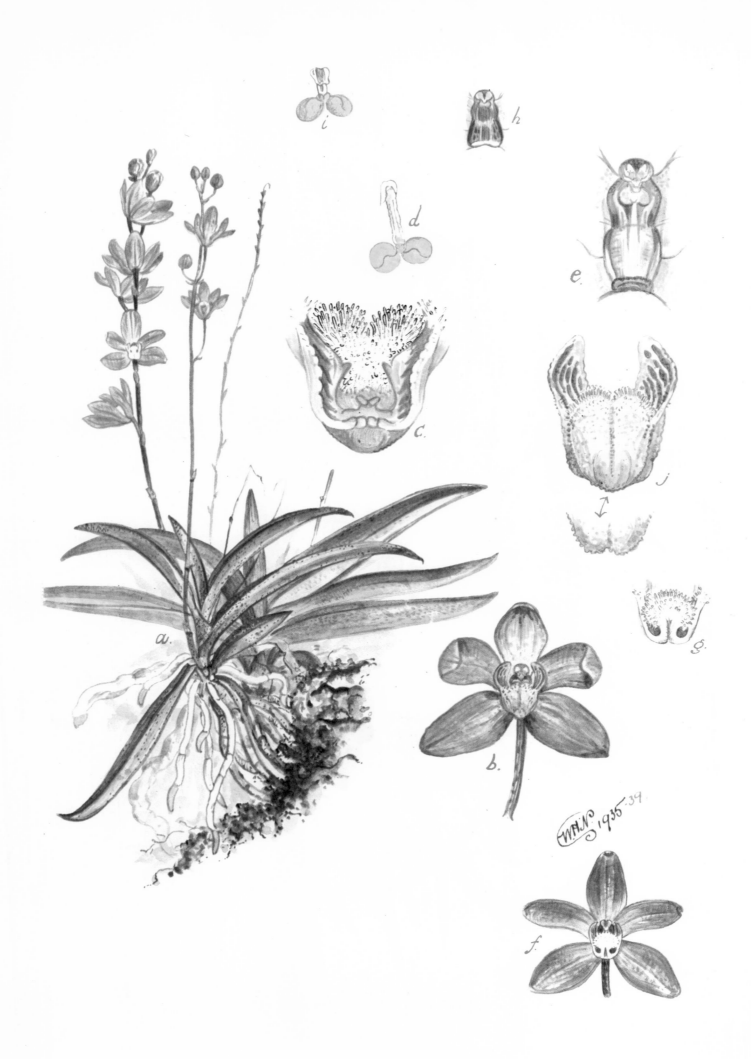

456 *Sarcochilus ceciliae* (see also p. 123)

(see also p. 123)

a Mt Fox, Qld, specimen **b** flower, from front **c** base of labellum, from rear, showing callus-plate **d** pollinia, showing the varying length of caudicle **e** column, from front
f Mt Fox flower, showing the characteristic surface of the mid-lobe **g** mid-lobe of same **h** column, from front **i** pollinia, showing varying length of caudicle
j labellum, from front, also showing variation of the dorsal spur
Fig. **a** natural size

457 *Sarcochilus ceciliae* (see also p. 123)

Very fine specimen plant from Tambourine North, Qld. When received, the budding racemes were just apparent. In bloom it was exactly as figured and was brought to this state of perfection in the author's heated glasshouse in Footscray, Vic.

Fig. natural size

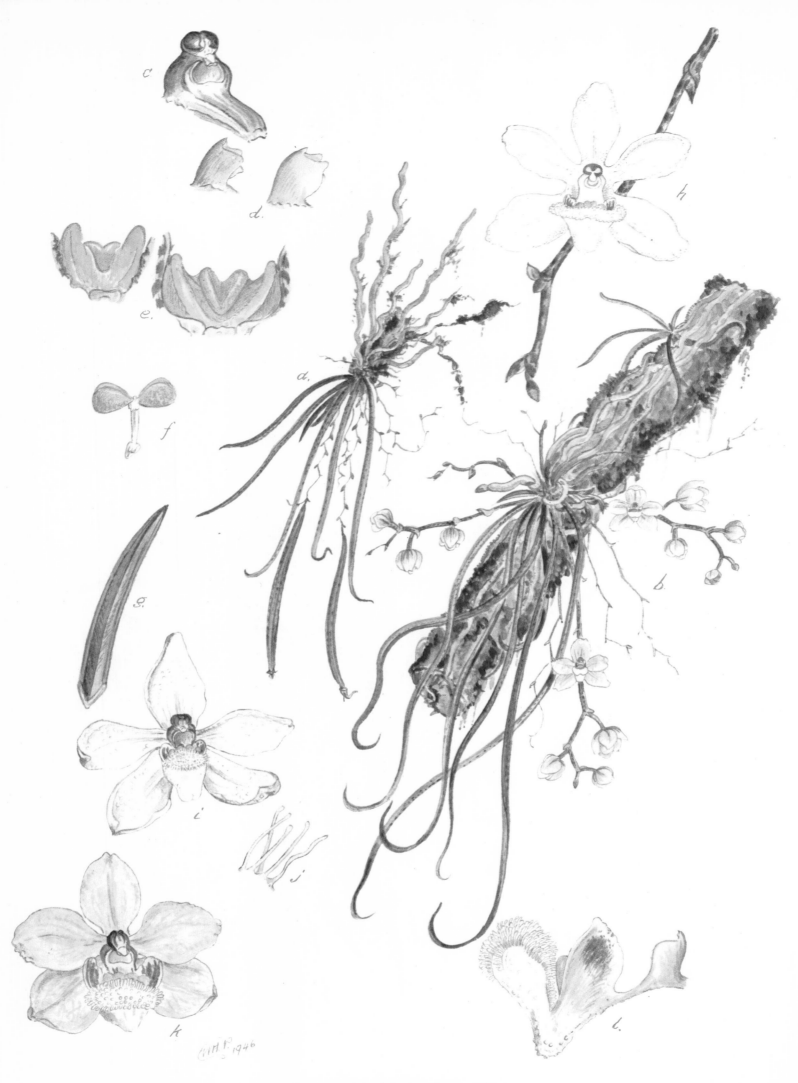

458 *Sarcochilus hillii* (see also p. 123)

(see also p. 123)

a plant with capsule attached from the New England Range, near Guy Fawkes, NSW **b** robust plant with flowers **c** column **d** columns, from side—anther removed **e** glands from labellum lamina **f** pollinia **g** cross-section of leaf showing channelled blade **h** flower of a southern Qld plant, from front **i** flower, from front **j** cilia, from labellum **k** typical flower, from front **l** labellum and column, from side

Figs **a, b** natural size

459 *Sarcochilus olivaceus* (see also p. 123)

a typical plant from Tambourine North, Qld   **b** flower, from rear   **c** labellum of NSW specimen, from front   **d** flower, from rear   **e** labellum, from rear   **f** labellum, from front   **g** labellum, from side   **h** capsule with seed   **i** column, from front   **j** pollinia
Figs **a, h** natural size

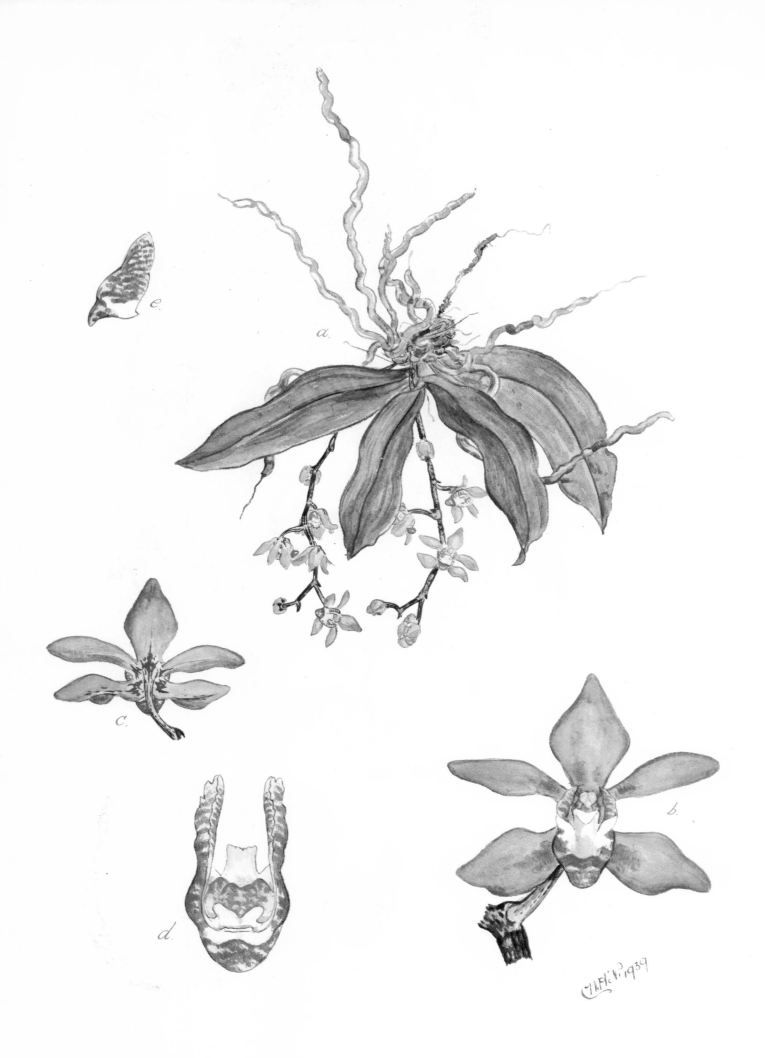

460 *Sarcochilus olivaceus* var. *borealis* (see also p. 124)

a flowering plant **b** flower, from front **c** flower, from rear **d** labellum, from rear **e** labellum, from side
Fig. **a** natural size

461 *Sarcochilus dilatatus* (see also p. 124)

a specimen from Mt French, Qld **b** flower, from front **c** column, from front **d** rostellum **e** pollinia **f** labellum, from rear—lobes removed **g** labellum, from side
h dorsal sepal
Fig. **a** natural size

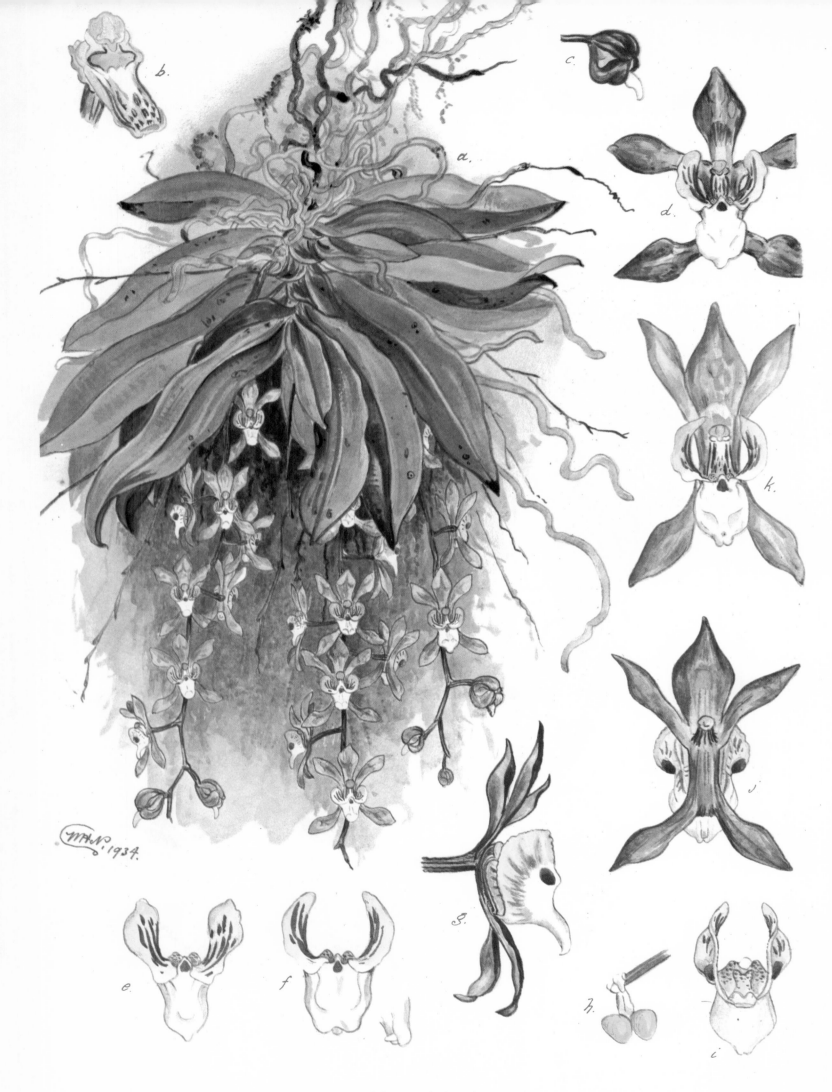

462 *Sarcochilus australis* (see also p. 124)

a typical plant with flowers   b column, from front   c bud   d flower of robust form from Fern Tree Gully, Vic.   e labellum (typical form), from front   f labellum from the robust form, from front; also figure showing the base, from side   g flower, from side   h pollinia extracted on a needle point   i labellum, from rear   j flower, from rear
k flower of the typical form
Fig. a natural size

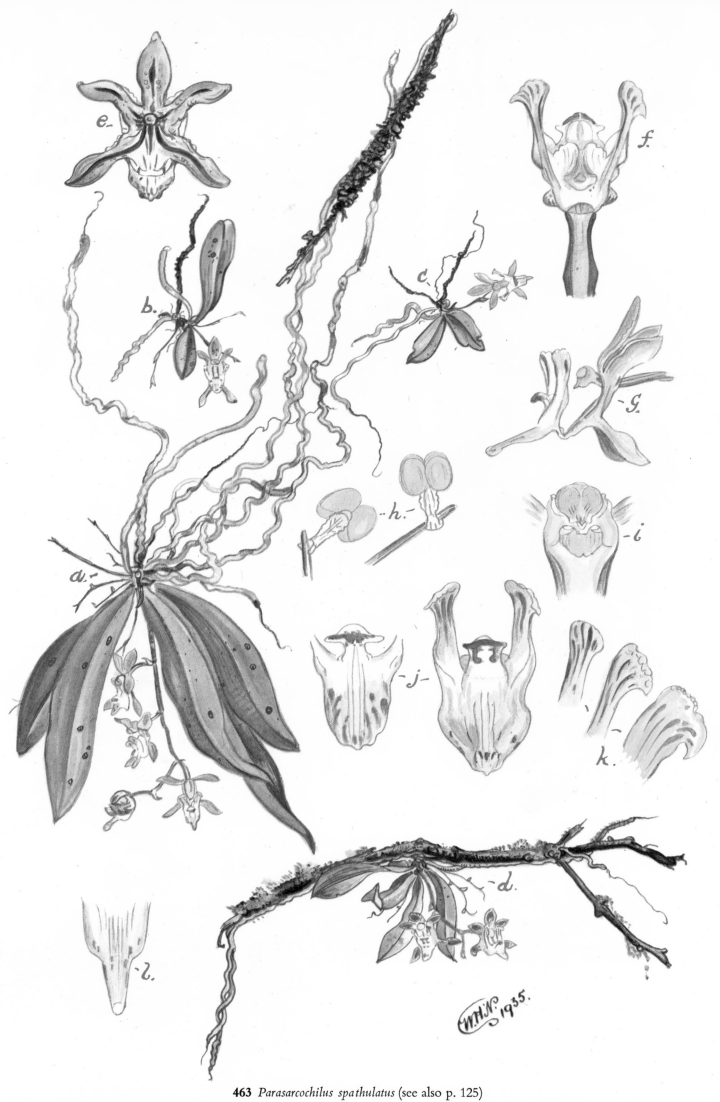

463 *Parasarcochilus spathulatus* (see also p. 125)

a   b   c   d flowering specimens   **e** flower, showing the reverse markings   **f** labellum, from above, showing attachment   **g** flower, from side   **h** pollinia, two views   **i** column
j   k labella, showing variation in the shape of the lobes, etc.   **l** narrow keel from labellum mid-lobe
Figs **a–d** natural size

464 *Parasarcochilus weinthalii* (see also p. 125)

a plant in full bloom **b** flower, from rear **c** labellum, from rear **d** flower, from front **e** labellum, from side **f** column, from side **g** pollinia
Fig. **a** natural size

465 *Parasarcochilus weinthalii* (see also p. 125)

a flowering plants **b** flower, from front **c** labellum, from rear **d** flower, from rear **e** column, from side **f** pollinia **g** labellum, from side
Fig. **a** natural size

466 *Mobilabium hamatum* (see also p. 125)

a comparatively small plant with racemes **b** flower, from front **c** flower, from side **d** labellum, from rear **e** labellum, from side **f** pollinia **g** labellum, from side, dissected to show solid, fleshy sac **h** column, from front and side

Fig. **a** natural size

467 *Peristeranthus hillii* (see also p. 125)

a small plant **b** robust plant in bloom **c d** flowers, from front **e** column, from front **f** column, from side **g** labellum and column, from side **h** labellum, from above **i** pollinia

Figs **a, b** natural size

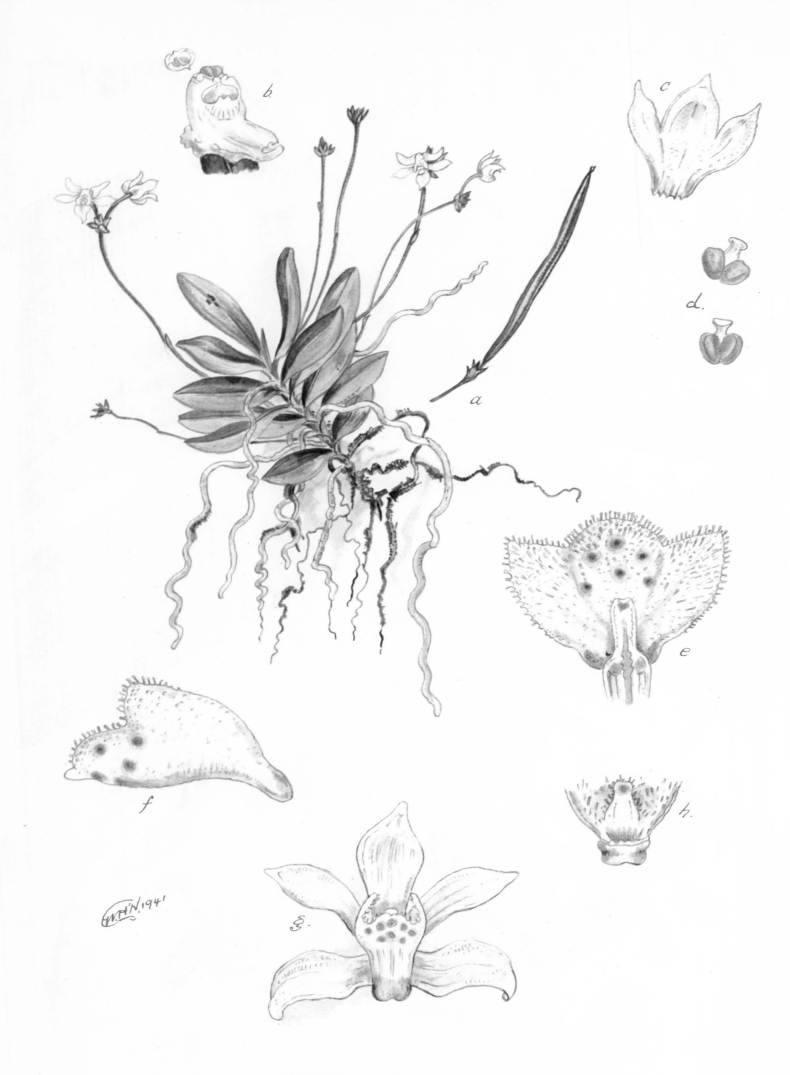

468 *Thrixspermum congestum* (see also p. 126)

a typical plant with flowers; also capsule **b** column, with anther removed to show pollinia in position **c** conjoined dorsal sepal and petals **d** pollinia, two views **e** labellum, from above, spread out **f** labellum, from side **g** flower, from front **h** appendage at base of labellum lamina
Fig. **a** natural size

469 *Plectorrhiza tridentata* (see also p. 126)

a typical plant **b** flower from northern Qld plant **c** flower from Vic. plant **d** pollinia **e** pollinia from northern Qld flower **f** flower, from side **g** spur, dissected to show interior **h** rostellum **i** column, from side **j** labellum, from rear

Fig. **a** natural size

471 *Plectorrhiza brevilabris* (see also p. 127)

a Mt Fox, Qld, plant **b** flower, from front **c** labellum and column, from side **d** **e** labellum glands **f** capsule **g** pollinia
Fig. **a** natural size

472 *Pomatocalpa macphersonii* (see also p. 127)

a Mt Fox, Qld, plant with capsules b flowers c capsules of seed d flower, from front e pollinia f column, from side g column, from front
h labellum, from side i flower, from side—anther removed
Figs a–c natural size

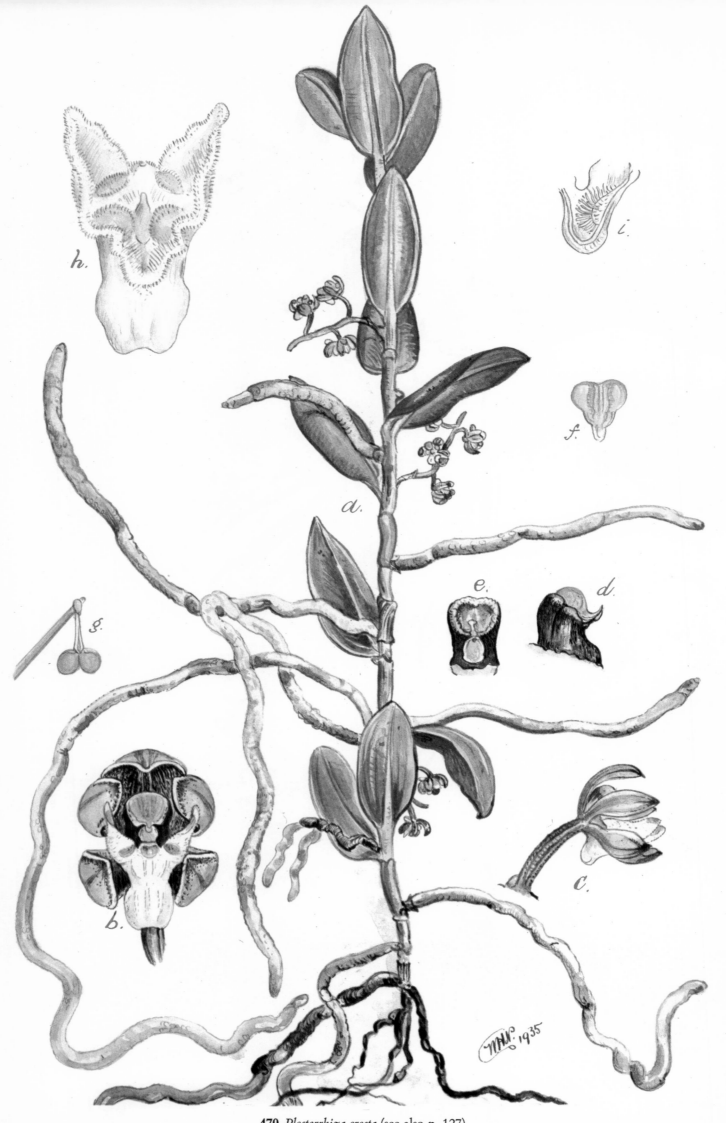

470 *Plectorrhiza erecta* (see also p. 127)

a typical plant **b** flower, from front **c** flower, from side **d** column, from side **e** column, from front—anther, etc. removed **f** anther **g** pollinia **h** labellum, from rear
i spur, dissected to show interior
Fig. **a** natural size

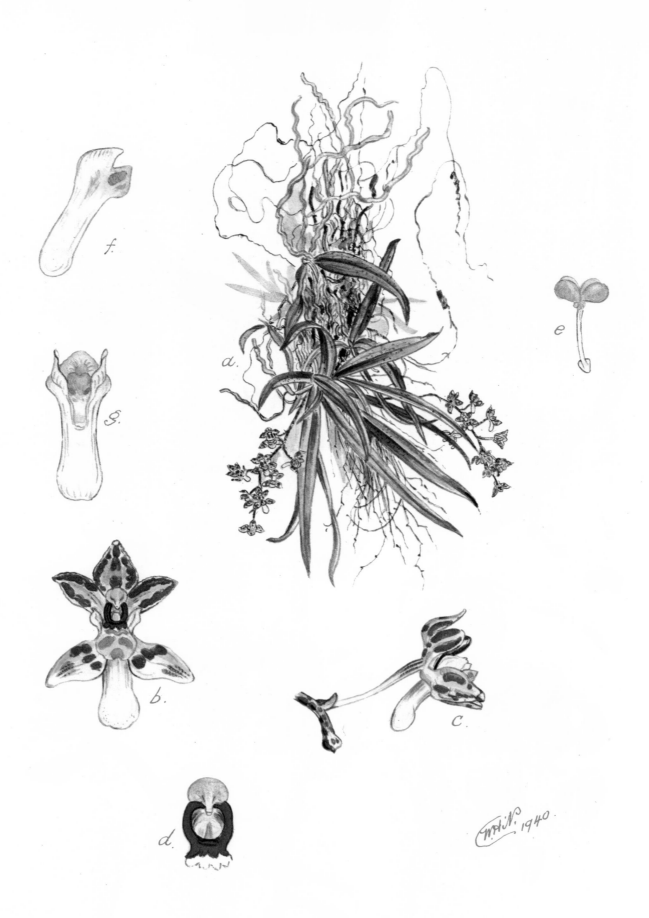

473 *Schistotylus purpuratus* (see also p. 128)

a typical plant **b** flower, from front **c** flower, from side **d** column, from front **e** pollinia **f** labellum, from side **g** labellum, from above
Fig. **a** natural size

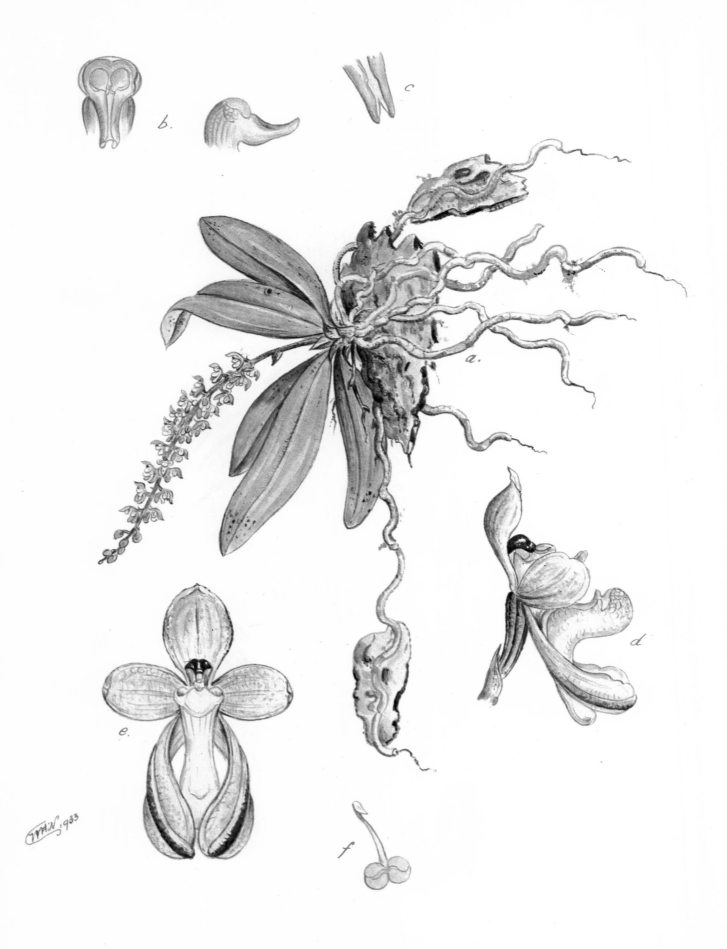

474 *Saccolabiopsis armitii* (see also p. 128)

a sturdy plant with raceme   **b** head of column, from front and side—anther removed to show pollinia in position   **c** apex of rostellum   **d** flower, from side   **e** flower, from front   **f** pollinia

Fig. **a** natural size

475 *Papillilabium beckleri* (see also p. 128)

a b typical plants **c** swollen root-tip **d** unexpanded flower, from front **e** flower, from front **f** flower, from side; also spur, cut to show interior **g** pollinia
Figs **a, b** natural size

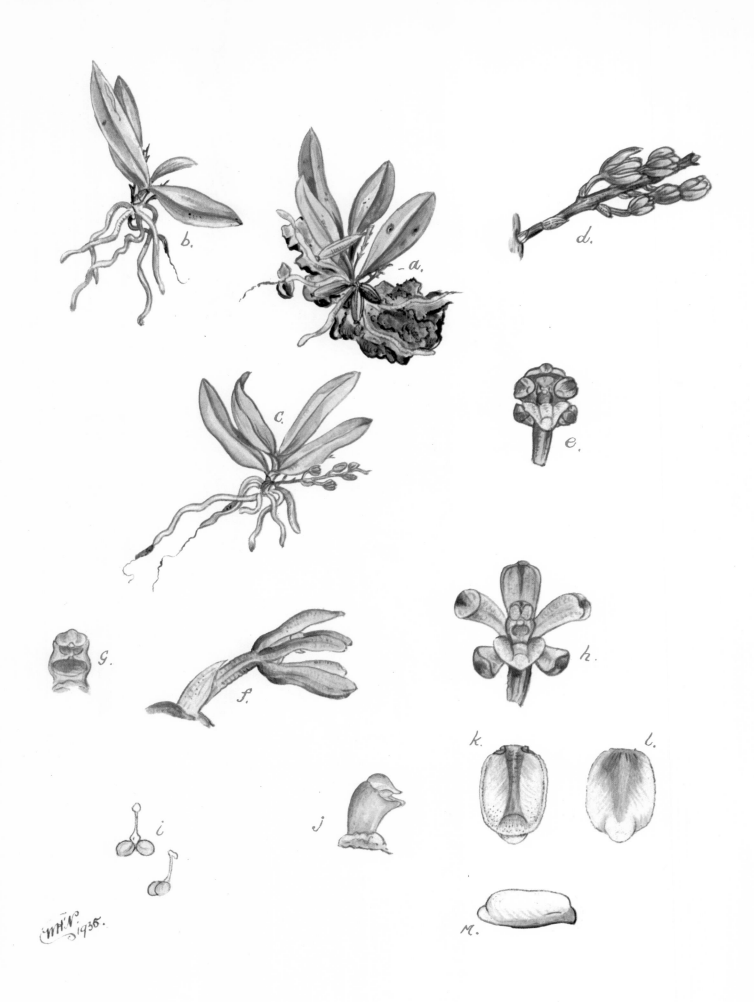

476 *Drymoanthus minutus* (see also p. 129)

a plant with capsules b the same plant twelve months later c two years later, with raceme of flowers d raceme e flower about to expand its segments f flower, from side
g column, from front h flower, fully expanded i pollinia j column, from side k labellum, from above l labellum, from below m labellum, from side
Figs a–c natural size

Units of Measurement and Abbreviations

Generally dimensions are in the metric system, and in certain cases the equivalent in feet or inches is included.

Australian states

NSW	New South Wales	NT	Northern Territory	Qld	Queensland
SA	South Australia	Tas.	Tasmania	Vic.	Victoria
WA	Western Australia				

All countries other than New Zealand (NZ) are spelled in full.

Citatory abbreviations

Authors' names are abbreviated as in current botanical literature, thus *R.Br.* for Robert Brown, *Benth.* for George Bentham, *Hook.f.* for J. D. Hooker (son of W. J. Hooker). Modern botanists generally have their surnames written in full, with initials.

Abbreviations of titles of botanical publications are based on those of the *World List of Scientific Publications Published in the Years 1900–1960*, 4th edn, edited by P. Brown and G. B. Stratton (1963–5).

Other abbreviations and Latin expressions

cum icon.	together with an illustration	pro parte	in part
ed.	edition; edited by	sens.	in the sense of
Ed.	editors of this book	ser.	series
et al.	and others	sp., spp.	species (sing. and pl.)
f.	son	ssp.	subspecies
Fig., Figs	Figure, Figures	sub	under
l.c.	in the place cited	t.	plate
non	not	ut tabula separata	as a separate plate
opp.	opposite	var.	variety

Glossary

actinomorphic — radially symmetrical, i.e. divisible into two identical halves by any plane passing through the centre

adnate — attached along the whole length

anterior — the parts of an organ furthest from an axis or stem on which it grows

antero-lateral — anterior and at the side

anticous — on the anterior side

apiculate — with a small sharp, but not stiff, point

arcuate — arched; bent like a bow

articulate — jointed

auriculate — with a small ear-like appendage

bicalcarate — with two spurs

bifarious — arranged in two rows

bifurcate — twice forked or branched

botryoidal — resembling a bunch of grapes

callus (plural calli) — a thickening; often found on the labellum. In *Caladenia* they are numerous, stalked, and with thickened heads. In *Prasophyllum* they take the form of a plate, called the *callus plate*. In *Microtis* they are often called *callosities*

campanulate — bell-shaped

canaliculate — with longitudinal grooves

capitulum — inflorescence with flowers compacted into a dense cluster

carinate — with a keel

cauda — a tail-like appendage

caudicle — a strap-like structure connecting the pollinia to the viscid disc of the rostellum

cauline — borne on the stem

chelate — shaped like a lobster's claw

circinnate — rolled from the top downwards to form a coil; coiled into a ring

clavate — club-shaped

clinandrium — the depression on top of the column, on which the anther rests

complicate — folded upon itself

connate — united, especially referring to like-parts

coriaceous — of a leathery texture

corymbiform — with the shape or appearance of a corymb

crenulate — bordered by very small rounded teeth

cruciform — shaped like a cross

cucullate — arched over to form a hood

cuneate — wedge-shaped

cuspidate — terminating in a sharp rigid point

cymbiform — boat-shaped

decurrent — with the base continuous along the stem in the form of a wing

decurved — curved or bent downward

dilatation — a widening or expansion into a blade

disc — the sticky gland of the rostellum, by means of which the pollinia become attached to an insect; also the middle portion of the labellum, usually between the bases of the lateral lobes and the base of the mid-lobe (used only in reference to the sub-tribe *Sarcanthinae*)

distal — the free end of a part, as distinct from the attached end

distichous — regularly arranged in two opposite rows

divaricate — widely diverging

dorsum — the back of an organ

emarginate — with a notch at the apex

endemic — denoting those genera or species which are restricted to one particular area

ensiform — sword-shaped

epigeal — on the surface of the soil

equitant — younger leaves overlapped by older ones, especially applying to leaves which are folded along the middle

erose — as though bitten or gnawed off

falcate — sickle-shaped

flabelliform — fan-like

flagelliform — whip-like

foveolar — having small depressions or pits

fugacious — fading or withering soon after opening

furcate — forked

furfuraceous — scurfy or mealy

fusiform — spindle-shaped; tapering gradually towards each end

galea — a helmet; the hood formed by union of the dorsal sepal and lateral petals in *Pterostylis*

gibbous — humped or projecting into a pouch-like swelling

gynostemium — the column formed by union of the stamens and style

hirsute — with rather coarse and stiff hair

imbricate — overlapping

incumbent — resting or leaning upon another surface, as distinct from erect

incurved — turned inward or towards the upper side

inflexed — bent or turned abruptly inward

involute — with edges rolled inward or towards the upper side

lamellate — composed of thin plates

leaf-fistula — the opening in a hollow leaf, through which the stem emerges

lenticular — lens-shaped

ligulate — strap-shaped

linguiform — tongue-shaped

lobule — a small lobe

lorate — strap-shaped

mentum — a chin; an extension formed by the union of the column foot and bases of lateral sepals

mesial — on the middle line of a part

monopodial — habit of growth of a plant in which growth is continued from year to year by the same apical growing point

monotypic — referring to a genus with a single species

mucronate — terminated by a short sharp point, emerging suddenly from a rounded apex

obfalcate — inversely sickle-shaped, i.e. becoming broader towards the tip

operculate — furnished with a lid

papillae — minute wart-like glands or protuberances

patelliform — shaped like a saucer or dish

patent — spreading

pectinate — resembling the teeth of a comb

peltate — attached to a leaf by its lower surface instead of its margin

penicillate — brush-like; arranged like a tuft of hair

plicate — folded like a closed fan

porrect — directed forward and downward

posterior	the parts of an organ closest to an axis or stem on which it grows
proximal	the attached end of a part, as distinct from the free end
puberulous	slightly hairy
pulvinate	cushion- or pad-shaped
pyriform	pear-shaped
quadrate	square or nearly so
radical	springing from the root
reclinate	turned or bent downward
recomplicate	folded back on itself, and then folded again
recurved	turned backward or towards the lower side
reflexed	turned down or bent back abruptly
resupinate	having the flower reversed, so that the parts usually lowest have become uppermost
retinaculum	the attachment of stipitate pollinia to the rostellum
retroflex	bent or turned backward
retuse	with a shallow notch in a rounded apex
revolute	with edges rolled downward or towards the lower side
rostrum	a beak or beak-like extension
rugose	wrinkled
rugulose	somewhat wrinkled
runcinate	with large saw-like teeth pointing backward
scarious	dry, thin, and membranous
sectile	divided into small parts
semilunar	shaped like a half-moon or crescent
seta	a bristle or stiff hair
stipitate	borne on a short stalk
subulate	awl-shaped
sympodial	habit of growth of a plant in which the growing point terminates in an inflorescence or dies each year, growth being continued by a new lateral growth
tomentose	densely covered with short soft matted hairs
tumid	inflated or swollen
turbinate	top-shaped, like an inverted cone
uncinate	hooked or barbed at the apex
undulate	wavy on the edges
unguiculate	contracted at the base into a claw or narrow stalk
valvate	meeting along the edge, without overlapping
villous	with shaggy hairs
zygomorphic	bilaterally symmetrical, i.e. divisible into two identical halves by only one plane passing through the centre

Additional Reading

Select list

Black, J. M., *Flora of South Australia*, Government Printer, Adelaide, 2nd ed., 1943–57.

Dockrill, A. W., *Australasian Sarcanthinae*, Australasian Native Orchid Society, Sydney, 1967.

Erickson, R., *Orchids of W.A.*, Lamb, Perth, 2nd ed., 1965.

Ewart, A. J., *Flora of Victoria*, Government Printer, Melbourne, 1931.

Firth, M. J., *Native orchids of Tasmania*, published by the author, Devonport, 1965.

Rupp, H. M. R., *The orchids of New South Wales*, Government Printer, for the National Herbarium, Sydney, 1943.

Willis, J. H., *A handbook to plants in Victoria*, vol. 1, Melbourne University Press, Melbourne, 1962.

Other books

Allan, H. H., *Flora of New Zealand*, Government Printer, Wellington, NZ, 1961– . A subsequent volume should deal with orchids.

Backer, C. A., and Bakhuizen van den Brink jnr, R. C., *Flora of Java*, vol. 3, Noordhoff, Groningen, Netherlands, 1968.

Barrett, C., *Gems of the Bush. Sun nature book No. 5*, Sun News-Pictorial, Melbourne, 1934.

Beadle, N. C. W., Evans, O. D., and Carolin, R. C., *Handbook of vascular plants of the Sydney district and Blue Mountains*, published by the authors, Armidale, NSW, 1962.

Beard, J. S. (ed.), *Descriptive catalogue of West Australian plants*, Society for Growing Australian Plants, Sydney, 1965.

Blackall, W. E., *How to know Western Australian wildflowers*, vol. 1, ed. B. J. Grieve, University of Western Australia Press, 1959.

Curtis, W. M., *The student's flora of Tasmania*, Government Printer, Hobart, 1956– . A subsequent volume should deal with orchids.

Debenham, C. N., *The language of botany*, Society for Growing Australian Plants, Sydney, 1963.

Dockrill, A. W., *A checklist of the orchidaceous plants of North Queensland*, North Queensland Naturalists' Club, Cairns, 1966.

Eichler, H., *Supplement to J. M. Black's Flora of South Australia*, Government Printer, Adelaide, 1965.

FitzGerald, R. D., *Australian orchids*, vols 1 and 2, ? Government Printer, Sydney, 1875–1894. A number of Herbarium and State Libraries in Australia have copies.

Galbraith, J., *Wildflowers of Victoria*, Longmans, Melbourne, 3rd ed., 1967.

George, A. S., *Orchids of Western Australia*, Westviews, Perth, 1969.

Gray, C. E., *Victorian native orchids*, vol. 1, Longmans, Melbourne, 1966.

Harman, C. W., *Orchids of Green Mountains (Lamington National Park, Queensland)*, printed by Smith & Paterson, Brisbane, 1968.

Holttum, R. E., *A revised flora of Malaya*, vol. 1, *Orchids of Malaya*, Government Printing Office, Singapore, 2nd ed., 1957.

Hunt, T. E., *A census of South Queensland orchids*, printed by R. G. Gillies, Brisbane, ? 1948.

Pelloe, E. H., *West Australian orchids*, published by the author, Perth, 1930.

Pescott, E. E., *The orchids of Victoria*, Horticultural Press, Melbourne, 1928.

Pijl, L. van der, and Dodson, C. H., *Orchid flowers: Their pollination and evolution*, University of Miami Press, Florida, USA, 1967.

Rogers, R. S., *An introduction to the study of South Australian orchids*, Government Printer, Adelaide, published by Education Dept, Adelaide, 1911.

Rupp, H. M. R., *Guide to the orchids of New South Wales*, 1930.

Withner, C. L. (ed.), *The orchids: A scientific survey*, The Ronald Press, New York, USA, 1959.

Journals

Annals of the Missouri Botanical Garden, St Louis, Missouri (See vol. 47: 25–68 (1960) for an excellent article entitled 'Classification and phylogeny in Orchidaceae', by R. L. Dressler and C. H. Dodson.)

Australian Orchid Review, Sydney.

Australian Plants, Sydney.

North Queensland Naturalist, Cairns.

Orchadian, Sydney.

Queensland Naturalist, Brisbane.

South Australian Naturalist, Adelaide.

Transactions of the Royal Society of New Zealand, Wellington.

Victorian Naturalist, Melbourne.

Western Australian Naturalist, Perth.

Wild Life: Australian nature magazine, Melbourne.

Index

Page numbers in italics indicate major entries, numbers in bold type refer to Plates. Synonyms are in italics.